COLLECTOR'S EDITION

Fruits Basket

NATS

6

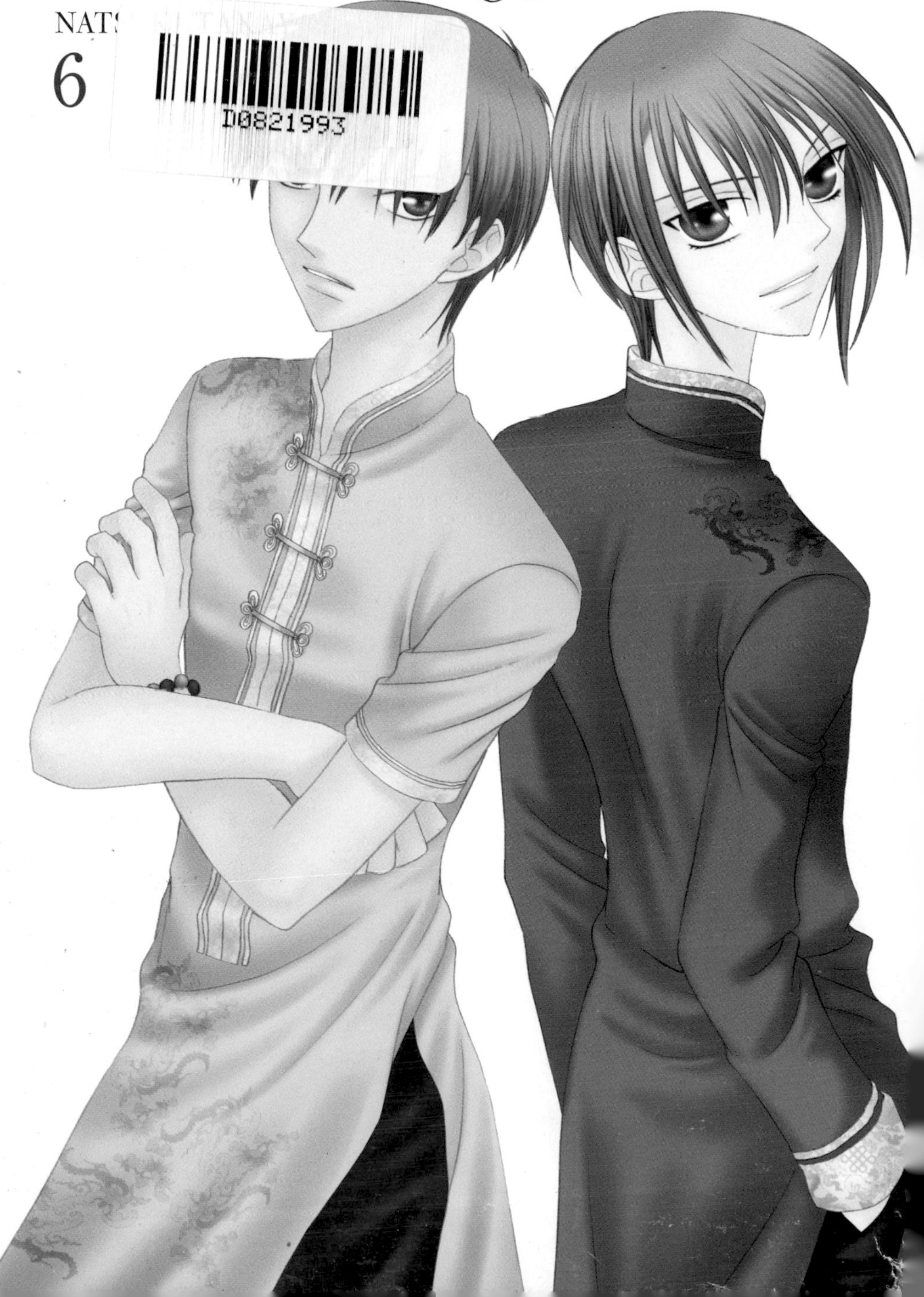

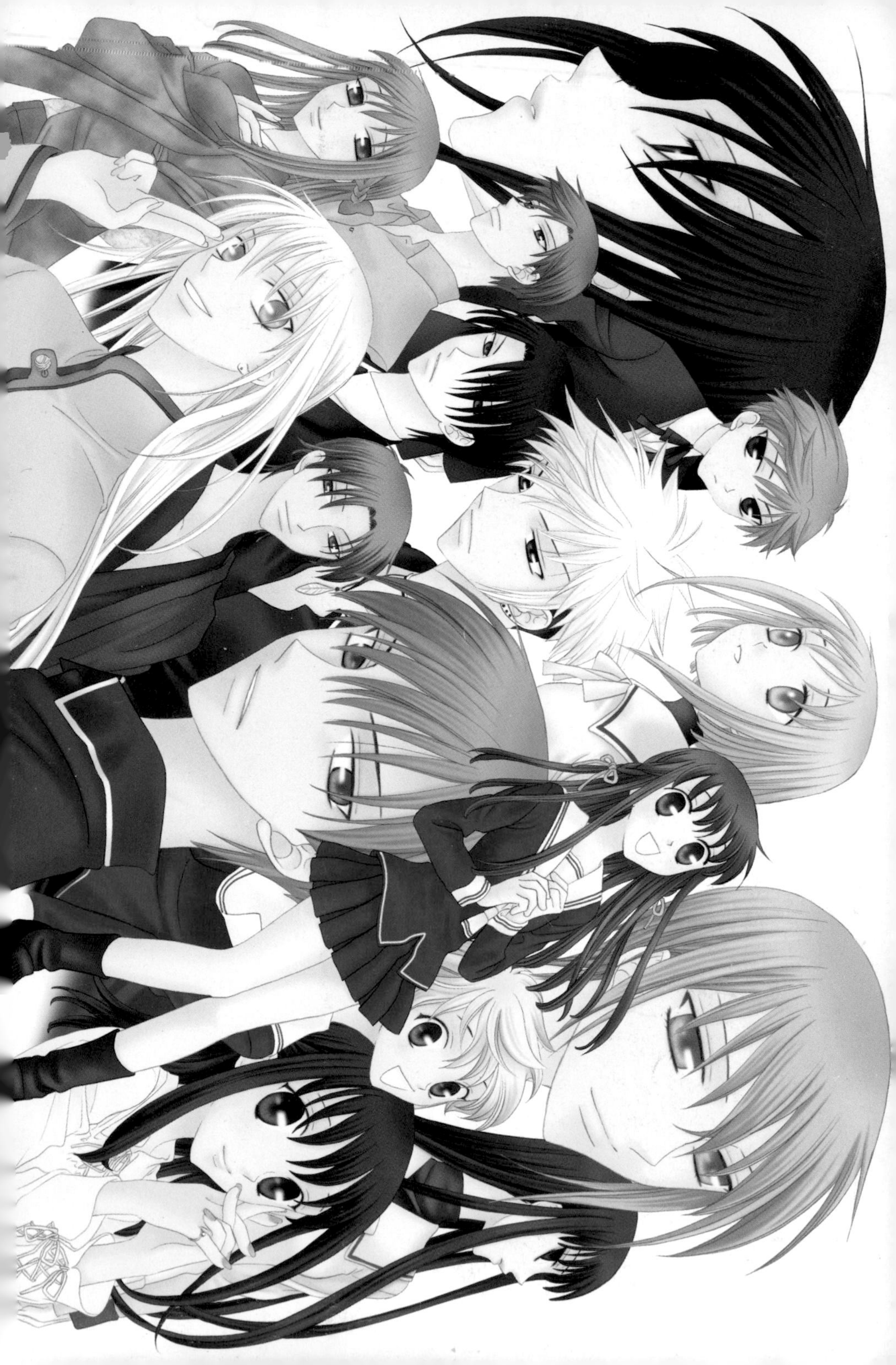

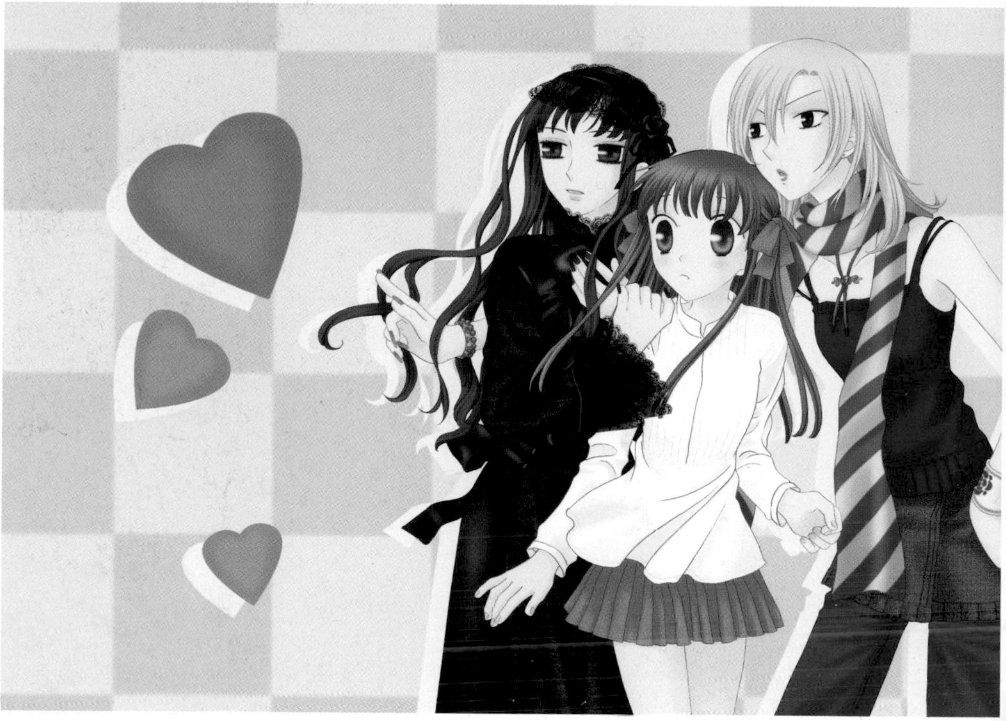

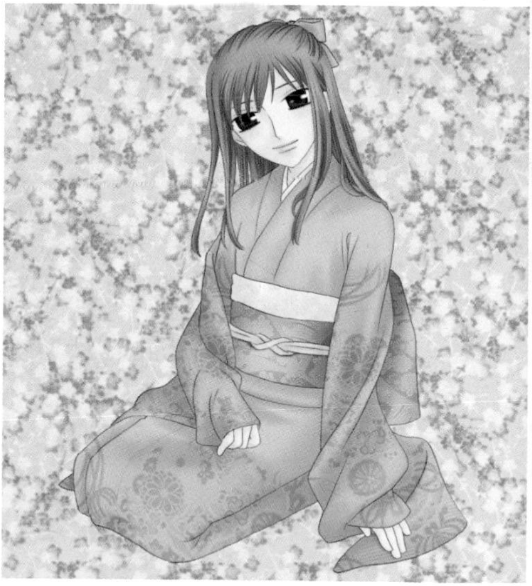

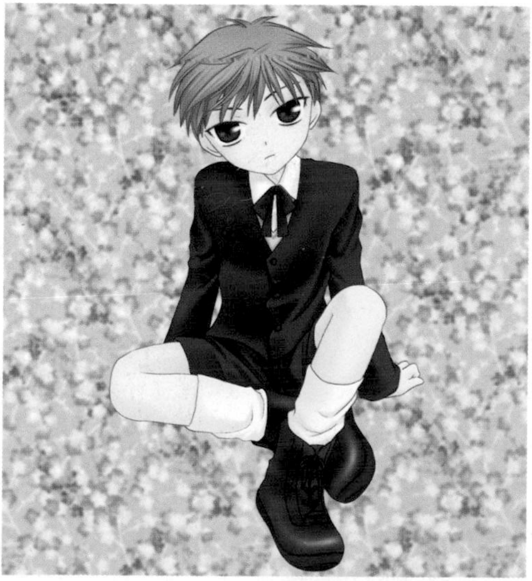

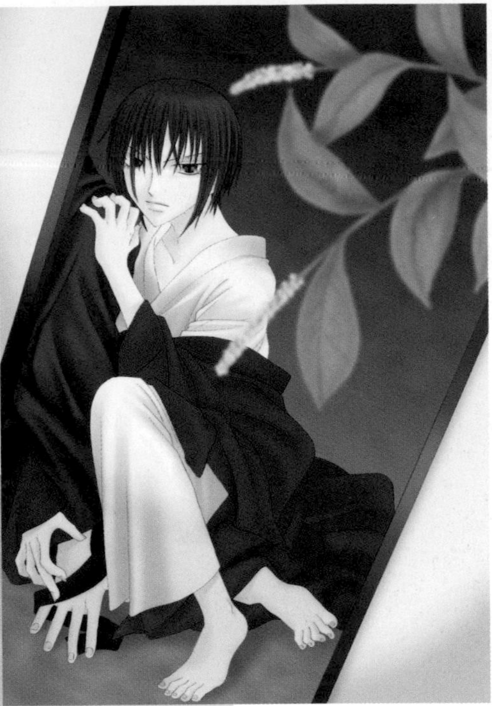
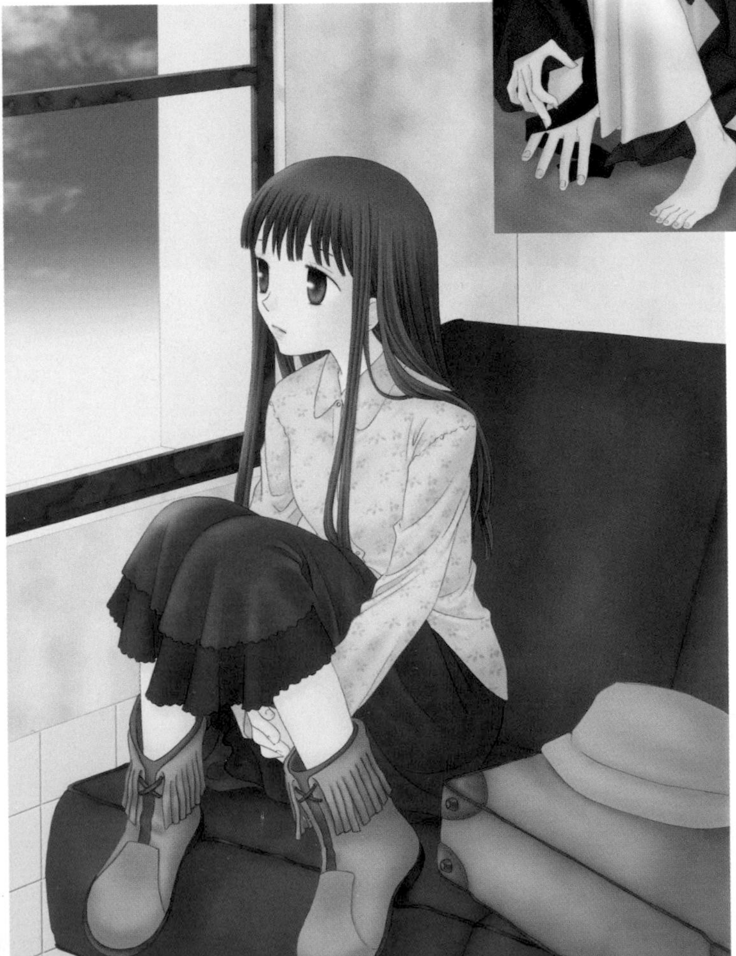

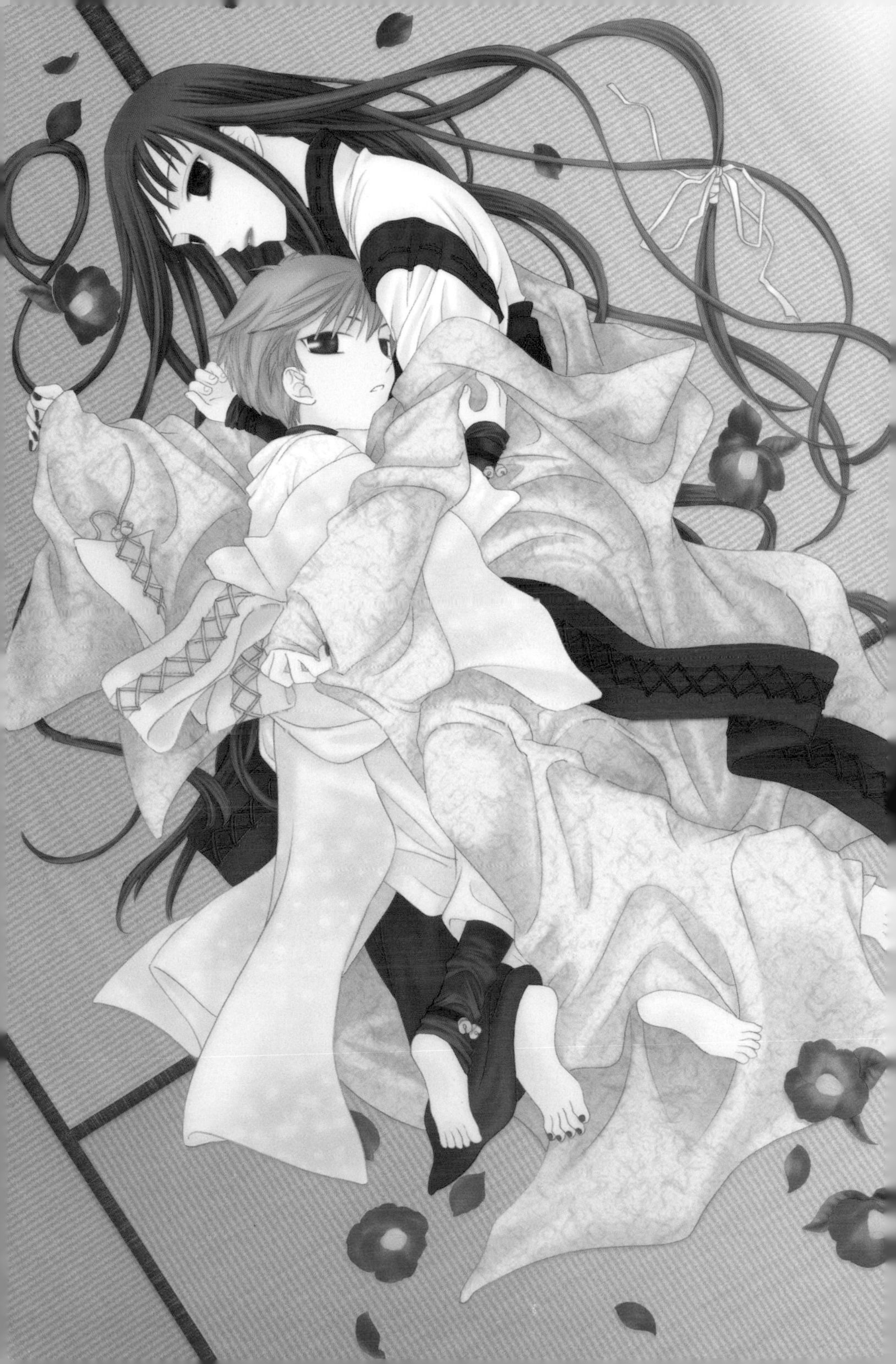

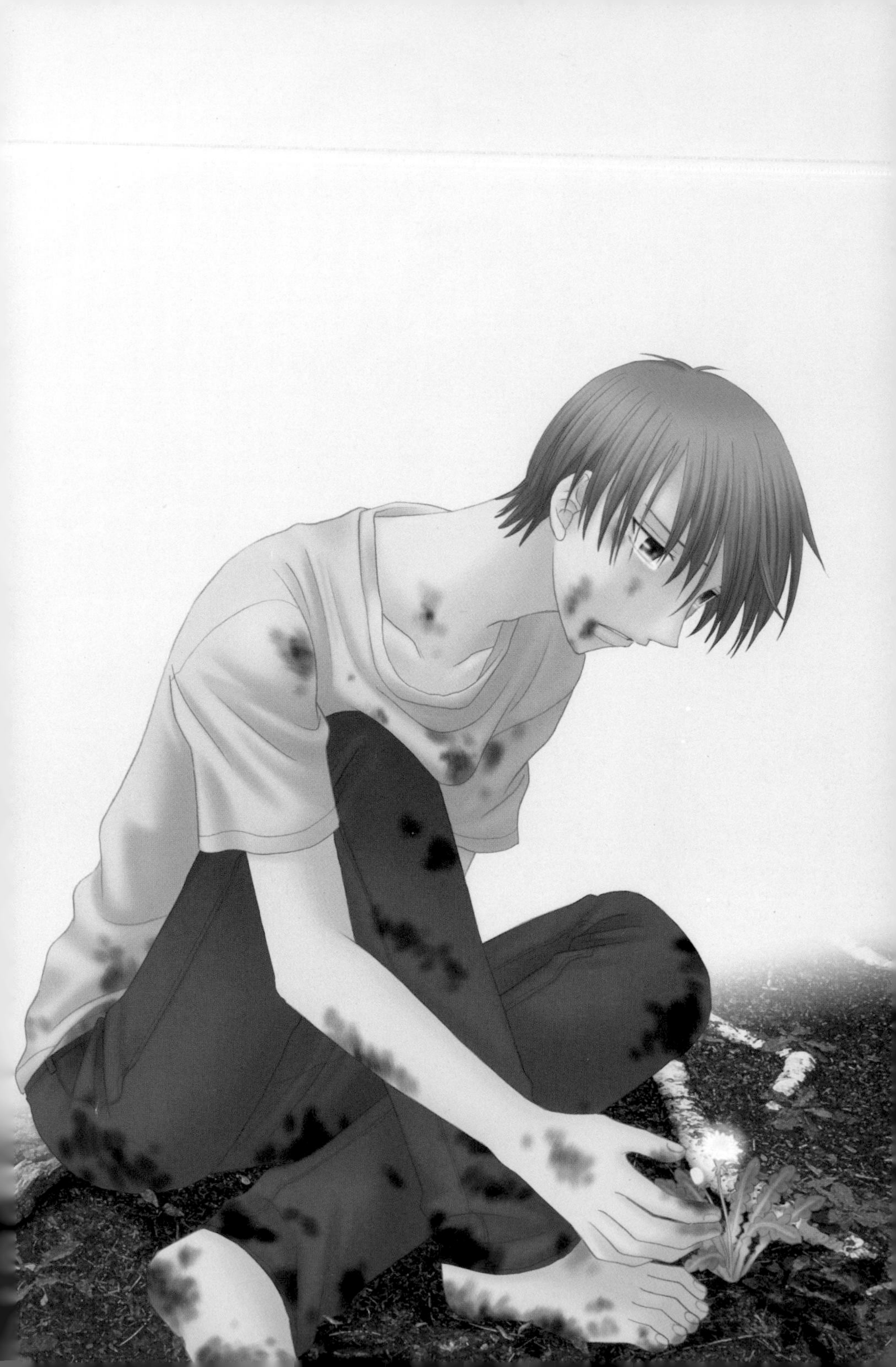

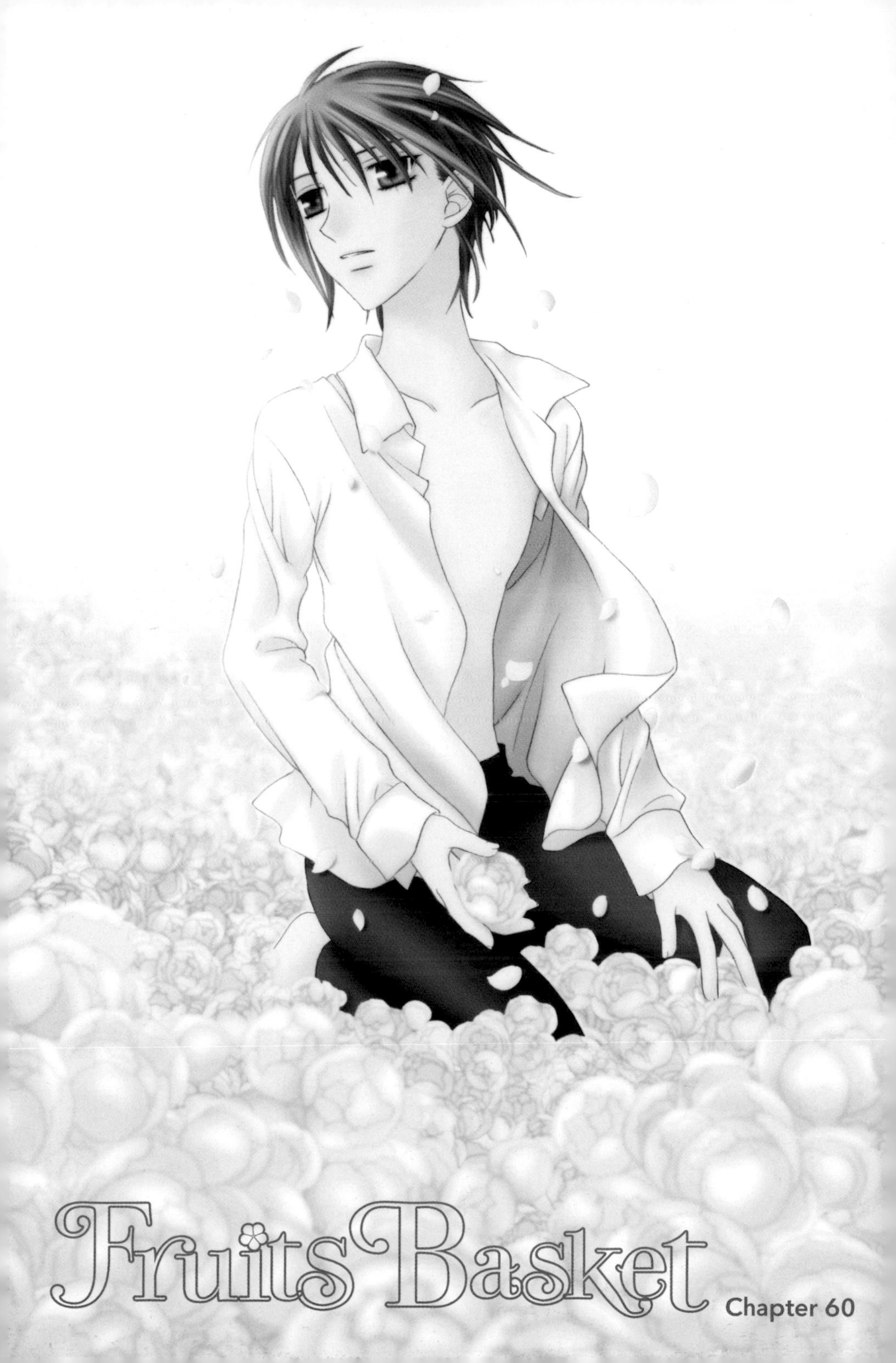
Fruits Basket
Chapter 60

TABLE OF CONTENTS

COLLECTOR'S EDITION

Fruits Basket 6

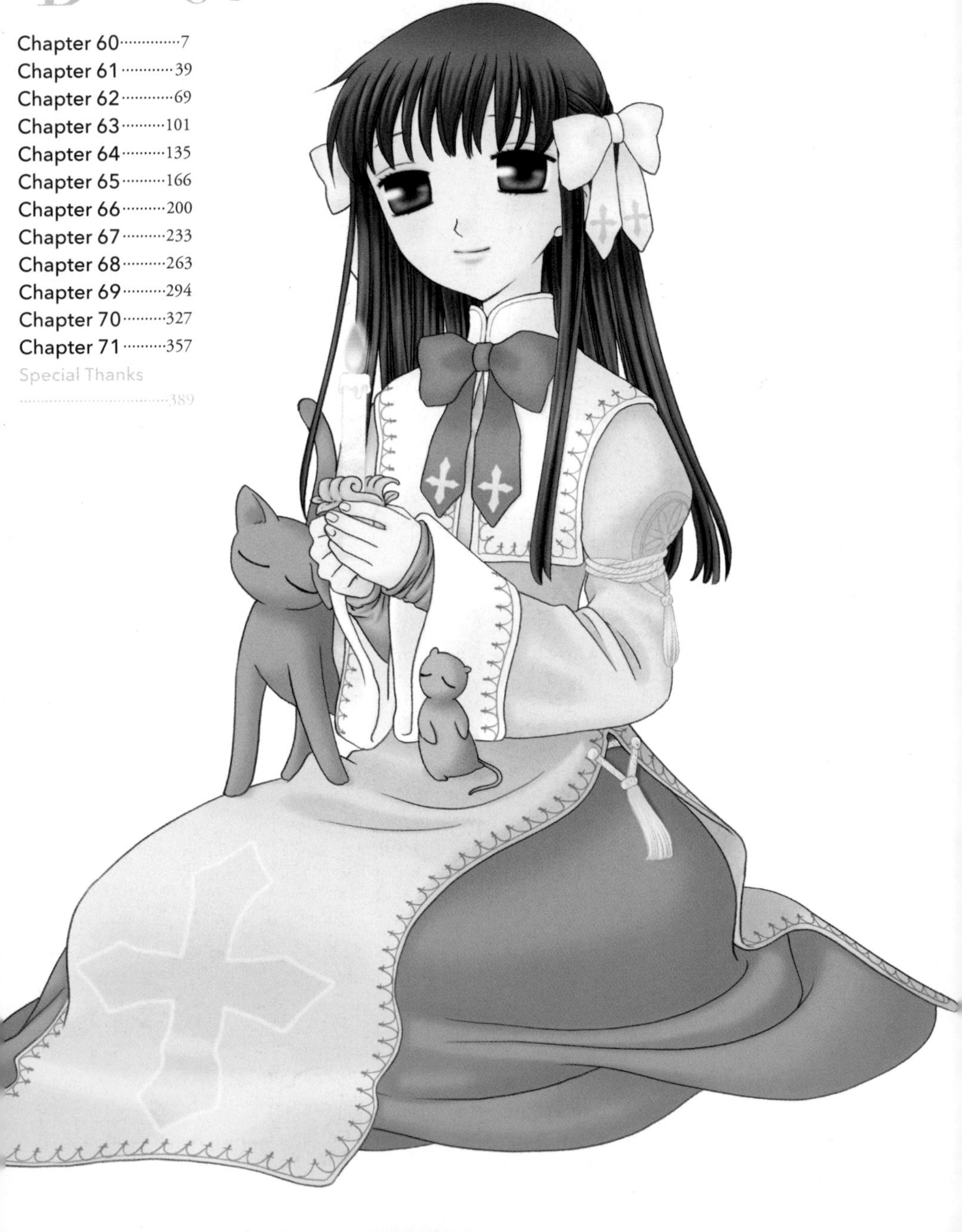

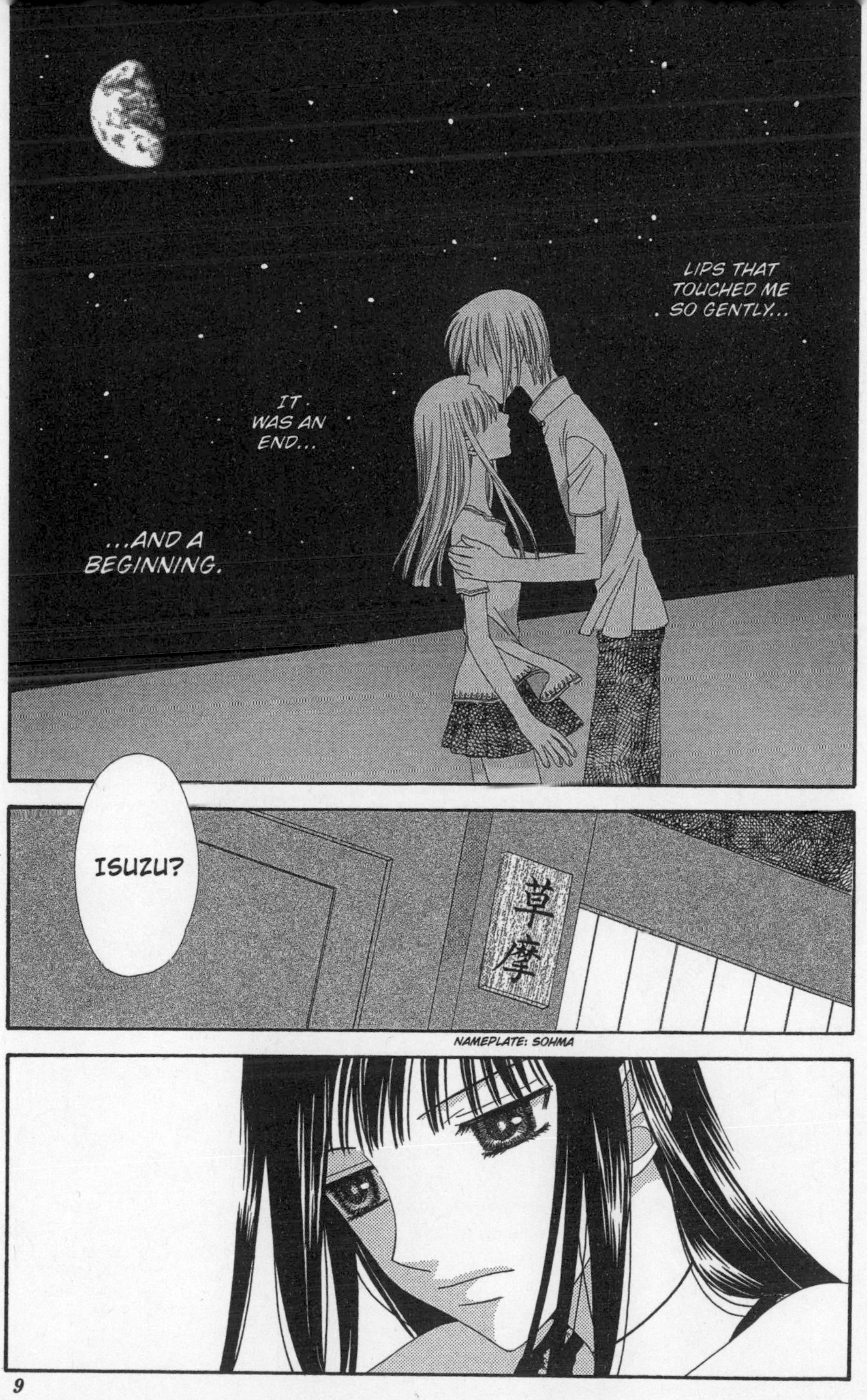
LIPS THAT TOUCHED ME SO GENTLY...
IT WAS AN END...
...AND A BEGINNING.
ISUZU?
草摩
NAMEPLATE: SOHMA

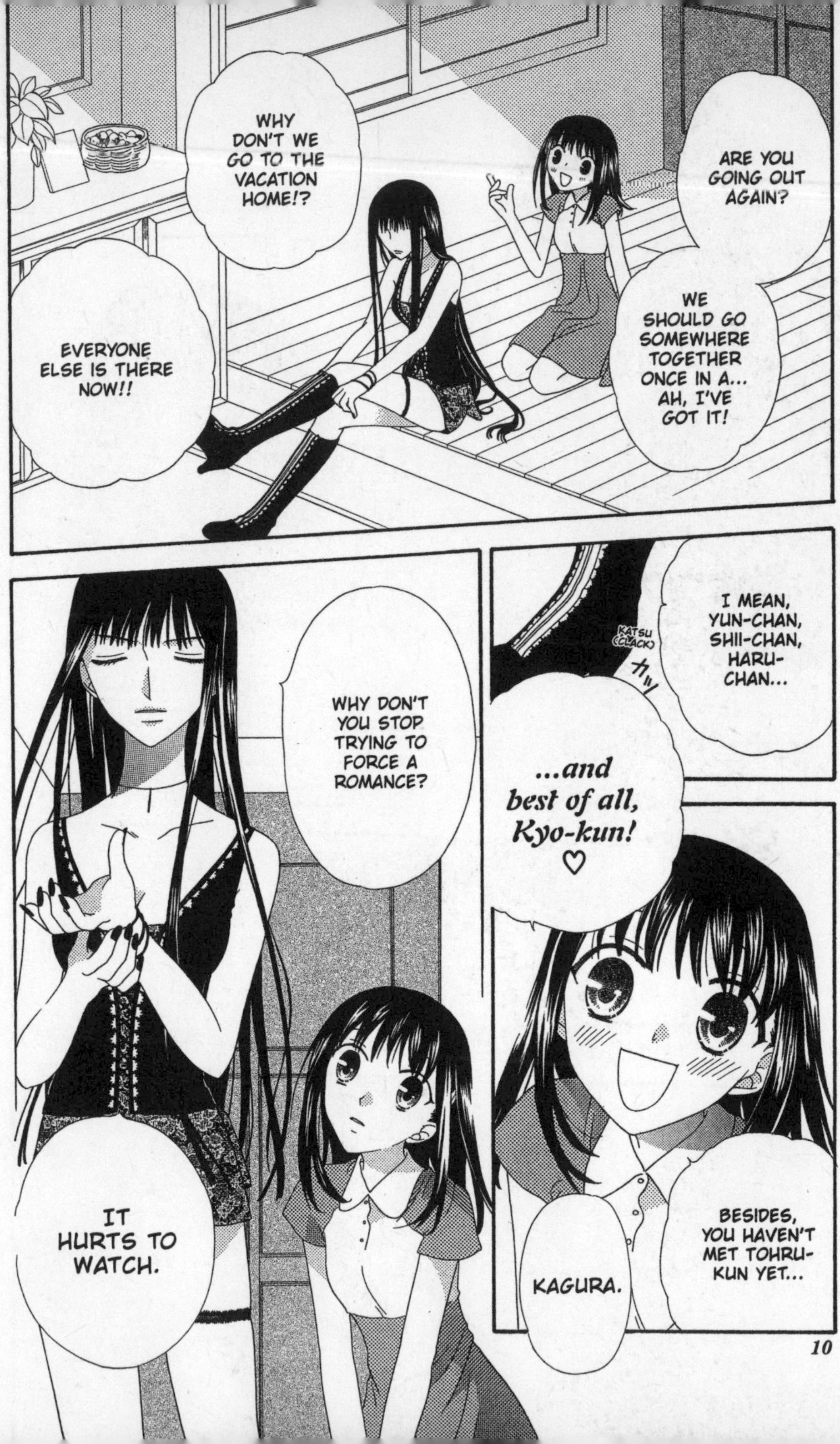

ARE YOU GOING OUT AGAIN?
WE SHOULD GO SOMEWHERE TOGETHER ONCE IN A... AH, I'VE GOT IT!
WHY DON'T WE GO TO THE VACATION HOME!?
EVERYONE ELSE IS THERE NOW!!
I MEAN, YUN-CHAN, SHII-CHAN, HARU-CHAN...
KATSU (CLACK)
カッ
...and best of all, Kyo-kun! ♡
BESIDES, YOU HAVEN'T MET TOHRU-KUN YET...
KAGURA.
WHY DON'T YOU STOP TRYING TO FORCE A ROMANCE?
IT HURTS TO WATCH.

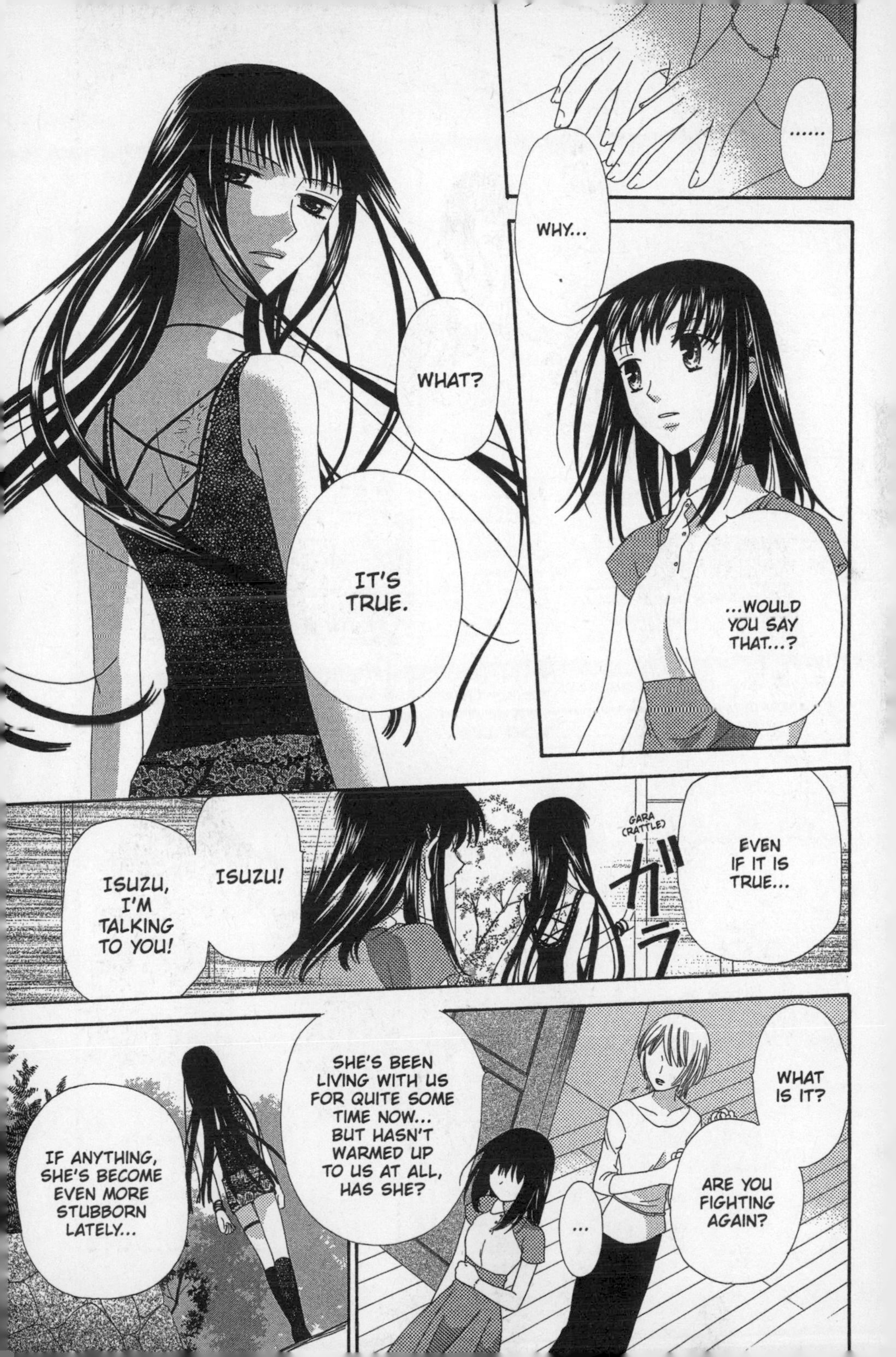
......
WHY...
...WOULD YOU SAY THAT...?
WHAT?
IT'S TRUE.
EVEN IF IT IS TRUE...
GARA (RATTLE)
ガラ
ISUZU!
ISUZU, I'M TALKING TO YOU!
WHAT IS IT?
ARE YOU FIGHTING AGAIN?
...
SHE'S BEEN LIVING WITH US FOR QUITE SOME TIME NOW... BUT HASN'T WARMED UP TO US AT ALL, HAS SHE?
IF ANYTHING, SHE'S BECOME EVEN MORE STUBBORN LATELY...

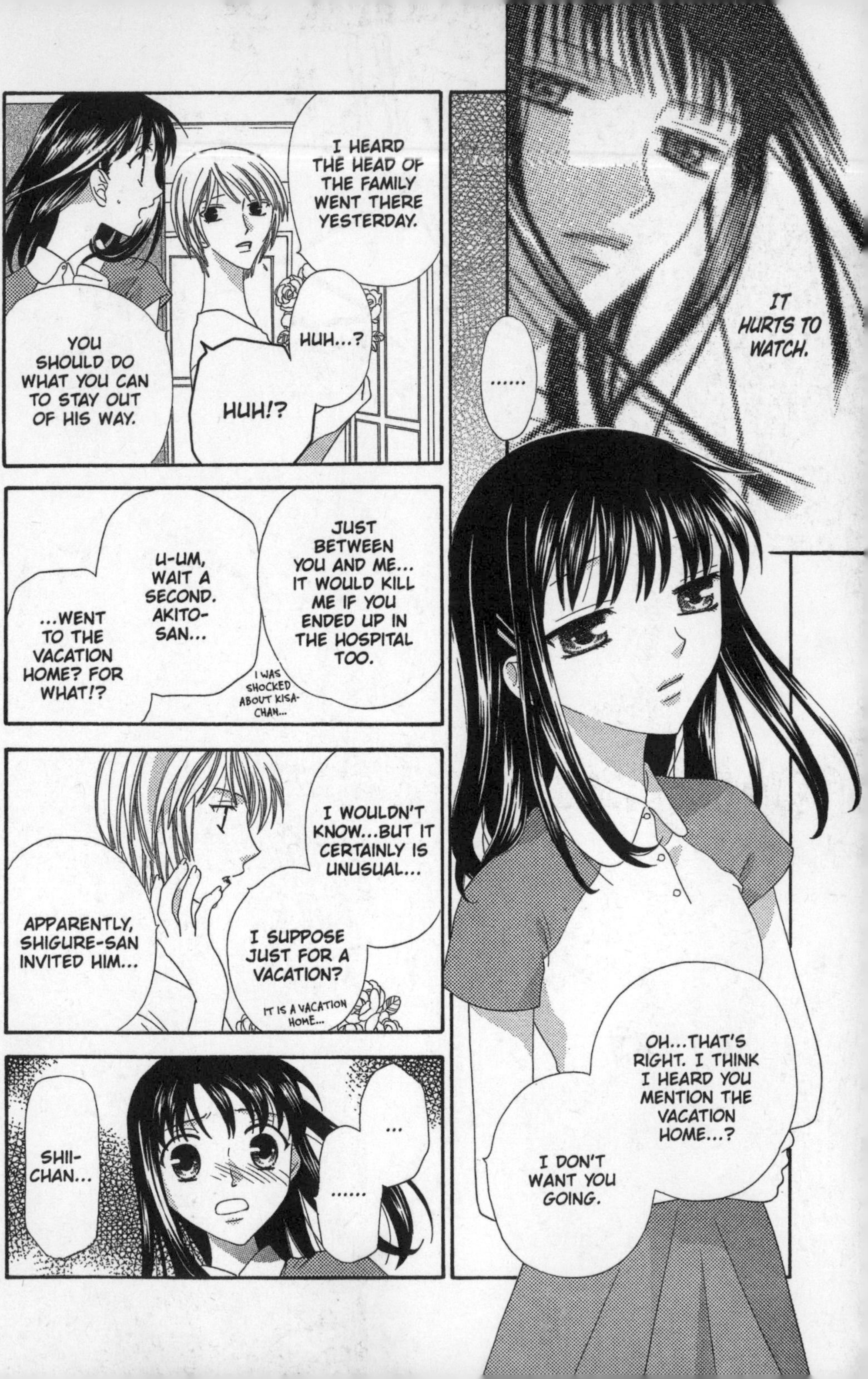

IT HURTS TO WATCH.
......
OH...THAT'S RIGHT. I THINK I HEARD YOU MENTION THE VACATION HOME...?
I DON'T WANT YOU GOING.
I HEARD THE HEAD OF THE FAMILY WENT THERE YESTERDAY.
HUH...?
HUH!?
YOU SHOULD DO WHAT YOU CAN TO STAY OUT OF HIS WAY.
JUST BETWEEN YOU AND ME... IT WOULD KILL ME IF YOU ENDED UP IN THE HOSPITAL TOO.
I WAS SHOCKED ABOUT KISA-CHAN...
U-UM, WAIT A SECOND. AKITO-SAN...
...WENT TO THE VACATION HOME? FOR WHAT!?
I WOULDN'T KNOW...BUT IT CERTAINLY IS UNUSUAL...
I SUPPOSE JUST FOR A VACATION?
IT IS A VACATION HOME...
APPARENTLY, SHIGURE-SAN INVITED HIM...
...
......
SHII-CHAN...

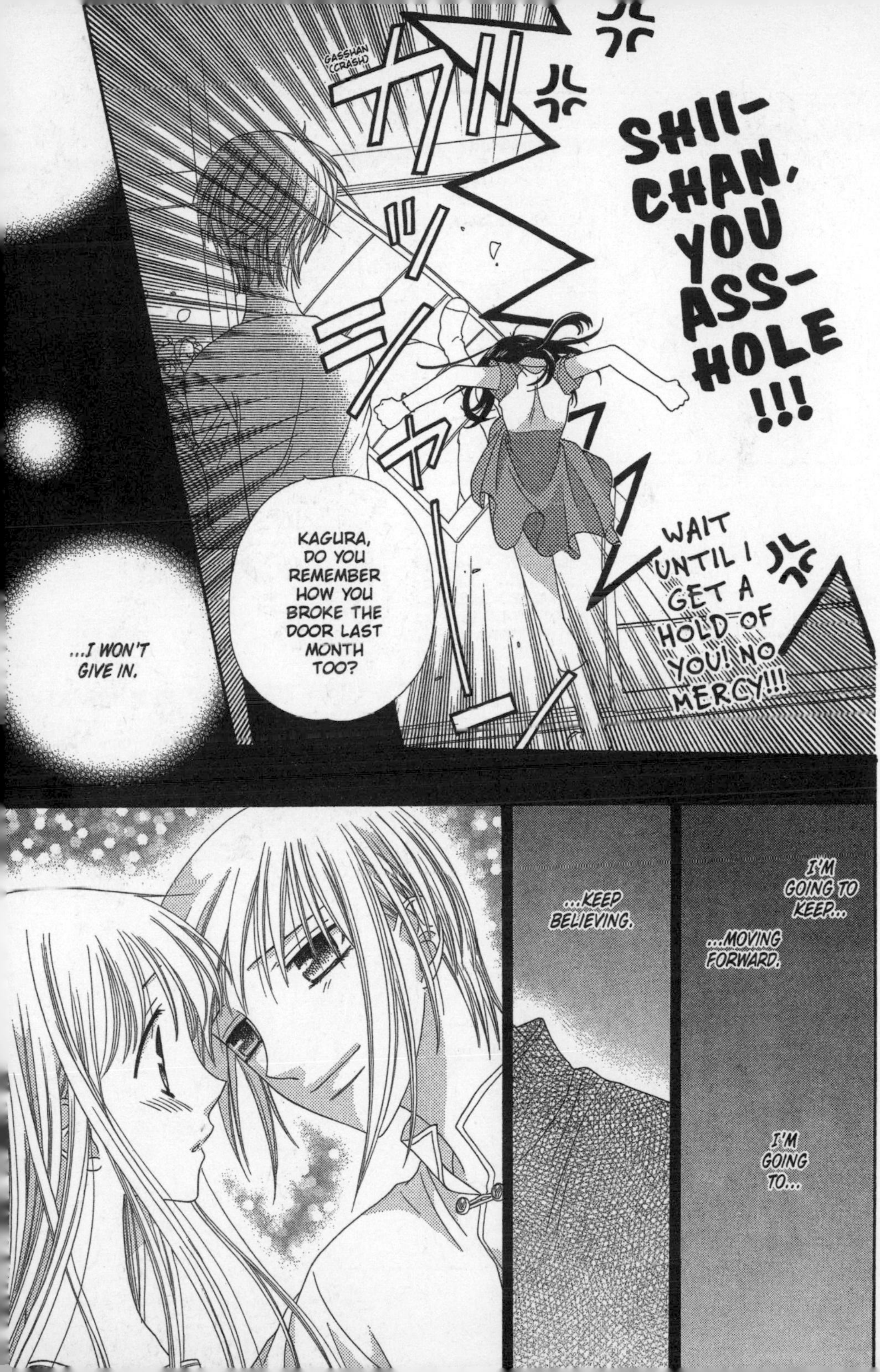
SHII-CHAN, YOU ASS-HOLE!!!
GASSHAN (CRASH)
WAIT UNTIL I GET A HOLD OF YOU! NO MERCY!!!
KAGURA, DO YOU REMEMBER HOW YOU BROKE THE DOOR LAST MONTH TOO?
...I WON'T GIVE IN.
I'M GOING TO KEEP...
...MOVING FORWARD.
I'M GOING TO...
...KEEP BELIEVING.

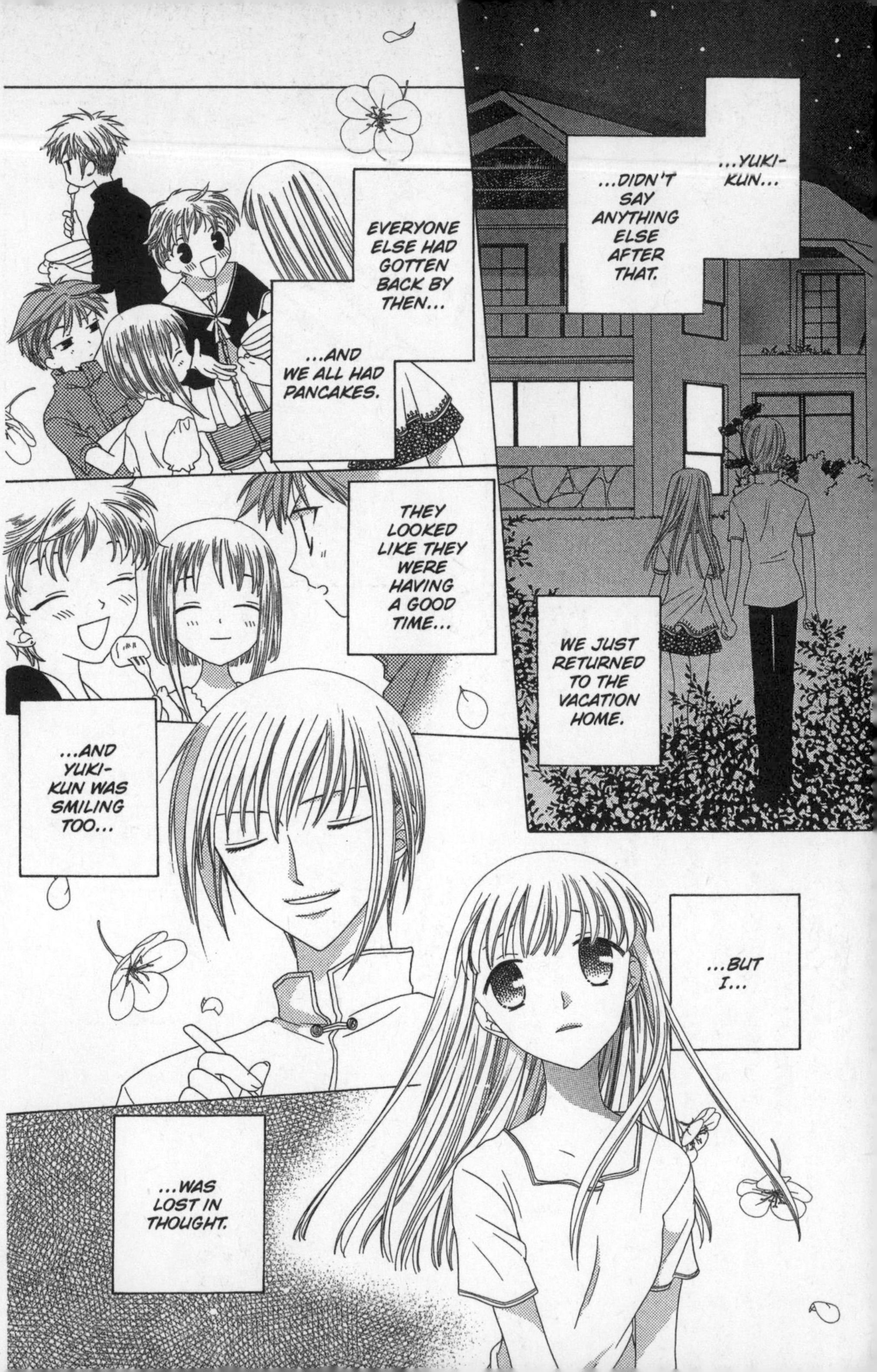
...YUKI-KUN...
...DIDN'T SAY ANYTHING ELSE AFTER THAT.
WE JUST RETURNED TO THE VACATION HOME.
EVERYONE ELSE HAD GOTTEN BACK BY THEN...
...AND WE ALL HAD PANCAKES.
THEY LOOKED LIKE THEY WERE HAVING A GOOD TIME...
...AND YUKI-KUN WAS SMILING TOO...
...BUT I...
...WAS LOST IN THOUGHT.

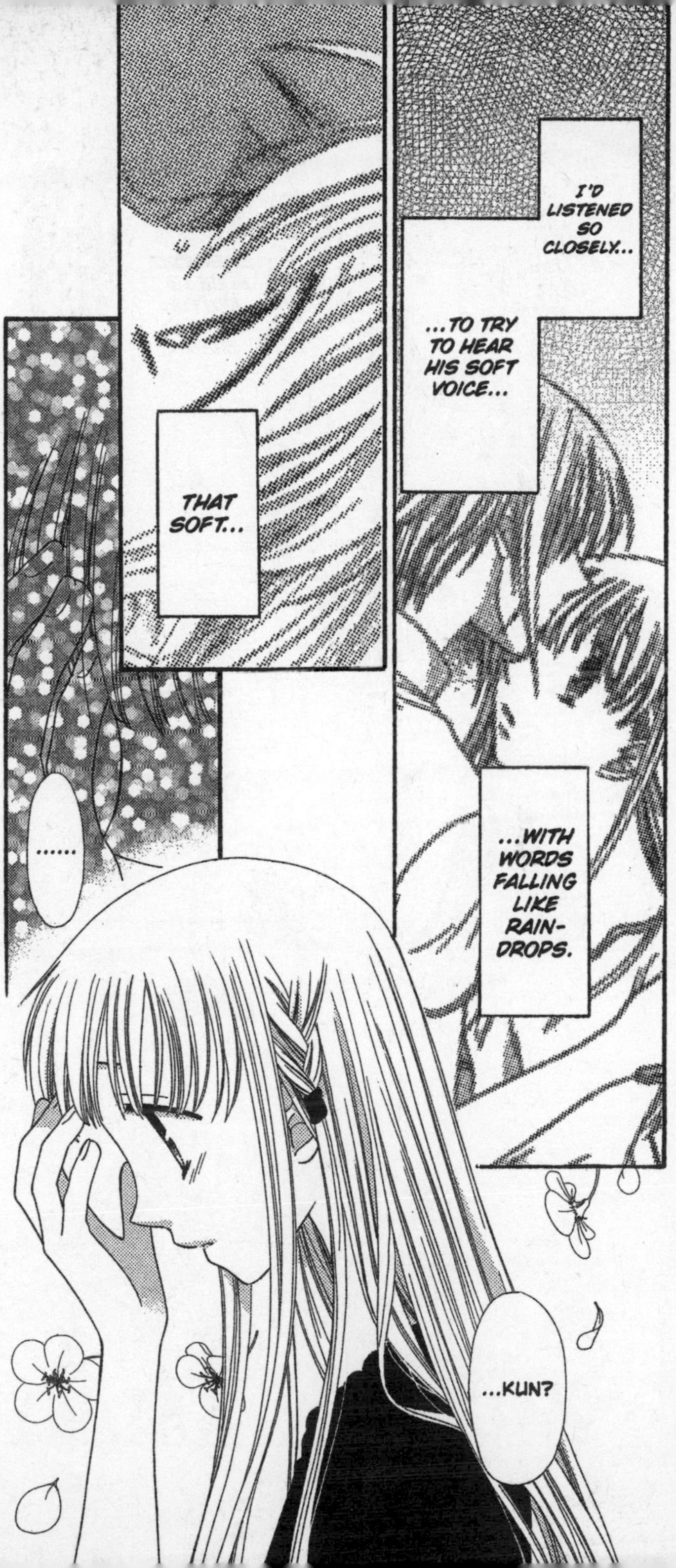
I'D LISTENED SO CLOSELY...
...TO TRY TO HEAR HIS SOFT VOICE...
...WITH WORDS FALLING LIKE RAIN-DROPS.
THAT SOFT...
......
...KUN?
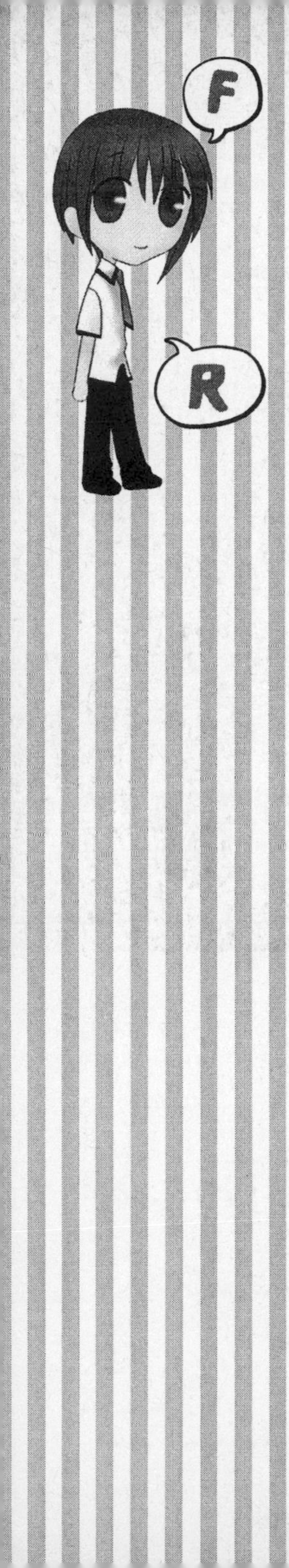
F
R

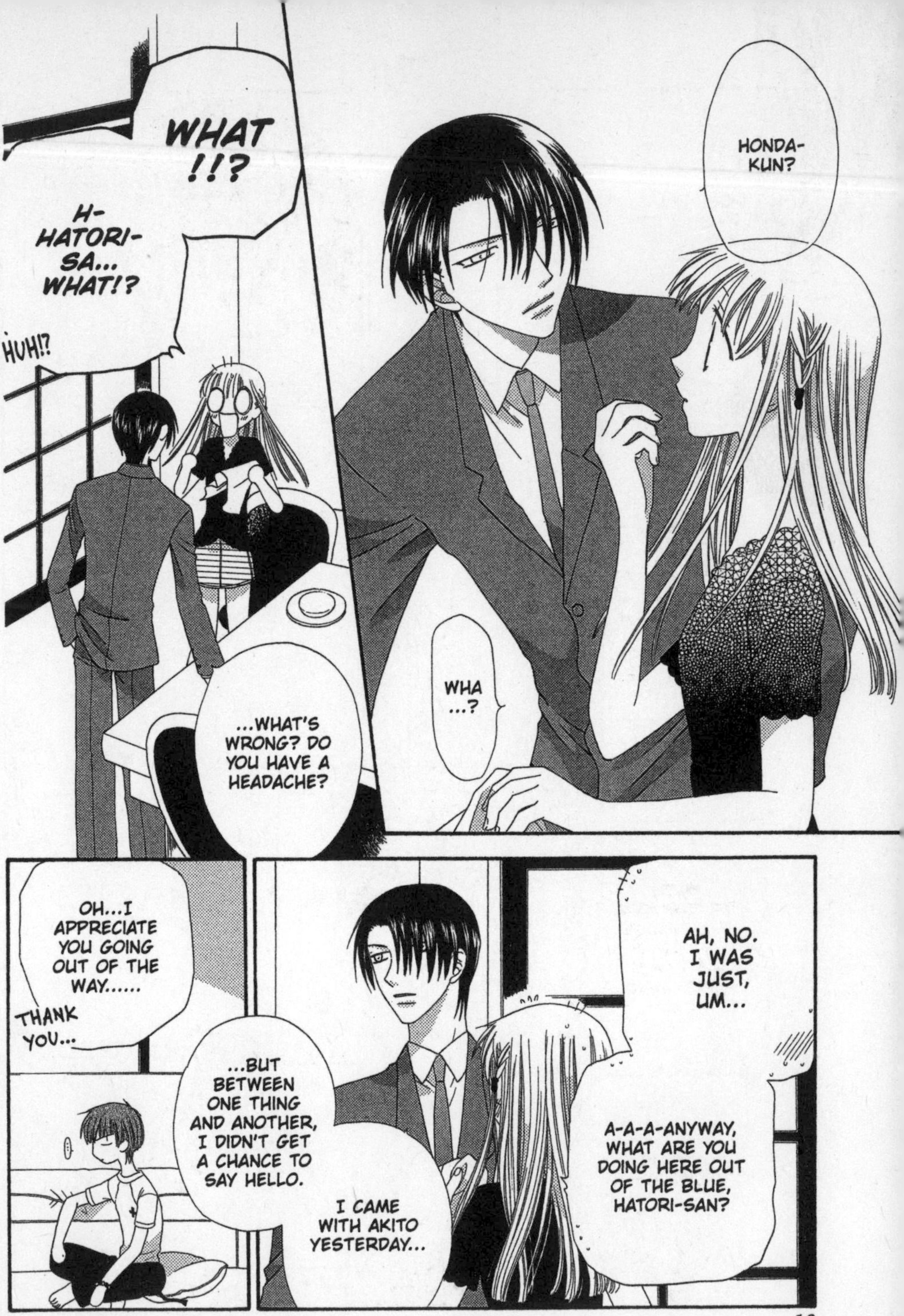
HONDA-KUN?
WHA...?
...WHAT'S WRONG? DO YOU HAVE A HEADACHE?
WHAT!!?
H-HATORI-SA... WHAT!?
HUH!?
AH, NO. I WAS JUST, UM...
A-A-A-ANYWAY, WHAT ARE YOU DOING HERE OUT OF THE BLUE, HATORI-SAN?
I CAME WITH AKITO YESTERDAY...
...BUT BETWEEN ONE THING AND ANOTHER, I DIDN'T GET A CHANCE TO SAY HELLO.
OH...I APPRECIATE YOU GOING OUT OF THE WAY......
THANK YOU...
...

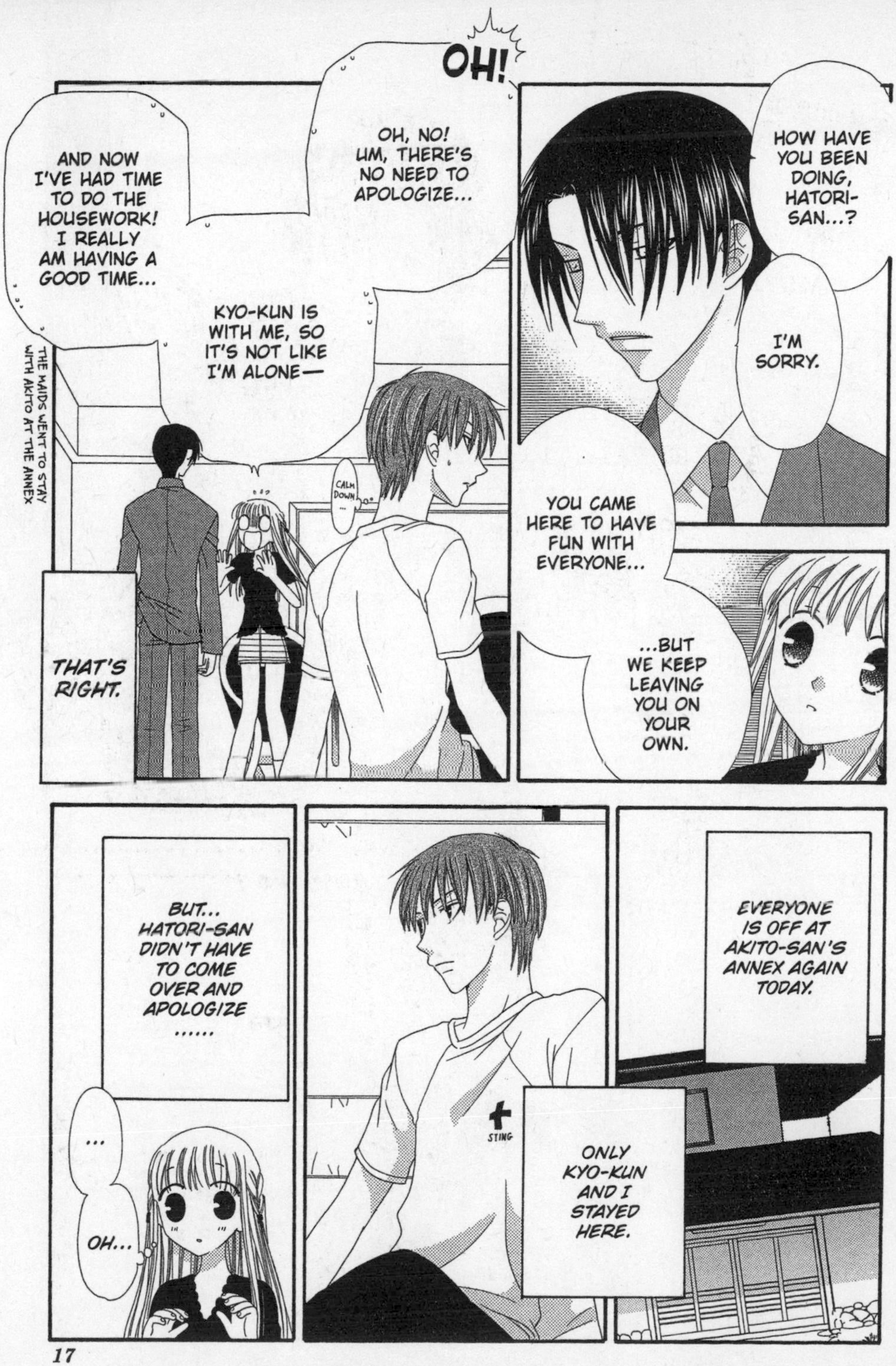
HOW HAVE YOU BEEN DOING, HATORI-SAN...?
I'M SORRY.
YOU CAME HERE TO HAVE FUN WITH EVERYONE...
...BUT WE KEEP LEAVING YOU ON YOUR OWN.
OH!
OH, NO! UM, THERE'S NO NEED TO APOLOGIZE...
AND NOW I'VE HAD TIME TO DO THE HOUSEWORK! I REALLY AM HAVING A GOOD TIME...
KYO-KUN IS WITH ME, SO IT'S NOT LIKE I'M ALONE—
CALM DOWN ...
THE MAIDS WENT TO STAY WITH AKITO AT THE ANNEX
THAT'S RIGHT.
EVERYONE IS OFF AT AKITO-SAN'S ANNEX AGAIN TODAY.
ONLY KYO-KUN AND I STAYED HERE.
STING
BUT... HATORI-SAN DIDN'T HAVE TO COME OVER AND APOLOGIZE ......
...
OH...

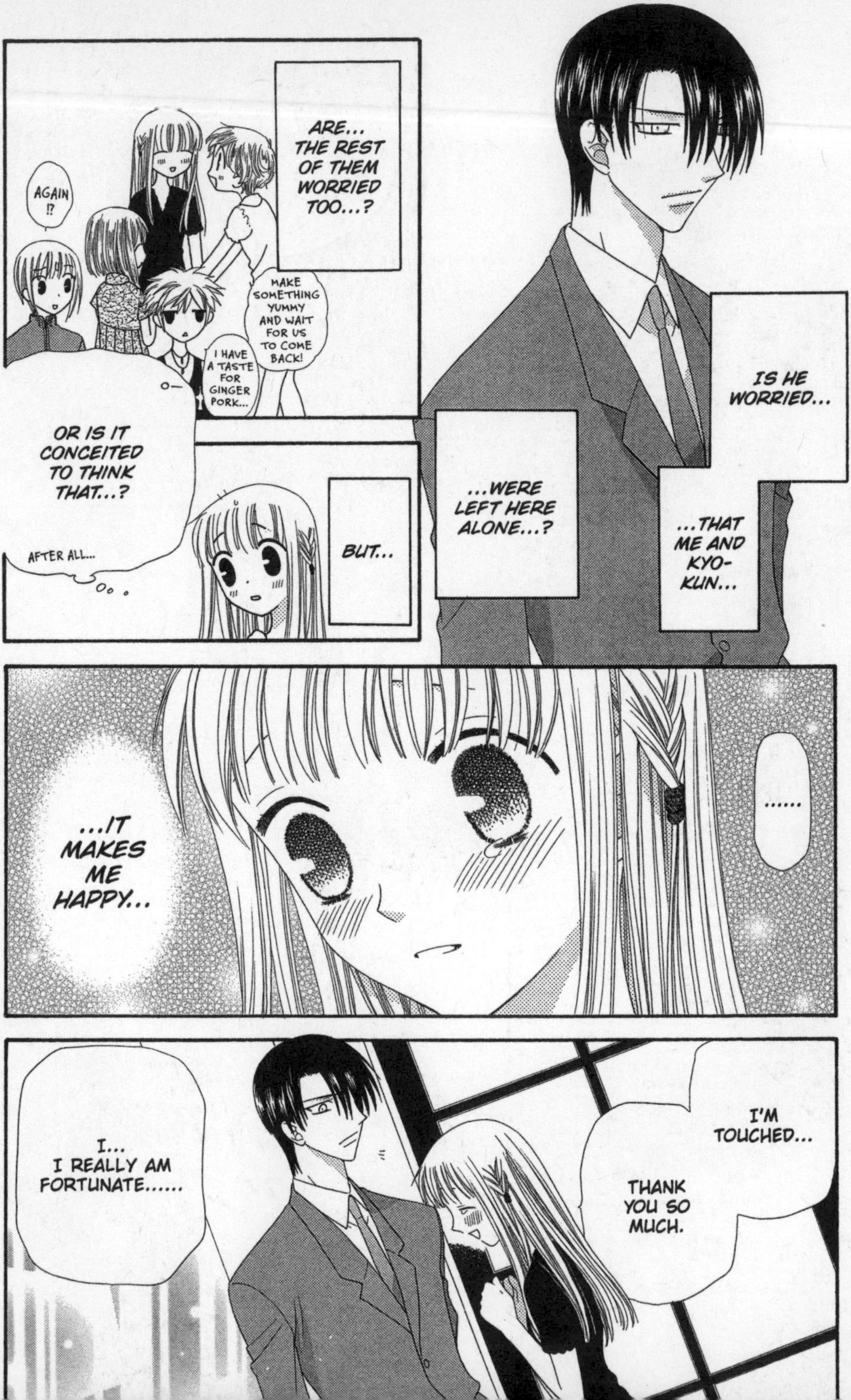
IS HE WORRIED...
...THAT ME AND KYO-KUN...
...WERE LEFT HERE ALONE...?
ARE... THE REST OF THEM WORRIED TOO...?
MAKE SOMETHING YUMMY AND WAIT FOR US TO COME BACK!
AGAIN !?
I HAVE A TASTE FOR GINGER PORK...
BUT...
OR IS IT CONCEITED TO THINK THAT...?
AFTER ALL...
......
...IT MAKES ME HAPPY...
I'M TOUCHED...
THANK YOU SO MUCH.
I... I REALLY AM FORTUNATE......

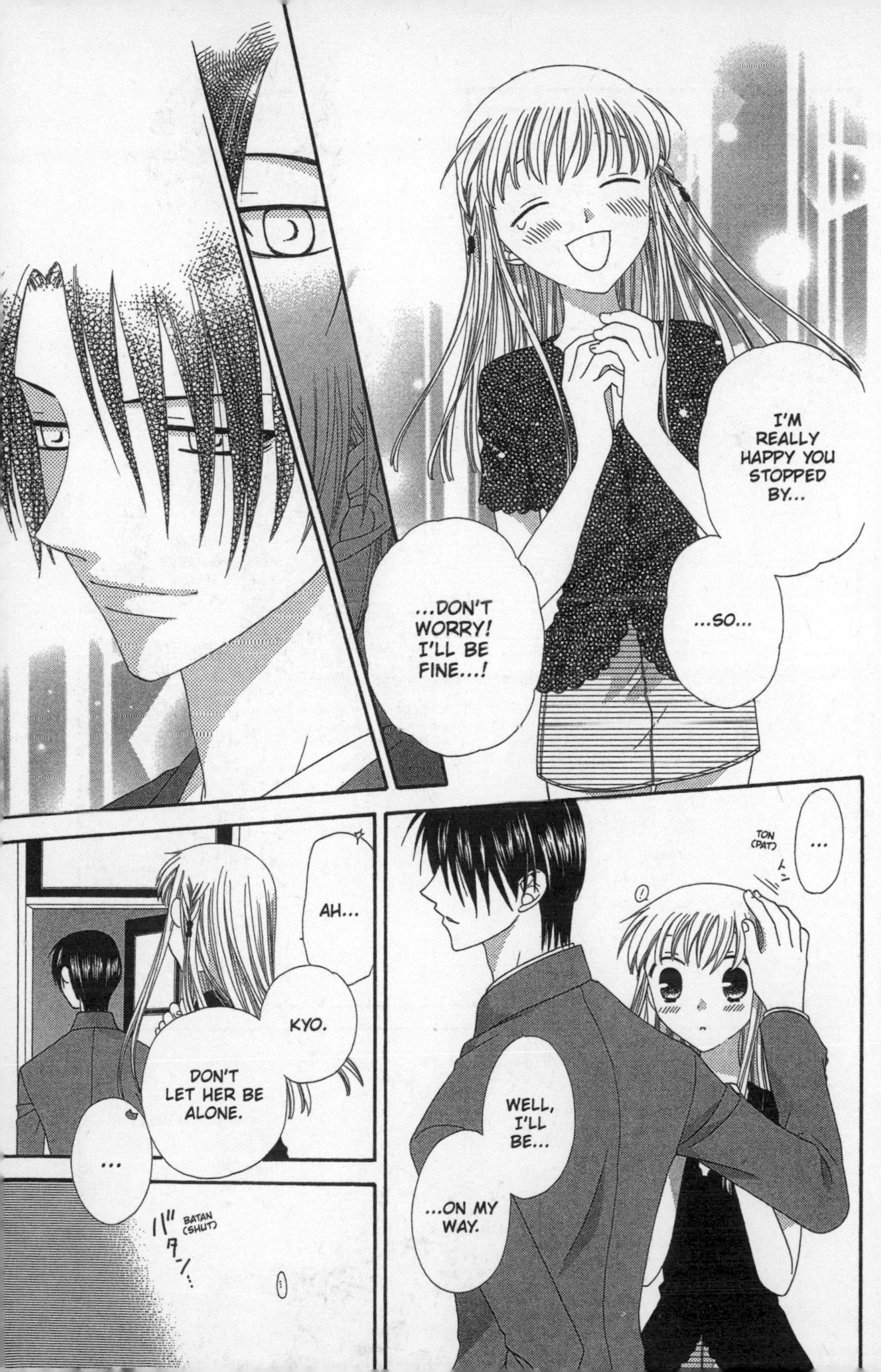
I'M REALLY HAPPY YOU STOPPED BY...
...SO...
...DON'T WORRY! I'LL BE FINE...!
TON (PAT)
...
WELL, I'LL BE...
...ON MY WAY.
AH...
KYO.
DON'T LET HER BE ALONE.
...
BATAN (SHUT)

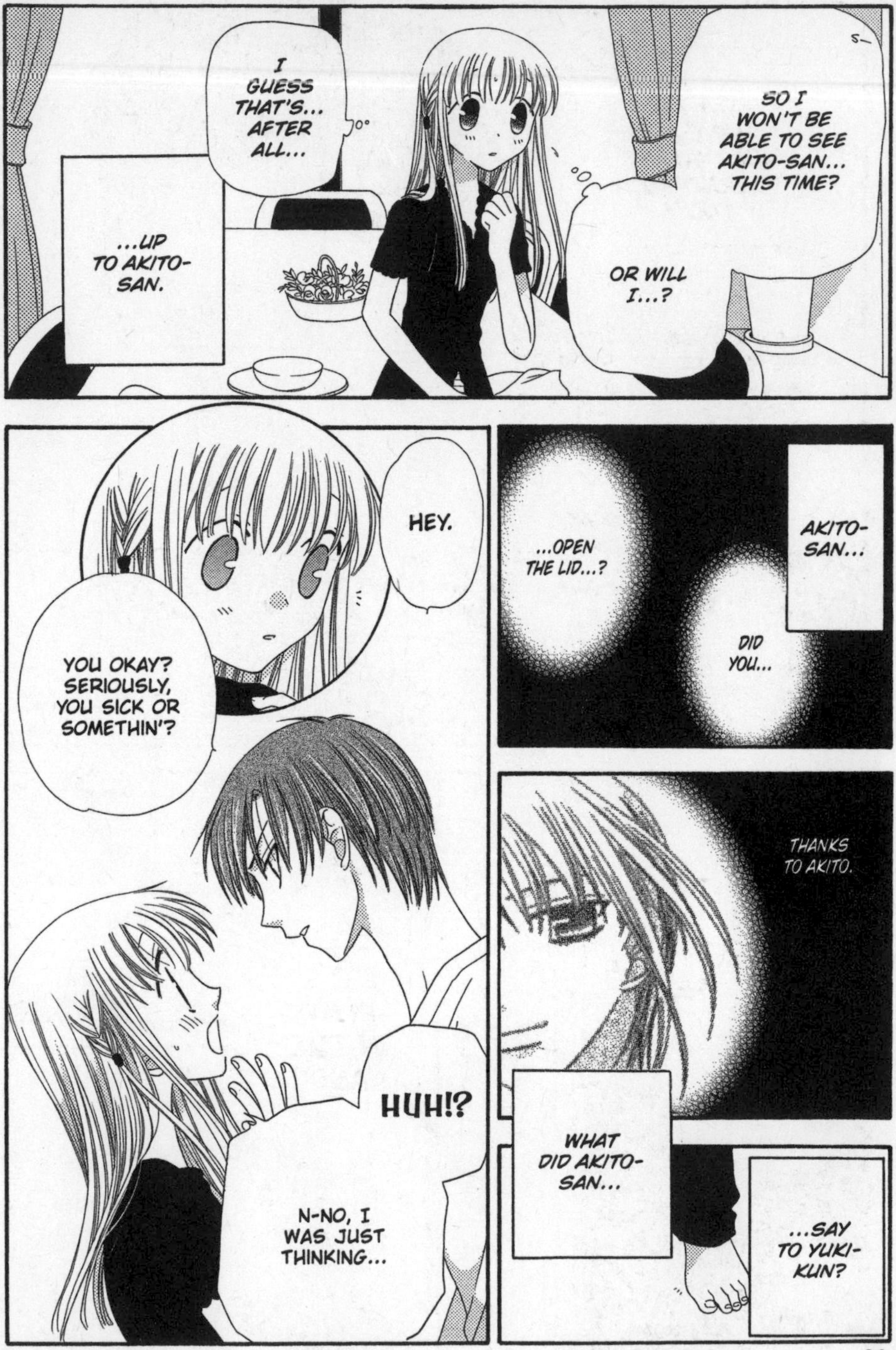
S–
SO I WON'T BE ABLE TO SEE AKITO-SAN... THIS TIME?
I GUESS THAT'S... AFTER ALL...
OR WILL I...?
...UP TO AKITO-SAN.
AKITO-SAN...
DID YOU...
...OPEN THE LID...?
THANKS TO AKITO.
WHAT DID AKITO-SAN...
...SAY TO YUKI-KUN?
HEY.
YOU OKAY? SERIOUSLY, YOU SICK OR SOMETHIN'?
HUH!?
N-NO, I WAS JUST THINKING...

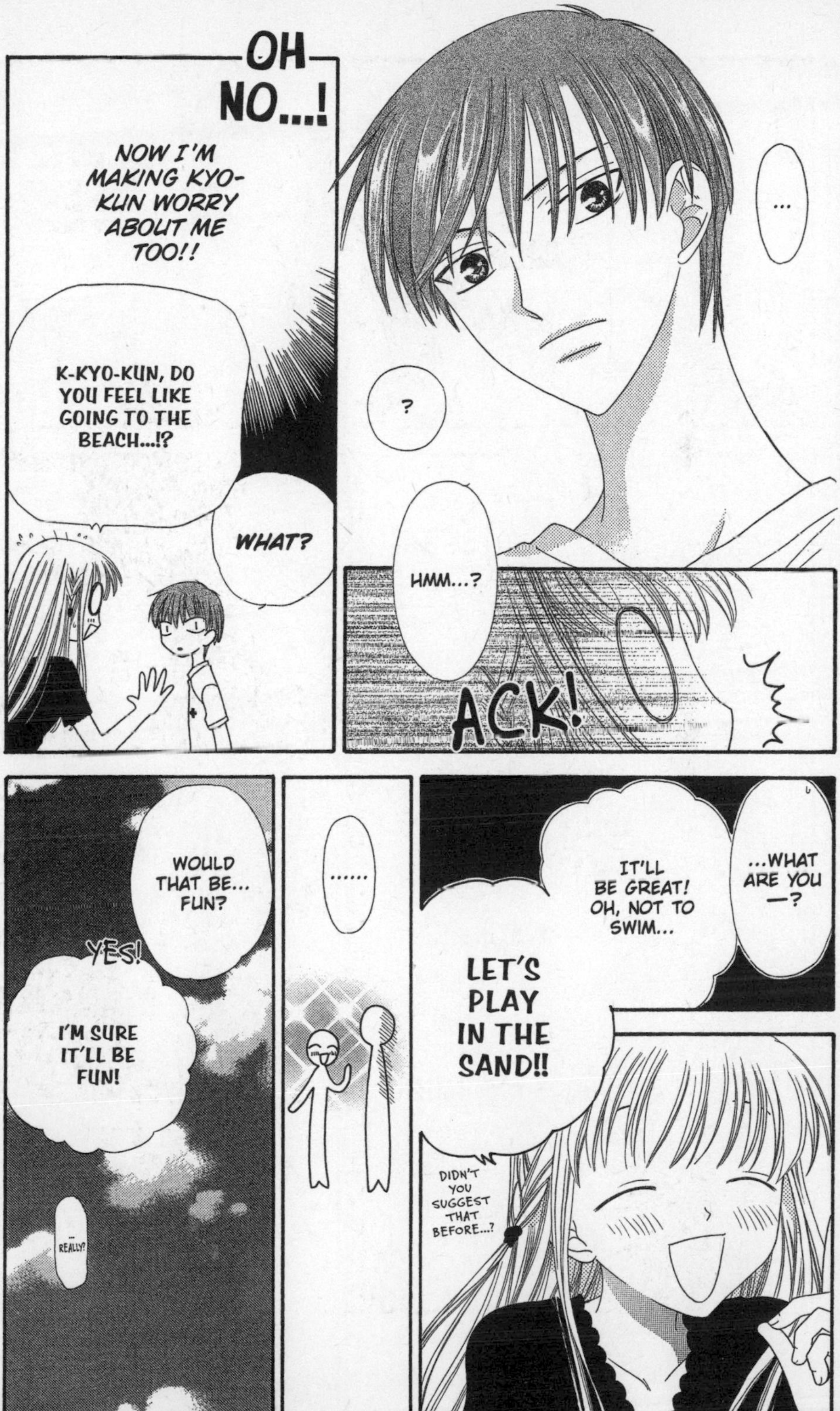
...
?
HMM...?
ACK!
OH NO...!
NOW I'M MAKING KYO-KUN WORRY ABOUT ME TOO!!
K-KYO-KUN, DO YOU FEEL LIKE GOING TO THE BEACH...!?
WHAT?
...WHAT ARE YOU—?
IT'LL BE GREAT! OH, NOT TO SWIM...
LET'S PLAY IN THE SAND!!
DIDN'T YOU SUGGEST THAT BEFORE...?
......
WOULD THAT BE... FUN?
YES!
I'M SURE IT'LL BE FUN!
...REALLY?

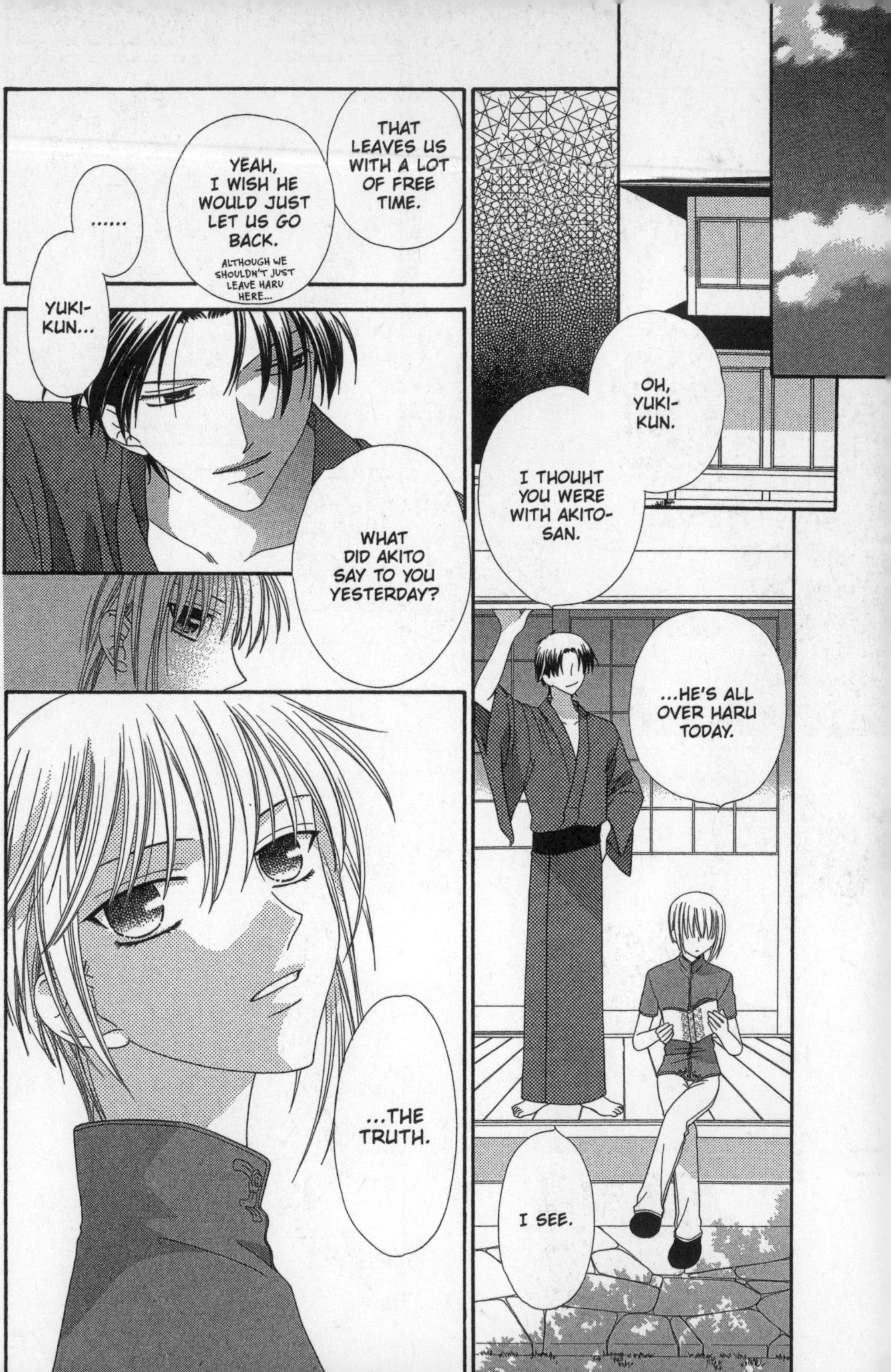
OH, YUKI-KUN.
I THOUHT YOU WERE WITH AKITO-SAN.
...HE'S ALL OVER HARU TODAY.
I SEE.
THAT LEAVES US WITH A LOT OF FREE TIME.
YEAH, I WISH HE WOULD JUST LET US GO BACK.
ALTHOUGH WE SHOULDN'T JUST LEAVE HARU HERE...
......
YUKI-KUN...
WHAT DID AKITO SAY TO YOU YESTERDAY?
...THE TRUTH.

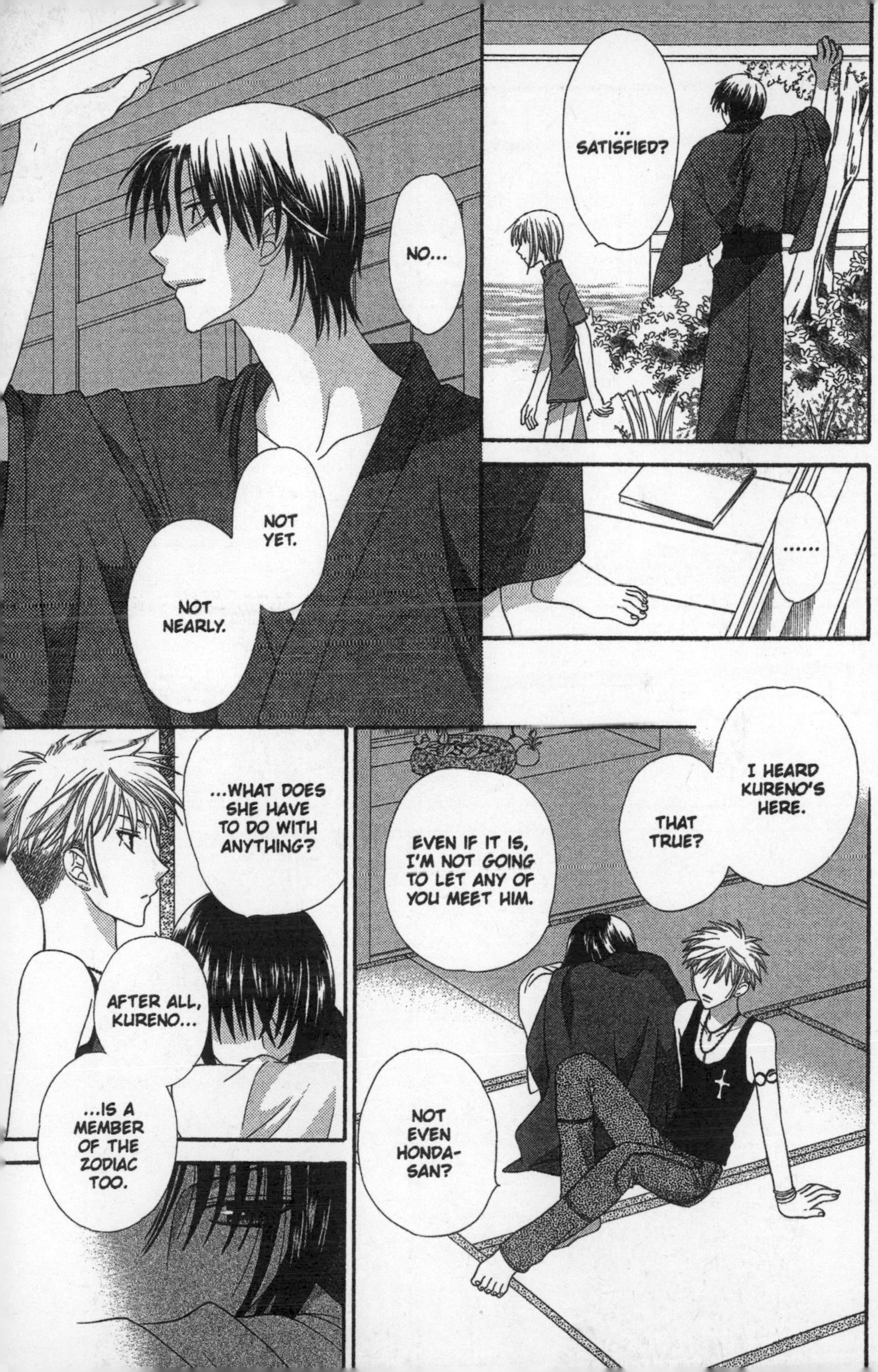
...SATISFIED?
......
NO...
NOT YET.
NOT NEARLY.
I HEARD KURENO'S HERE.
THAT TRUE?
EVEN IF IT IS, I'M NOT GOING TO LET ANY OF YOU MEET HIM.
NOT EVEN HONDA-SAN?
...WHAT DOES SHE HAVE TO DO WITH ANYTHING?
AFTER ALL, KURENO...
...IS A MEMBER OF THE ZODIAC TOO.

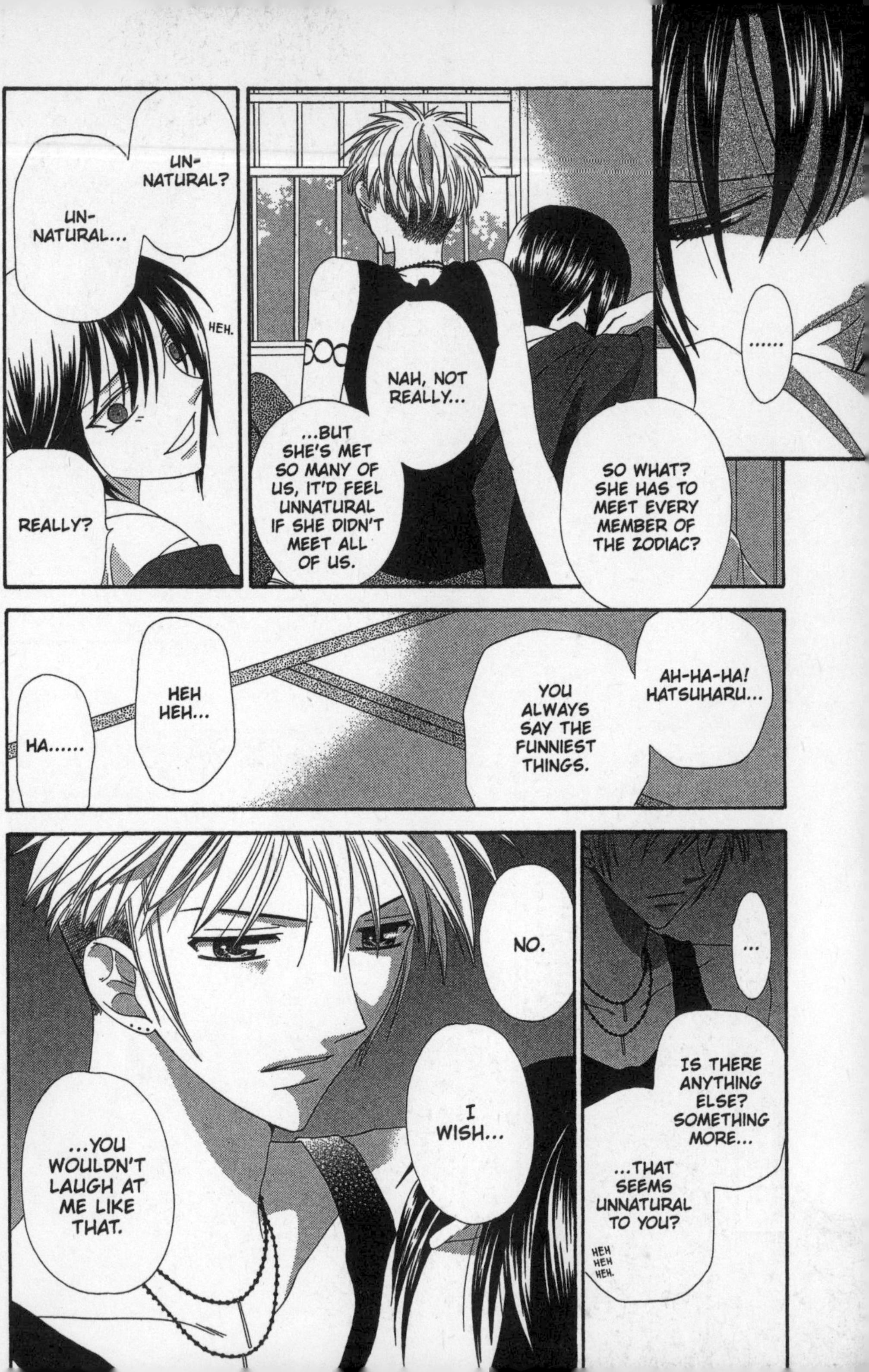
......
SO WHAT? SHE HAS TO MEET EVERY MEMBER OF THE ZODIAC?
NAH, NOT REALLY...
...BUT SHE'S MET SO MANY OF US, IT'D FEEL UNNATURAL IF SHE DIDN'T MEET ALL OF US.
UN-NATURAL?
UN-NATURAL...
HEH.
REALLY?
AH-HA-HA! HATSUHARU...
YOU ALWAYS SAY THE FUNNIEST THINGS.
HEH HEH...
HA......
...
IS THERE ANYTHING ELSE? SOMETHING MORE...
...THAT SEEMS UNNATURAL TO YOU?
HEH HEH HEH.
NO.
I WISH...
...YOU WOULDN'T LAUGH AT ME LIKE THAT.

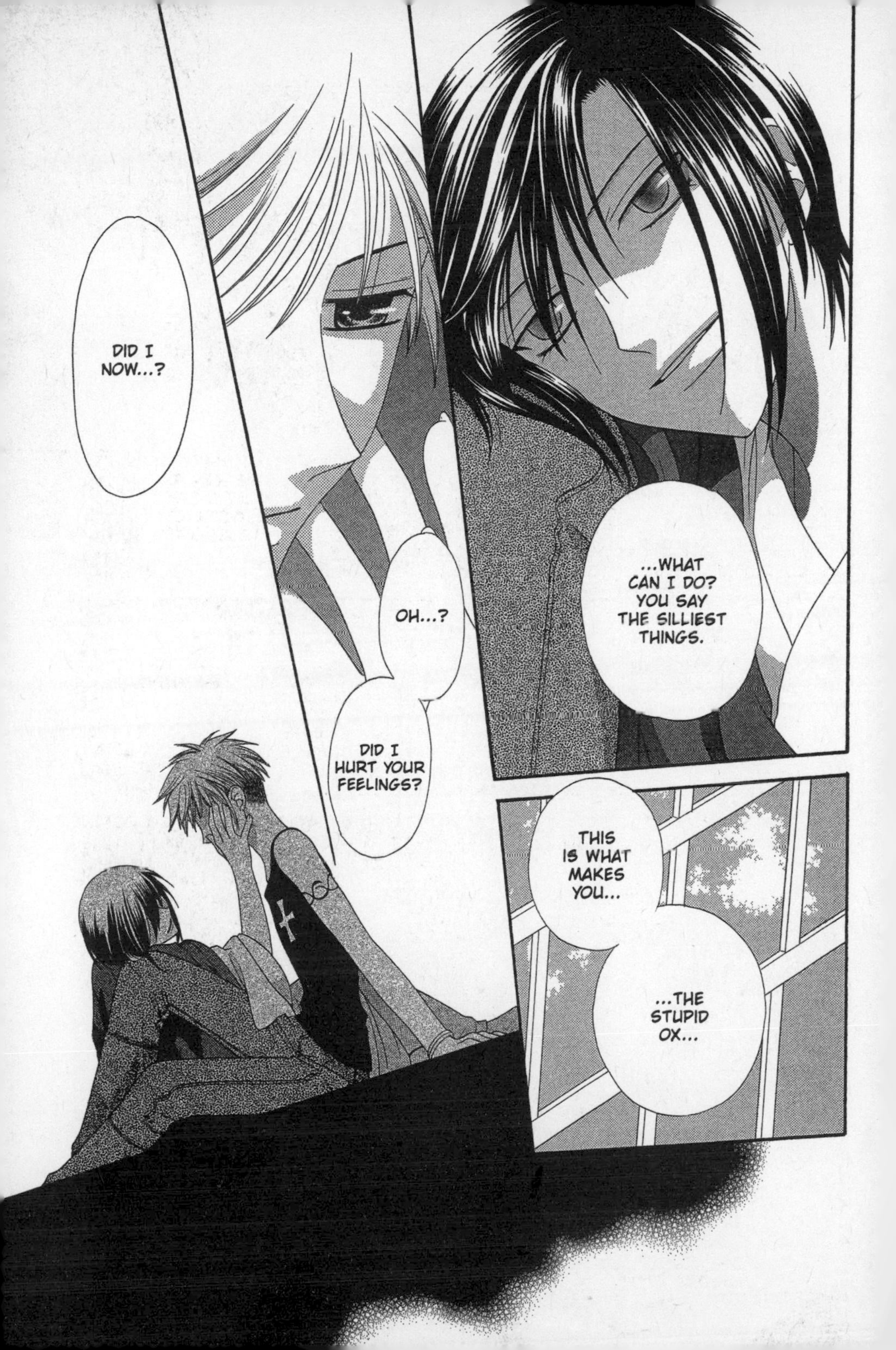
...WHAT CAN I DO? YOU SAY THE SILLIEST THINGS.
OH...?
DID I HURT YOUR FEELINGS?
DID I NOW...?
THIS IS WHAT MAKES YOU...
...THE STUPID OX...

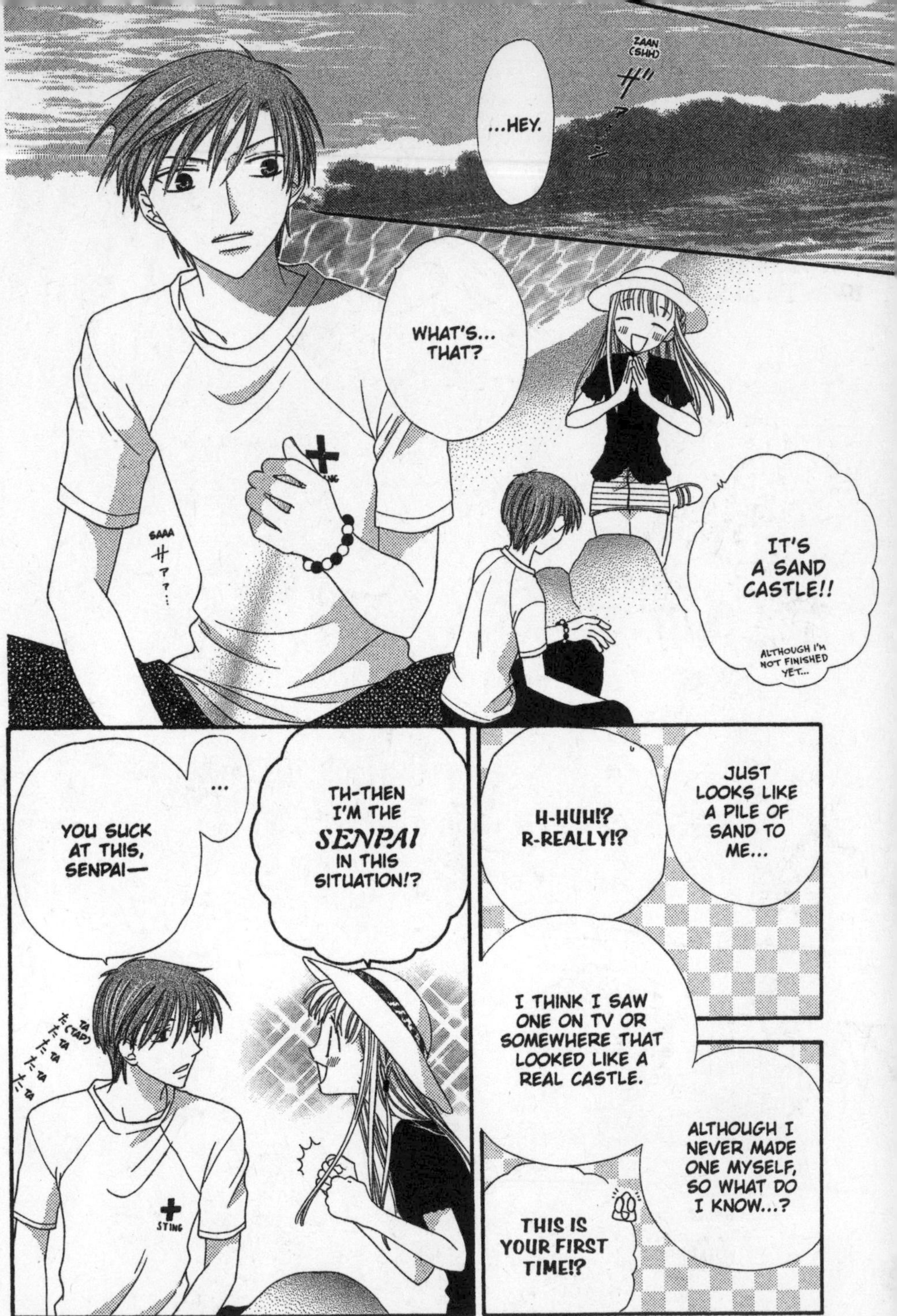
ZAAN (SHH)
...HEY.
WHAT'S... THAT?
IT'S A SAND CASTLE!!
ALTHOUGH I'M NOT FINISHED YET...
SAAA
JUST LOOKS LIKE A PILE OF SAND TO ME...
H-HUH!? R-REALLY!?
I THINK I SAW ONE ON TV OR SOMEWHERE THAT LOOKED LIKE A REAL CASTLE.
ALTHOUGH I NEVER MADE ONE MYSELF, SO WHAT DO I KNOW...?
THIS IS YOUR FIRST TIME!?
TH-THEN I'M THE *SENPAI* IN THIS SITUATION!?
...
YOU SUCK AT THIS, SENPAI—
TA (TAP)

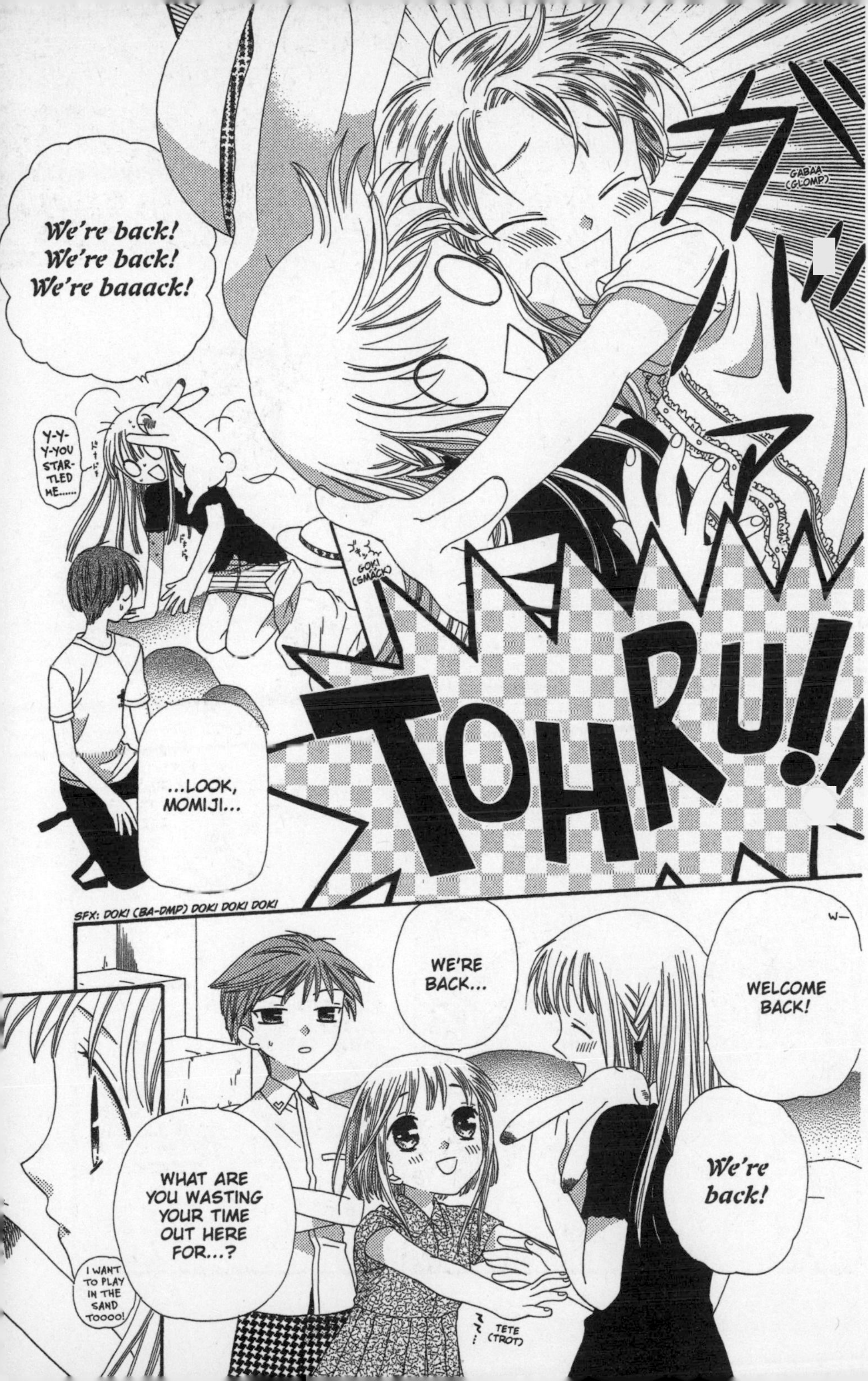
GABAA (GLOMP)
TOHRU!!
We're back! We're back! We're baaack!
Y-Y-Y-YOU STARTLED ME......
GOKI (SMACK)
...LOOK, MOMIJI...
SFX: DOKI (BA-DMP) DOKI DOKI DOKI
W—
WELCOME BACK!
WE'RE BACK...
We're back!
WHAT ARE YOU WASTING YOUR TIME OUT HERE FOR...?
I WANT TO PLAY IN THE SAND TOOOO!
TETE (TROT)

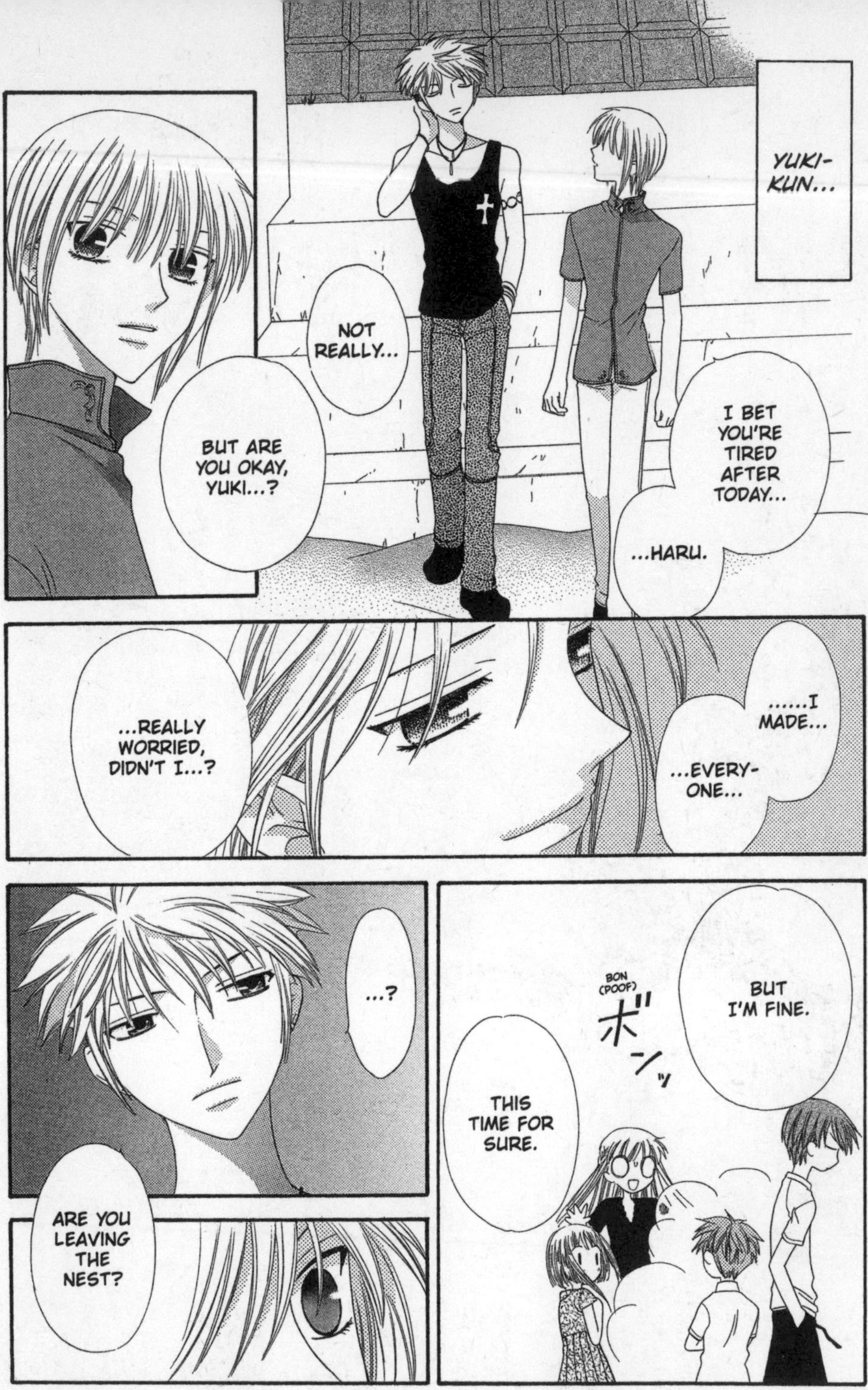
YUKI-KUN...
I BET YOU'RE TIRED AFTER TODAY...
...HARU.
NOT REALLY...
BUT ARE YOU OKAY, YUKI...?
......I MADE...
...EVERY-ONE...
...REALLY WORRIED, DIDN'T I...?
BUT I'M FINE.
BON (POOF)
ボンッ
THIS TIME FOR SURE.
...?
ARE YOU LEAVING THE NEST?

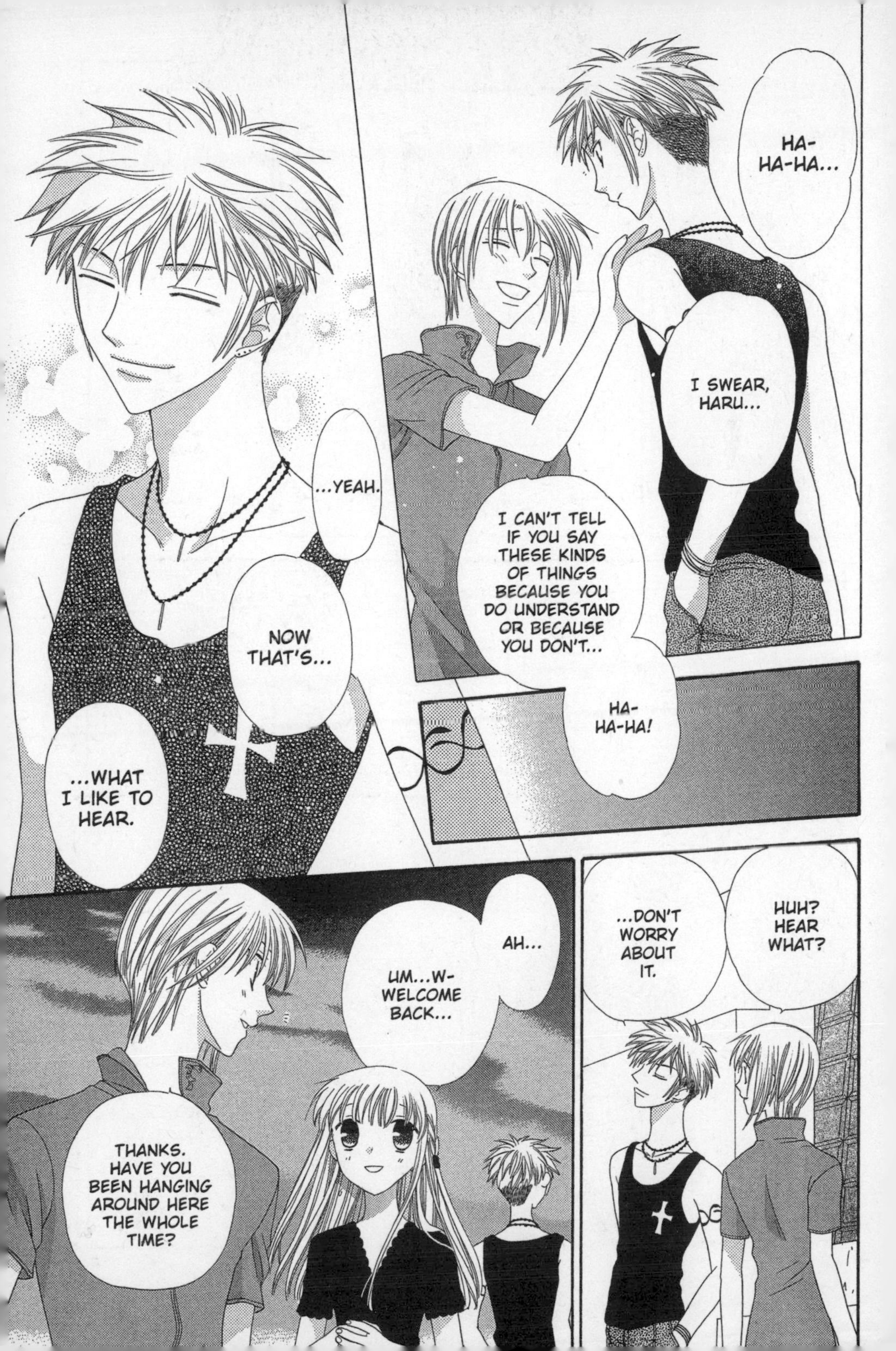
HA-HA-HA...
I SWEAR, HARU...
I CAN'T TELL IF YOU SAY THESE KINDS OF THINGS BECAUSE YOU DO UNDERSTAND OR BECAUSE YOU DON'T...
HA-HA-HA!
...YEAH.
NOW THAT'S...
...WHAT I LIKE TO HEAR.
HUH? HEAR WHAT?
...DON'T WORRY ABOUT IT.
AH...
UM...W-WELCOME BACK...
THANKS. HAVE YOU BEEN HANGING AROUND HERE THE WHOLE TIME?

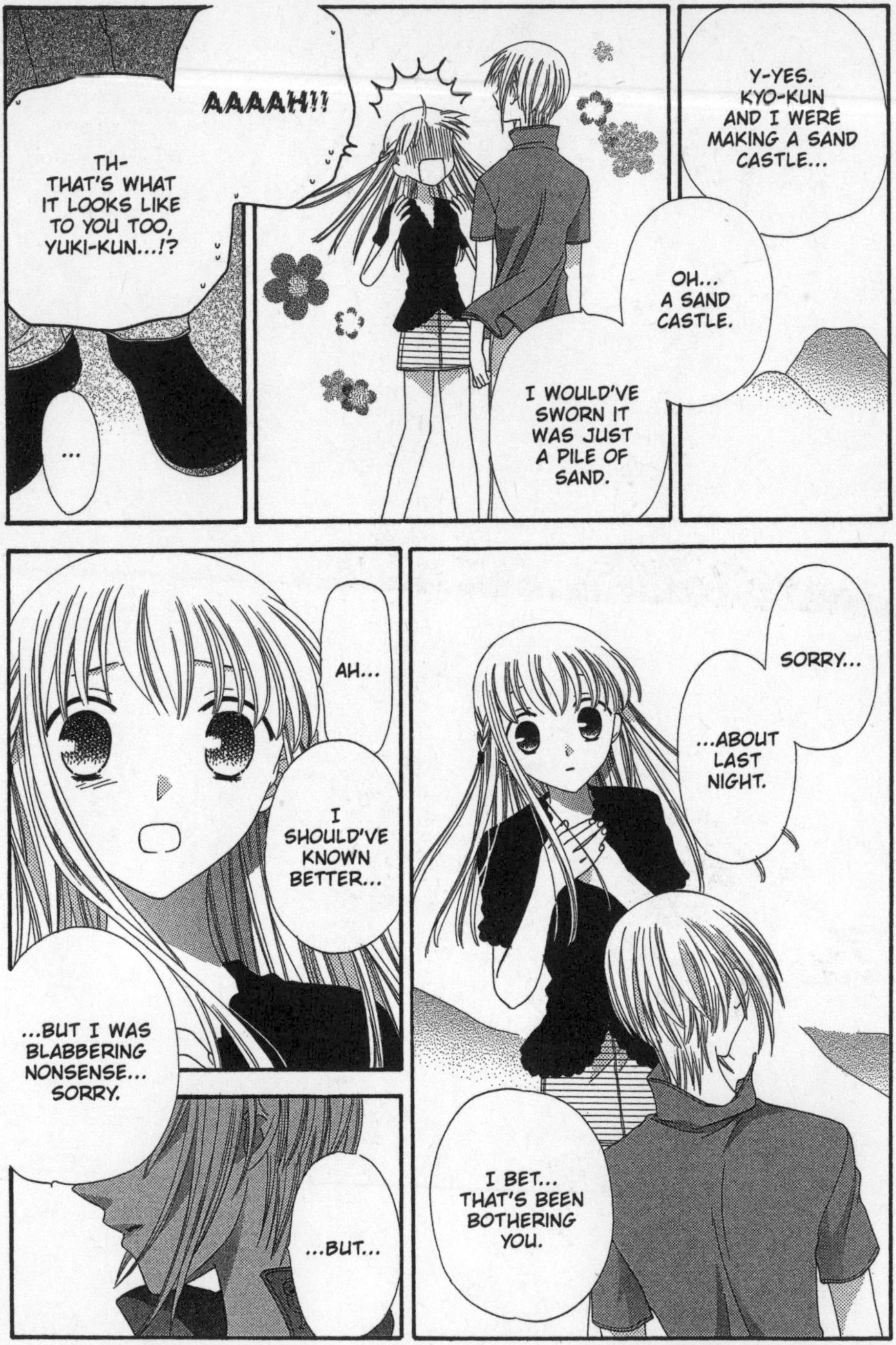
Y-YES. KYO-KUN AND I WERE MAKING A SAND CASTLE...
OH... A SAND CASTLE.
I WOULD'VE SWORN IT WAS JUST A PILE OF SAND.
AAAAH!!
TH- THAT'S WHAT IT LOOKS LIKE TO YOU TOO, YUKI-KUN...!?
...
SORRY...
...ABOUT LAST NIGHT.
I BET... THAT'S BEEN BOTHERING YOU.
AH...
I SHOULD'VE KNOWN BETTER...
...BUT I WAS BLABBERING NONSENSE... SORRY.
...BUT...

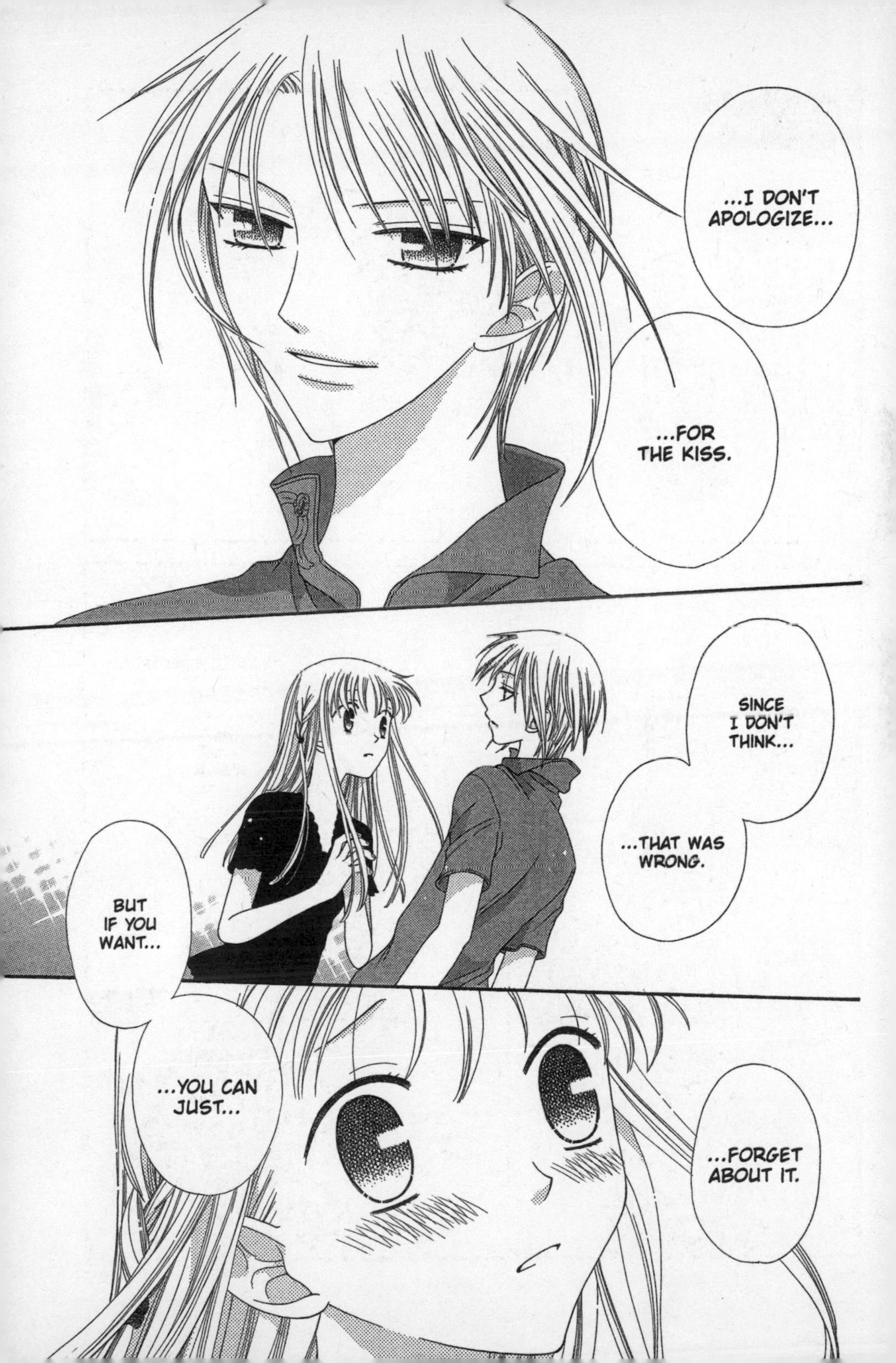
...I DON'T APOLOGIZE...
...FOR THE KISS.
SINCE I DON'T THINK...
...THAT WAS WRONG.
BUT IF YOU WANT...
...YOU CAN JUST...
...FORGET ABOUT IT.

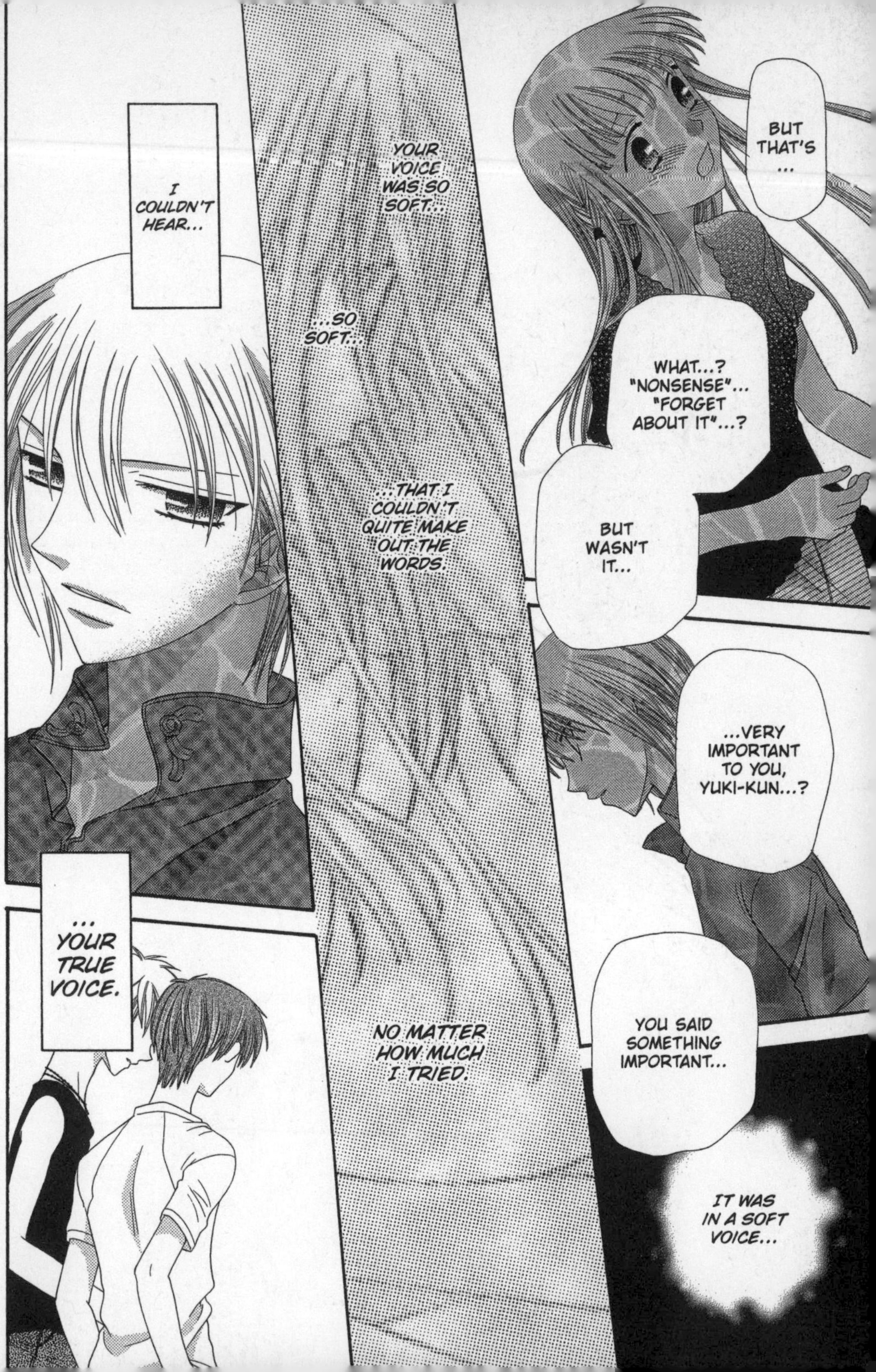
BUT THAT'S...
WHAT...? "NONSENSE"... "FORGET ABOUT IT"...?
BUT WASN'T IT...
...VERY IMPORTANT TO YOU, YUKI-KUN...?
YOU SAID SOMETHING IMPORTANT...
IT WAS IN A SOFT VOICE...
YOUR VOICE WAS SO SOFT...
...SO SOFT...
...THAT I COULDN'T QUITE MAKE OUT THE WORDS.
NO MATTER HOW MUCH I TRIED.
I COULDN'T HEAR...
...YOUR TRUE VOICE.

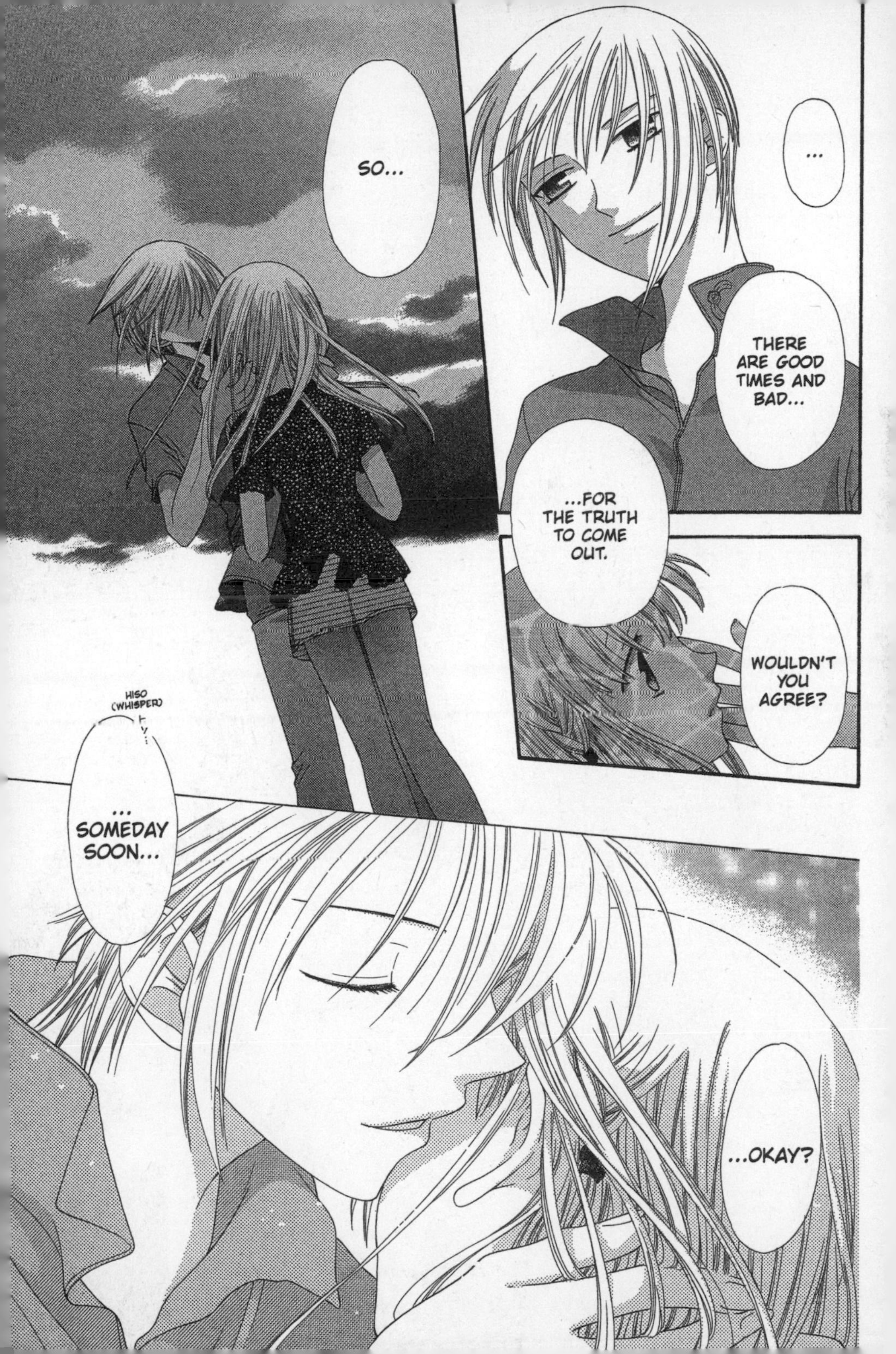

...
THERE ARE GOOD TIMES AND BAD...
...FOR THE TRUTH TO COME OUT.
WOULDN'T YOU AGREE?
SO...
HISO (WHISPER)
... SOMEDAY SOON...
...OKAY?

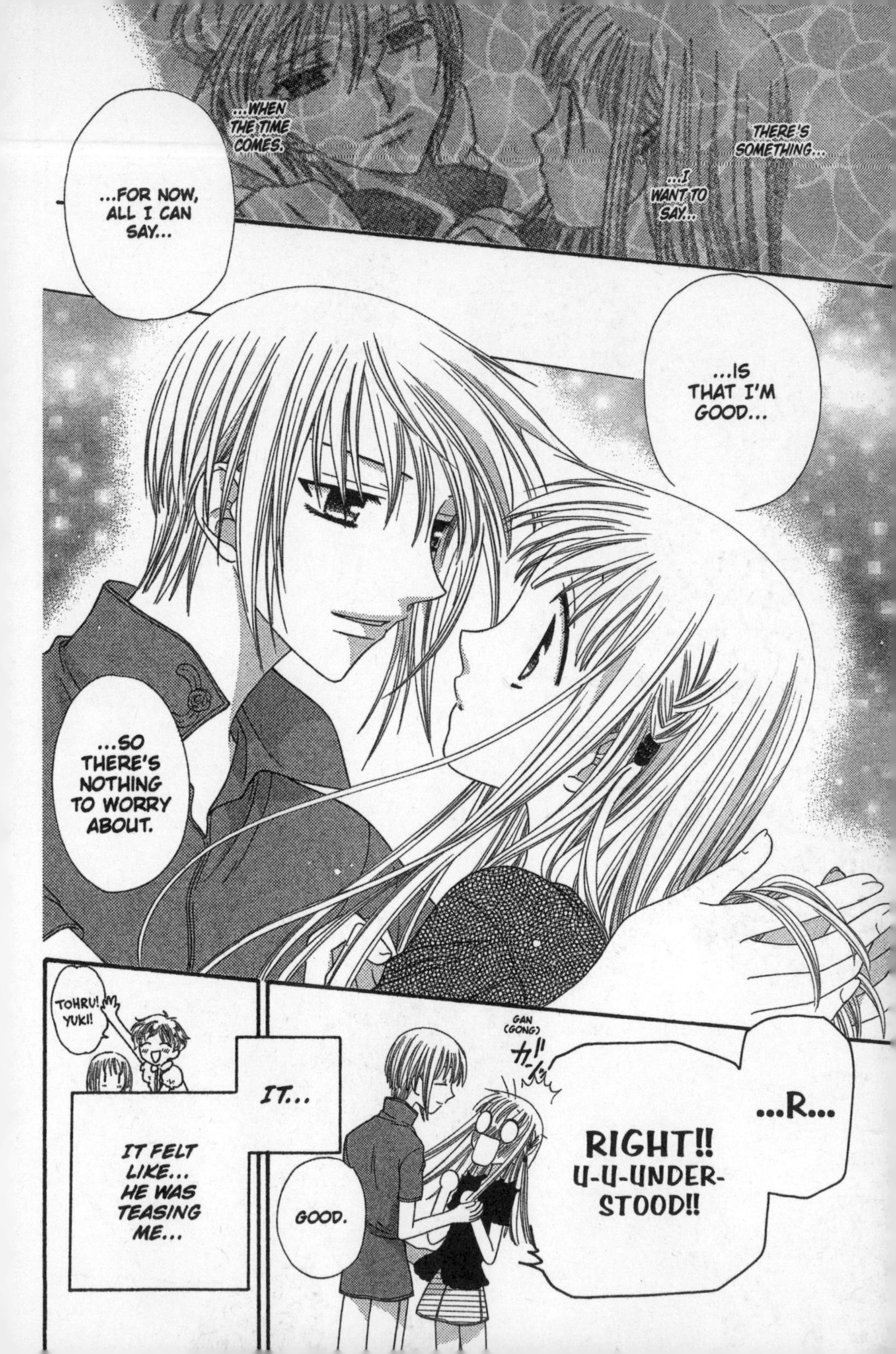
THERE'S SOMETHING...
...I WANT TO SAY...
...WHEN THE TIME COMES.
...FOR NOW, ALL I CAN SAY...
...IS THAT I'M GOOD...
...SO THERE'S NOTHING TO WORRY ABOUT.
GAN (GONG)
...R...
RIGHT!! U-U-UNDER-STOOD!!
GOOD.
TOHRU! YUKI!
IT...
IT FELT LIKE... HE WAS TEASING ME...

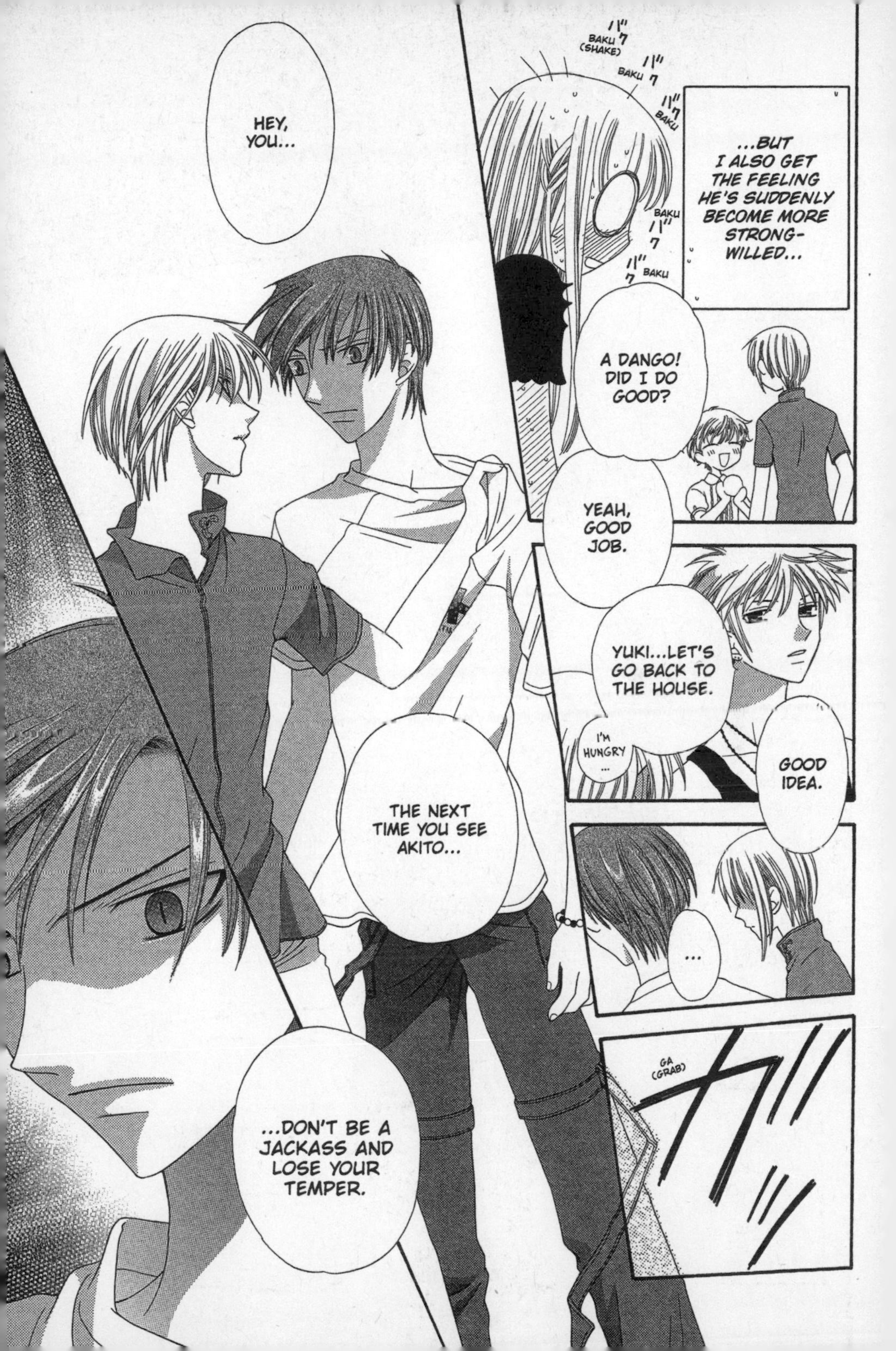

BAKU (SHAKE)
BAKU
BAKU
...BUT I ALSO GET THE FEELING HE'S SUDDENLY BECOME MORE STRONG-WILLED...
BAKU
BAKU
A DANGO! DID I DO GOOD?
YEAH, GOOD JOB.
YUKI...LET'S GO BACK TO THE HOUSE.
GOOD IDEA.
I'M HUNGRY...
...
GA (GRAB)
HEY, YOU...
THE NEXT TIME YOU SEE AKITO...
...DON'T BE A JACKASS AND LOSE YOUR TEMPER.

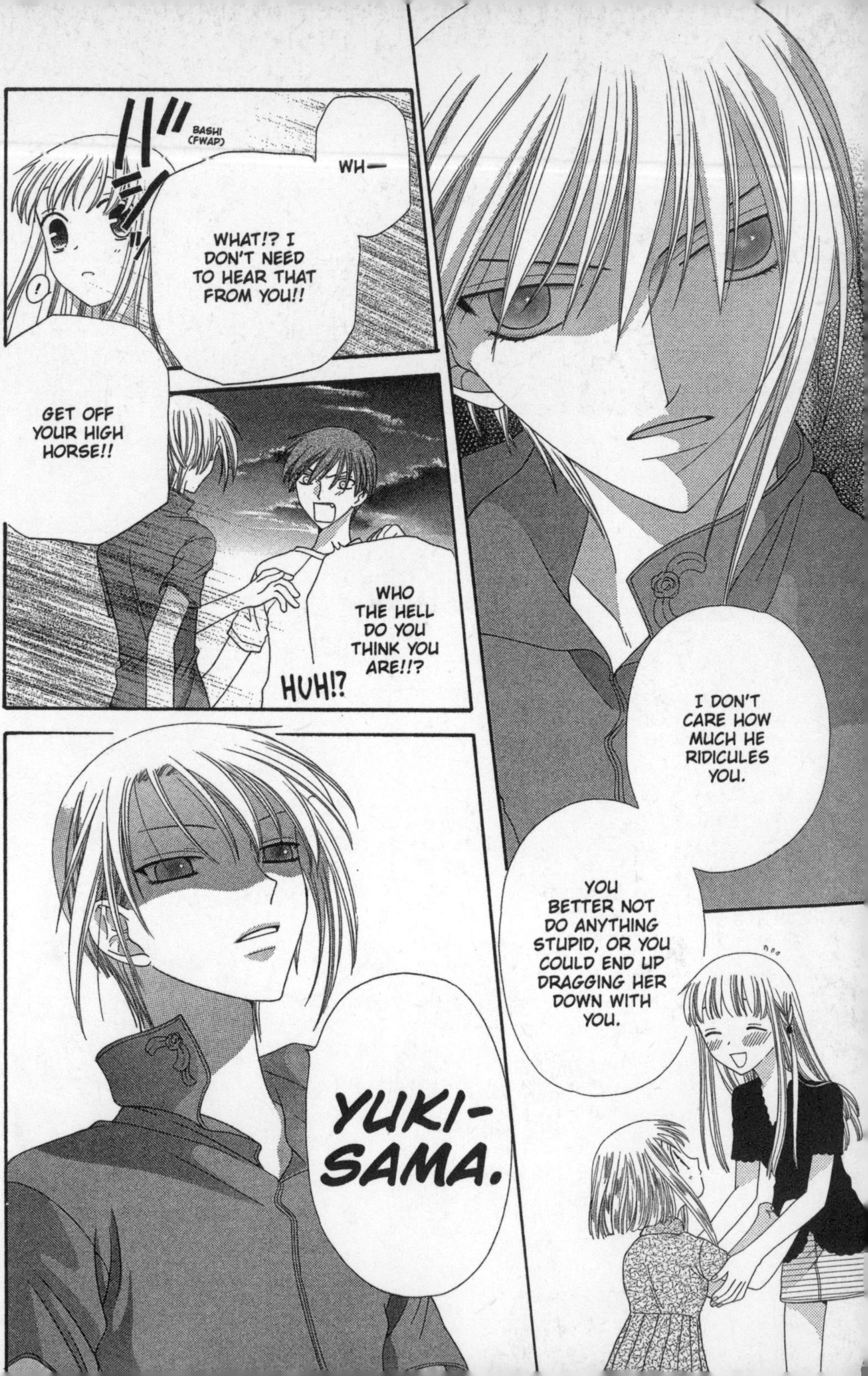
I DON'T CARE HOW MUCH HE RIDICULES YOU.
YOU BETTER NOT DO ANYTHING STUPID, OR YOU COULD END UP DRAGGING HER DOWN WITH YOU.
BASHI (FWAP)
WH—
WHAT!? I DON'T NEED TO HEAR THAT FROM YOU!!
WHO THE HELL DO YOU THINK YOU ARE!!?
HUH!?
GET OFF YOUR HIGH HORSE!!
YUKI-SAMA.

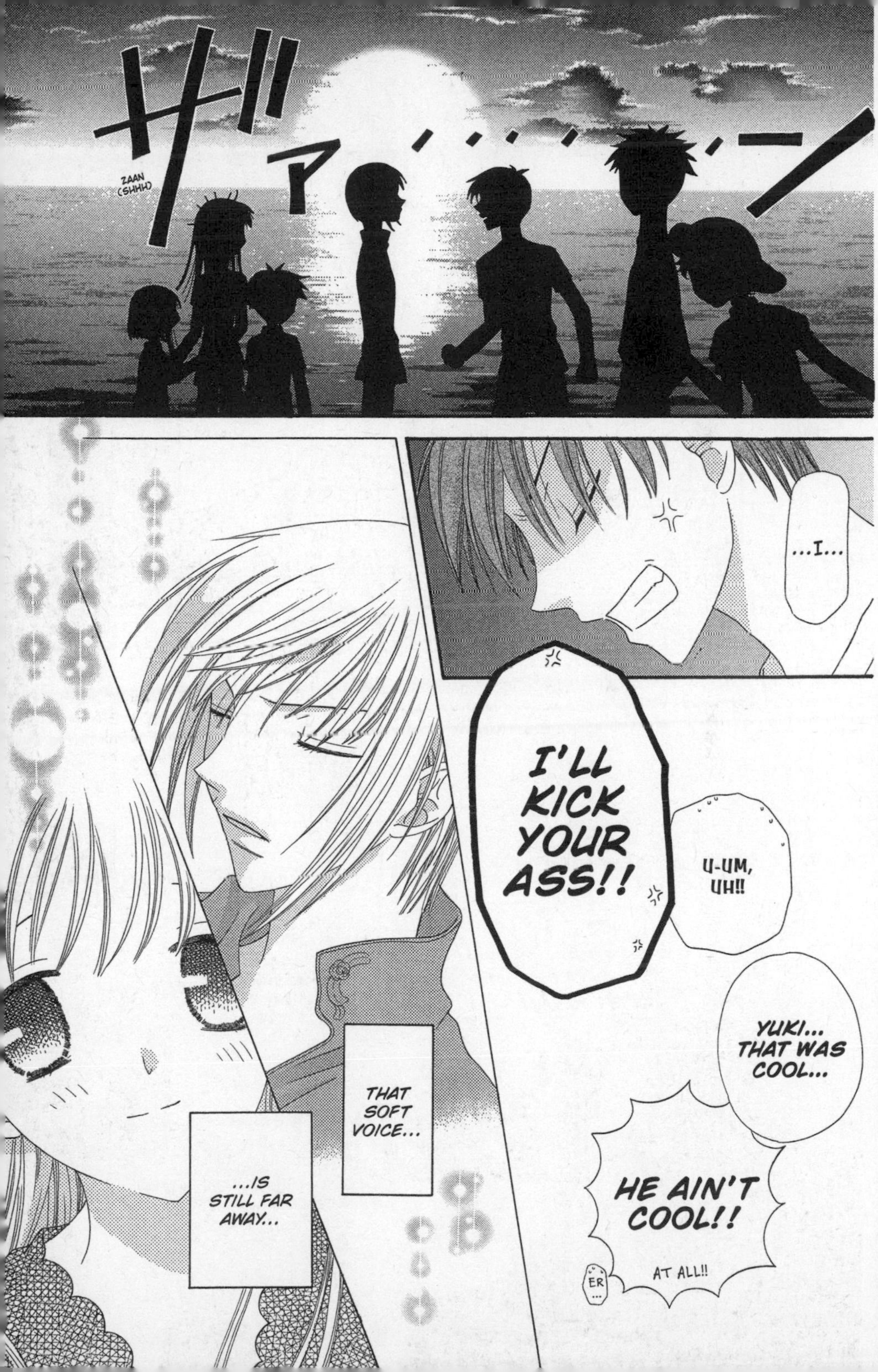
ZAAN (SHHH)
...I...
I'LL KICK YOUR ASS!!
U-UM, UH!!
YUKI... THAT WAS COOL...
HE AIN'T COOL!!
AT ALL!!
ER...
THAT SOFT VOICE...
...IS STILL FAR AWAY...

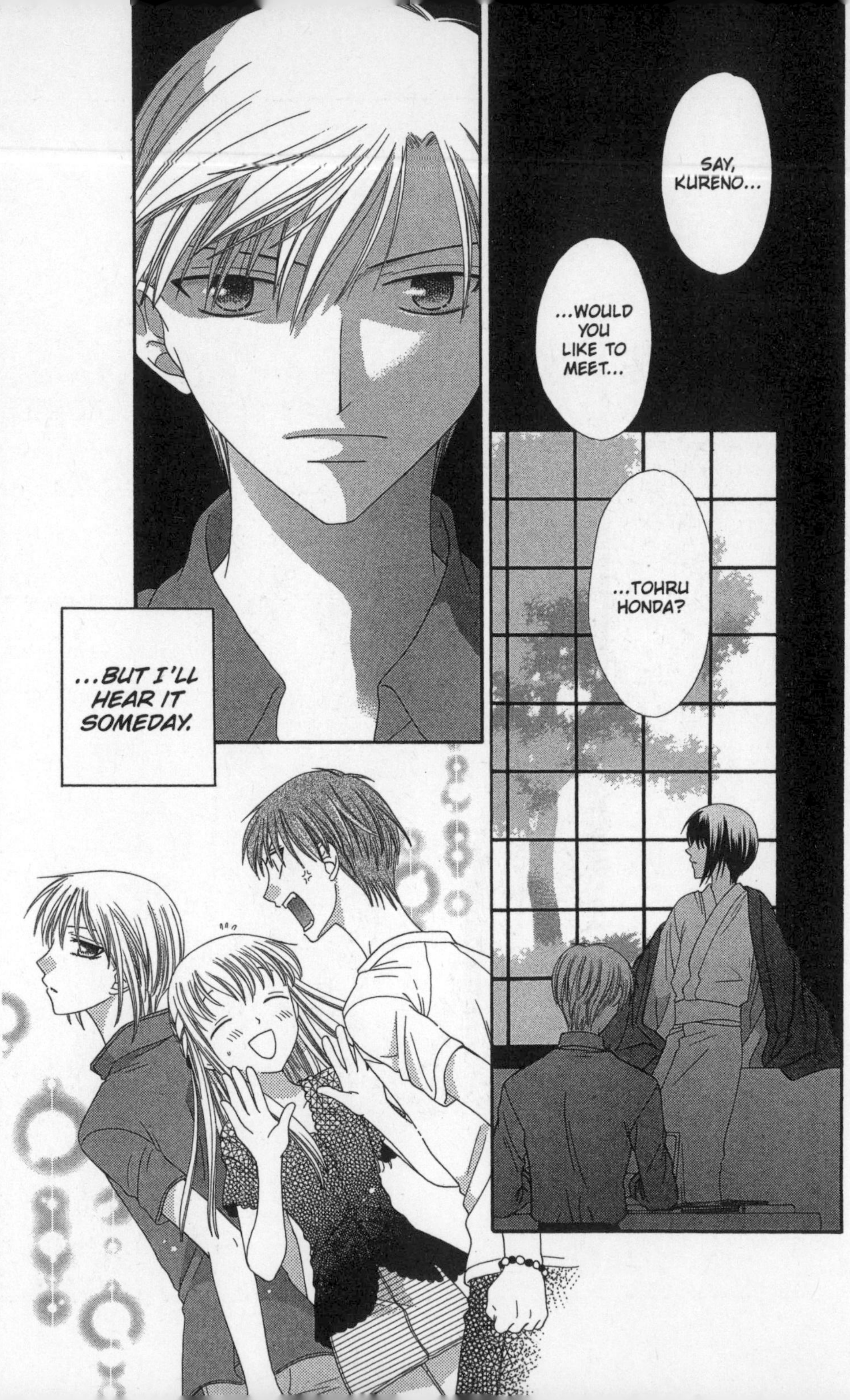
SAY, KURENO...
...WOULD YOU LIKE TO MEET...
...TOHRU HONDA?
...BUT I'LL HEAR IT SOMEDAY.

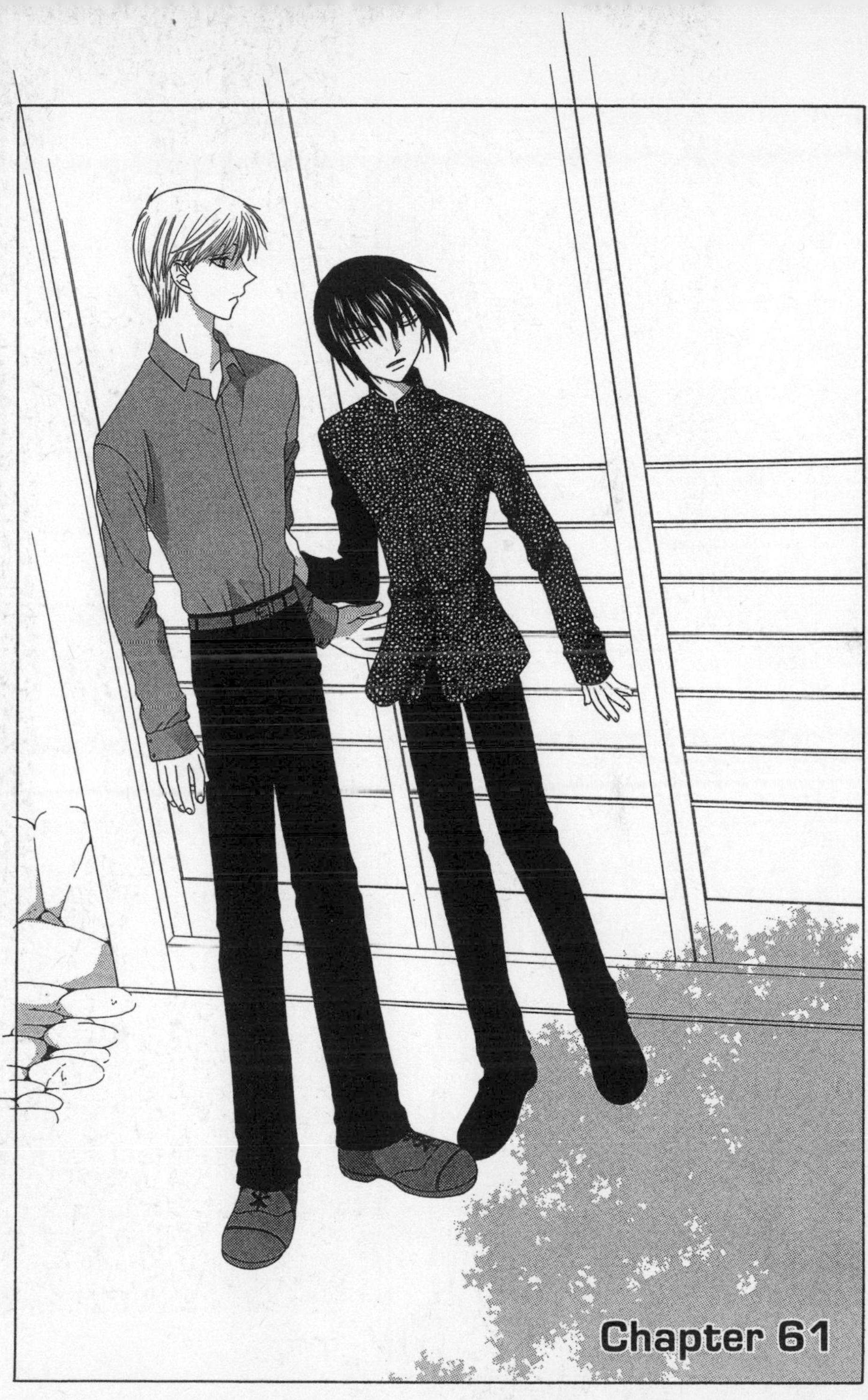
Chapter 61

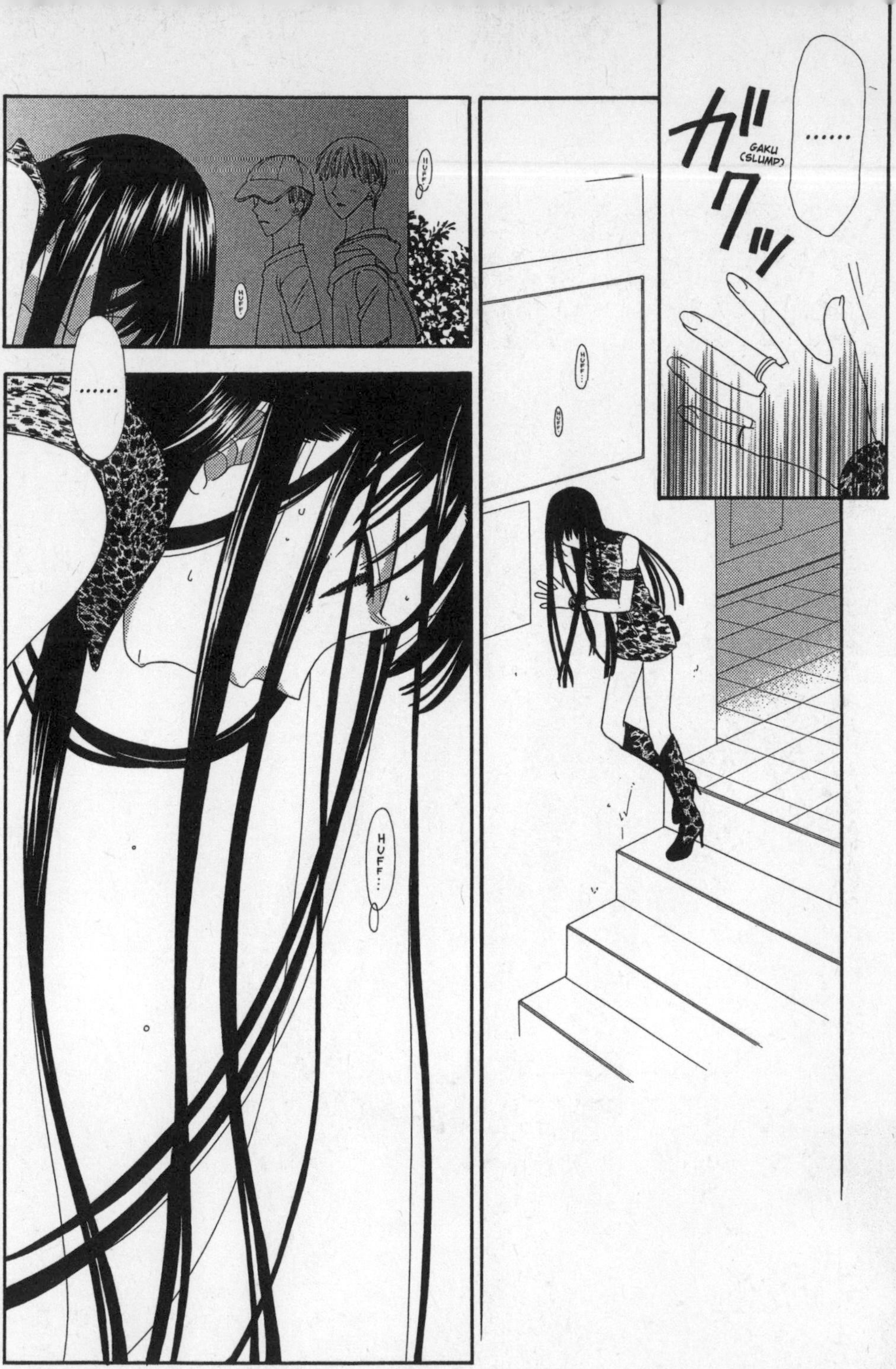

……
ガクッ
GAKU (SLUMP)
HUFF...
HUFF
HUFF
HUFF
……
HUFF...

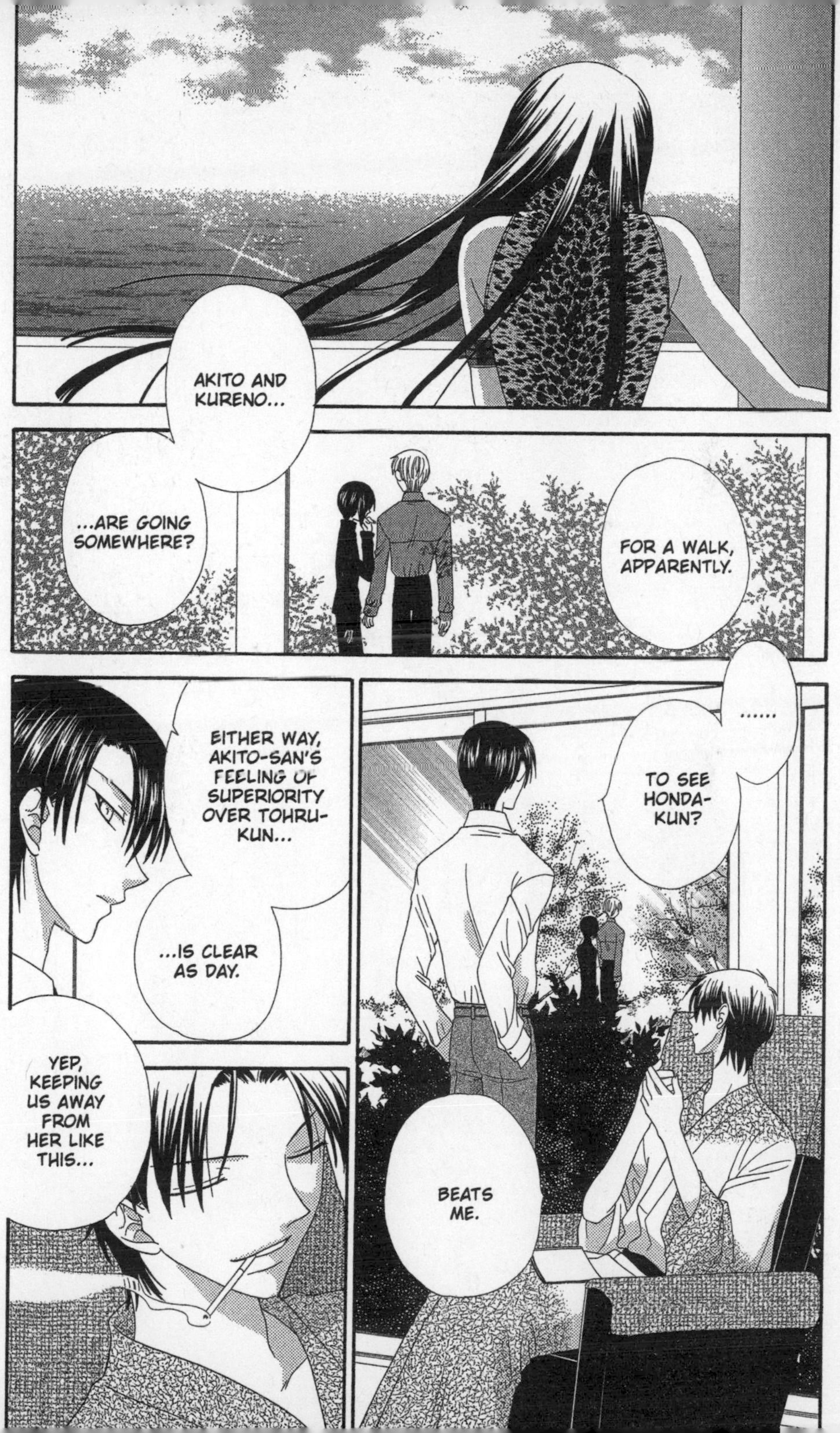
AKITO AND KURENO...
...ARE GOING SOMEWHERE?
FOR A WALK, APPARENTLY.
......
TO SEE HONDA-KUN?
BEATS ME.
EITHER WAY, AKITO-SAN'S FEELING OF SUPERIORITY OVER TOHRU-KUN...
...IS CLEAR AS DAY.
YEP, KEEPING US AWAY FROM HER LIKE THIS...

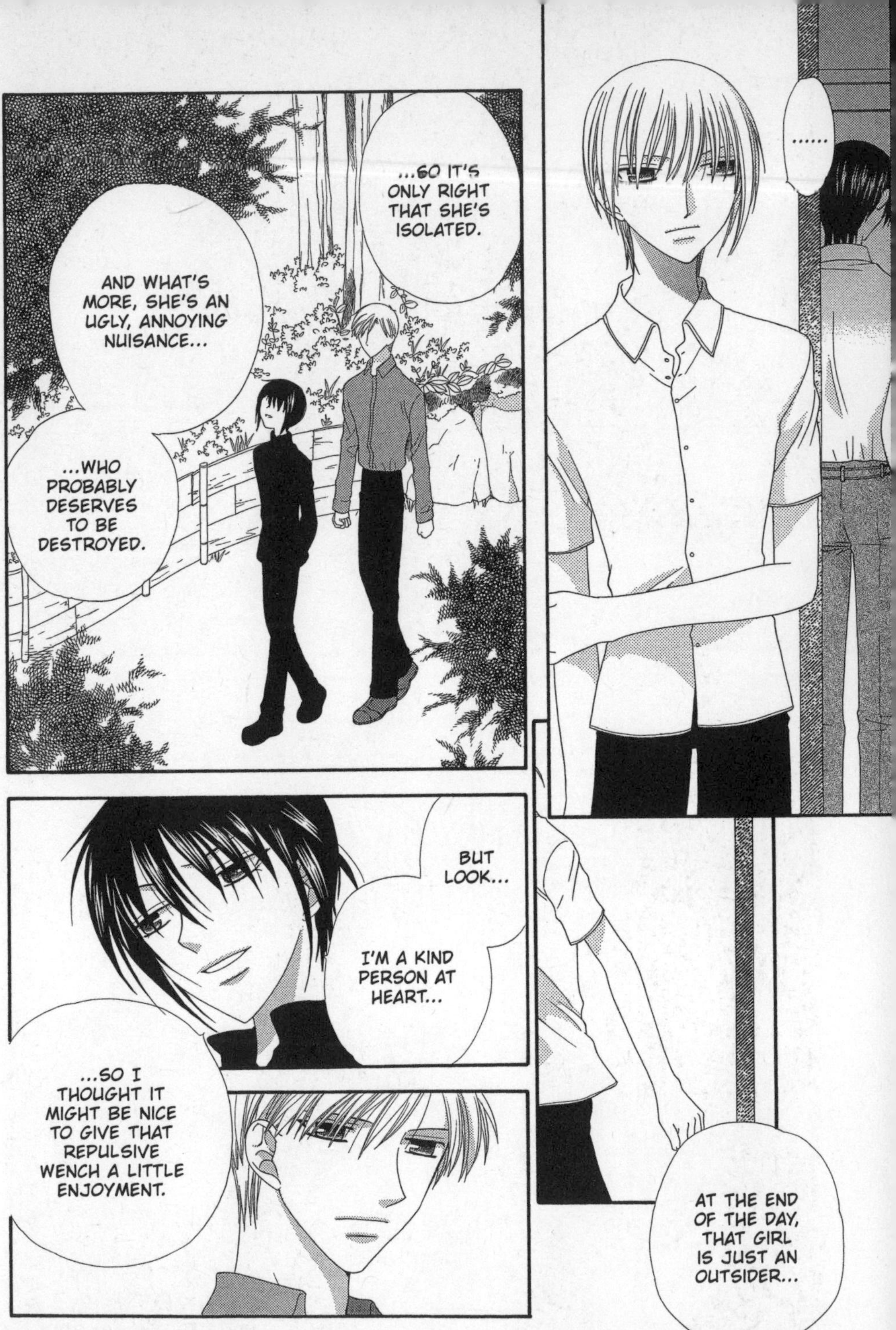
......
...SO IT'S ONLY RIGHT THAT SHE'S ISOLATED.
AND WHAT'S MORE, SHE'S AN UGLY, ANNOYING NUISANCE...
...WHO PROBABLY DESERVES TO BE DESTROYED.
AT THE END OF THE DAY, THAT GIRL IS JUST AN OUTSIDER...
BUT LOOK...
I'M A KIND PERSON AT HEART...
...SO I THOUGHT IT MIGHT BE NICE TO GIVE THAT REPULSIVE WENCH A LITTLE ENJOYMENT.

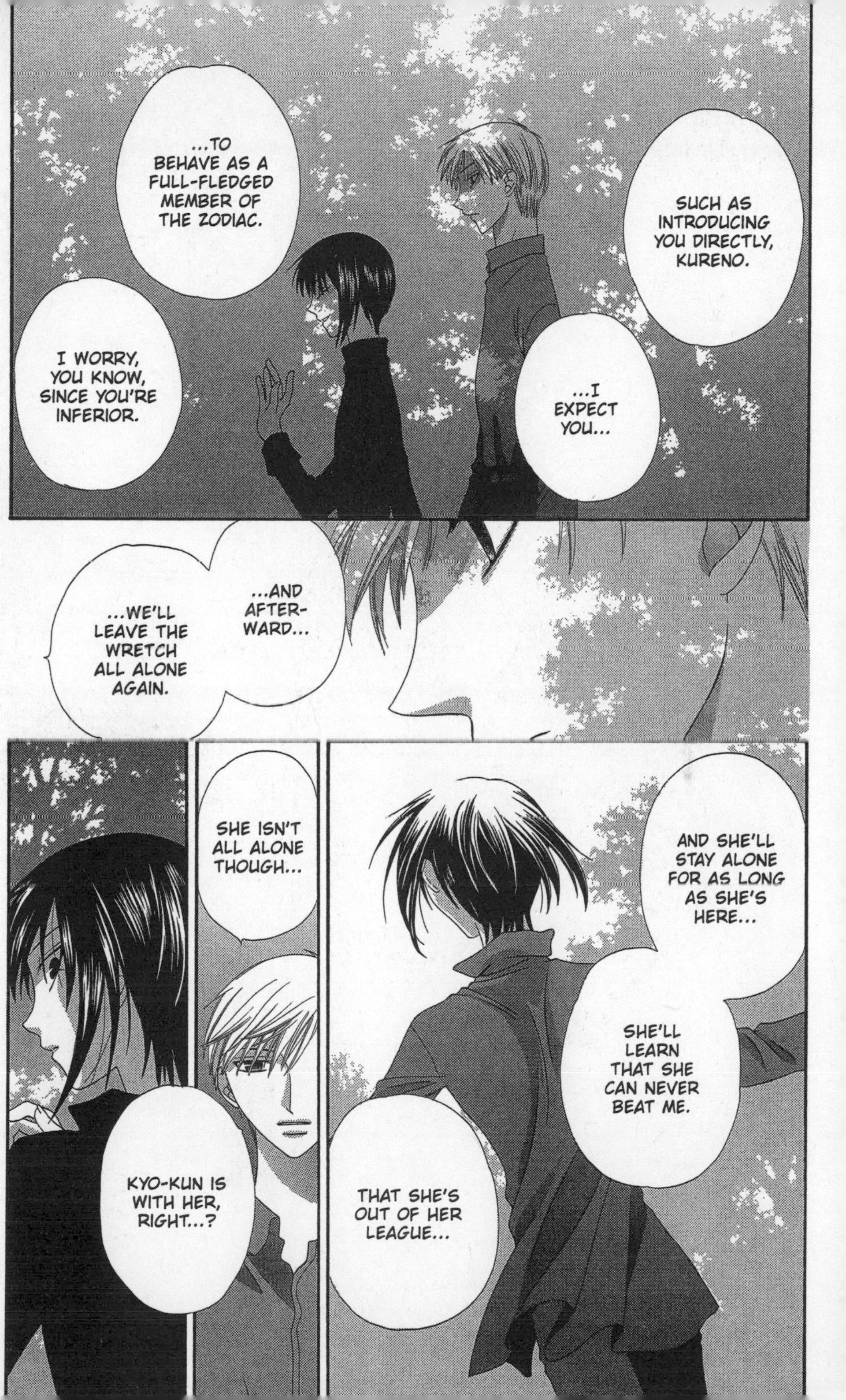
SUCH AS INTRODUCING YOU DIRECTLY, KURENO.
...I EXPECT YOU...
...TO BEHAVE AS A FULL-FLEDGED MEMBER OF THE ZODIAC.
I WORRY, YOU KNOW, SINCE YOU'RE INFERIOR.
...AND AFTER-WARD...
...WE'LL LEAVE THE WRETCH ALL ALONE AGAIN.
AND SHE'LL STAY ALONE FOR AS LONG AS SHE'S HERE...
SHE'LL LEARN THAT SHE CAN NEVER BEAT ME.
THAT SHE'S OUT OF HER LEAGUE...
SHE ISN'T ALL ALONE THOUGH...
KYO-KUN IS WITH HER, RIGHT...?

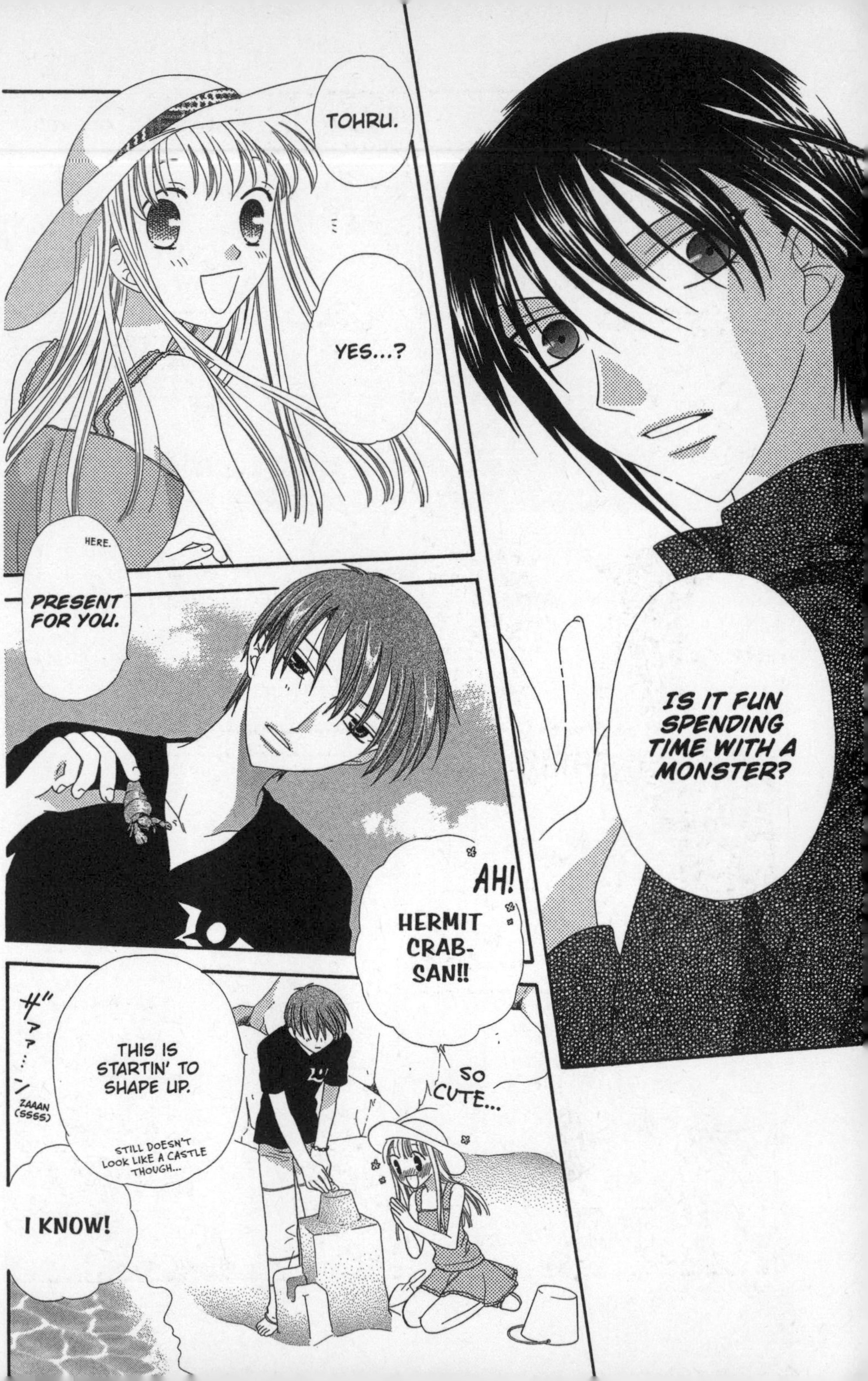
IS IT FUN SPENDING TIME WITH A MONSTER?
TOHRU.
YES...?
HERE.
PRESENT FOR YOU.
AH!
HERMIT CRAB-SAN!!
SO CUTE...
THIS IS STARTIN' TO SHAPE UP.
STILL DOESN'T LOOK LIKE A CASTLE THOUGH...
ザァァ…ン
ZAAAN (SSSS)
I KNOW!

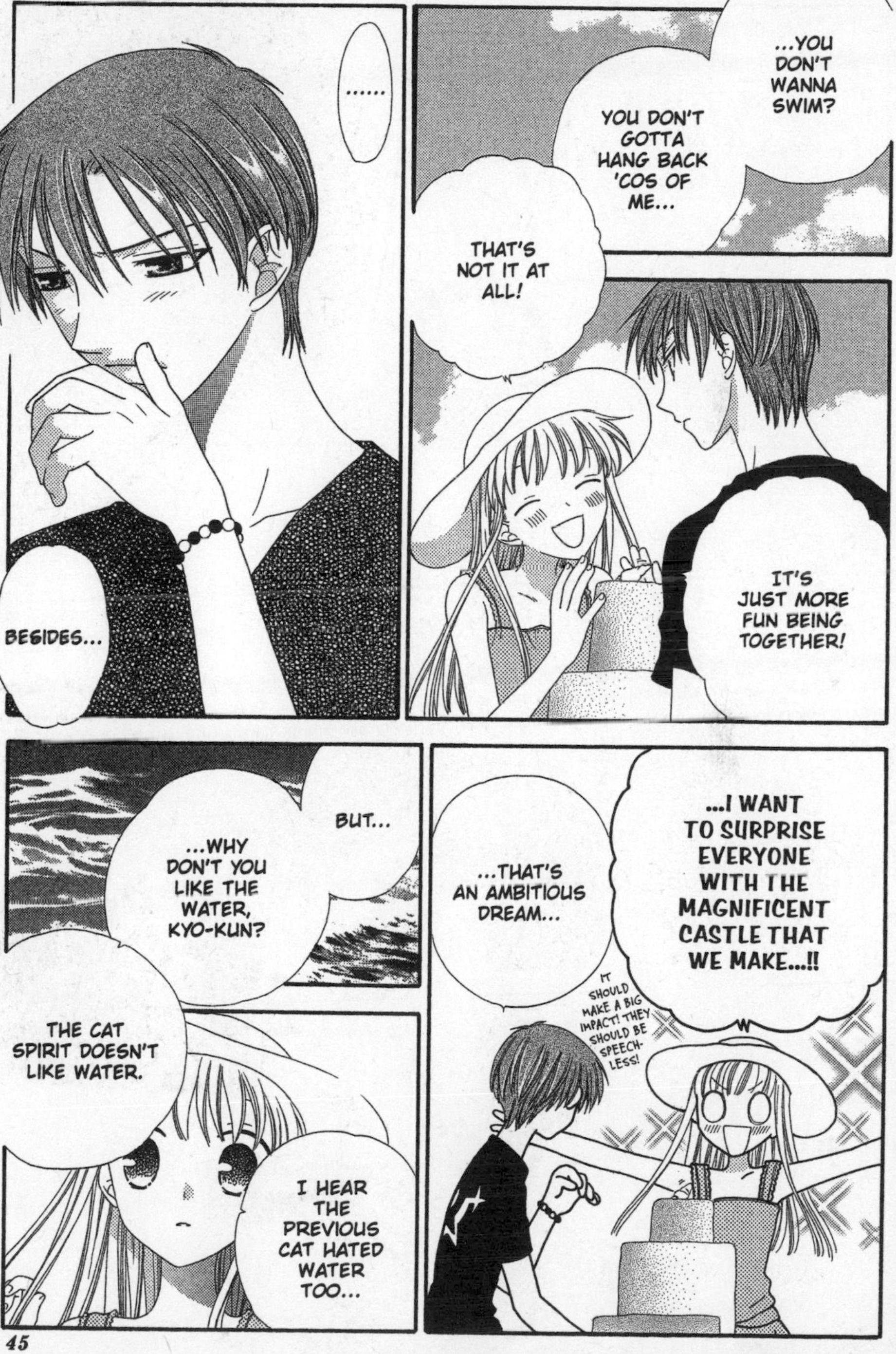
...YOU DON'T WANNA SWIM?
YOU DON'T GOTTA HANG BACK 'COS OF ME...
THAT'S NOT IT AT ALL!
IT'S JUST MORE FUN BEING TOGETHER!
......
BESIDES...
...I WANT TO SURPRISE EVERYONE WITH THE MAGNIFICENT CASTLE THAT WE MAKE...!!
IT SHOULD MAKE A BIG IMPACT! THEY SHOULD BE SPEECHLESS!
...THAT'S AN AMBITIOUS DREAM...
BUT...
...WHY DON'T YOU LIKE THE WATER, KYO-KUN?
THE CAT SPIRIT DOESN'T LIKE WATER.
I HEAR THE PREVIOUS CAT HATED WATER TOO...

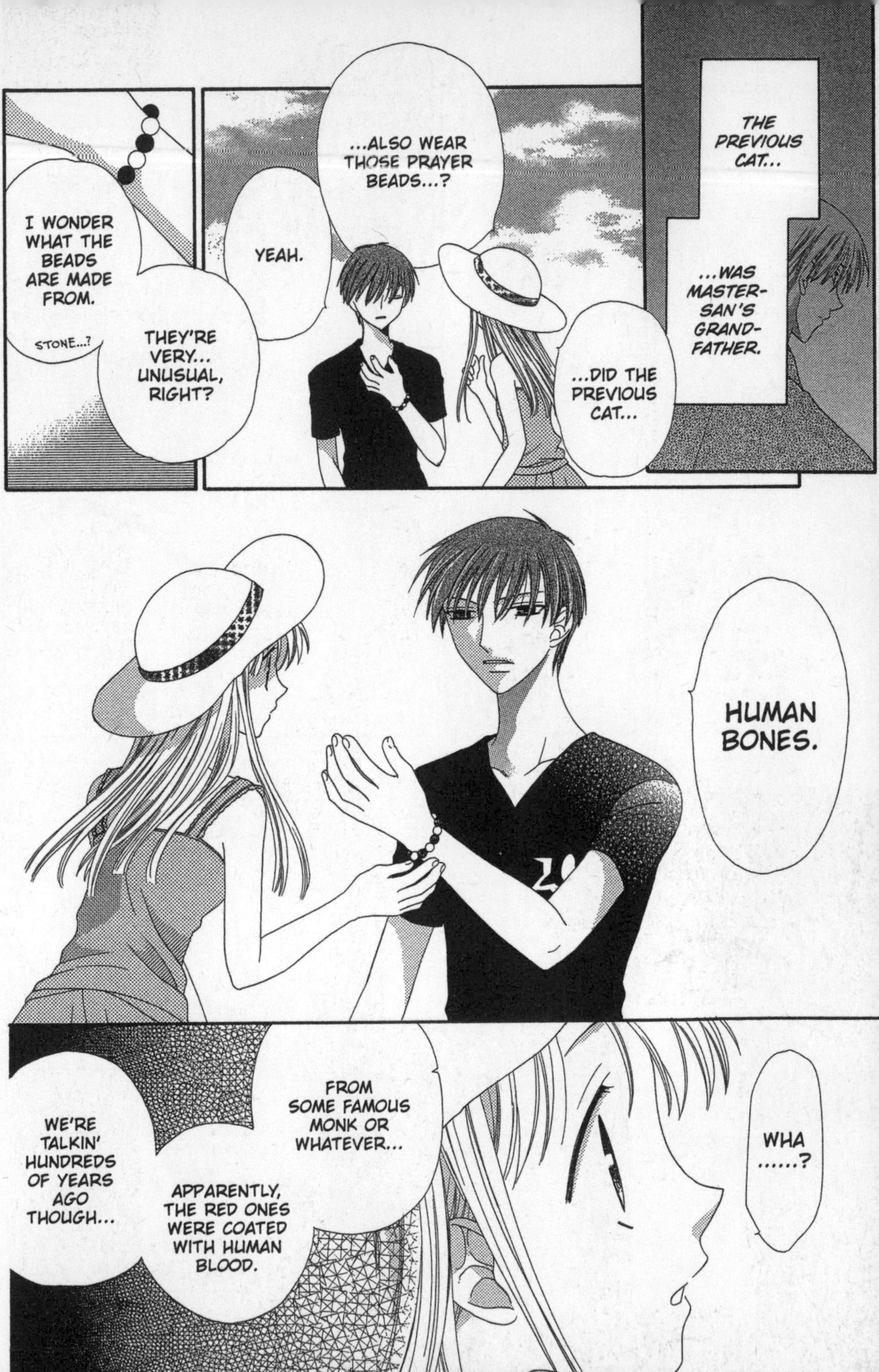
THE PREVIOUS CAT...
...WAS MASTER-SAN'S GRANDFATHER.
...DID THE PREVIOUS CAT...
...ALSO WEAR THOSE PRAYER BEADS...?
YEAH.
I WONDER WHAT THE BEADS ARE MADE FROM.
THEY'RE VERY... UNUSUAL, RIGHT?
STONE...?
HUMAN BONES.
WHA ......?
FROM SOME FAMOUS MONK OR WHATEVER...
APPARENTLY, THE RED ONES WERE COATED WITH HUMAN BLOOD.
WE'RE TALKIN' HUNDREDS OF YEARS AGO THOUGH...

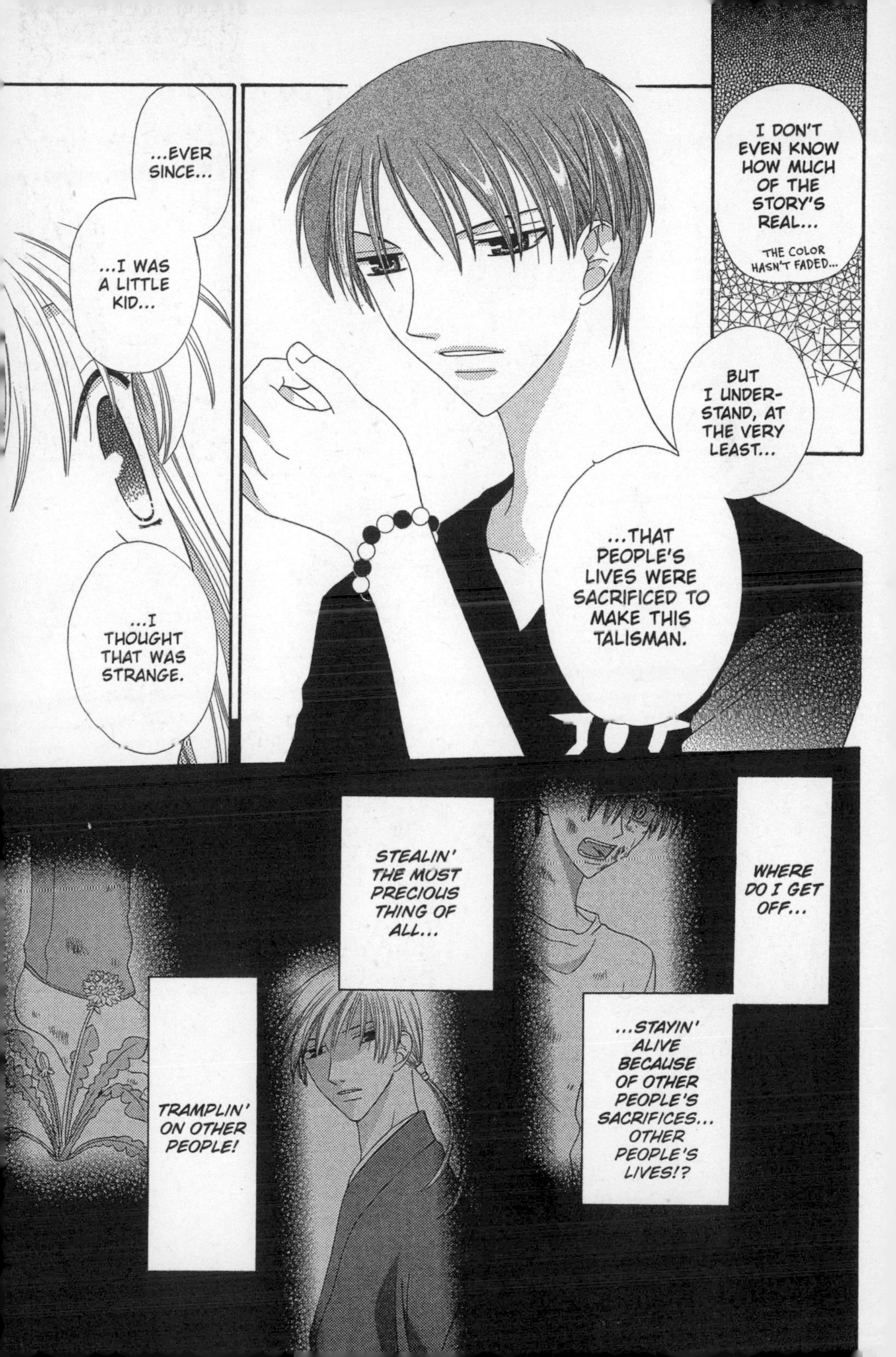
I DON'T EVEN KNOW HOW MUCH OF THE STORY'S REAL...
THE COLOR HASN'T FADED...
BUT I UNDERSTAND, AT THE VERY LEAST...
...THAT PEOPLE'S LIVES WERE SACRIFICED TO MAKE THIS TALISMAN.
...EVER SINCE...
...I WAS A LITTLE KID...
...I THOUGHT THAT WAS STRANGE.
WHERE DO I GET OFF...
STEALIN' THE MOST PRECIOUS THING OF ALL...
TRAMPLIN' ON OTHER PEOPLE!
...STAYIN' ALIVE BECAUSE OF OTHER PEOPLE'S SACRIFICES... OTHER PEOPLE'S LIVES!?

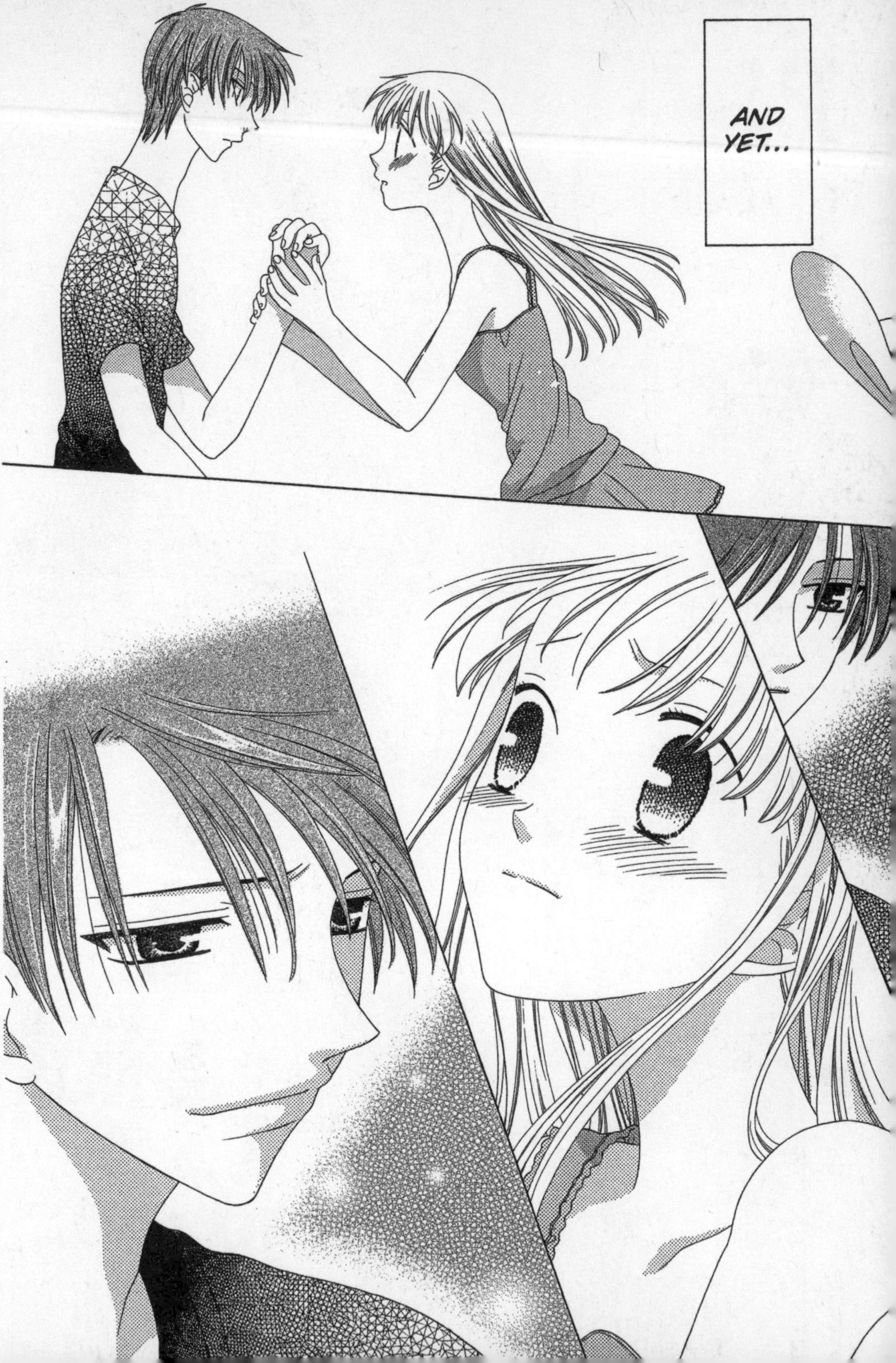
AND YET...

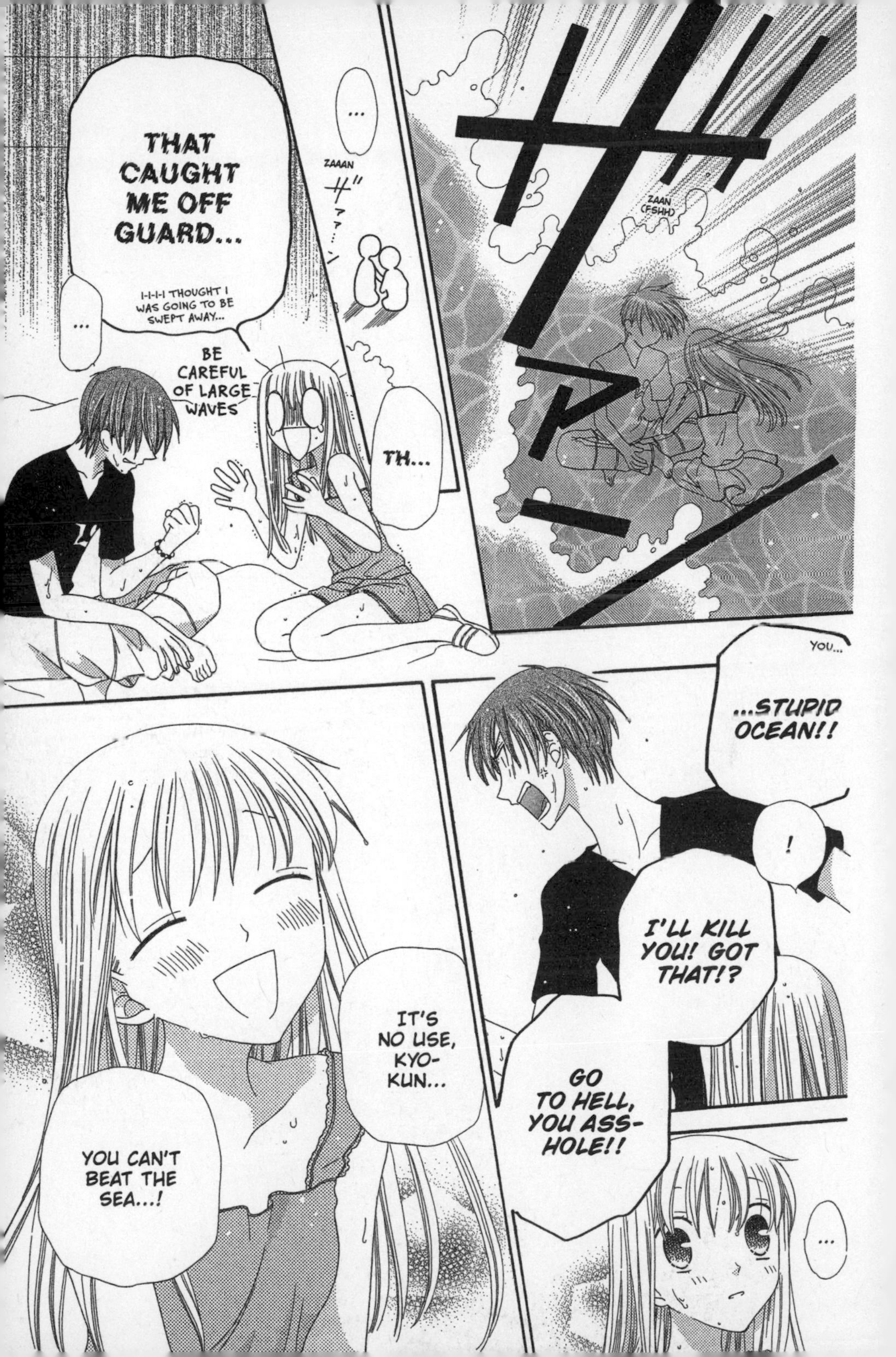
ZAAN (FSHH)
...
ZAAAN
TH...
THAT CAUGHT ME OFF GUARD...
I-I-I-I THOUGHT I WAS GOING TO BE SWEPT AWAY...
BE CAREFUL OF LARGE WAVES
...
YOU...
...STUPID OCEAN!!
!
I'LL KILL YOU! GOT THAT!?
GO TO HELL, YOU ASS-HOLE!!
...
IT'S NO USE, KYO-KUN...
YOU CAN'T BEAT THE SEA...!

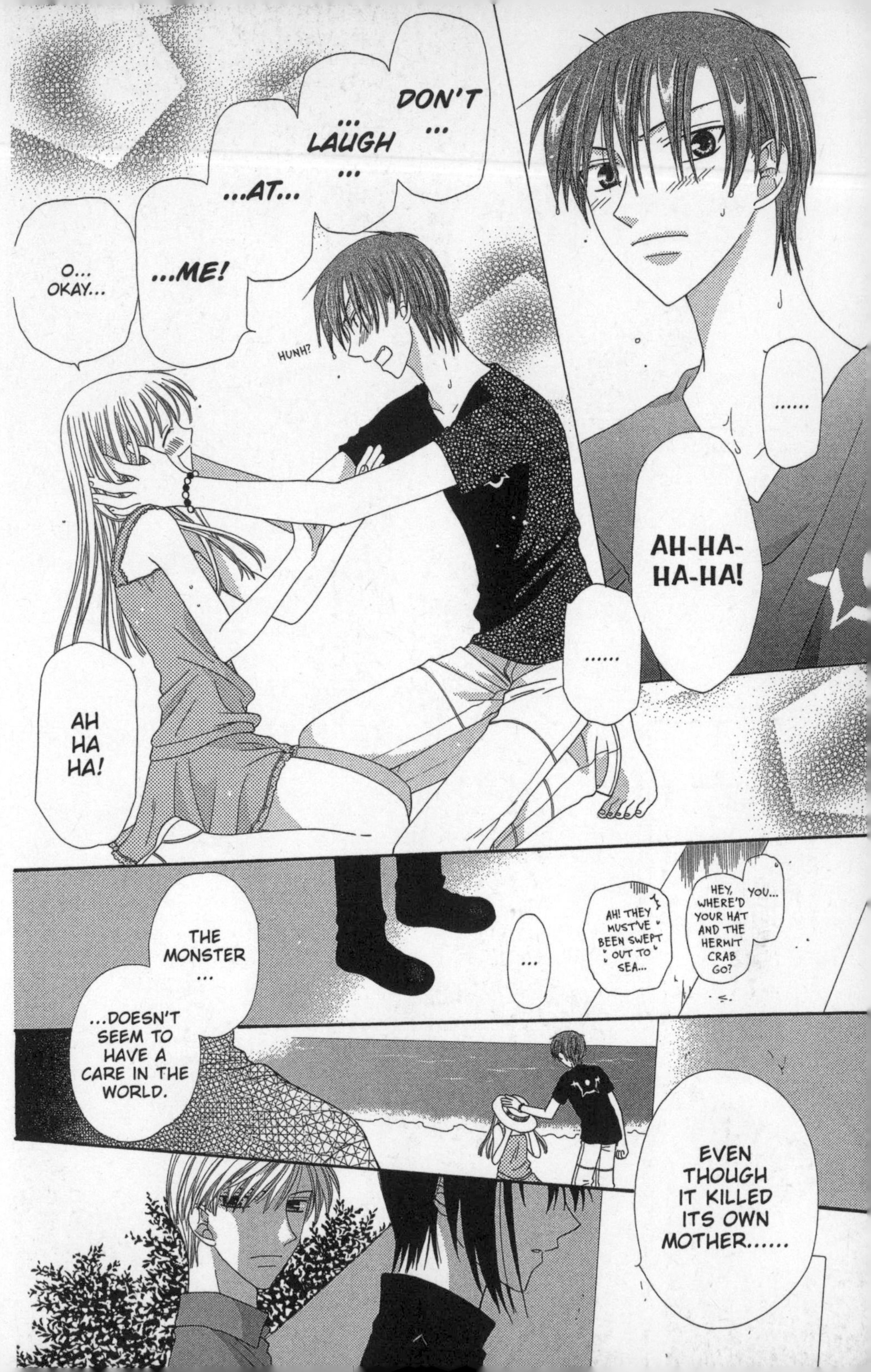
......
AH-HA-HA-HA!
DON'T ... LAUGH ... ...AT...
...ME!
O... OKAY...
HUNH?
AH HA HA!
......
HEY, YOU... WHERE'D YOUR HAT AND THE HERMIT CRAB GO?
AH! THEY MUST'VE BEEN SWEPT OUT TO SEA...
...
THE MONSTER ...
...DOESN'T SEEM TO HAVE A CARE IN THE WORLD.
EVEN THOUGH IT KILLED ITS OWN MOTHER......

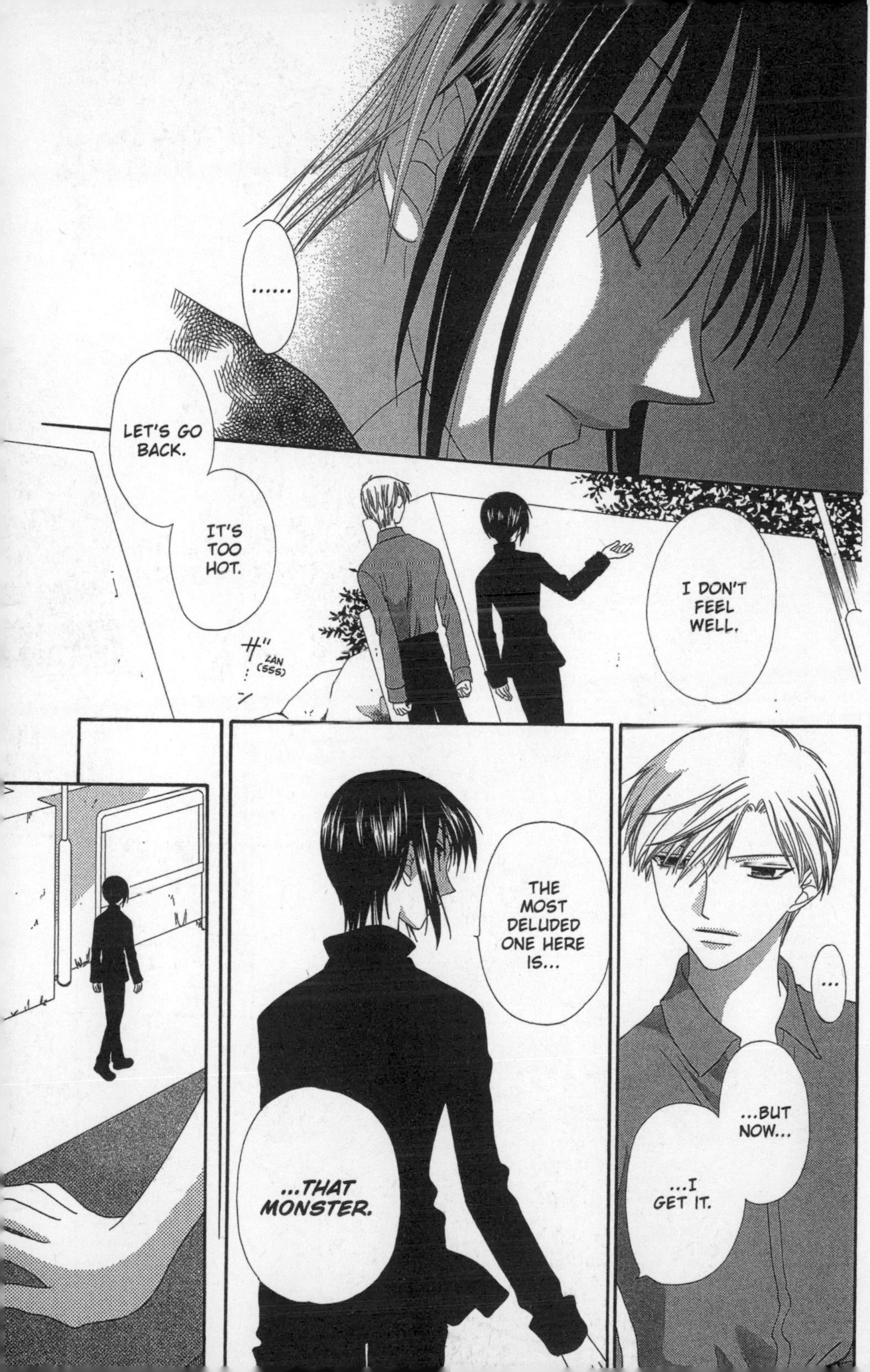
......
LET'S GO BACK.
IT'S TOO HOT.
I DON'T FEEL WELL.
ZAN (SSS)
...
...BUT NOW...
...I GET IT.
THE MOST DELUDED ONE HERE IS...
...THAT MONSTER.

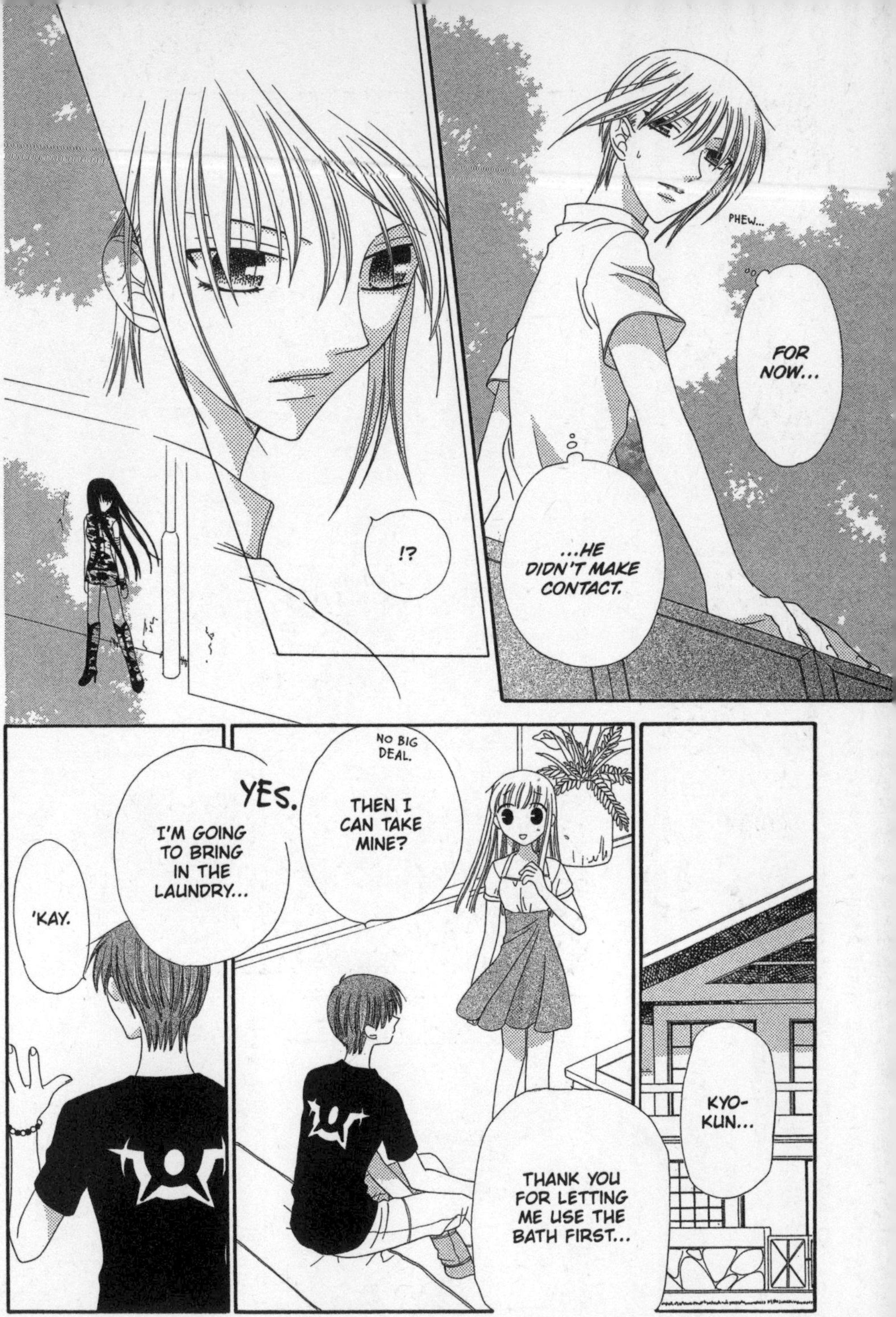
PHEW...
FOR NOW...
...HE DIDN'T MAKE CONTACT.
!?
KYO-KUN...
THANK YOU FOR LETTING ME USE THE BATH FIRST...
NO BIG DEAL.
THEN I CAN TAKE MINE?
YES.
I'M GOING TO BRING IN THE LAUNDRY...
'KAY.

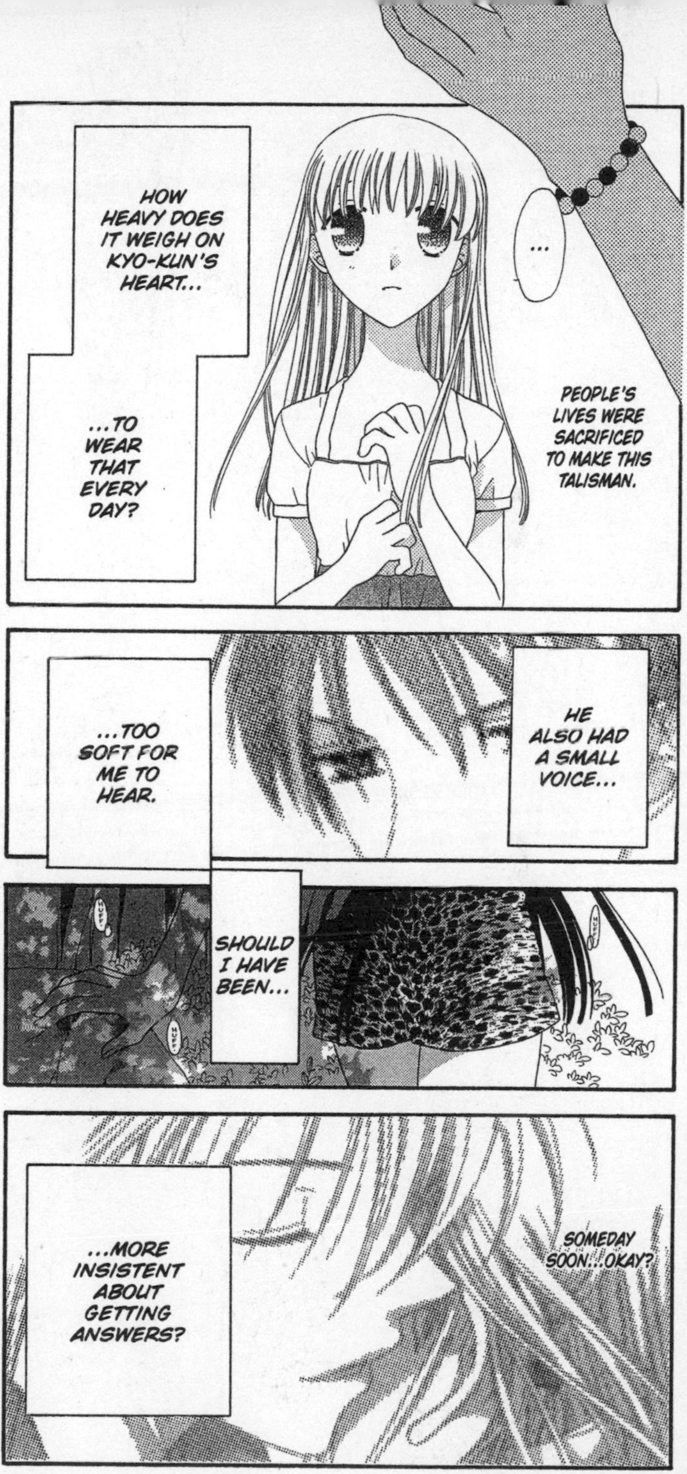
...
PEOPLE'S LIVES WERE SACRIFICED TO MAKE THIS TALISMAN.
HOW HEAVY DOES IT WEIGH ON KYO-KUN'S HEART...
...TO WEAR THAT EVERY DAY?
HE ALSO HAD A SMALL VOICE...
...TOO SOFT FOR ME TO HEAR.
SHOULD I HAVE BEEN...
SOMEDAY SOON...OKAY?
...MORE INSISTENT ABOUT GETTING ANSWERS?
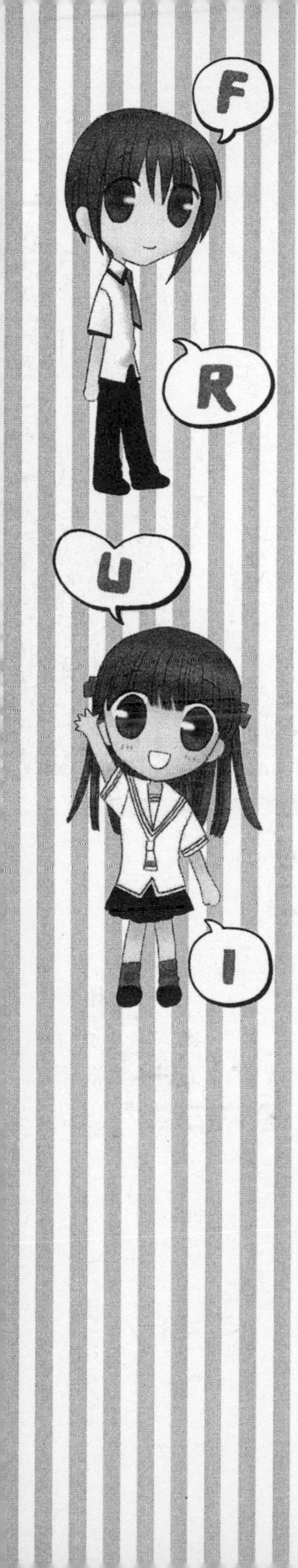
F
R
U
I

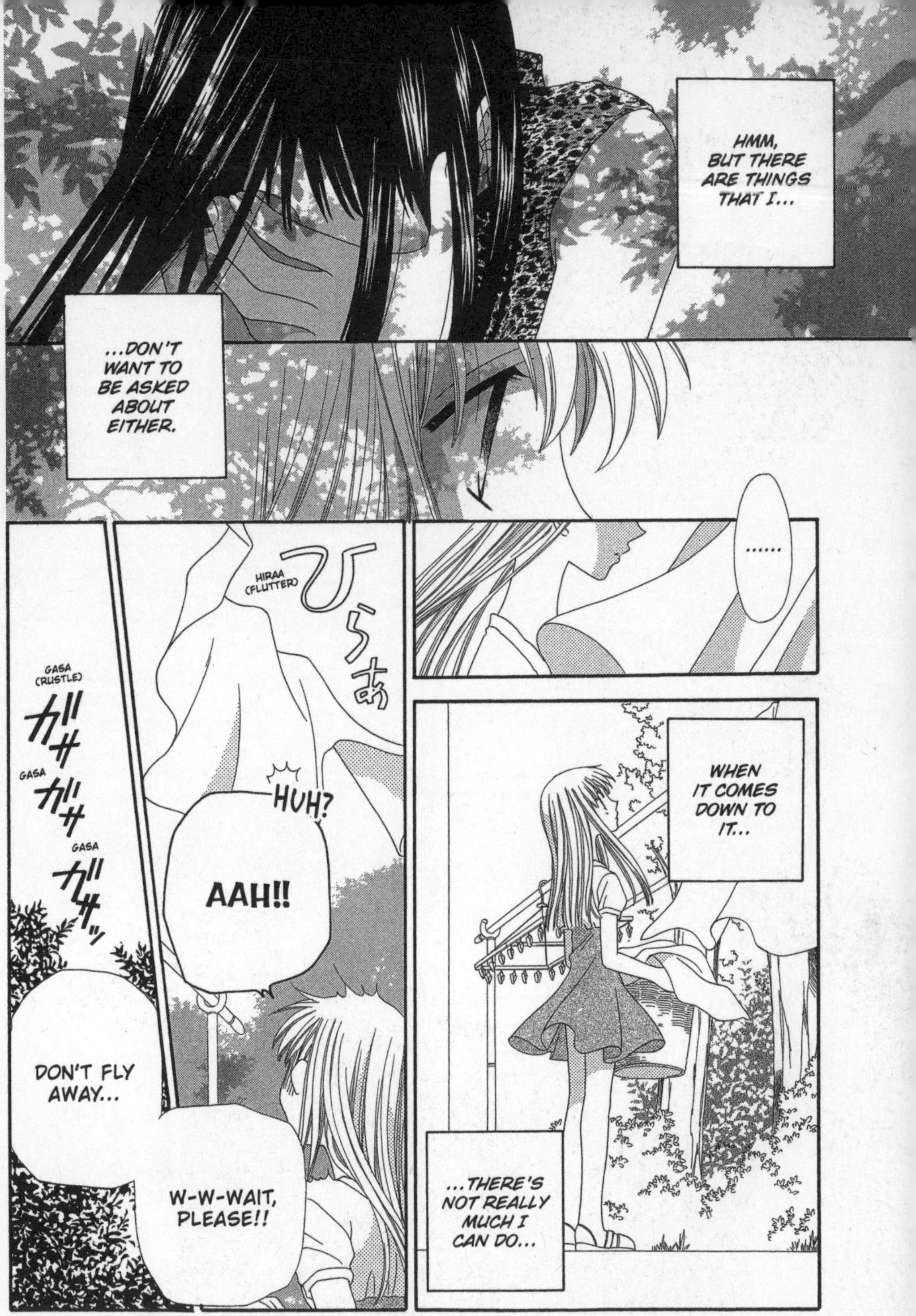
HMM, BUT THERE ARE THINGS THAT I...
...DON'T WANT TO BE ASKED ABOUT EITHER.
......
WHEN IT COMES DOWN TO IT...
...THERE'S NOT REALLY MUCH I CAN DO...
ひらあ
HIRAA (FLUTTER)
HUH?
AAH!!
ガサ
GASA (RUSTLE)
ガサ
GASA
ガザッ
GASA
DON'T FLY AWAY...
W-W-WAIT, PLEASE!!

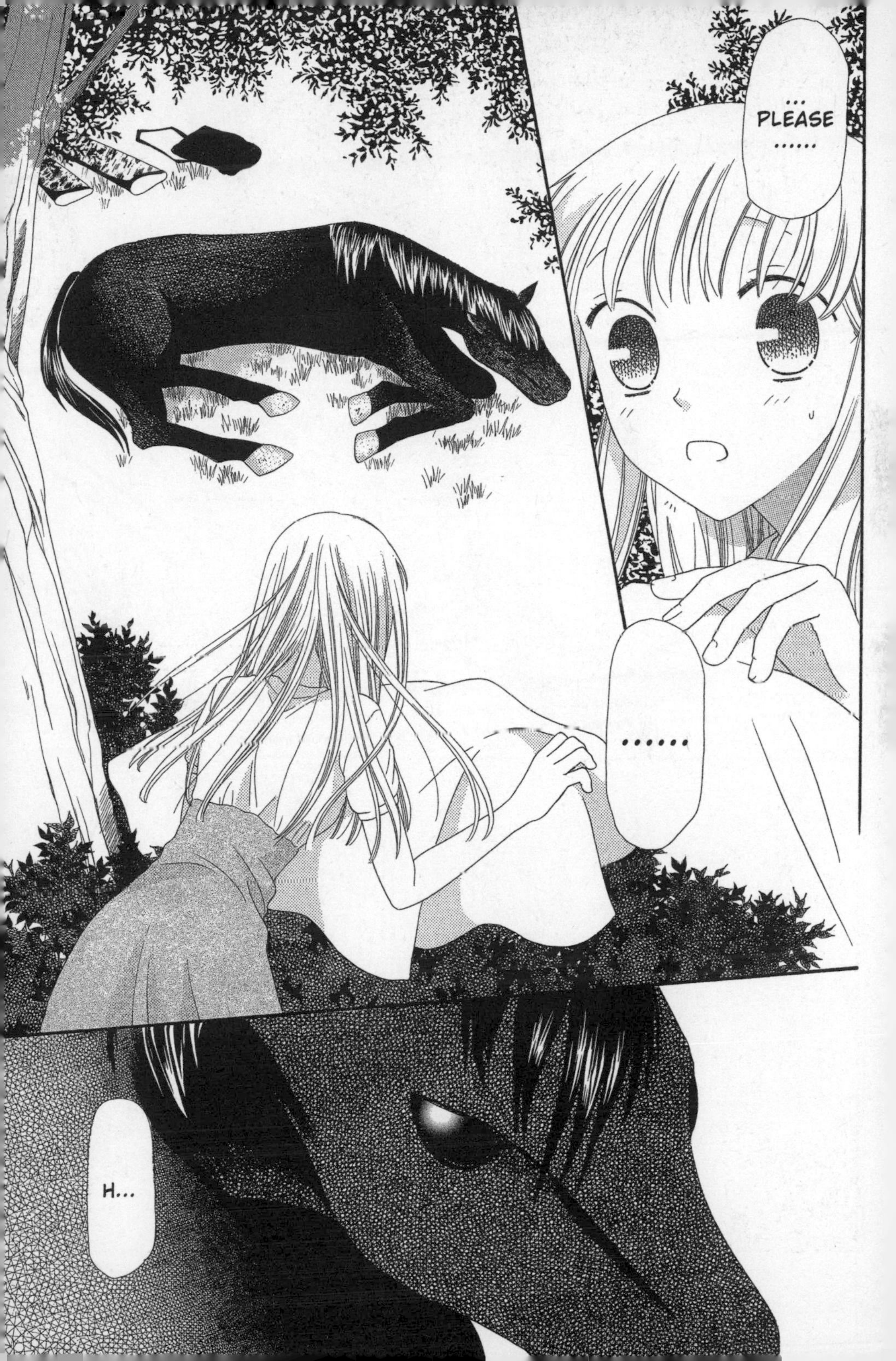
... PLEASE ......
......
H...

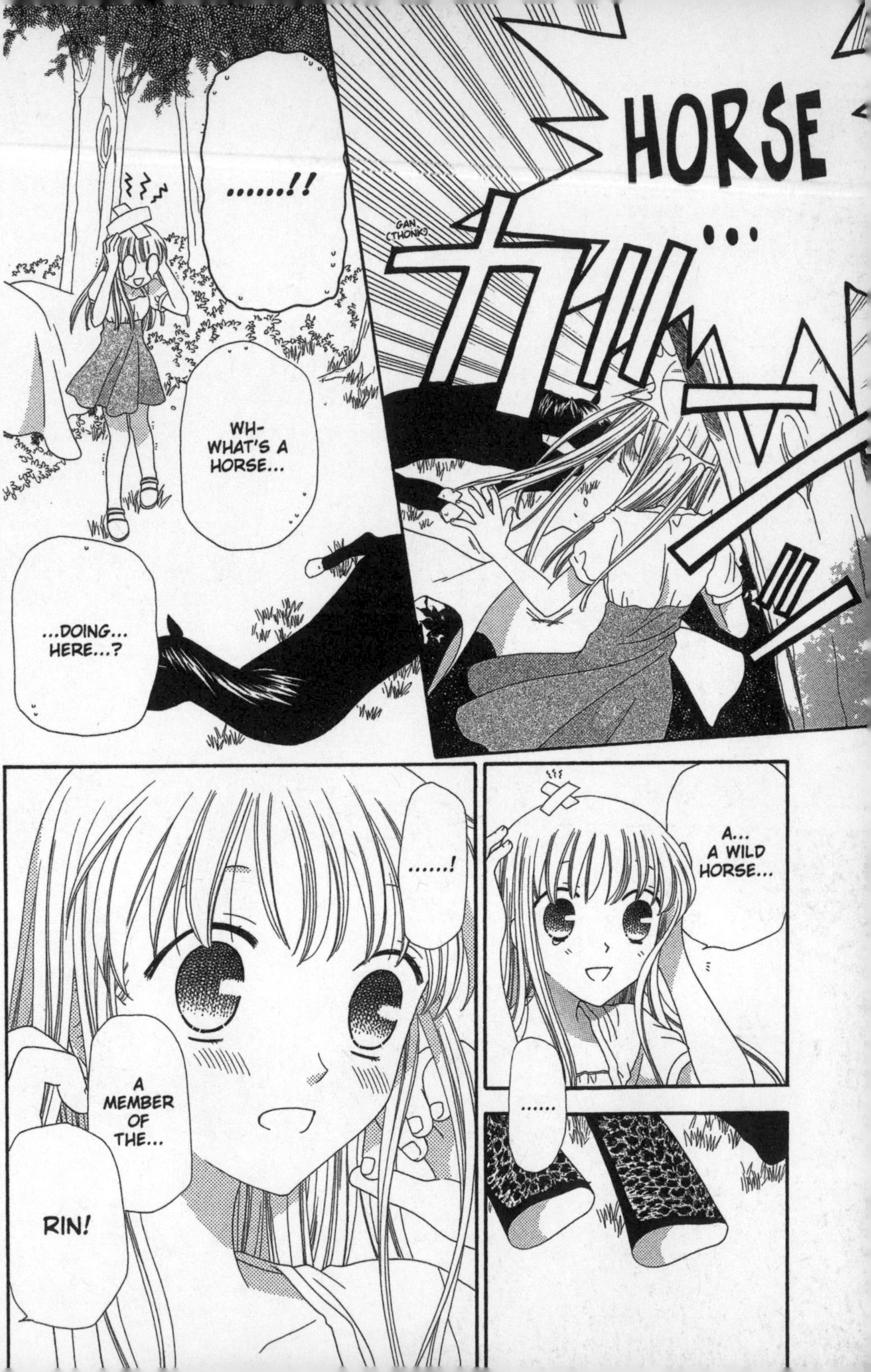
HORSE...
GAN (THONK)
......!!
WH- WHAT'S A HORSE...
...DOING... HERE...?
A... A WILD HORSE...
......
......!
A MEMBER OF THE...
RIN!

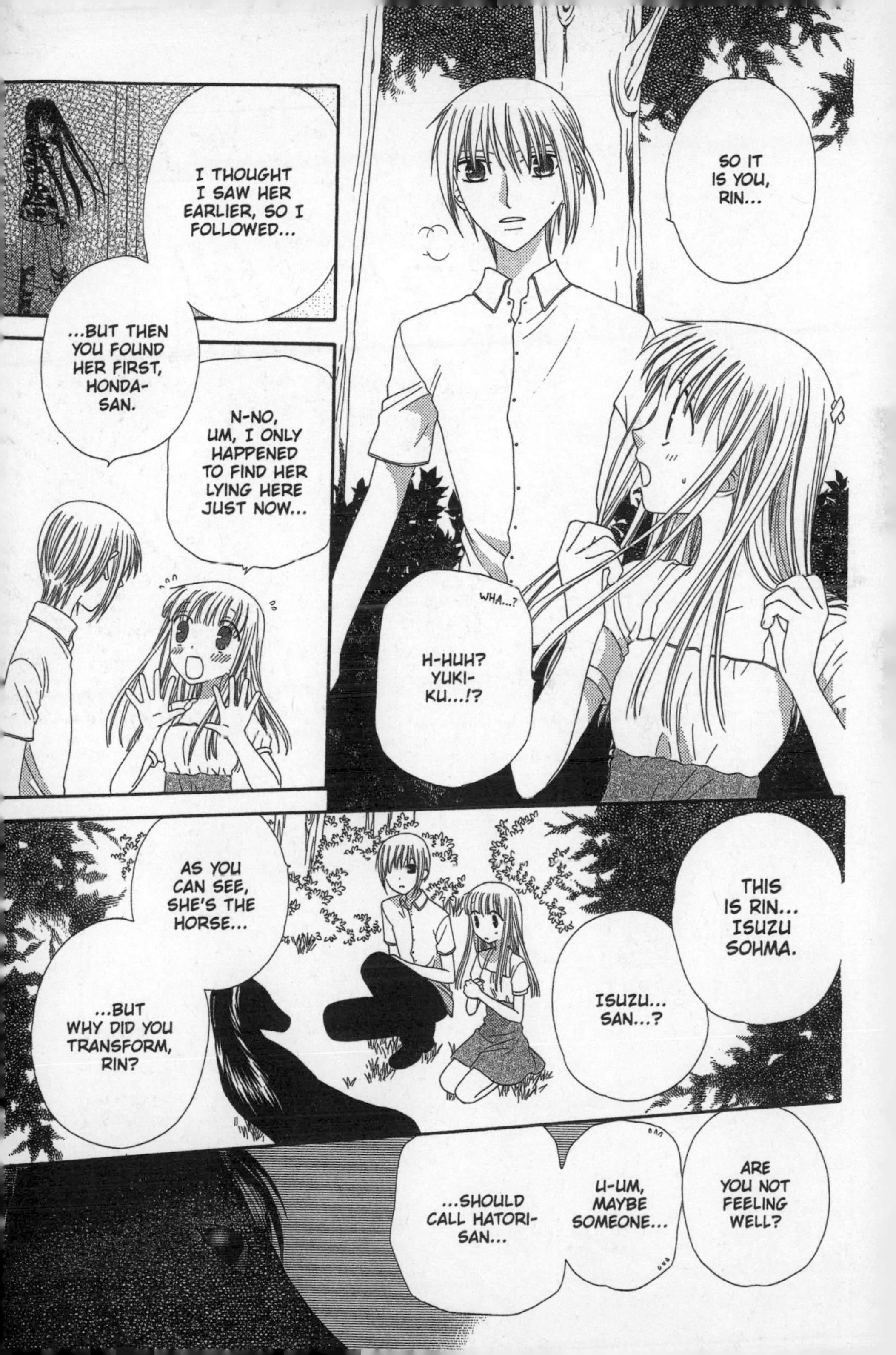
SO IT IS YOU, RIN...
WHA...?
H-HUH? YUKI-KU...!?
I THOUGHT I SAW HER EARLIER, SO I FOLLOWED...
...BUT THEN YOU FOUND HER FIRST, HONDA-SAN.
N-NO, UM, I ONLY HAPPENED TO FIND HER LYING HERE JUST NOW...
THIS IS RIN... ISUZU SOHMA.
ISUZU... SAN...?
AS YOU CAN SEE, SHE'S THE HORSE...
...BUT WHY DID YOU TRANSFORM, RIN?
ARE YOU NOT FEELING WELL?
U-UM, MAYBE SOMEONE...
...SHOULD CALL HATORI-SAN...

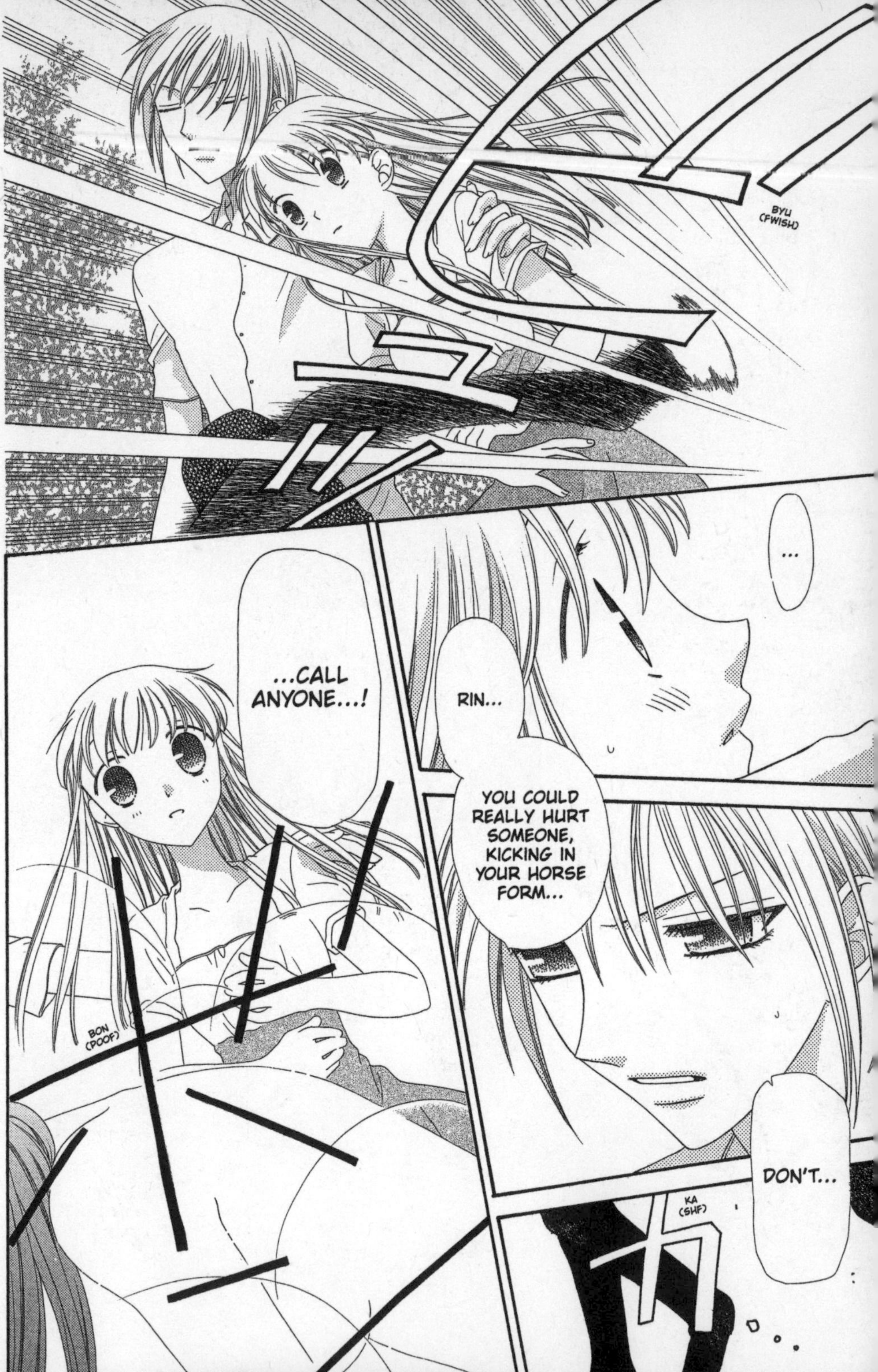
BYU (FWISH)
...
RIN...
YOU COULD REALLY HURT SOMEONE, KICKING IN YOUR HORSE FORM...
DON'T...
KA (SHF)
...CALL ANYONE...!
BON (POOF)

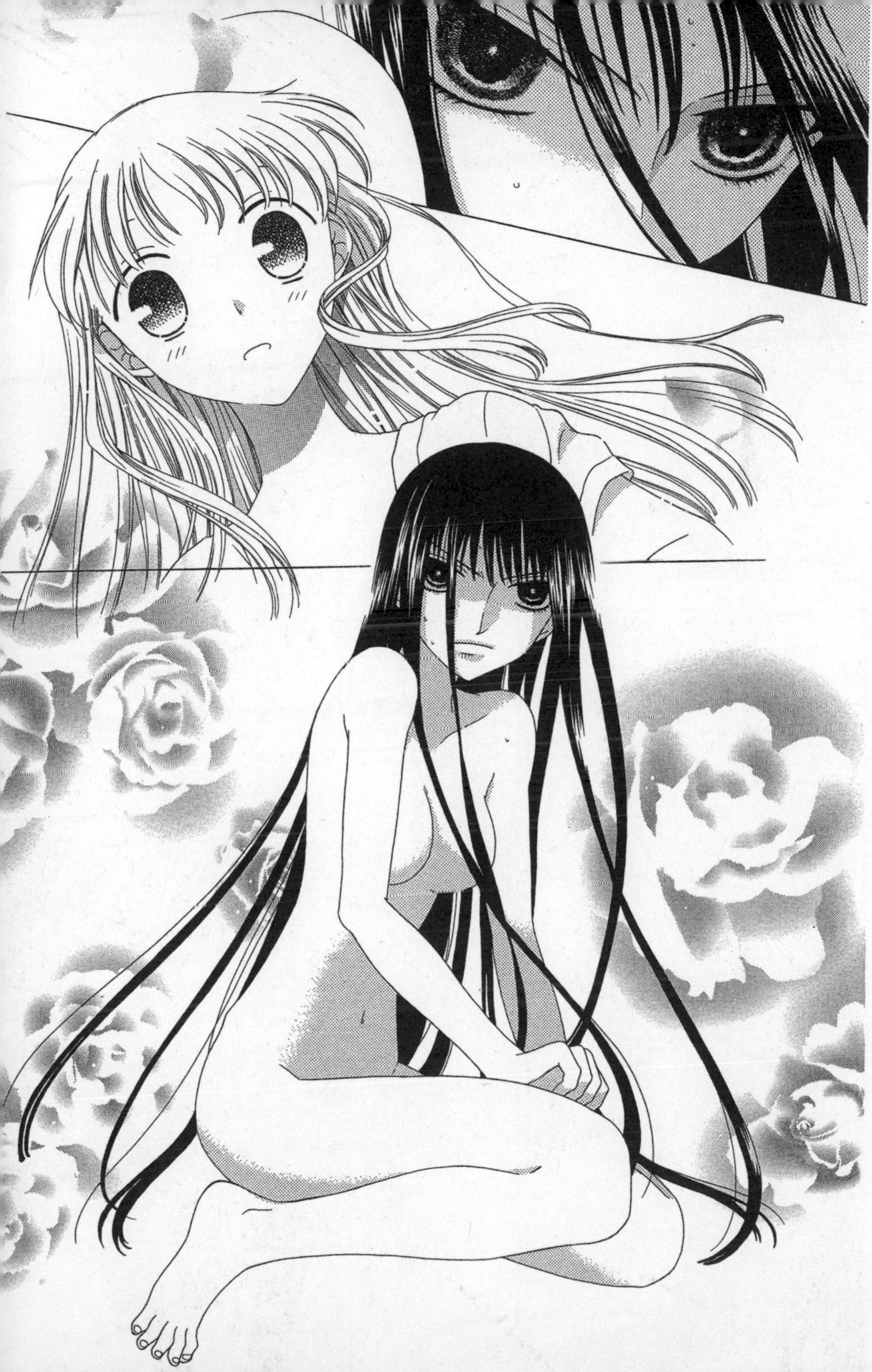

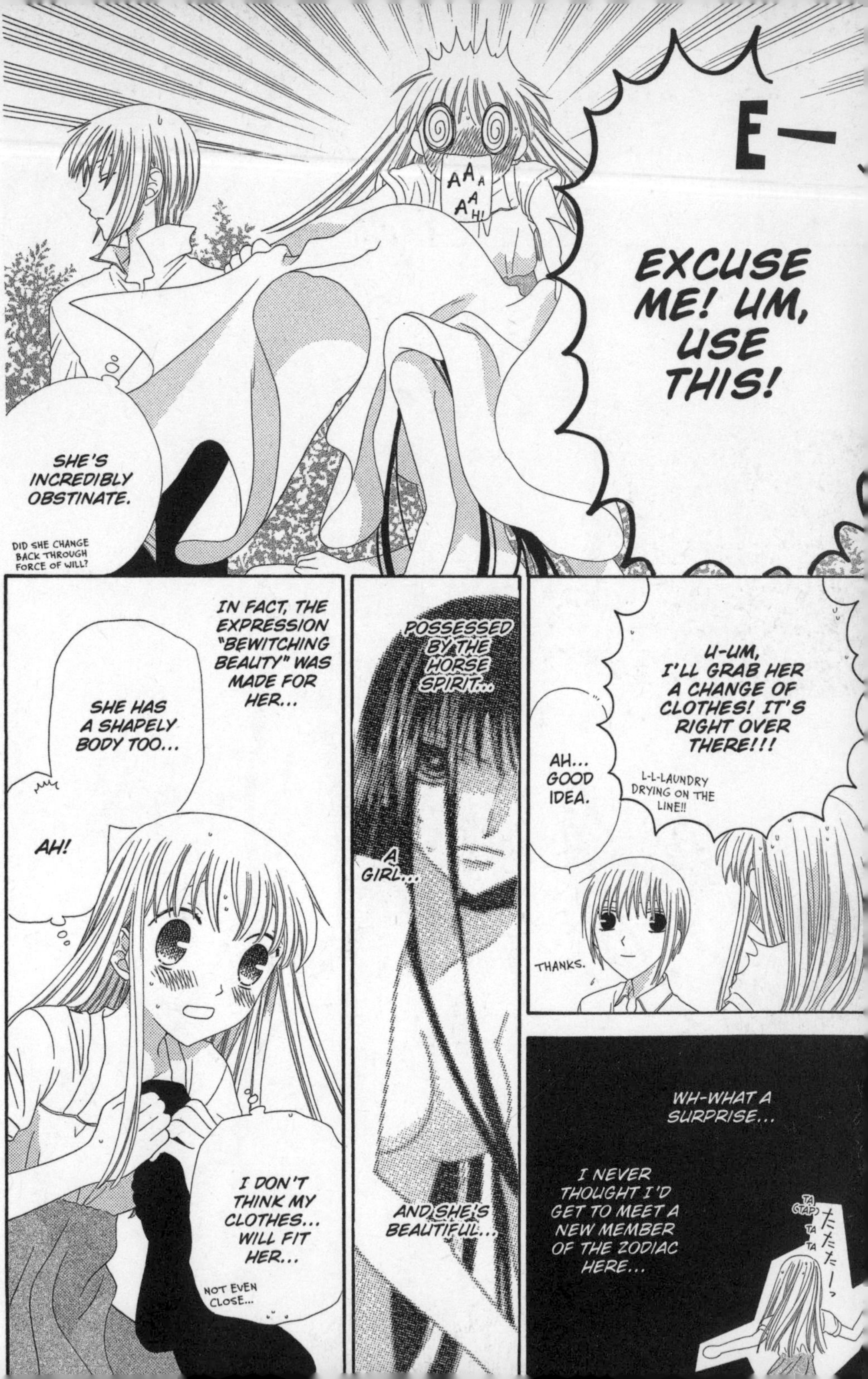
E—
EXCUSE ME! UM, USE THIS!
AAAAAH!
SHE'S INCREDIBLY OBSTINATE.
DID SHE CHANGE BACK THROUGH FORCE OF WILL?
U-UM, I'LL GRAB HER A CHANGE OF CLOTHES! IT'S RIGHT OVER THERE!!!
L-L-LAUNDRY DRYING ON THE LINE!!
AH... GOOD IDEA.
THANKS.
WH-WHAT A SURPRISE...
I NEVER THOUGHT I'D GET TO MEET A NEW MEMBER OF THE ZODIAC HERE...
TA (TAP) TA TA
たたたーっ
POSSESSED BY THE HORSE SPIRIT...
A GIRL...
AND SHE'S BEAUTIFUL...
IN FACT, THE EXPRESSION "BEWITCHING BEAUTY" WAS MADE FOR HER...
SHE HAS A SHAPELY BODY TOO...
AH!
I DON'T THINK MY CLOTHES... WILL FIT HER...
NOT EVEN CLOSE...

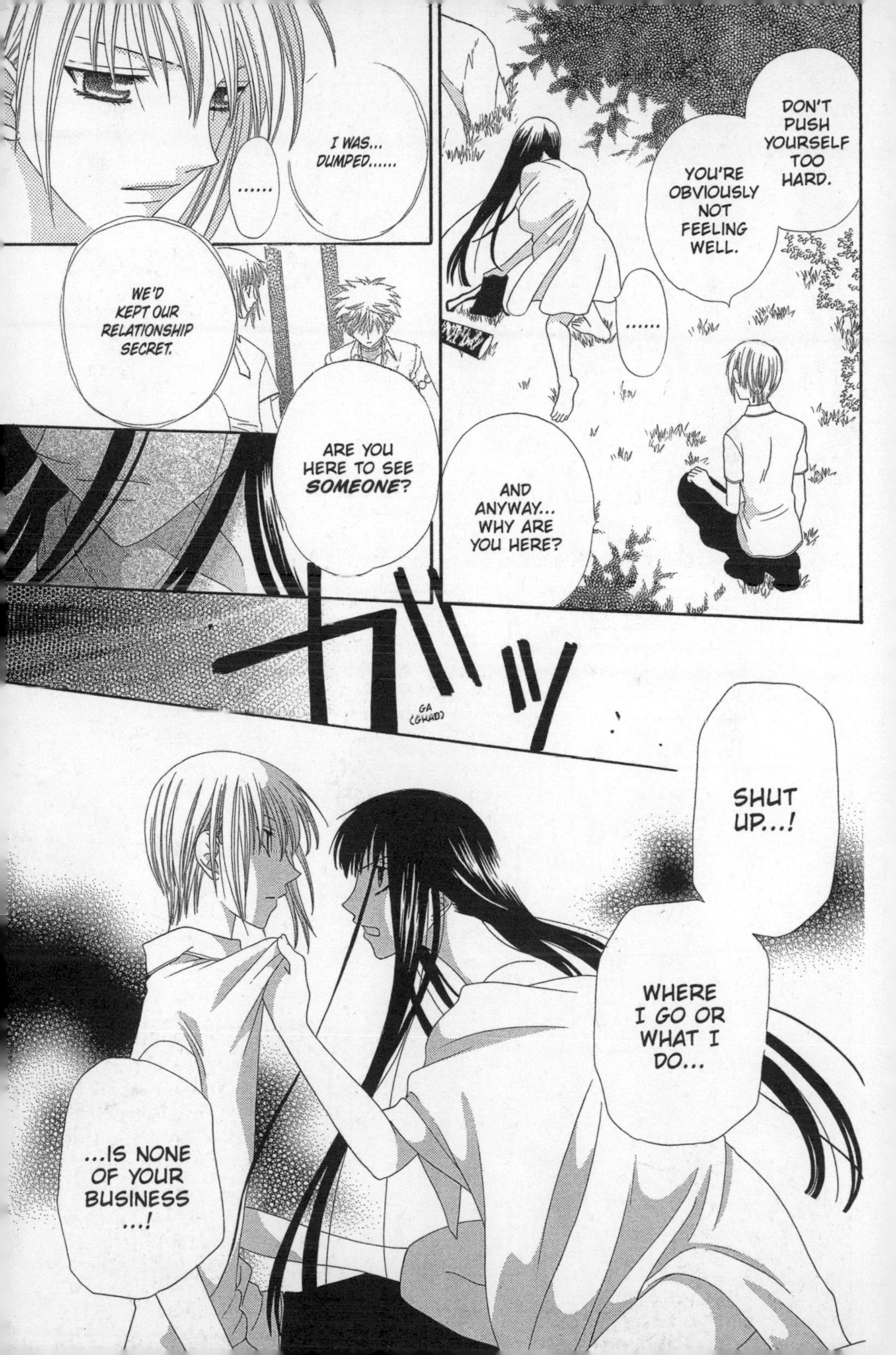

DON'T PUSH YOURSELF TOO HARD.
YOU'RE OBVIOUSLY NOT FEELING WELL.
......
AND ANYWAY... WHY ARE YOU HERE?
I WAS... DUMPED......
......
WE'D KEPT OUR RELATIONSHIP SECRET.
ARE YOU HERE TO SEE *SOMEONE*?
GA (GRAB)
SHUT UP...!
WHERE I GO OR WHAT I DO...
...IS NONE OF YOUR BUSINESS ...!

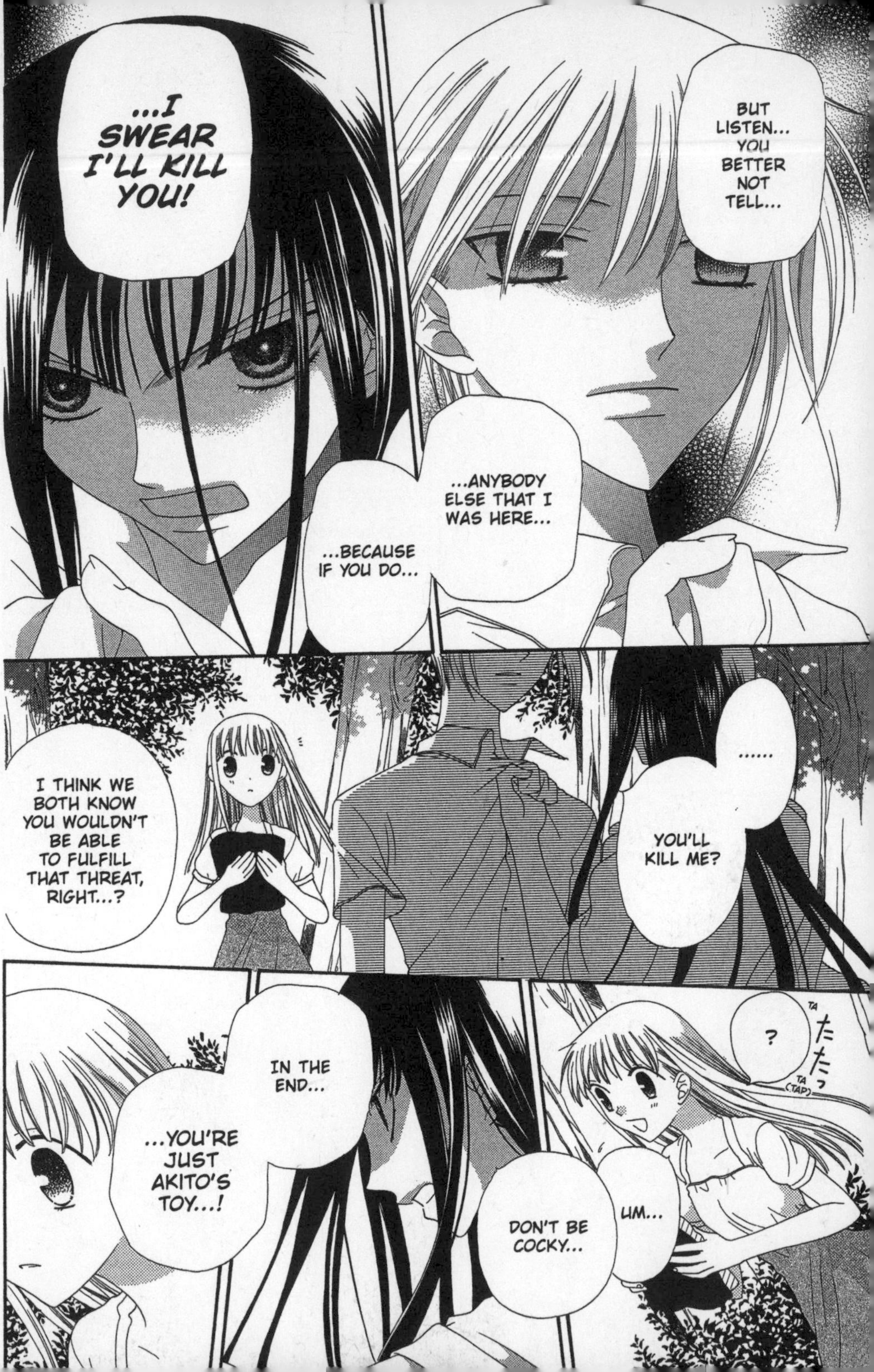
BUT LISTEN... YOU BETTER NOT TELL...
...ANYBODY ELSE THAT I WAS HERE...
...BECAUSE IF YOU DO...
...I SWEAR I'LL KILL YOU!
......
YOU'LL KILL ME?
I THINK WE BOTH KNOW YOU WOULDN'T BE ABLE TO FULFILL THAT THREAT, RIGHT...?
?
たたっ
TA TA (TAP)
UM...
DON'T BE COCKY...
IN THE END...
...YOU'RE JUST AKITO'S TOY...!

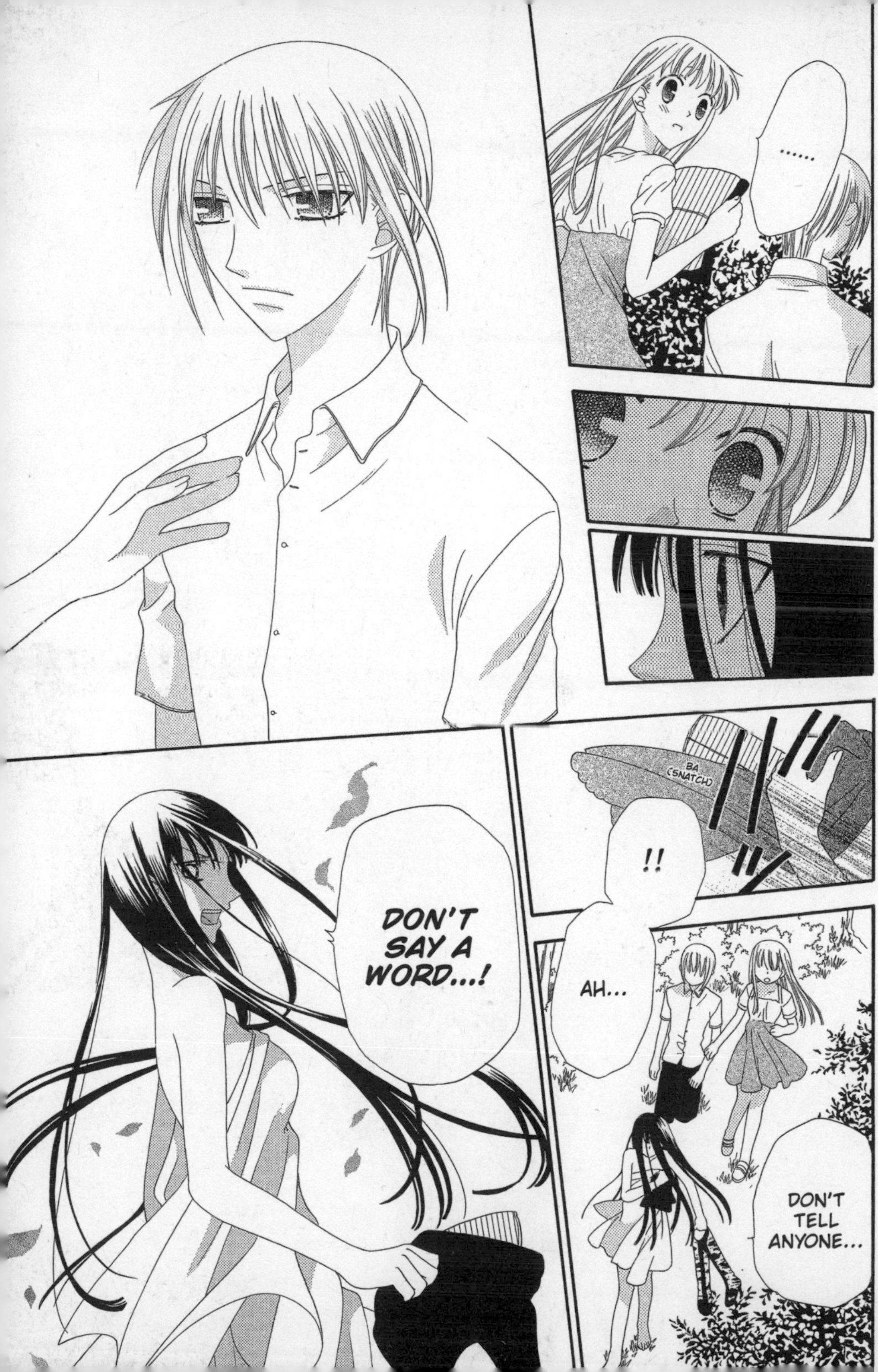
......
BA (SNATCH)
!!
AH...
DON'T TELL ANYONE...
DON'T SAY A WORD...!

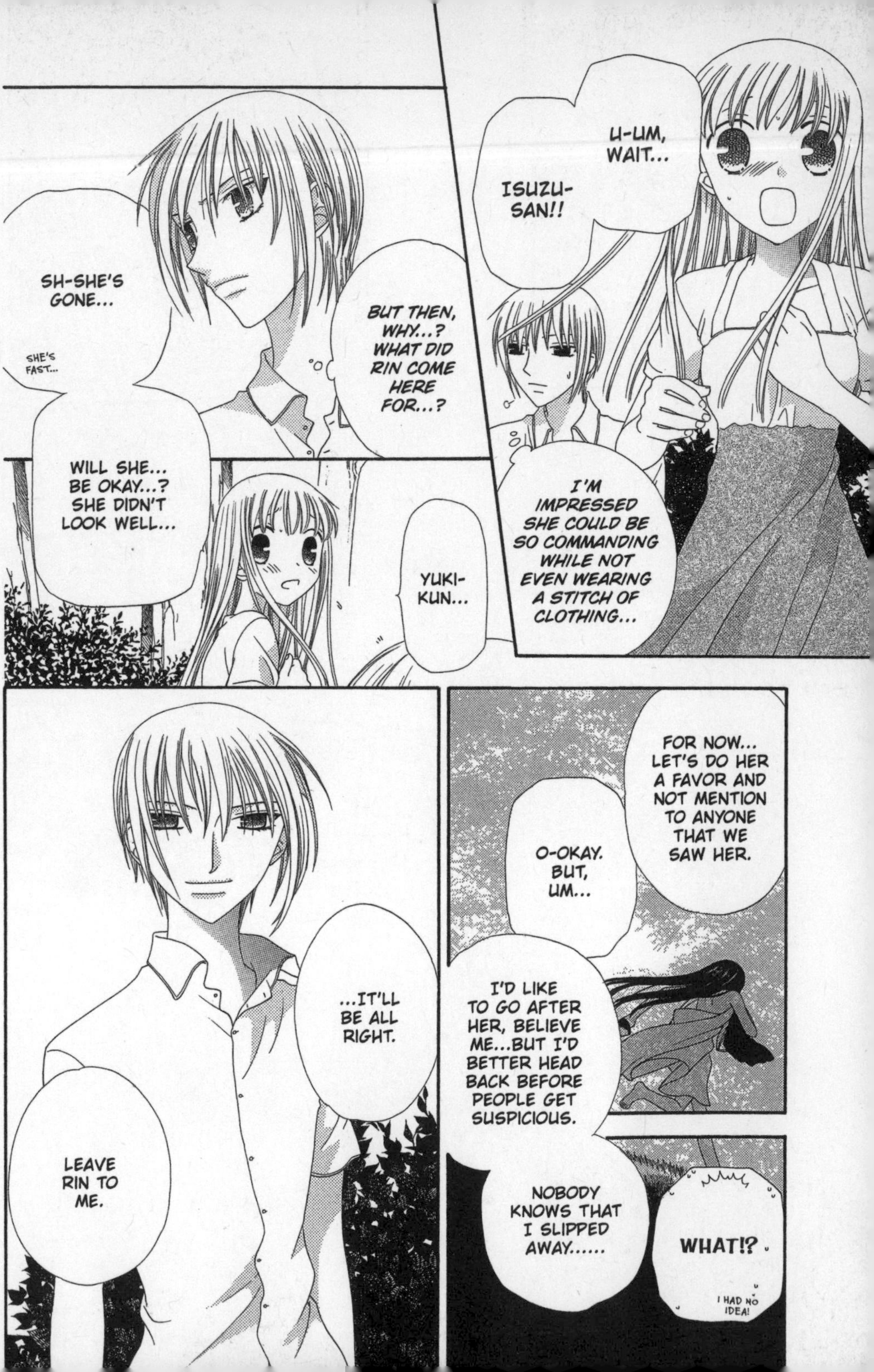
U-UM, WAIT...
ISUZU-SAN!!
I'M IMPRESSED SHE COULD BE SO COMMANDING WHILE NOT EVEN WEARING A STITCH OF CLOTHING...
SH-SHE'S GONE...
SHE'S FAST...
BUT THEN, WHY...? WHAT DID RIN COME HERE FOR...?
WILL SHE... BE OKAY...? SHE DIDN'T LOOK WELL...
YUKI-KUN...
FOR NOW... LET'S DO HER A FAVOR AND NOT MENTION TO ANYONE THAT WE SAW HER.
O-OKAY. BUT, UM...
I'D LIKE TO GO AFTER HER, BELIEVE ME...BUT I'D BETTER HEAD BACK BEFORE PEOPLE GET SUSPICIOUS.
NOBODY KNOWS THAT I SLIPPED AWAY......
WHAT!?
I HAD NO IDEA!
...IT'LL BE ALL RIGHT.
LEAVE RIN TO ME.

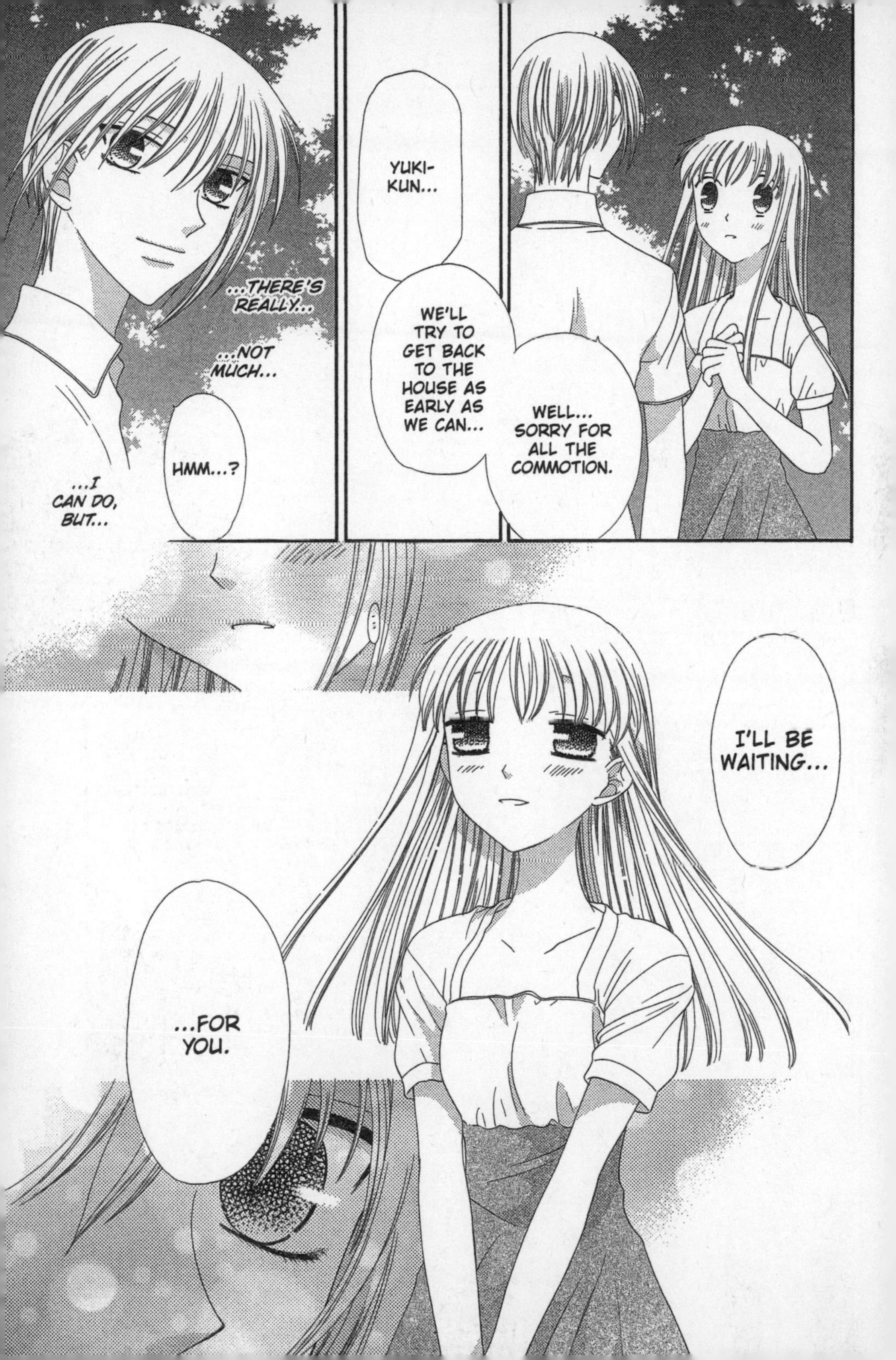
WELL... SORRY FOR ALL THE COMMOTION.
WE'LL TRY TO GET BACK TO THE HOUSE AS EARLY AS WE CAN...
YUKI-KUN...
...THERE'S REALLY...
...NOT MUCH...
HMM...?
...I CAN DO, BUT...
I'LL BE WAITING...
...FOR YOU.

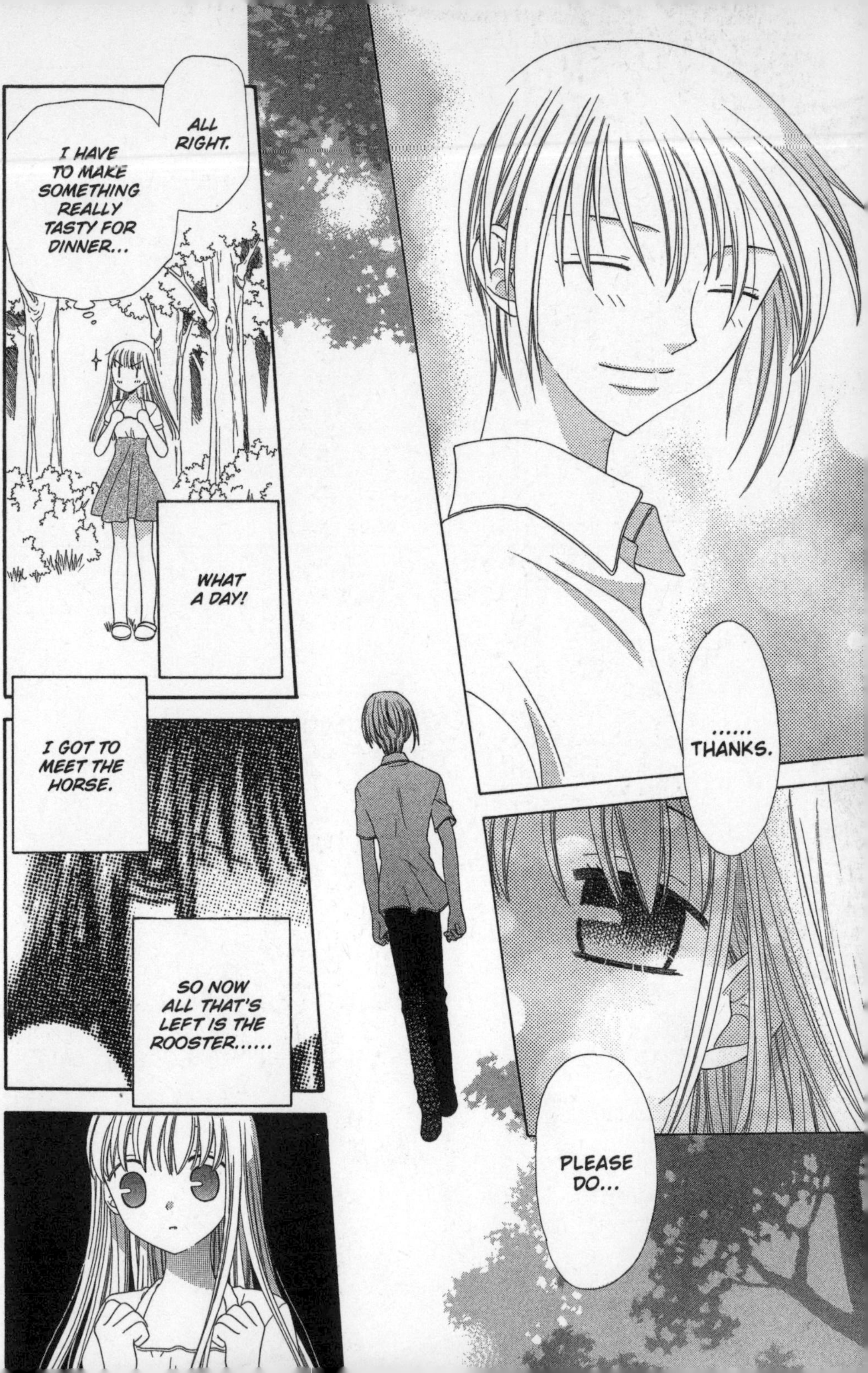
......THANKS.
PLEASE DO...
ALL RIGHT.
I HAVE TO MAKE SOMETHING REALLY TASTY FOR DINNER...
WHAT A DAY!
I GOT TO MEET THE HORSE.
SO NOW ALL THAT'S LEFT IS THE ROOSTER......

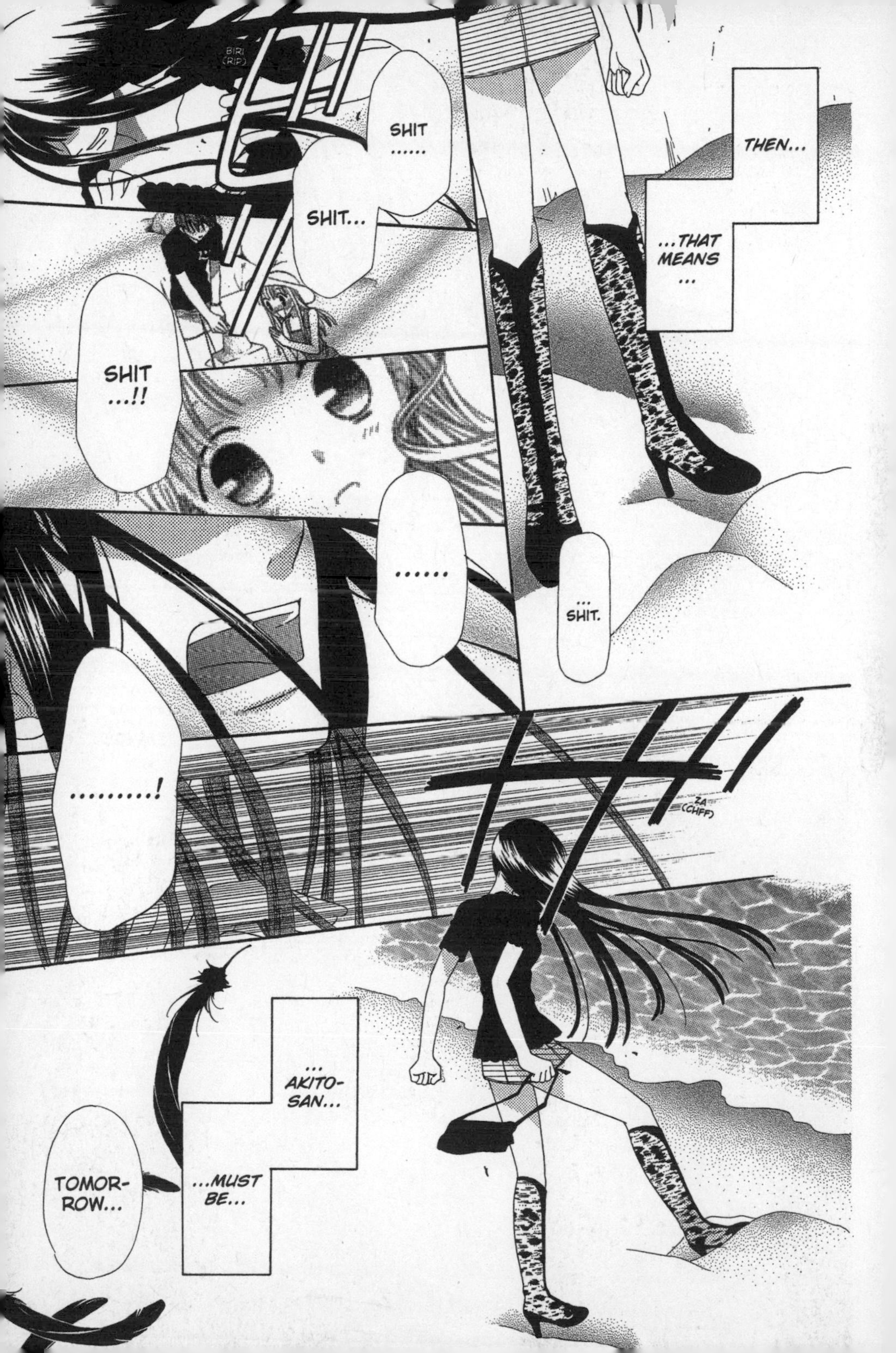
THEN...
...THAT MEANS ...
... SHIT.
BIRI (RIP)
SHIT ......
SHIT...
SHIT ...!!
......
.........!
ZA (CHFF)
... AKITO-SAN...
...MUST BE...
TOMOR-ROW...

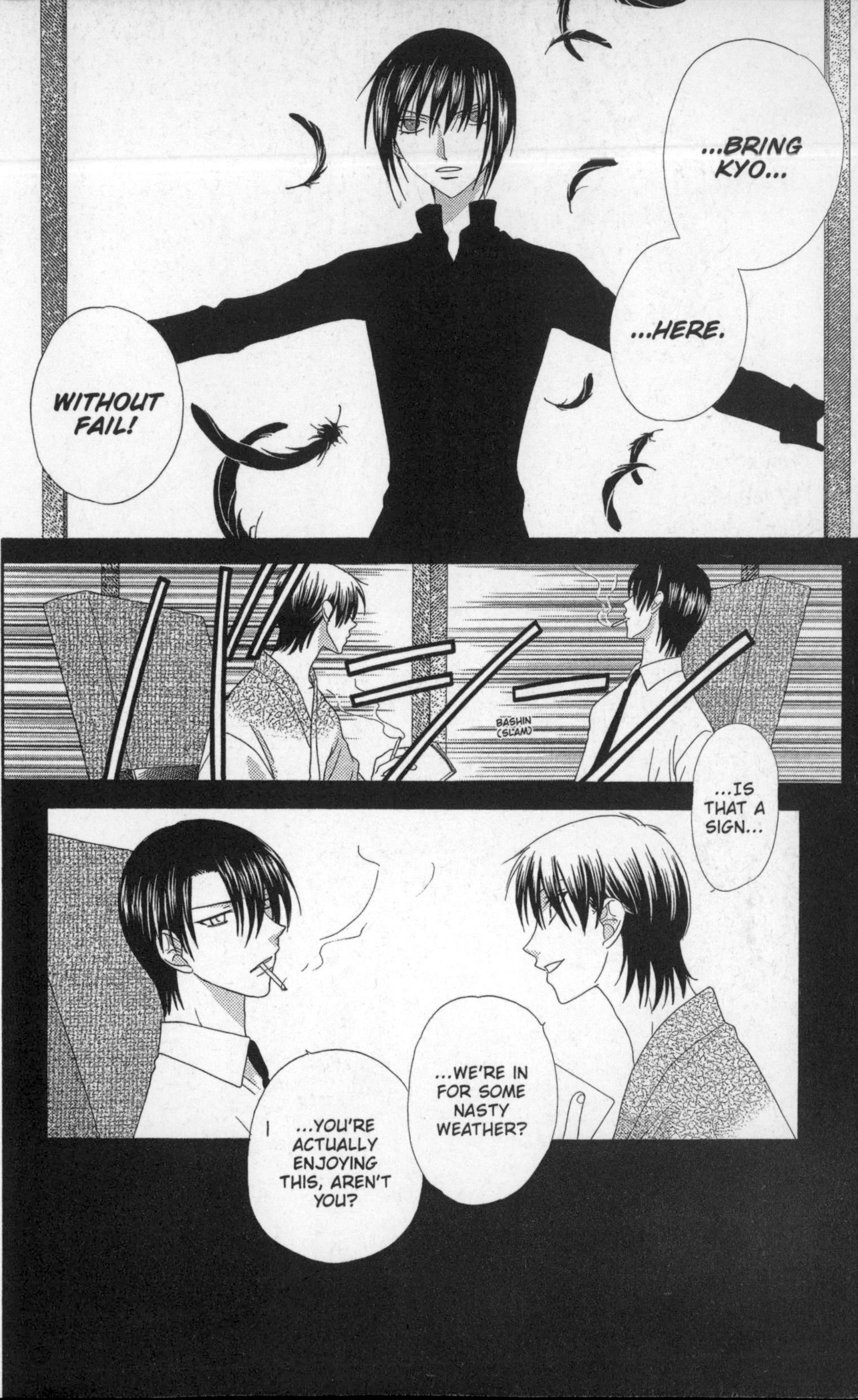
...BRING KYO...
...HERE.
WITHOUT FAIL!
BASHIN (SLAM)
...IS THAT A SIGN...
...WE'RE IN FOR SOME NASTY WEATHER?
...YOU'RE ACTUALLY ENJOYING THIS, AREN'T YOU?

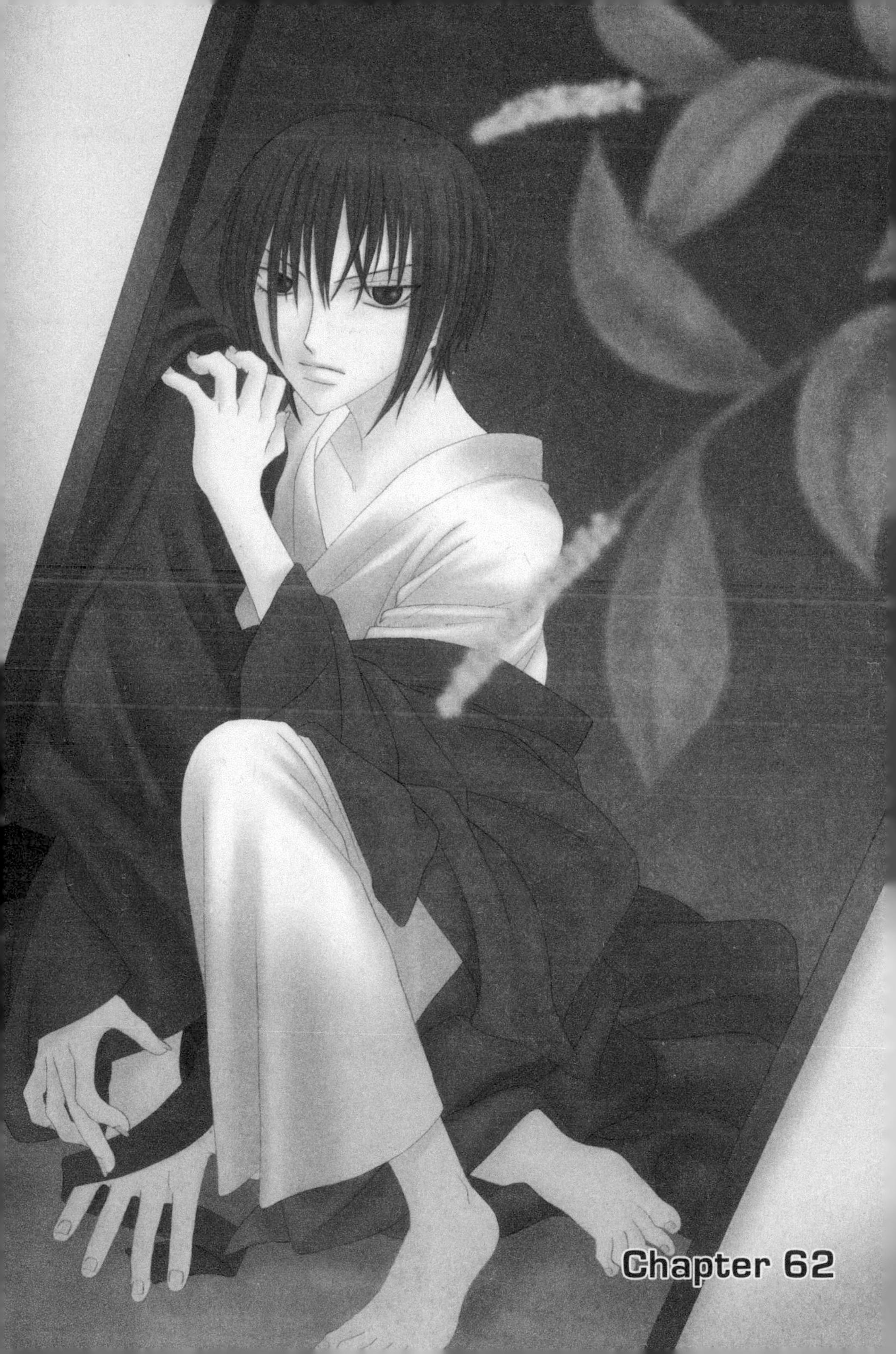

Chapter 62

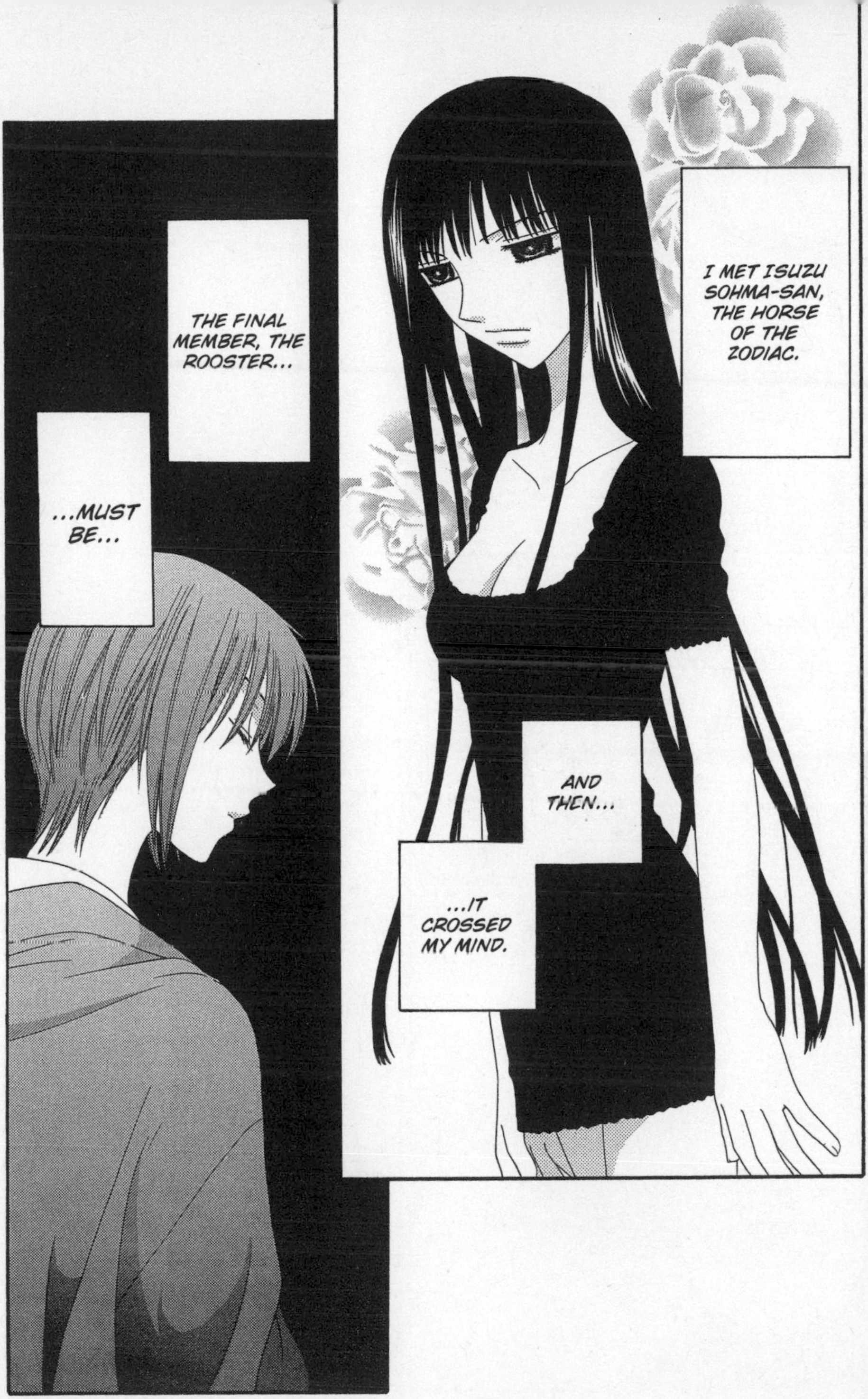
I MET ISUZU SOHMA-SAN, THE HORSE OF THE ZODIAC.
AND THEN...
...IT CROSSED MY MIND.
THE FINAL MEMBER, THE ROOSTER...
...MUST BE...

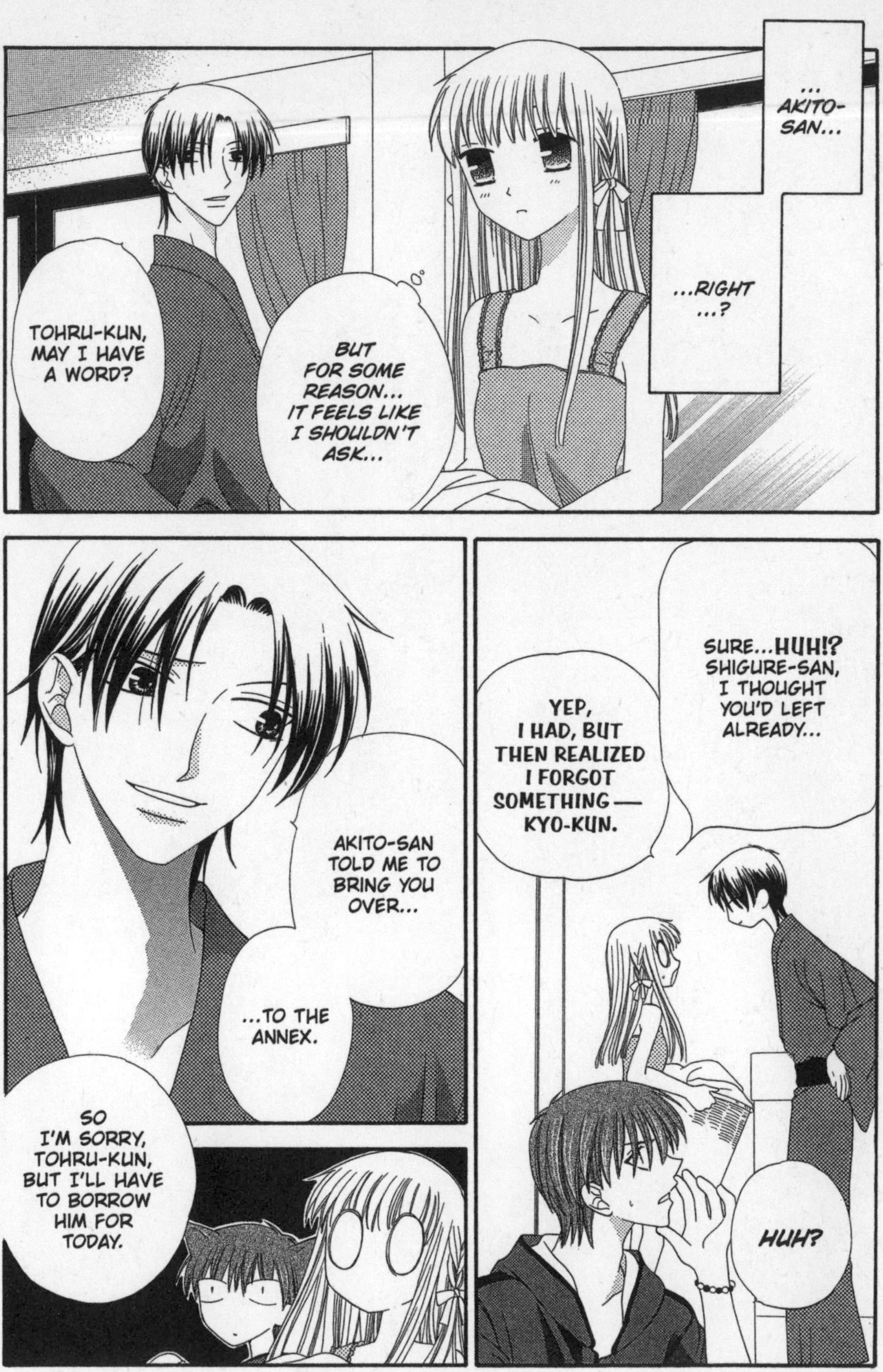
...AKITO-SAN...
...RIGHT...?
BUT FOR SOME REASON... IT FEELS LIKE I SHOULDN'T ASK...
TOHRU-KUN, MAY I HAVE A WORD?
SURE...HUH!? SHIGURE-SAN, I THOUGHT YOU'D LEFT ALREADY...
YEP, I HAD, BUT THEN REALIZED I FORGOT SOMETHING—KYO-KUN.
HUH?
AKITO-SAN TOLD ME TO BRING YOU OVER...
...TO THE ANNEX.
SO I'M SORRY, TOHRU-KUN, BUT I'LL HAVE TO BORROW HIM FOR TODAY.

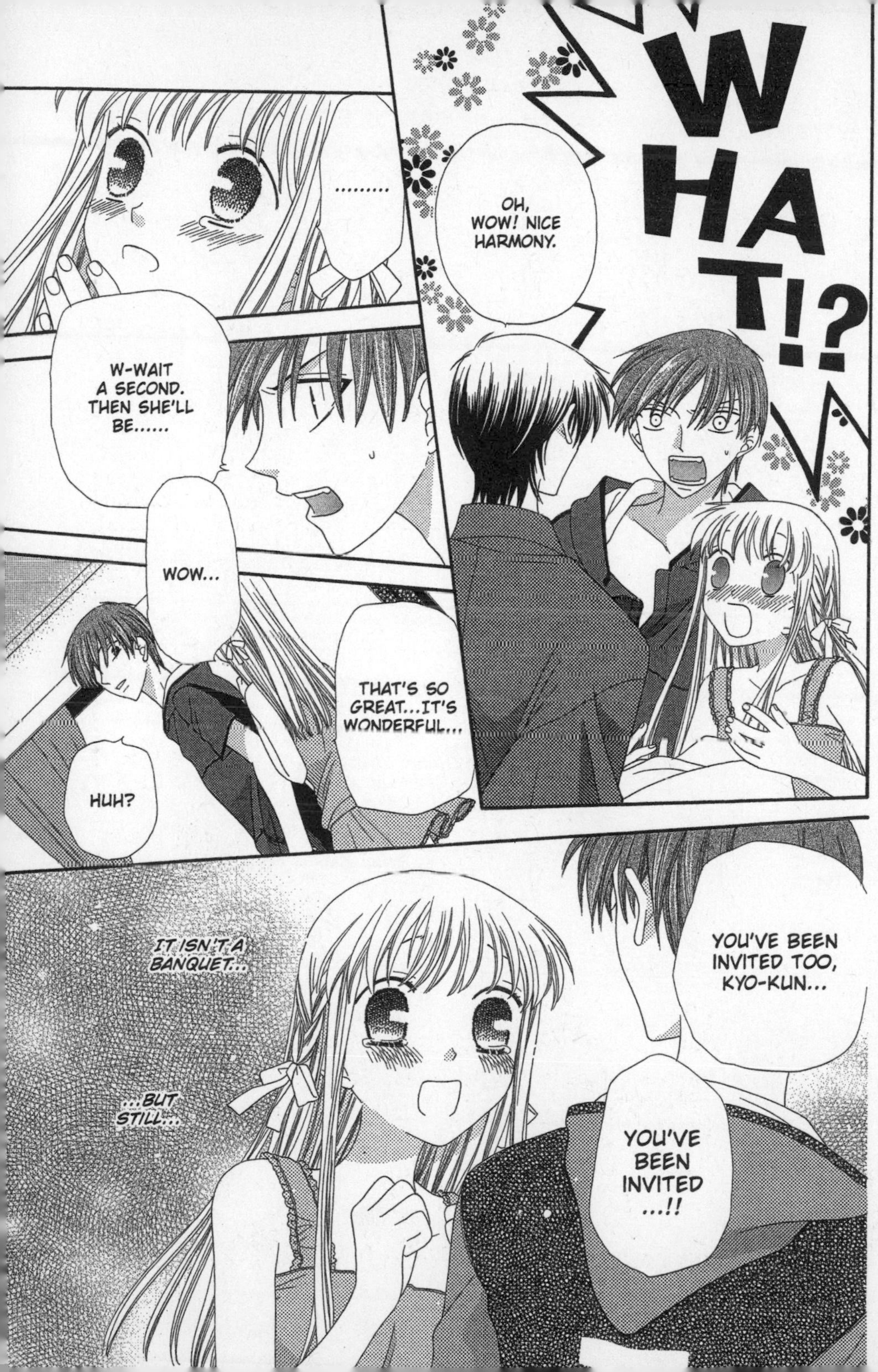
WHAT!?
OH, WOW! NICE HARMONY.
....
W-WAIT A SECOND. THEN SHE'LL BE......
WOW...
THAT'S SO GREAT...IT'S WONDERFUL...
HUH?
YOU'VE BEEN INVITED TOO, KYO-KUN...
YOU'VE BEEN INVITED ...!!
IT ISN'T A BANQUET...
...BUT STILL...

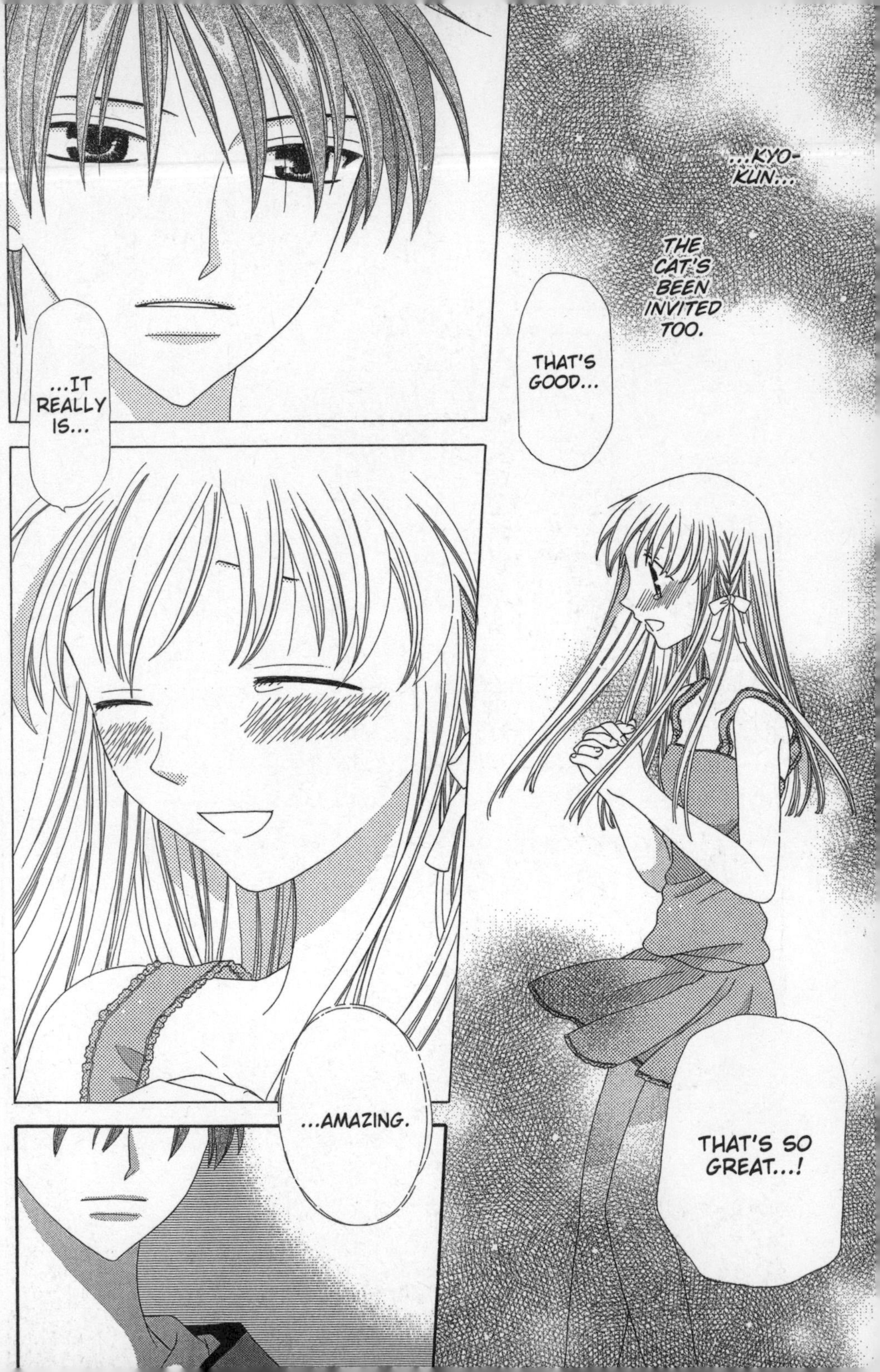
...KYO-KUN...
THE CAT'S BEEN INVITED TOO.
THAT'S GOOD...
THAT'S SO GREAT...!
...IT REALLY IS...
...AMAZING.

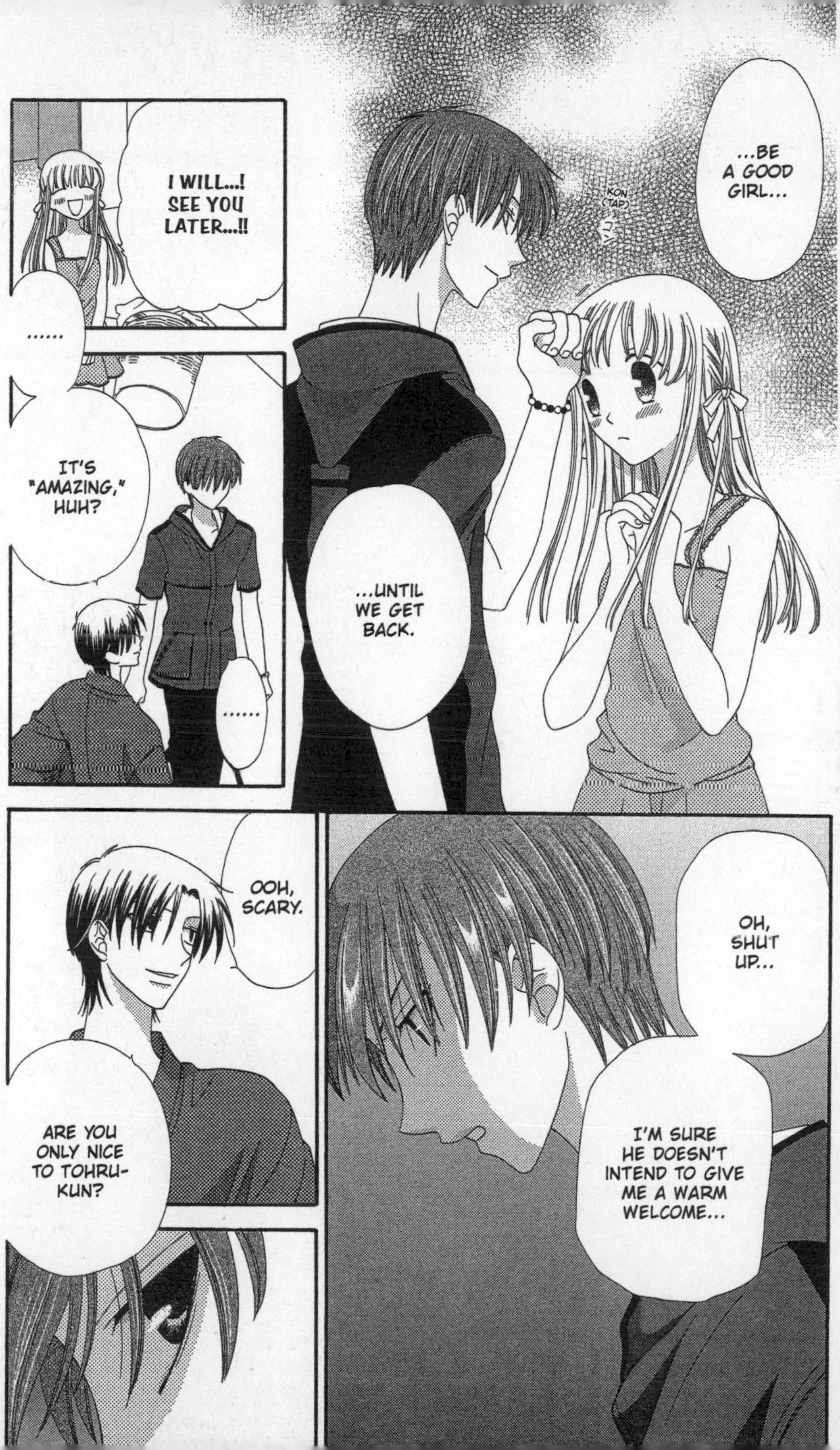
...BE A GOOD GIRL...
KON (TAP)
...UNTIL WE GET BACK.
I WILL...! SEE YOU LATER...!!
......
IT'S "AMAZING," HUH?
......
OH, SHUT UP...
I'M SURE HE DOESN'T INTEND TO GIVE ME A WARM WELCOME...
OOH, SCARY.
ARE YOU ONLY NICE TO TOHRU-KUN?

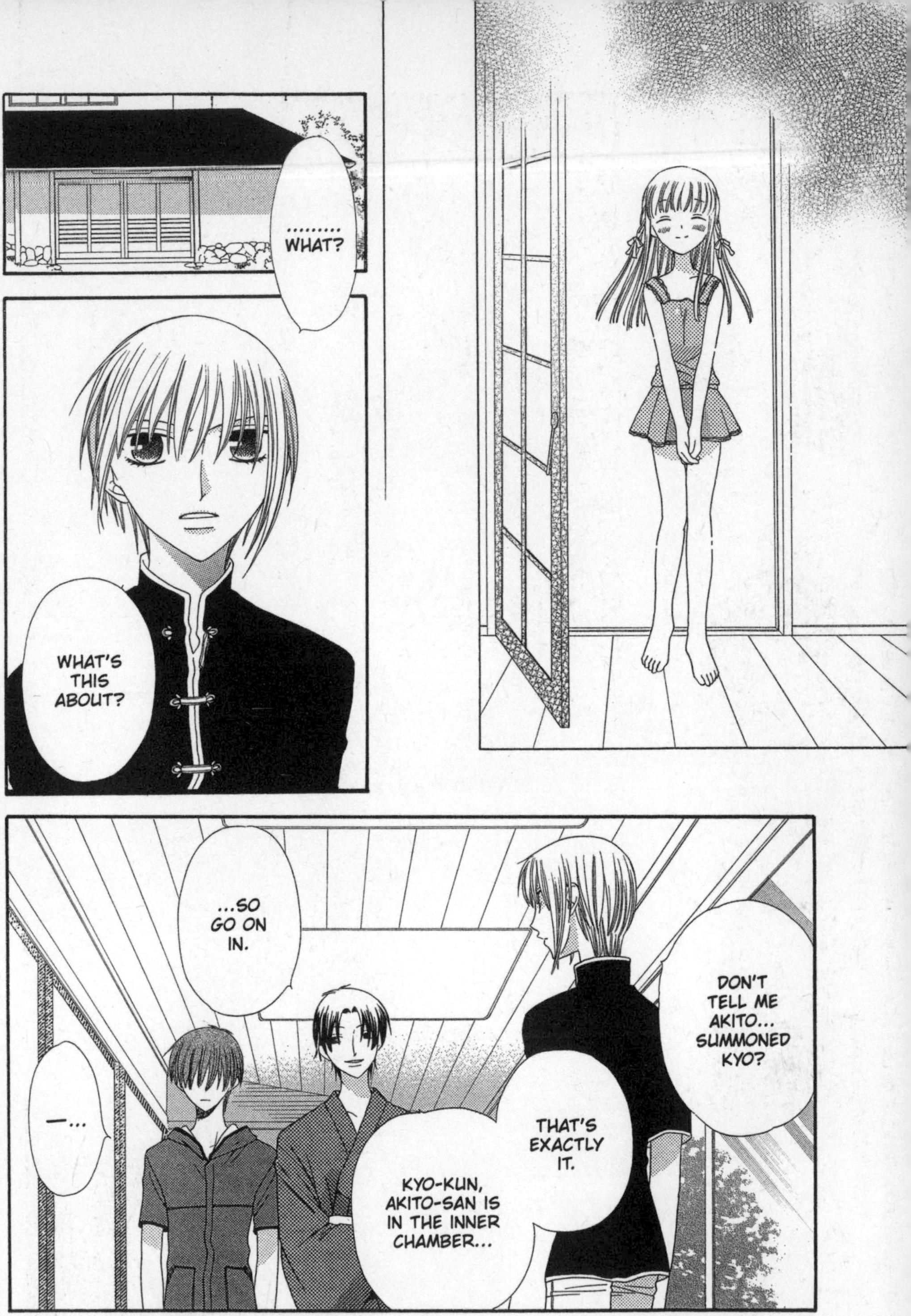
....
WHAT?
WHAT'S THIS ABOUT?
DON'T TELL ME AKITO... SUMMONED KYO?
THAT'S EXACTLY IT.
KYO-KUN, AKITO-SAN IS IN THE INNER CHAMBER...
...SO GO ON IN.
—...

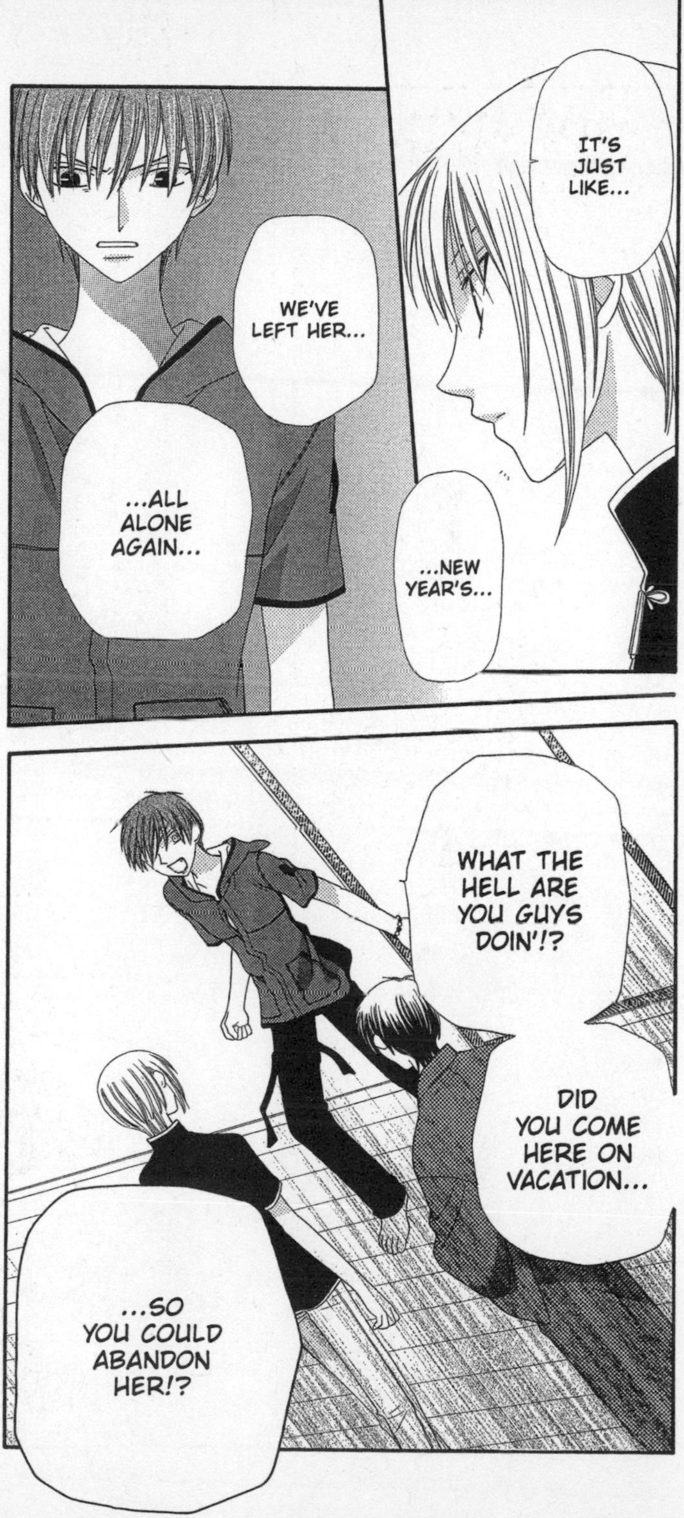
IT'S JUST LIKE...
...NEW YEAR'S...
WE'VE LEFT HER...
...ALL ALONE AGAIN...
WHAT THE HELL ARE YOU GUYS DOIN'!?
DID YOU COME HERE ON VACATION...
...SO YOU COULD ABANDON HER!?
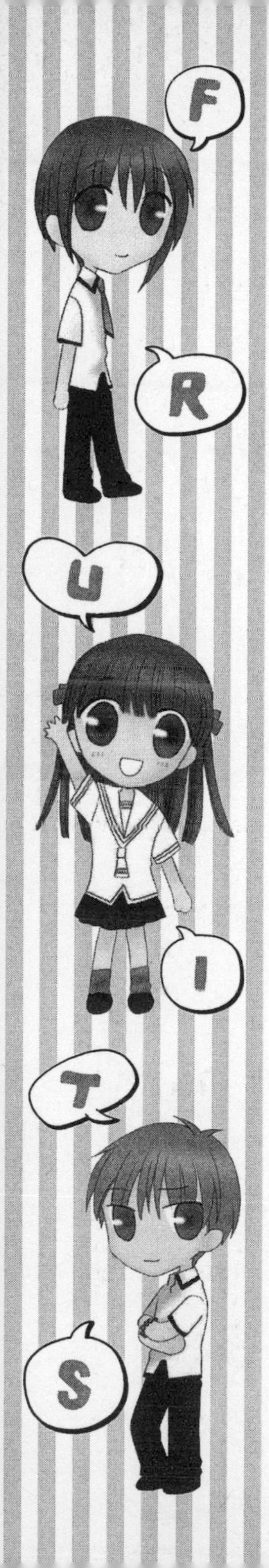
F
R
U
I
T
S

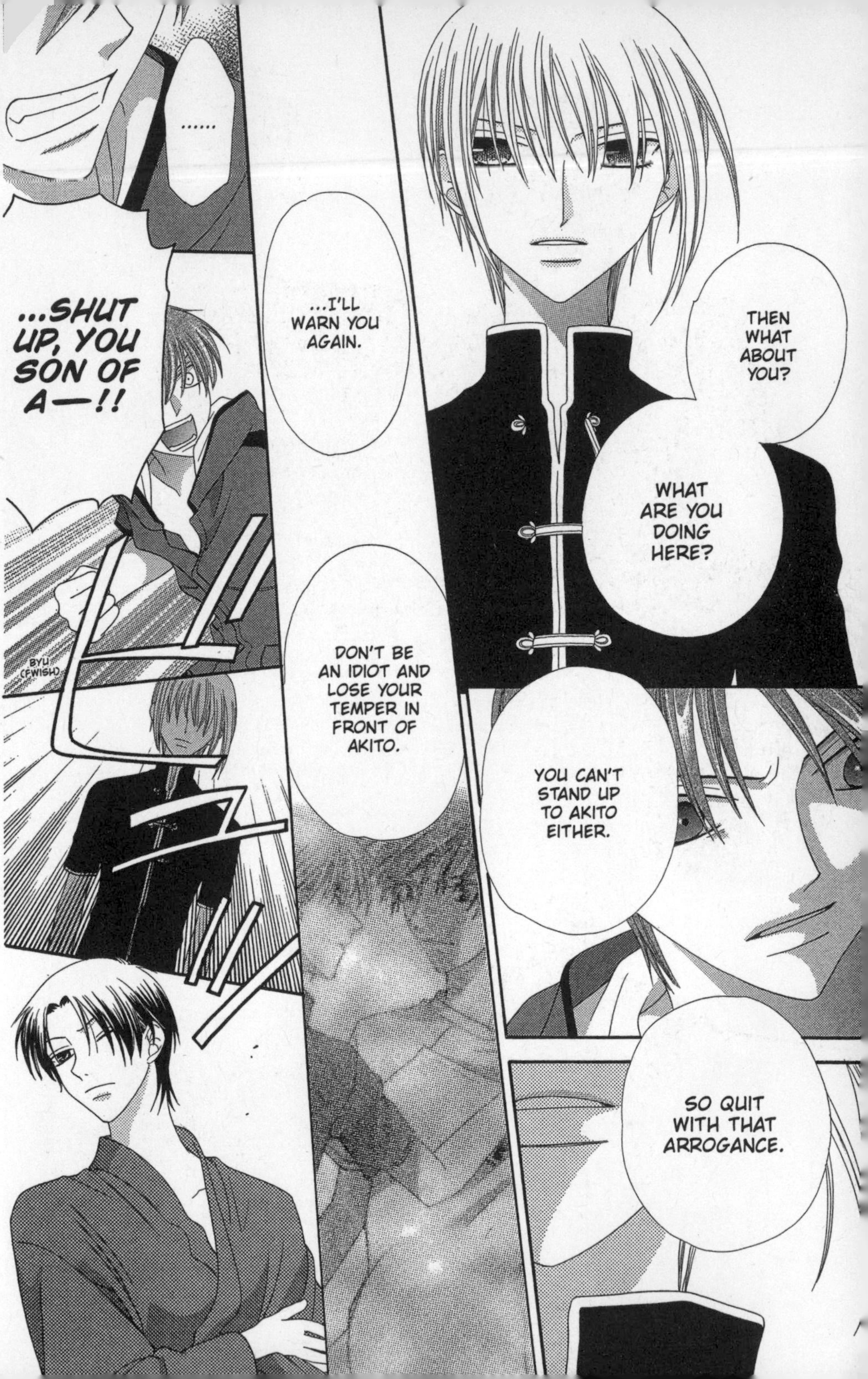
...I'LL WARN YOU AGAIN.
DON'T BE AN IDIOT AND LOSE YOUR TEMPER IN FRONT OF AKITO.
THEN WHAT ABOUT YOU?
WHAT ARE YOU DOING HERE?
YOU CAN'T STAND UP TO AKITO EITHER.
SO QUIT WITH THAT ARROGANCE.
......
...SHUT UP, YOU SON OF A—!!
BYU (FWISH)

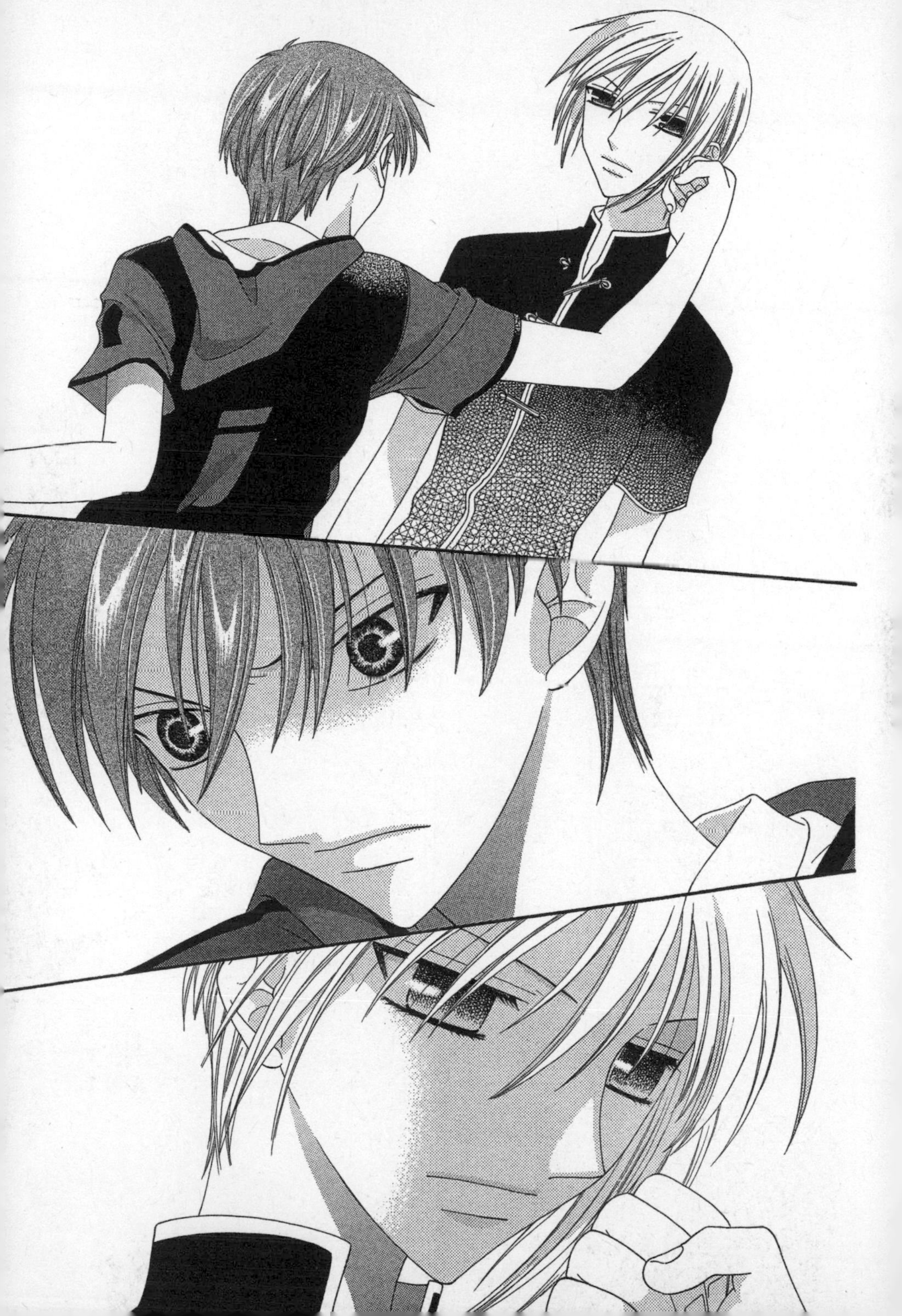

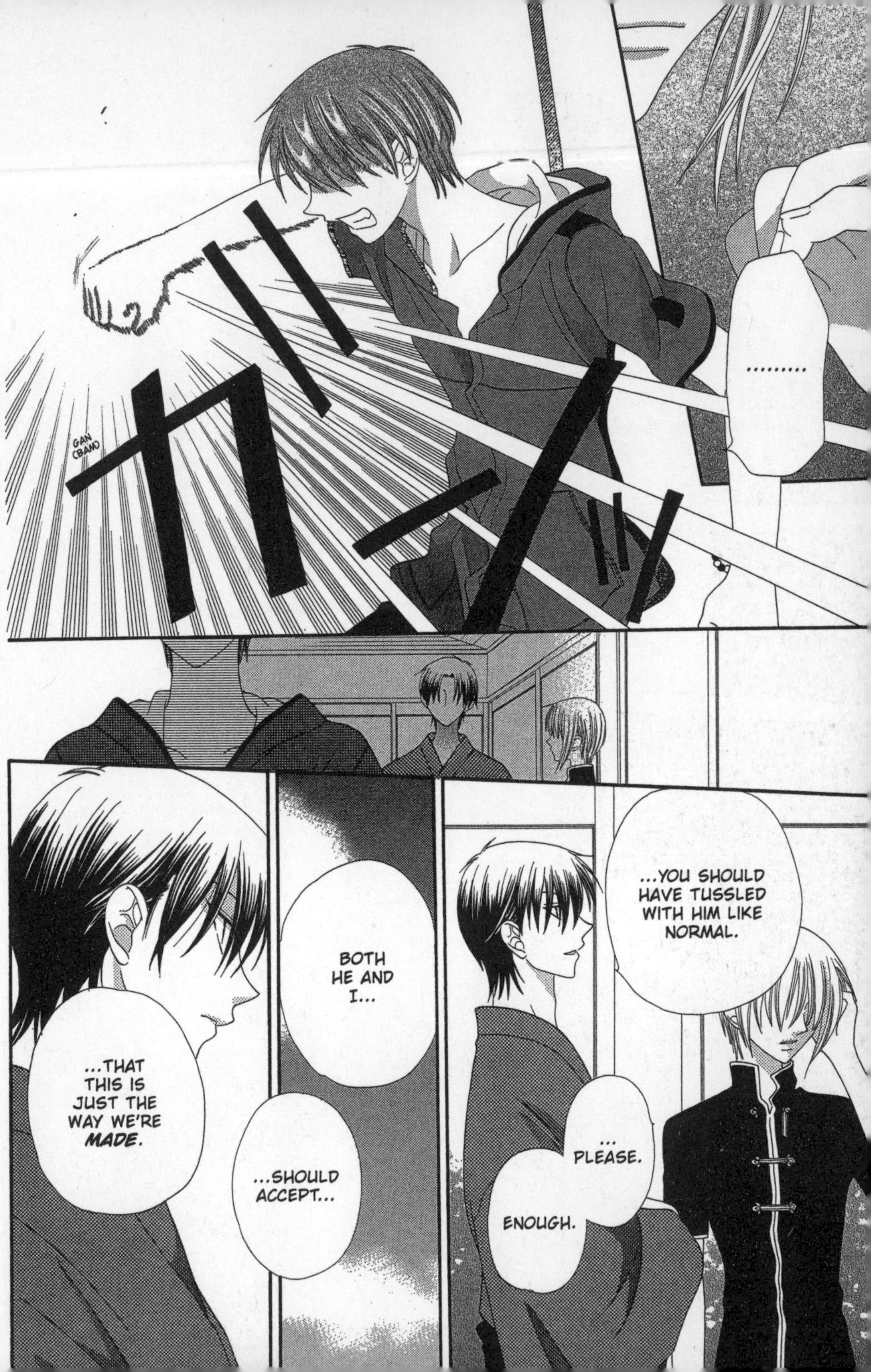
....
GAN (BAM)
...YOU SHOULD HAVE TUSSLED WITH HIM LIKE NORMAL.
... PLEASE.
ENOUGH.
BOTH HE AND I...
...SHOULD ACCEPT...
...THAT THIS IS JUST THE WAY WE'RE *MADE*.

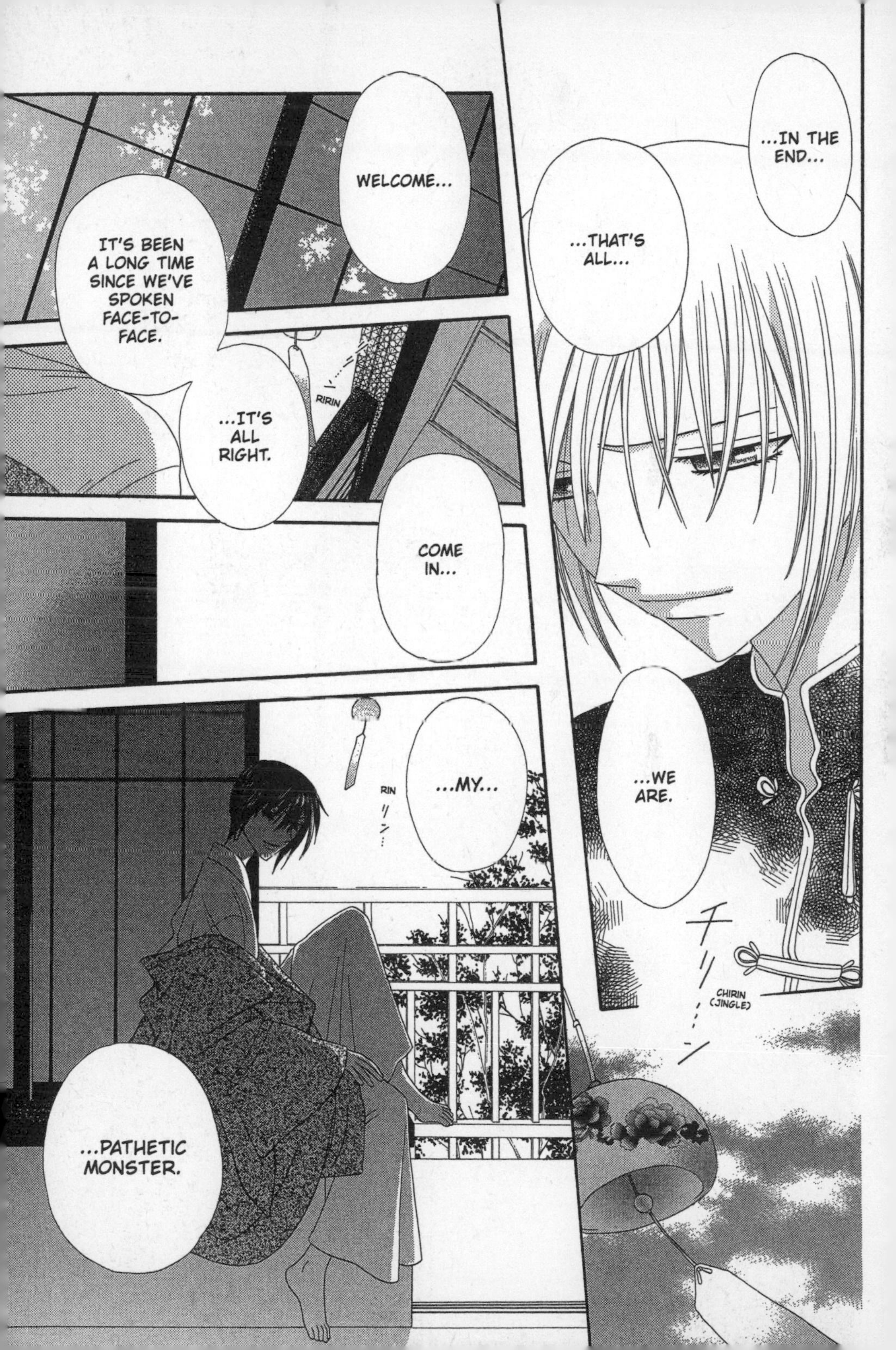

...IN THE END...
...THAT'S ALL...
...WE ARE.
CHIRIN (JINGLE)
WELCOME...
IT'S BEEN A LONG TIME SINCE WE'VE SPOKEN FACE-TO-FACE.
RIRIN
...IT'S ALL RIGHT.
COME IN...
...MY...
RIN
...PATHETIC MONSTER.

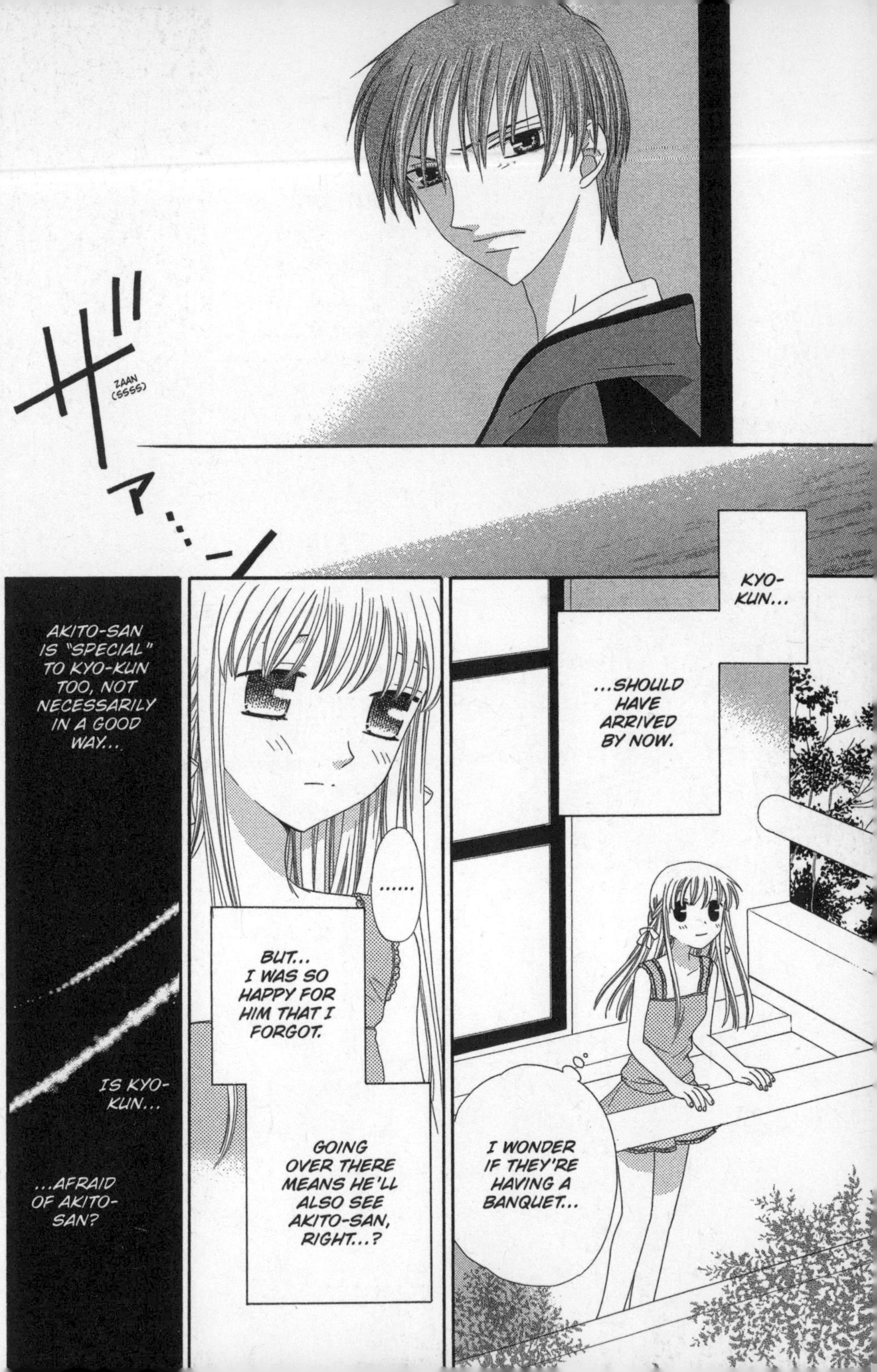
ザァ…ー
ZAAN (SSSSS)
KYO-KUN...
...SHOULD HAVE ARRIVED BY NOW.
I WONDER IF THEY'RE HAVING A BANQUET...
......
BUT... I WAS SO HAPPY FOR HIM THAT I FORGOT.
GOING OVER THERE MEANS HE'LL ALSO SEE AKITO-SAN, RIGHT...?
AKITO-SAN IS "SPECIAL" TO KYO-KUN TOO, NOT NECESSARILY IN A GOOD WAY...
IS KYO-KUN...
...AFRAID OF AKITO-SAN?

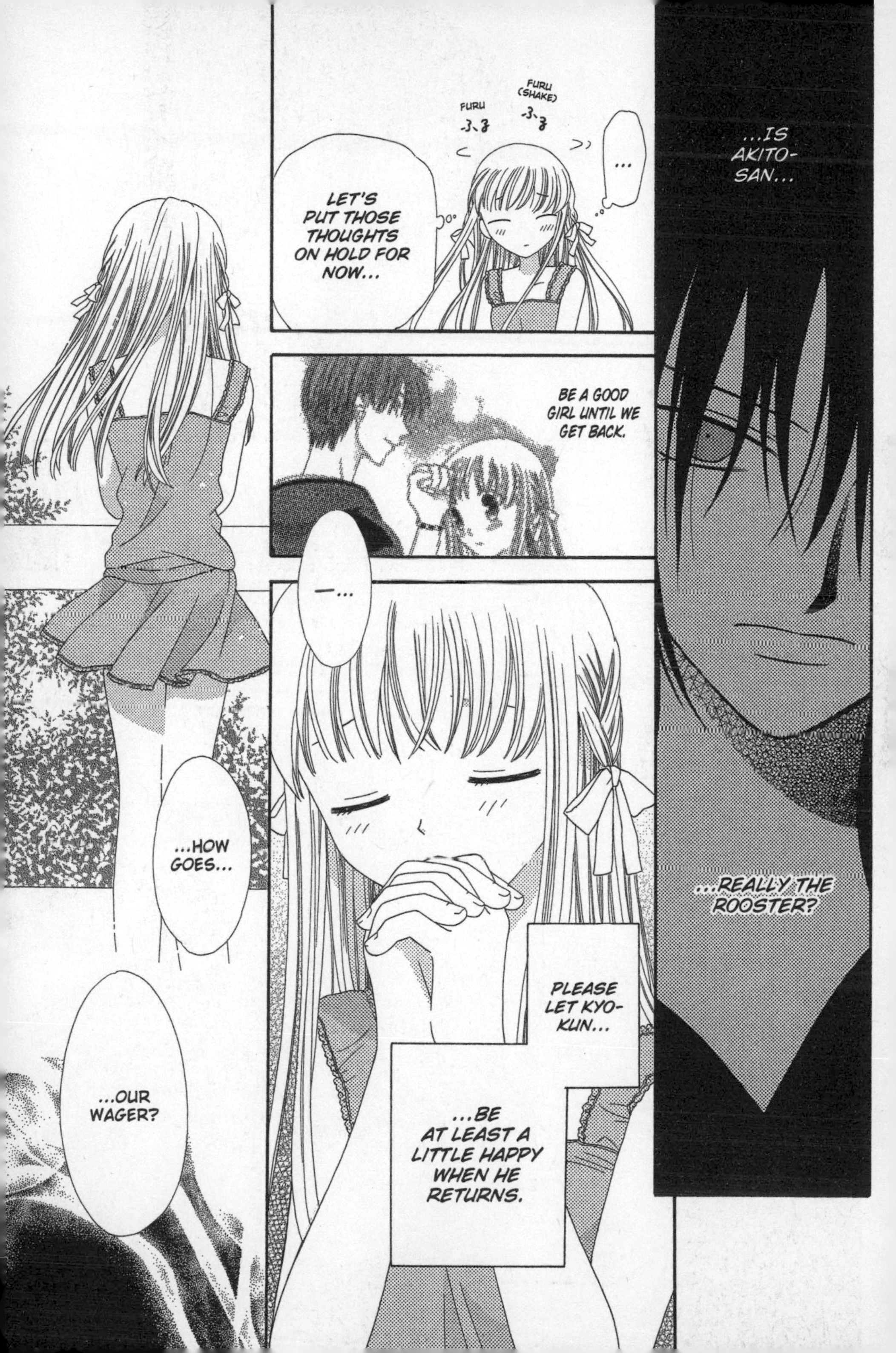

...IS AKITO-SAN...
...REALLY THE ROOSTER?
FURU (SHAKE)
FURU
...
LET'S PUT THOSE THOUGHTS ON HOLD FOR NOW...
BE A GOOD GIRL UNTIL WE GET BACK.
—...
PLEASE LET KYO-KUN...
...BE AT LEAST A LITTLE HAPPY WHEN HE RETURNS.
...HOW GOES...
...OUR WAGER?

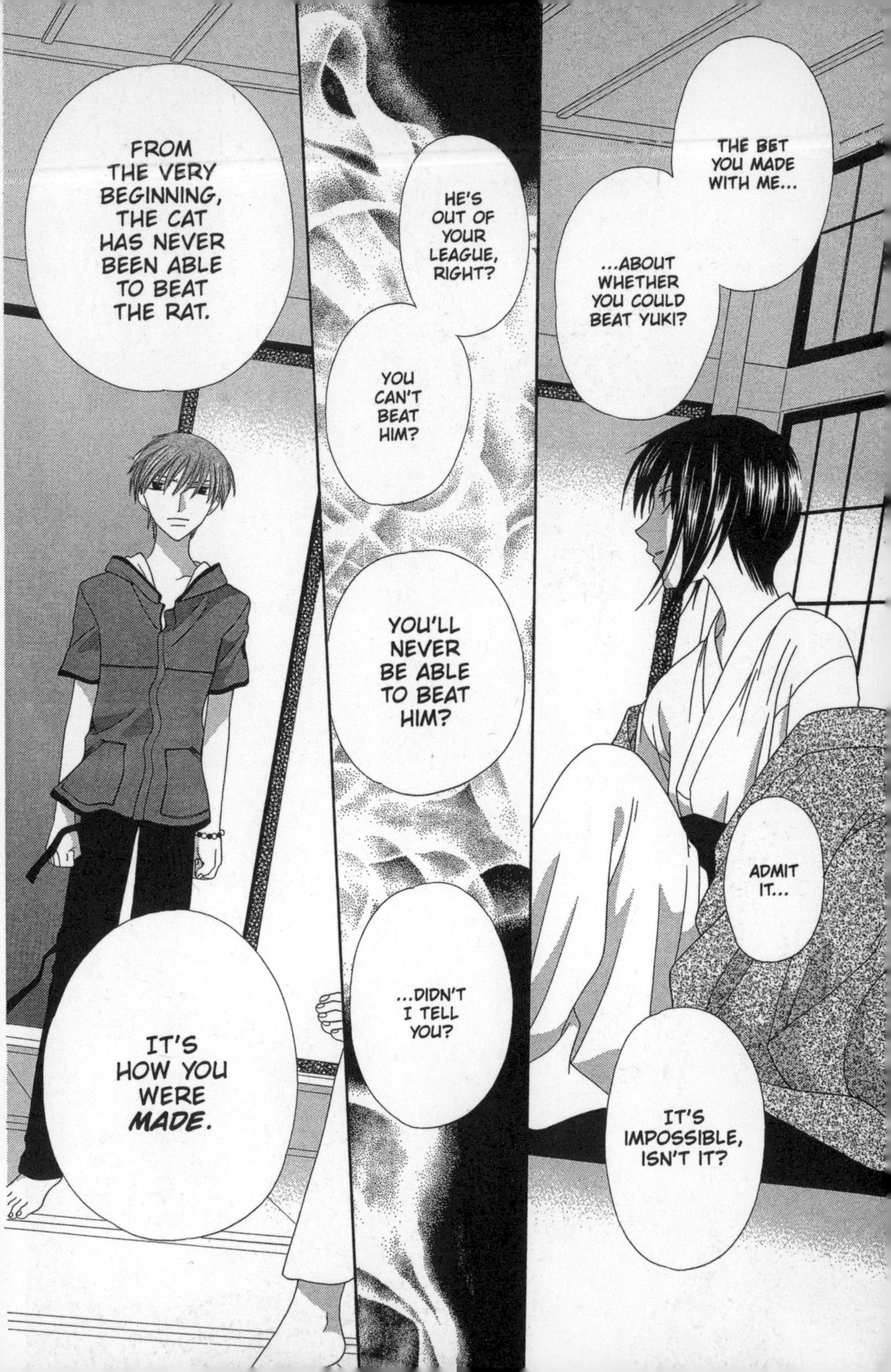
THE BET YOU MADE WITH ME...
...ABOUT WHETHER YOU COULD BEAT YUKI?
ADMIT IT...
IT'S IMPOSSIBLE, ISN'T IT?
HE'S OUT OF YOUR LEAGUE, RIGHT?
YOU CAN'T BEAT HIM?
YOU'LL NEVER BE ABLE TO BEAT HIM?
...DIDN'T I TELL YOU?
FROM THE VERY BEGINNING, THE CAT HAS NEVER BEEN ABLE TO BEAT THE RAT.
IT'S HOW YOU WERE *MADE*.

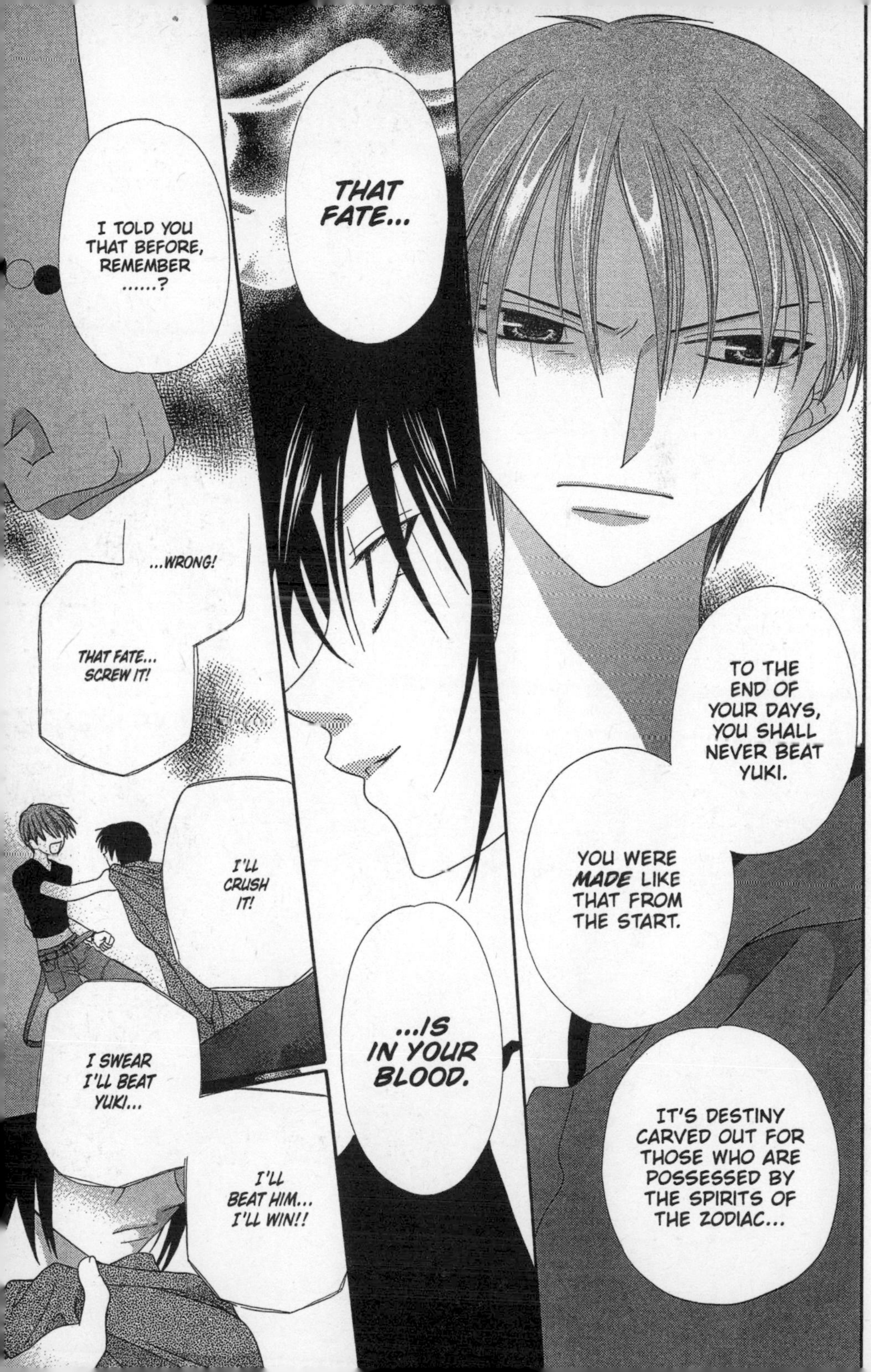
TO THE END OF YOUR DAYS, YOU SHALL NEVER BEAT YUKI.
YOU WERE MADE LIKE THAT FROM THE START.
IT'S DESTINY CARVED OUT FOR THOSE WHO ARE POSSESSED BY THE SPIRITS OF THE ZODIAC...
THAT FATE...
...IS IN YOUR BLOOD.
I TOLD YOU THAT BEFORE, REMEMBER ......?
...WRONG!
THAT FATE... SCREW IT!
I'LL CRUSH IT!
I SWEAR I'LL BEAT YUKI...
I'LL BEAT HIM... I'LL WIN!!

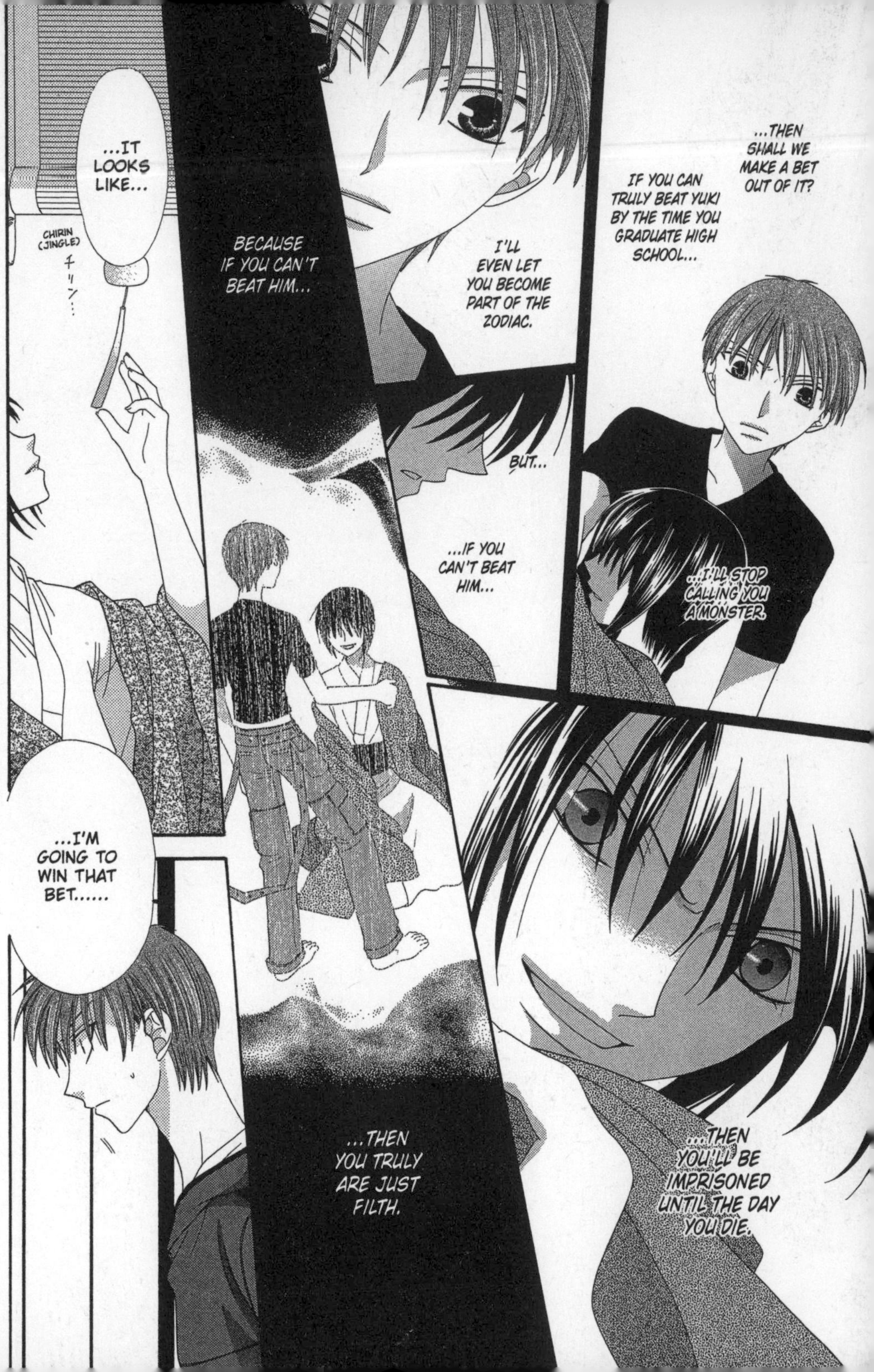
...THEN SHALL WE MAKE A BET OUT OF IT?
IF YOU CAN TRULY BEAT YUKI BY THE TIME YOU GRADUATE HIGH SCHOOL...
I'LL EVEN LET YOU BECOME PART OF THE ZODIAC.
...I'LL STOP CALLING YOU A MONSTER.
BUT...
...IF YOU CAN'T BEAT HIM...
...THEN YOU'LL BE IMPRISONED UNTIL THE DAY YOU DIE.
BECAUSE IF YOU CAN'T BEAT HIM...
...THEN YOU TRULY ARE JUST FILTH.
...IT LOOKS LIKE...
CHIRIN (JINGLE)
チリン…
...I'M GOING TO WIN THAT BET......

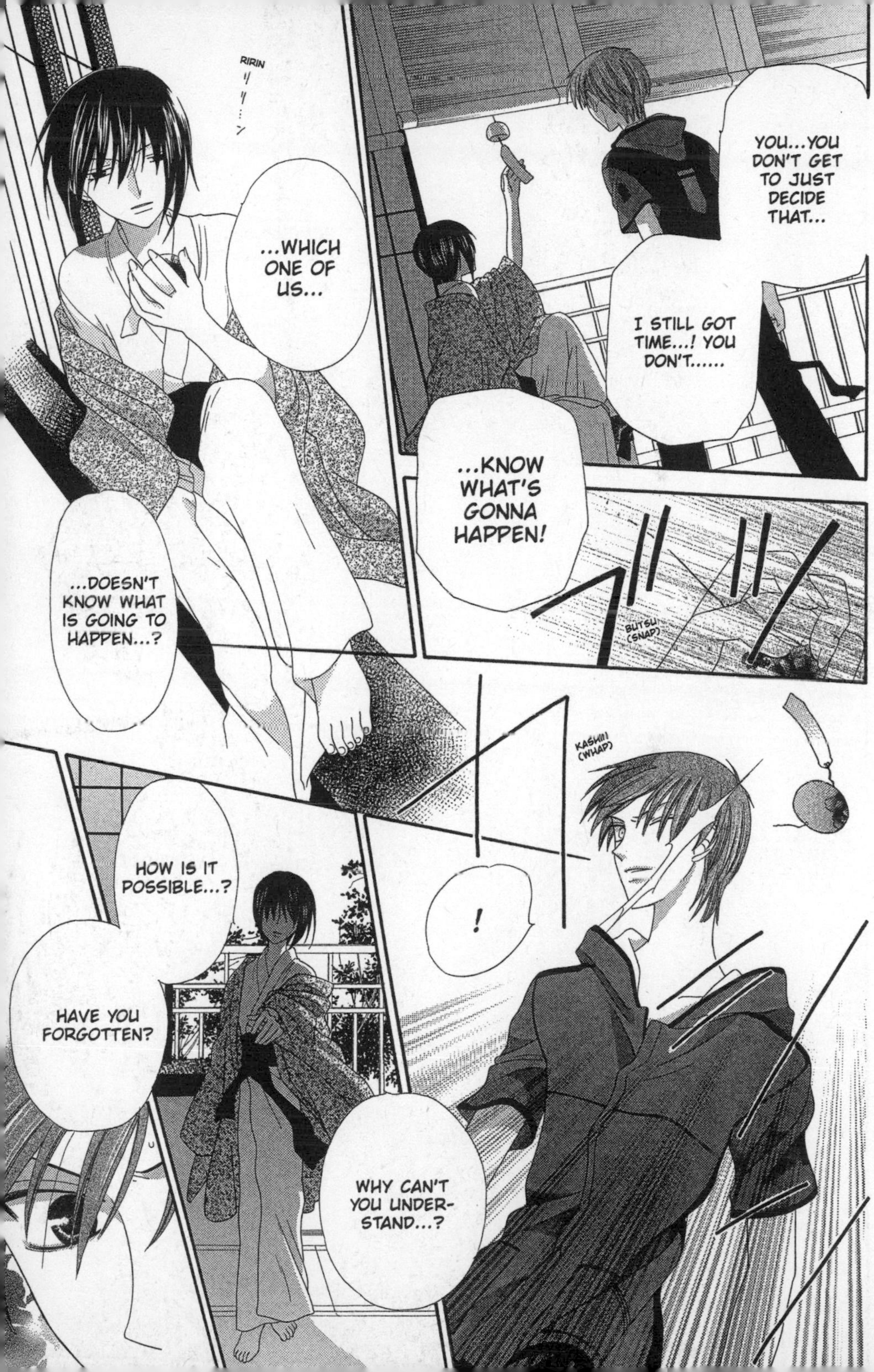
YOU...YOU DON'T GET TO JUST DECIDE THAT...
I STILL GOT TIME...! YOU DON'T......
...KNOW WHAT'S GONNA HAPPEN!
BUTSU (SNAP)
RIRIN
リリ…ン
...WHICH ONE OF US...
...DOESN'T KNOW WHAT IS GOING TO HAPPEN...?
KASHIN (WHAP)
!
HOW IS IT POSSIBLE...?
HAVE YOU FORGOTTEN?
WHY CAN'T YOU UNDER-STAND...?

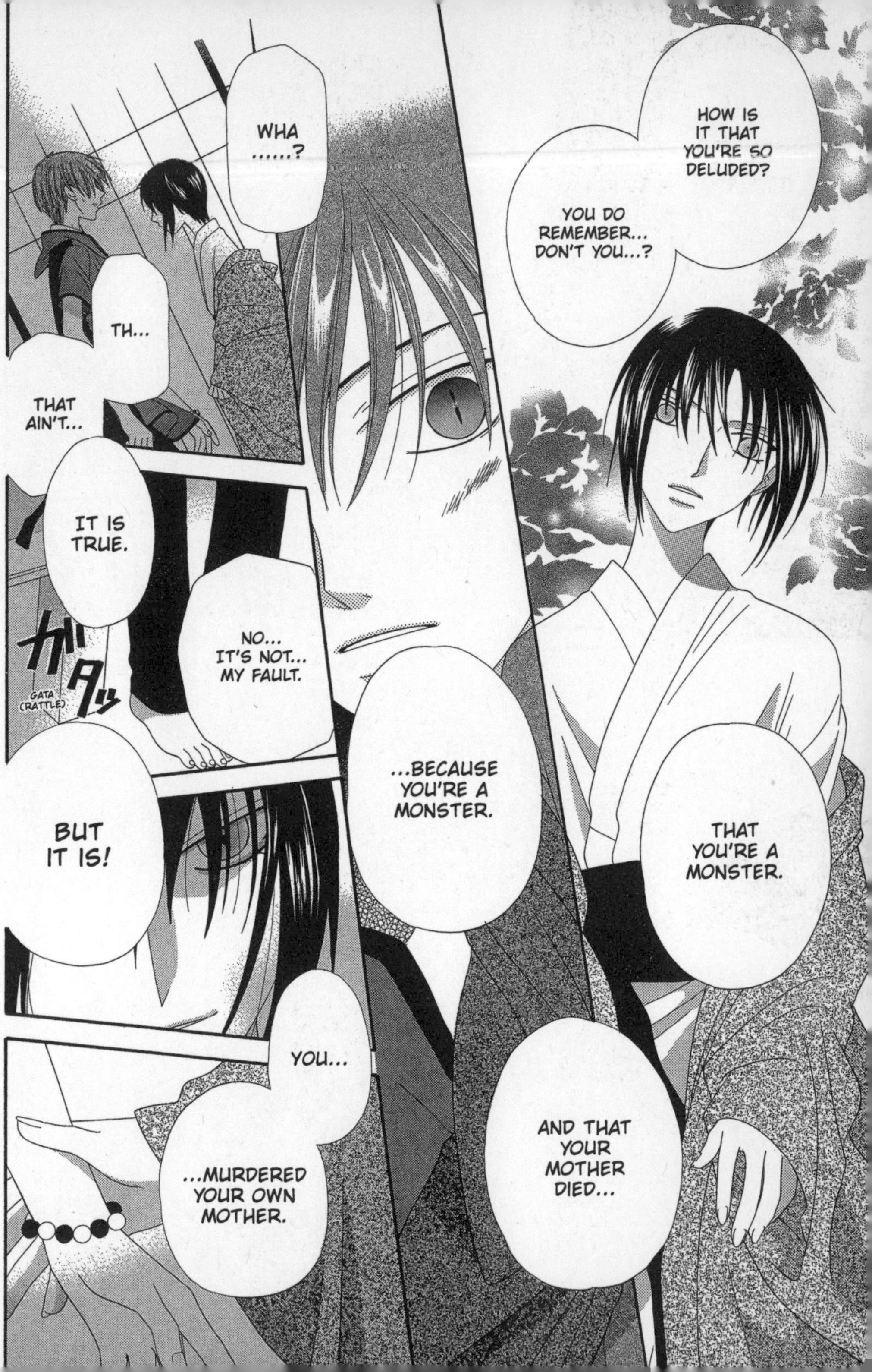
HOW IS IT THAT YOU'RE SO DELUDED?
YOU DO REMEMBER... DON'T YOU...?
WHA ......?
THAT YOU'RE A MONSTER.
AND THAT YOUR MOTHER DIED...
...BECAUSE YOU'RE A MONSTER.
TH...
THAT AIN'T...
NO... IT'S NOT... MY FAULT.
IT IS TRUE.
ガタッ
GATA (RATTLE)
BUT IT IS!
YOU...
...MURDERED YOUR OWN MOTHER.

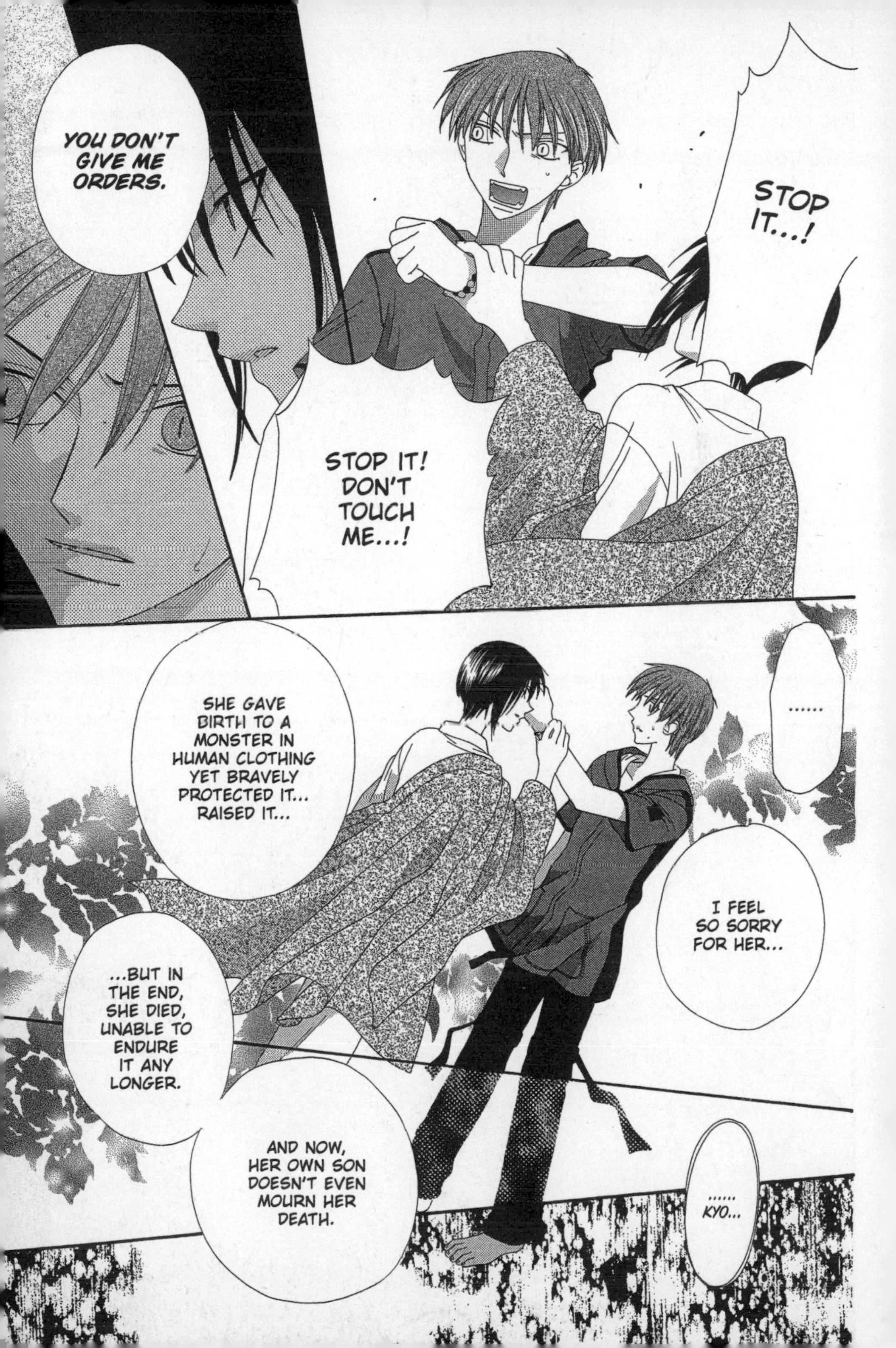
STOP IT...!
STOP IT! DON'T TOUCH ME...!
YOU DON'T GIVE ME ORDERS.
......
SHE GAVE BIRTH TO A MONSTER IN HUMAN CLOTHING YET BRAVELY PROTECTED IT... RAISED IT...
...BUT IN THE END, SHE DIED, UNABLE TO ENDURE IT ANY LONGER.
AND NOW, HER OWN SON DOESN'T EVEN MOURN HER DEATH.
I FEEL SO SORRY FOR HER...
...... KYO...

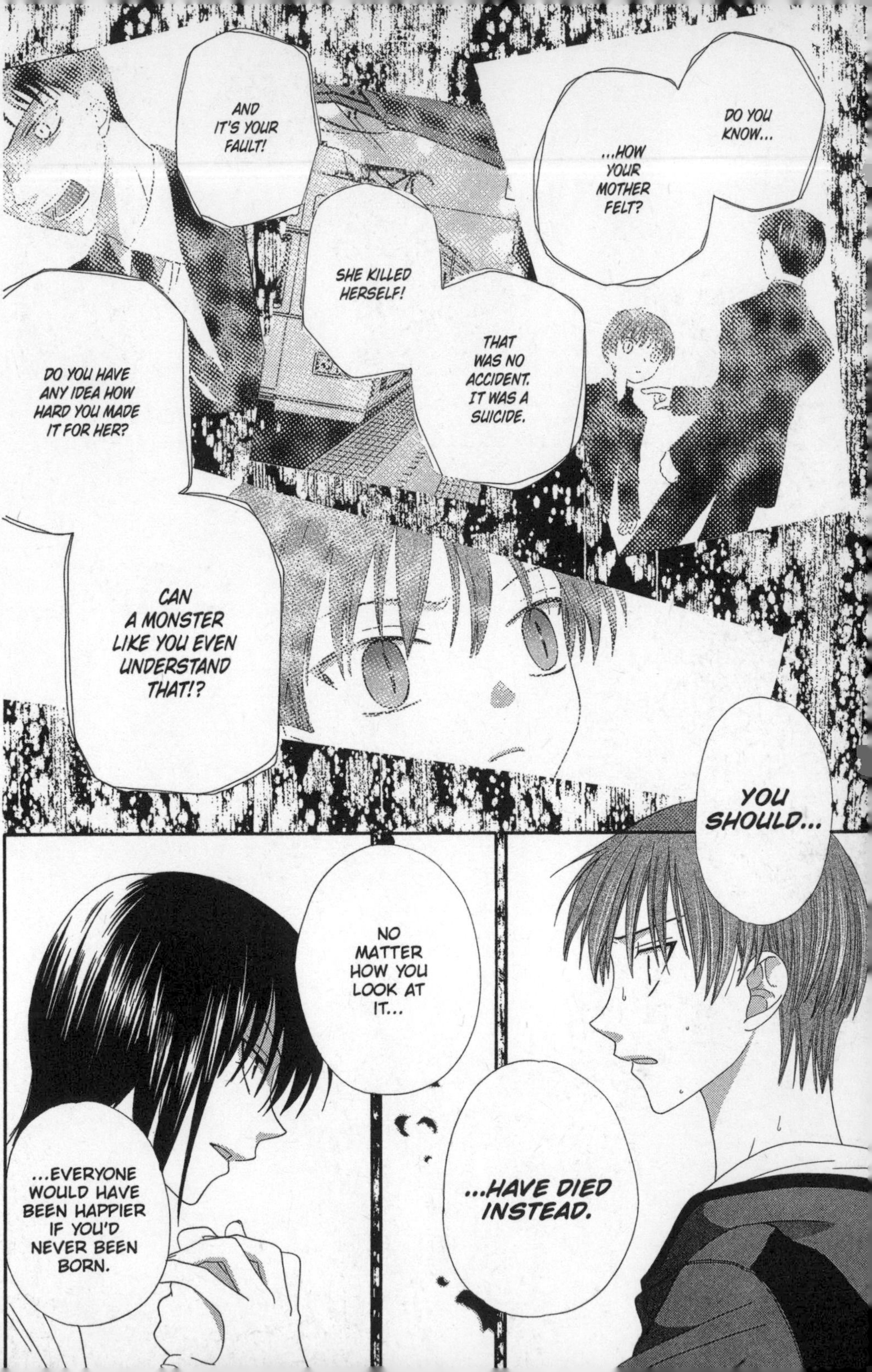
DO YOU KNOW...
...HOW YOUR MOTHER FELT?
SHE KILLED HERSELF!
THAT WAS NO ACCIDENT. IT WAS A SUICIDE.
AND IT'S YOUR FAULT!
DO YOU HAVE ANY IDEA HOW HARD YOU MADE IT FOR HER?
CAN A MONSTER LIKE YOU EVEN UNDERSTAND THAT!?
YOU SHOULD...
...HAVE DIED INSTEAD.
NO MATTER HOW YOU LOOK AT IT...
...EVERYONE WOULD HAVE BEEN HAPPIER IF YOU'D NEVER BEEN BORN.

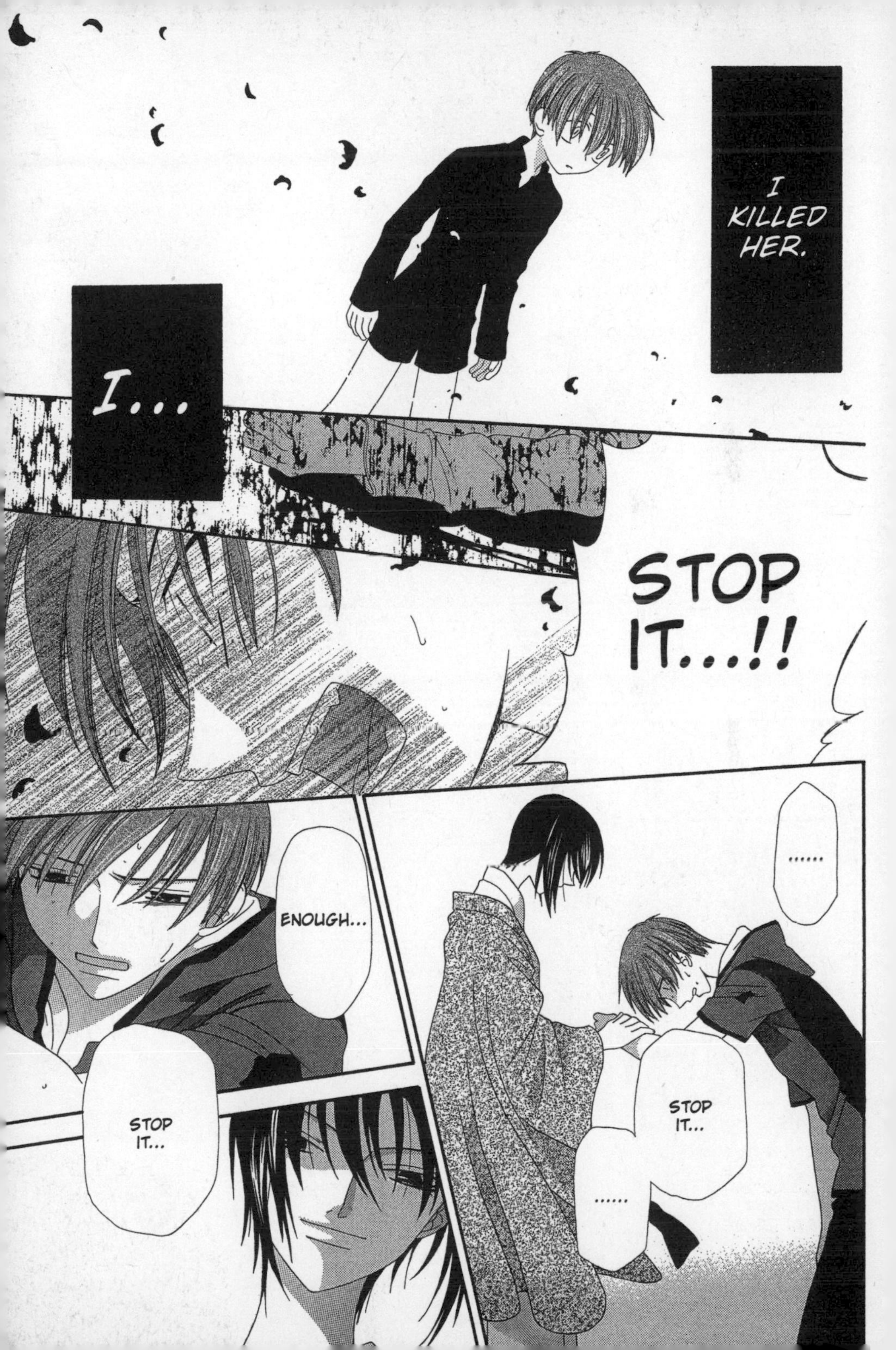
I KILLED HER.
I...
STOP IT...!!
......
STOP IT...
......
ENOUGH...
STOP IT...

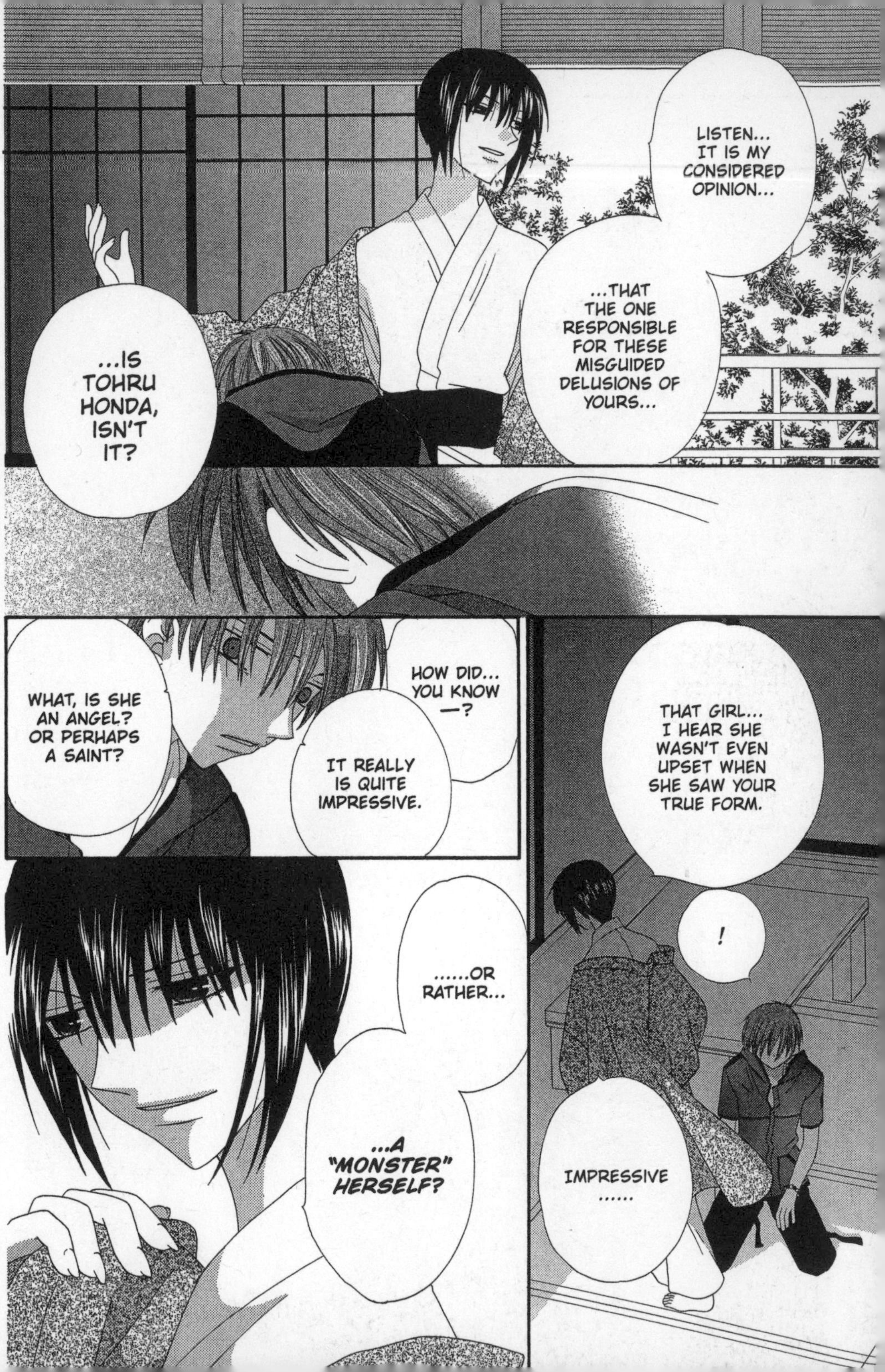

LISTEN... IT IS MY CONSIDERED OPINION...
...THAT THE ONE RESPONSIBLE FOR THESE MISGUIDED DELUSIONS OF YOURS...
...IS TOHRU HONDA, ISN'T IT?
THAT GIRL... I HEAR SHE WASN'T EVEN UPSET WHEN SHE SAW YOUR TRUE FORM.
!
IMPRESSIVE ......
HOW DID... YOU KNOW —?
IT REALLY IS QUITE IMPRESSIVE.
WHAT, IS SHE AN ANGEL? OR PERHAPS A SAINT?
......OR RATHER...
...A ***"MONSTER" HERSELF?***

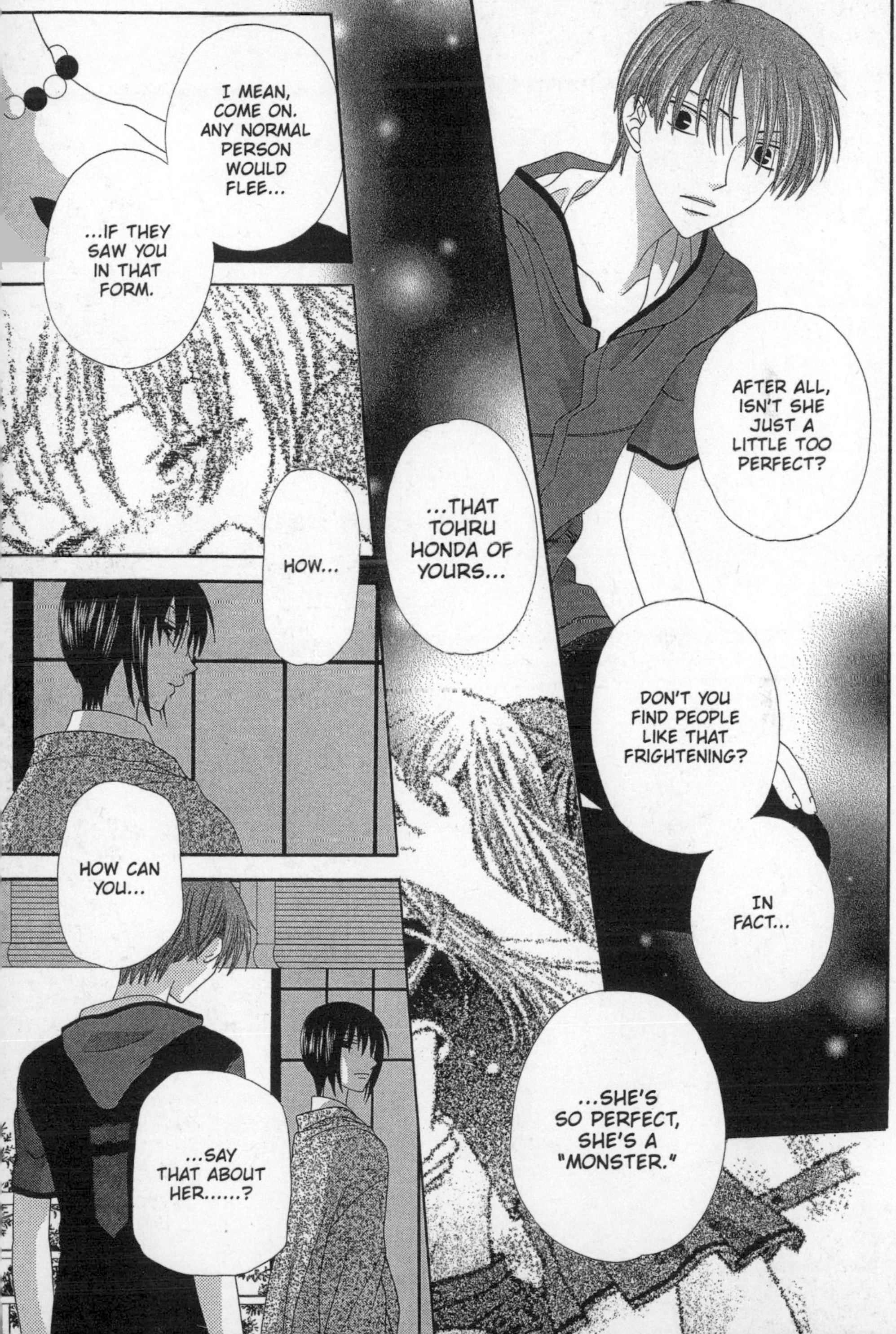
I MEAN, COME ON. ANY NORMAL PERSON WOULD FLEE...
...IF THEY SAW YOU IN THAT FORM.
...THAT TOHRU HONDA OF YOURS...
AFTER ALL, ISN'T SHE JUST A LITTLE TOO PERFECT?
DON'T YOU FIND PEOPLE LIKE THAT FRIGHTENING?
IN FACT...
...SHE'S SO PERFECT, SHE'S A "MONSTER."
HOW...
HOW CAN YOU...
...SAY THAT ABOUT HER......?

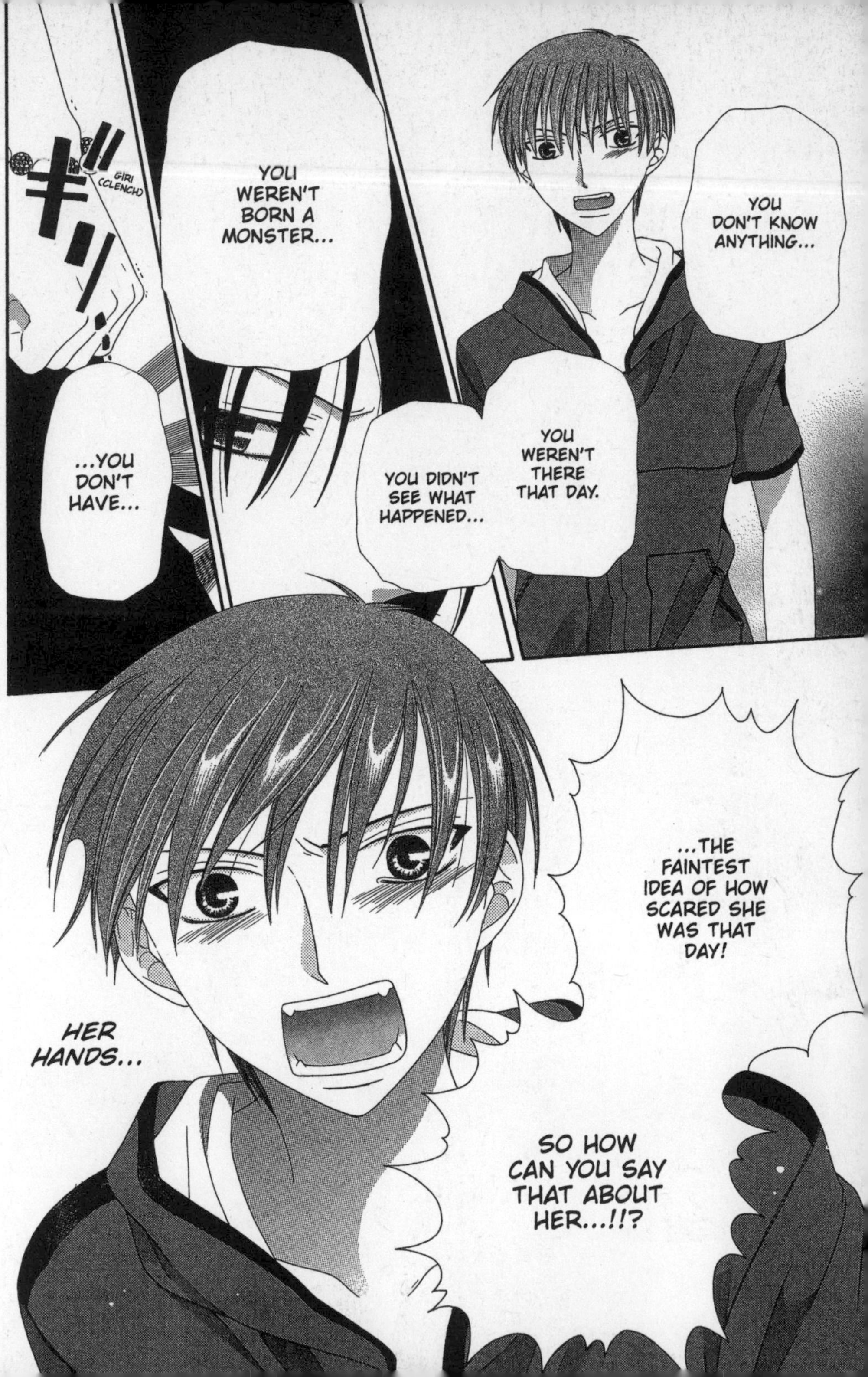
YOU DON'T KNOW ANYTHING...
YOU WEREN'T THERE THAT DAY.
YOU DIDN'T SEE WHAT HAPPENED...
YOU WEREN'T BORN A MONSTER...
GIRI (CLENCH)
...YOU DON'T HAVE...
...THE FAINTEST IDEA OF HOW SCARED SHE WAS THAT DAY!
SO HOW CAN YOU SAY THAT ABOUT HER...!!?
HER HANDS...

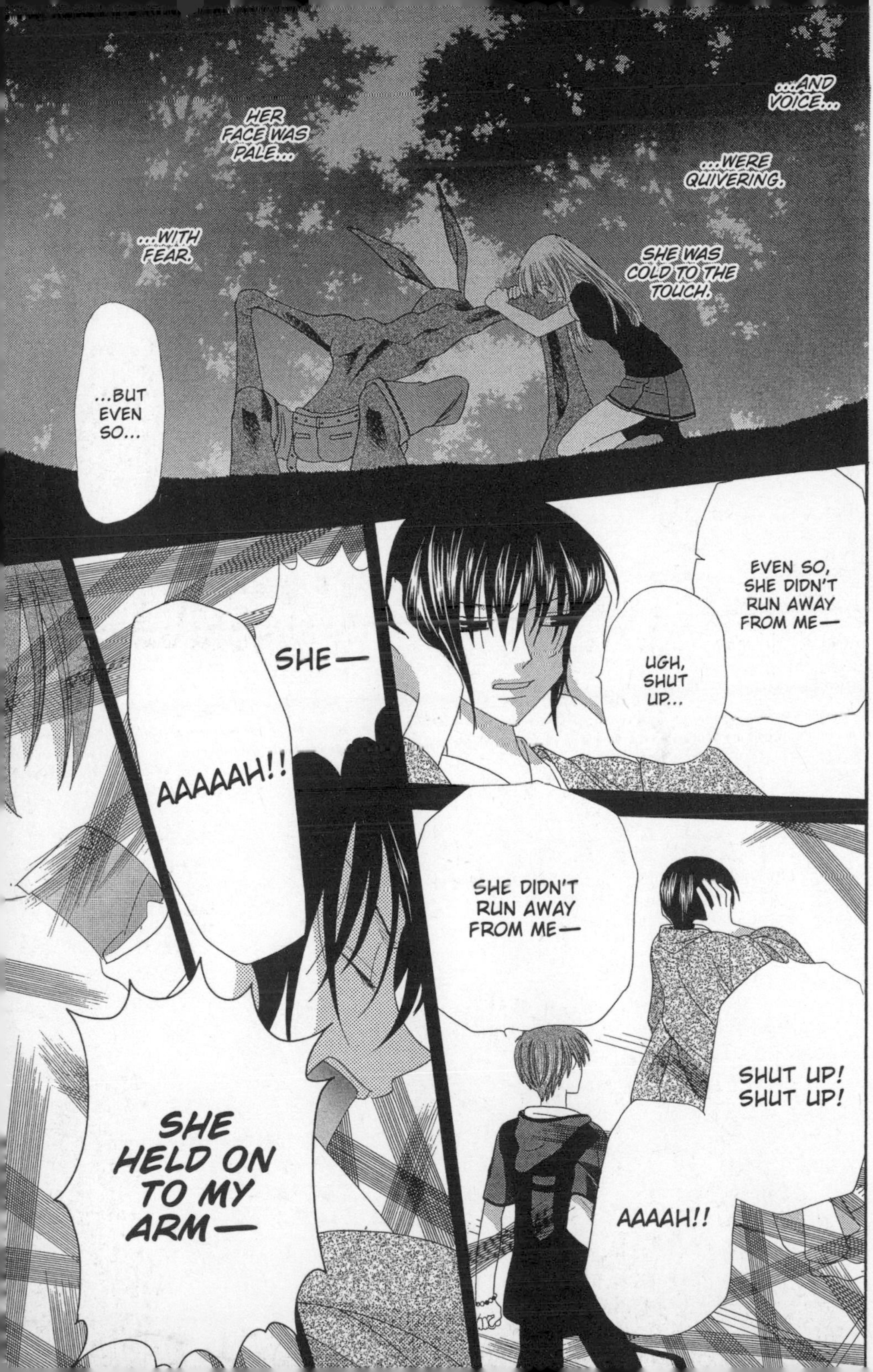

HER FACE WAS PALE...
...AND VOICE...
...WERE QUIVERING.
...WITH FEAR.
SHE WAS COLD TO THE TOUCH.
...BUT EVEN SO...
EVEN SO, SHE DIDN'T RUN AWAY FROM ME—
UGH, SHUT UP...
SHE DIDN'T RUN AWAY FROM ME—
SHUT UP! SHUT UP!
AAAAH!!
SHE—
AAAAAH!!
SHE HELD ON TO MY ARM—

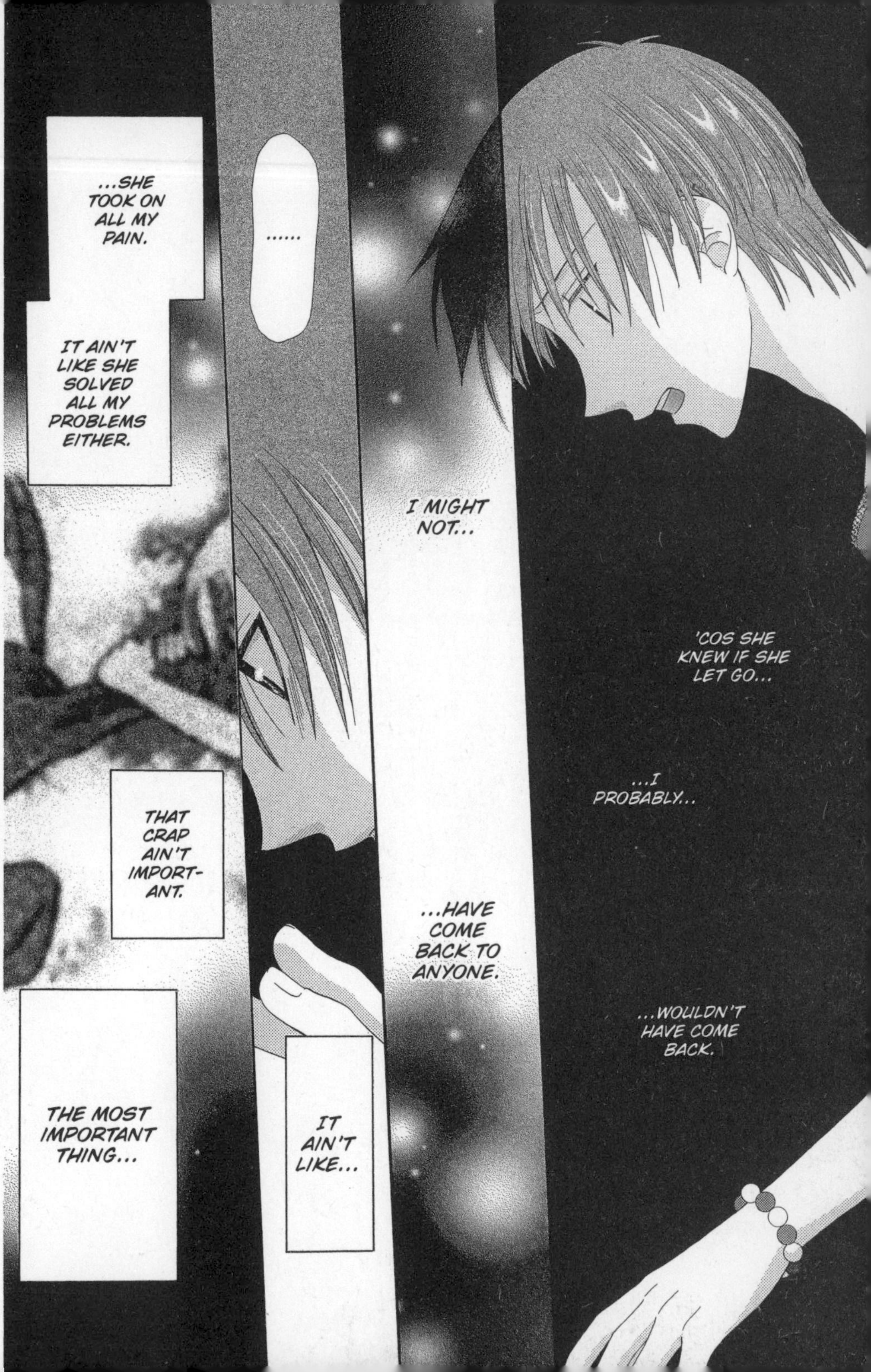
'COS SHE KNEW IF SHE LET GO...
...I PROBABLY...
...WOULDN'T HAVE COME BACK.
I MIGHT NOT...
...HAVE COME BACK TO ANYONE.
......
IT AIN'T LIKE...
...SHE TOOK ON ALL MY PAIN.
IT AIN'T LIKE SHE SOLVED ALL MY PROBLEMS EITHER.
THAT CRAP AIN'T IMPORT-ANT.
THE MOST IMPORTANT THING...

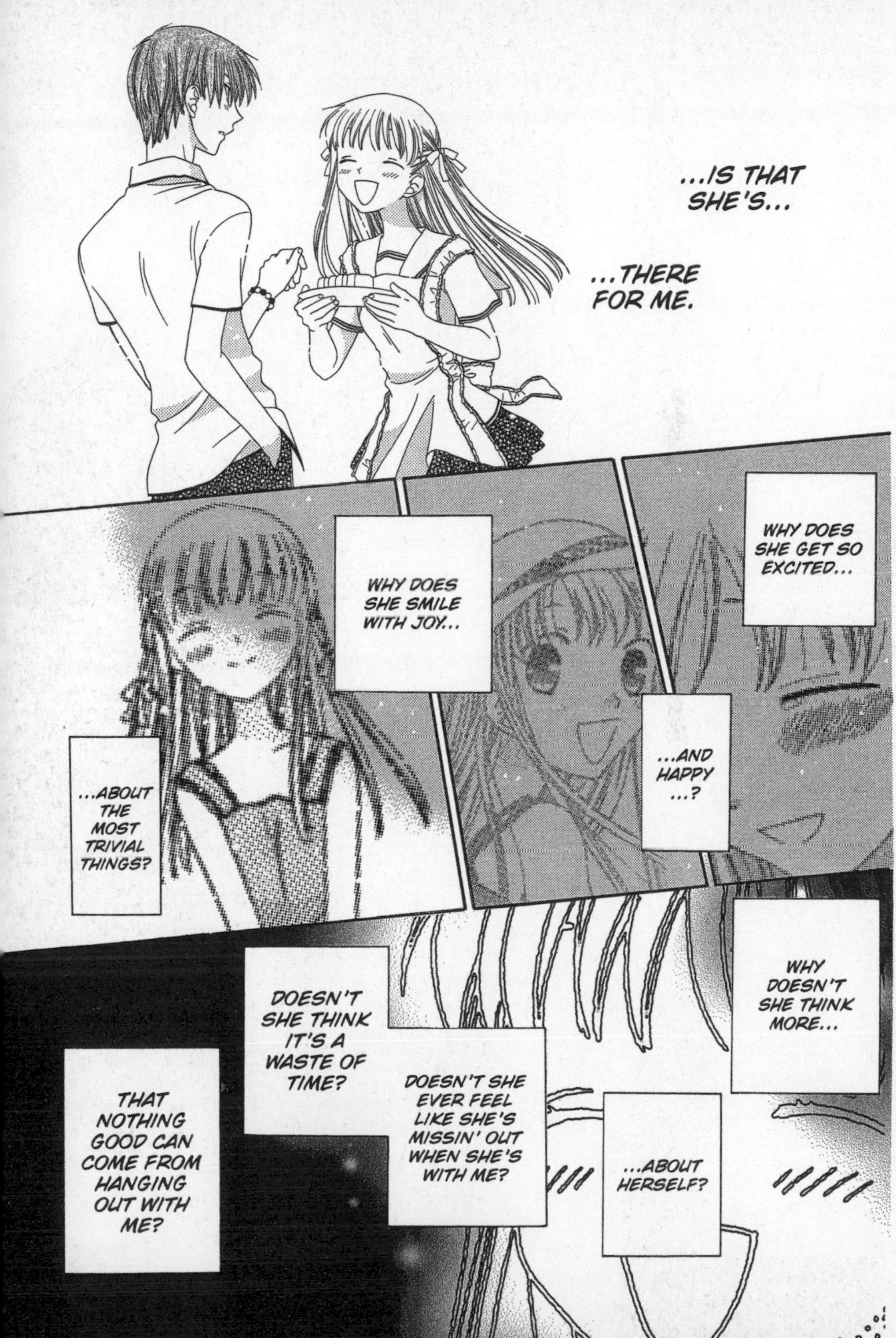

...IS THAT SHE'S...
...THERE FOR ME.
WHY DOES SHE GET SO EXCITED...
...AND HAPPY ...?
WHY DOES SHE SMILE WITH JOY...
...ABOUT THE MOST TRIVIAL THINGS?
WHY DOESN'T SHE THINK MORE...
...ABOUT HERSELF?
DOESN'T SHE THINK IT'S A WASTE OF TIME?
DOESN'T SHE EVER FEEL LIKE SHE'S MISSIN' OUT WHEN SHE'S WITH ME?
THAT NOTHING GOOD CAN COME FROM HANGING OUT WITH ME?

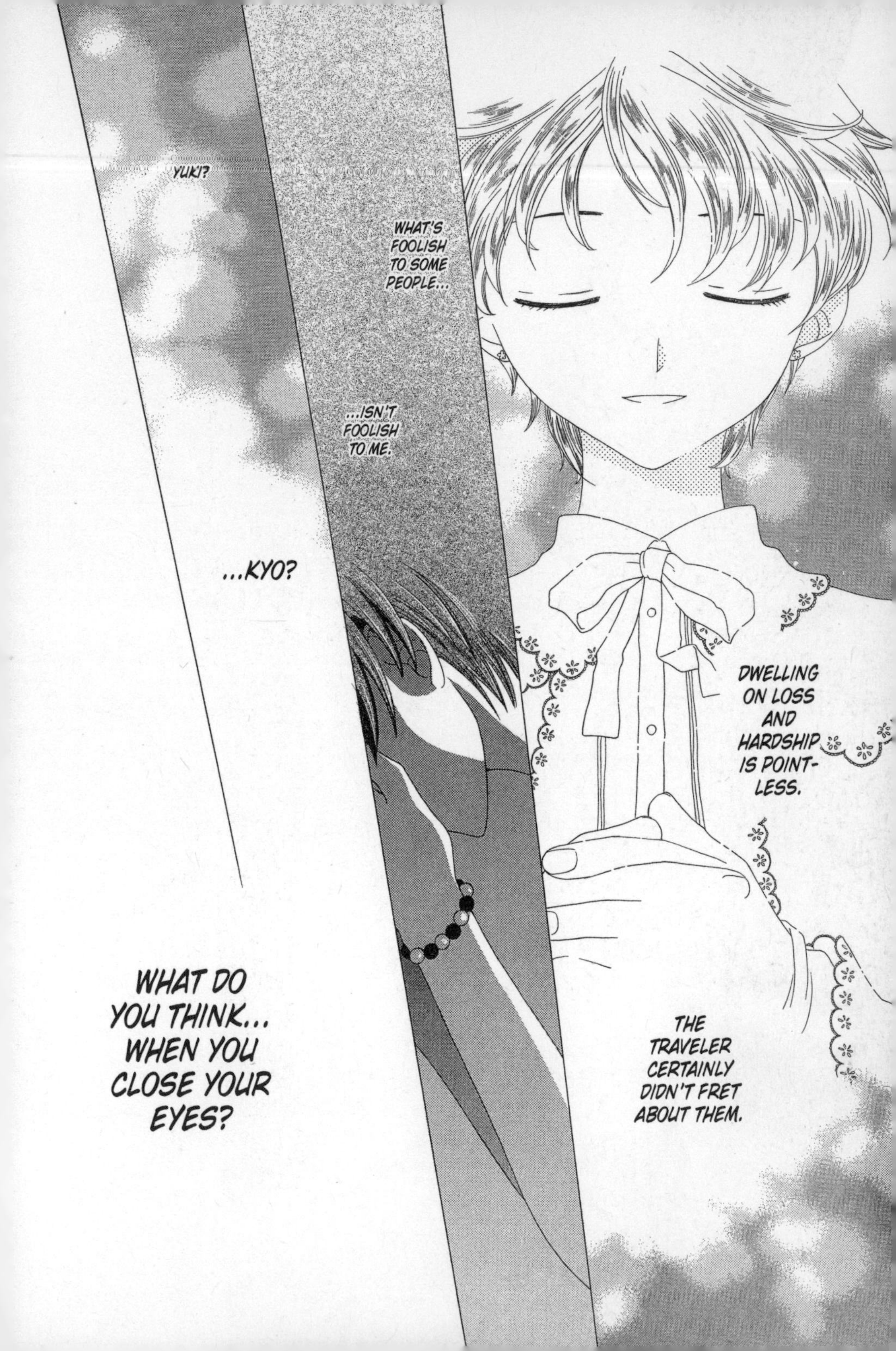
DWELLING ON LOSS AND HARDSHIP IS POINTLESS.
THE TRAVELER CERTAINLY DIDN'T FRET ABOUT THEM.
WHAT'S FOOLISH TO SOME PEOPLE...
...ISN'T FOOLISH TO ME.
YUKI?
...KYO?
WHAT DO YOU THINK... WHEN YOU CLOSE YOUR EYES?

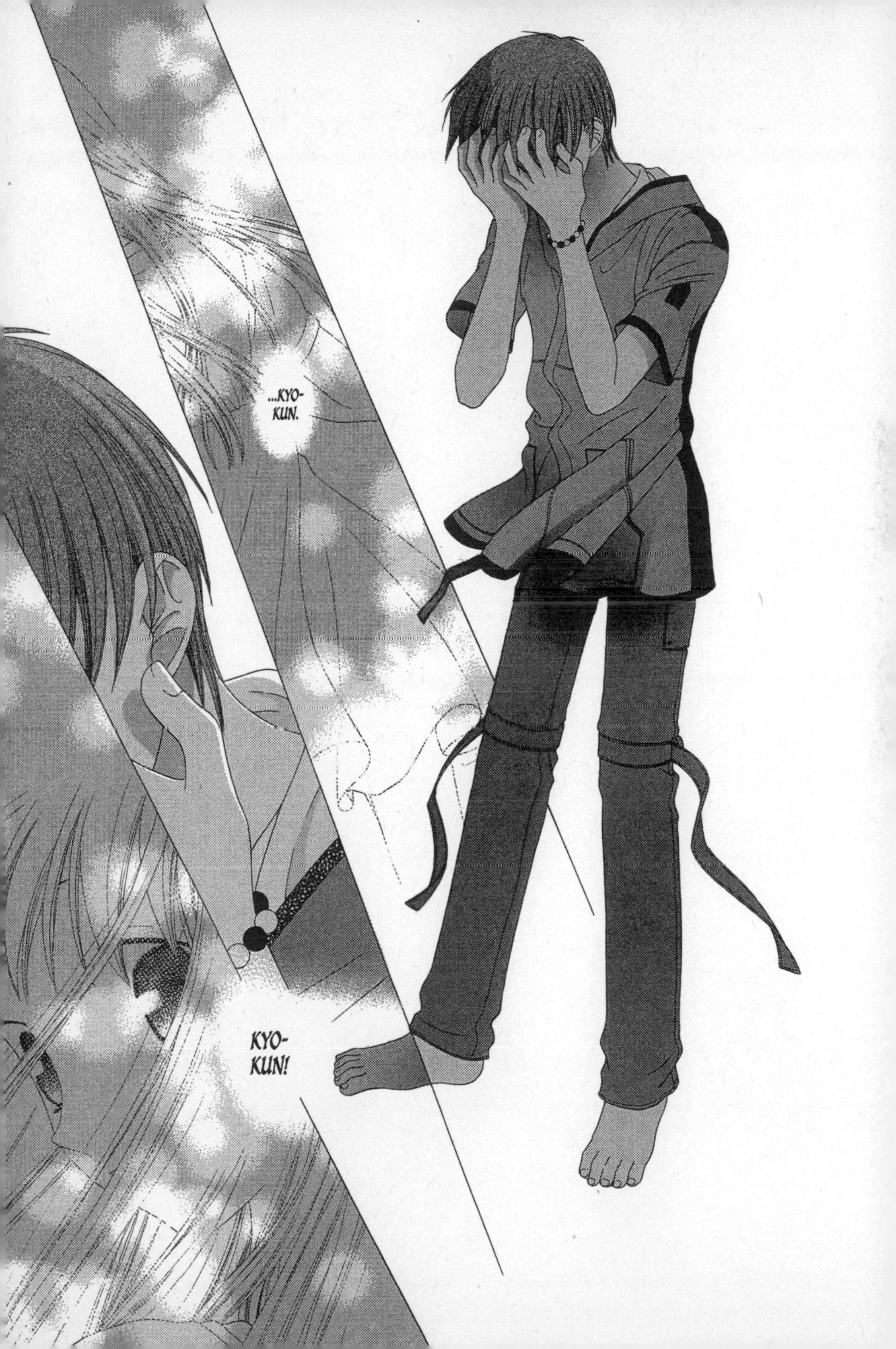
...KYO-KUN.
KYO-KUN!

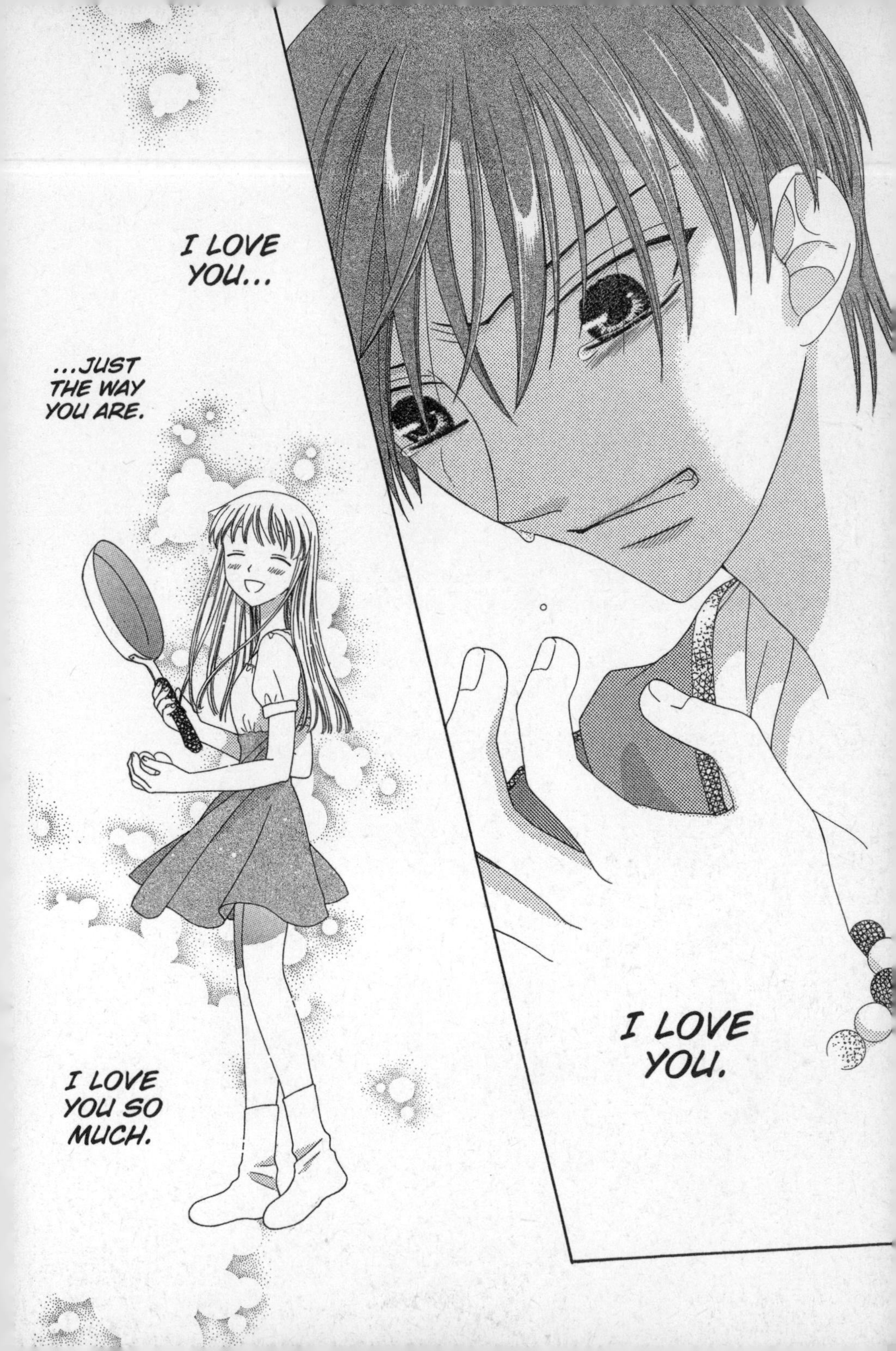
I LOVE YOU.
I LOVE YOU...
...JUST THE WAY YOU ARE.
I LOVE YOU SO MUCH.

Chapter 63

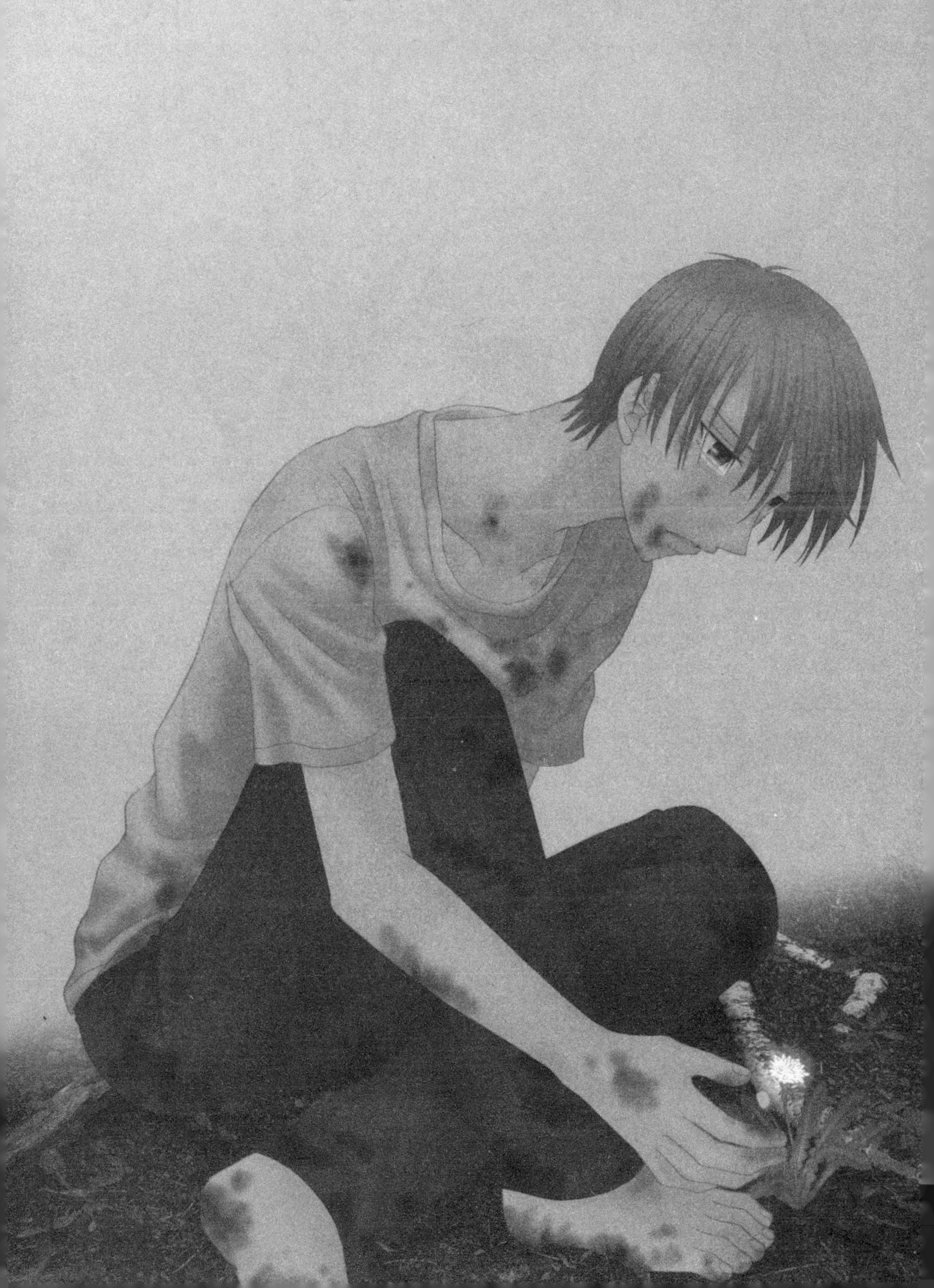

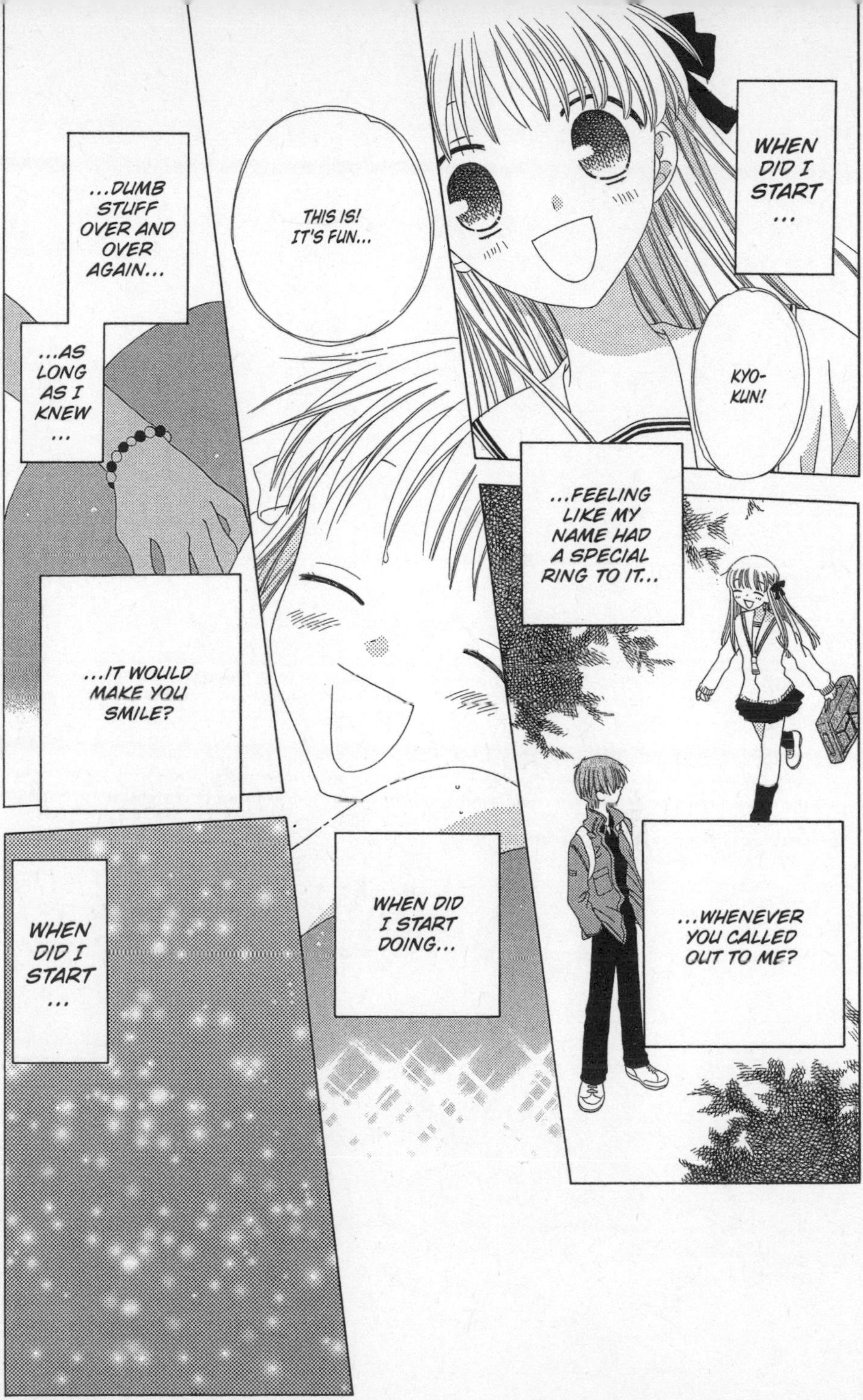
WHEN DID I START ...
KYO-KUN!
...FEELING LIKE MY NAME HAD A SPECIAL RING TO IT...
...WHENEVER YOU CALLED OUT TO ME?
THIS IS! IT'S FUN...
WHEN DID I START DOING...
...DUMB STUFF OVER AND OVER AGAIN...
...AS LONG AS I KNEW ...
...IT WOULD MAKE YOU SMILE?
WHEN DID I START ...

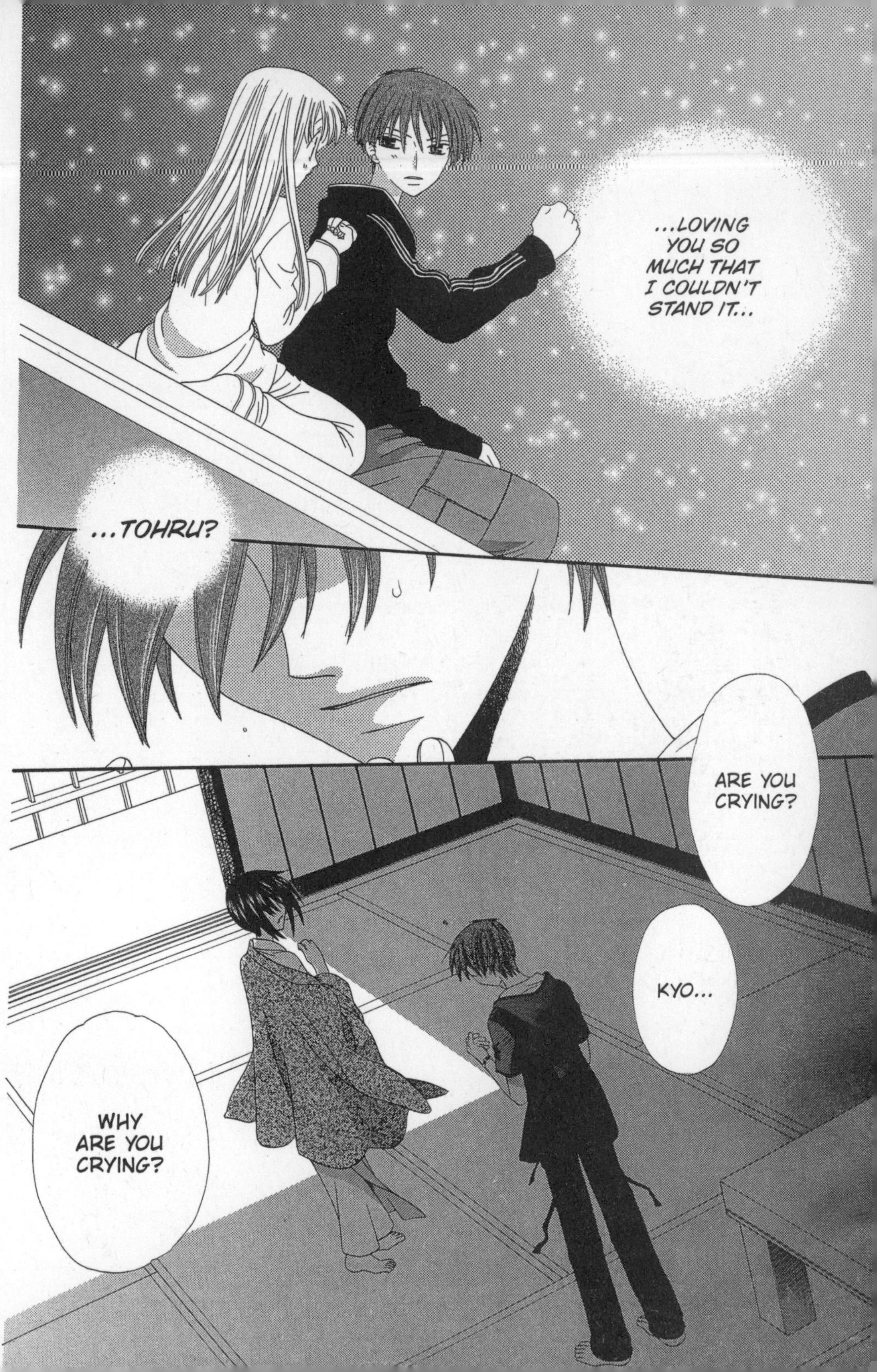
...LOVING YOU SO MUCH THAT I COULDN'T STAND IT...
...TOHRU?
ARE YOU CRYING?
KYO...
WHY ARE YOU CRYING?

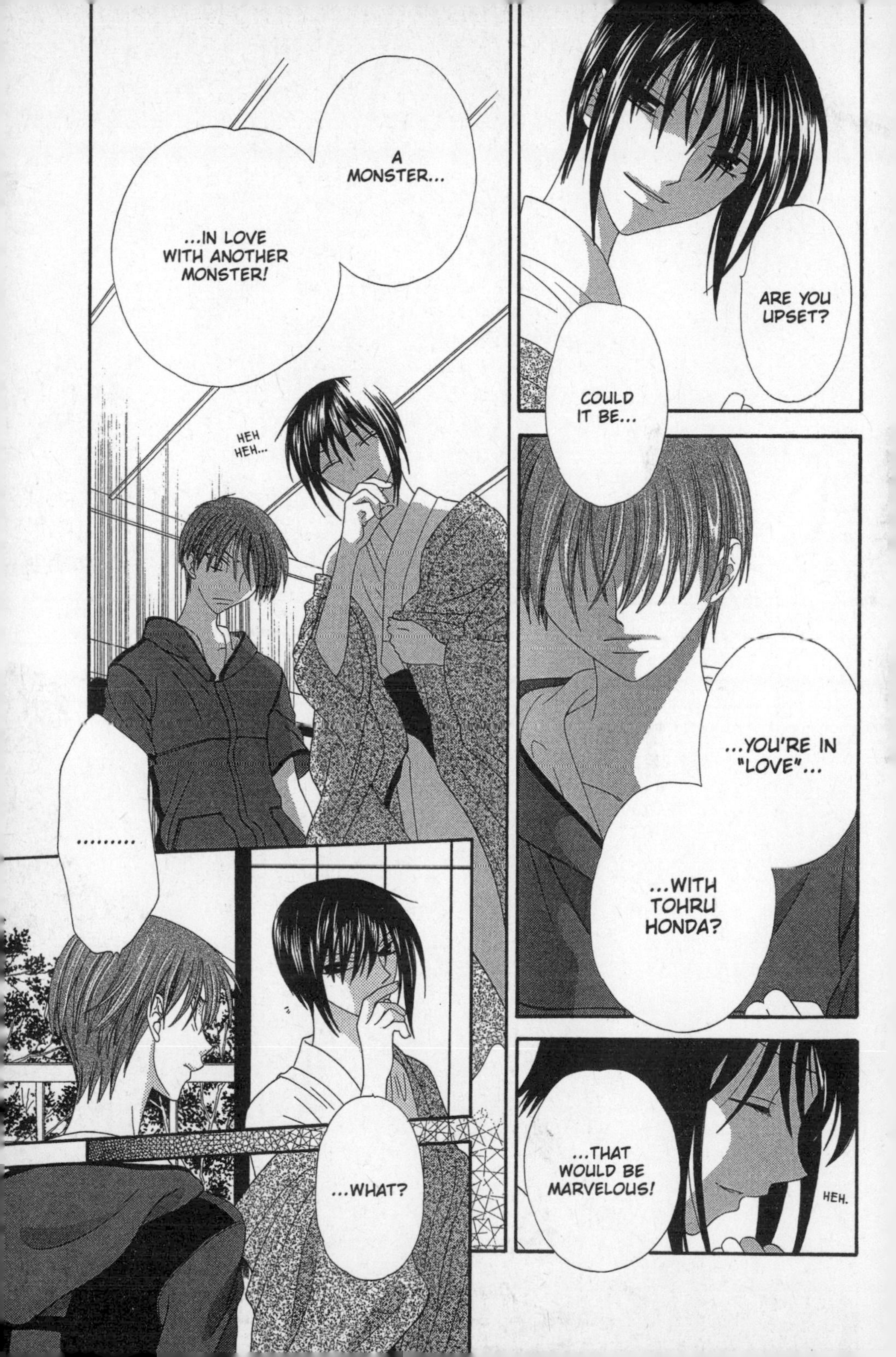

ARE YOU UPSET?
COULD IT BE...
...YOU'RE IN "LOVE"...
...WITH TOHRU HONDA?
...THAT WOULD BE MARVELOUS!
HEH.
A MONSTER...
...IN LOVE WITH ANOTHER MONSTER!
HEH HEH...
....
...WHAT?

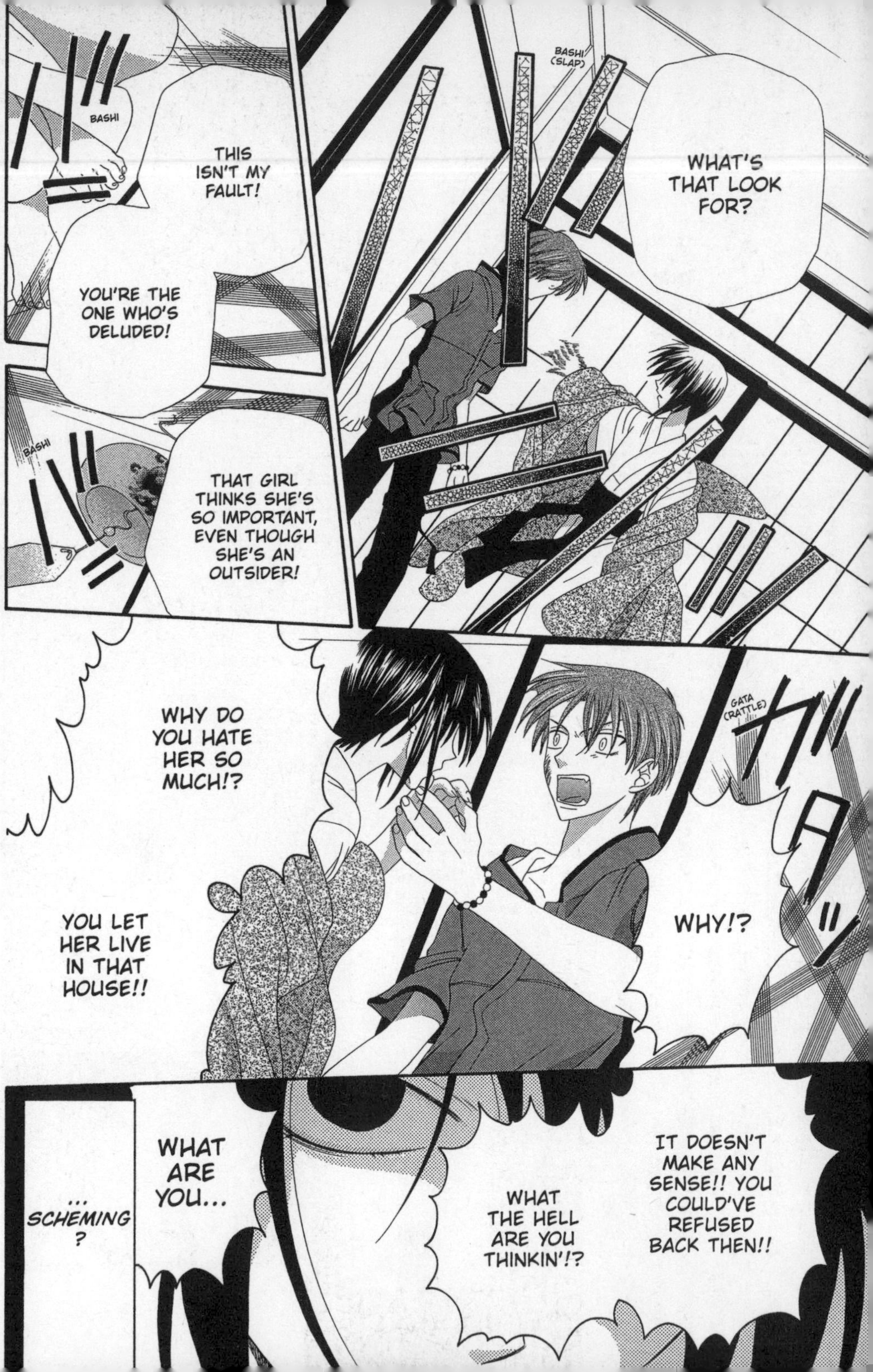
BASHI (SLAP)
WHAT'S THAT LOOK FOR?
BASHI
THIS ISN'T MY FAULT!
YOU'RE THE ONE WHO'S DELUDED!
BASHI
THAT GIRL THINKS SHE'S SO IMPORTANT, EVEN THOUGH SHE'S AN OUTSIDER!
GATA (RATTLE)
WHY!?
WHY DO YOU HATE HER SO MUCH!?
YOU LET HER LIVE IN THAT HOUSE!!
IT DOESN'T MAKE ANY SENSE!! YOU COULD'VE REFUSED BACK THEN!!
WHAT THE HELL ARE YOU THINKIN'!?
WHAT ARE YOU...
... SCHEMING?

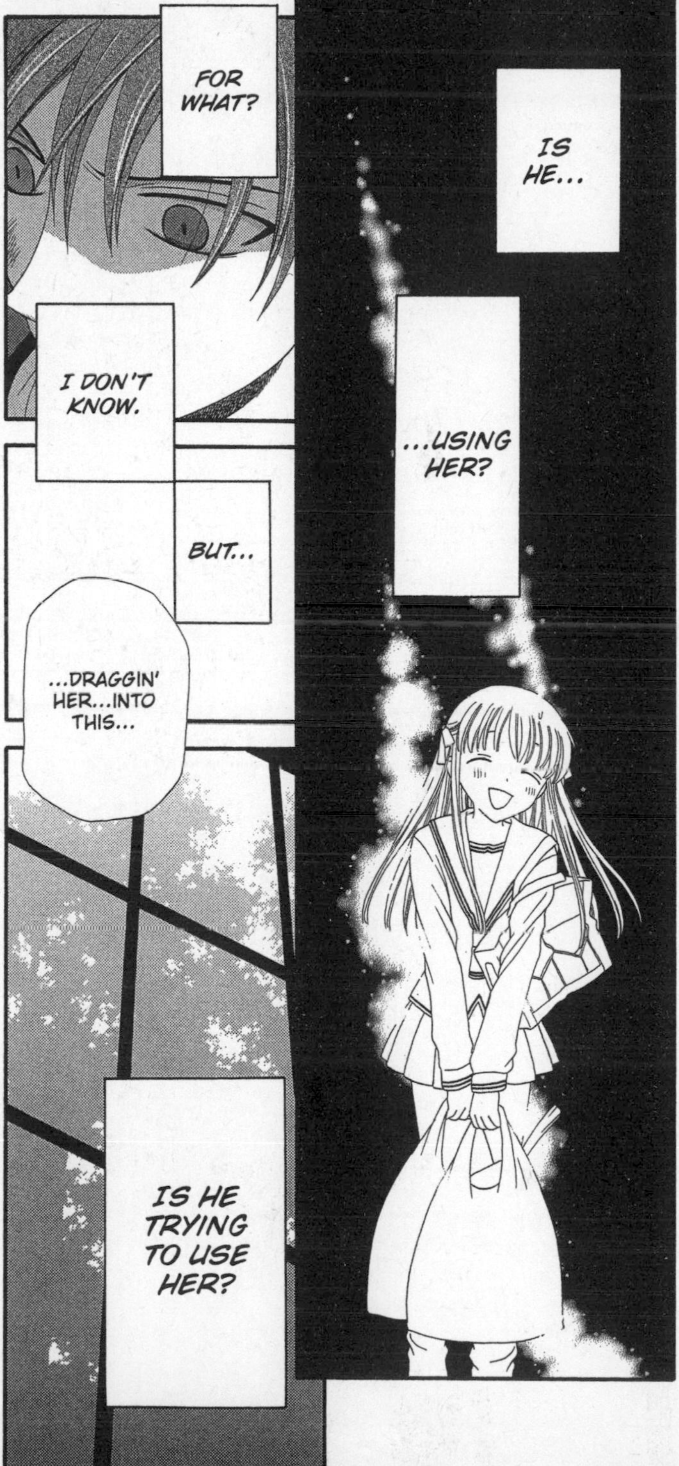
IS HE...
...USING HER?
FOR WHAT?
I DON'T KNOW.
BUT...
...DRAGGIN' HER...INTO THIS...
IS HE TRYING TO USE HER?

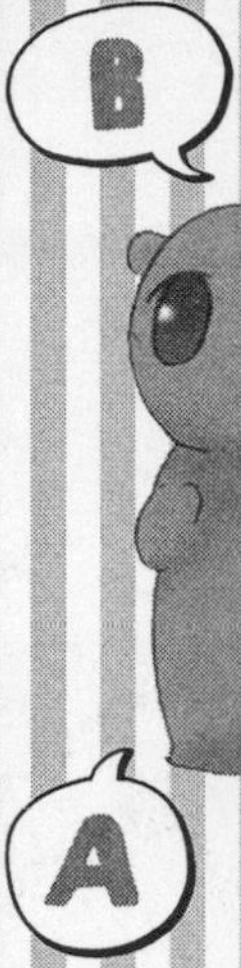
B
A

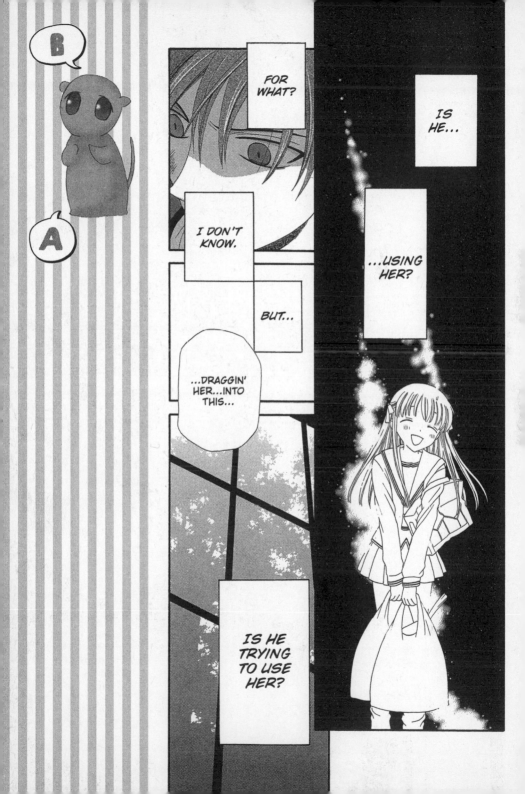

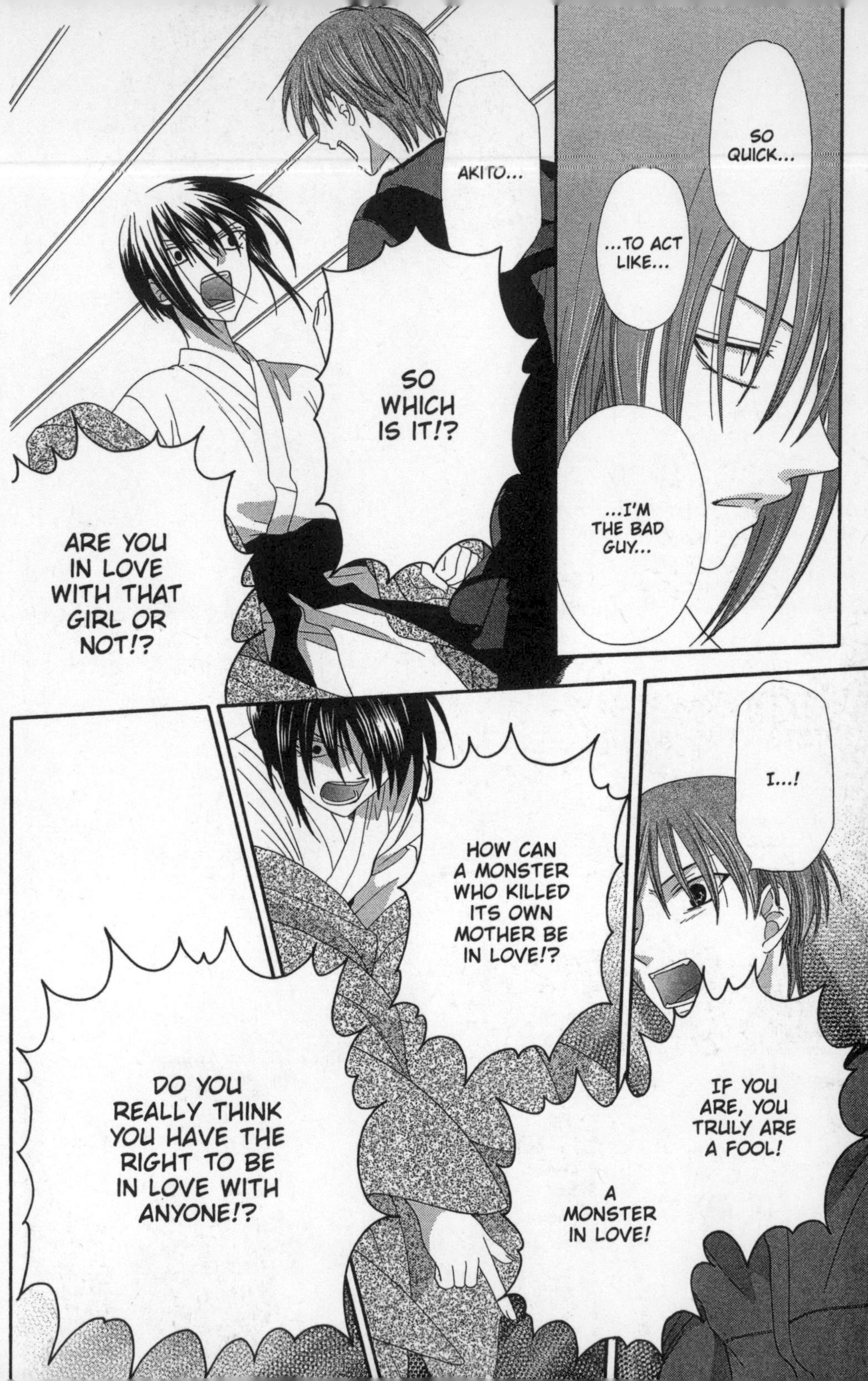
SO QUICK...
...TO ACT LIKE...
...I'M THE BAD GUY...
AKITO...
SO WHICH IS IT!?
ARE YOU IN LOVE WITH THAT GIRL OR NOT!?
I...!
HOW CAN A MONSTER WHO KILLED ITS OWN MOTHER BE IN LOVE!?
IF YOU ARE, YOU TRULY ARE A FOOL!
A MONSTER IN LOVE!
DO YOU REALLY THINK YOU HAVE THE RIGHT TO BE IN LOVE WITH ANYONE!?

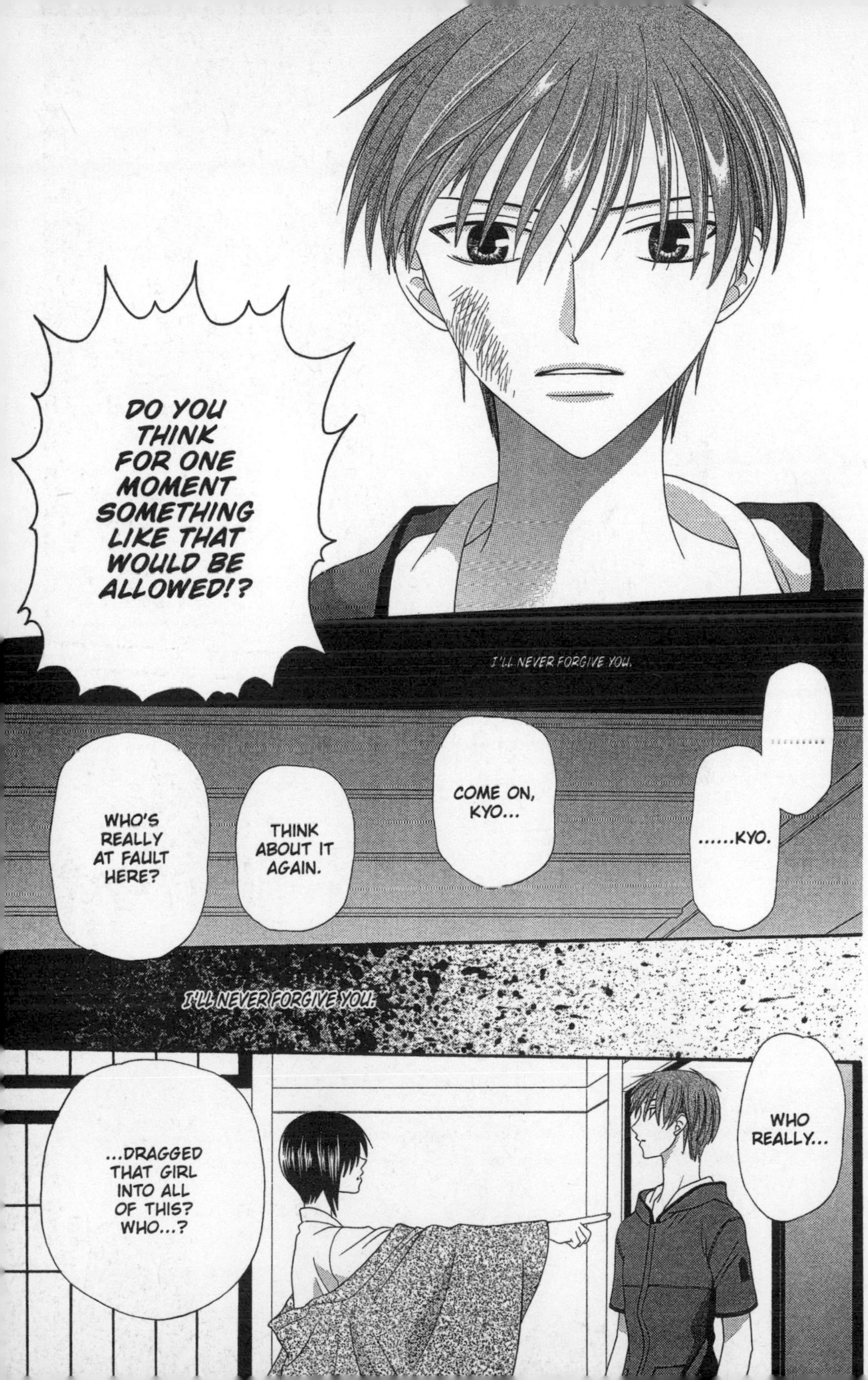
DO YOU THINK FOR ONE MOMENT SOMETHING LIKE THAT WOULD BE ALLOWED!?
I'LL NEVER FORGIVE YOU.
....
......KYO.
COME ON, KYO...
THINK ABOUT IT AGAIN.
WHO'S REALLY AT FAULT HERE?
I'LL NEVER FORGIVE YOU.
WHO REALLY...
...DRAGGED THAT GIRL INTO ALL OF THIS? WHO...?

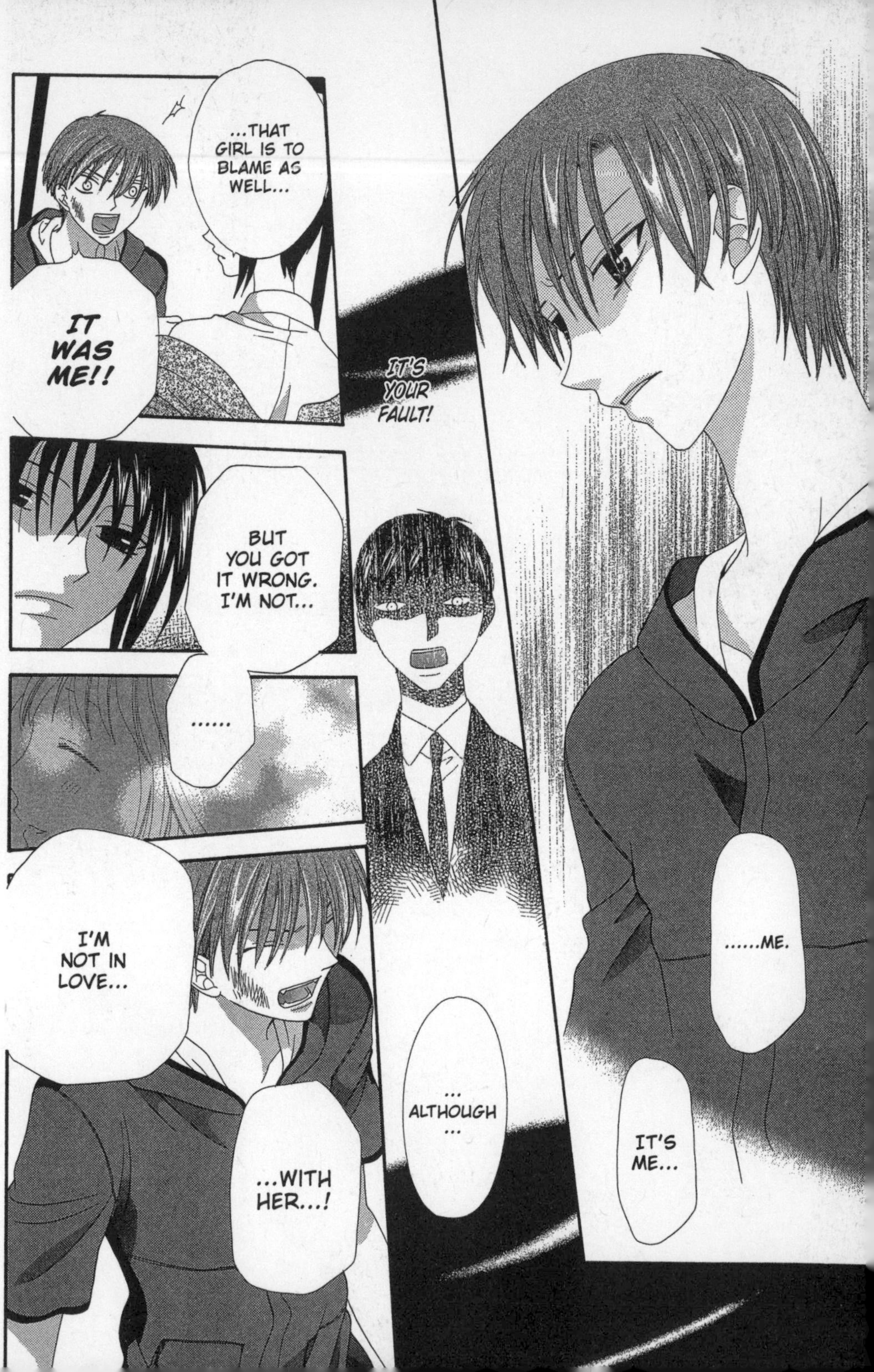
......ME.
IT'S ME...
IT'S YOUR FAULT!
...ALTHOUGH...
...THAT GIRL IS TO BLAME AS WELL...
IT WAS ME!!
BUT YOU GOT IT WRONG. I'M NOT...
......
I'M NOT IN LOVE...
...WITH HER...!

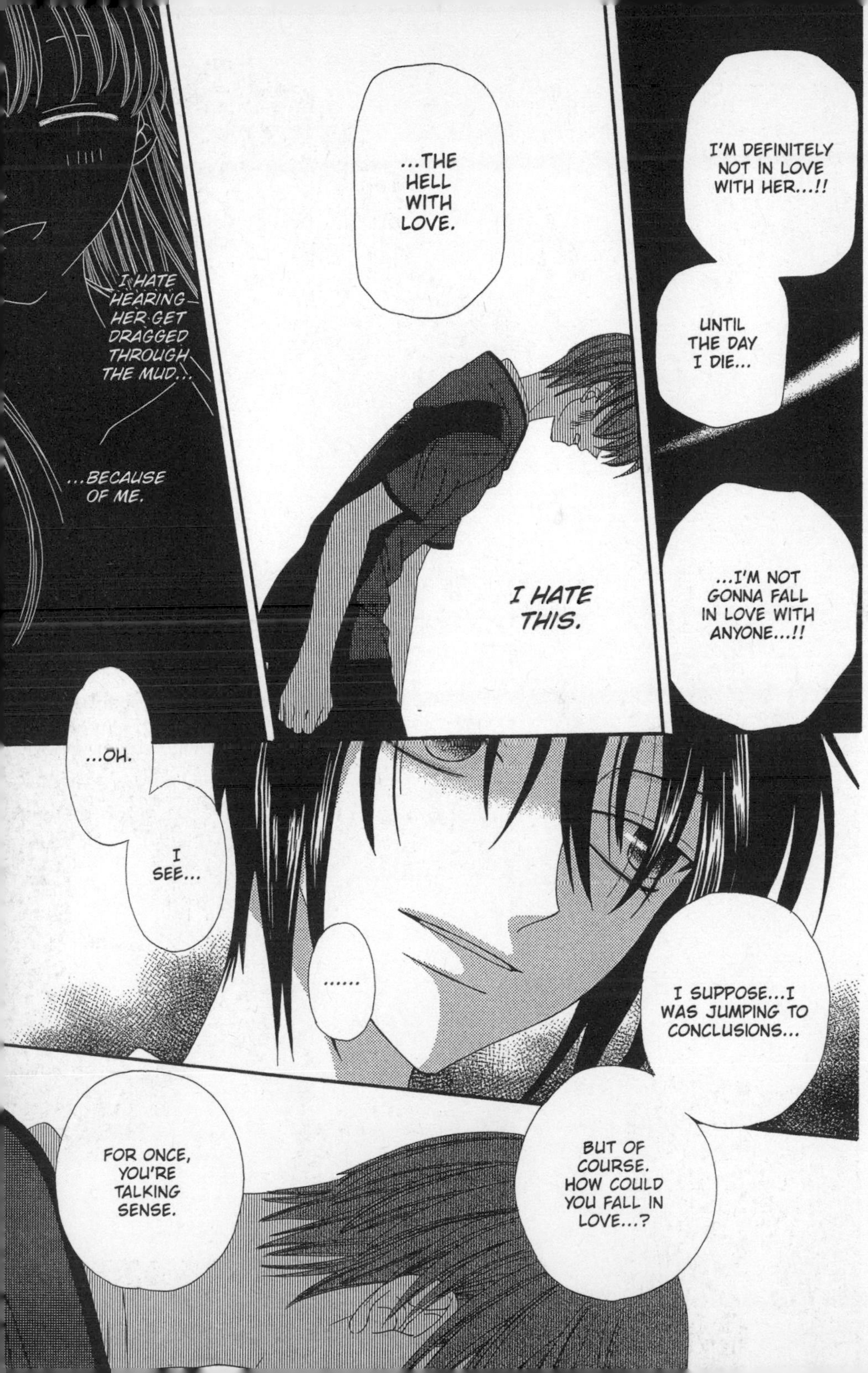
I'M DEFINITELY NOT IN LOVE WITH HER...!!
UNTIL THE DAY I DIE...
...I'M NOT GONNA FALL IN LOVE WITH ANYONE...!!
...THE HELL WITH LOVE.
I HATE THIS.
I HATE HEARING HER GET DRAGGED THROUGH THE MUD...
...BECAUSE OF ME.
...OH.
I SEE...
......
I SUPPOSE...I WAS JUMPING TO CONCLUSIONS...
BUT OF COURSE. HOW COULD YOU FALL IN LOVE...?
FOR ONCE, YOU'RE TALKING SENSE.

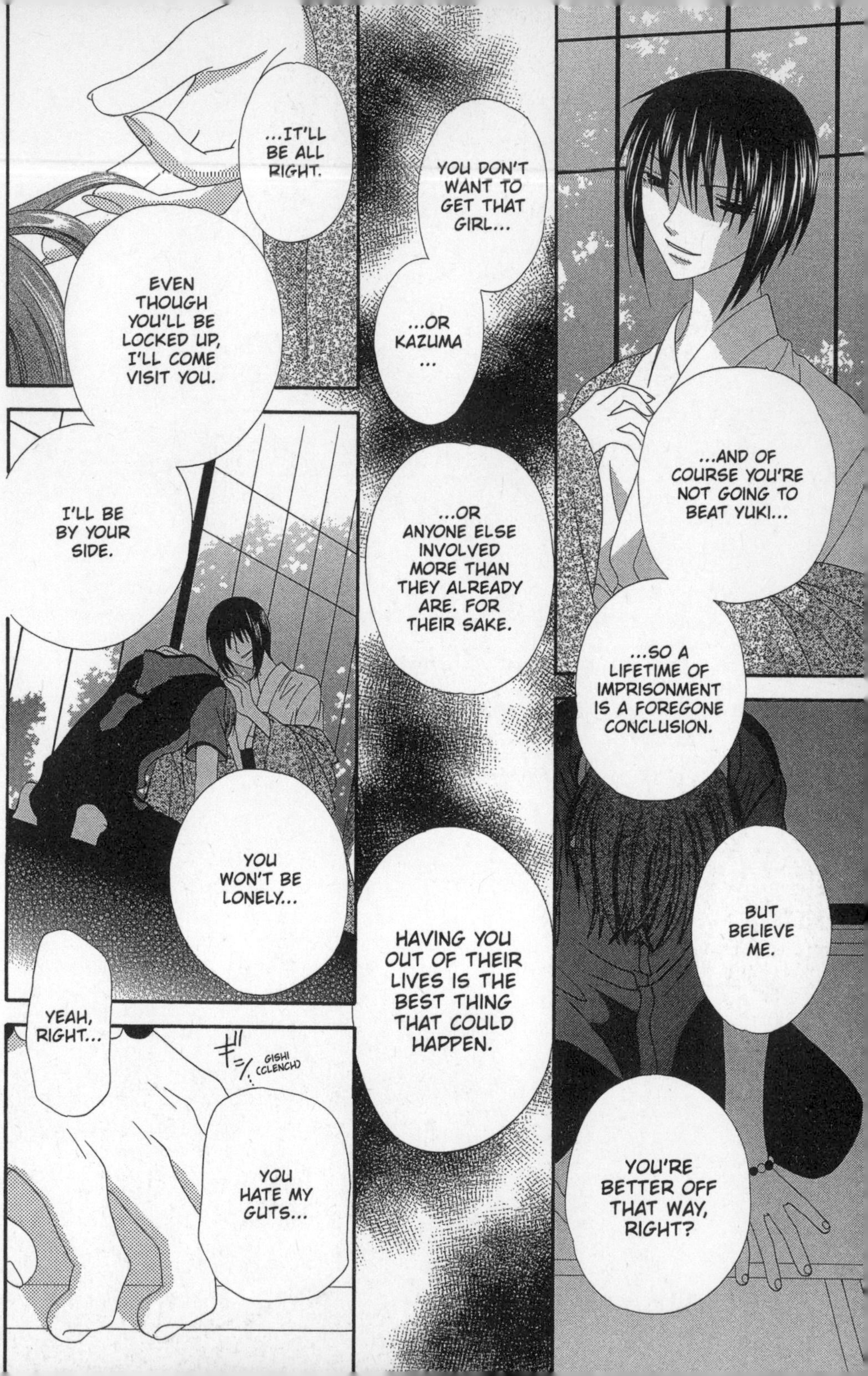
...AND OF COURSE YOU'RE NOT GOING TO BEAT YUKI...
...SO A LIFETIME OF IMPRISONMENT IS A FOREGONE CONCLUSION.
BUT BELIEVE ME.
YOU'RE BETTER OFF THAT WAY, RIGHT?
YOU DON'T WANT TO GET THAT GIRL...
...OR KAZUMA...
...OR ANYONE ELSE INVOLVED MORE THAN THEY ALREADY ARE. FOR THEIR SAKE.
HAVING YOU OUT OF THEIR LIVES IS THE BEST THING THAT COULD HAPPEN.
...IT'LL BE ALL RIGHT.
EVEN THOUGH YOU'LL BE LOCKED UP, I'LL COME VISIT YOU.
I'LL BE BY YOUR SIDE.
YOU WON'T BE LONELY...
ギリ GISHI (CLENCH)
YEAH, RIGHT...
YOU HATE MY GUTS...

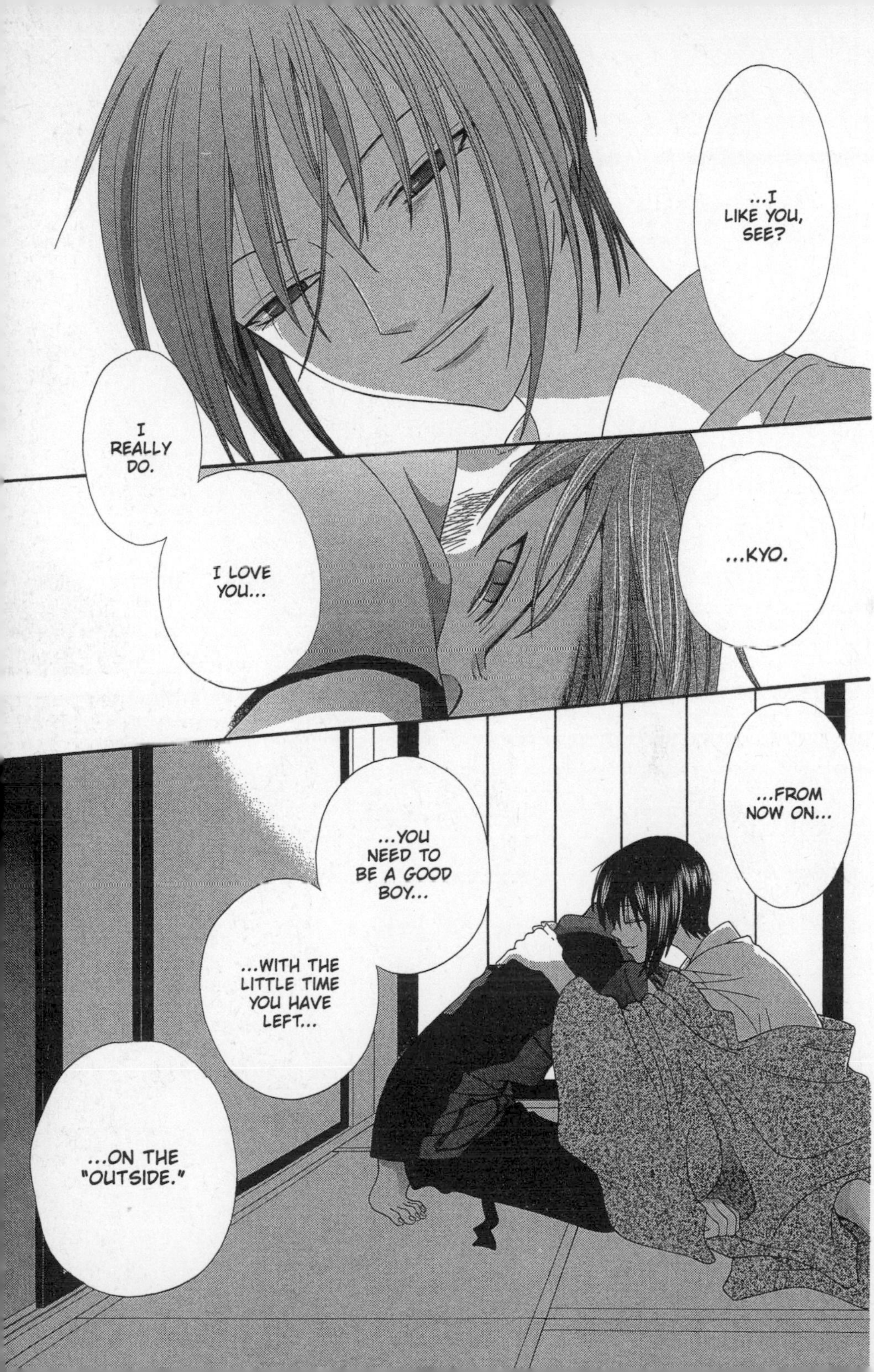

...I LIKE YOU, SEE?
I REALLY DO.
...KYO.
I LOVE YOU...
...FROM NOW ON...
...YOU NEED TO BE A GOOD BOY...
...WITH THE LITTLE TIME YOU HAVE LEFT...
...ON THE "OUTSIDE."

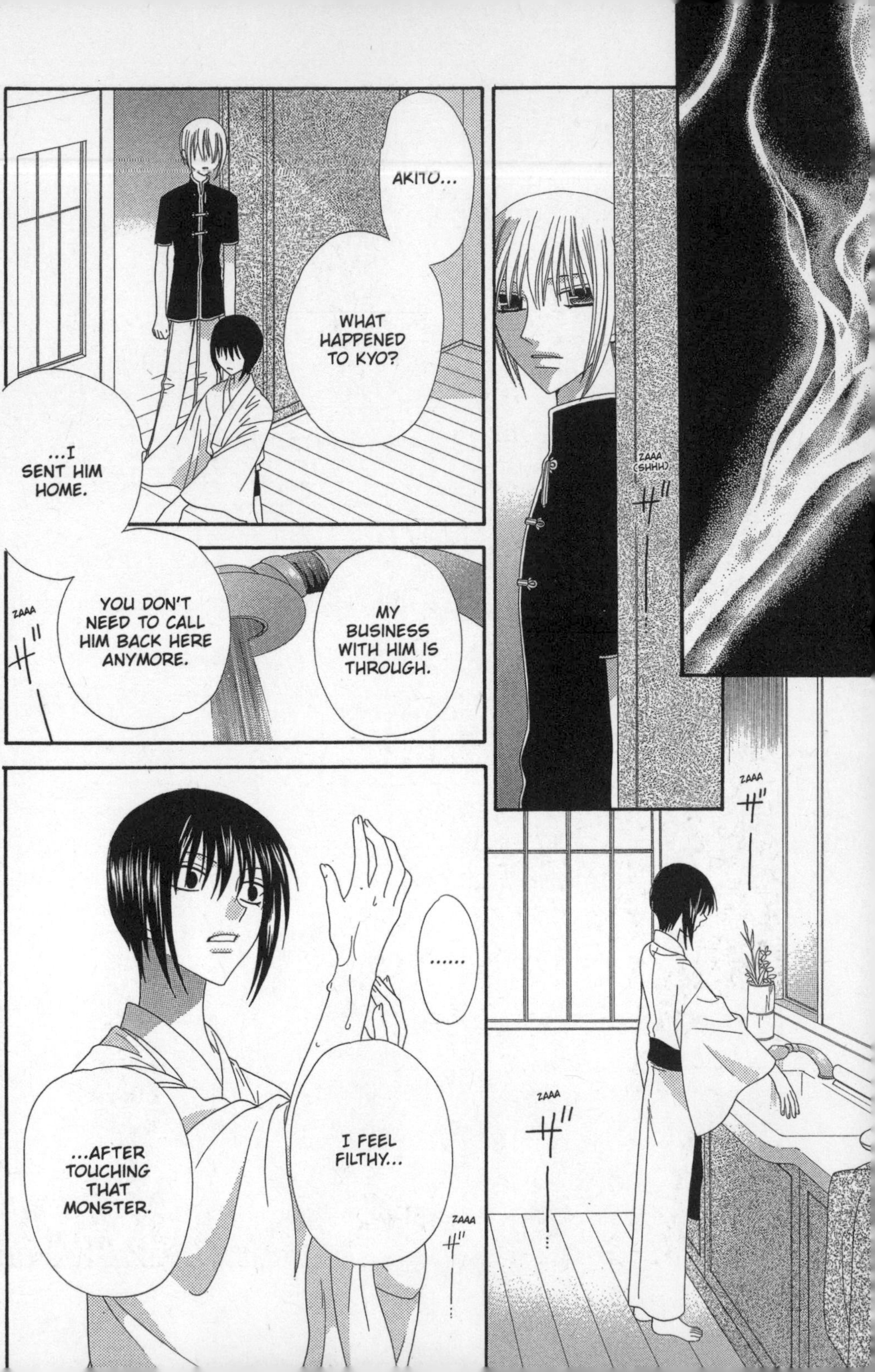
ZAAA (SHHH)
AKITO...
WHAT HAPPENED TO KYO?
...I SENT HIM HOME.
MY BUSINESS WITH HIM IS THROUGH.
YOU DON'T NEED TO CALL HIM BACK HERE ANYMORE.
ZAAA
ZAAA
ZAAA
......
I FEEL FILTHY...
...AFTER TOUCHING THAT MONSTER.
ZAAA

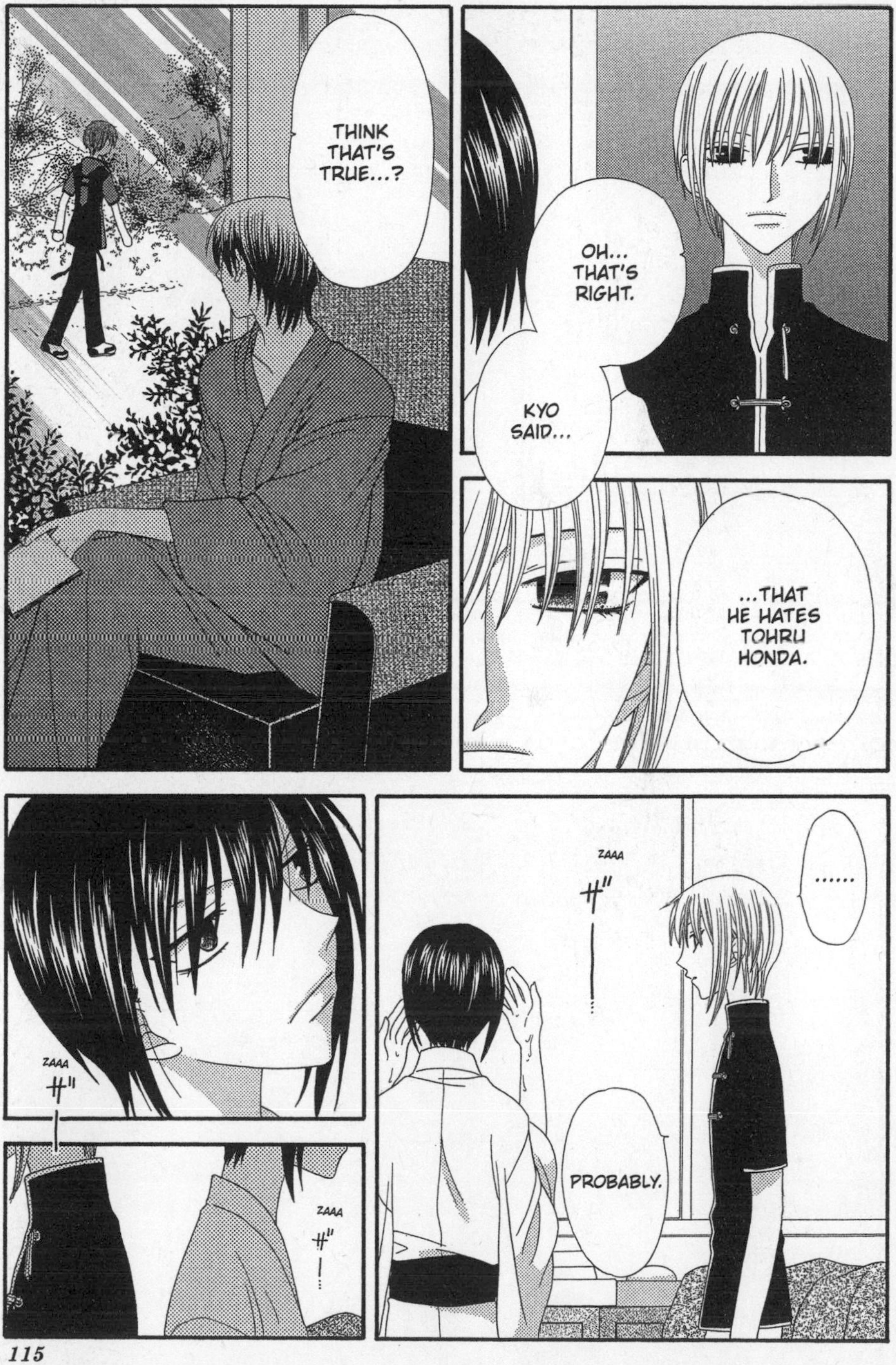
OH... THAT'S RIGHT.
KYO SAID...
...THAT HE HATES TOHRU HONDA.
THINK THAT'S TRUE...?
......
ZAAA
ザー
PROBABLY.
ZAAA
ザー
ZAAA
ザー

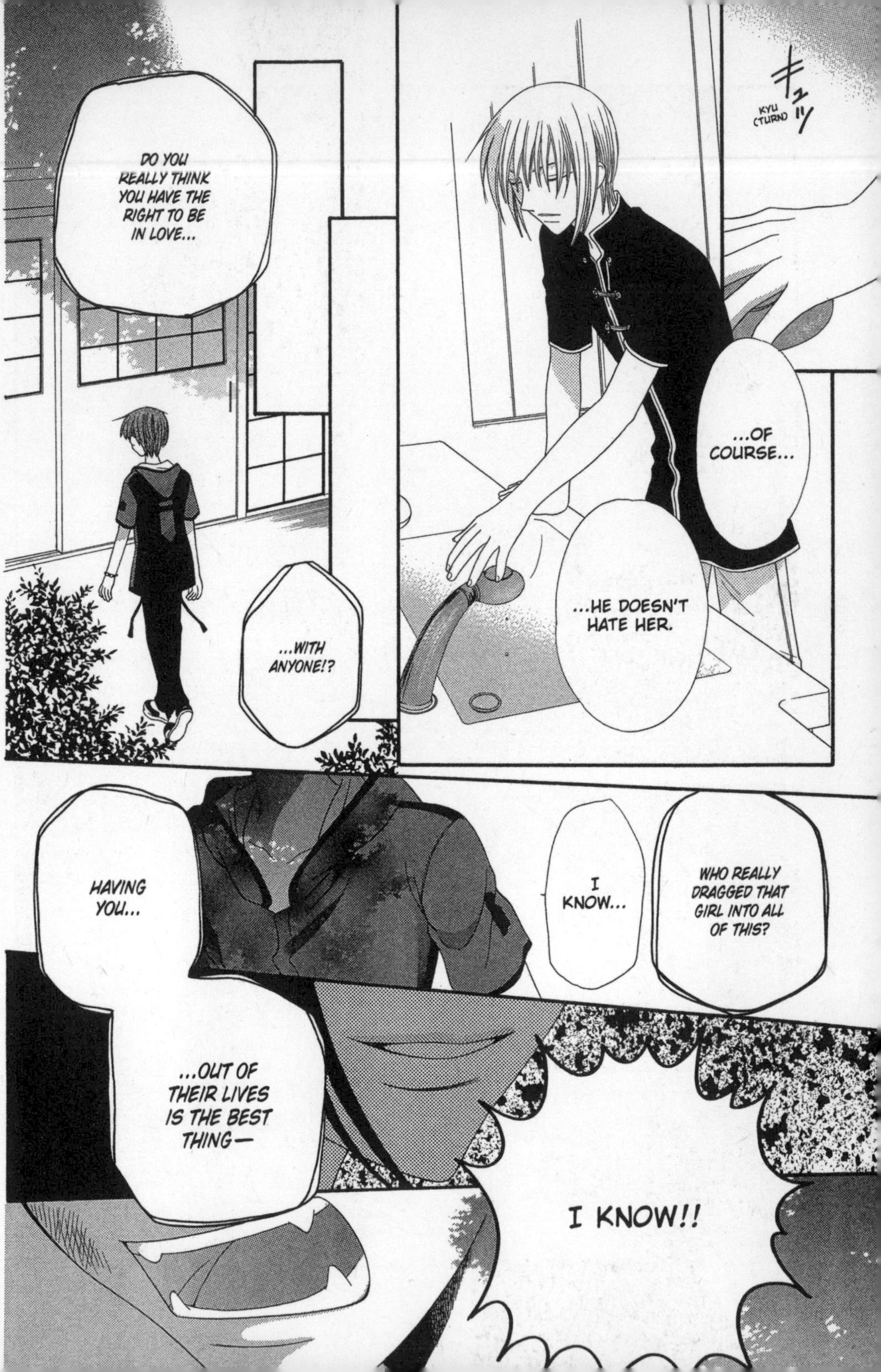
KYU (TURN)
...OF COURSE...
...HE DOESN'T HATE HER.
DO YOU REALLY THINK YOU HAVE THE RIGHT TO BE IN LOVE...
...WITH ANYONE!?
WHO REALLY DRAGGED THAT GIRL INTO ALL OF THIS?
I KNOW...
HAVING YOU...
...OUT OF THEIR LIVES IS THE BEST THING—
I KNOW!!

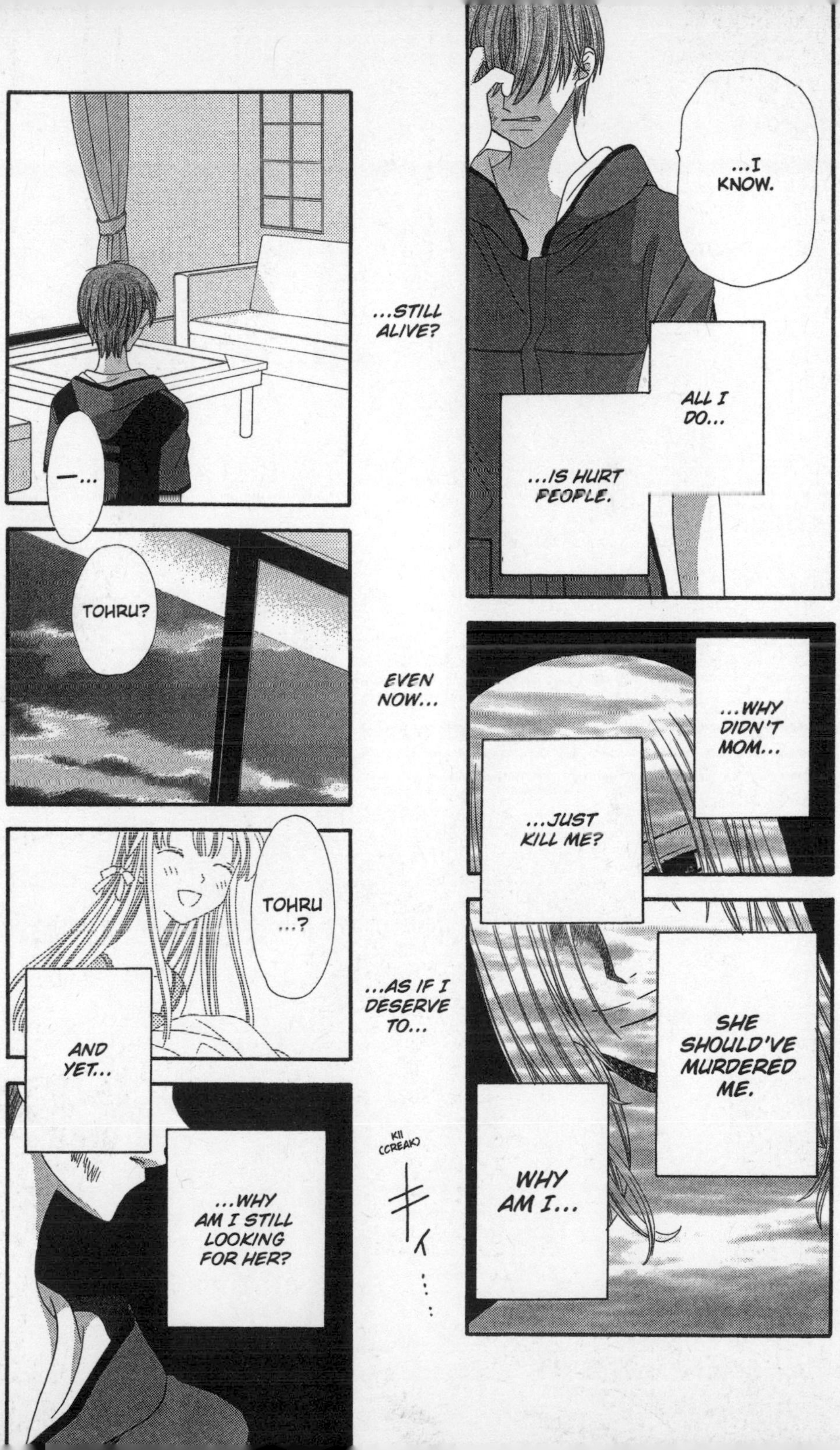
...I KNOW.
ALL I DO...
...IS HURT PEOPLE.
...WHY DIDN'T MOM...
...JUST KILL ME?
SHE SHOULD'VE MURDERED ME.
WHY AM I...
...STILL ALIVE?
EVEN NOW...
...AS IF I DESERVE TO...
KII (CREAK)
—...
TOHRU?
TOHRU ...?
AND YET...
...WHY AM I STILL LOOKING FOR HER?

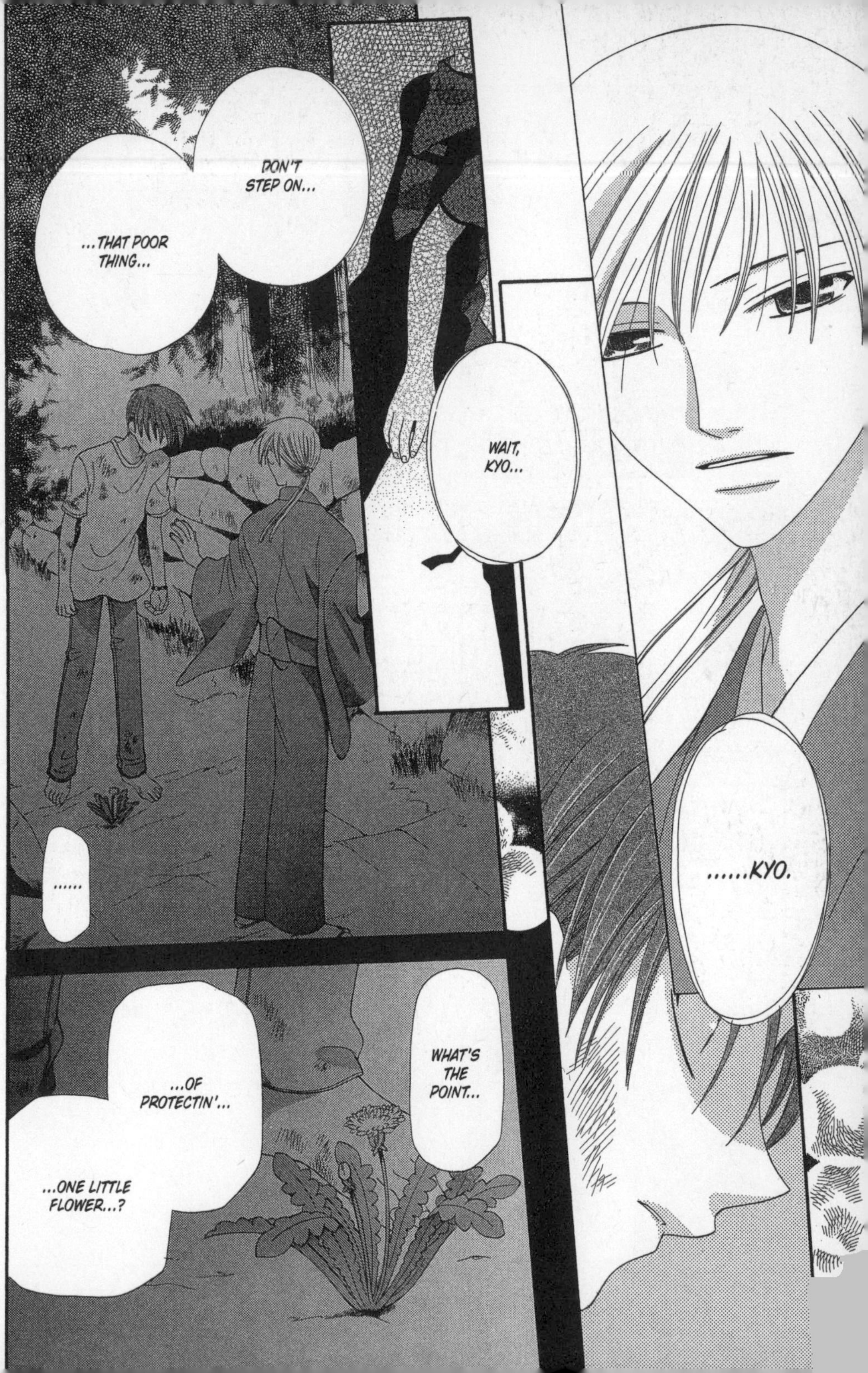
......KYO.
DON'T STEP ON...
...THAT POOR THING...
WAIT, KYO...
......
WHAT'S THE POINT...
...OF PROTECTIN'...
...ONE LITTLE FLOWER...?

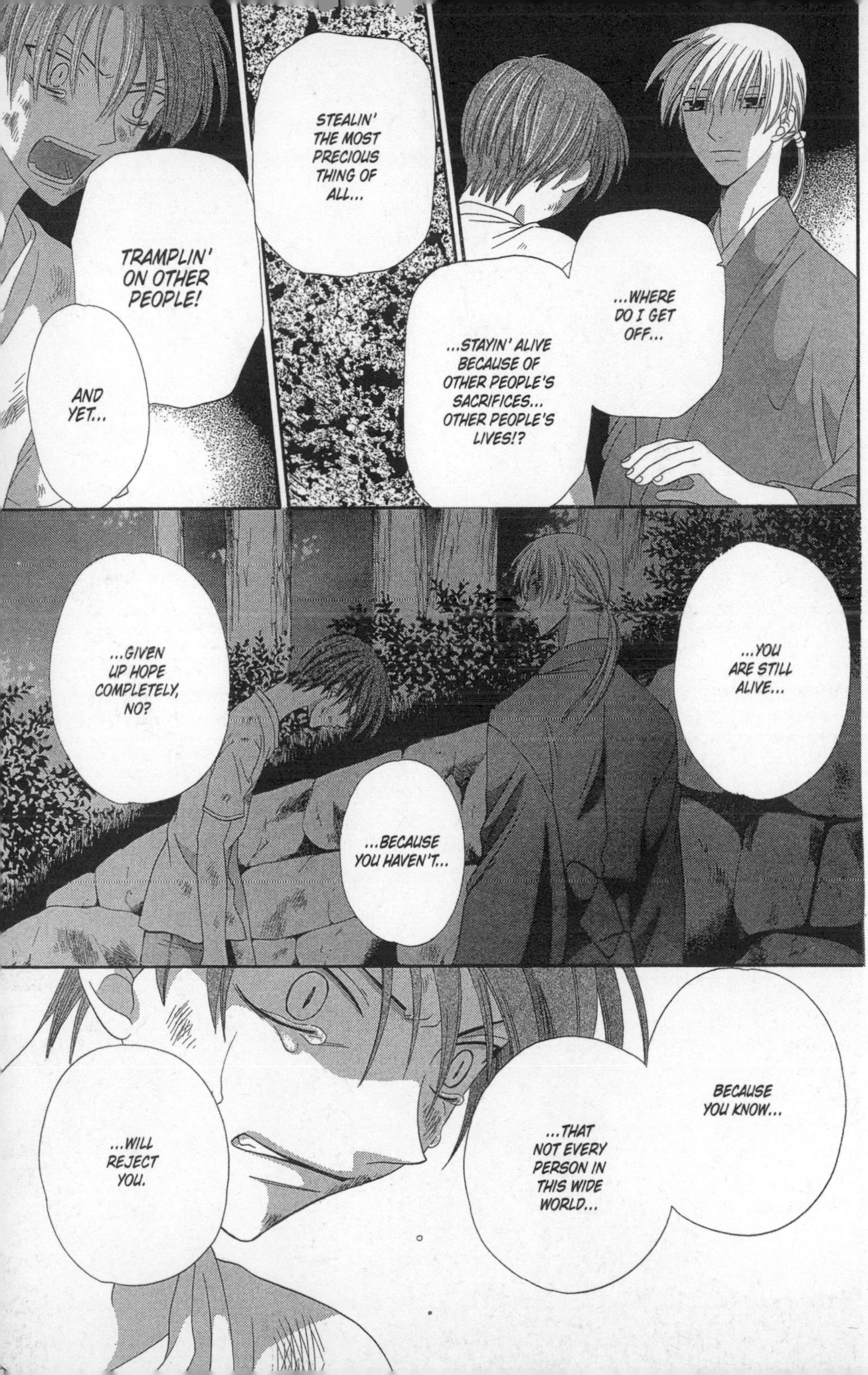
...WHERE DO I GET OFF...
...STAYIN' ALIVE BECAUSE OF OTHER PEOPLE'S SACRIFICES... OTHER PEOPLE'S LIVES!?
STEALIN' THE MOST PRECIOUS THING OF ALL...
TRAMPLIN' ON OTHER PEOPLE!
AND YET...
...YOU ARE STILL ALIVE...
...BECAUSE YOU HAVEN'T...
...GIVEN UP HOPE COMPLETELY, NO?
BECAUSE YOU KNOW...
...THAT NOT EVERY PERSON IN THIS WIDE WORLD...
...WILL REJECT YOU.

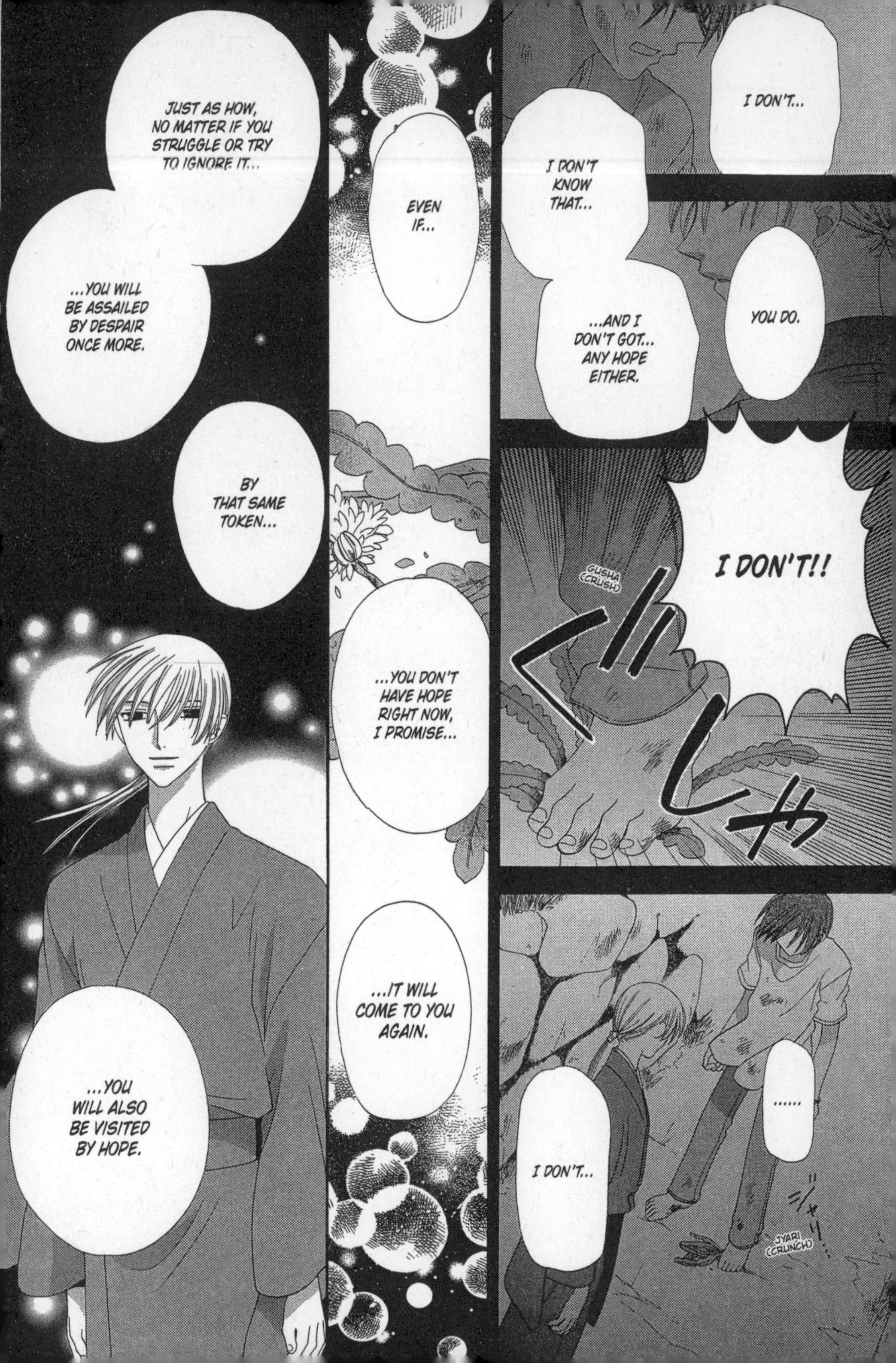
I DON'T...
I DON'T KNOW THAT...
YOU DO.
...AND I DON'T GOT... ANY HOPE EITHER.
I DON'T!!
GUSHA (CRUSH)
......
I DON'T...
JYARI (CRUNCH)
EVEN IF...
...YOU DON'T HAVE HOPE RIGHT NOW, I PROMISE...
...IT WILL COME TO YOU AGAIN.
JUST AS HOW, NO MATTER IF YOU STRUGGLE OR TRY TO IGNORE IT...
...YOU WILL BE ASSAILED BY DESPAIR ONCE MORE.
BY THAT SAME TOKEN...
...YOU WILL ALSO BE VISITED BY HOPE.

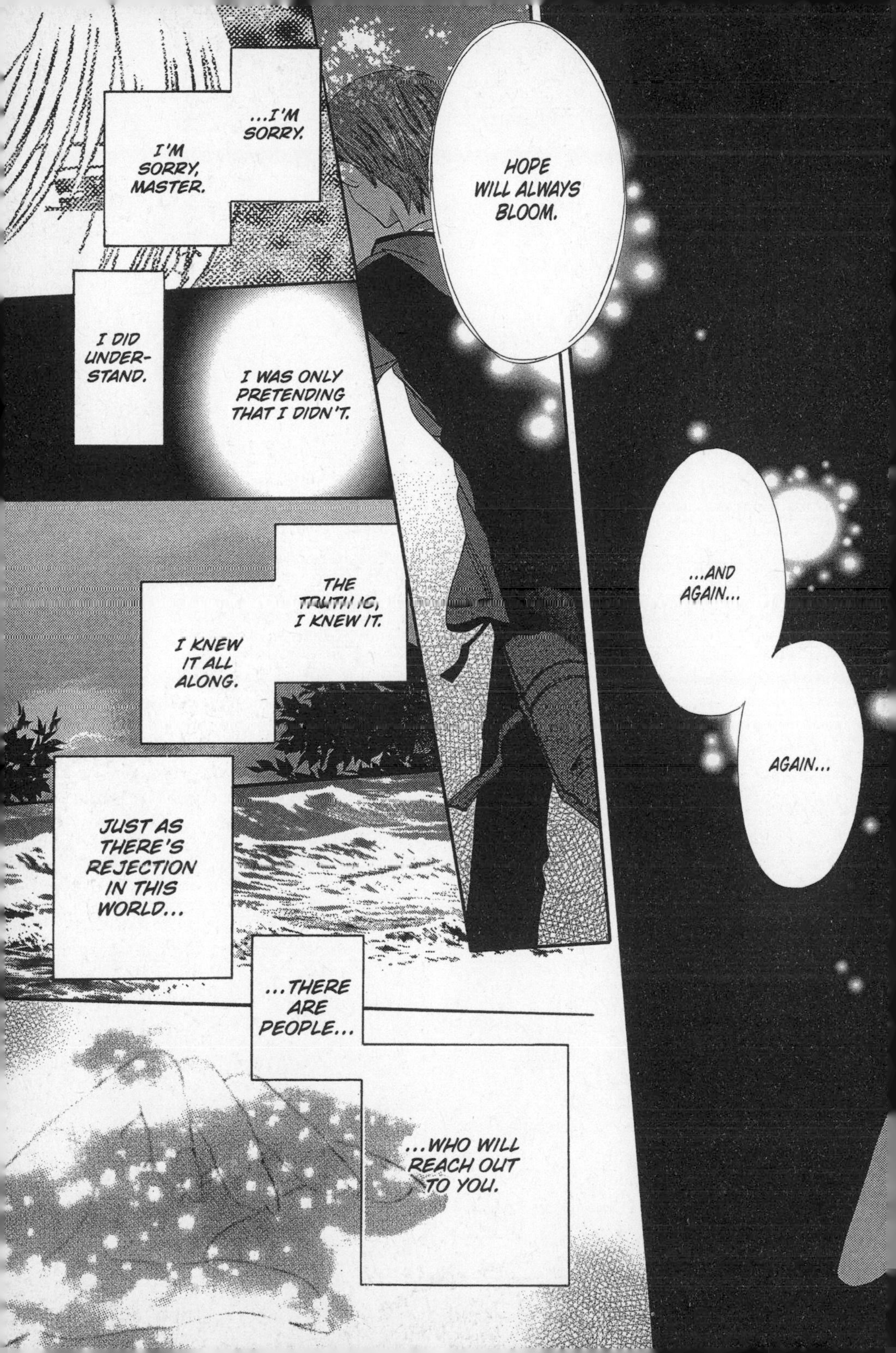
HOPE WILL ALWAYS BLOOM.
...AND AGAIN...
AGAIN...
...I'M SORRY.
I'M SORRY, MASTER.
I DID UNDER-STAND.
I WAS ONLY PRETENDING THAT I DIDN'T.
THE TRUTH IS, I KNEW IT.
I KNEW IT ALL ALONG.
JUST AS THERE'S REJECTION IN THIS WORLD...
...THERE ARE PEOPLE...
...WHO WILL REACH OUT TO YOU.

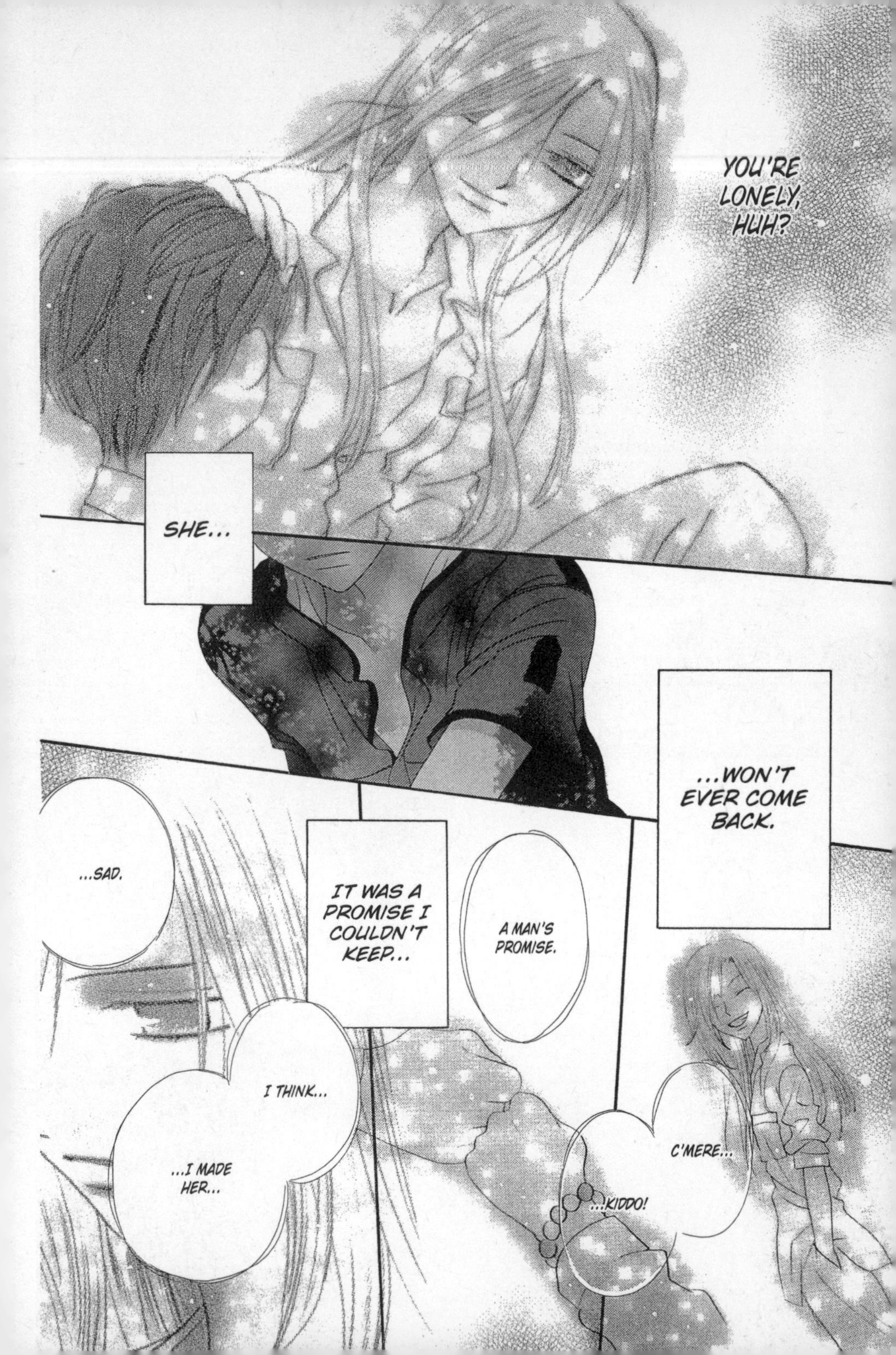
YOU'RE LONELY, HUH?
SHE...
...WON'T EVER COME BACK.
C'MERE...
...KIDDO!
A MAN'S PROMISE.
IT WAS A PROMISE I COULDN'T KEEP...
I THINK...
...I MADE HER...
...SAD.

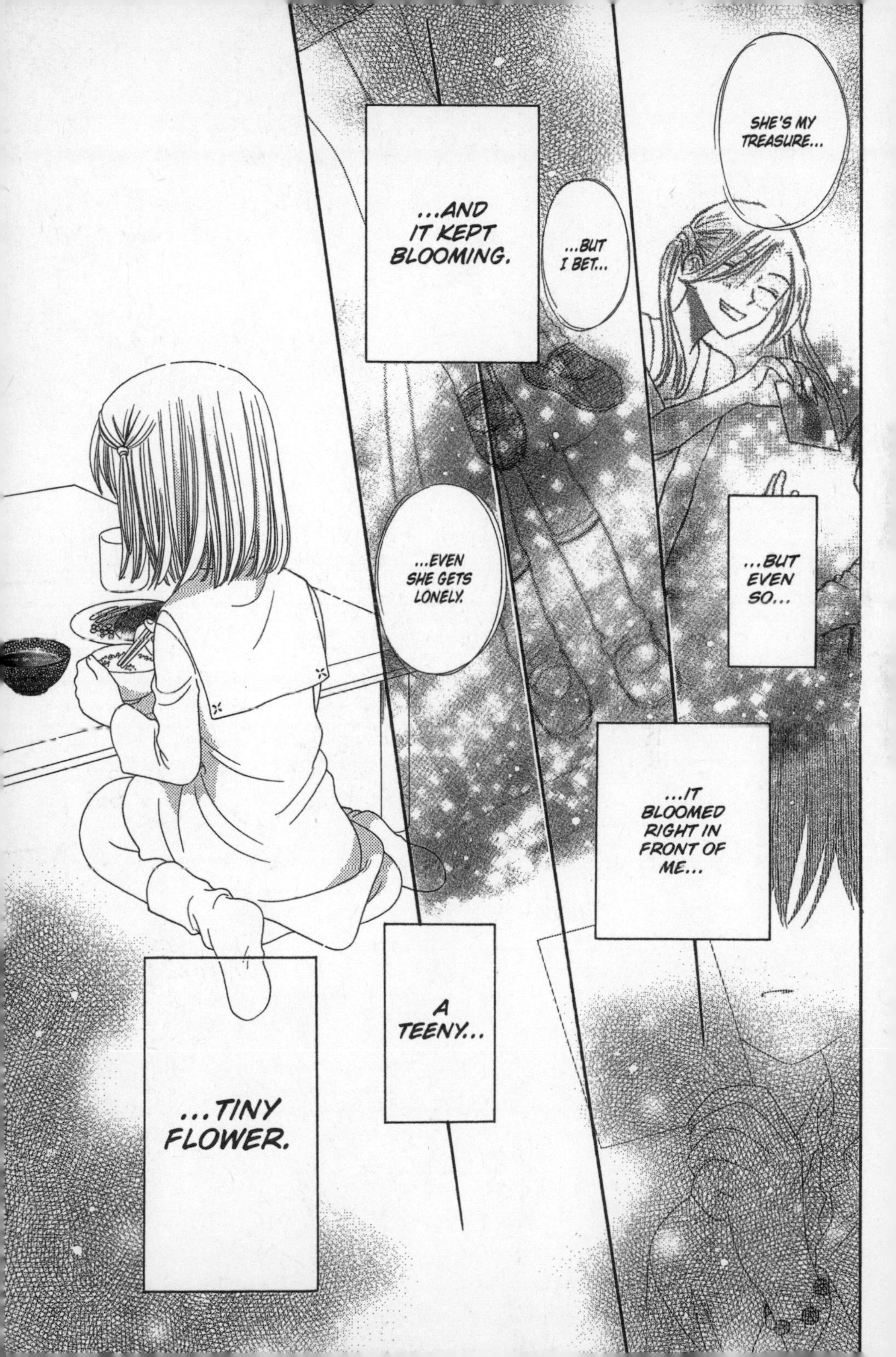
SHE'S MY TREASURE...
...BUT I BET...
...EVEN SHE GETS LONELY.
...BUT EVEN SO...
...IT BLOOMED RIGHT IN FRONT OF ME...
...AND IT KEPT BLOOMING.
A TEENY...
...TINY FLOWER.

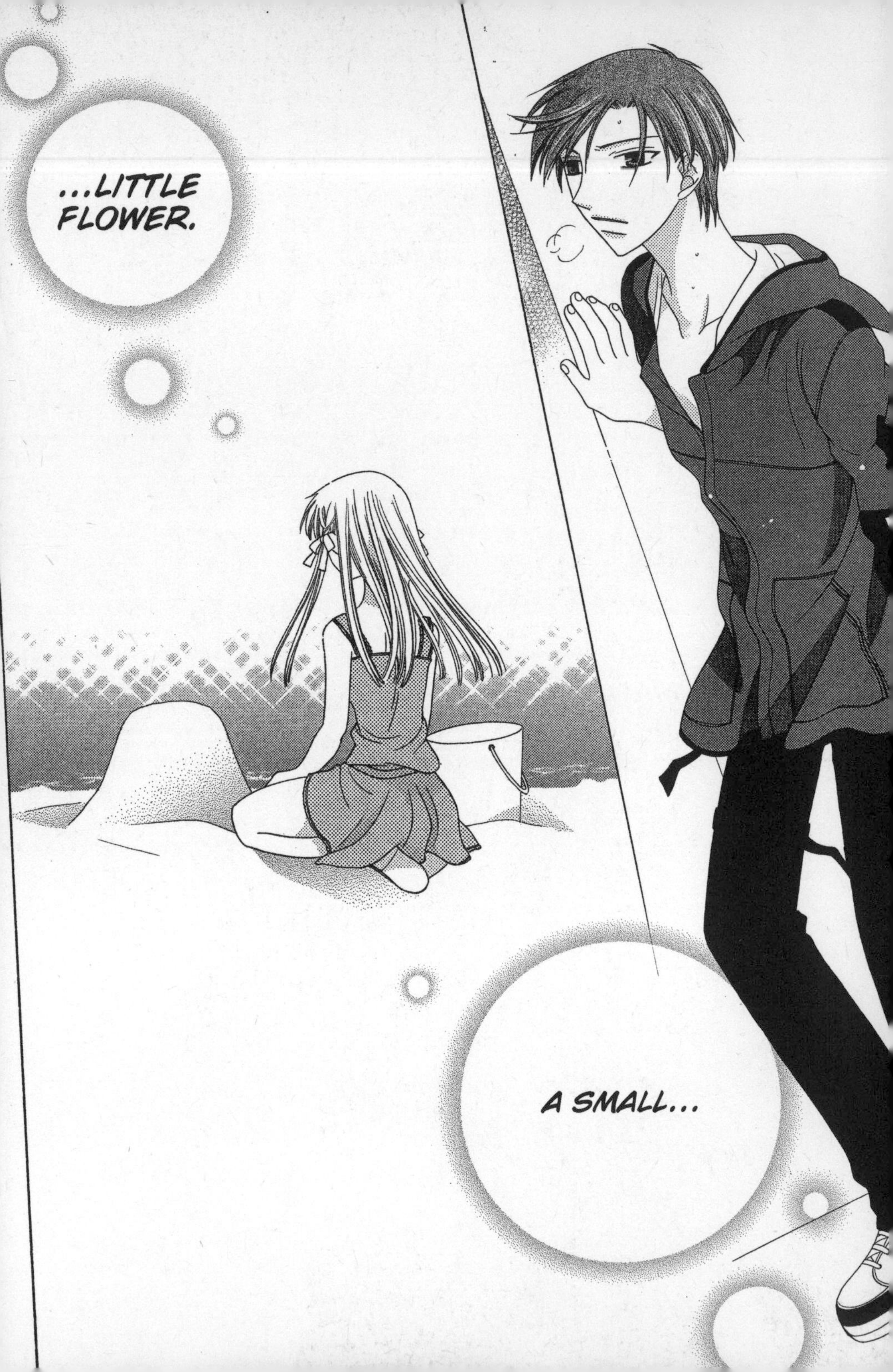
A SMALL...
...LITTLE FLOWER.

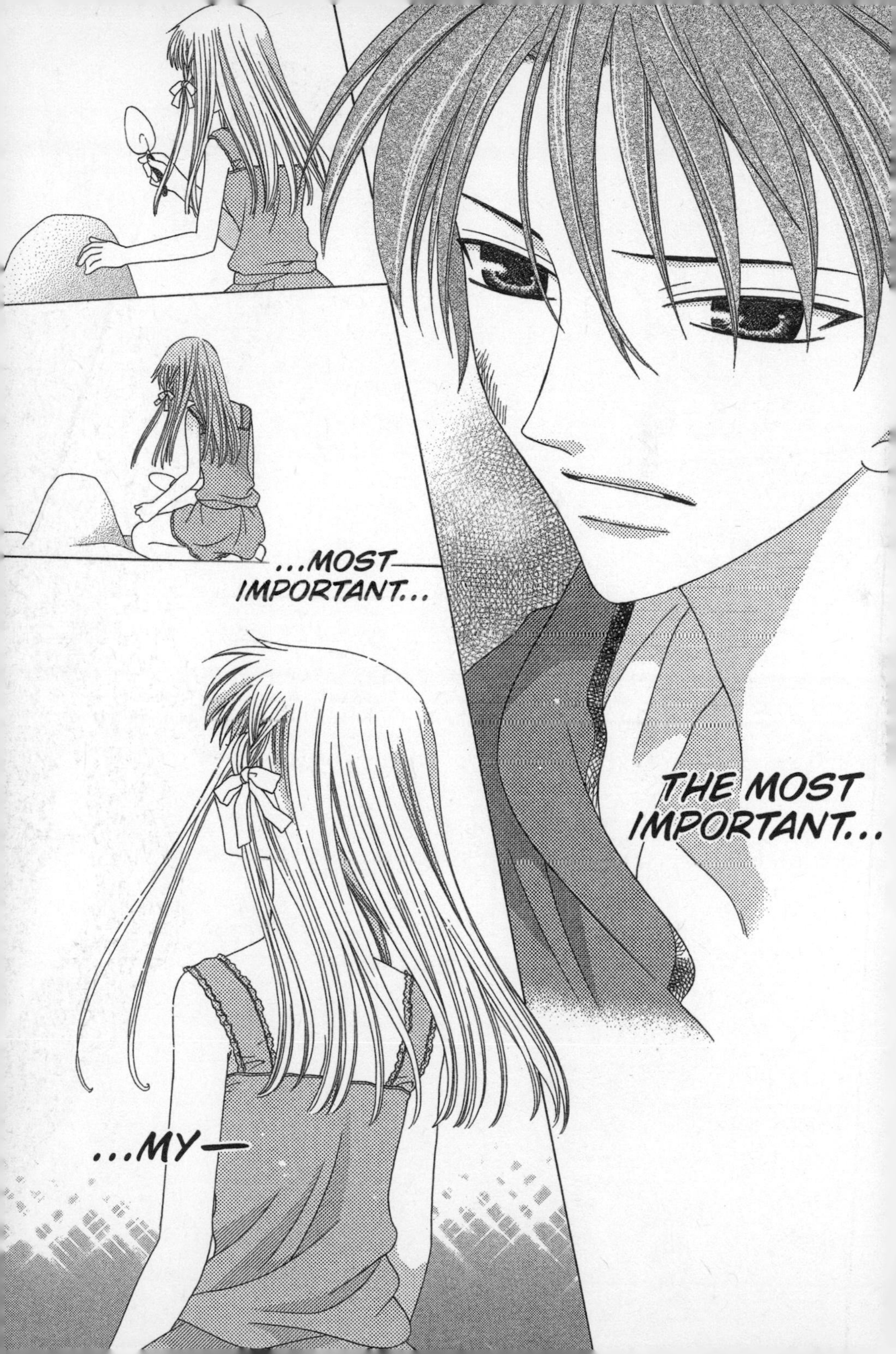
THE MOST IMPORTANT...
...MOST IMPORTANT...
...MY—

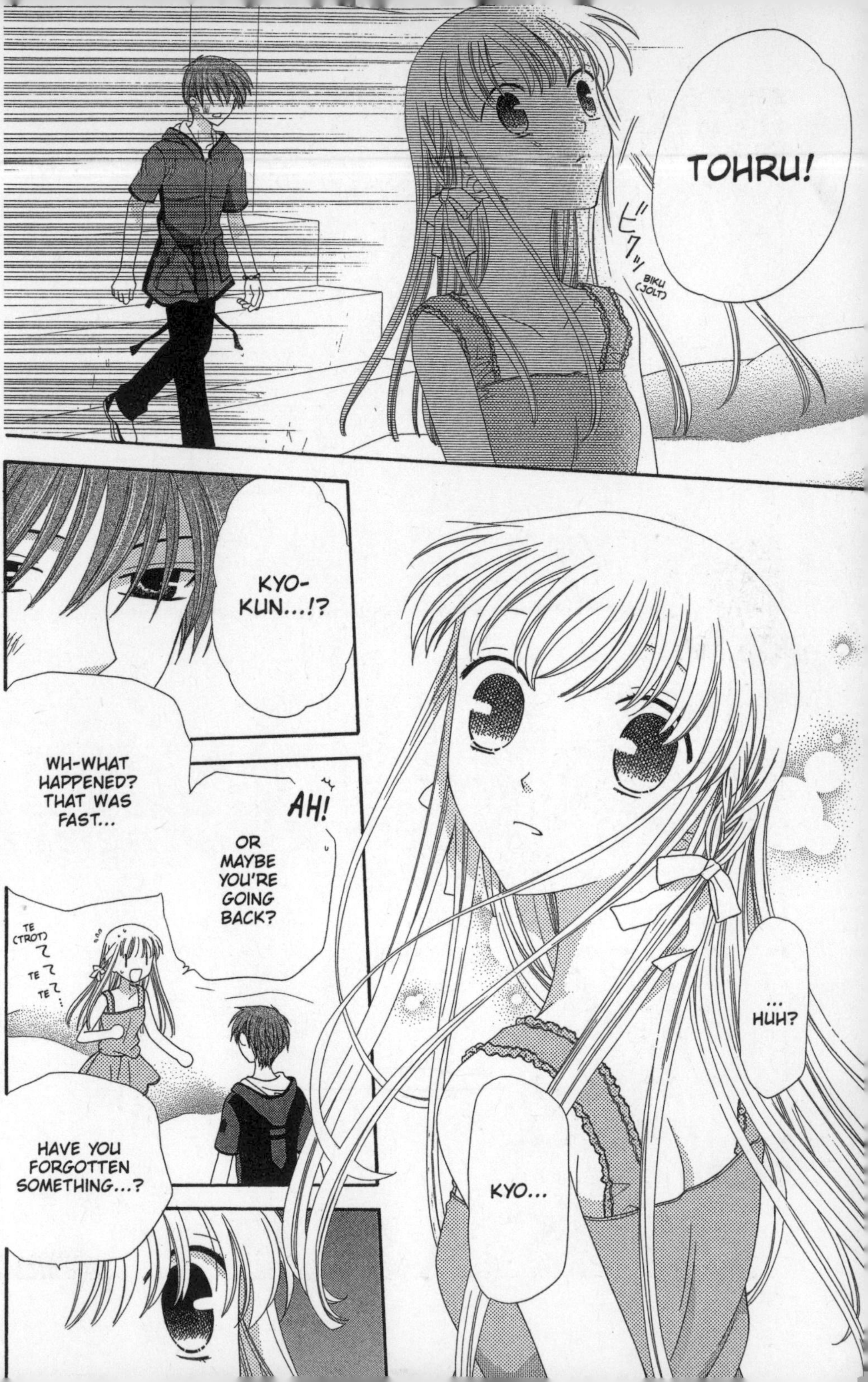
TOHRU!
ビクッ
BIKU (JOLT)
... HUH?
KYO...
KYO-KUN...!?
WH-WHAT HAPPENED? THAT WAS FAST...
AH!
OR MAYBE YOU'RE GOING BACK?
TE (TROT) TE TE...
HAVE YOU FORGOTTEN SOMETHING...?

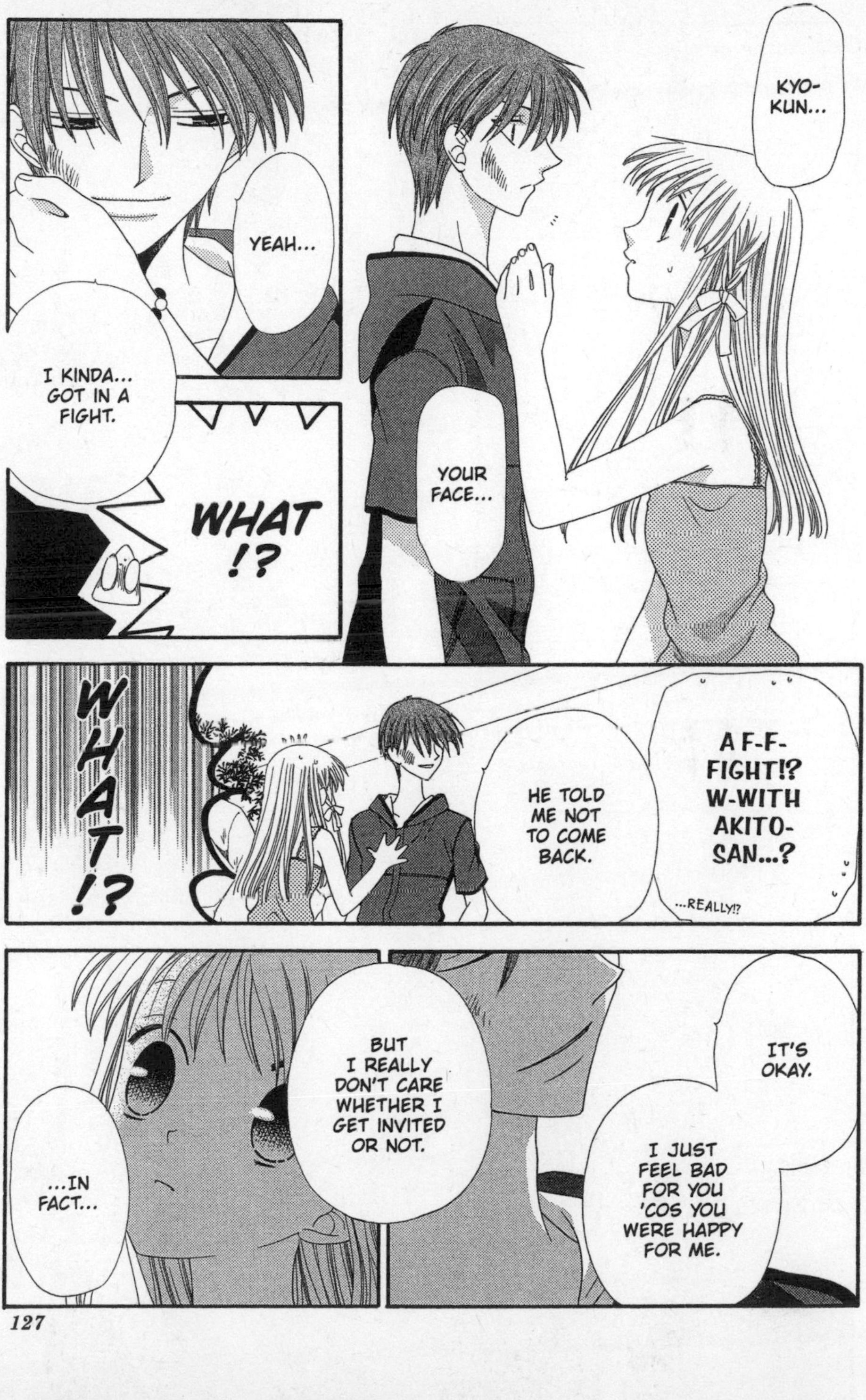
KYO-KUN...
YOUR FACE...
YEAH...
I KINDA... GOT IN A FIGHT.
WHAT!?
A F-F-FIGHT!? W-WITH AKITO-SAN...?
...REALLY!?
HE TOLD ME NOT TO COME BACK.
WHAT!?
IT'S OKAY.
I JUST FEEL BAD FOR YOU 'COS YOU WERE HAPPY FOR ME.
BUT I REALLY DON'T CARE WHETHER I GET INVITED OR NOT.
...IN FACT...

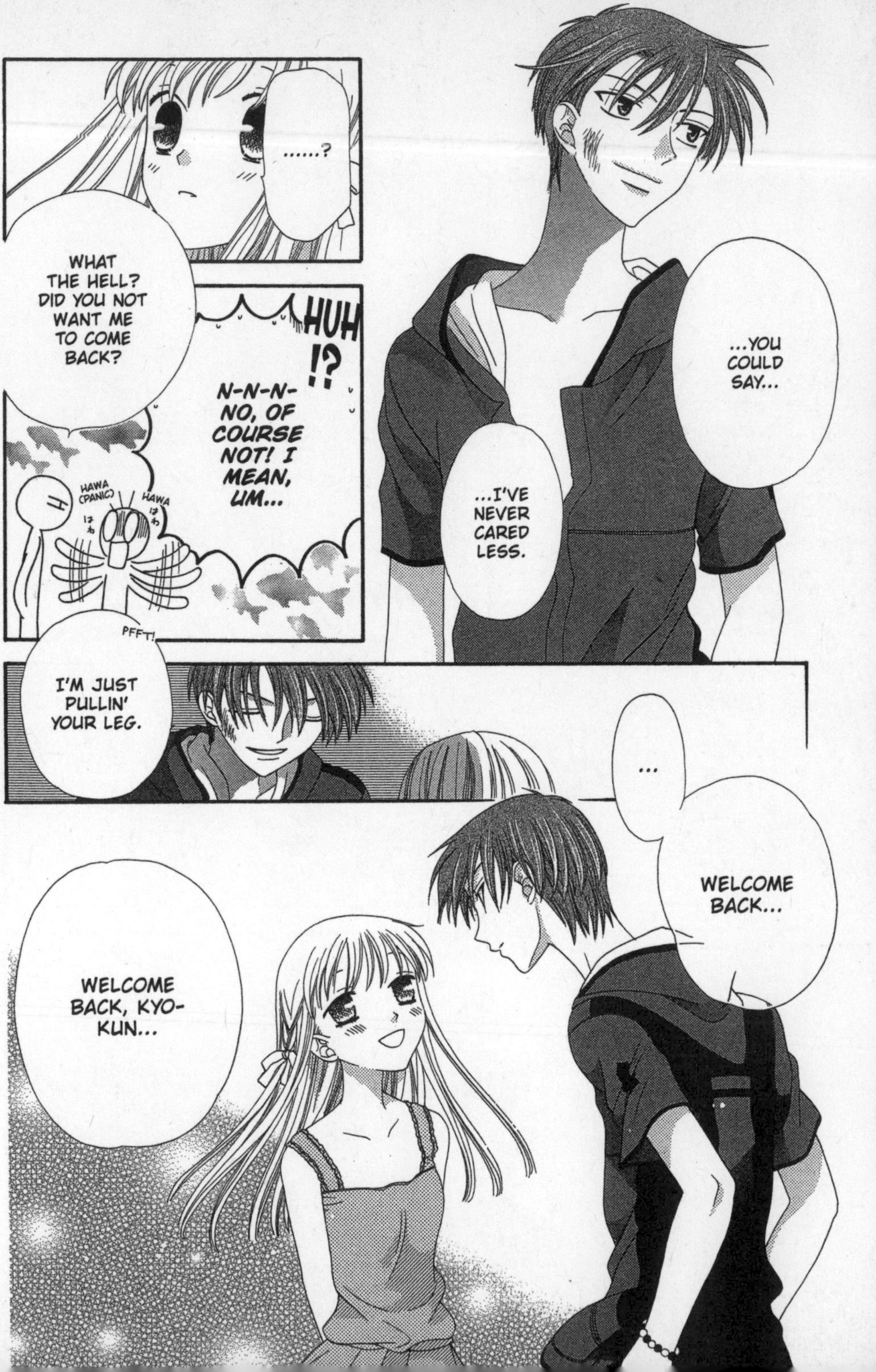

...YOU COULD SAY...
...I'VE NEVER CARED LESS.
......?
WHAT THE HELL? DID YOU NOT WANT ME TO COME BACK?
HUH !?
N-N-N-NO, OF COURSE NOT! I MEAN, UM...
HAWA (PANIC)
HAWA
PFFT!
I'M JUST PULLIN' YOUR LEG.
...
WELCOME BACK...
WELCOME BACK, KYO-KUN...

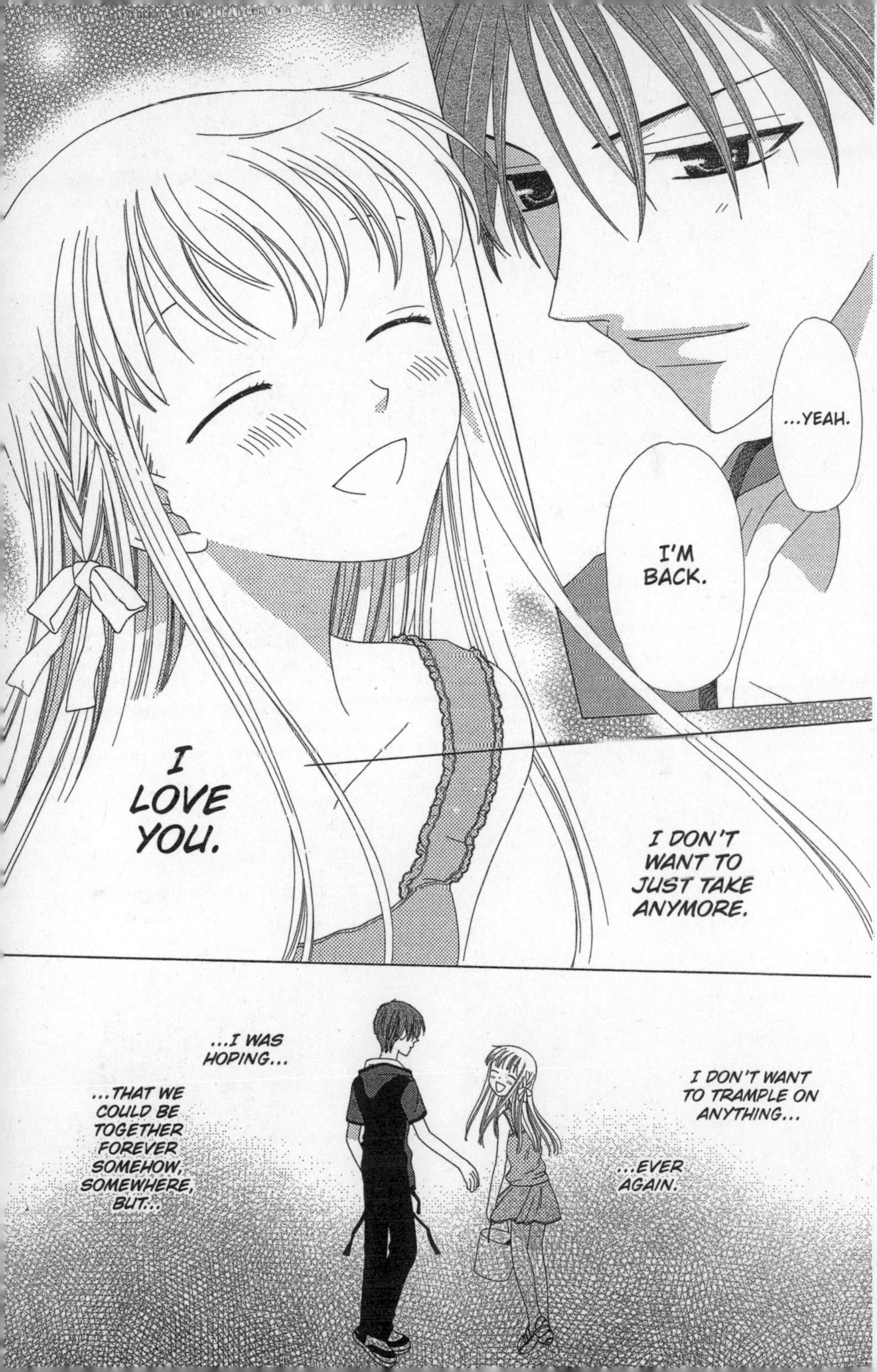
...YEAH.
I'M BACK.
I DON'T WANT TO JUST TAKE ANYMORE.
I LOVE YOU.
I DON'T WANT TO TRAMPLE ON ANYTHING...
...EVER AGAIN.
...I WAS HOPING...
...THAT WE COULD BE TOGETHER FOREVER SOMEHOW, SOMEWHERE, BUT...

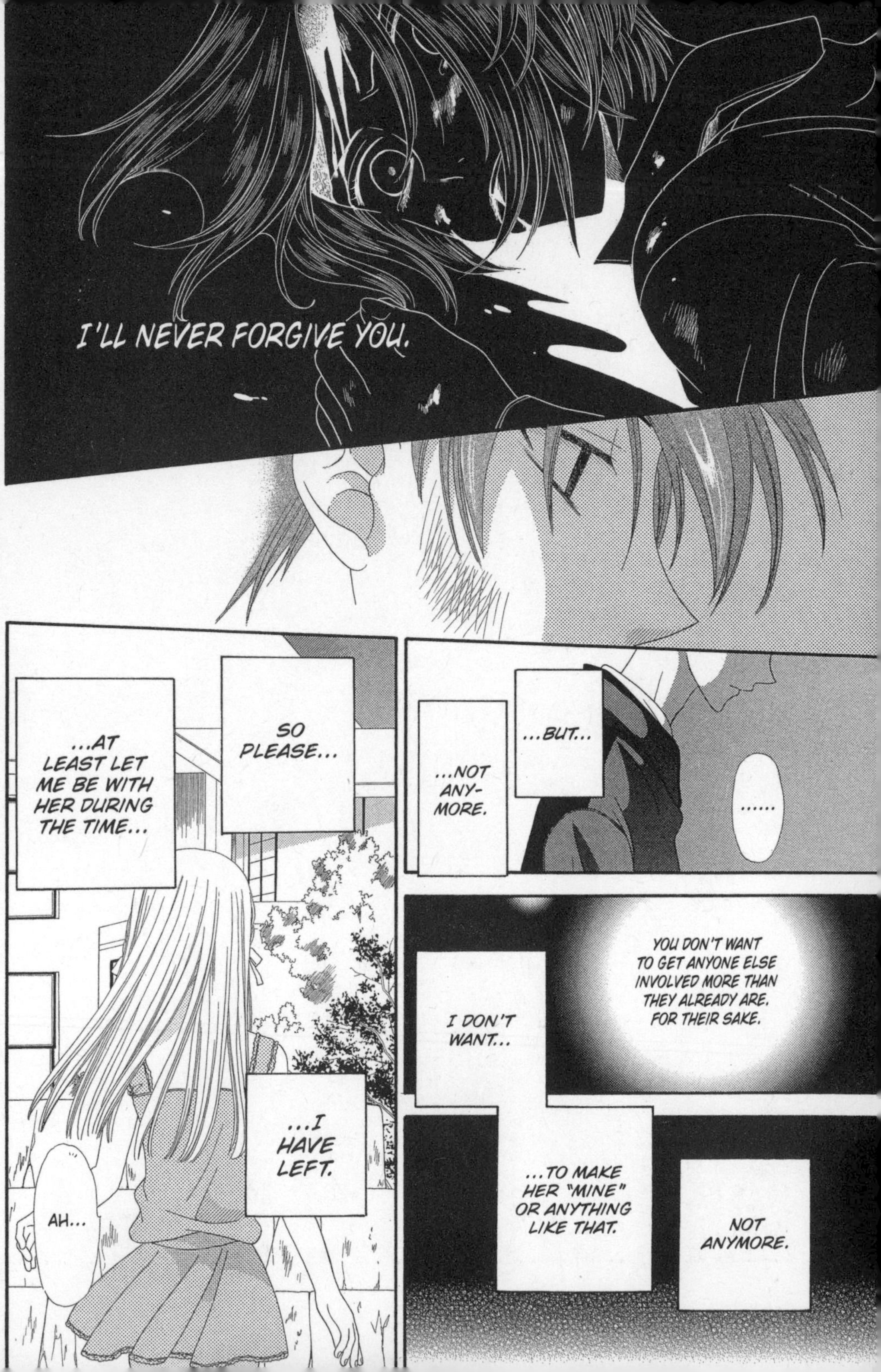
I'LL NEVER FORGIVE YOU.
......
...BUT...
...NOT ANY-MORE.
YOU DON'T WANT TO GET ANYONE ELSE INVOLVED MORE THAN THEY ALREADY ARE. FOR THEIR SAKE.
I DON'T WANT...
...TO MAKE HER "MINE" OR ANYTHING LIKE THAT.
NOT ANYMORE.
SO PLEASE...
...AT LEAST LET ME BE WITH HER DURING THE TIME...
...I HAVE LEFT.
AH...

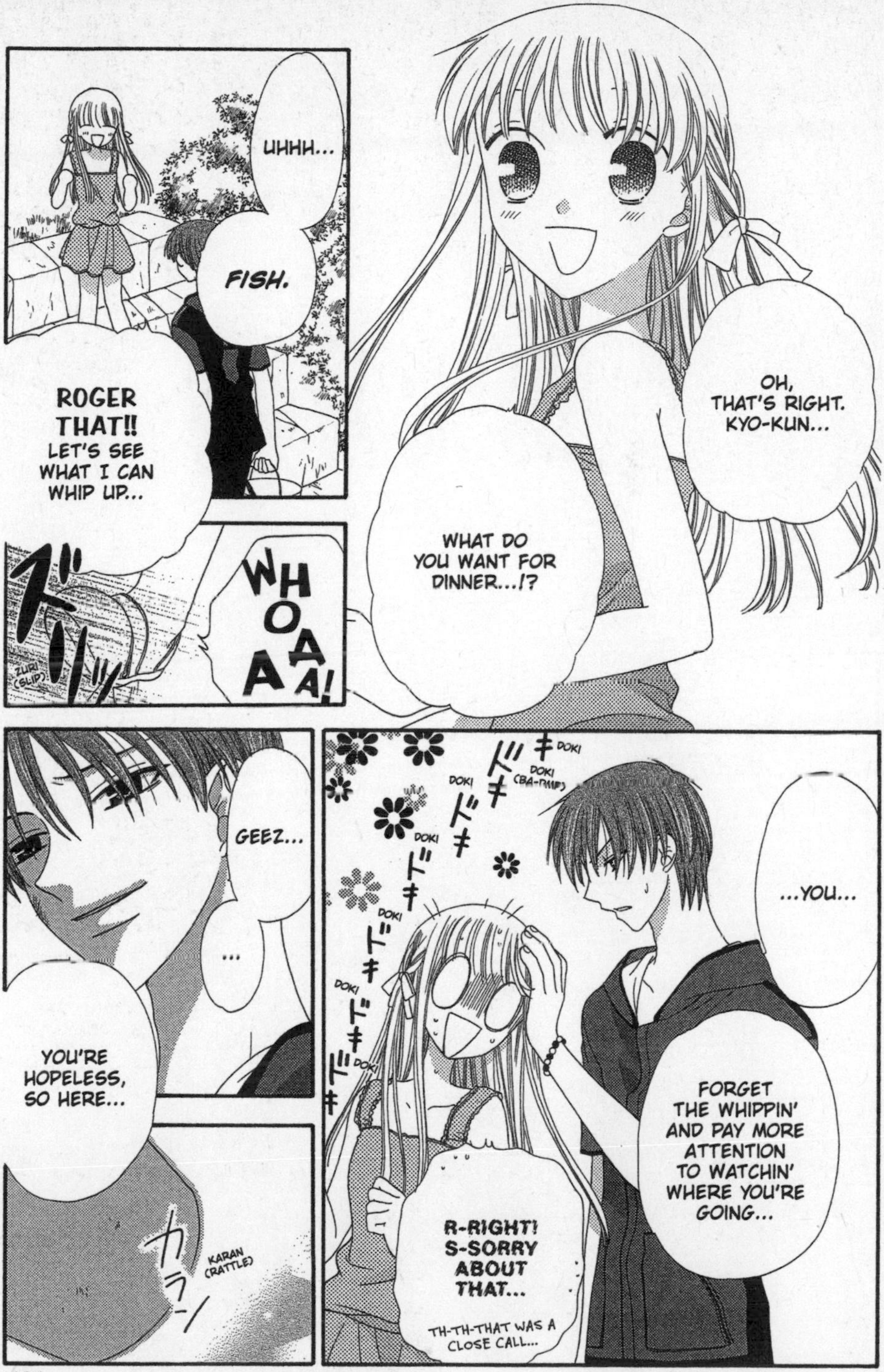
OH, THAT'S RIGHT. KYO-KUN...
WHAT DO YOU WANT FOR DINNER...!?
UHHH...
FISH.
ROGER THAT!! LET'S SEE WHAT I CAN WHIP UP...
WHOAAA!
ZURI (SLIP)
DOKI DOKI (BA-DMP) DOKI DOKI DOKI DOKI DOKI
...YOU...
FORGET THE WHIPPIN' AND PAY MORE ATTENTION TO WATCHIN' WHERE YOU'RE GOING...
R-RIGHT! S-SORRY ABOUT THAT...
TH-TH-THAT WAS A CLOSE CALL...
GEEZ...
...
YOU'RE HOPELESS, SO HERE...
KARAN (RATTLE)

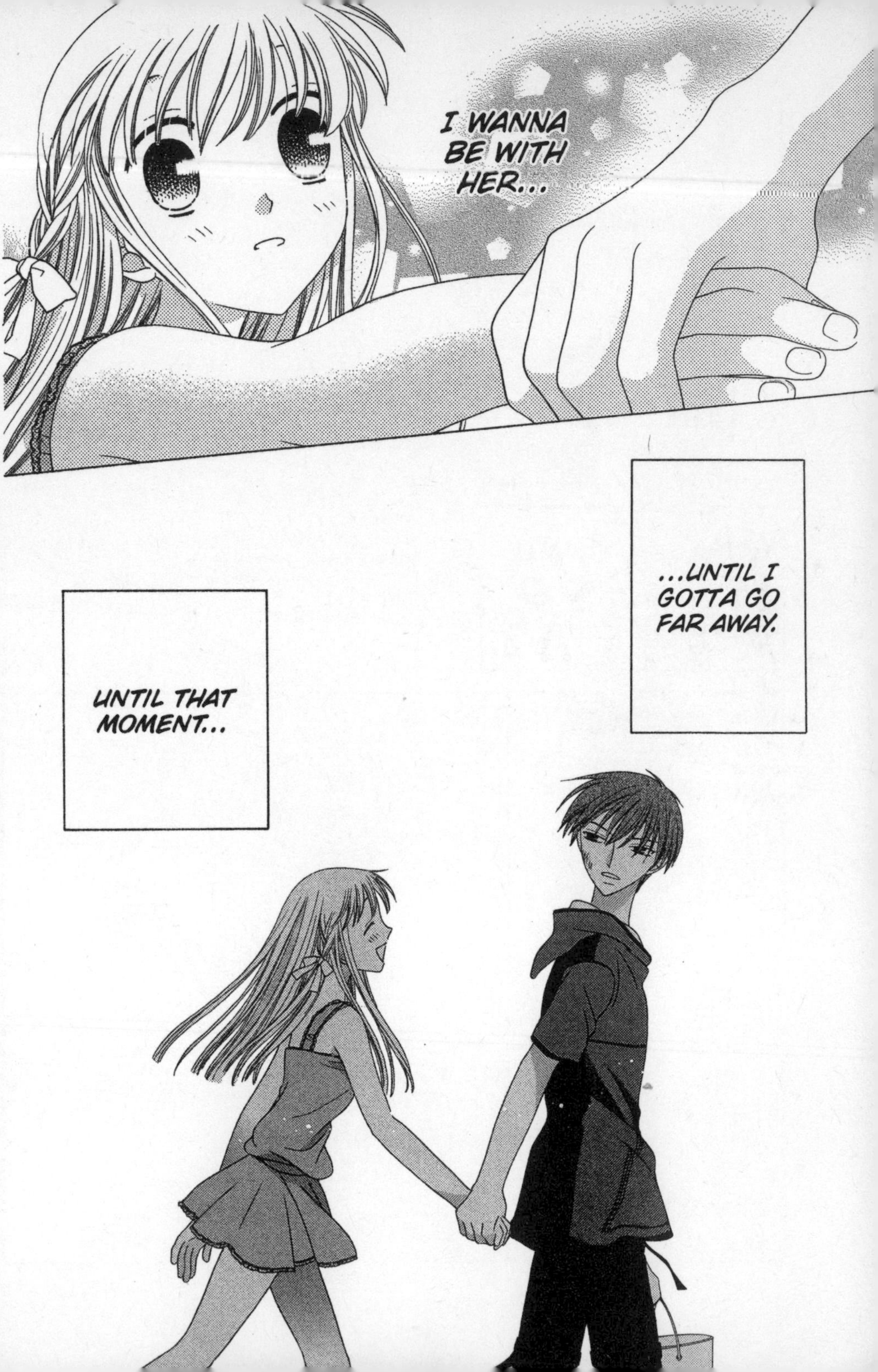
I WANNA BE WITH HER...
...UNTIL I GOTTA GO FAR AWAY.
UNTIL THAT MOMENT...

COLLECTOR'S EDITION

Fruits Basket

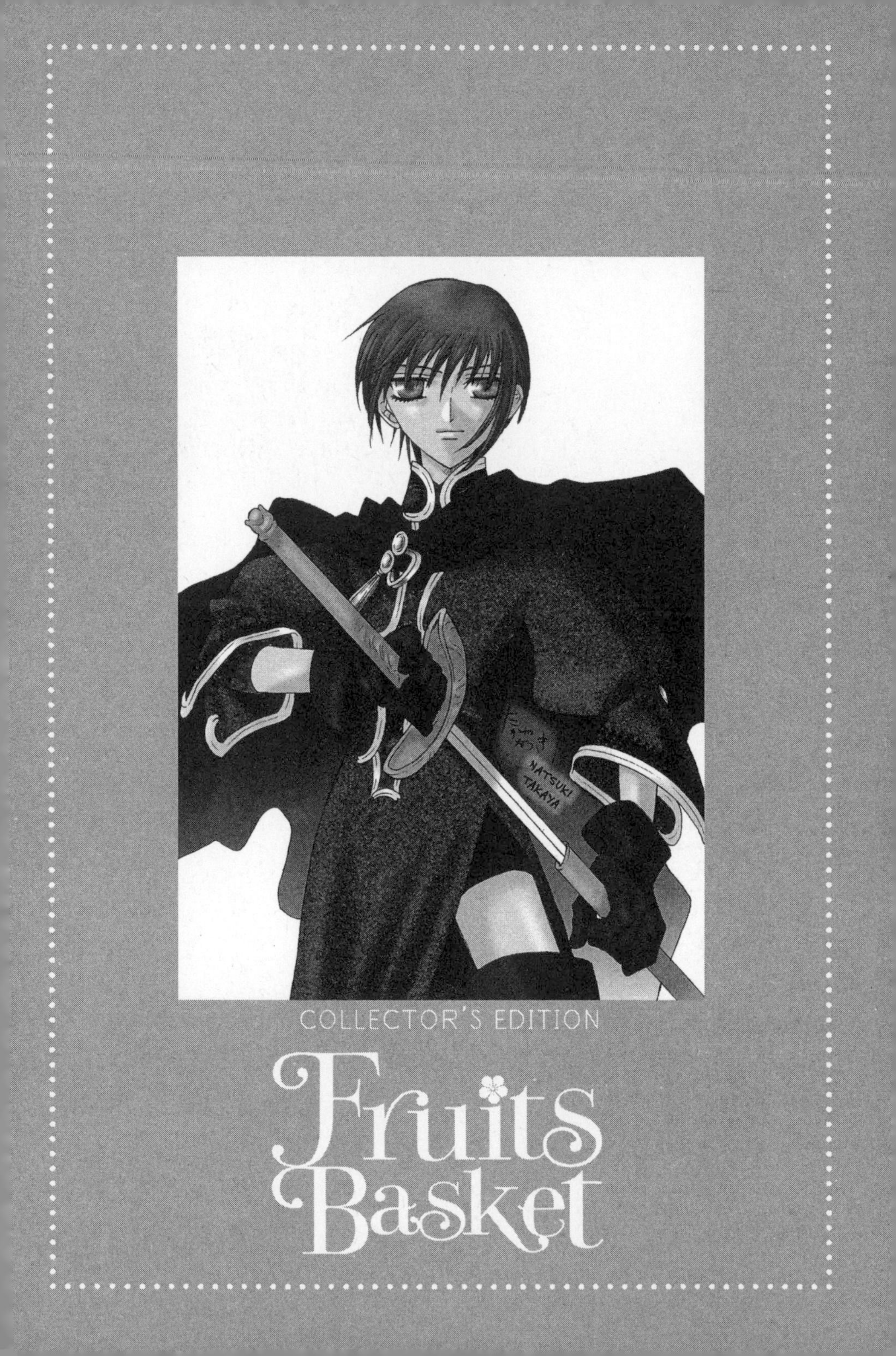
NATSUKI
TAKAYA

COLLECTOR'S EDITION

Fruits Basket

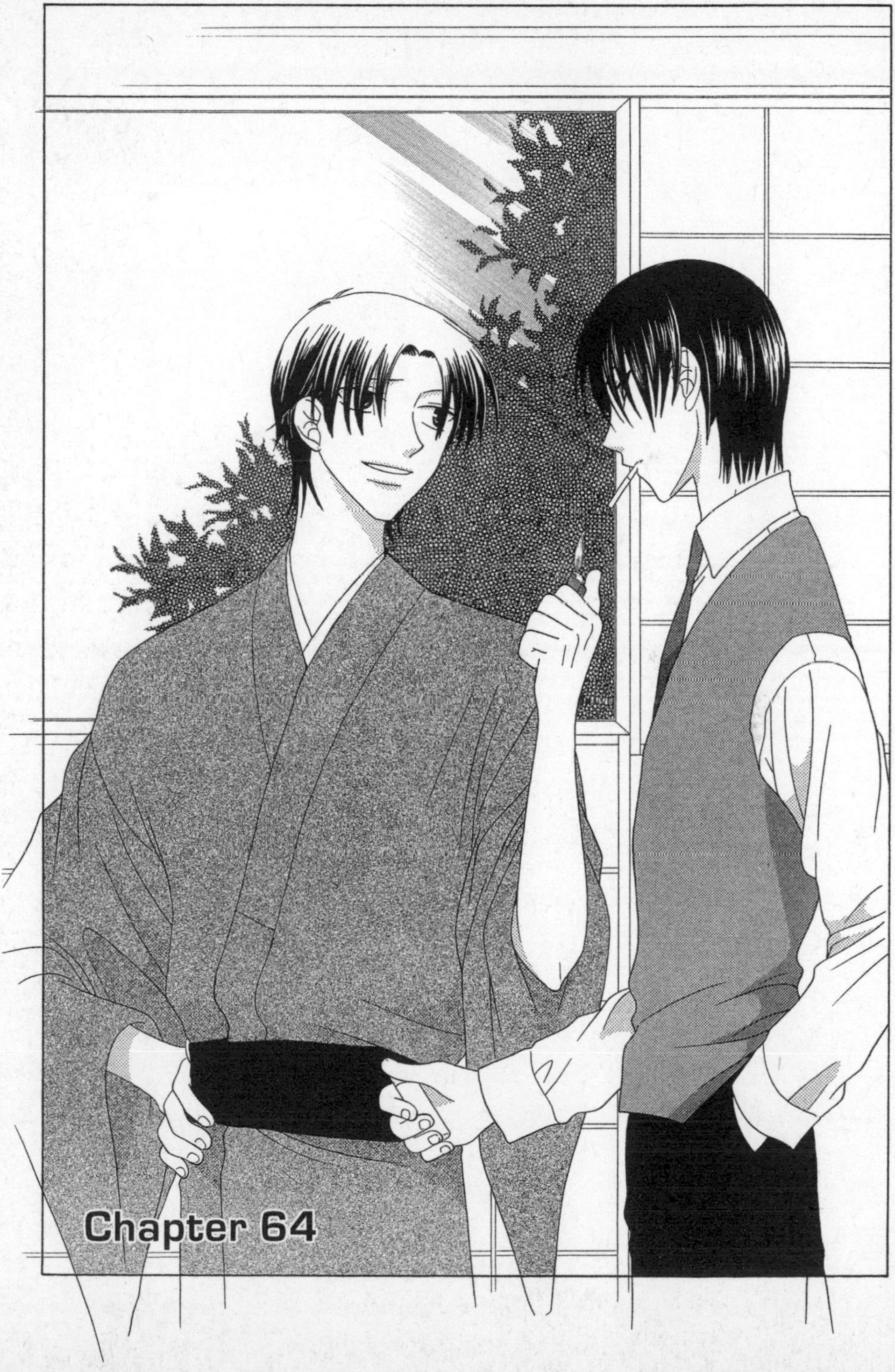
Chapter 64

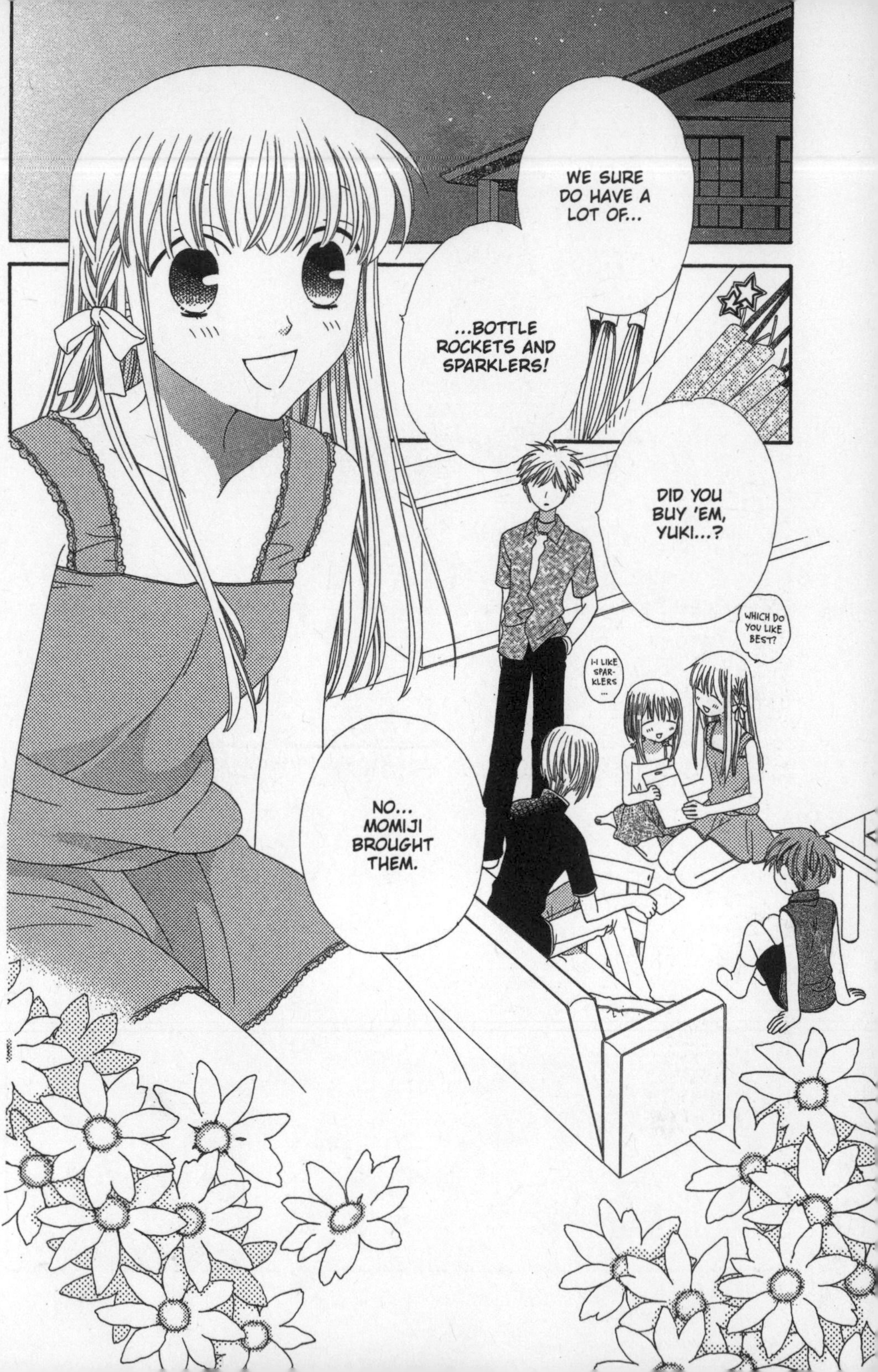
WE SURE DO HAVE A LOT OF...
...BOTTLE ROCKETS AND SPARKLERS!
DID YOU BUY 'EM, YUKI...?
WHICH DO YOU LIKE BEST?
I-I LIKE SPARKLERS...
NO... MOMIJI BROUGHT THEM.

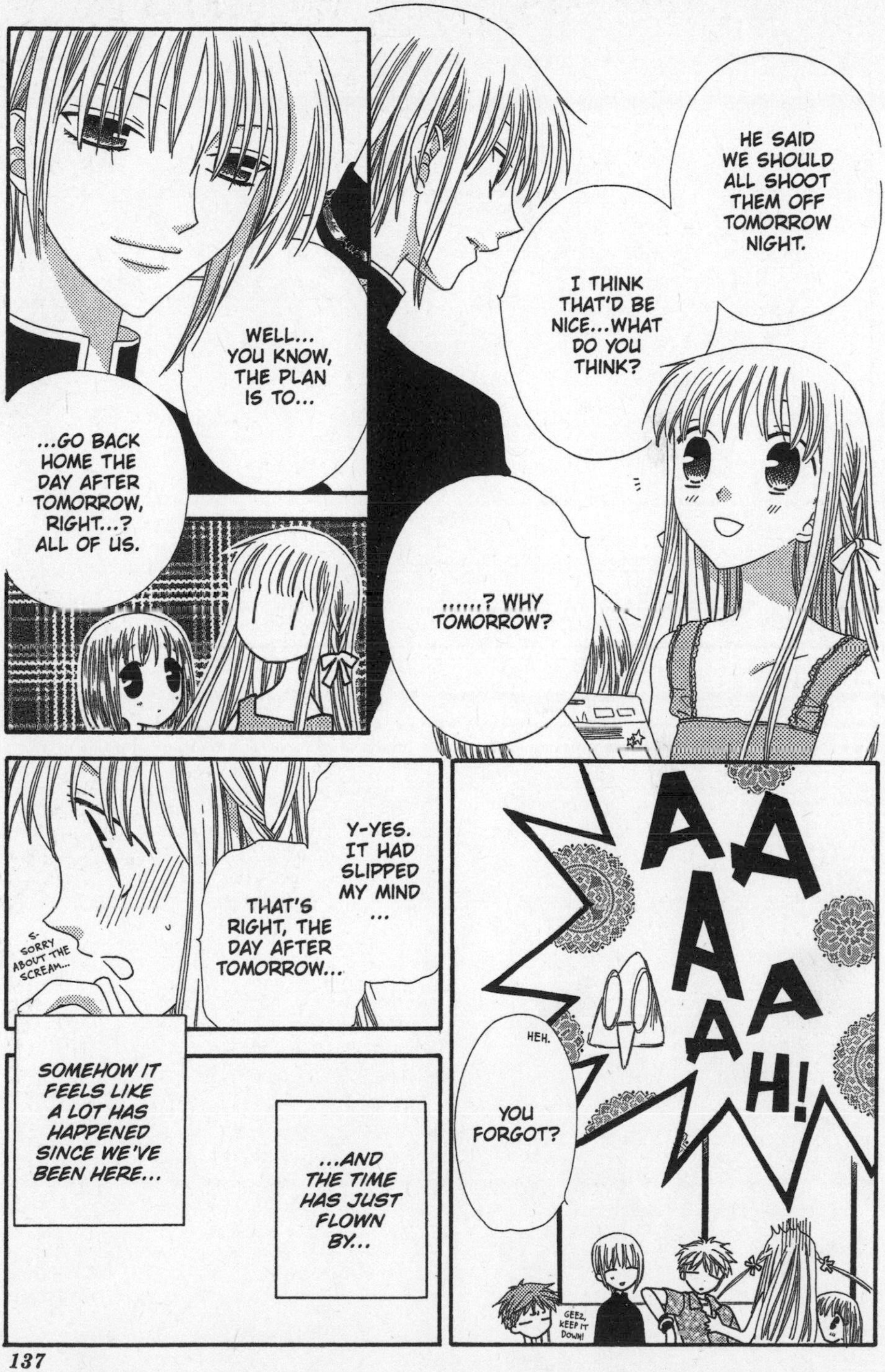
HE SAID WE SHOULD ALL SHOOT THEM OFF TOMORROW NIGHT.
I THINK THAT'D BE NICE...WHAT DO YOU THINK?
......? WHY TOMORROW?
WELL... YOU KNOW, THE PLAN IS TO...
...GO BACK HOME THE DAY AFTER TOMORROW, RIGHT...? ALL OF US.
AAAAAAH!
HEH.
YOU FORGOT?
GEEZ, KEEP IT DOWN!
Y-YES. IT HAD SLIPPED MY MIND ...
THAT'S RIGHT, THE DAY AFTER TOMORROW...
S-SORRY ABOUT THE SCREAM...
SOMEHOW IT FEELS LIKE A LOT HAS HAPPENED SINCE WE'VE BEEN HERE...
...AND THE TIME HAS JUST FLOWN BY...

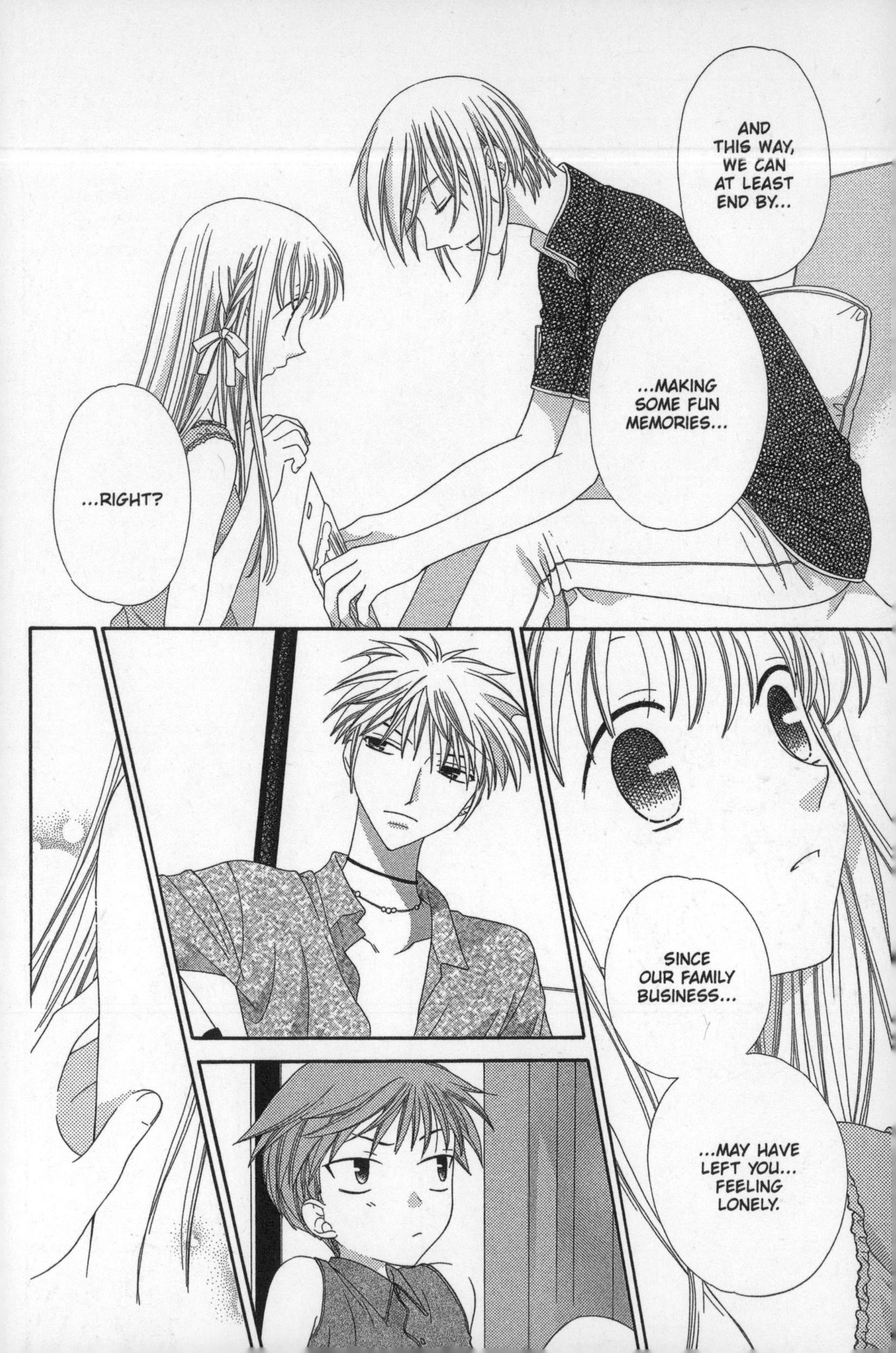
AND THIS WAY, WE CAN AT LEAST END BY...
...MAKING SOME FUN MEMORIES...
...RIGHT?
SINCE OUR FAMILY BUSINESS...
...MAY HAVE LEFT YOU... FEELING LONELY.

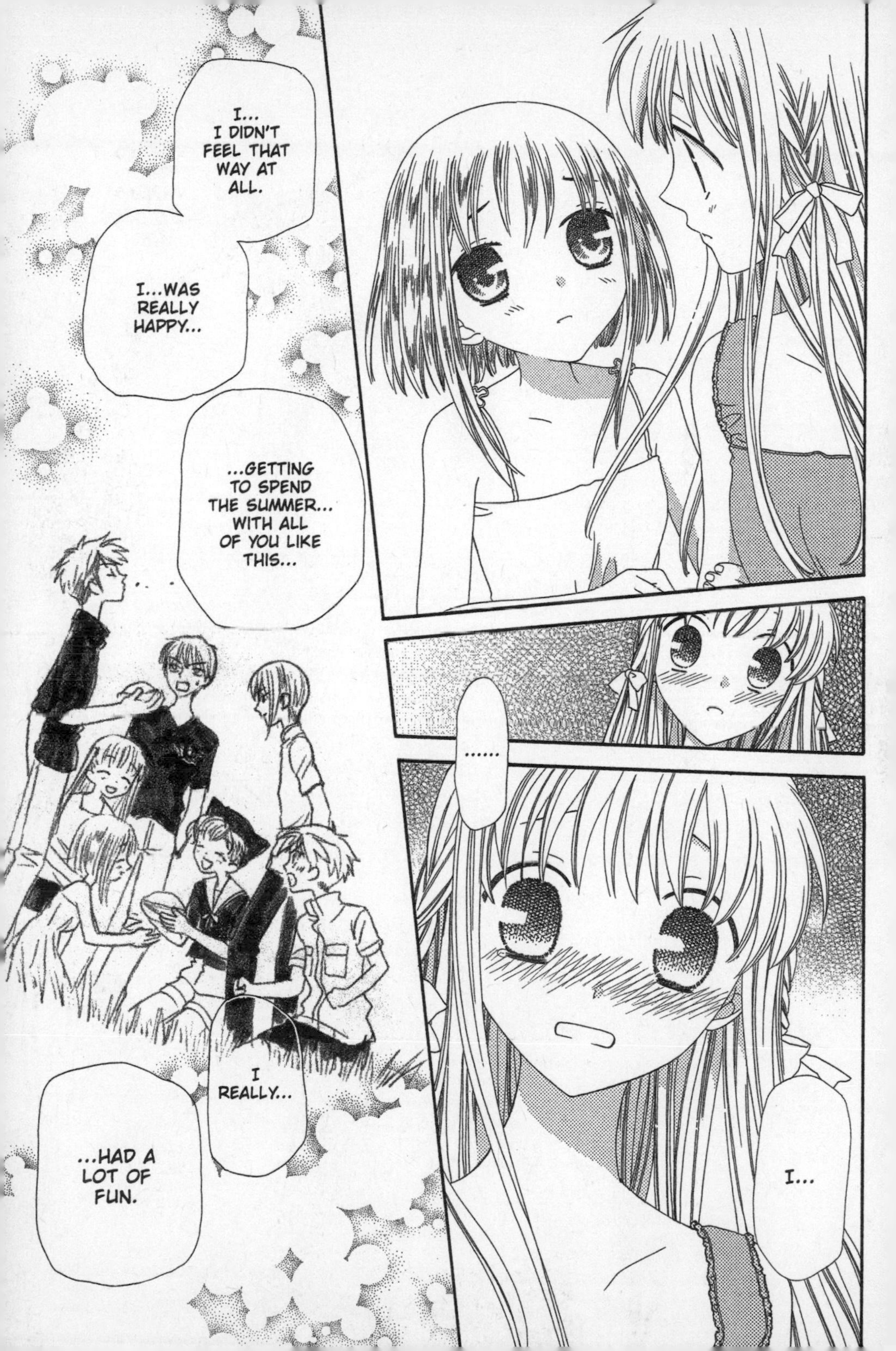
......
I...
I... I DIDN'T FEEL THAT WAY AT ALL.
I...WAS REALLY HAPPY...
...GETTING TO SPEND THE SUMMER... WITH ALL OF YOU LIKE THIS...
I REALLY...
...HAD A LOT OF FUN.

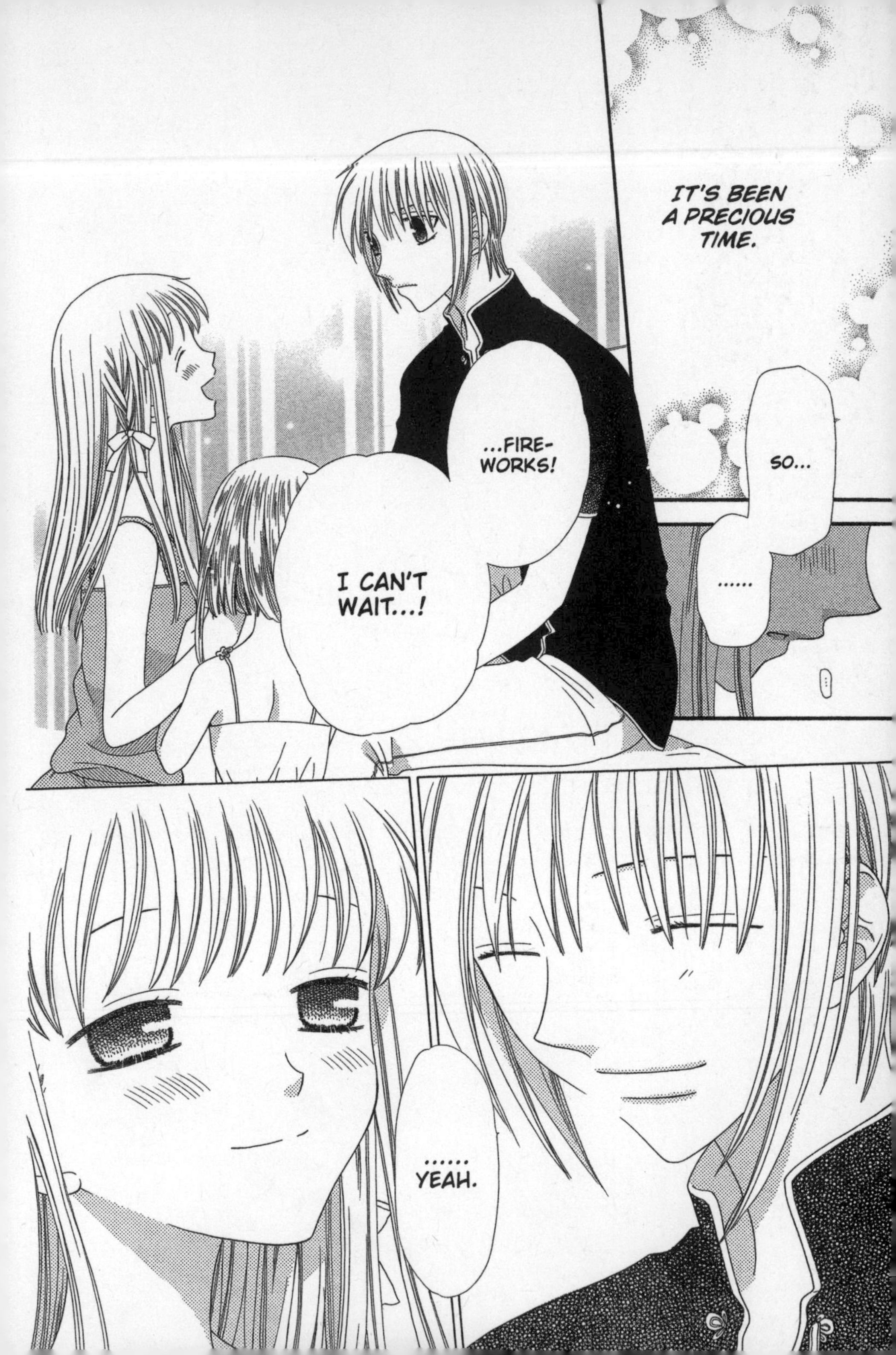
IT'S BEEN A PRECIOUS TIME.
SO...
......
...
...FIRE-WORKS!
I CAN'T WAIT...!
...... YEAH.

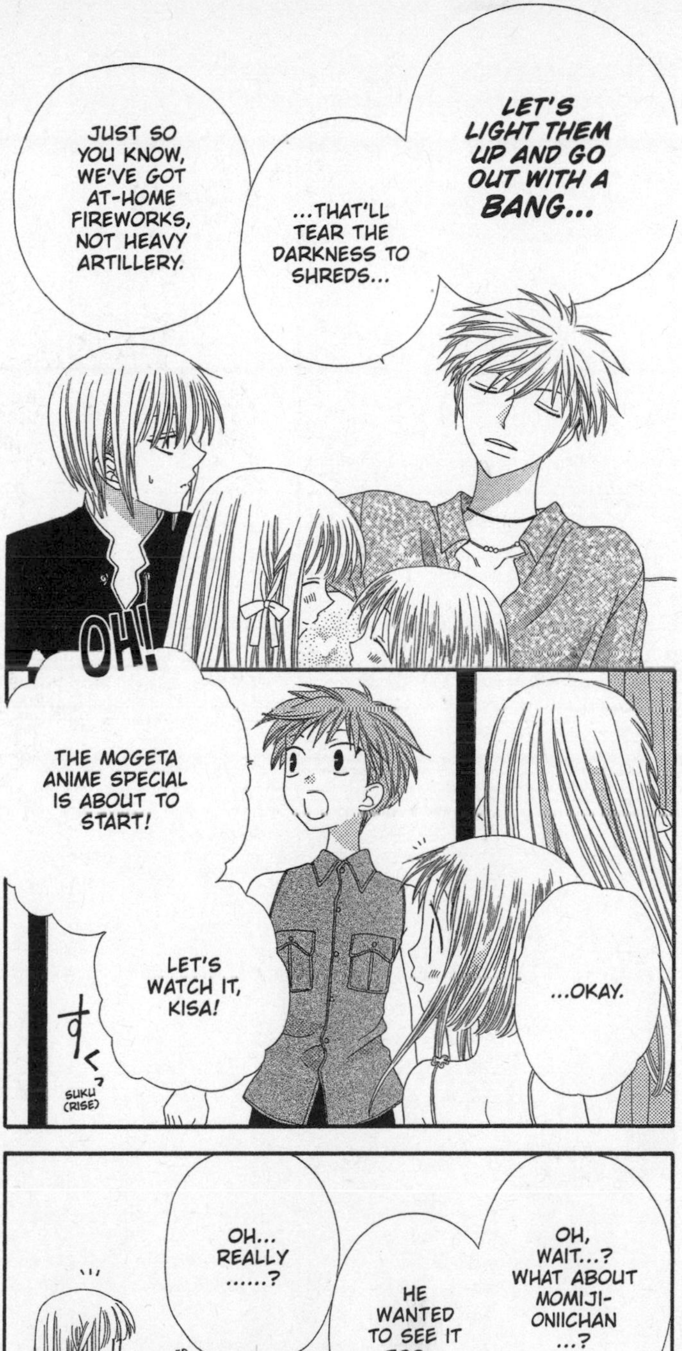
LET'S LIGHT THEM UP AND GO OUT WITH A BANG...
...THAT'LL TEAR THE DARKNESS TO SHREDS...
JUST SO YOU KNOW, WE'VE GOT AT-HOME FIREWORKS, NOT HEAVY ARTILLERY.
OH!
...OKAY.
THE MOGETA ANIME SPECIAL IS ABOUT TO START!
LET'S WATCH IT, KISA!
SUKU (RISE)
OH, WAIT...? WHAT ABOUT MOMIJI-ONIICHAN ...?
HE WANTED TO SEE IT TOO...
OH... REALLY ......?
I WANTED JUST THE TWO OF US...
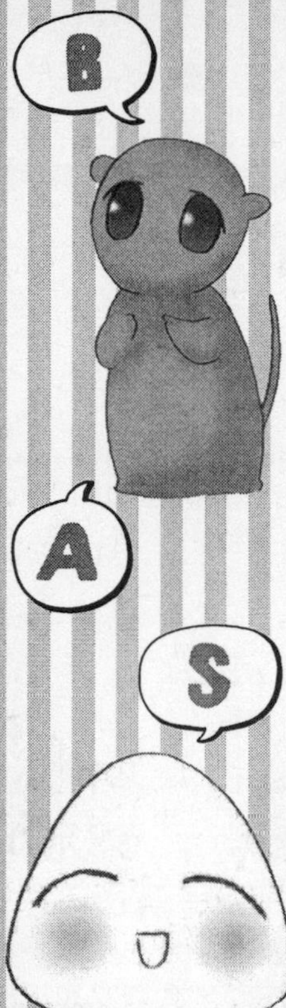
B
A
S
K

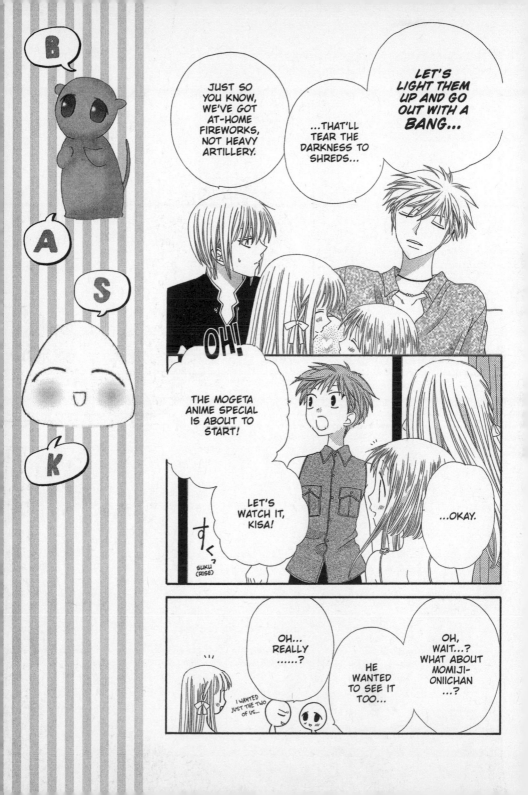

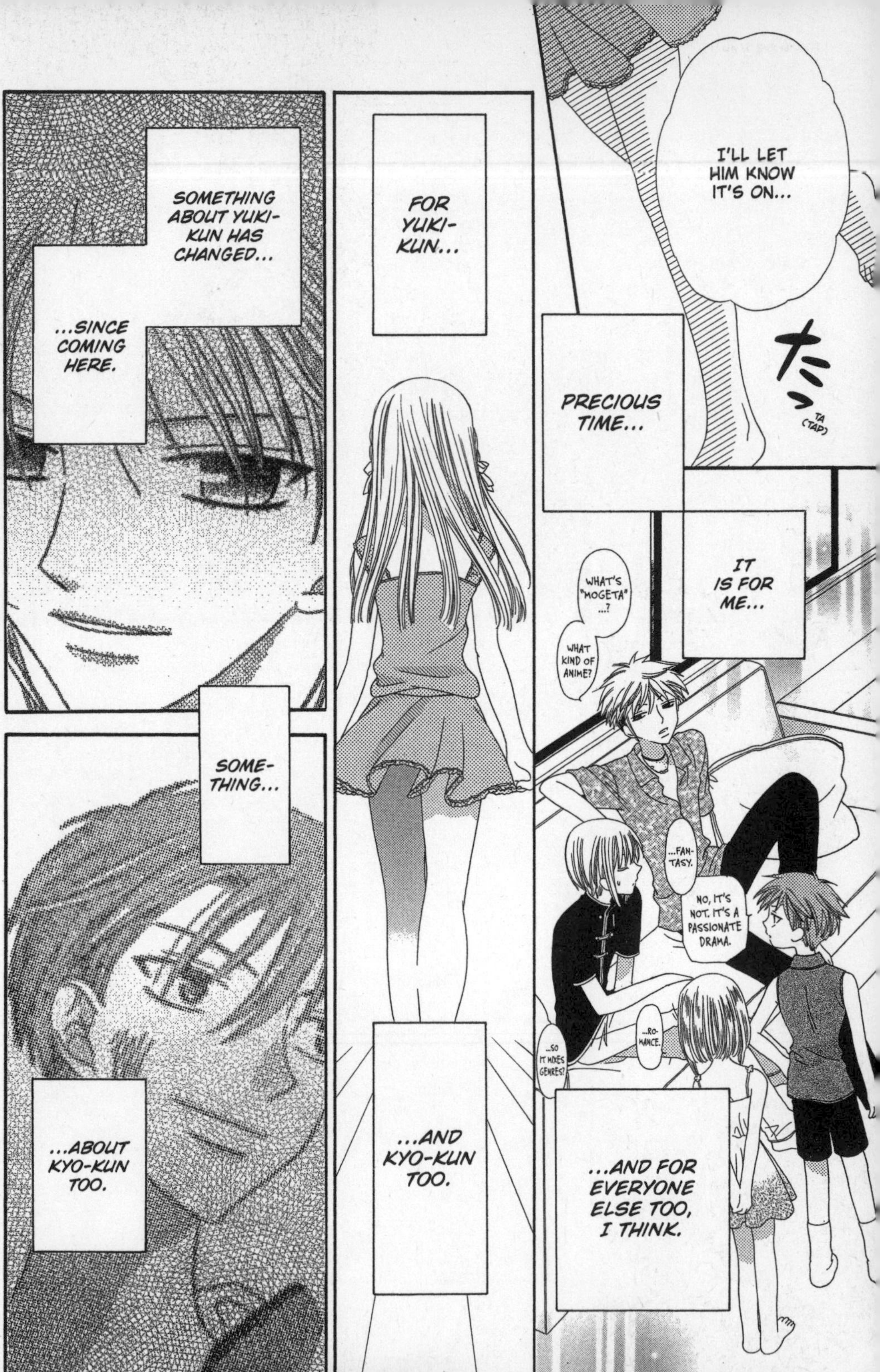
I'LL LET HIM KNOW IT'S ON...
たっ
TA (TAP)
PRECIOUS TIME...
IT IS FOR ME...
WHAT'S "MOGETA"...?
WHAT KIND OF ANIME?
...FAN-TASY.
NO, IT'S NOT. IT'S A PASSIONATE DRAMA.
...RO-MANCE.
...SO IT MIXES GENRES?
...AND FOR EVERYONE ELSE TOO, I THINK.
FOR YUKI-KUN...
...AND KYO-KUN TOO.
SOMETHING ABOUT YUKI-KUN HAS CHANGED...
...SINCE COMING HERE.
SOME-THING...
...ABOUT KYO-KUN TOO.

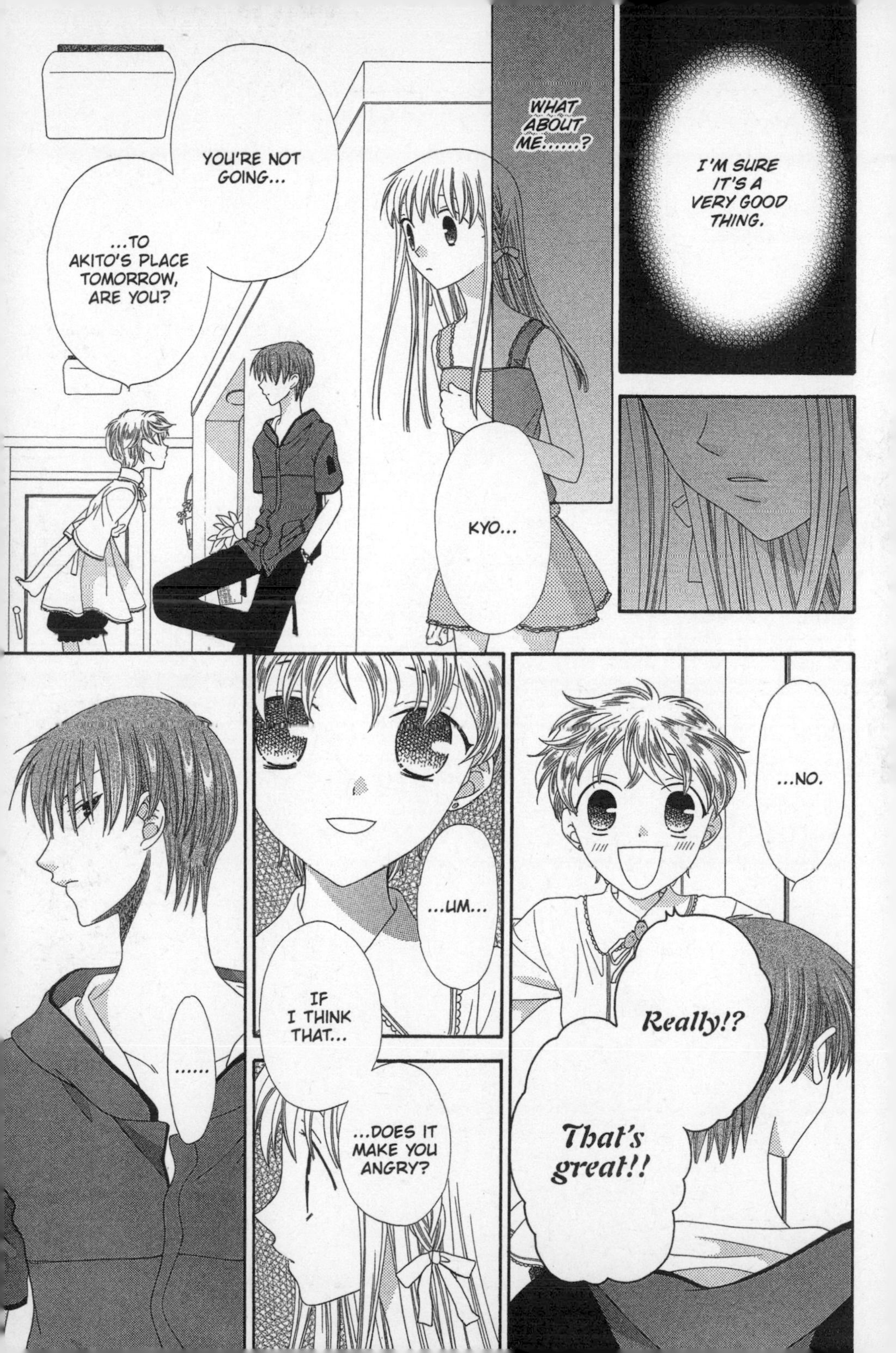
I'M SURE IT'S A VERY GOOD THING.
WHAT ABOUT ME......?
KYO...
YOU'RE NOT GOING...
...TO AKITO'S PLACE TOMORROW, ARE YOU?
...NO.
Really!?
That's great!!
...UM...
IF I THINK THAT...
...DOES IT MAKE YOU ANGRY?
......

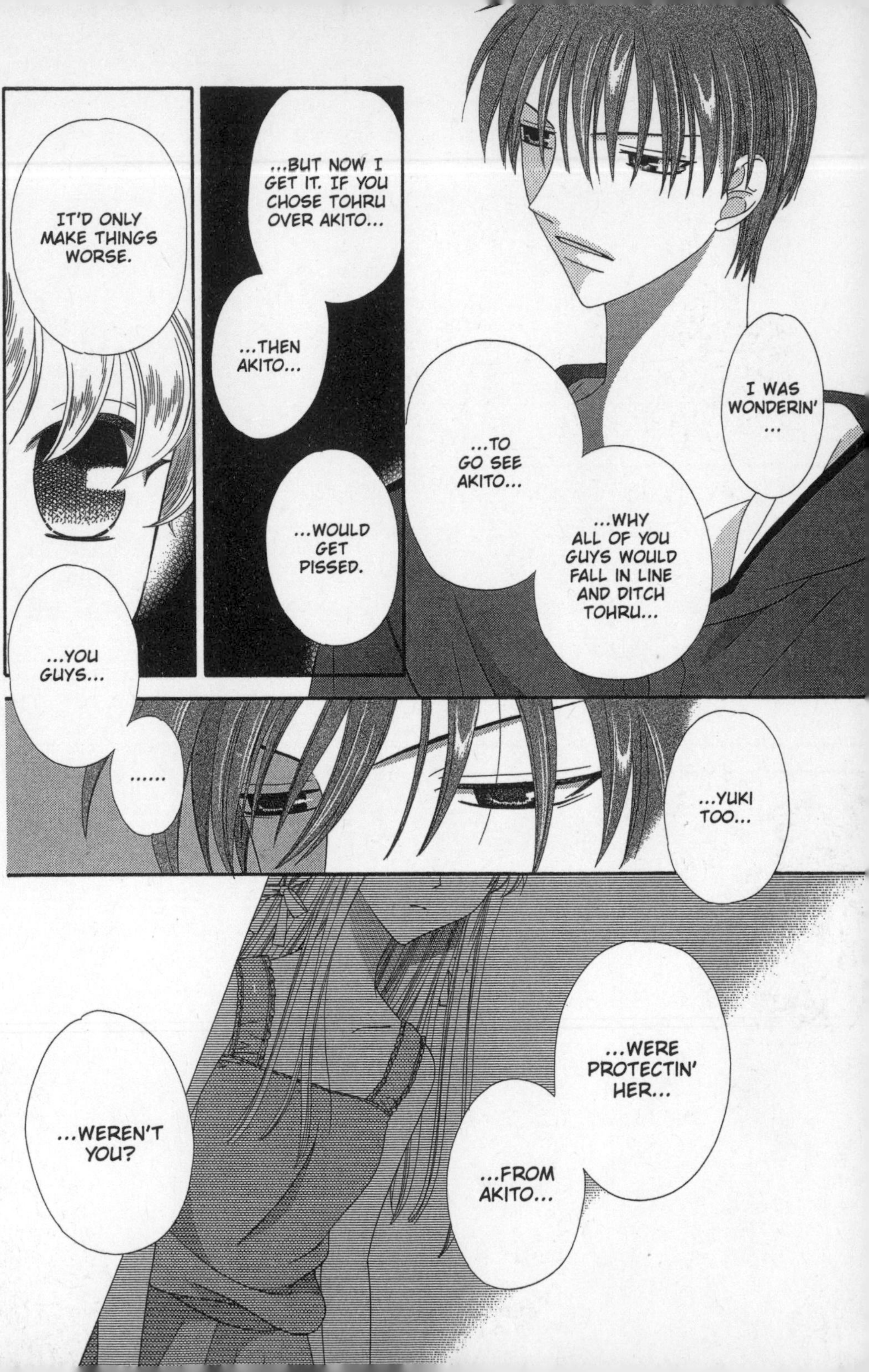
I WAS WONDERIN' ...
...WHY ALL OF YOU GUYS WOULD FALL IN LINE AND DITCH TOHRU...
...TO GO SEE AKITO...
...BUT NOW I GET IT. IF YOU CHOSE TOHRU OVER AKITO...
...THEN AKITO...
...WOULD GET PISSED.
IT'D ONLY MAKE THINGS WORSE.
...YOU GUYS...
...YUKI TOO...
......
...WERE PROTECTIN' HER...
...FROM AKITO...
...WEREN'T YOU?

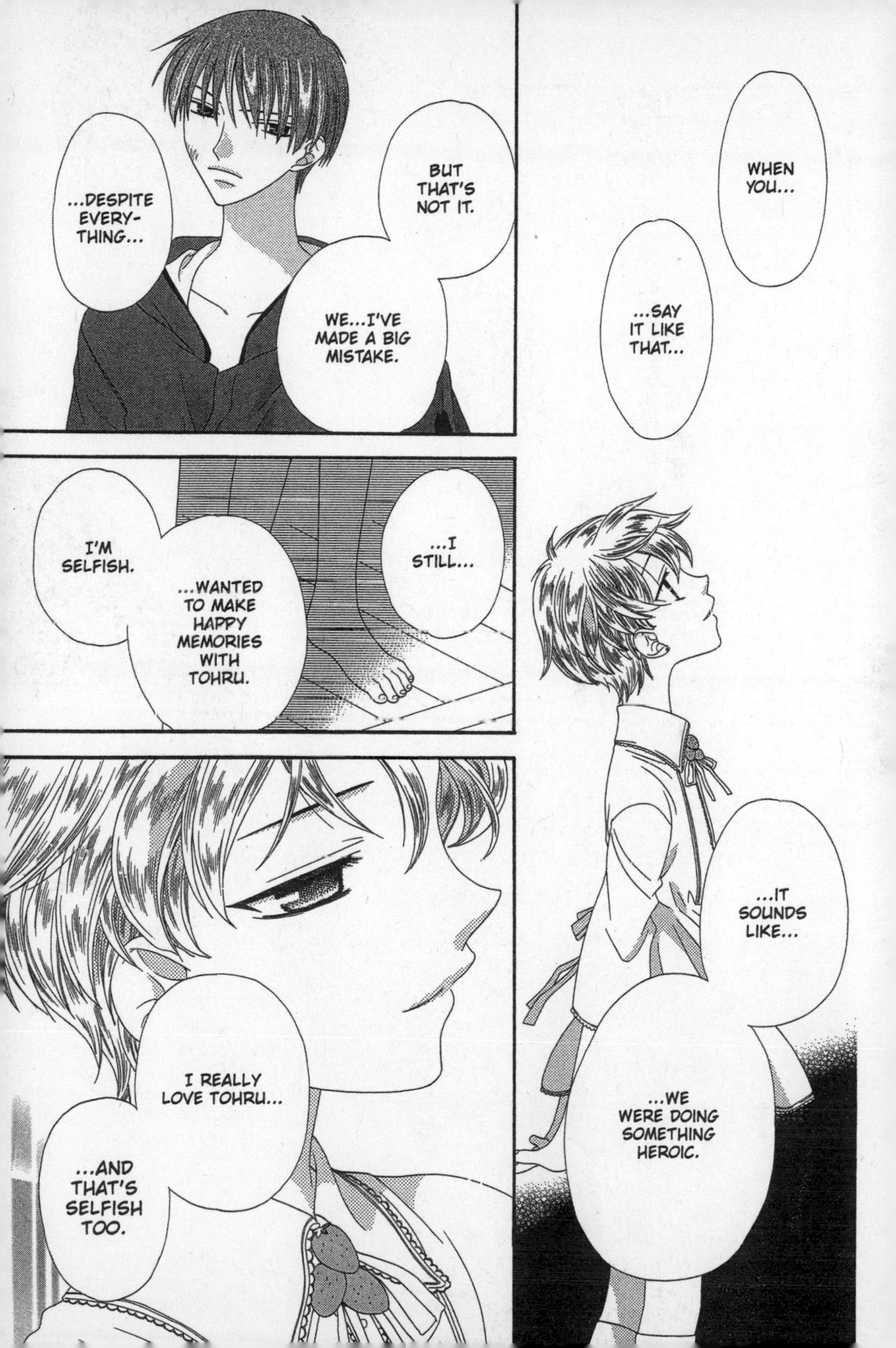

WHEN YOU...
...SAY IT LIKE THAT...
...IT SOUNDS LIKE...
...WE WERE DOING SOMETHING HEROIC.
BUT THAT'S NOT IT.
WE...I'VE MADE A BIG MISTAKE.
...DESPITE EVERYTHING...
...I STILL...
...WANTED TO MAKE HAPPY MEMORIES WITH TOHRU.
I'M SELFISH.
I REALLY LOVE TOHRU...
...AND THAT'S SELFISH TOO.

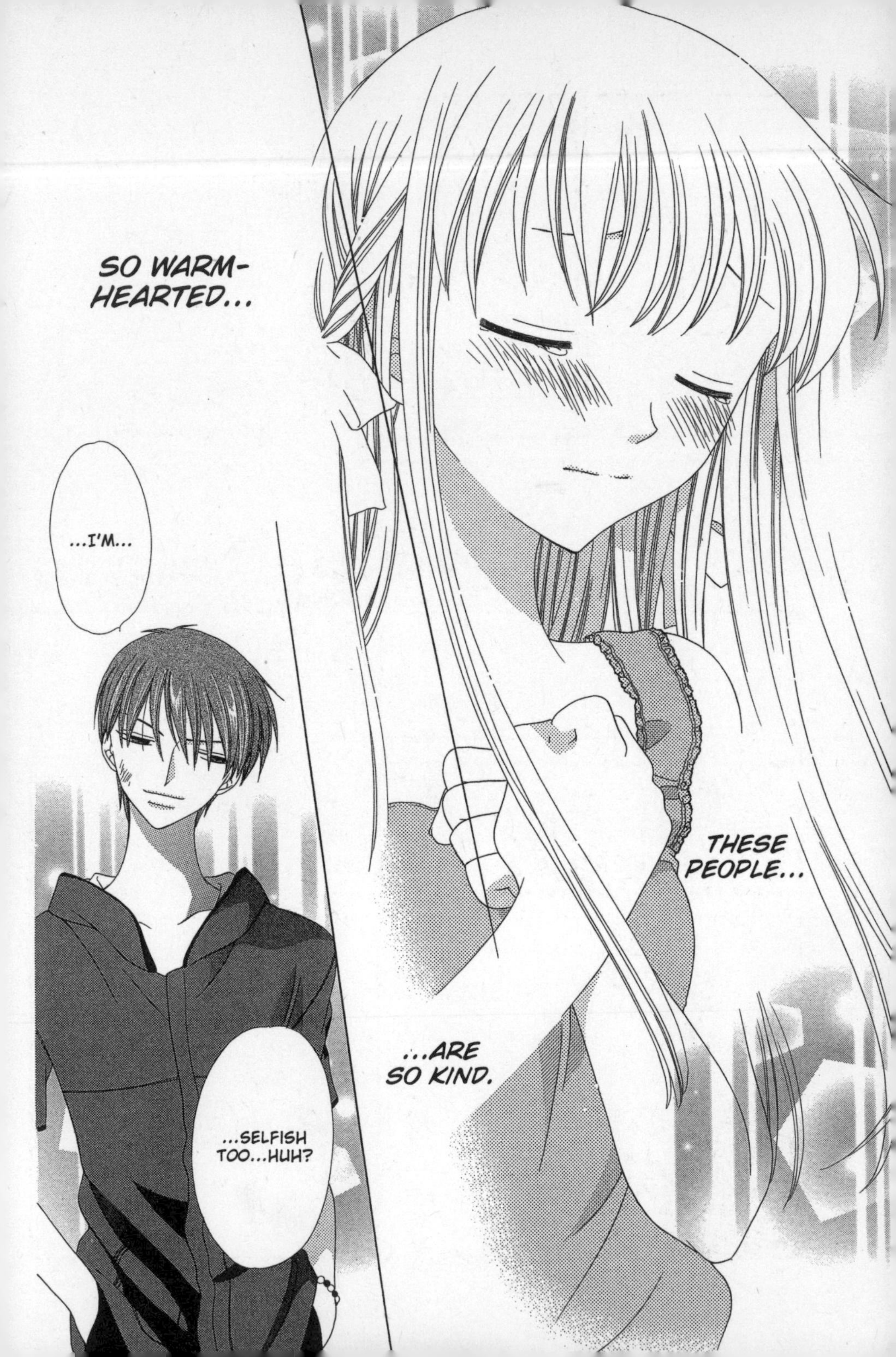
THESE PEOPLE...
...ARE SO KIND.
SO WARM-HEARTED...
...I'M...
...SELFISH TOO...HUH?

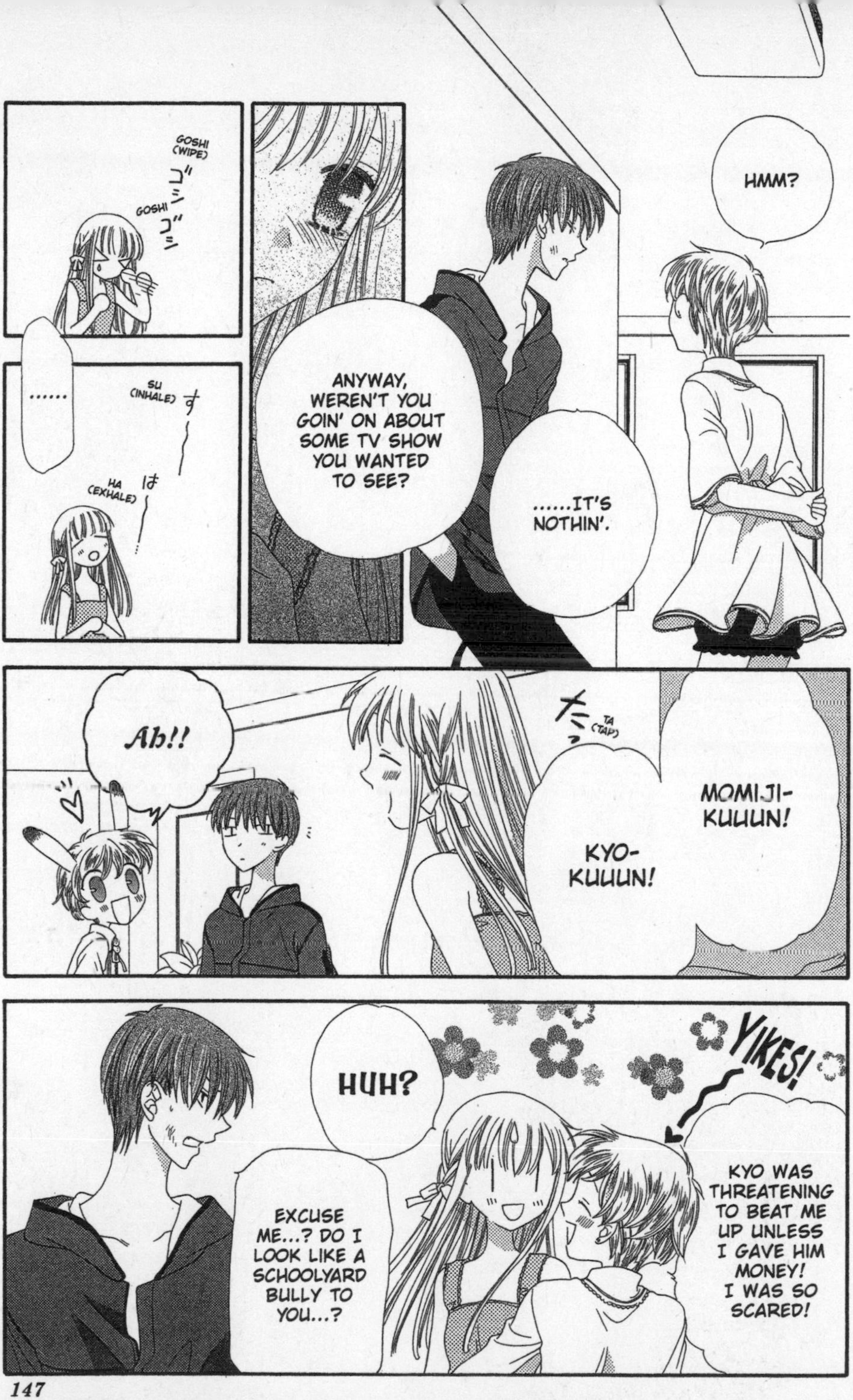
HMM?
......IT'S NOTHIN'.
ANYWAY, WEREN'T YOU GOIN' ON ABOUT SOME TV SHOW YOU WANTED TO SEE?
GOSHI (WIPE)
ゴシ
GOSHI
ゴシ
......
SU (INHALE)
す
HA (EXHALE)
は
MOMIJI-KUUUN!
KYO-KUUUN!
TA (TAP)
た
Ah!!
YIKES!
KYO WAS THREATENING TO BEAT ME UP UNLESS I GAVE HIM MONEY! I WAS SO SCARED!
HUH?
EXCUSE ME...? DO I LOOK LIKE A SCHOOLYARD BULLY TO YOU...?

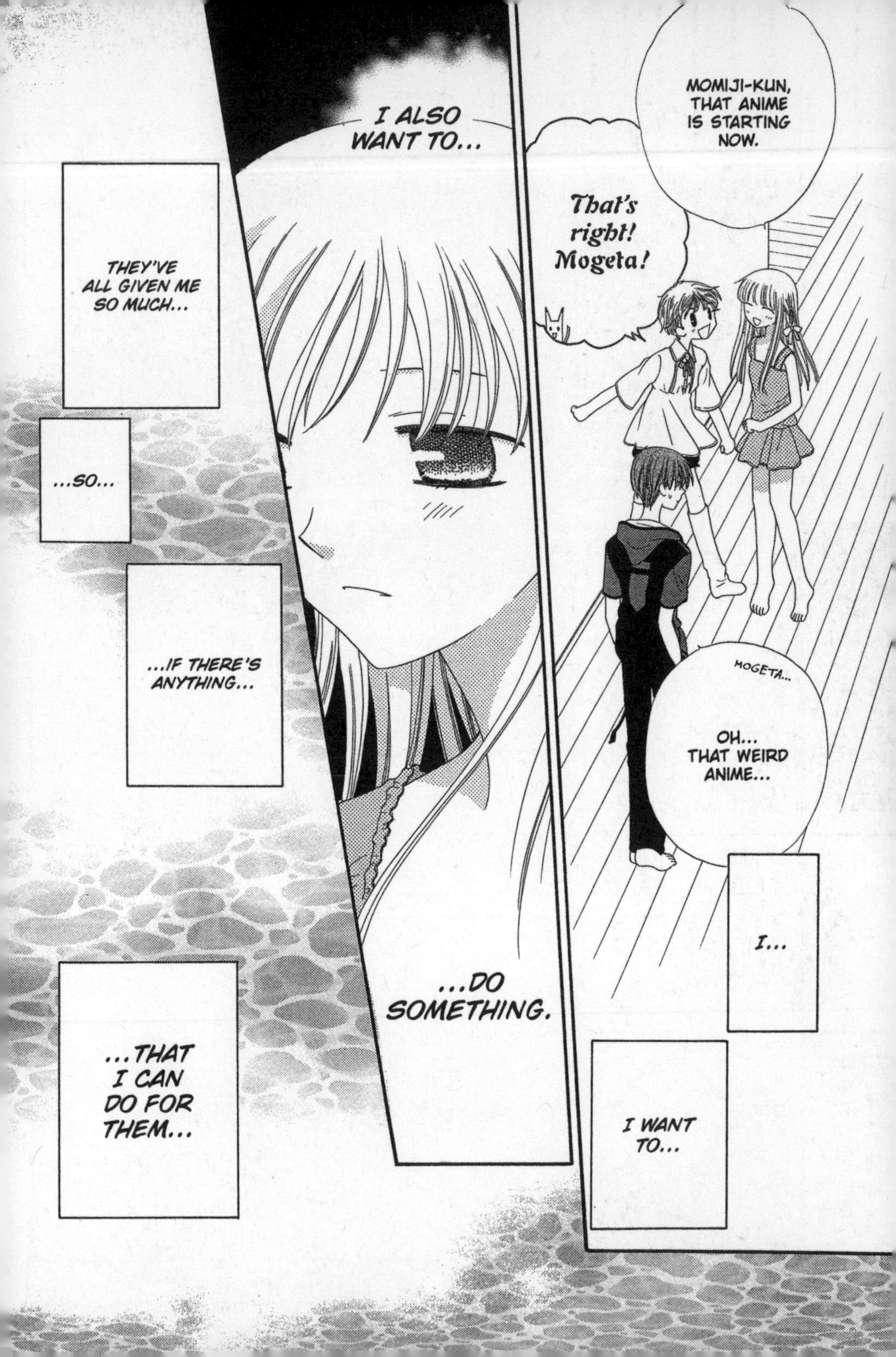
MOMIJI-KUN, THAT ANIME IS STARTING NOW.
That's right! Mogeta!
MOGETA...
OH... THAT WEIRD ANIME...
I...
I WANT TO...
I ALSO WANT TO...
...DO SOMETHING.
THEY'VE ALL GIVEN ME SO MUCH...
...SO...
...IF THERE'S ANYTHING...
...THAT I CAN DO FOR THEM...

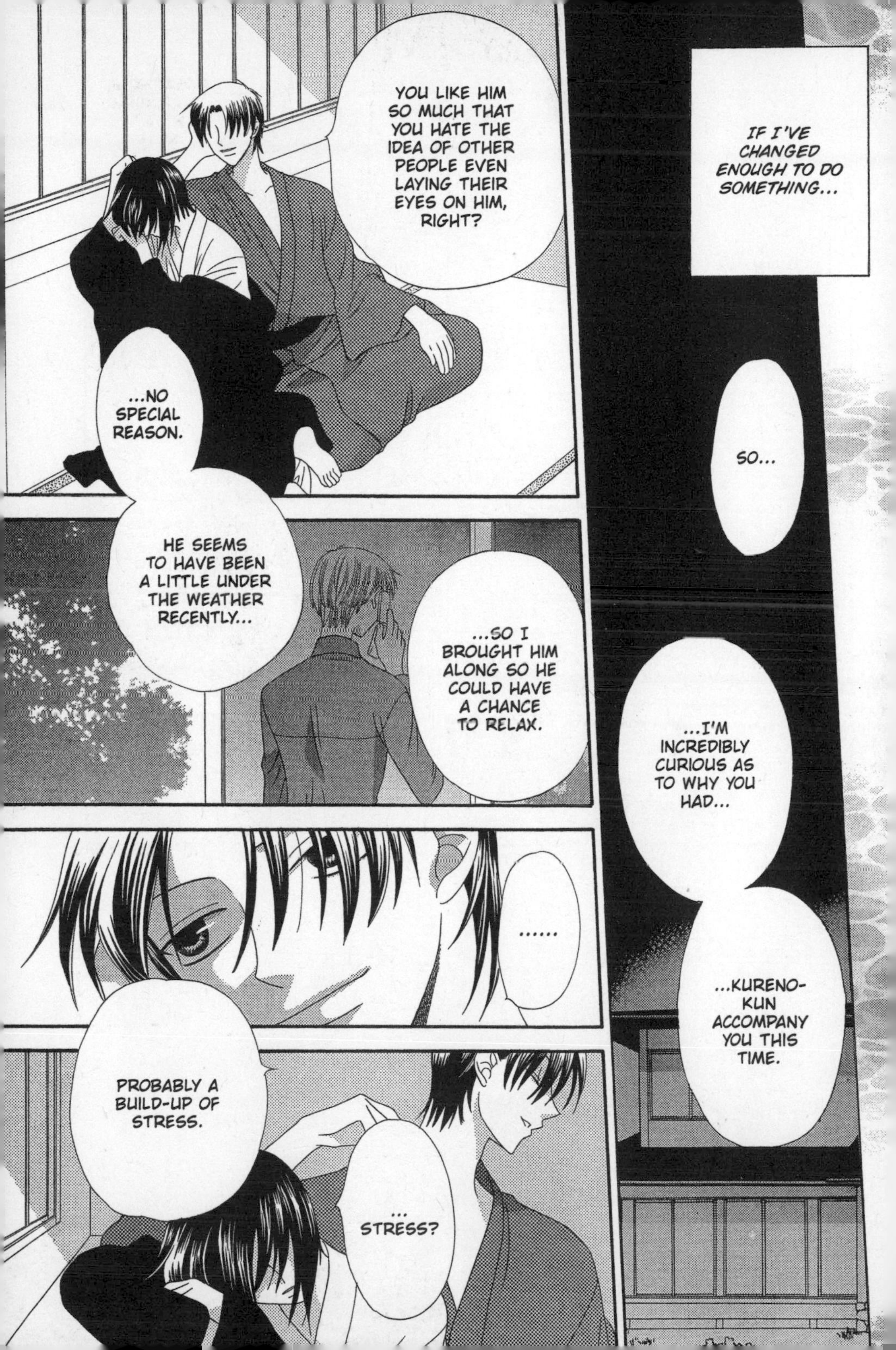
IF I'VE CHANGED ENOUGH TO DO SOMETHING...
SO...
...I'M INCREDIBLY CURIOUS AS TO WHY YOU HAD...
...KURENO-KUN ACCOMPANY YOU THIS TIME.
YOU LIKE HIM SO MUCH THAT YOU HATE THE IDEA OF OTHER PEOPLE EVEN LAYING THEIR EYES ON HIM, RIGHT?
...NO SPECIAL REASON.
HE SEEMS TO HAVE BEEN A LITTLE UNDER THE WEATHER RECENTLY...
...SO I BROUGHT HIM ALONG SO HE COULD HAVE A CHANCE TO RELAX.
......
PROBABLY A BUILD-UP OF STRESS.
... STRESS?

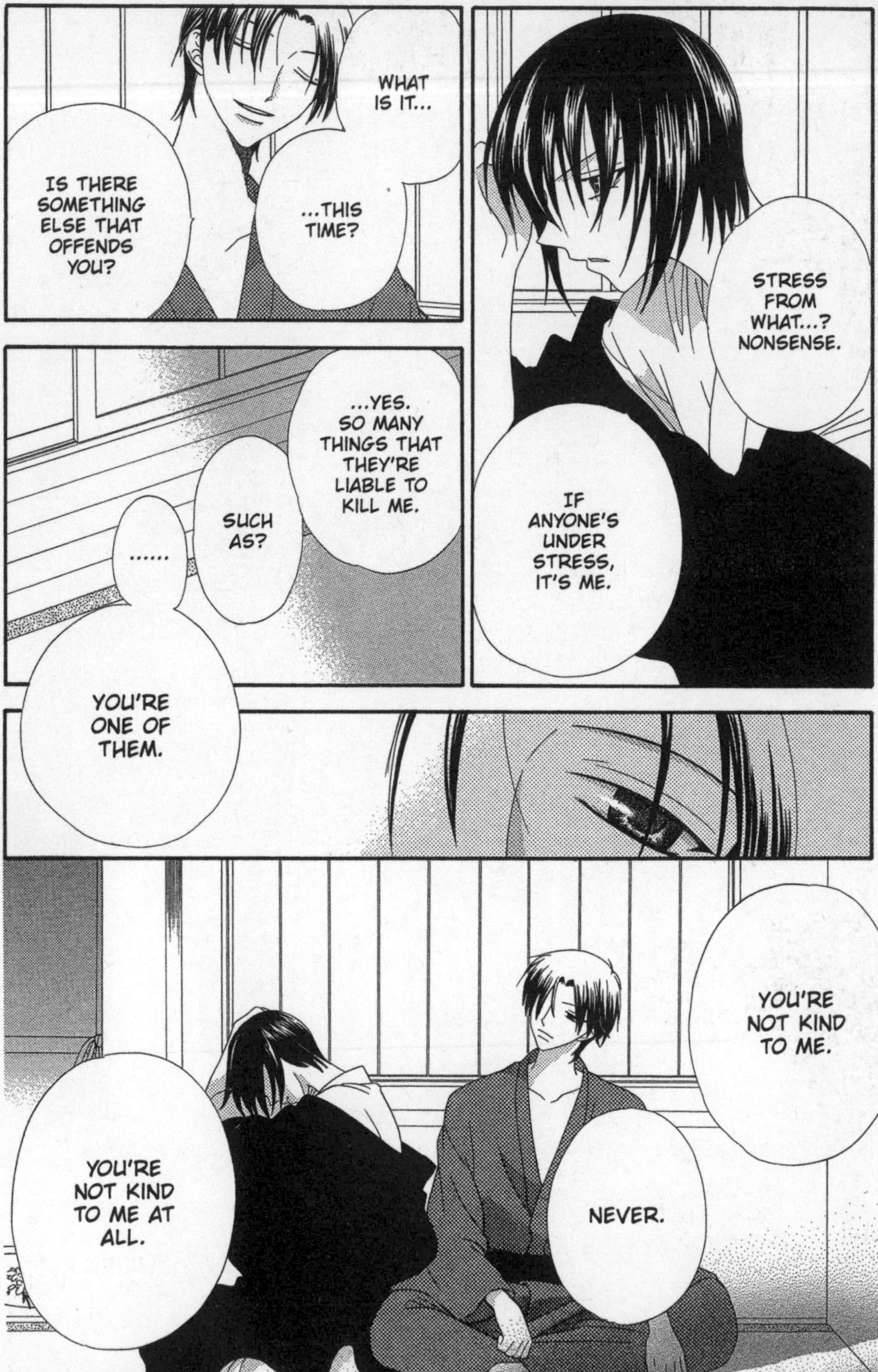
STRESS FROM WHAT...? NONSENSE.
IF ANYONE'S UNDER STRESS, IT'S ME.
WHAT IS IT...
...THIS TIME?
IS THERE SOMETHING ELSE THAT OFFENDS YOU?
...YES. SO MANY THINGS THAT THEY'RE LIABLE TO KILL ME.
SUCH AS?
......
YOU'RE ONE OF THEM.
YOU'RE NOT KIND TO ME.
NEVER.
YOU'RE NOT KIND TO ME AT ALL.

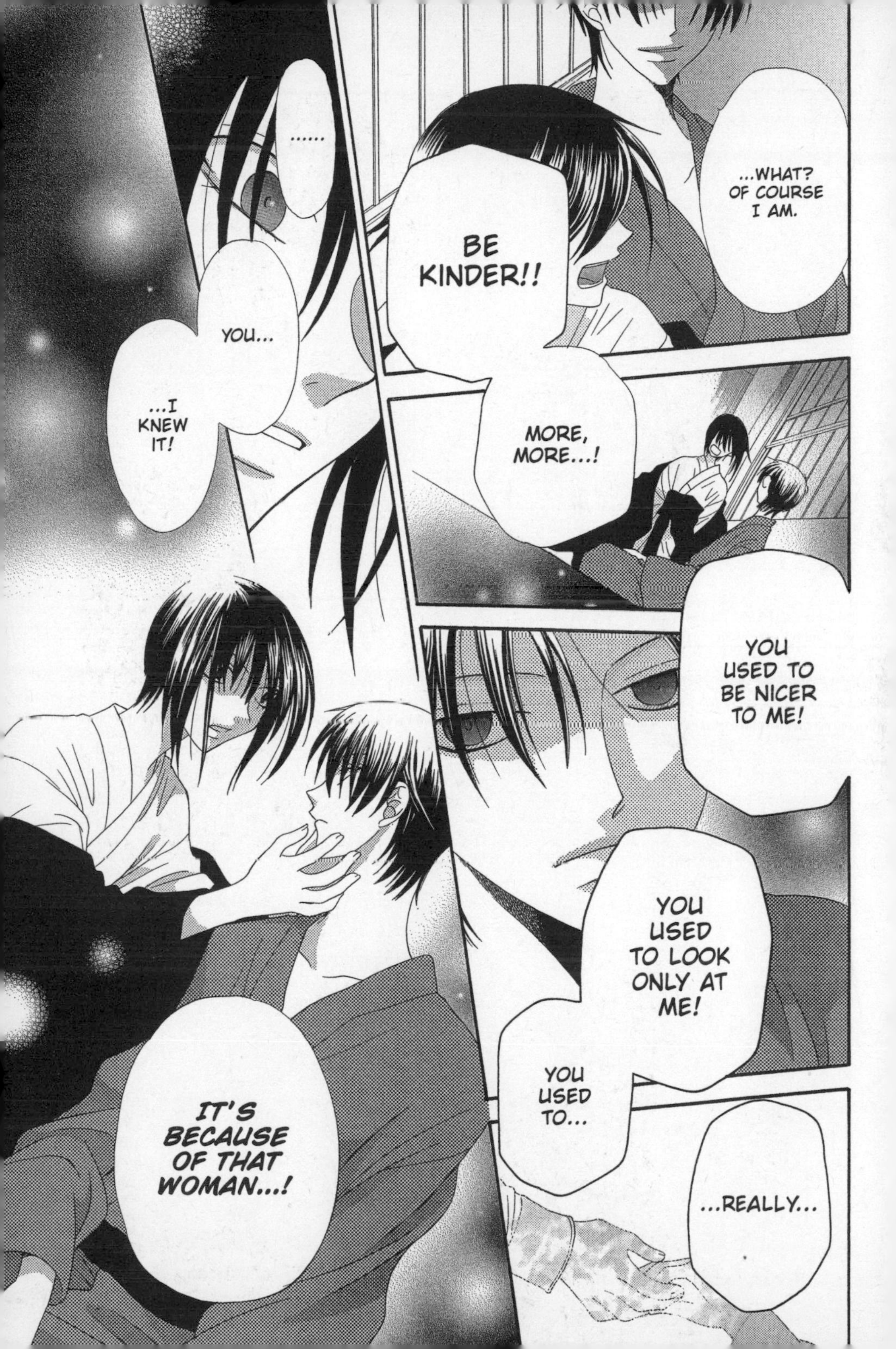
...WHAT? OF COURSE I AM.
BE KINDER!!
MORE, MORE...!
YOU USED TO BE NICER TO ME!
YOU USED TO LOOK ONLY AT ME!
YOU USED TO...
...REALLY...
......
YOU...
...I KNEW IT!
IT'S BECAUSE OF THAT WOMAN...!

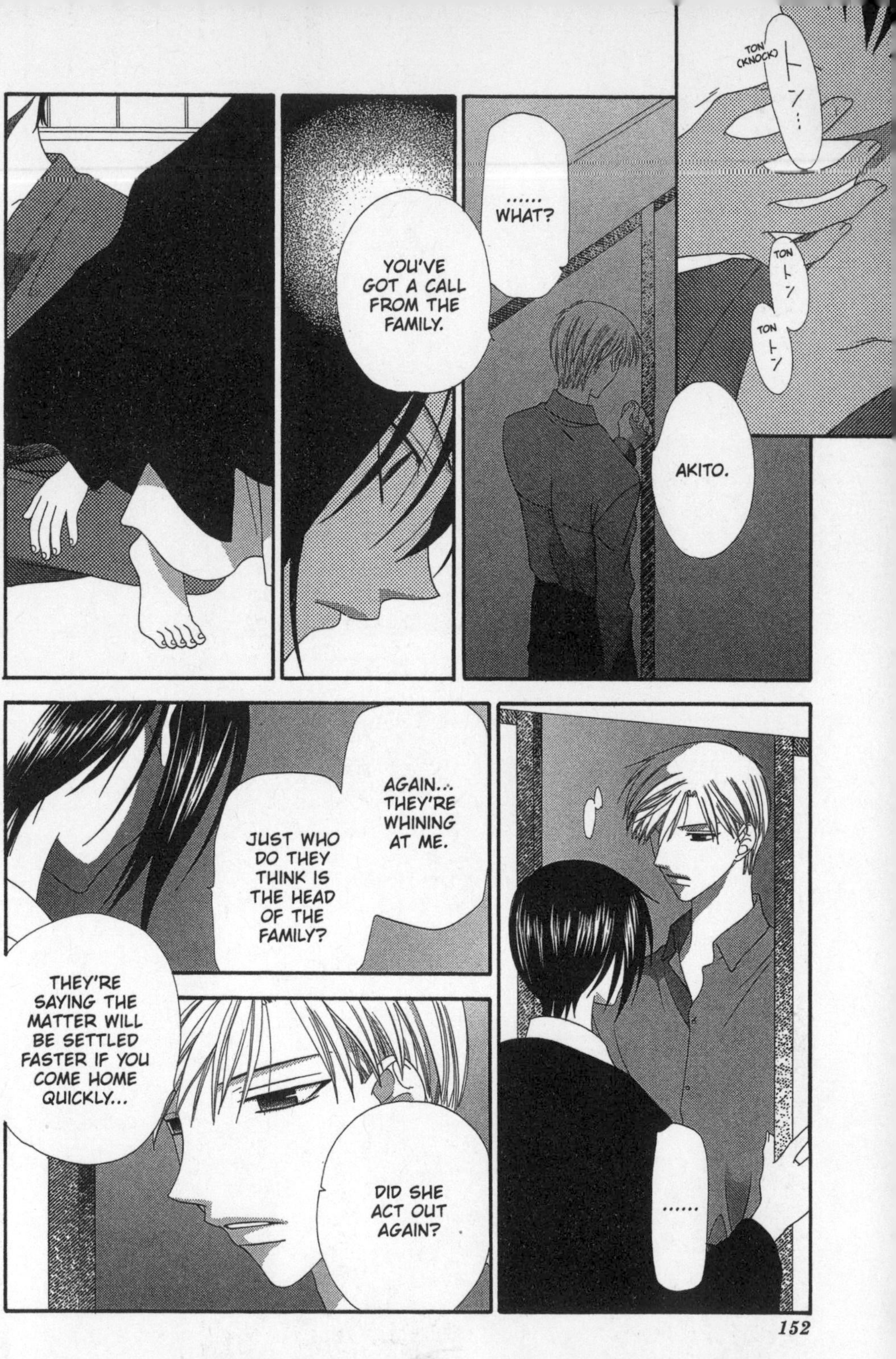
TON (KNOCK) トン…
TON トン
TON トン
AKITO.
......WHAT?
YOU'VE GOT A CALL FROM THE FAMILY.
......
AGAIN... THEY'RE WHINING AT ME.
JUST WHO DO THEY THINK IS THE HEAD OF THE FAMILY?
THEY'RE SAYING THE MATTER WILL BE SETTLED FASTER IF YOU COME HOME QUICKLY...
DID SHE ACT OUT AGAIN?

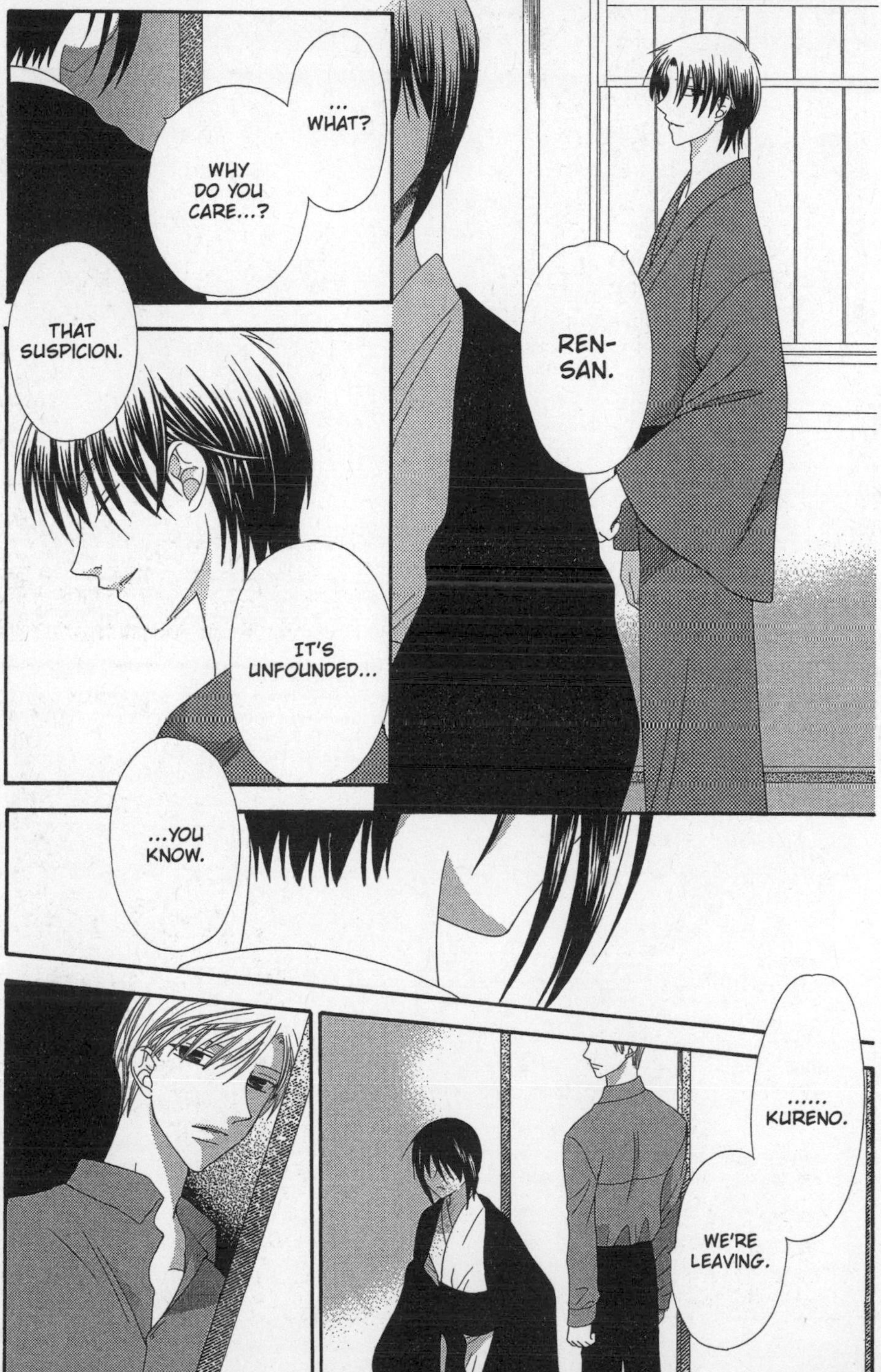
REN-SAN.
...WHAT?
WHY DO YOU CARE...?
THAT SUSPICION.
IT'S UNFOUNDED...
...YOU KNOW.
......KURENO.
WE'RE LEAVING.

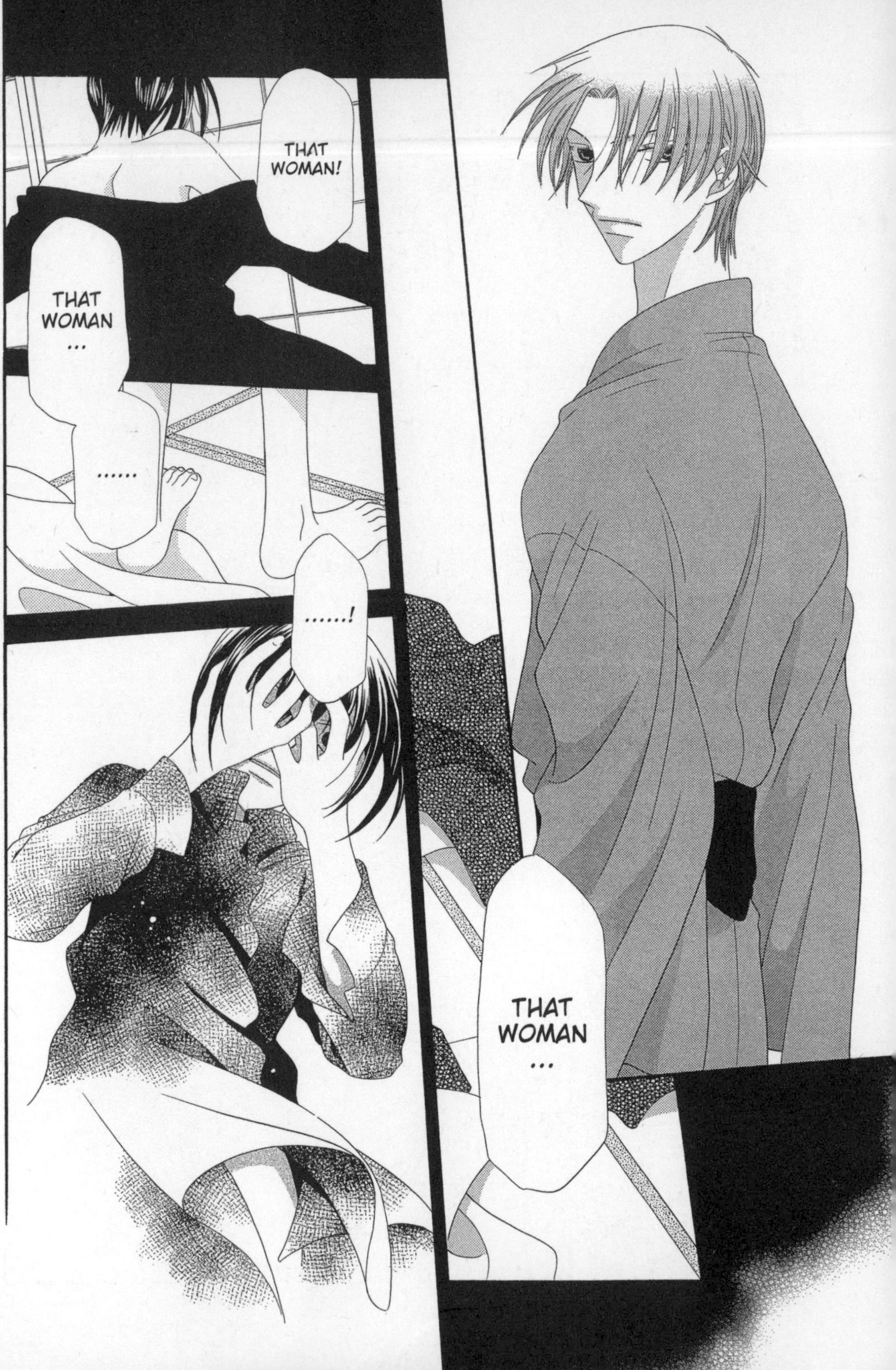
THAT WOMAN ...
THAT WOMAN!
THAT WOMAN ...
......
......!

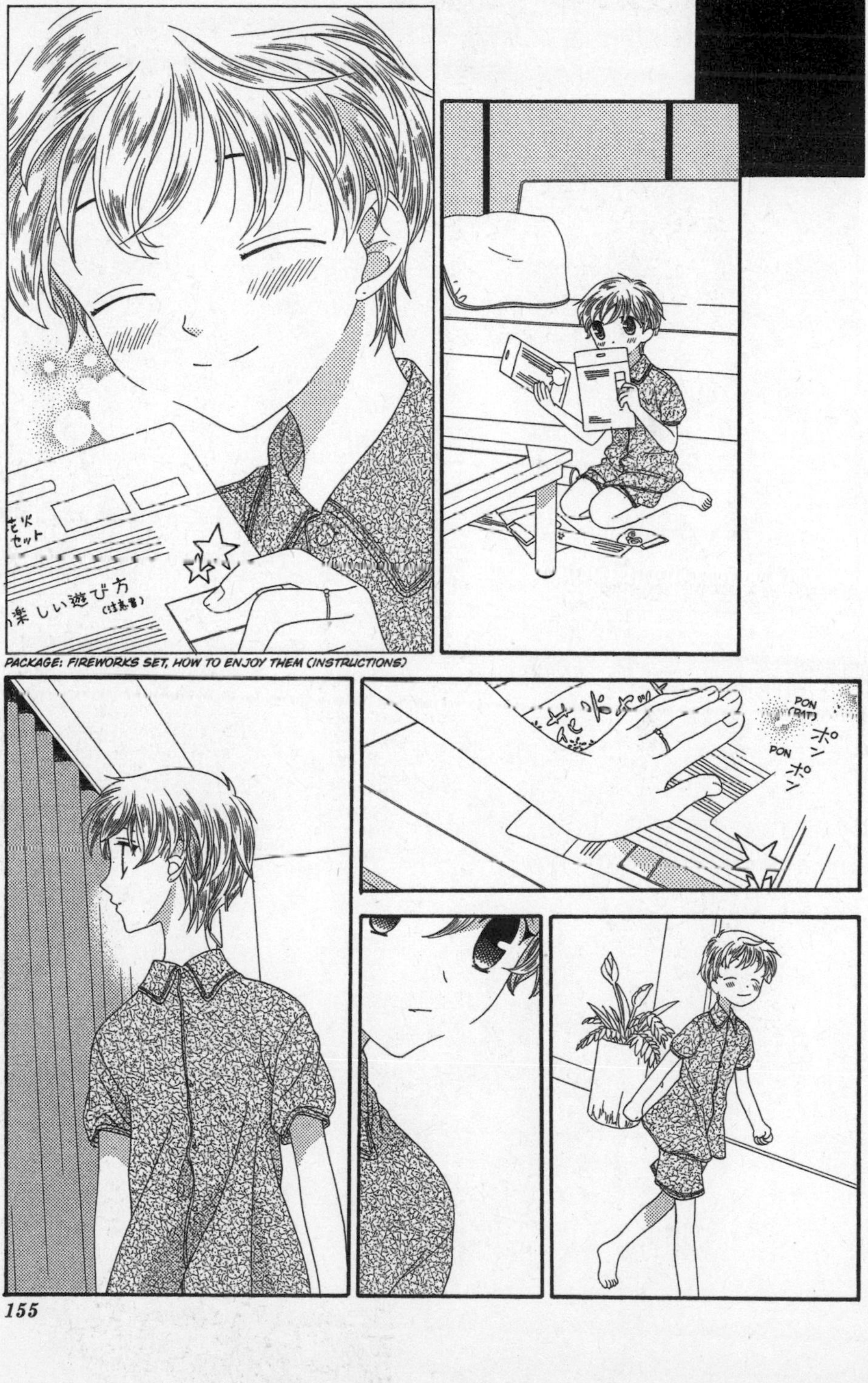
楽しい遊び方
PACKAGE: FIREWORKS SET, HOW TO ENJOY THEM (INSTRUCTIONS)
PON (PAT)
ポン
PON
ポン

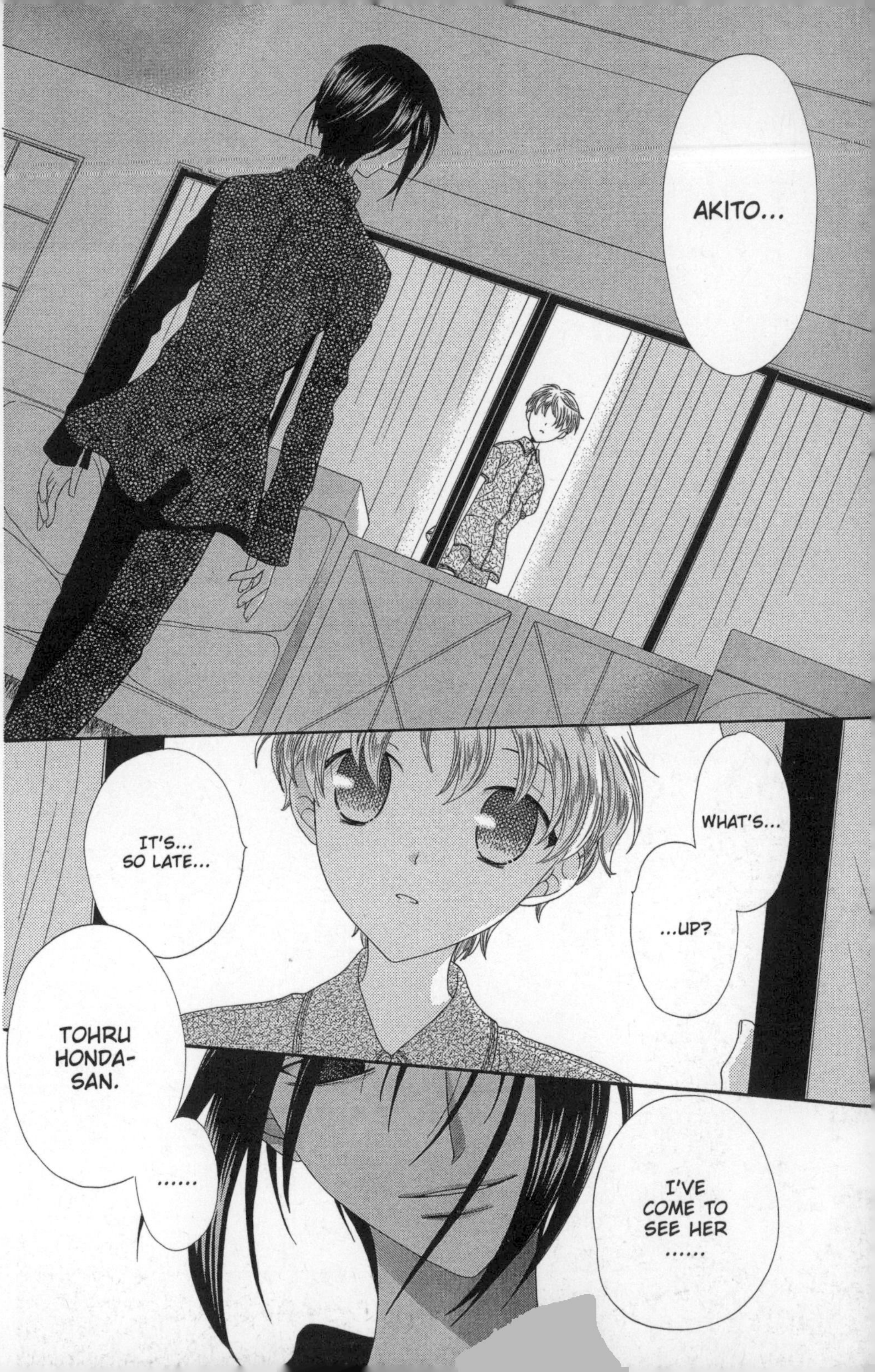
AKITO...
WHAT'S...
...UP?
IT'S... SO LATE...
I'VE COME TO SEE HER ......
TOHRU HONDA-SAN.
......

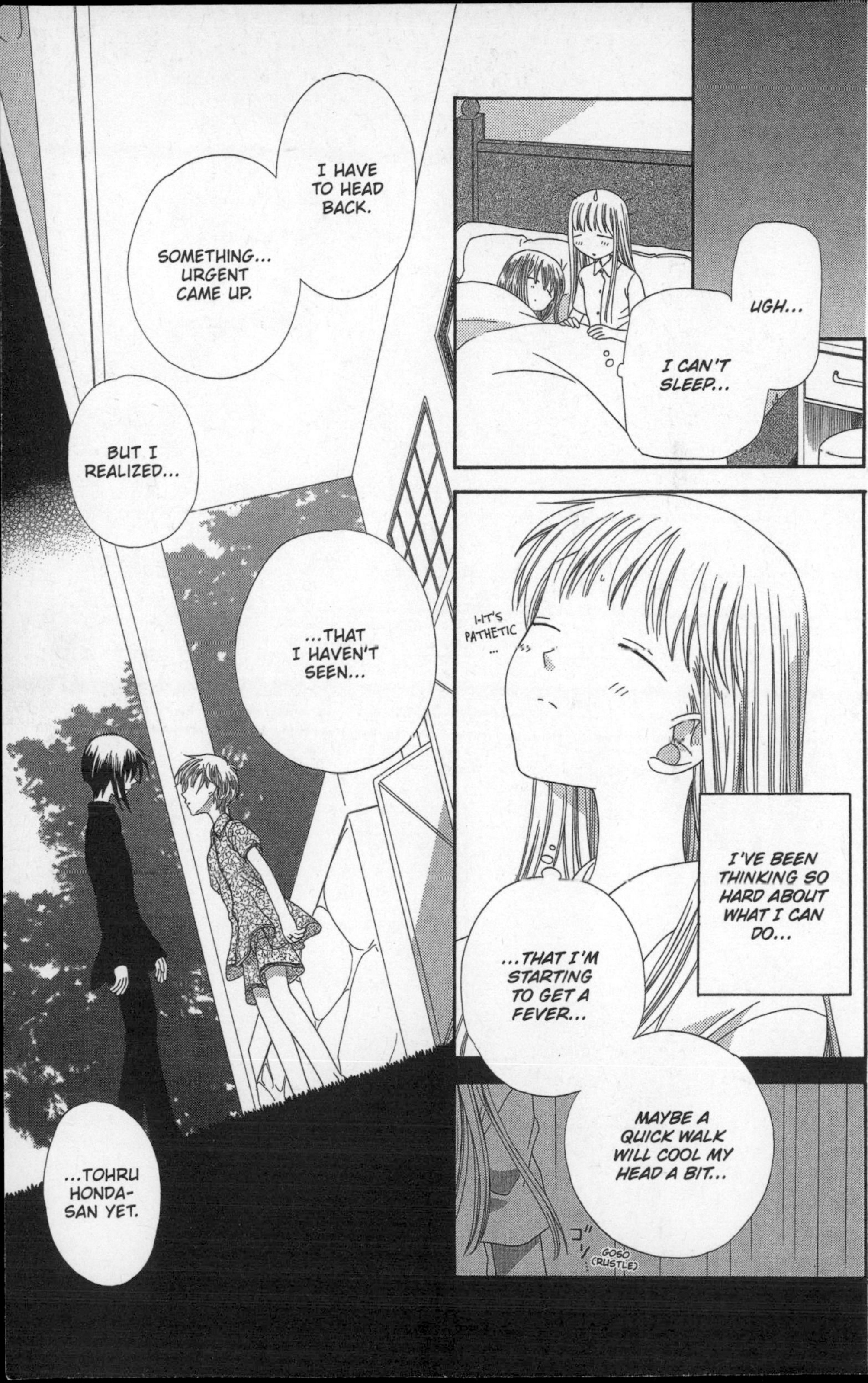
UGH...
I CAN'T SLEEP...
I-IT'S PATHETIC...
I'VE BEEN THINKING SO HARD ABOUT WHAT I CAN DO...
...THAT I'M STARTING TO GET A FEVER...
MAYBE A QUICK WALK WILL COOL MY HEAD A BIT...
GOSO (RUSTLE)
I HAVE TO HEAD BACK.
SOMETHING... URGENT CAME UP.
BUT I REALIZED...
...THAT I HAVEN'T SEEN...
...TOHRU HONDA-SAN YET.

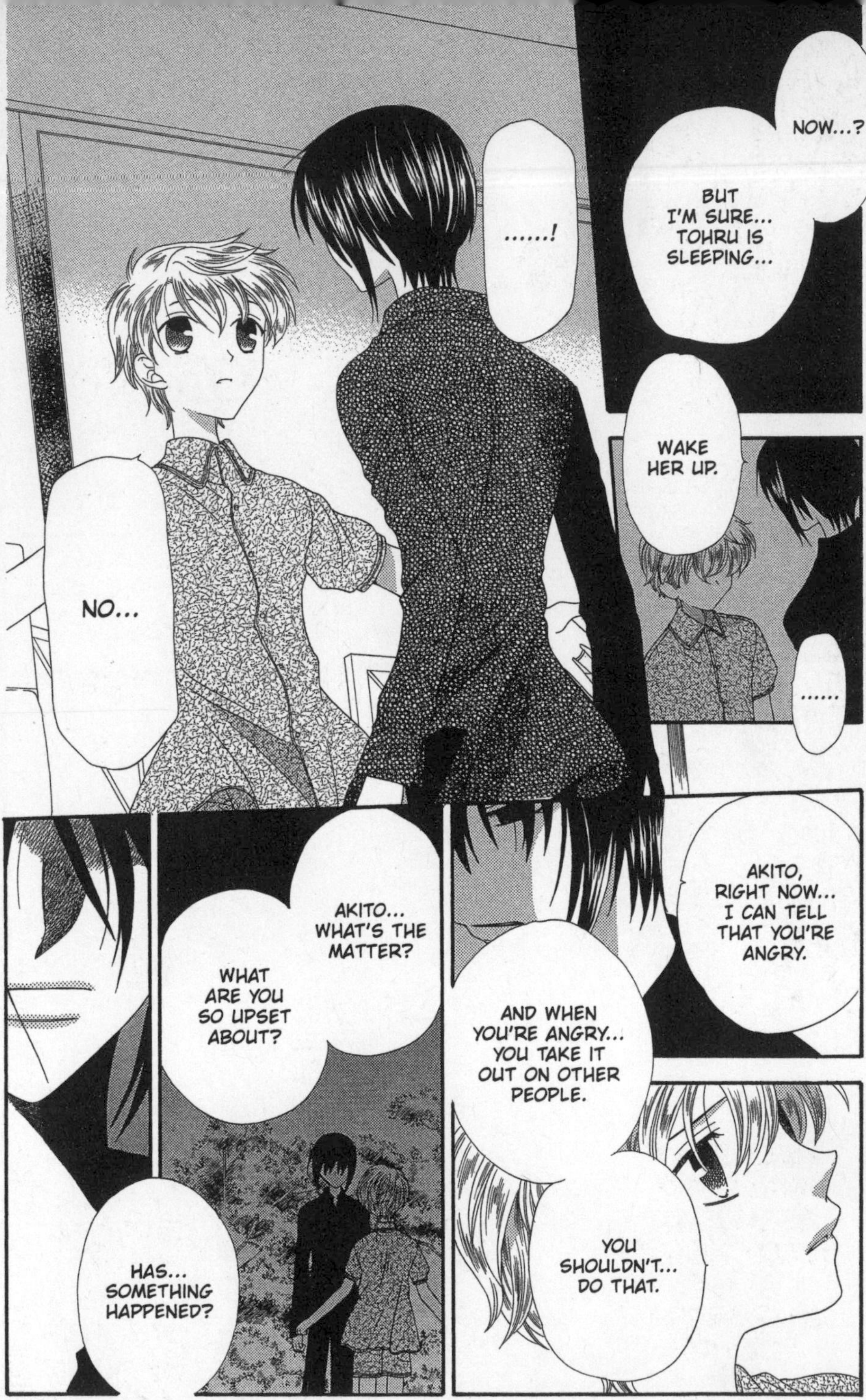
NOW...?
BUT I'M SURE... TOHRU IS SLEEPING...
WAKE HER UP.
......
......!
NO...
AKITO, RIGHT NOW... I CAN TELL THAT YOU'RE ANGRY.
AND WHEN YOU'RE ANGRY... YOU TAKE IT OUT ON OTHER PEOPLE.
YOU SHOULDN'T... DO THAT.
AKITO... WHAT'S THE MATTER?
WHAT ARE YOU SO UPSET ABOUT?
HAS... SOMETHING HAPPENED?

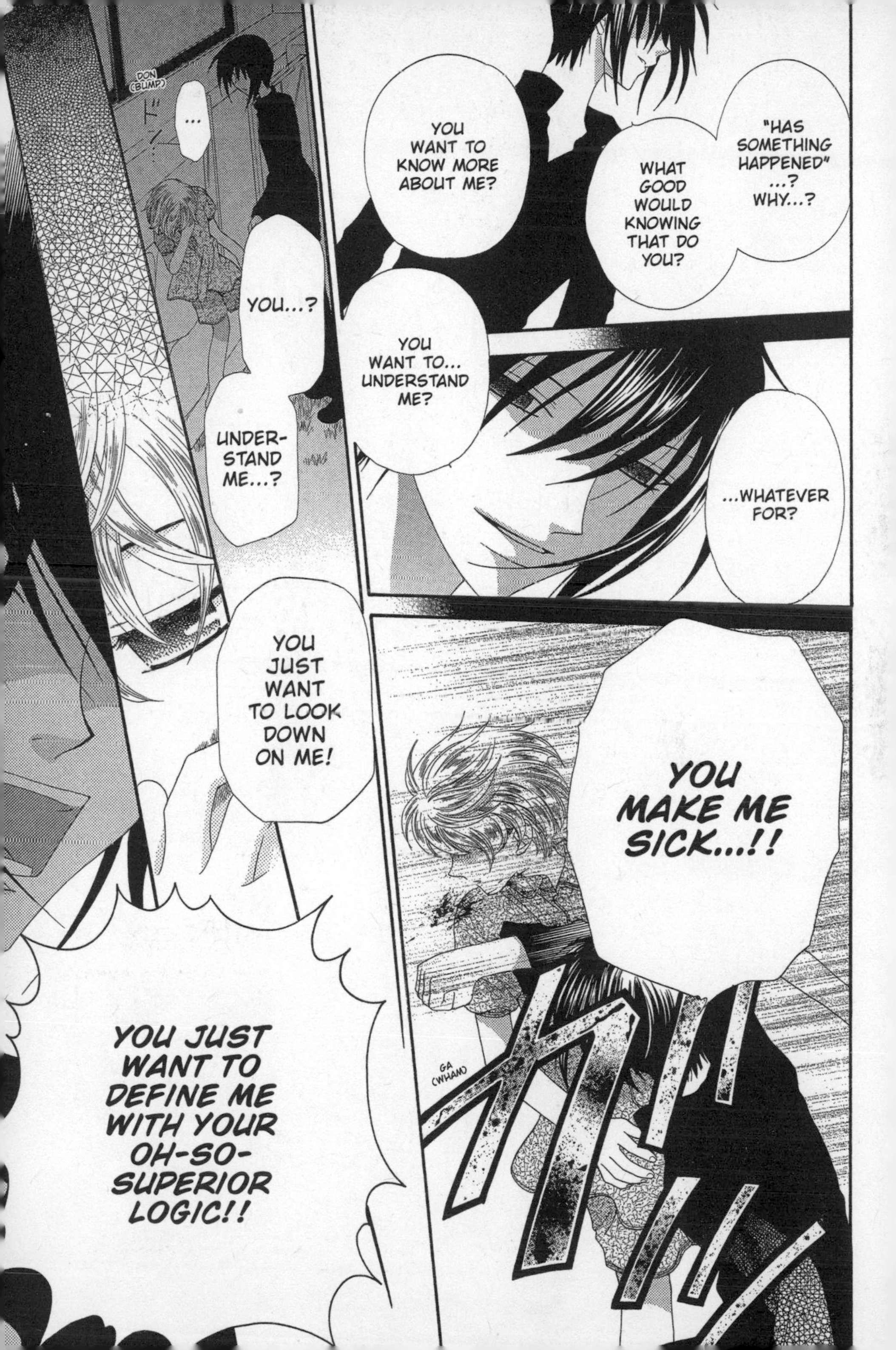
"HAS SOMETHING HAPPENED" ...? WHY...?
WHAT GOOD WOULD KNOWING THAT DO YOU?
YOU WANT TO KNOW MORE ABOUT ME?
YOU WANT TO... UNDERSTAND ME?
...WHATEVER FOR?
YOU MAKE ME SICK...!!
GA (WHAM)
DON (BUMP)
...
YOU...?
UNDER-STAND ME...?
YOU JUST WANT TO LOOK DOWN ON ME!
YOU JUST WANT TO DEFINE ME WITH YOUR OH-SO-SUPERIOR LOGIC!!

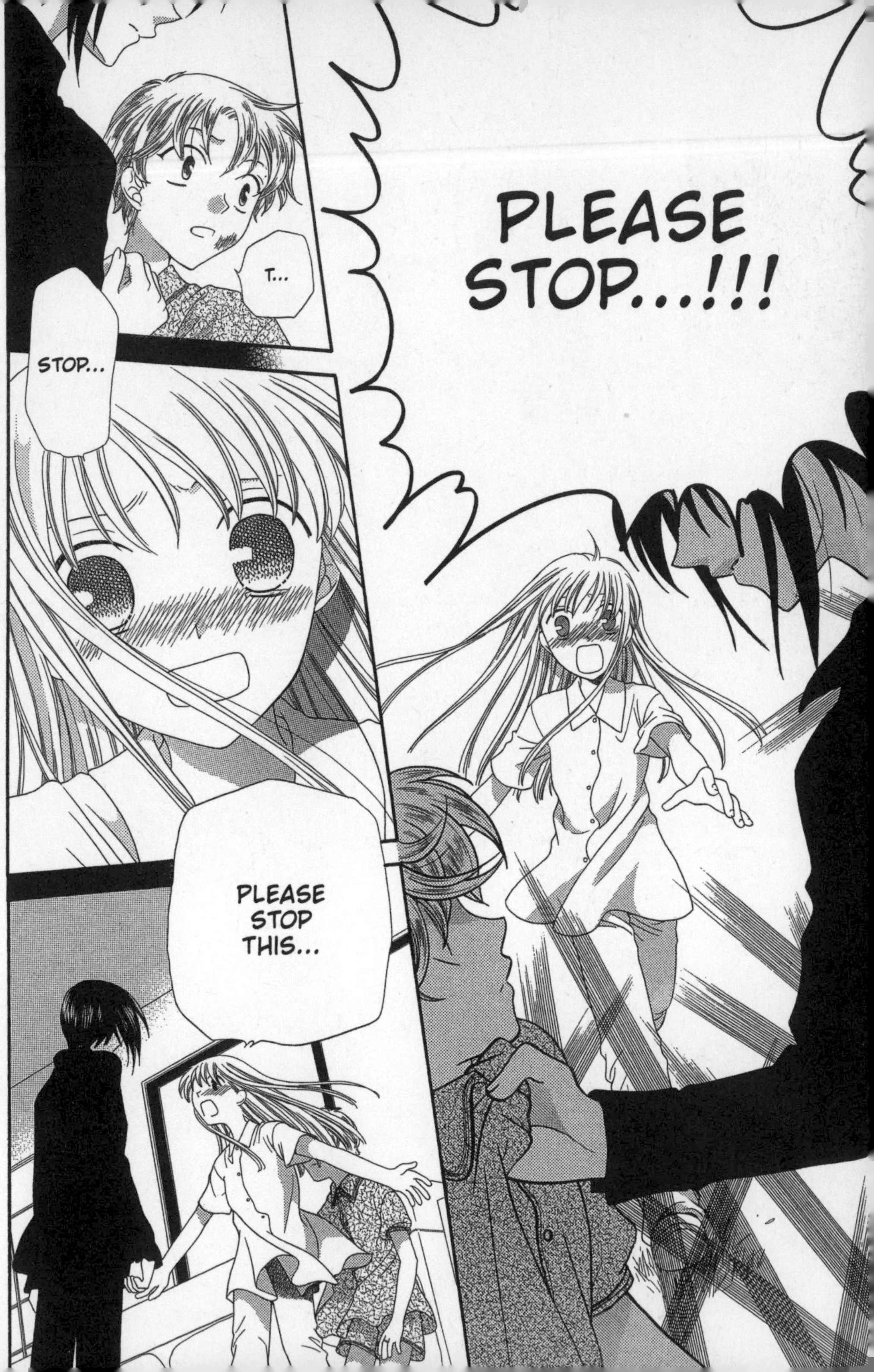
PLEASE STOP...!!!
T...
STOP...
PLEASE STOP THIS...

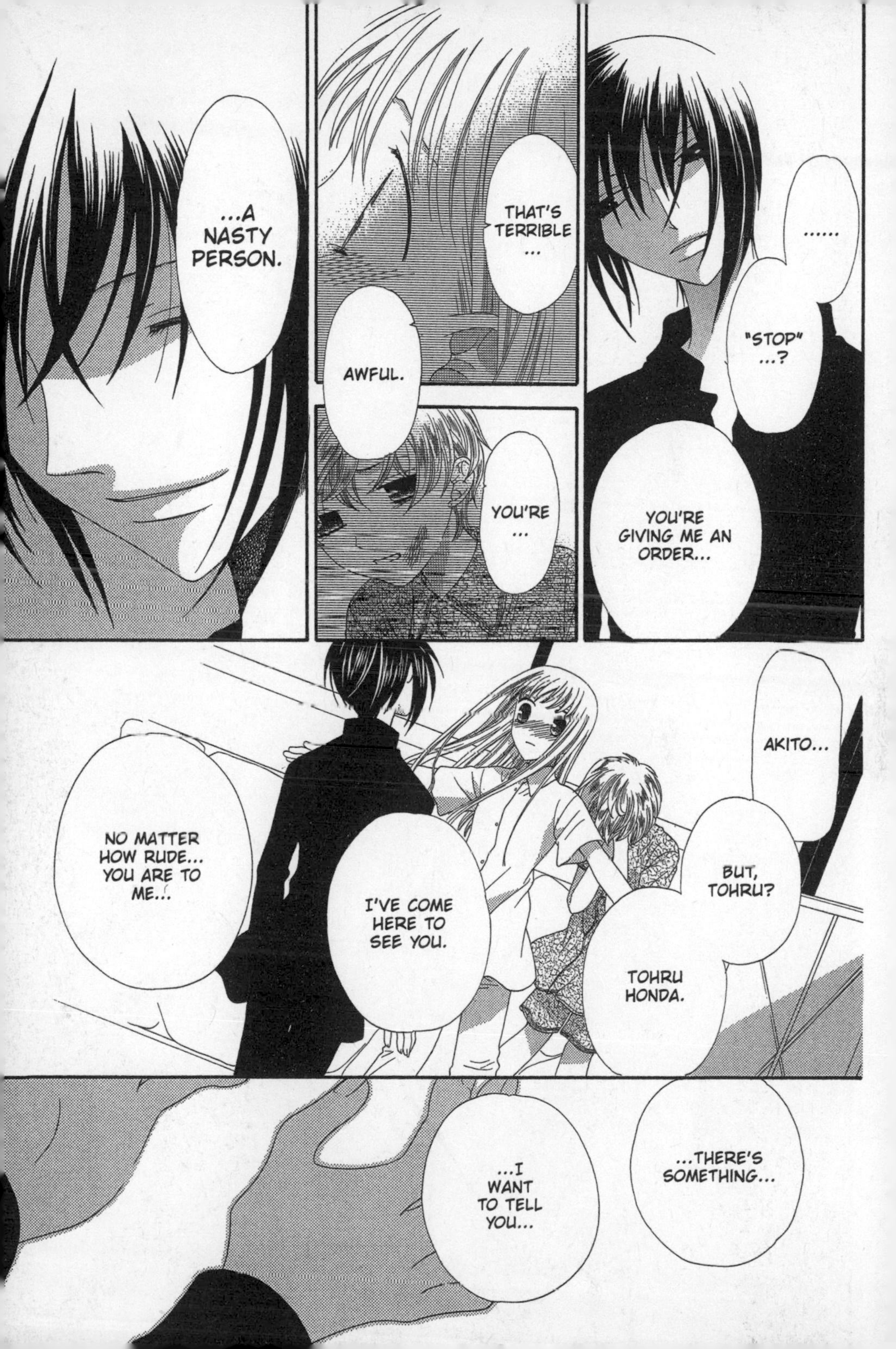
......
"STOP" ...?
YOU'RE GIVING ME AN ORDER...
THAT'S TERRIBLE ...
AWFUL.
YOU'RE ...
...A NASTY PERSON.
AKITO...
BUT, TOHRU?
TOHRU HONDA.
I'VE COME HERE TO SEE YOU.
NO MATTER HOW RUDE... YOU ARE TO ME...
...THERE'S SOMETHING...
...I WANT TO TELL YOU...

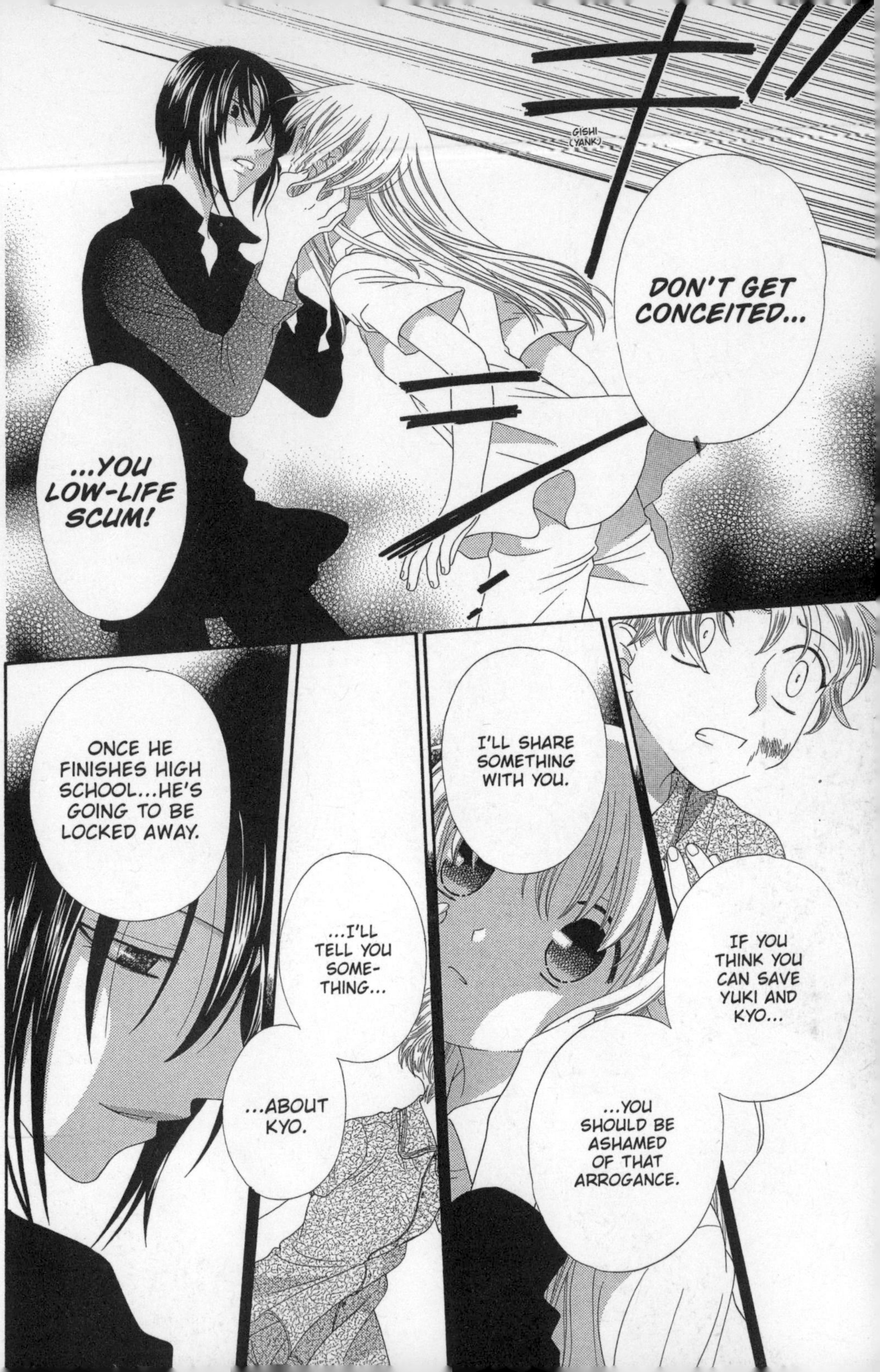
GISHI (YANK)
DON'T GET CONCEITED...
...YOU LOW-LIFE SCUM!
IF YOU THINK YOU CAN SAVE YUKI AND KYO...
...YOU SHOULD BE ASHAMED OF THAT ARROGANCE.
I'LL SHARE SOMETHING WITH YOU.
...I'LL TELL YOU SOME-THING...
...ABOUT KYO.
ONCE HE FINISHES HIGH SCHOOL...HE'S GOING TO BE LOCKED AWAY.

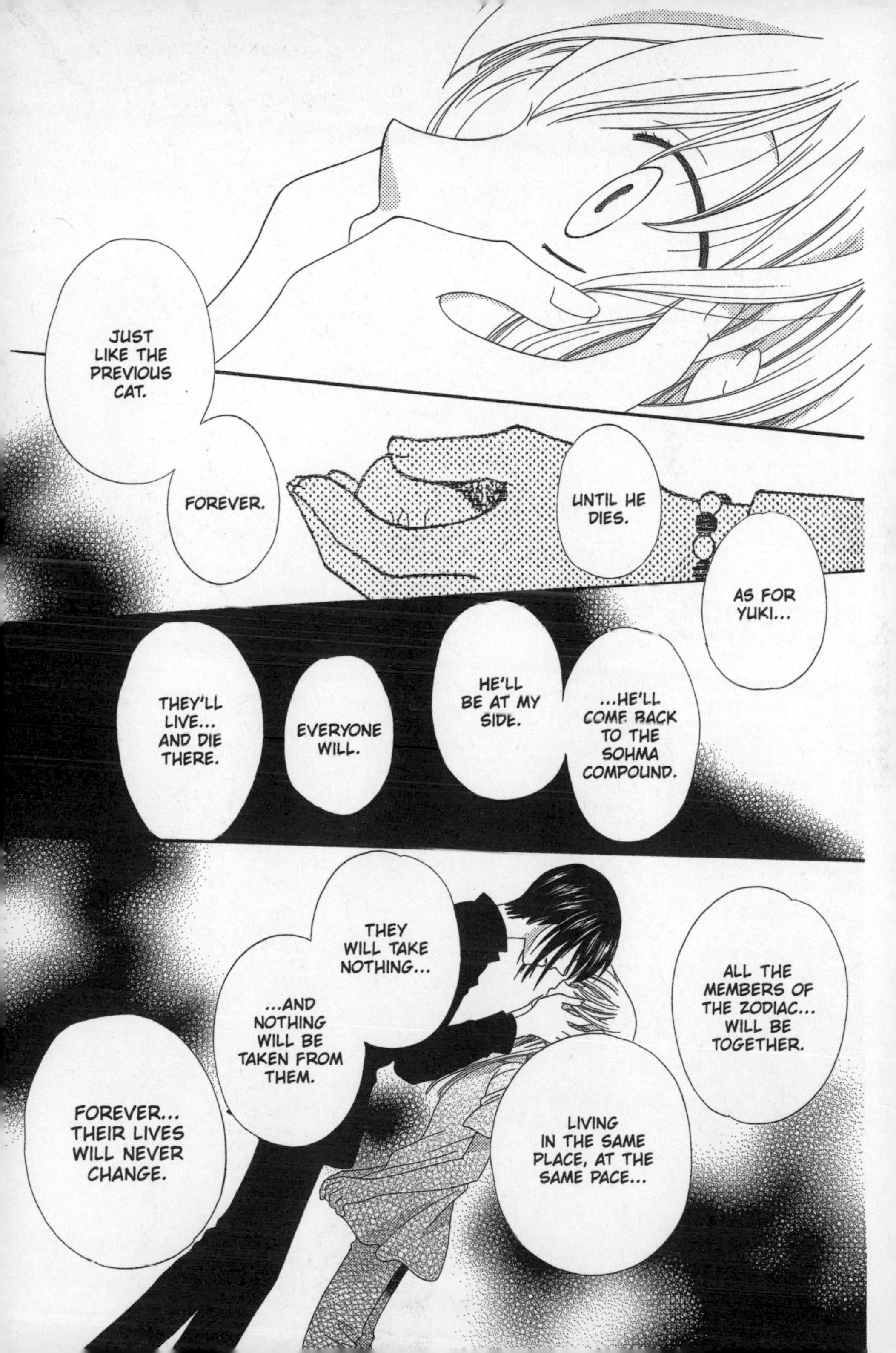
JUST LIKE THE PREVIOUS CAT.
UNTIL HE DIES.
FOREVER.
AS FOR YUKI...
...HE'LL COME BACK TO THE SOHMA COMPOUND.
HE'LL BE AT MY SIDE.
EVERYONE WILL.
THEY'LL LIVE... AND DIE THERE.
ALL THE MEMBERS OF THE ZODIAC... WILL BE TOGETHER.
LIVING IN THE SAME PLACE, AT THE SAME PACE...
THEY WILL TAKE NOTHING...
...AND NOTHING WILL BE TAKEN FROM THEM.
FOREVER... THEIR LIVES WILL NEVER CHANGE.

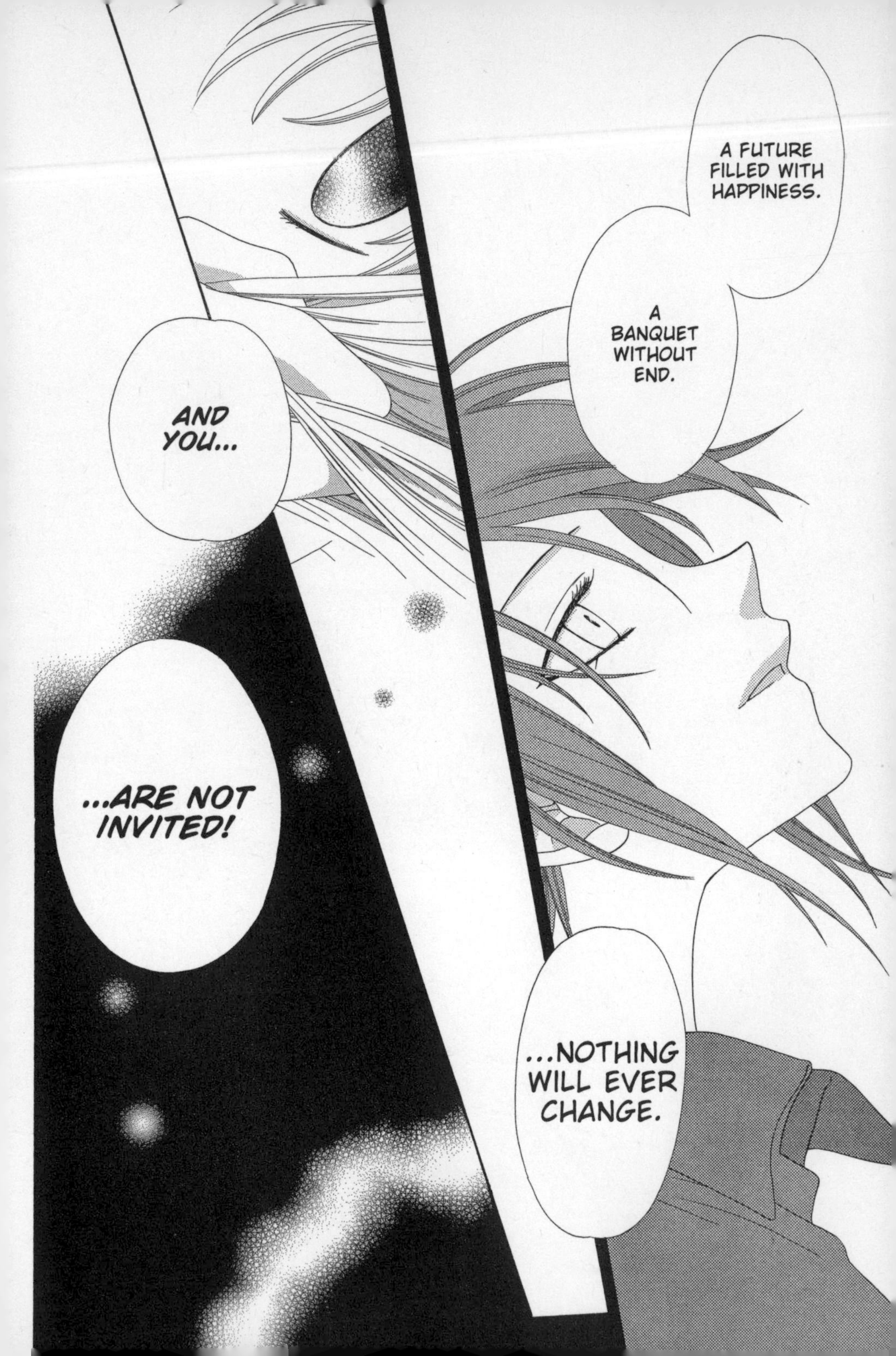
A FUTURE FILLED WITH HAPPINESS.
A BANQUET WITHOUT END.
AND YOU...
...NOTHING WILL EVER CHANGE.
...ARE NOT INVITED!

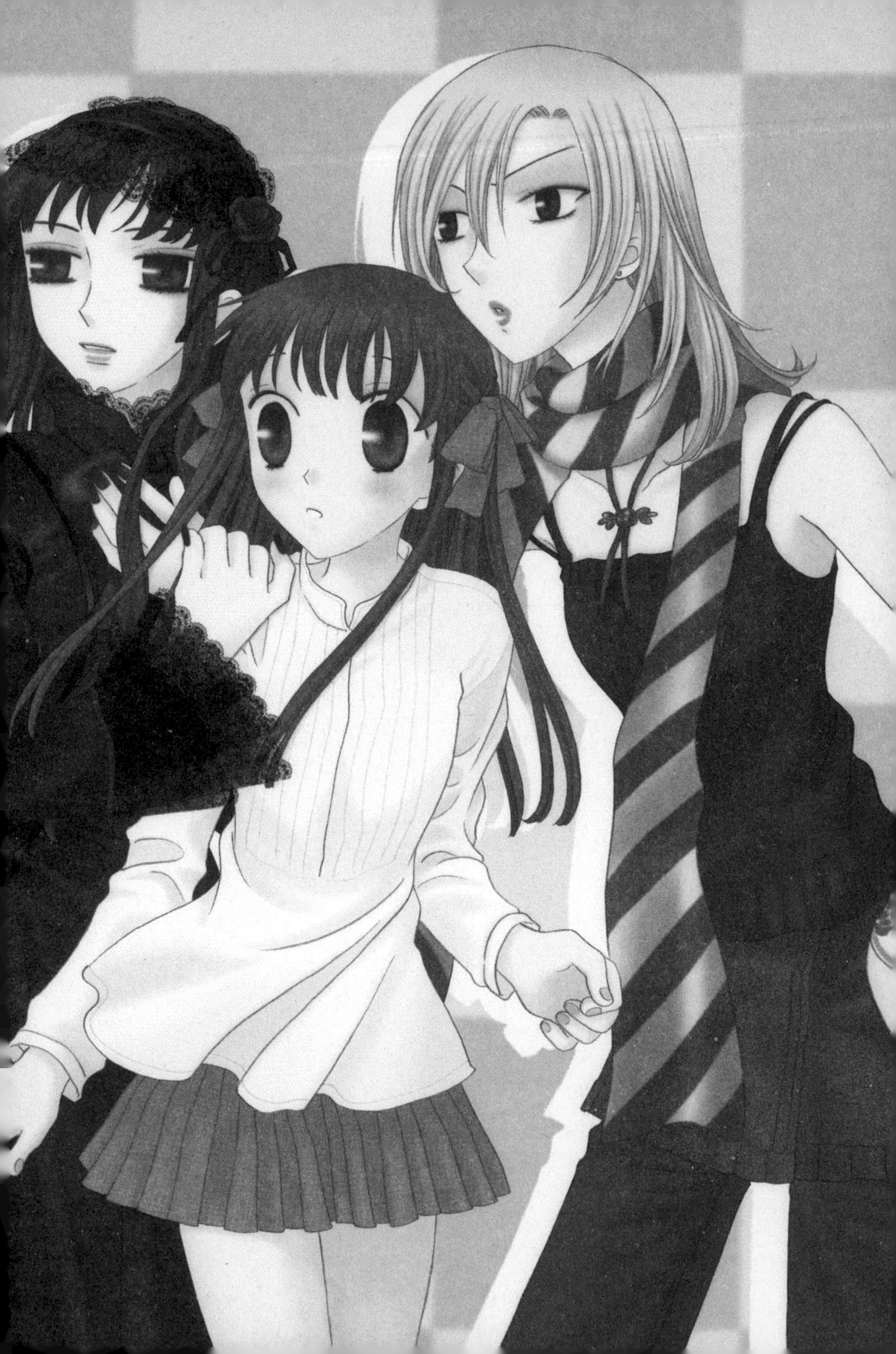

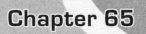

Chapter 65

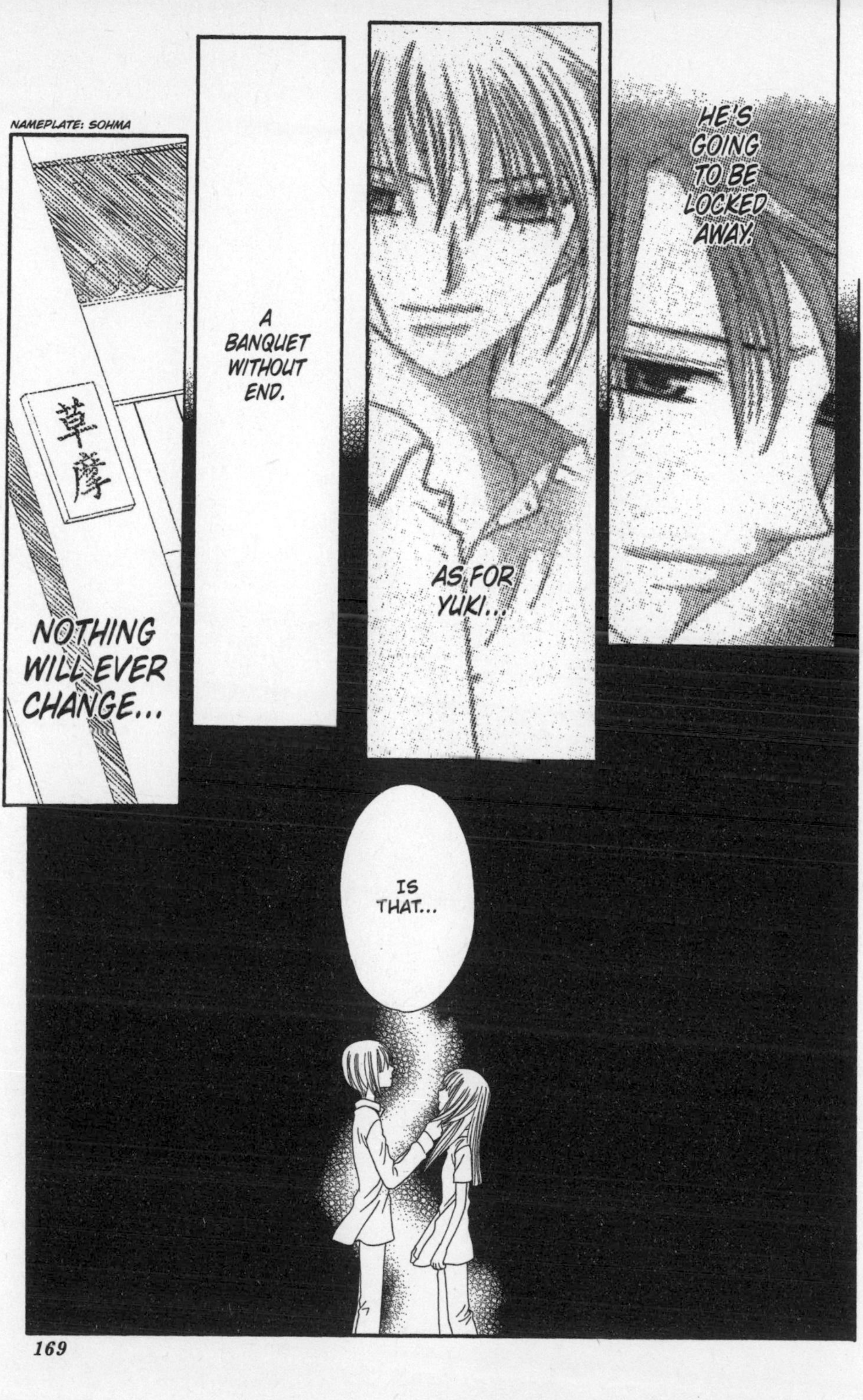
HE'S GOING TO BE LOCKED AWAY.
AS FOR YUKI...
A BANQUET WITHOUT END.
NAMEPLATE: SOHMA
草摩
NOTHING WILL EVER CHANGE...
IS THAT...

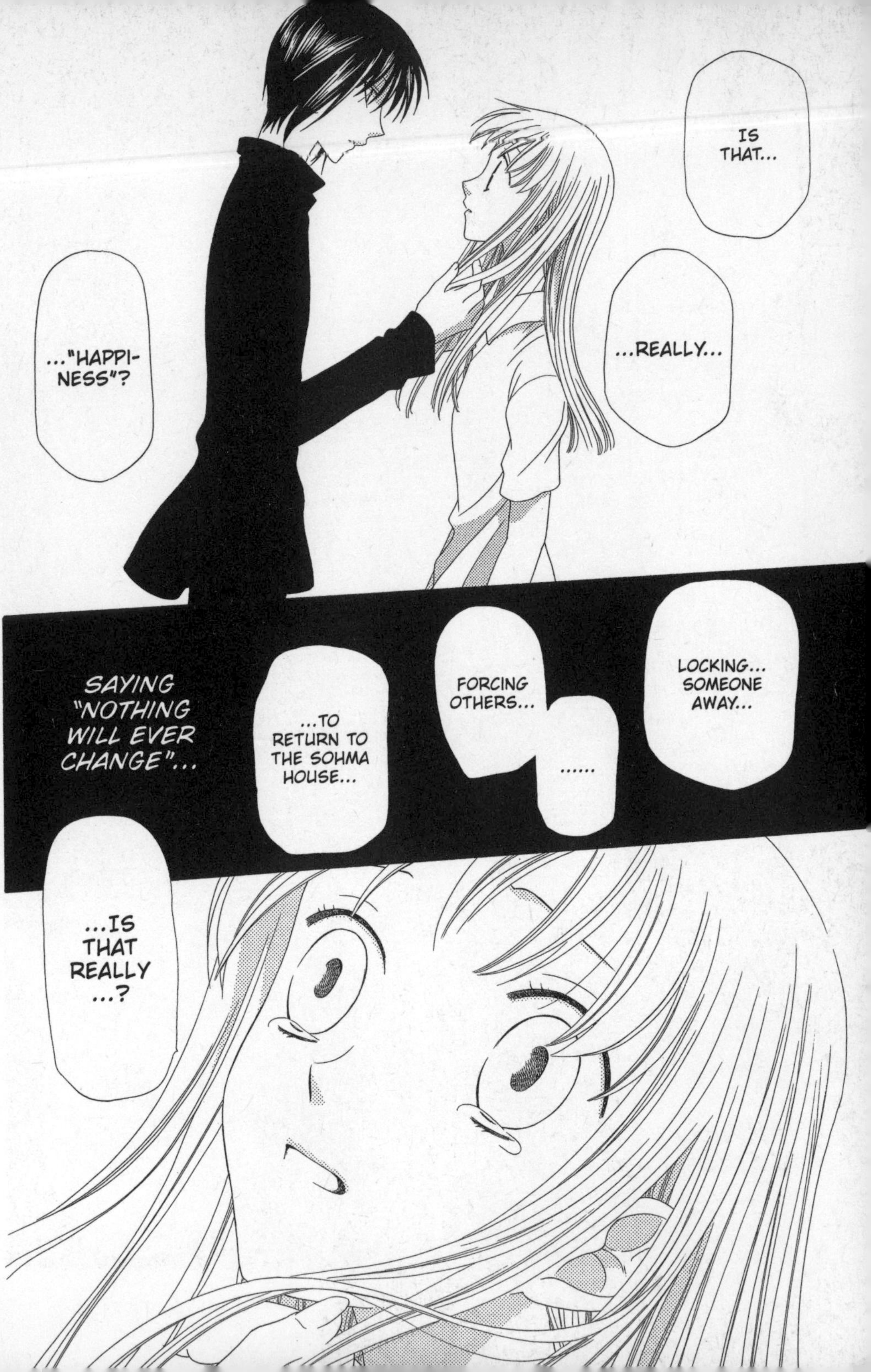
IS THAT...
...REALLY...
..."HAPPI-NESS"?
LOCKING... SOMEONE AWAY...
......
FORCING OTHERS...
...TO RETURN TO THE SOHMA HOUSE...
SAYING "NOTHING WILL EVER CHANGE"...
...IS THAT REALLY ...?

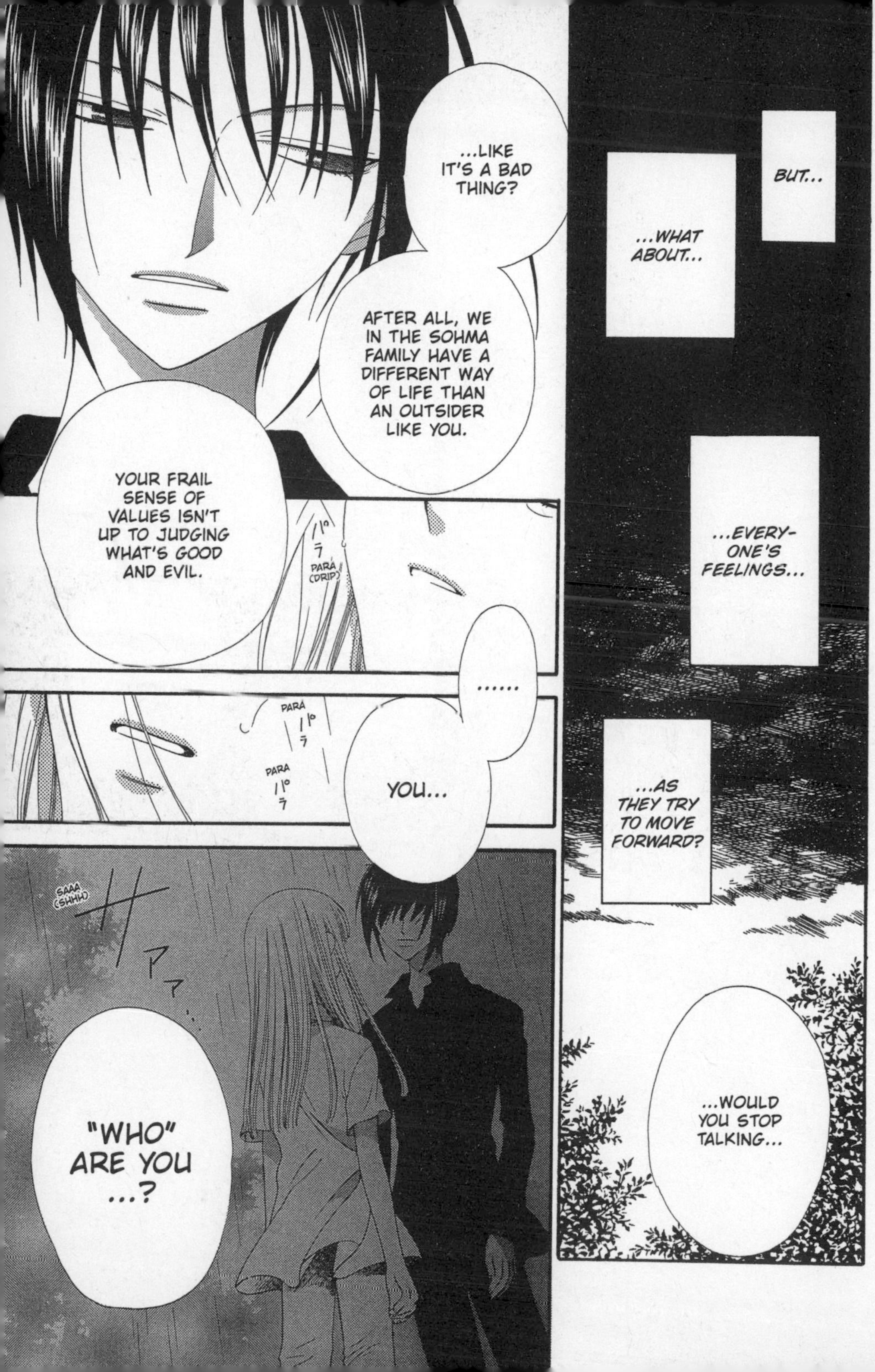
BUT...
...WHAT ABOUT...
...EVERY-ONE'S FEELINGS...
...AS THEY TRY TO MOVE FORWARD?
...WOULD YOU STOP TALKING...
...LIKE IT'S A BAD THING?
AFTER ALL, WE IN THE SOHMA FAMILY HAVE A DIFFERENT WAY OF LIFE THAN AN OUTSIDER LIKE YOU.
YOUR FRAIL SENSE OF VALUES ISN'T UP TO JUDGING WHAT'S GOOD AND EVIL.
PARA (DRIP)
......
PARA
PARA
YOU...
SAAA (SHHH)
"WHO" ARE YOU ...?

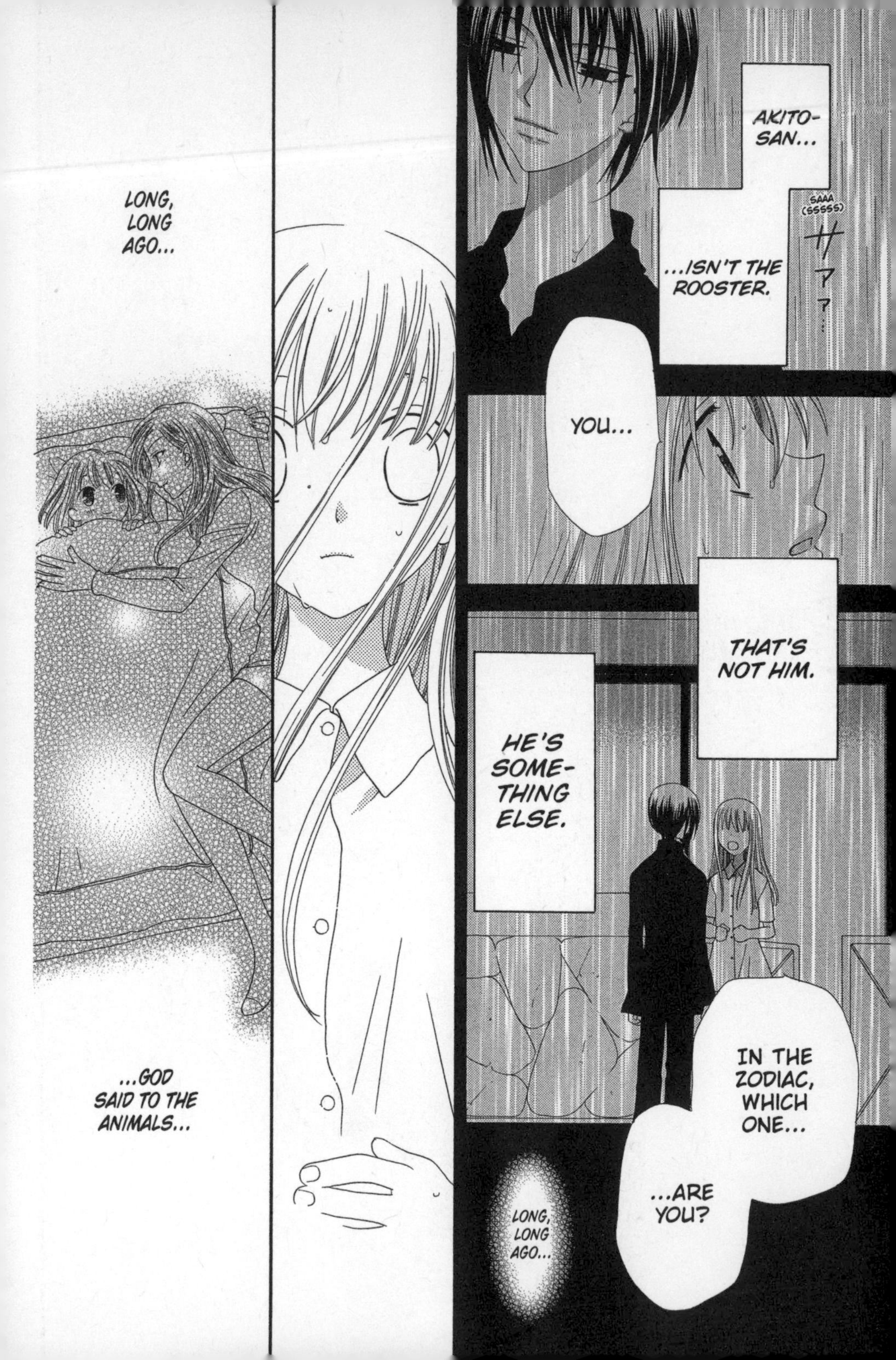
AKITO-SAN...
...ISN'T THE ROOSTER.
SAAA (SSSSS)
YOU...
THAT'S NOT HIM.
HE'S SOMETHING ELSE.
IN THE ZODIAC, WHICH ONE...
...ARE YOU?
LONG, LONG AGO...
LONG, LONG AGO...
...GOD SAID TO THE ANIMALS...

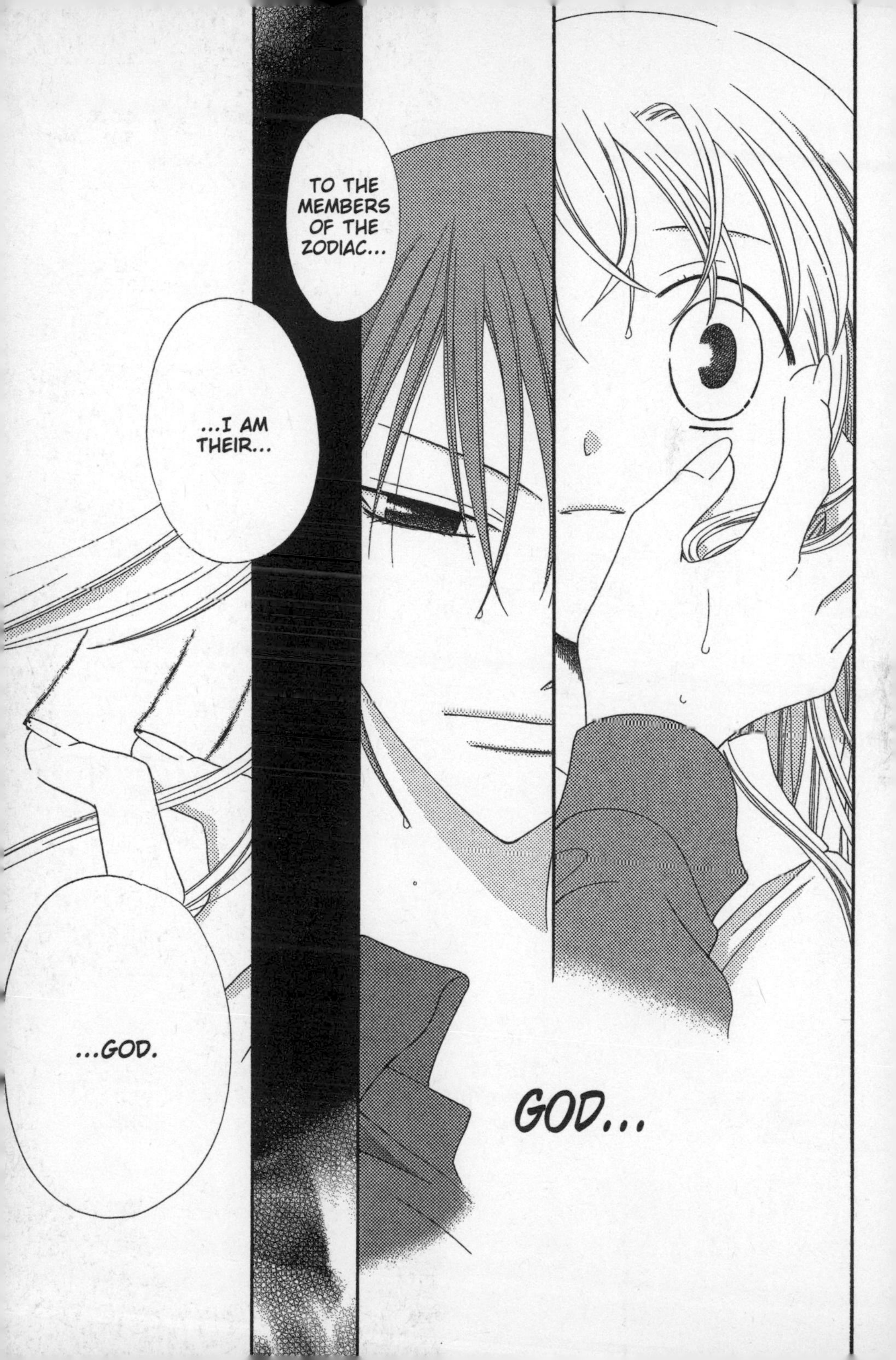
TO THE MEMBERS OF THE ZODIAC...
...I AM THEIR...
...GOD.
GOD...

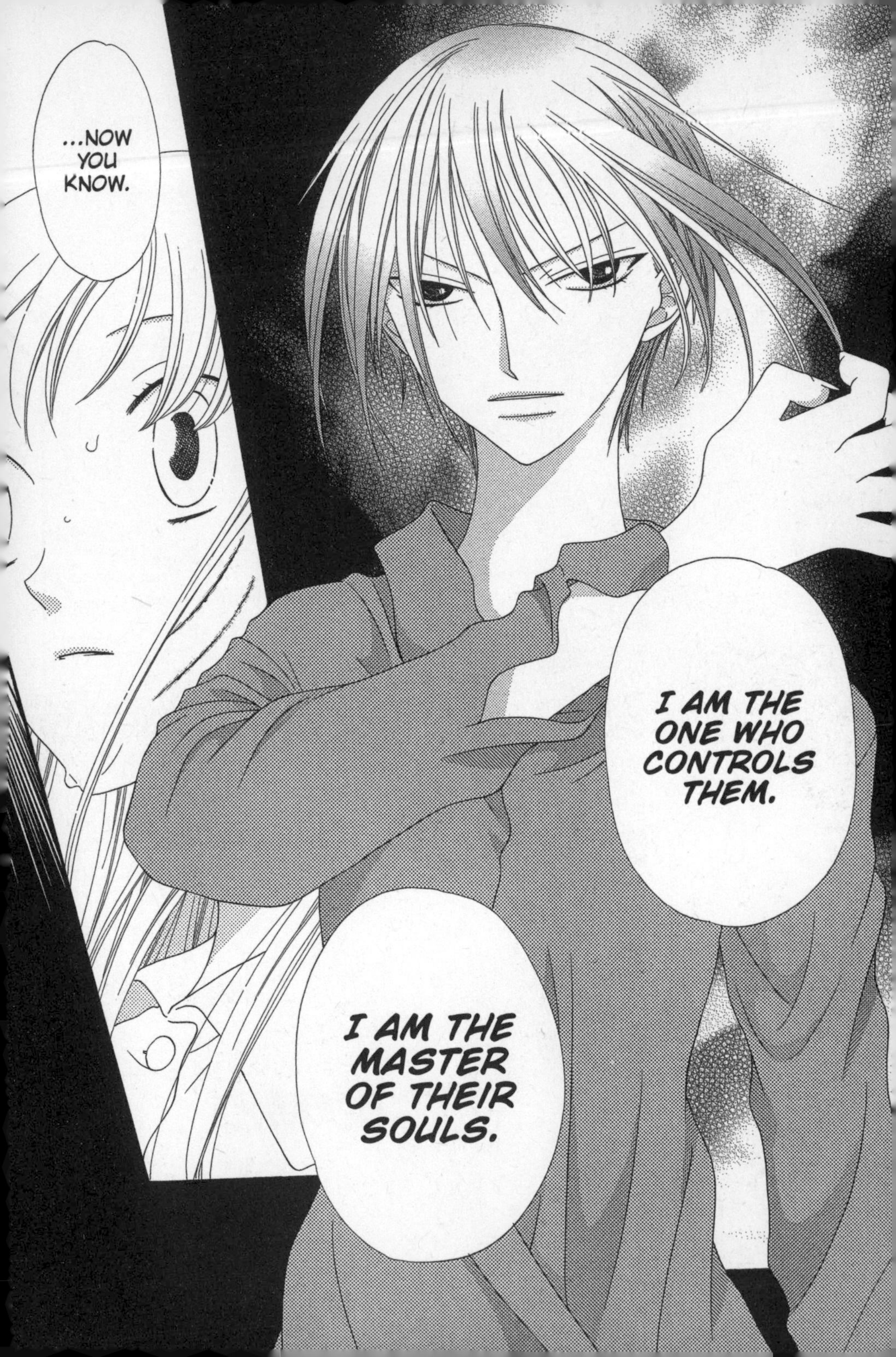
I AM THE ONE WHO CONTROLS THEM.
I AM THE MASTER OF THEIR SOULS.
...NOW YOU KNOW.

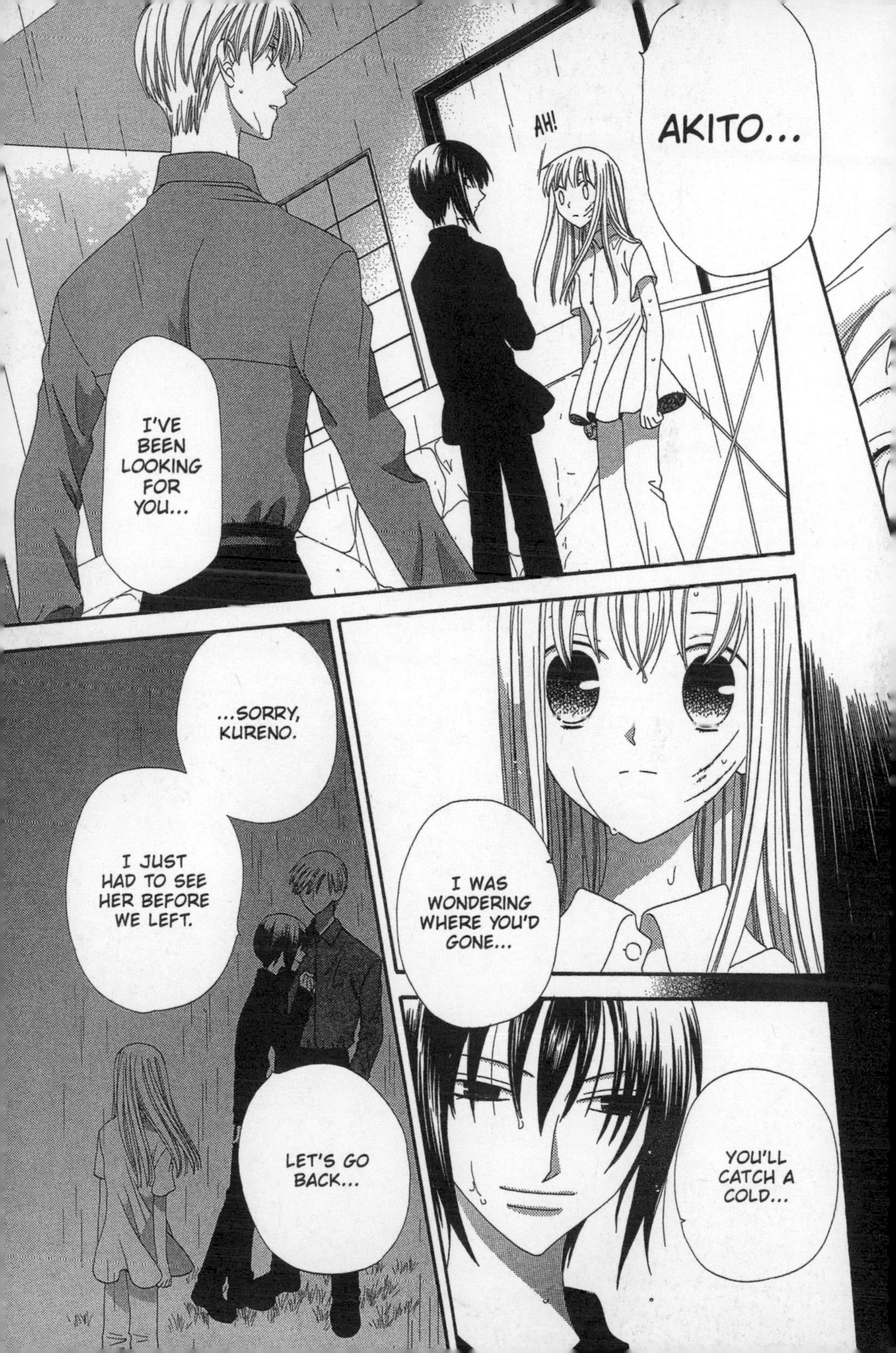
AKITO...
AH!
I'VE BEEN LOOKING FOR YOU...
I WAS WONDERING WHERE YOU'D GONE...
YOU'LL CATCH A COLD...
...SORRY, KURENO.
I JUST HAD TO SEE HER BEFORE WE LEFT.
LET'S GO BACK...

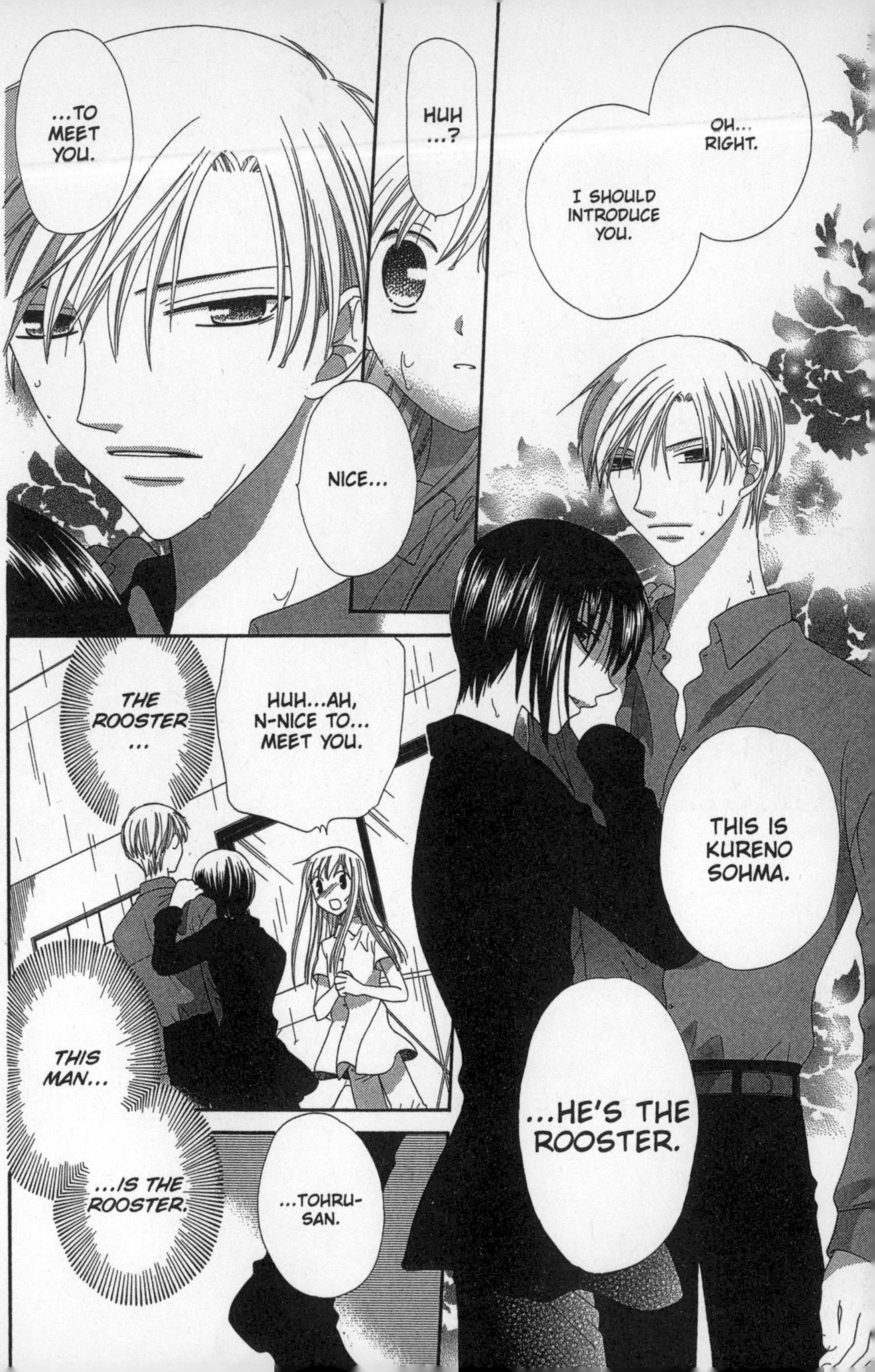
OH... RIGHT.
I SHOULD INTRODUCE YOU.
THIS IS KURENO SOHMA.
HUH ...?
NICE...
...TO MEET YOU.
...HE'S THE ROOSTER.
HUH...AH, N-NICE TO... MEET YOU.
THE ROOSTER ...
THIS MAN...
...IS THE ROOSTER.
...TOHRU-SAN.

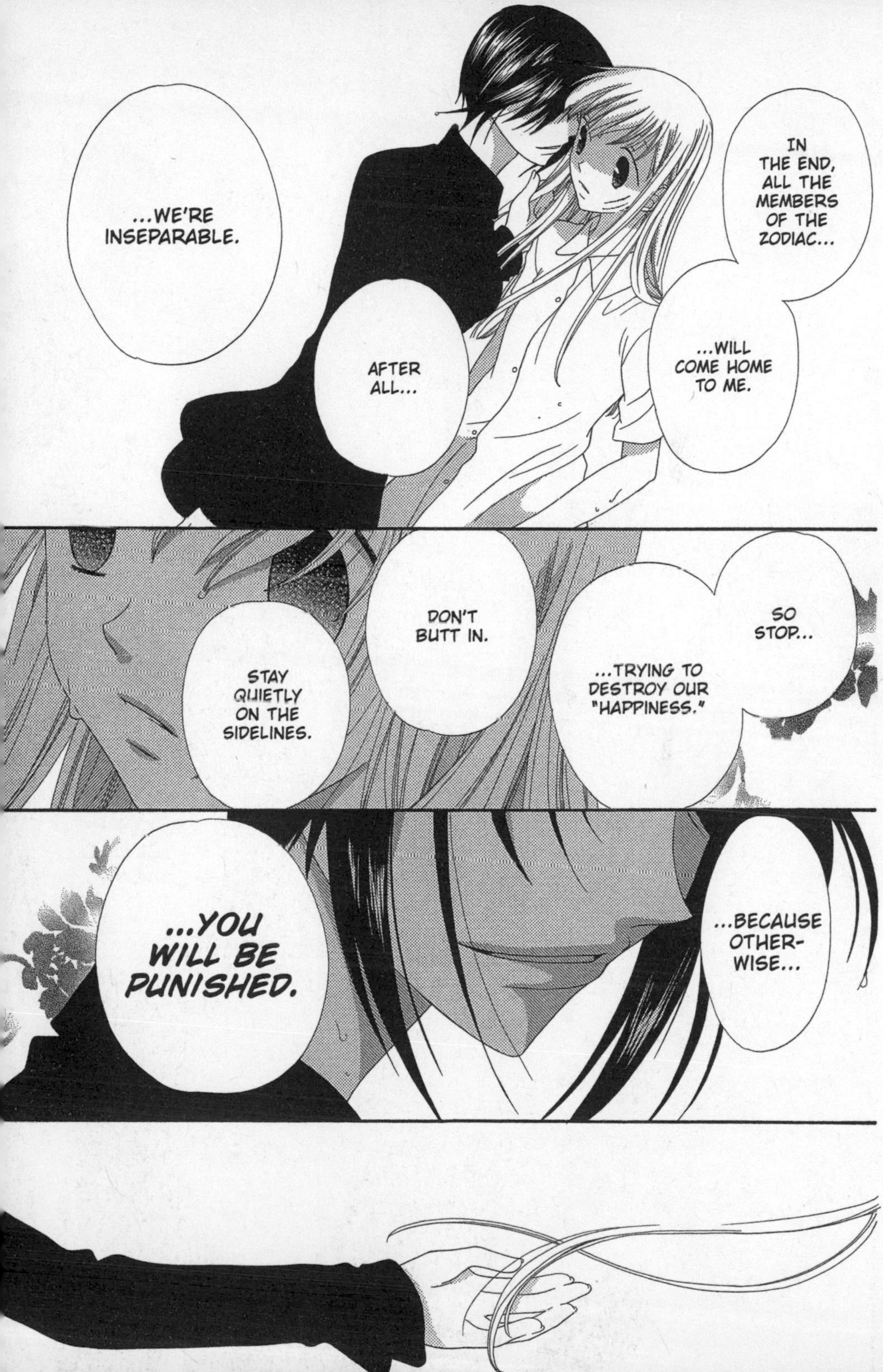
IN THE END, ALL THE MEMBERS OF THE ZODIAC...
...WILL COME HOME TO ME.
AFTER ALL...
...WE'RE INSEPARABLE.
SO STOP...
...TRYING TO DESTROY OUR "HAPPINESS."
DON'T BUTT IN.
STAY QUIETLY ON THE SIDELINES.
...BECAUSE OTHER-WISE...
...YOU WILL BE PUNISHED.

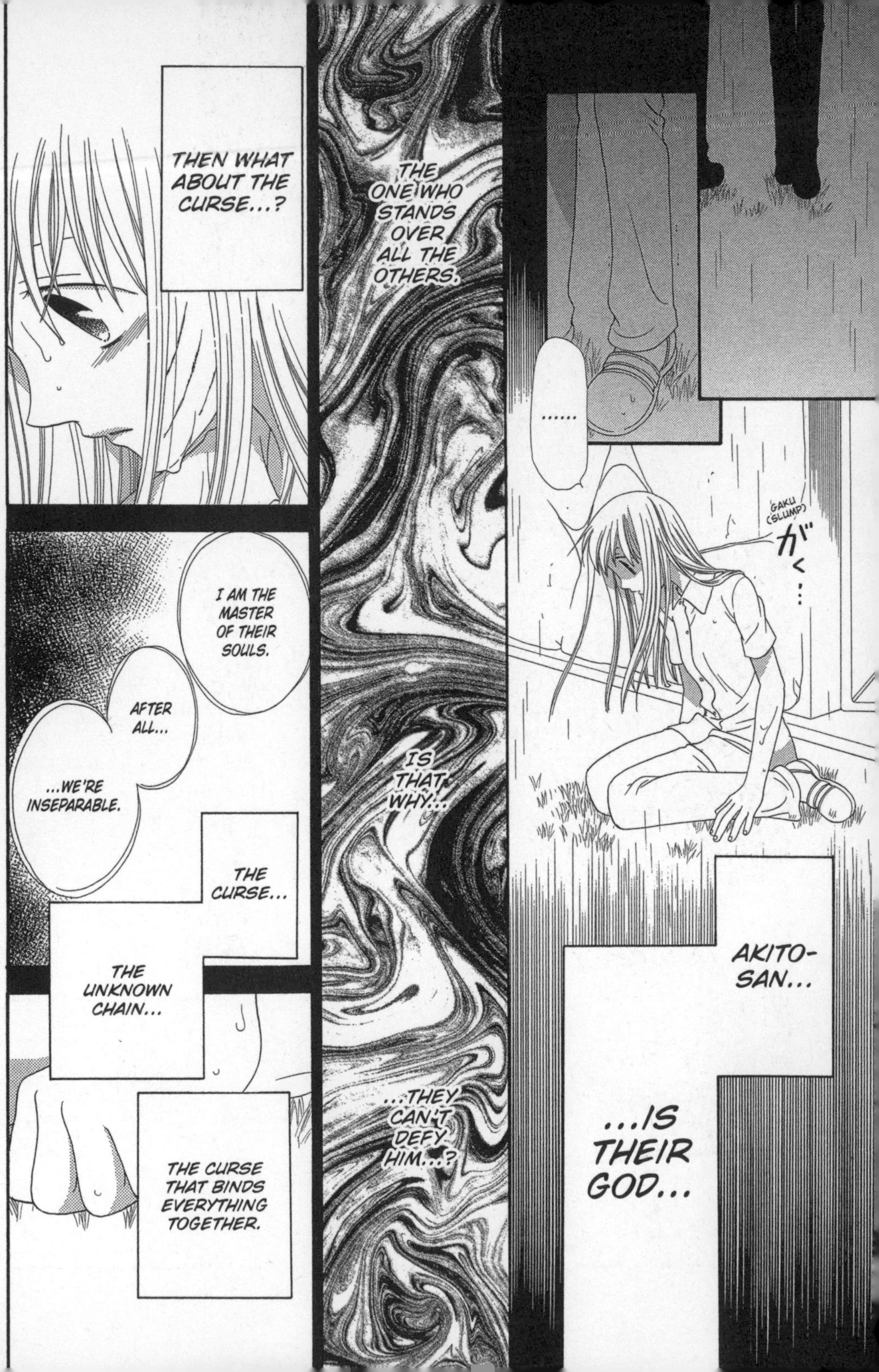
......
GAKU (SLUMP)
ガく…
AKITO-SAN...
...IS THEIR GOD...
THE ONE WHO STANDS OVER ALL THE OTHERS.
IS THAT WHY...
...THEY CAN'T DEFY HIM...?
THEN WHAT ABOUT THE CURSE...?
I AM THE MASTER OF THEIR SOULS.
AFTER ALL...
...WE'RE INSEPARABLE.
THE CURSE...
THE UNKNOWN CHAIN...
THE CURSE THAT BINDS EVERYTHING TOGETHER.

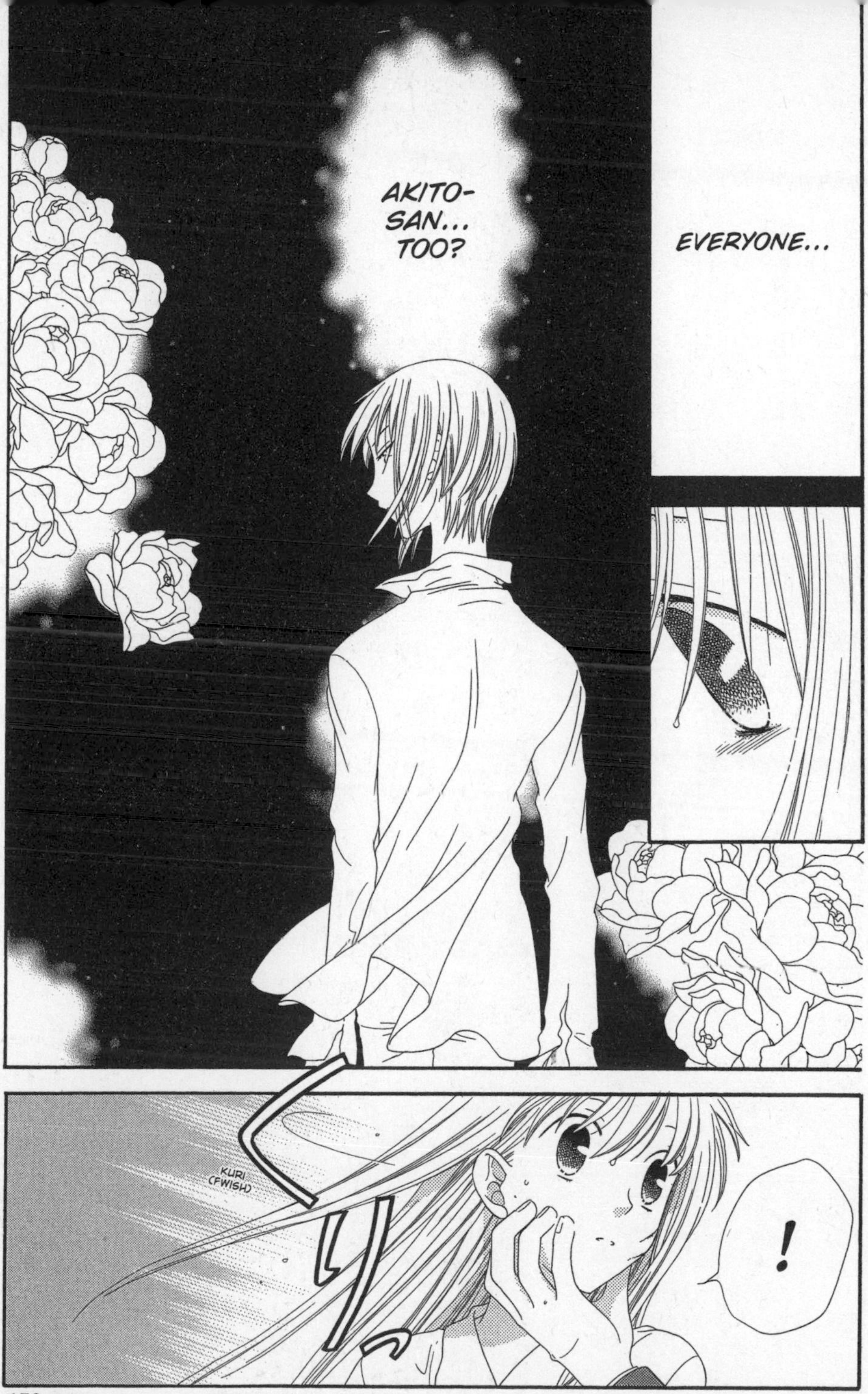
EVERYONE...
AKITO-SAN... TOO?
!
KURI (FWISH)

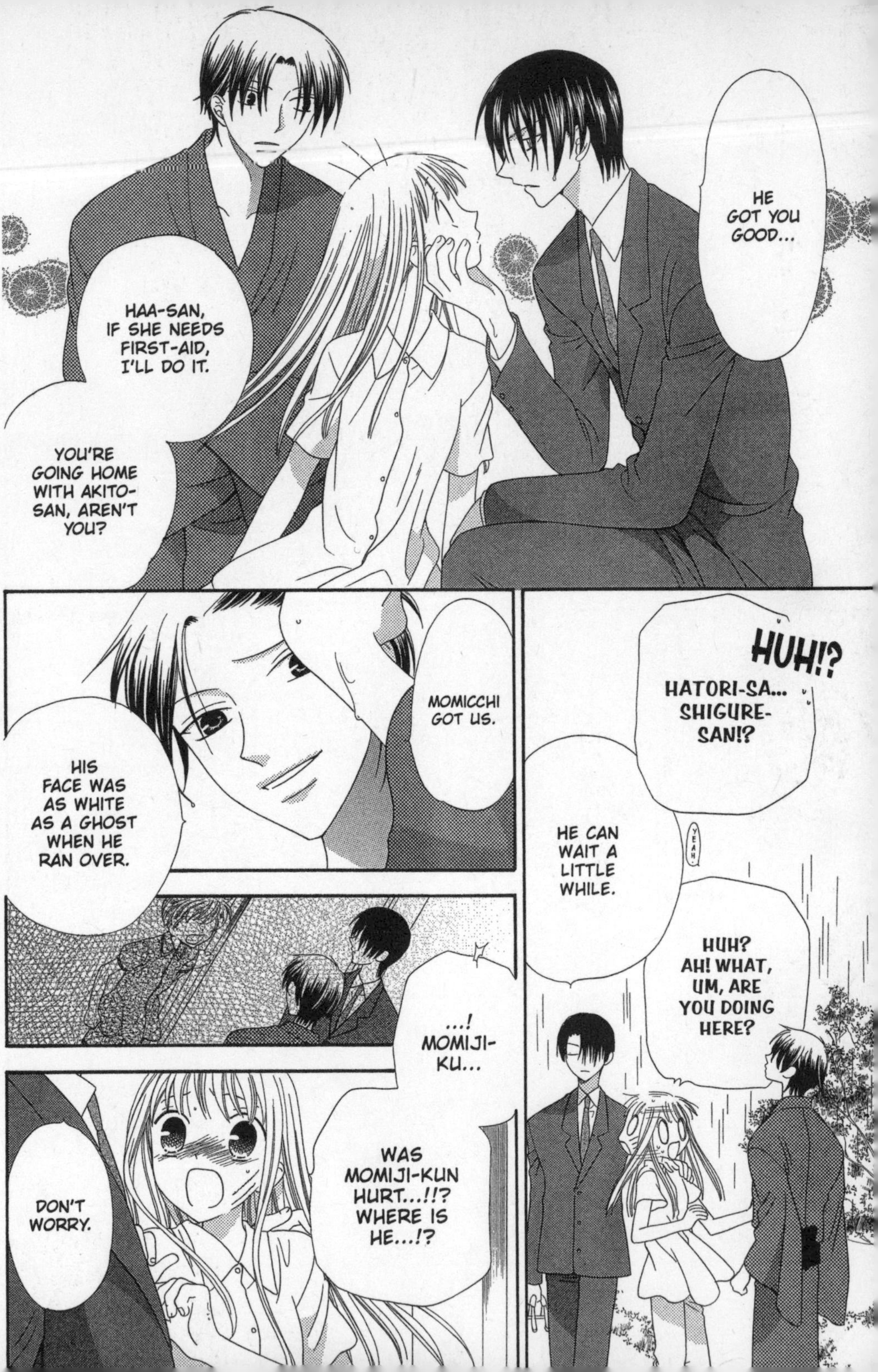
HE GOT YOU GOOD...
HAA-SAN, IF SHE NEEDS FIRST-AID, I'LL DO IT.
YOU'RE GOING HOME WITH AKITO-SAN, AREN'T YOU?
HUH!?
HATORI-SA... SHIGURE-SAN!?
HE CAN WAIT A LITTLE WHILE.
YEAH.
HUH? AH! WHAT, UM, ARE YOU DOING HERE?
MOMICCHI GOT US.
HIS FACE WAS AS WHITE AS A GHOST WHEN HE RAN OVER.
...! MOMIJI-KU...
WAS MOMIJI-KUN HURT...!!? WHERE IS HE...!?
DON'T WORRY.

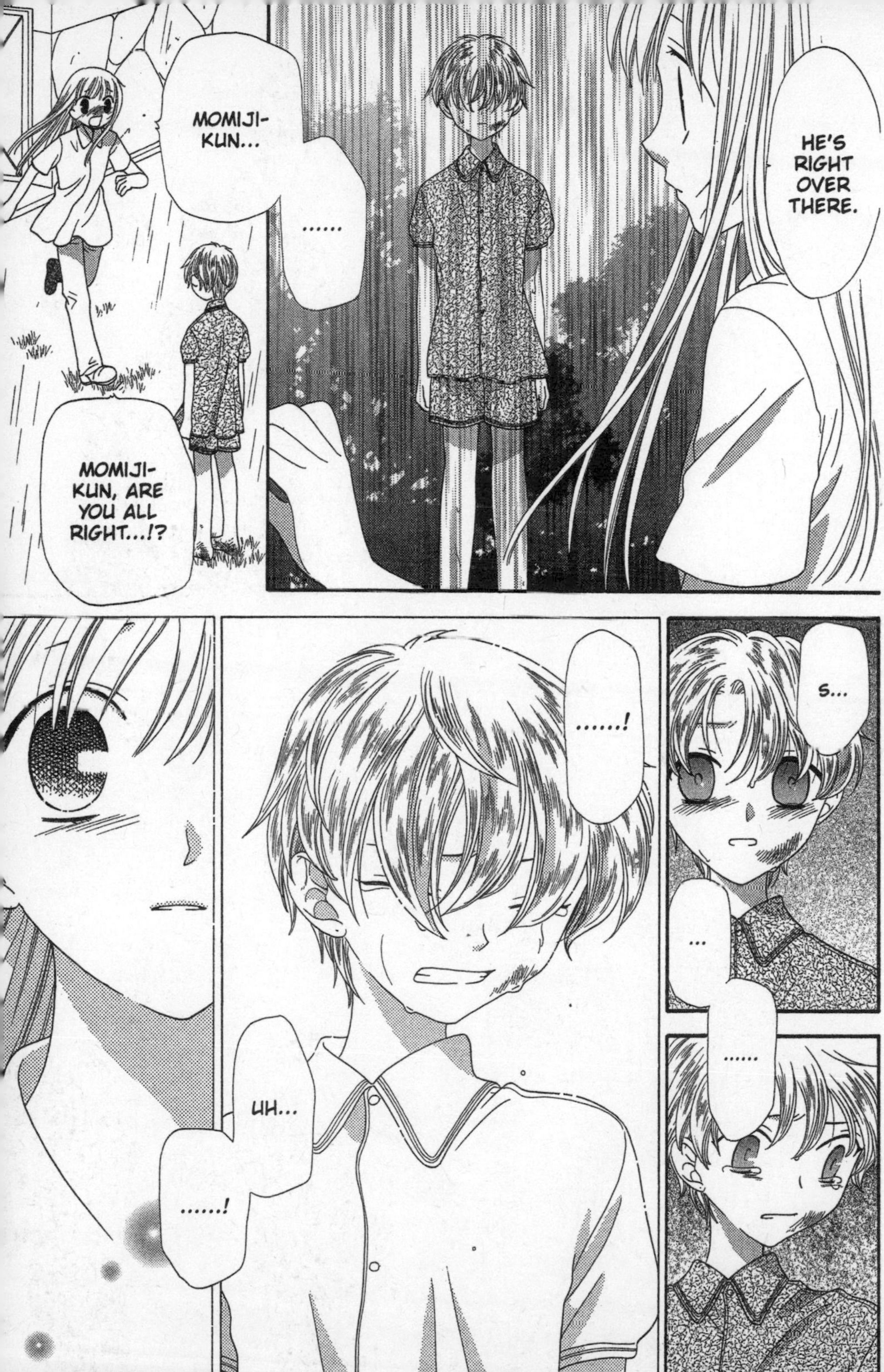

HE'S RIGHT OVER THERE.
MOMIJI-KUN...
......
MOMIJI-KUN, ARE YOU ALL RIGHT...!?
S...
...
......
......!
UH...
......!

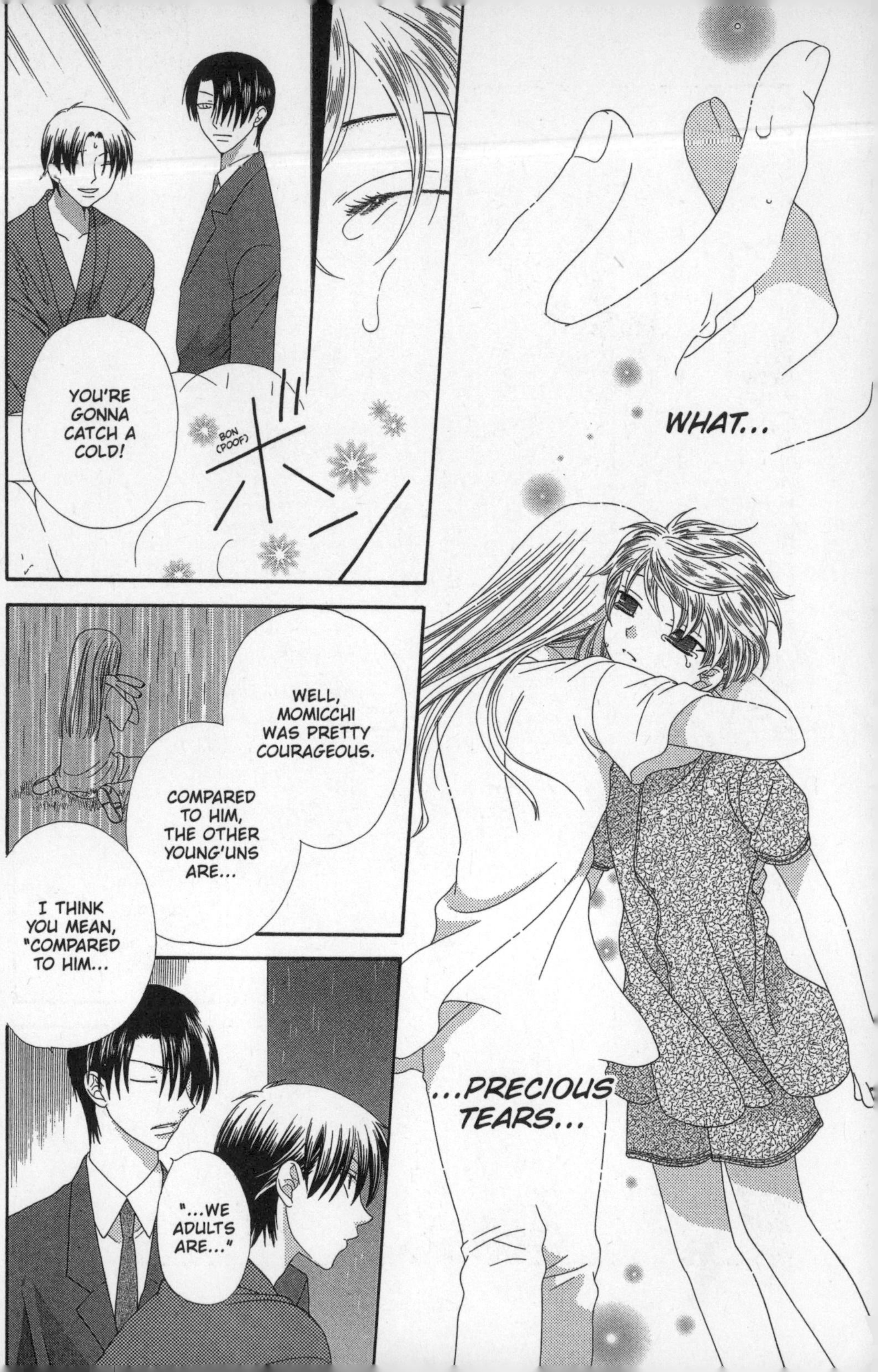
WHAT...
...PRECIOUS TEARS...
YOU'RE GONNA CATCH A COLD!
BON (POOF)
WELL, MOMICCHI WAS PRETTY COURAGEOUS.
COMPARED TO HIM, THE OTHER YOUNG'UNS ARE...
I THINK YOU MEAN, "COMPARED TO HIM...
"...WE ADULTS ARE..."

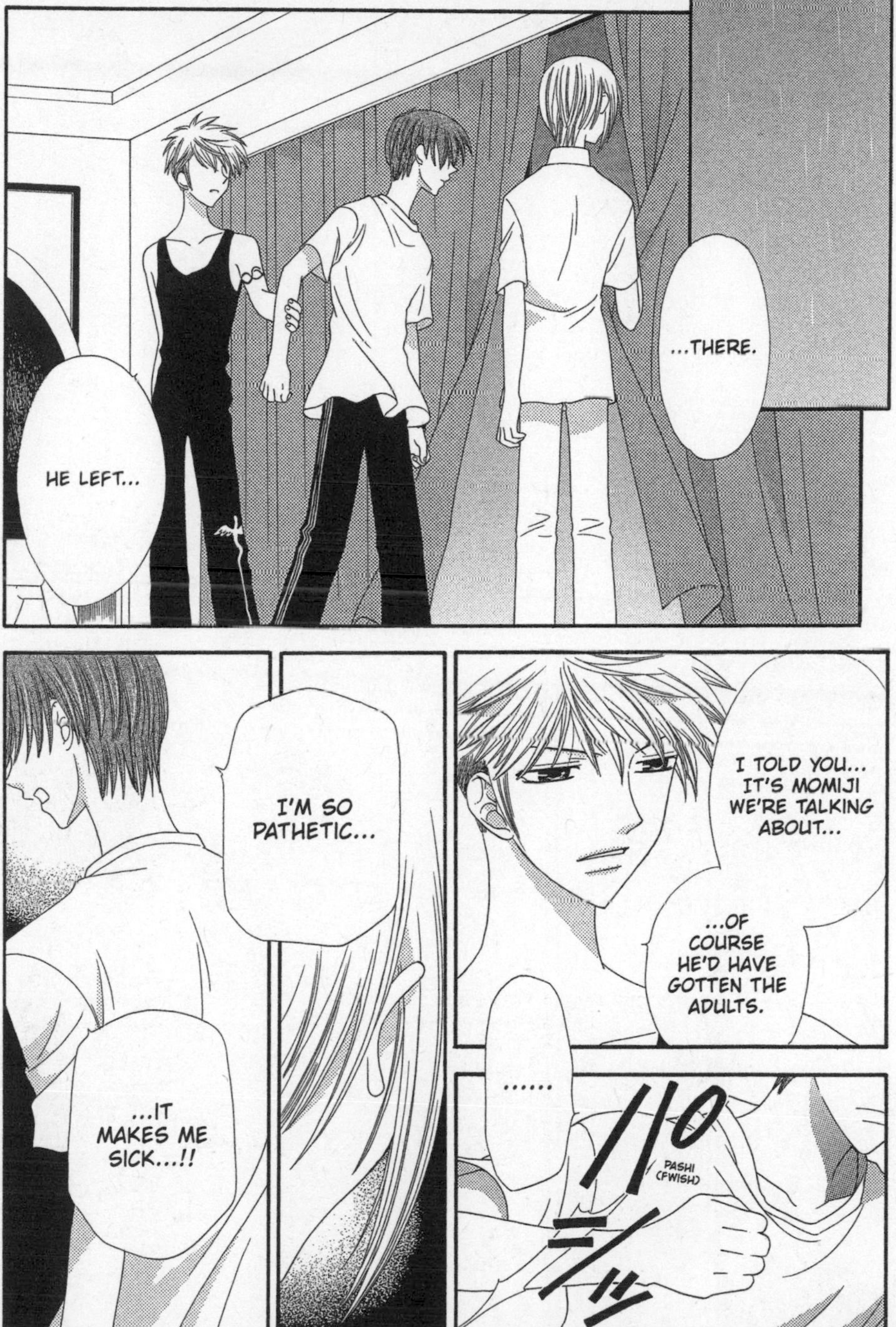
...THERE.
HE LEFT...
I TOLD YOU... IT'S MOMIJI WE'RE TALKING ABOUT...
...OF COURSE HE'D HAVE GOTTEN THE ADULTS.
......
PASHI (FWISH)
I'M SO PATHETIC...
...IT MAKES ME SICK...!!

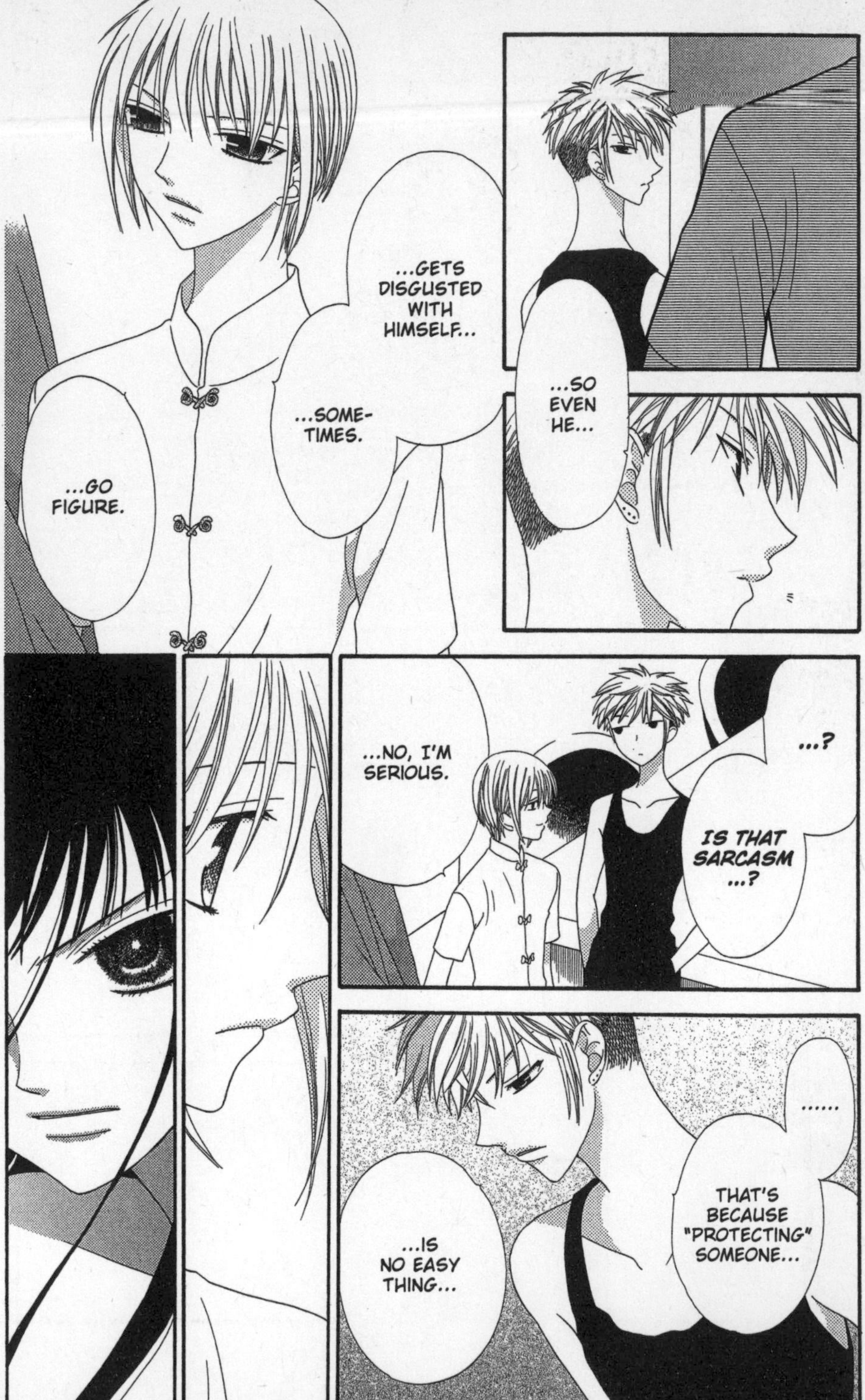
...SO EVEN HE...
...GETS DISGUSTED WITH HIMSELF...
...SOME-TIMES.
...GO FIGURE.
...?
IS THAT SARCASM ...?
...NO, I'M SERIOUS.
......
THAT'S BECAUSE "PROTECTING" SOMEONE...
...IS NO EASY THING...

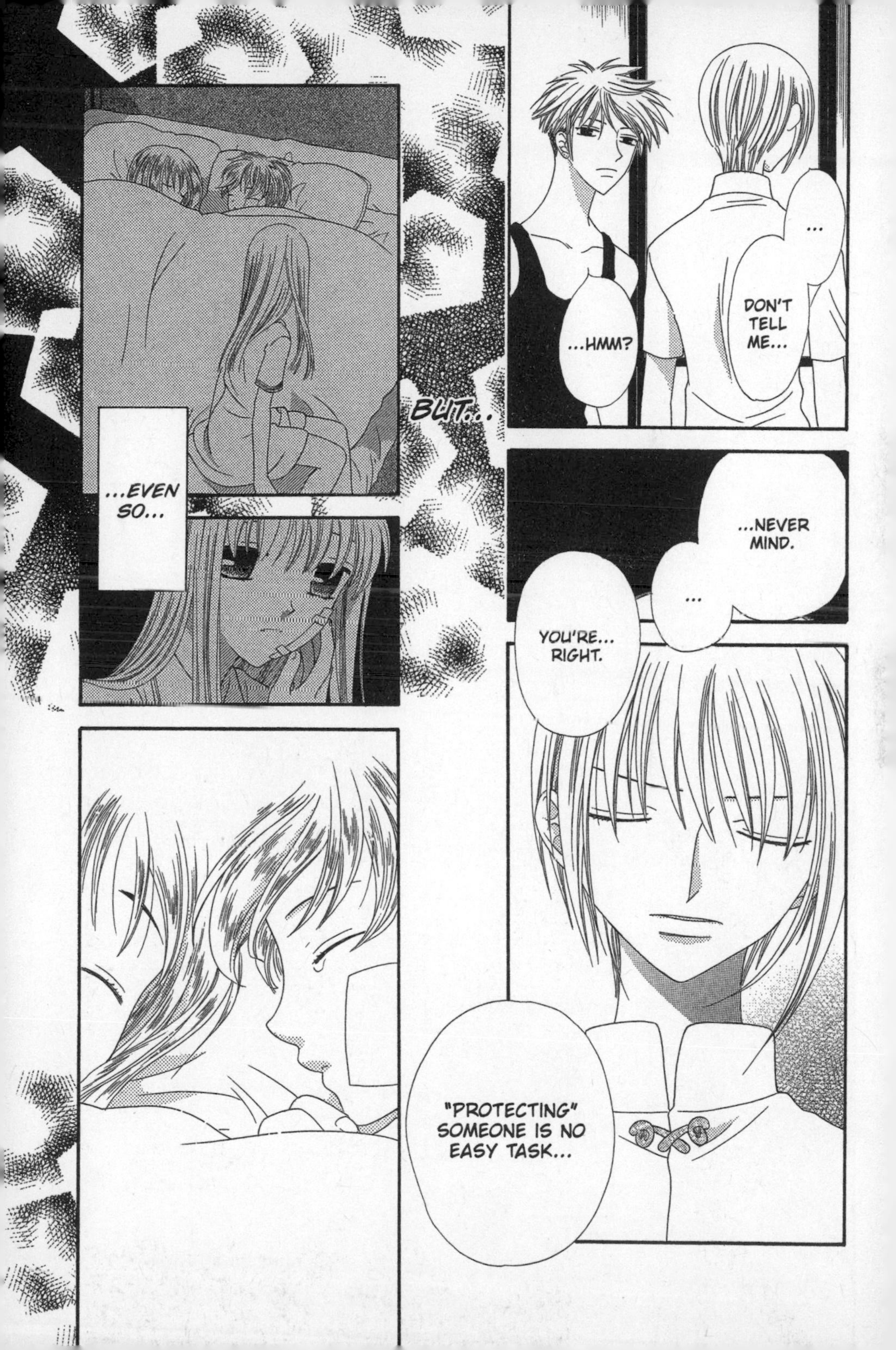
...
DON'T TELL ME...
...HMM?
...NEVER MIND.
...
YOU'RE... RIGHT.
"PROTECTING" SOMEONE IS NO EASY TASK...
BUT...
...EVEN SO...

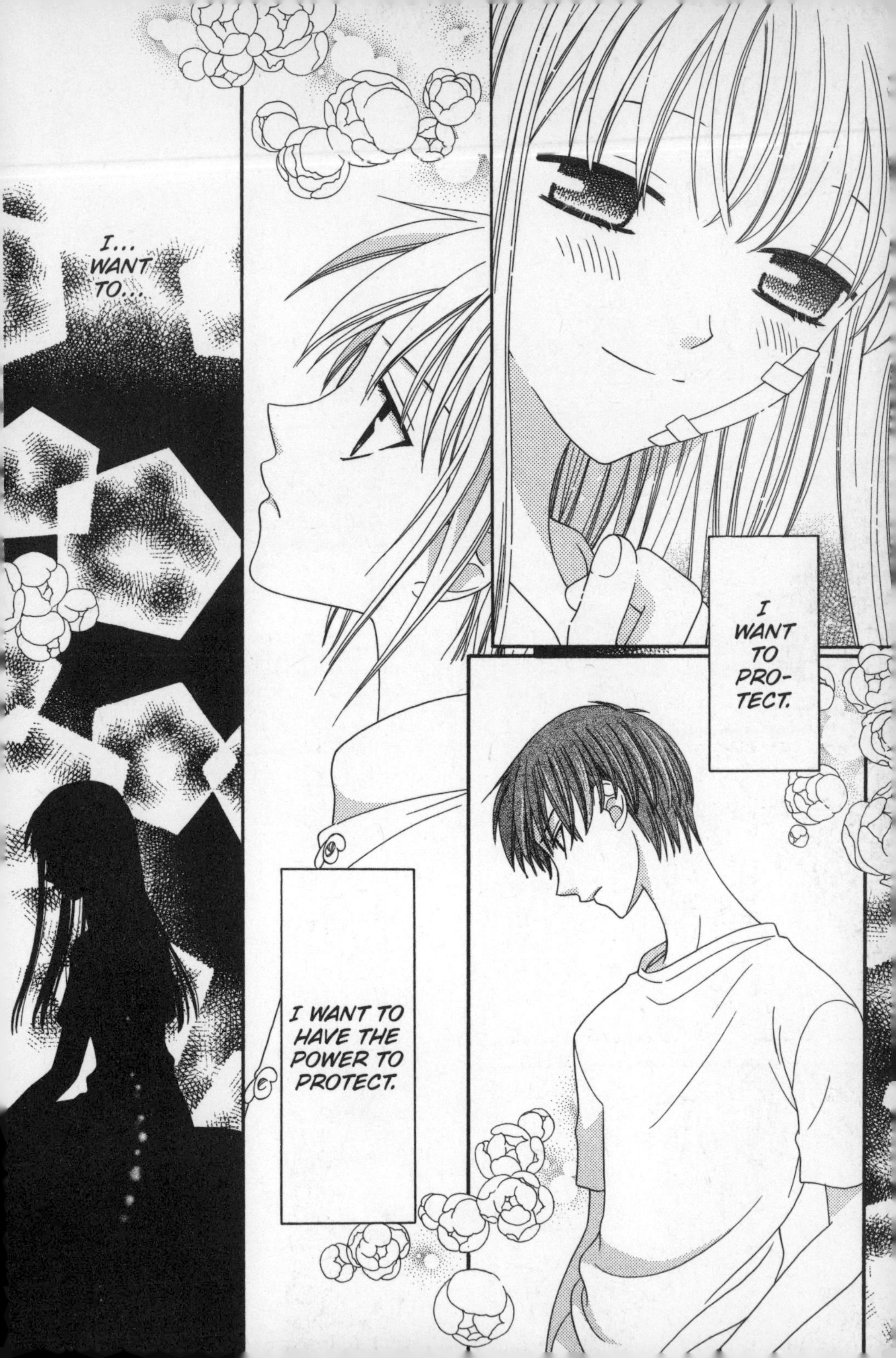
I WANT TO PRO-TECT.
I WANT TO HAVE THE POWER TO PROTECT.
I... WANT TO...

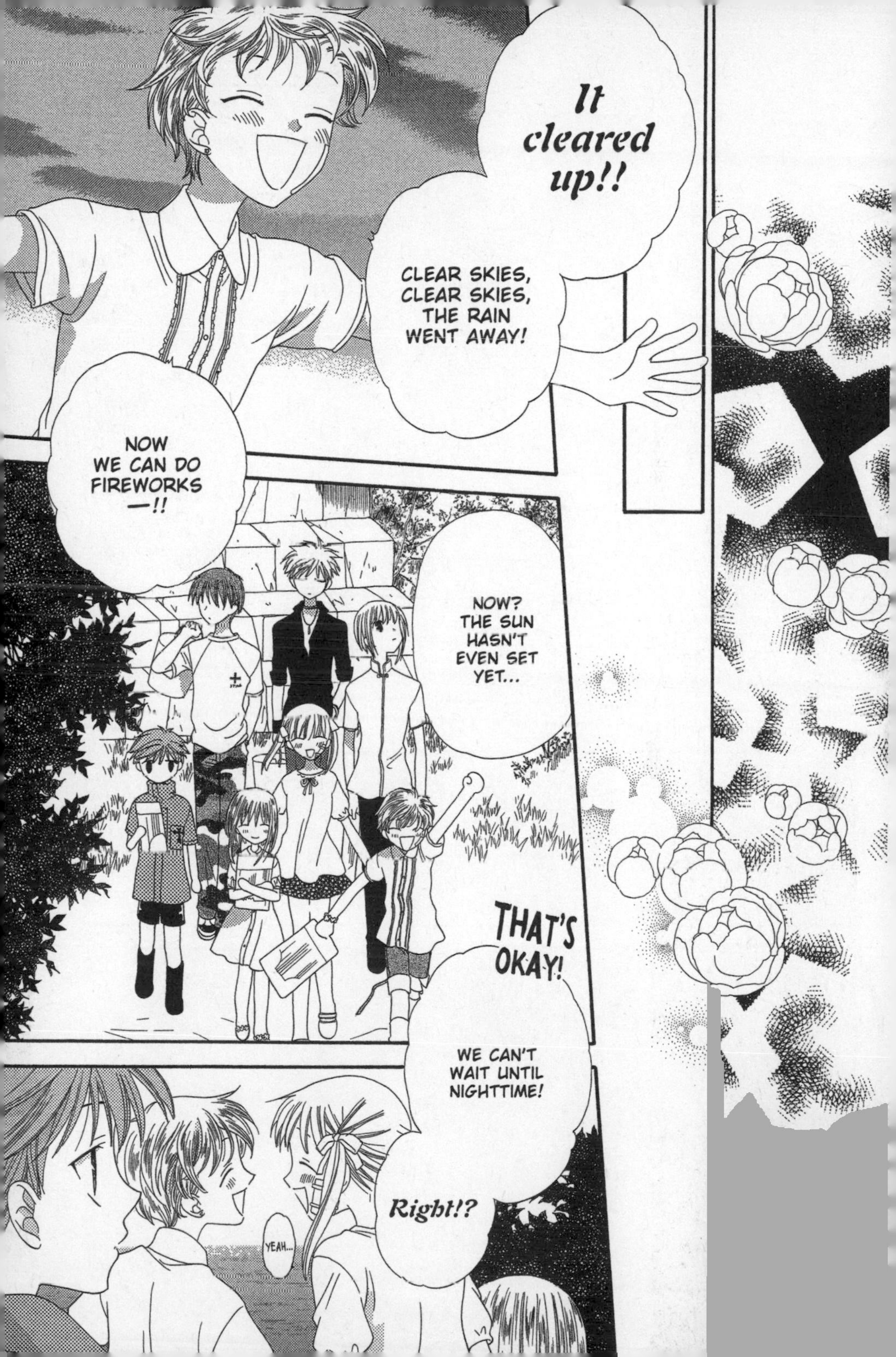
It cleared up!!
CLEAR SKIES, CLEAR SKIES, THE RAIN WENT AWAY!
NOW WE CAN DO FIREWORKS—!!
NOW? THE SUN HASN'T EVEN SET YET...
THAT'S OKAY!
WE CAN'T WAIT UNTIL NIGHTTIME!
Right!?
YEAH...

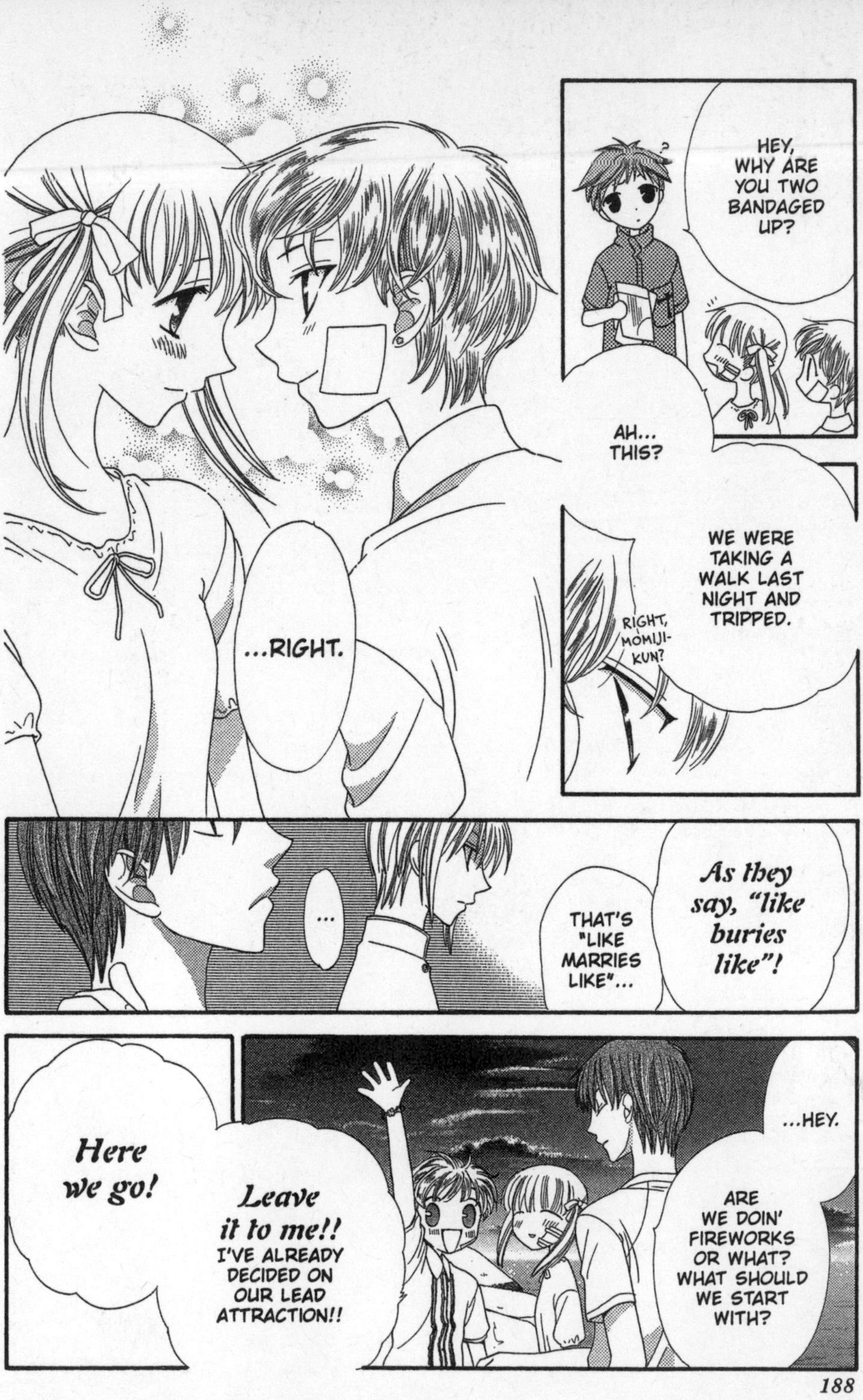
HEY, WHY ARE YOU TWO BANDAGED UP?
AH... THIS?
WE WERE TAKING A WALK LAST NIGHT AND TRIPPED.
RIGHT, MOMIJI-KUN?
...RIGHT.
As they say, "like buries like"!
THAT'S "LIKE MARRIES LIKE"...
...
...HEY.
ARE WE DOIN' FIREWORKS OR WHAT? WHAT SHOULD WE START WITH?
Leave it to me!! I'VE ALREADY DECIDED ON OUR LEAD ATTRACTION!!
Here we go!

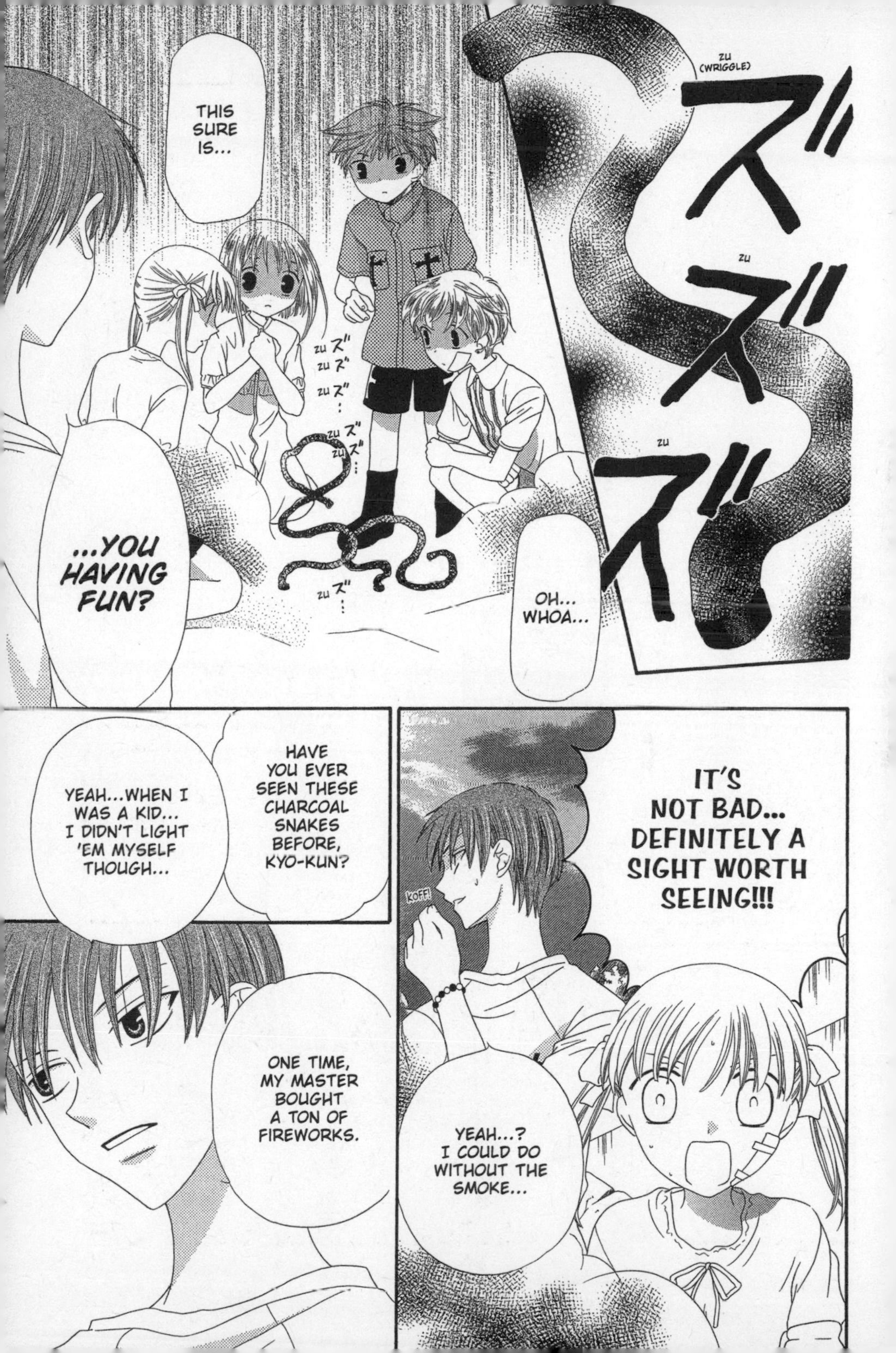

ZU (WRIGGLE)
ズ
ZU
ズ
ZU
ズ
THIS SURE IS...
ZU ズ ZU ズ ZU ズ...
ZU ズ ZU ズ...
ZU ズ...
OH... WHOA...
...YOU HAVING FUN?
IT'S NOT BAD... DEFINITELY A SIGHT WORTH SEEING!!!
KOFF!
YEAH...? I COULD DO WITHOUT THE SMOKE...
HAVE YOU EVER SEEN THESE CHARCOAL SNAKES BEFORE, KYO-KUN?
YEAH...WHEN I WAS A KID... I DIDN'T LIGHT 'EM MYSELF THOUGH...
ONE TIME, MY MASTER BOUGHT A TON OF FIREWORKS.

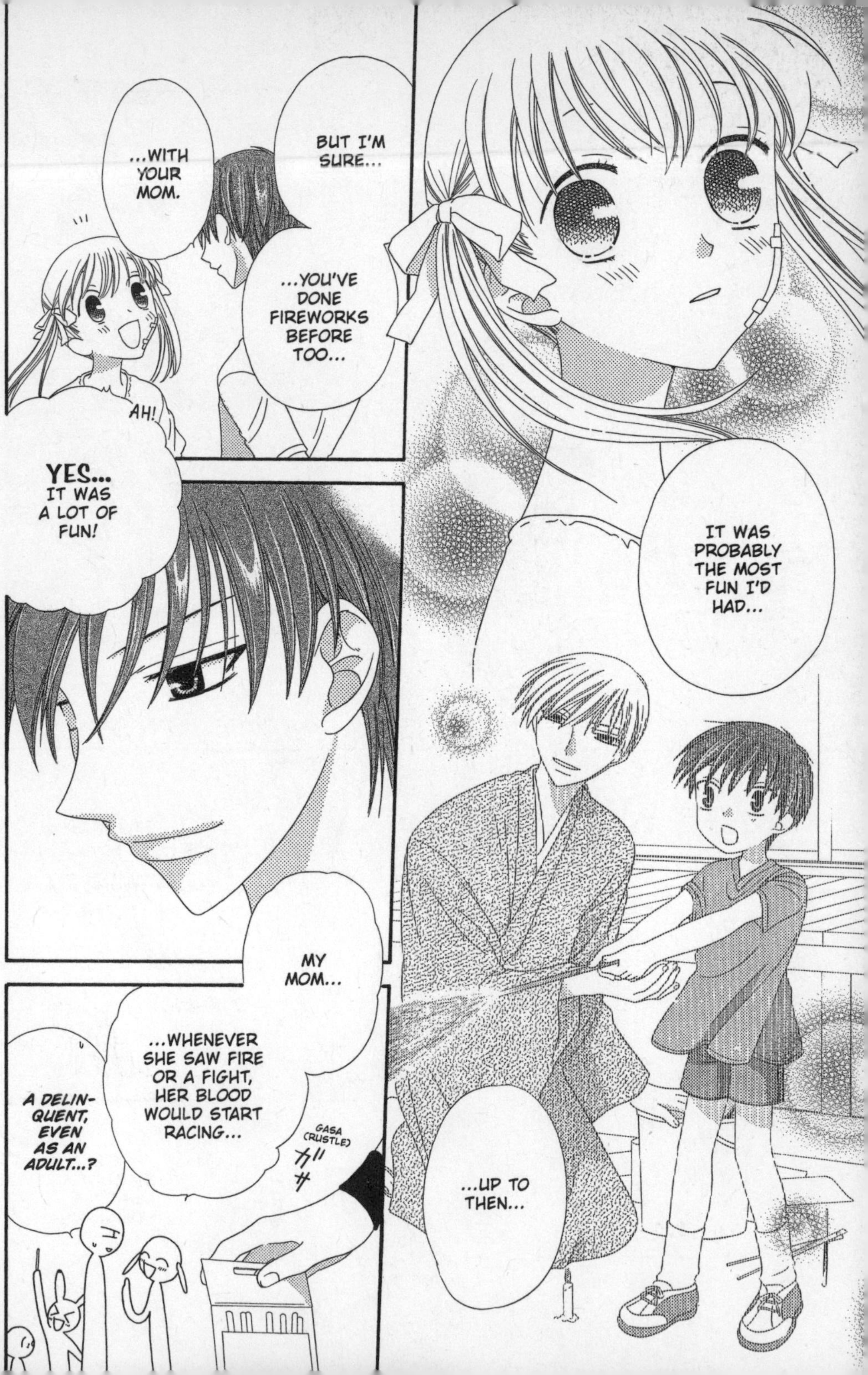
BUT I'M SURE...
...WITH YOUR MOM.
...YOU'VE DONE FIREWORKS BEFORE TOO...
AH!
YES... IT WAS A LOT OF FUN!
IT WAS PROBABLY THE MOST FUN I'D HAD...
...UP TO THEN...
MY MOM...
...WHENEVER SHE SAW FIRE OR A FIGHT, HER BLOOD WOULD START RACING...
GASA (RUSTLE)
A DELIN-QUENT, EVEN AS AN ADULT...?

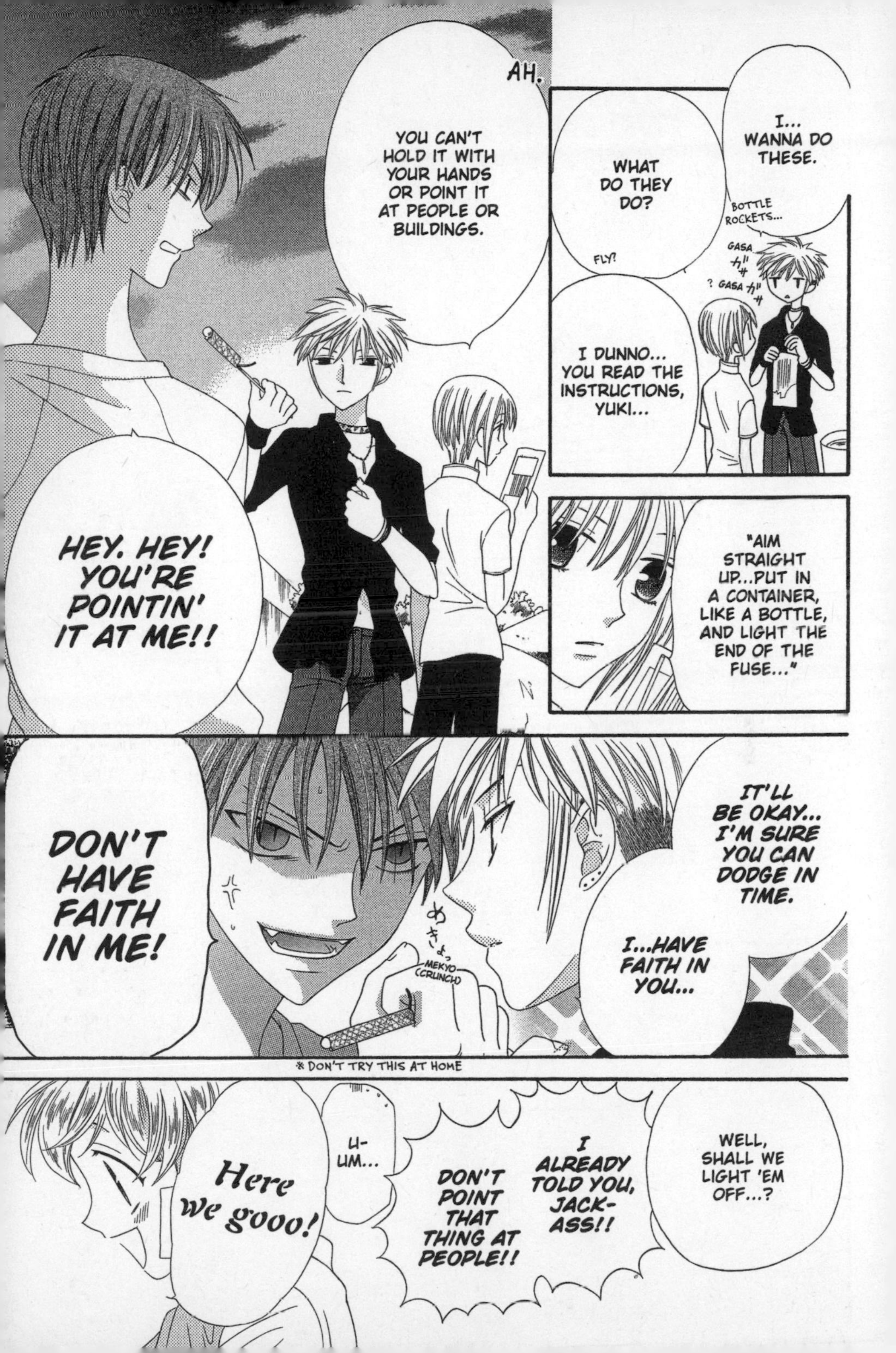
I... WANNA DO THESE.
BOTTLE ROCKETS...
WHAT DO THEY DO?
FLY?
GASA GASA
I DUNNO... YOU READ THE INSTRUCTIONS, YUKI...
?
"AIM STRAIGHT UP...PUT IN A CONTAINER, LIKE A BOTTLE, AND LIGHT THE END OF THE FUSE..."
AH.
YOU CAN'T HOLD IT WITH YOUR HANDS OR POINT IT AT PEOPLE OR BUILDINGS.
HEY. HEY! YOU'RE POINTIN' IT AT ME!!
IT'LL BE OKAY... I'M SURE YOU CAN DODGE IN TIME.
I...HAVE FAITH IN YOU...
DON'T HAVE FAITH IN ME!
MEKYO (CRUNCH)
※ DON'T TRY THIS AT HOME
WELL, SHALL WE LIGHT 'EM OFF...?
I ALREADY TOLD YOU, JACK-ASS!!
DON'T POINT THAT THING AT PEOPLE!!
U-UM...
Here we gooo!

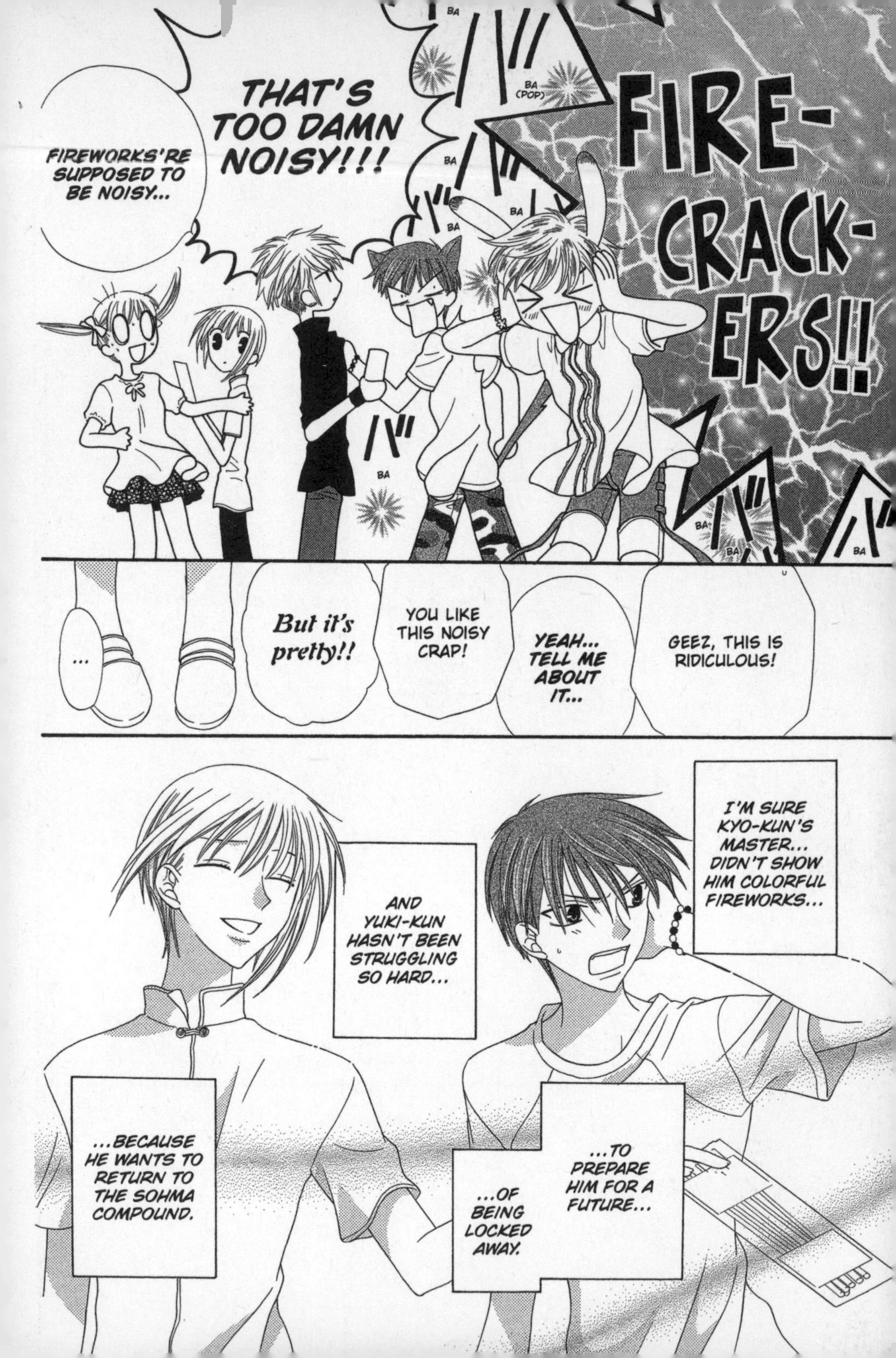
FIRE-CRACK-ERS!!
BA
BA (POP)
BA
BA
BA
BA
BA
BA
BA
THAT'S TOO DAMN NOISY!!!
FIREWORKS'RE SUPPOSED TO BE NOISY...
GEEZ, THIS IS RIDICULOUS!
YEAH... TELL ME ABOUT IT...
YOU LIKE THIS NOISY CRAP!
But it's pretty!!
...
I'M SURE KYO-KUN'S MASTER... DIDN'T SHOW HIM COLORFUL FIREWORKS...
...TO PREPARE HIM FOR A FUTURE...
...OF BEING LOCKED AWAY.
AND YUKI-KUN HASN'T BEEN STRUGGLING SO HARD...
...BECAUSE HE WANTS TO RETURN TO THE SOHMA COMPOUND.

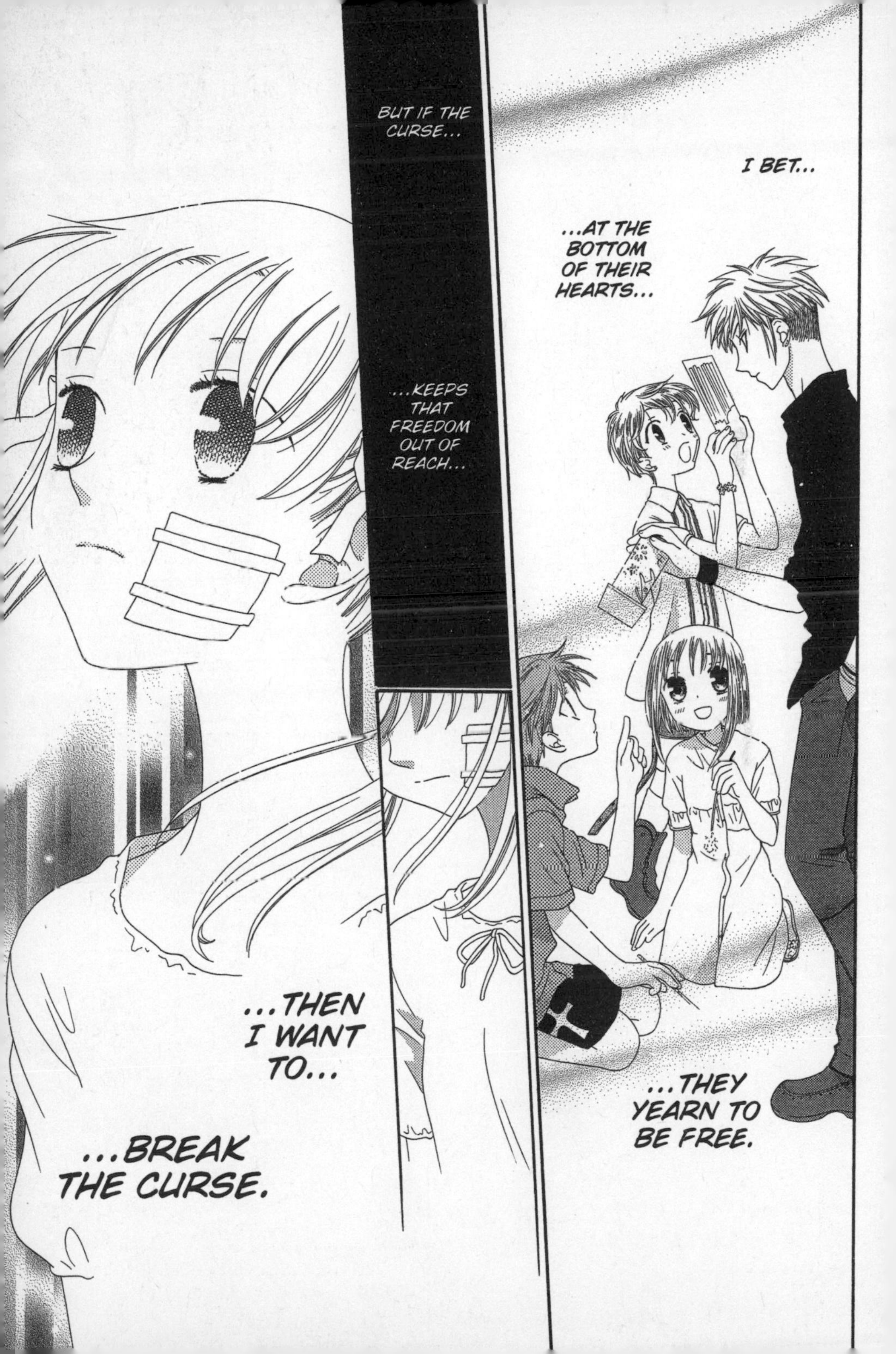
I BET...
...AT THE BOTTOM OF THEIR HEARTS...
...THEY YEARN TO BE FREE.
BUT IF THE CURSE...
...KEEPS THAT FREEDOM OUT OF REACH...
...THEN I WANT TO...
...BREAK THE CURSE.

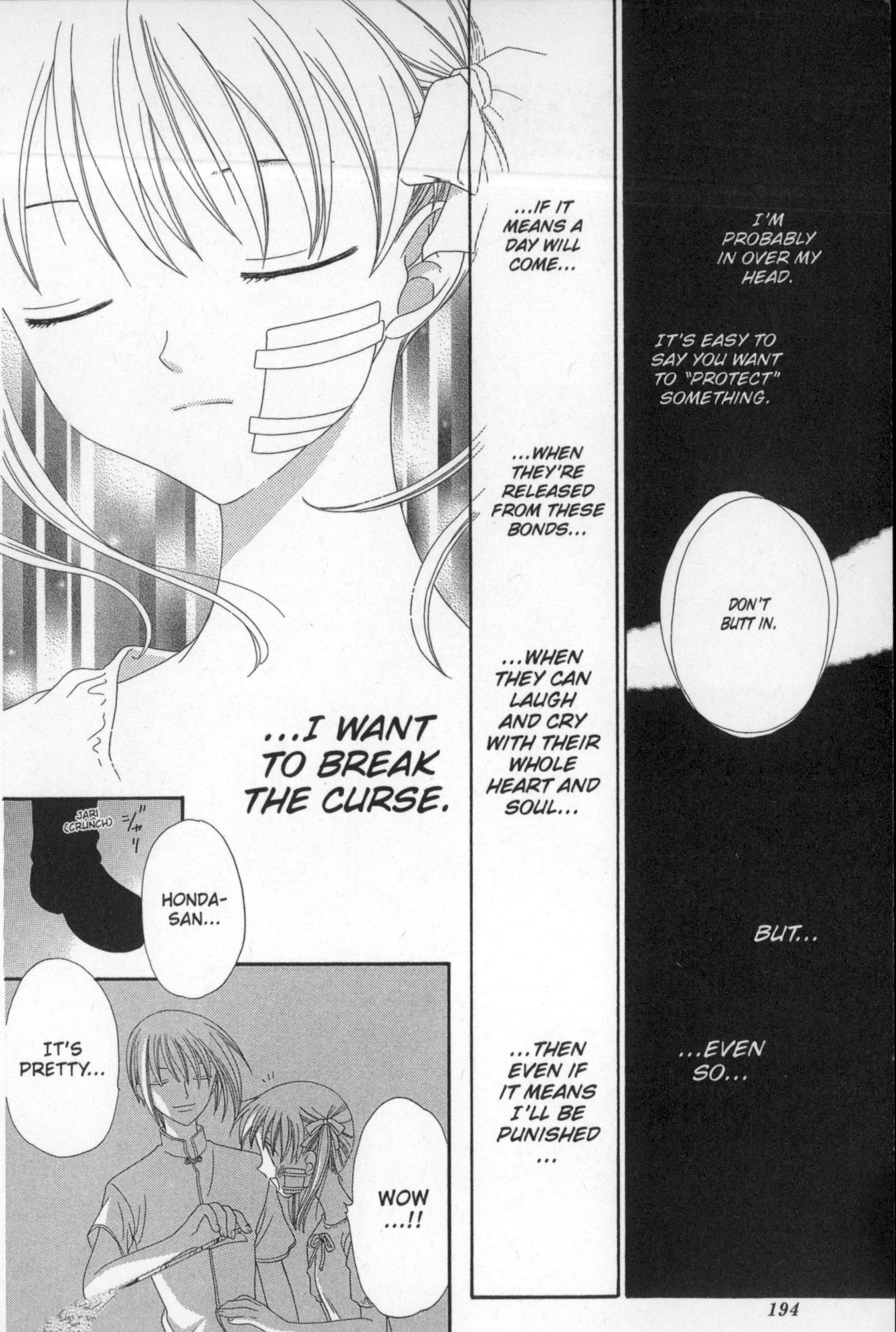
I'M PROBABLY IN OVER MY HEAD.
IT'S EASY TO SAY YOU WANT TO "PROTECT" SOMETHING.
DON'T BUTT IN.
BUT...
...EVEN SO...
...IF IT MEANS A DAY WILL COME...
...WHEN THEY'RE RELEASED FROM THESE BONDS...
...WHEN THEY CAN LAUGH AND CRY WITH THEIR WHOLE HEART AND SOUL...
...THEN EVEN IF IT MEANS I'LL BE PUNISHED...
...I WANT TO BREAK THE CURSE.
JARI (CRUNCH)
HONDA-SAN...
IT'S PRETTY...
WOW ...!!

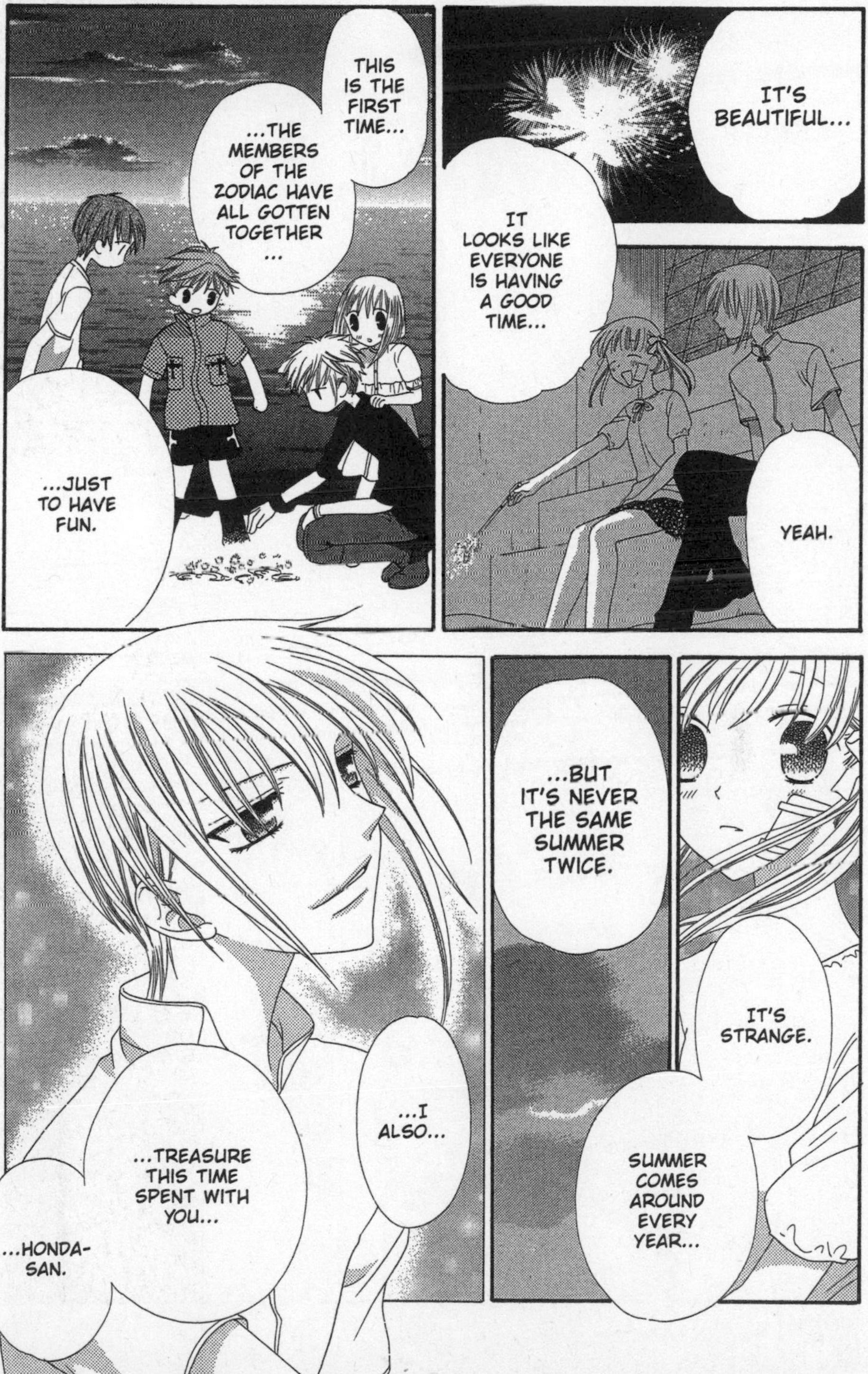
IT'S BEAUTIFUL...
IT LOOKS LIKE EVERYONE IS HAVING A GOOD TIME...
YEAH.
THIS IS THE FIRST TIME...
...THE MEMBERS OF THE ZODIAC HAVE ALL GOTTEN TOGETHER ...
...JUST TO HAVE FUN.
IT'S STRANGE.
SUMMER COMES AROUND EVERY YEAR...
...BUT IT'S NEVER THE SAME SUMMER TWICE.
...I ALSO...
...TREASURE THIS TIME SPENT WITH YOU...
...HONDA-SAN.

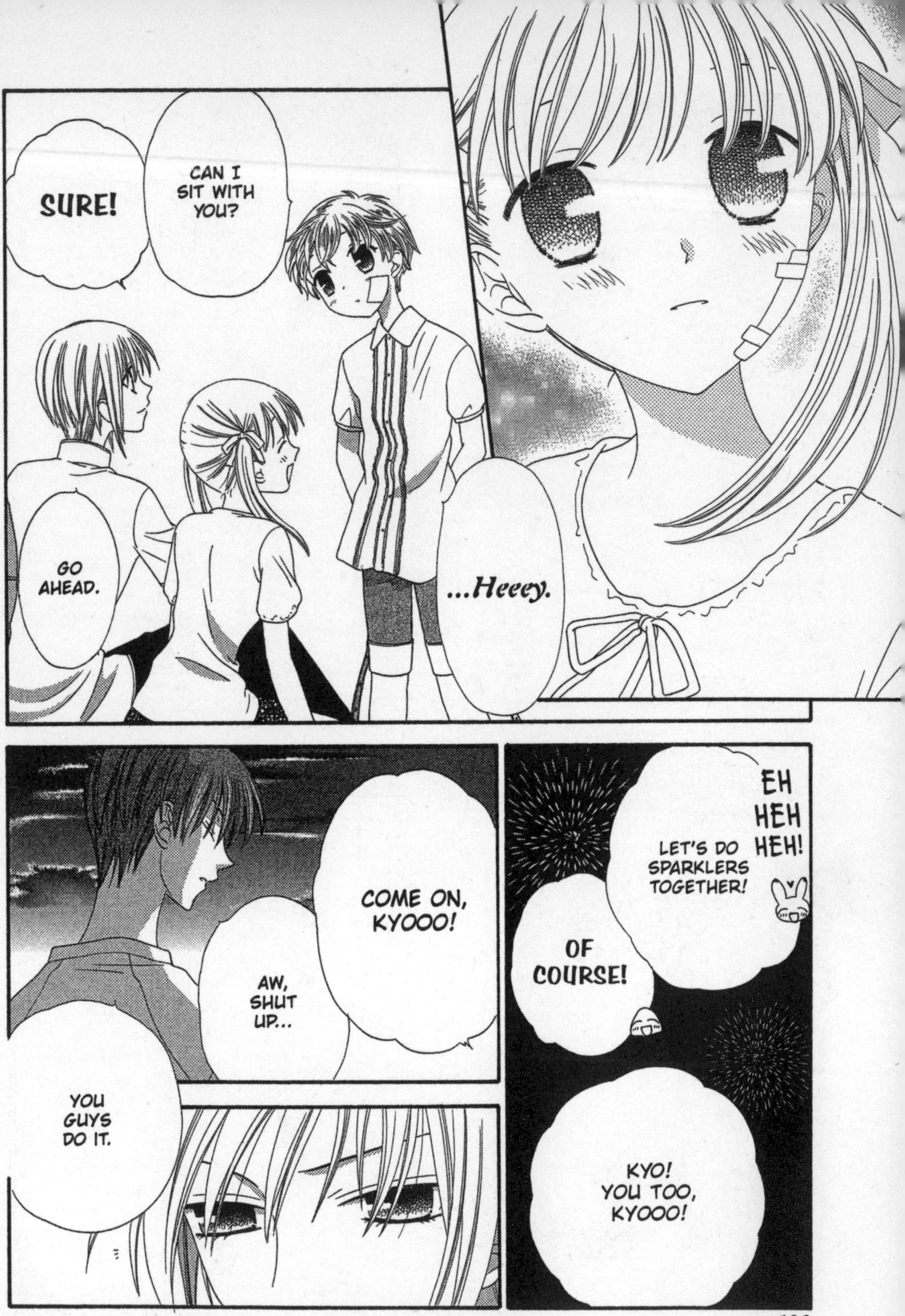
...Heeey.
CAN I SIT WITH YOU?
SURE!
GO AHEAD.
EH HEH HEH!
LET'S DO SPARKLERS TOGETHER!
OF COURSE!
KYO! YOU TOO, KYOOO!
COME ON, KYOOO!
AW, SHUT UP...
YOU GUYS DO IT.

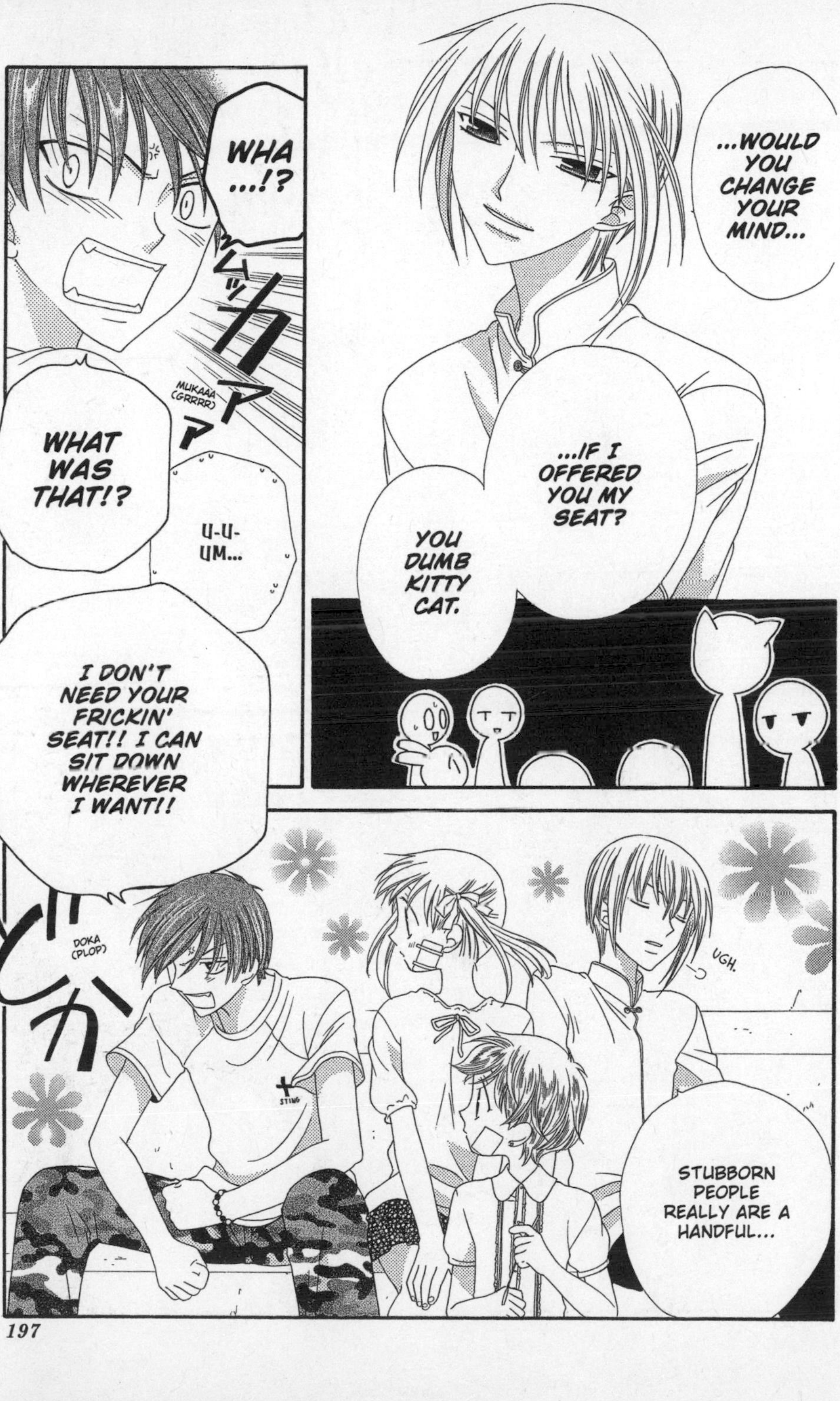

...WOULD YOU CHANGE YOUR MIND...
...IF I OFFERED YOU MY SEAT?
YOU DUMB KITTY CAT.
WHA ...!?
MUKAAA (GRRRR)
WHAT WAS THAT!?
U-U-UM...
I DON'T NEED YOUR FRICKIN' SEAT!! I CAN SIT DOWN WHEREVER I WANT!!
UGH.
STUBBORN PEOPLE REALLY ARE A HANDFUL...
DOKA (PLOP)
STING

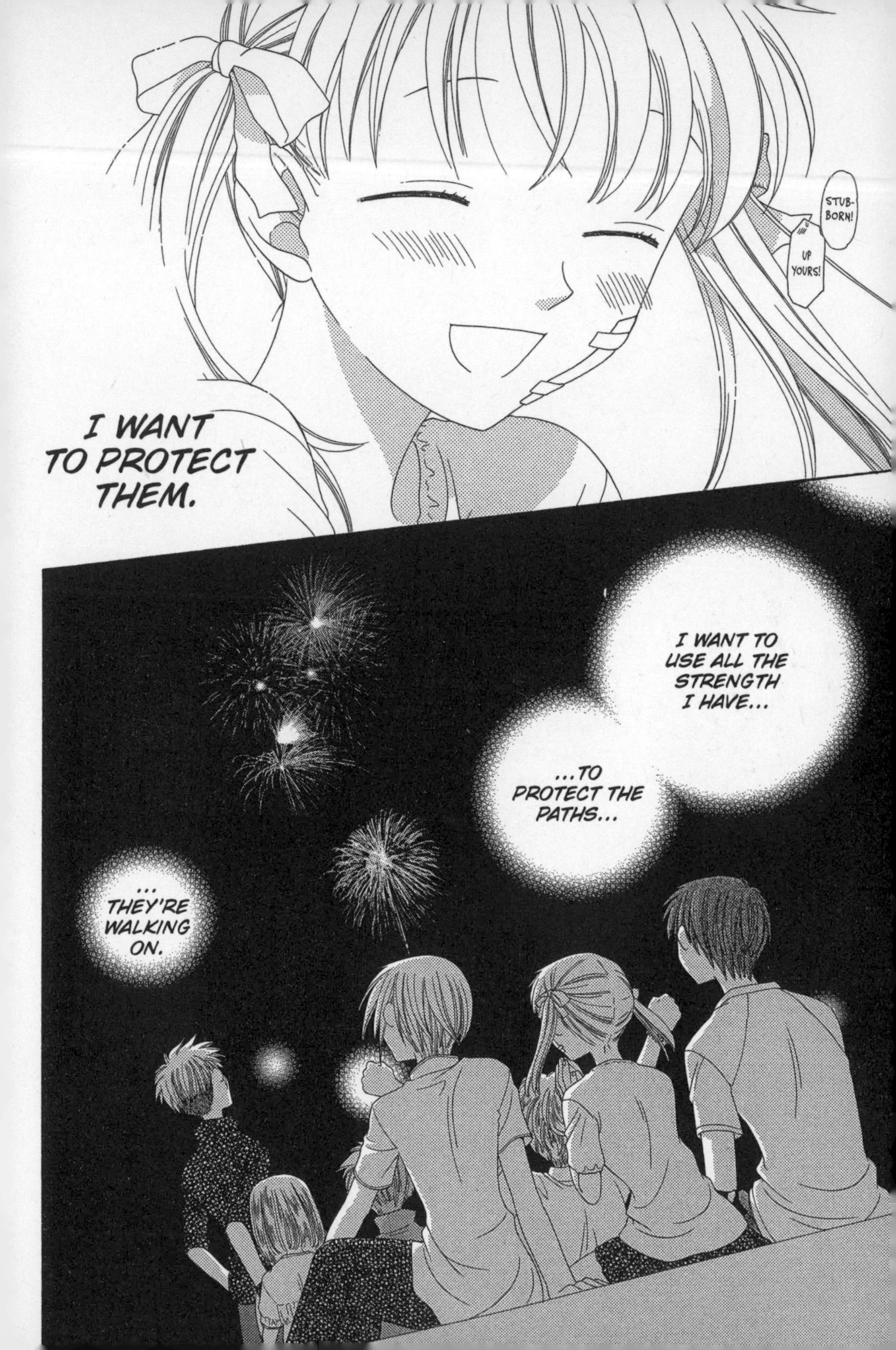
STUB-BORN!
UP YOURS!
I WANT TO PROTECT THEM.
I WANT TO USE ALL THE STRENGTH I HAVE...
...TO PROTECT THE PATHS...
...THEY'RE WALKING ON.

COLLECTOR'S EDITION

Fruits Basket

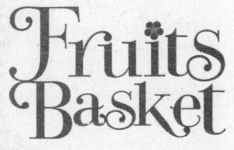

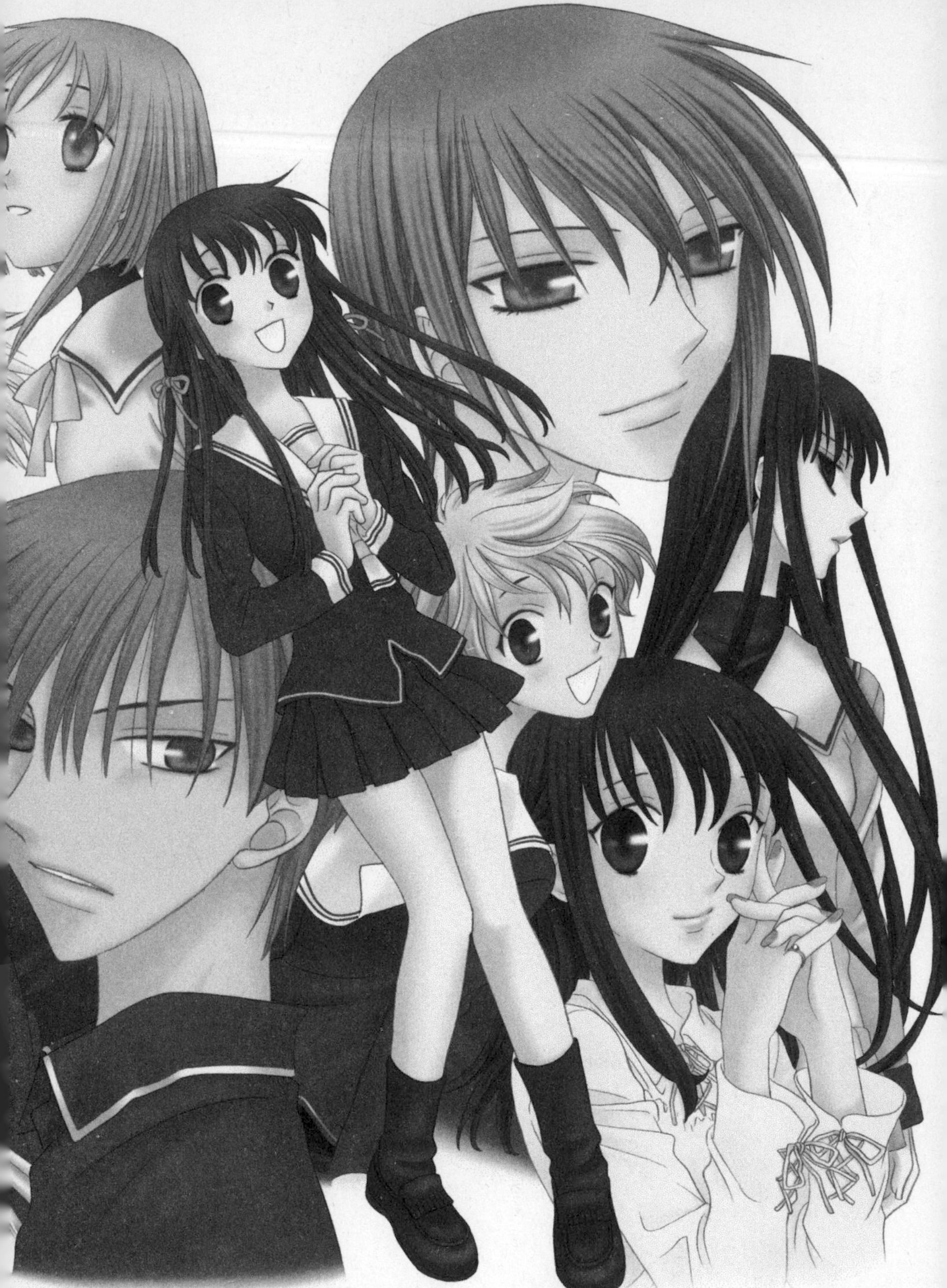

Chapter 66

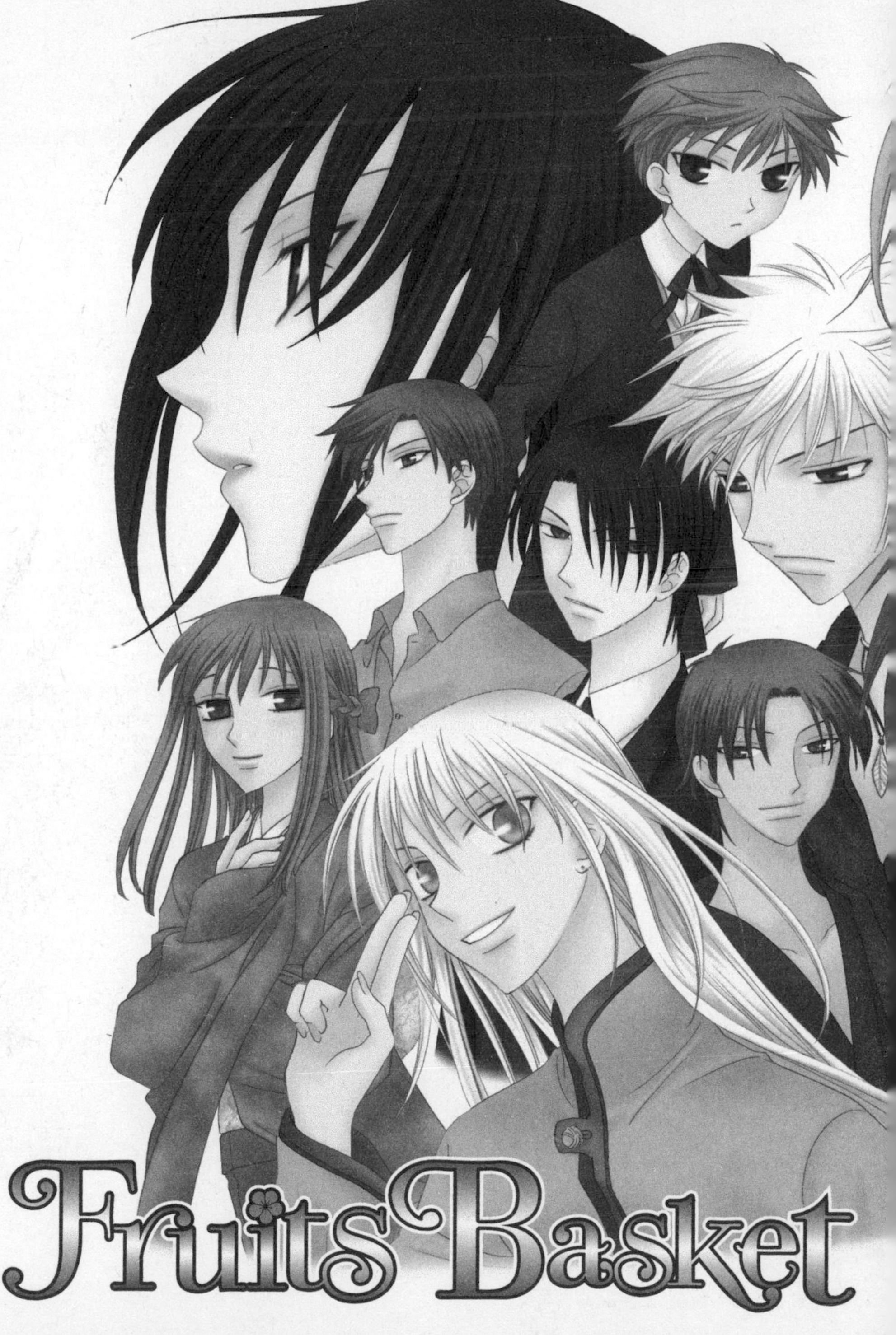
Fruits Basket

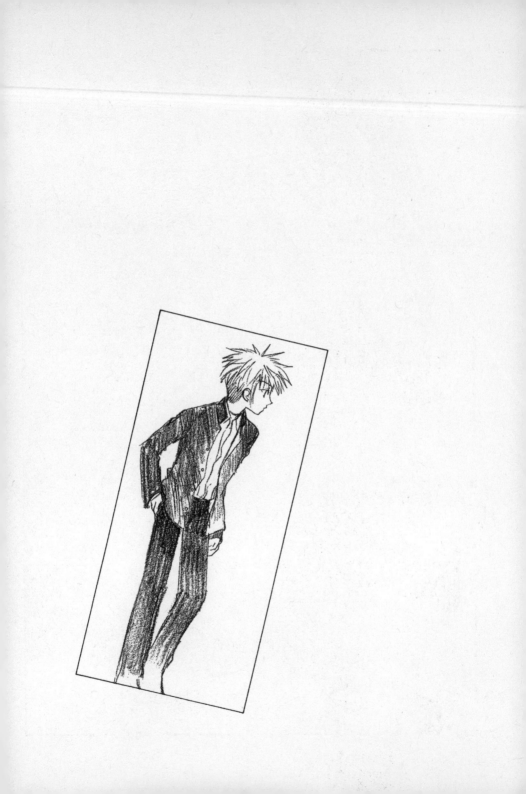

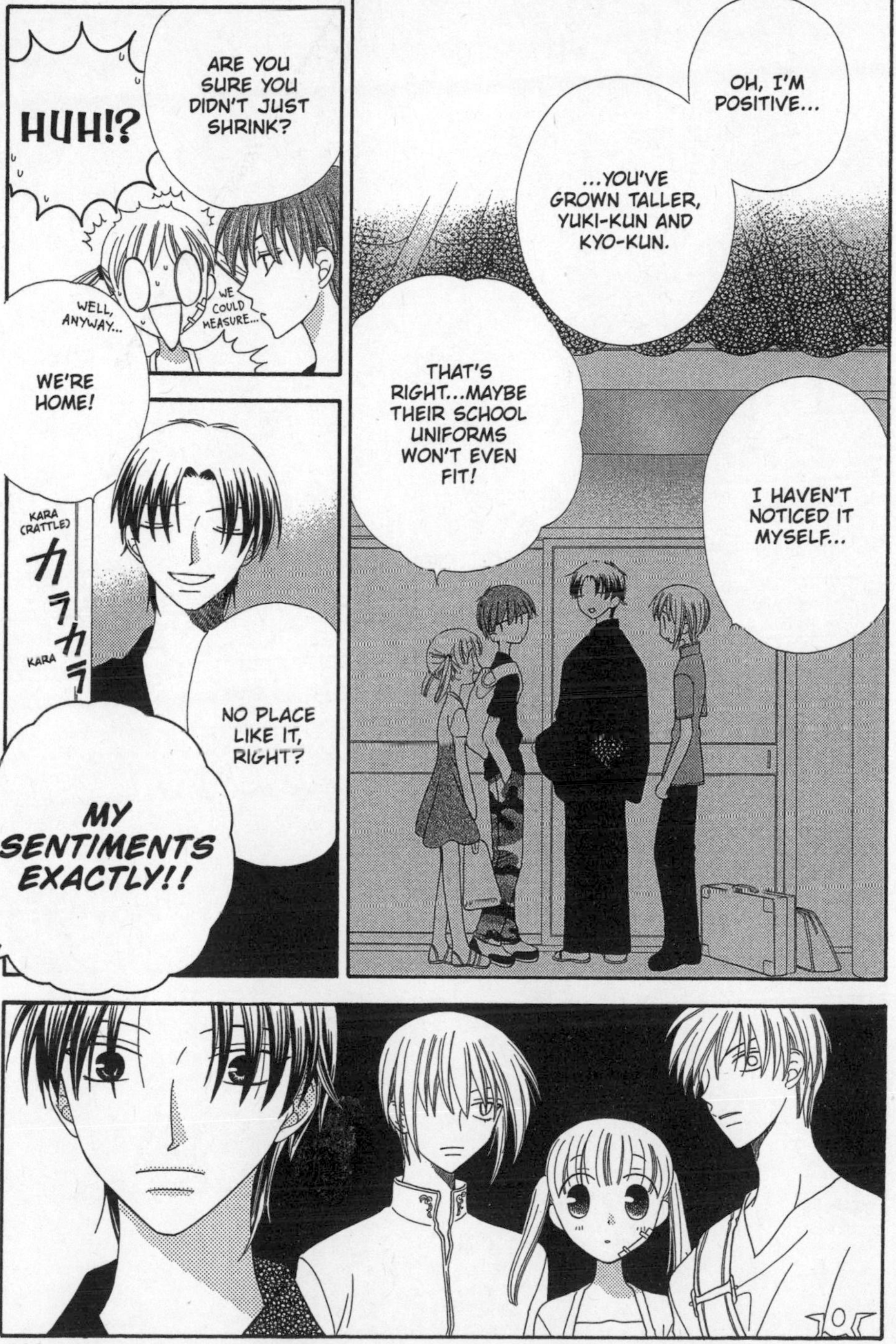
OH, I'M POSITIVE...
...YOU'VE GROWN TALLER, YUKI-KUN AND KYO-KUN.
I HAVEN'T NOTICED IT MYSELF...
THAT'S RIGHT...MAYBE THEIR SCHOOL UNIFORMS WON'T EVEN FIT!
ARE YOU SURE YOU DIDN'T JUST SHRINK?
HUH!?
WE COULD MEASURE...
WELL, ANYWAY...
WE'RE HOME!
KARA (RATTLE)
カラ
KARA
カラ
NO PLACE LIKE IT, RIGHT?
MY SENTIMENTS EXACTLY!!

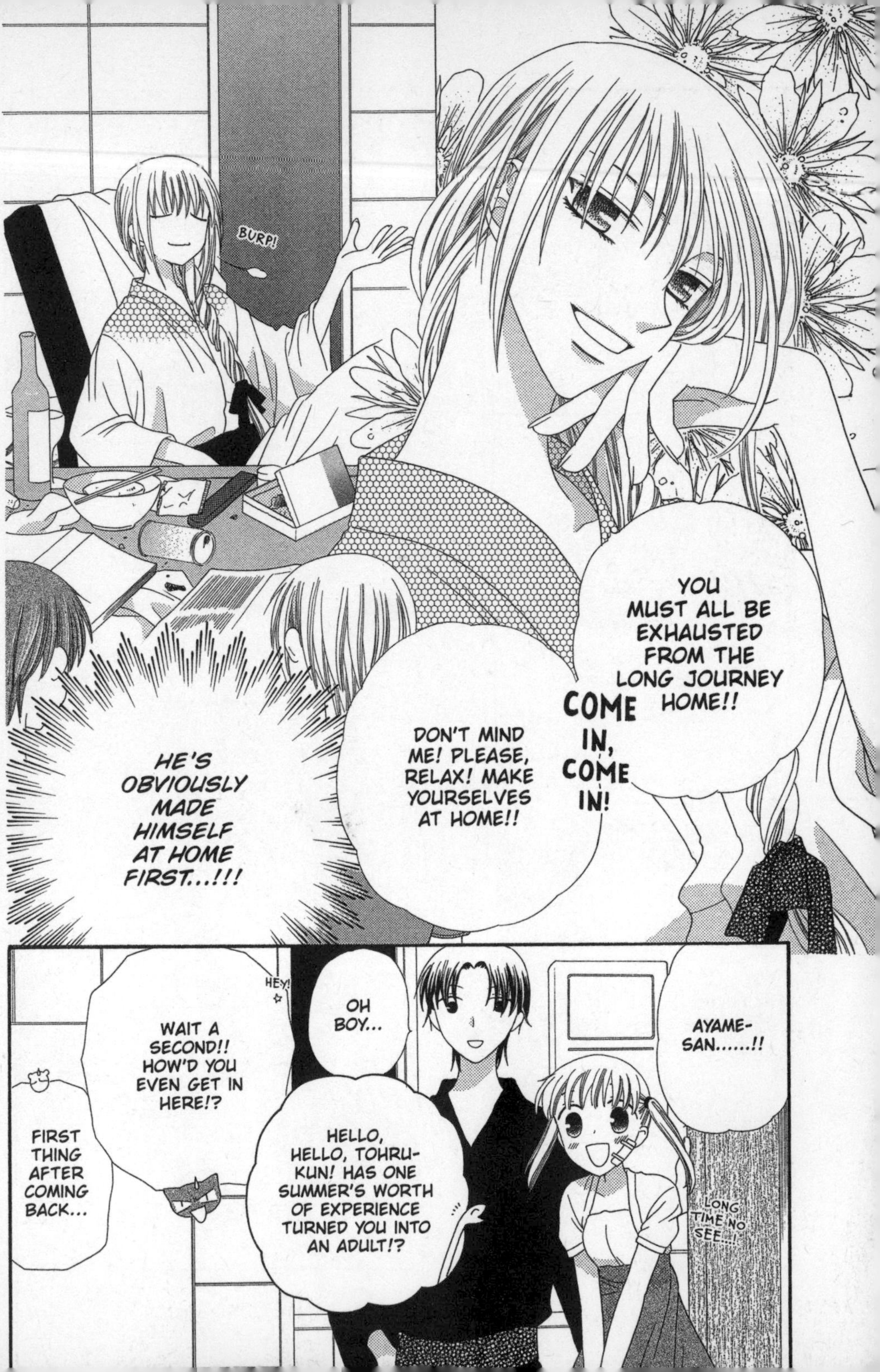
YOU MUST ALL BE EXHAUSTED FROM THE LONG JOURNEY HOME!!
COME IN, COME IN!
DON'T MIND ME! PLEASE, RELAX! MAKE YOURSELVES AT HOME!!
BURP!
HE'S OBVIOUSLY MADE HIMSELF AT HOME FIRST...!!!
AYAME-SAN......!!
LONG TIME NO SEE...
OH BOY...
HELLO, HELLO, TOHRU-KUN! HAS ONE SUMMER'S WORTH OF EXPERIENCE TURNED YOU INTO AN ADULT!?
HEY!
WAIT A SECOND!! HOW'D YOU EVEN GET IN HERE!?
FIRST THING AFTER COMING BACK...

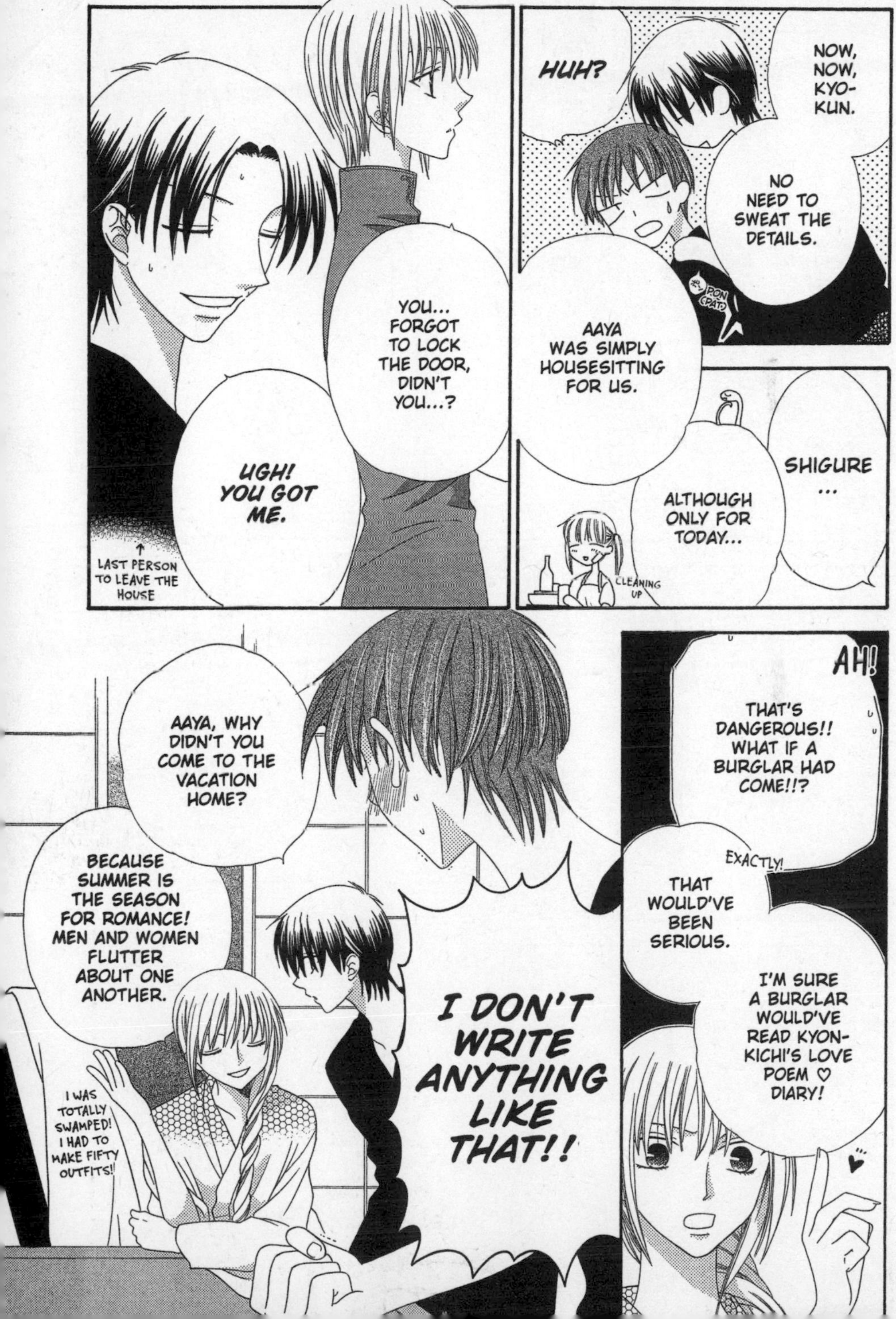
NOW, NOW, KYO-KUN.
NO NEED TO SWEAT THE DETAILS.
HUH?
PON (PAT)
AAYA WAS SIMPLY HOUSESITTING FOR US.
SHIGURE...
ALTHOUGH ONLY FOR TODAY...
CLEANING UP
YOU... FORGOT TO LOCK THE DOOR, DIDN'T YOU...?
UGH! YOU GOT ME.
LAST PERSON TO LEAVE THE HOUSE
AH!
THAT'S DANGEROUS!! WHAT IF A BURGLAR HAD COME!!?
EXACTLY!
THAT WOULD'VE BEEN SERIOUS.
I'M SURE A BURGLAR WOULD'VE READ KYON-KICHI'S LOVE POEM ♡ DIARY!
I DON'T WRITE ANYTHING LIKE THAT!!
AAYA, WHY DIDN'T YOU COME TO THE VACATION HOME?
BECAUSE SUMMER IS THE SEASON FOR ROMANCE! MEN AND WOMEN FLUTTER ABOUT ONE ANOTHER.
I WAS TOTALLY SWAMPED! I HAD TO MAKE FIFTY OUTFITS!

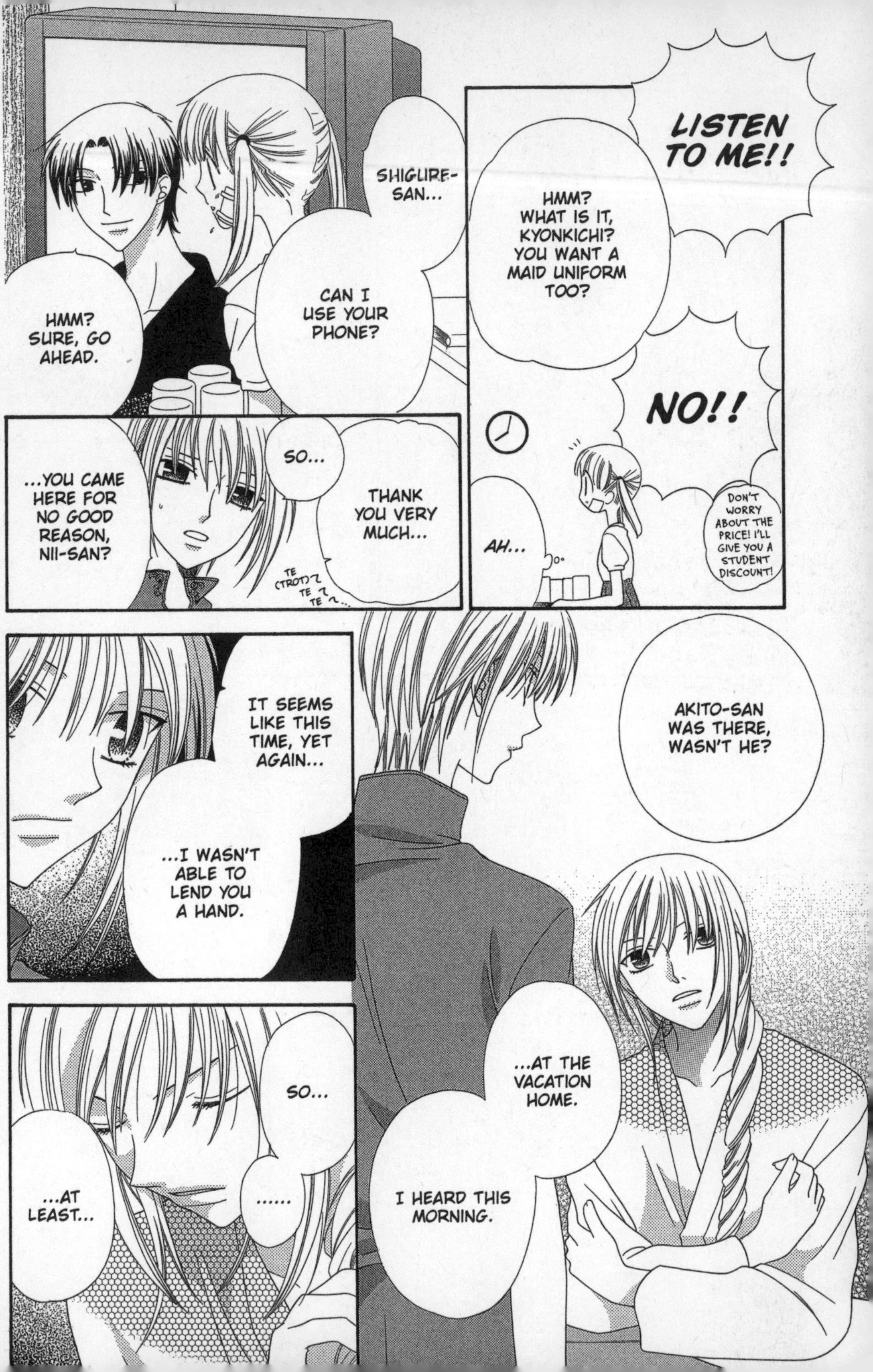
LISTEN TO ME!!
HMM? WHAT IS IT, KYONKICHI? YOU WANT A MAID UNIFORM TOO?
NO!!
DON'T WORRY ABOUT THE PRICE! I'LL GIVE YOU A STUDENT DISCOUNT!
AH...
SHIGURE-SAN...
CAN I USE YOUR PHONE?
HMM? SURE, GO AHEAD.
SO...
THANK YOU VERY MUCH...
TE (TROT) TE TE...
...YOU CAME HERE FOR NO GOOD REASON, NII-SAN?
AKITO-SAN WAS THERE, WASN'T HE?
...AT THE VACATION HOME.
I HEARD THIS MORNING.
IT SEEMS LIKE THIS TIME, YET AGAIN...
...I WASN'T ABLE TO LEND YOU A HAND.
SO...
......
...AT LEAST...

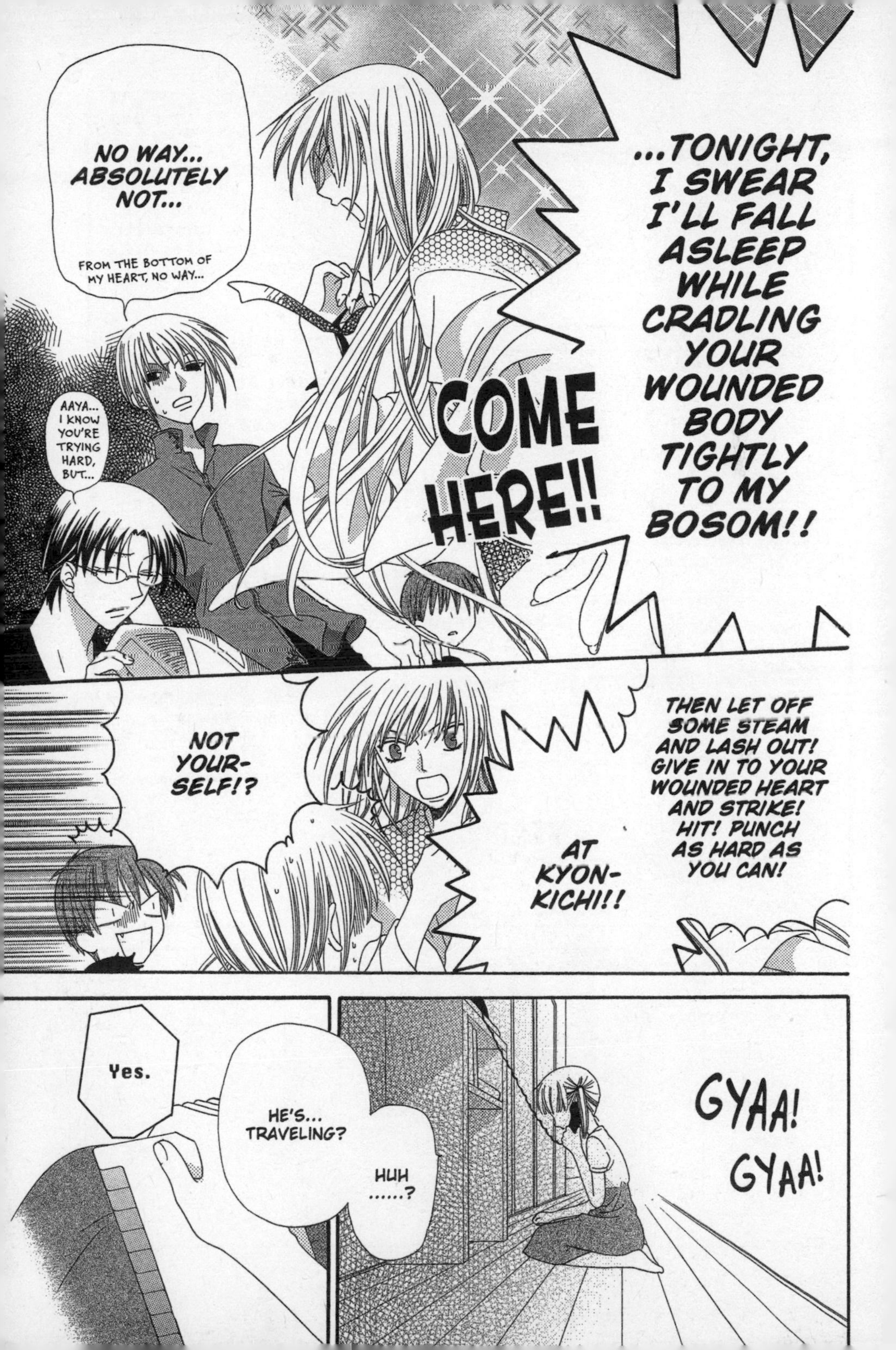
...TONIGHT, I SWEAR I'LL FALL ASLEEP WHILE CRADLING YOUR WOUNDED BODY TIGHTLY TO MY BOSOM!!
COME HERE!!
NO WAY... ABSOLUTELY NOT...
FROM THE BOTTOM OF MY HEART, NO WAY...
AAYA... I KNOW YOU'RE TRYING HARD, BUT...
THEN LET OFF SOME STEAM AND LASH OUT! GIVE IN TO YOUR WOUNDED HEART AND STRIKE! HIT! PUNCH AS HARD AS YOU CAN!
AT KYON-KICHI!!
NOT YOURSELF!?
GYAA!
GYAA!
HUH ......?
HE'S... TRAVELING?
Yes.

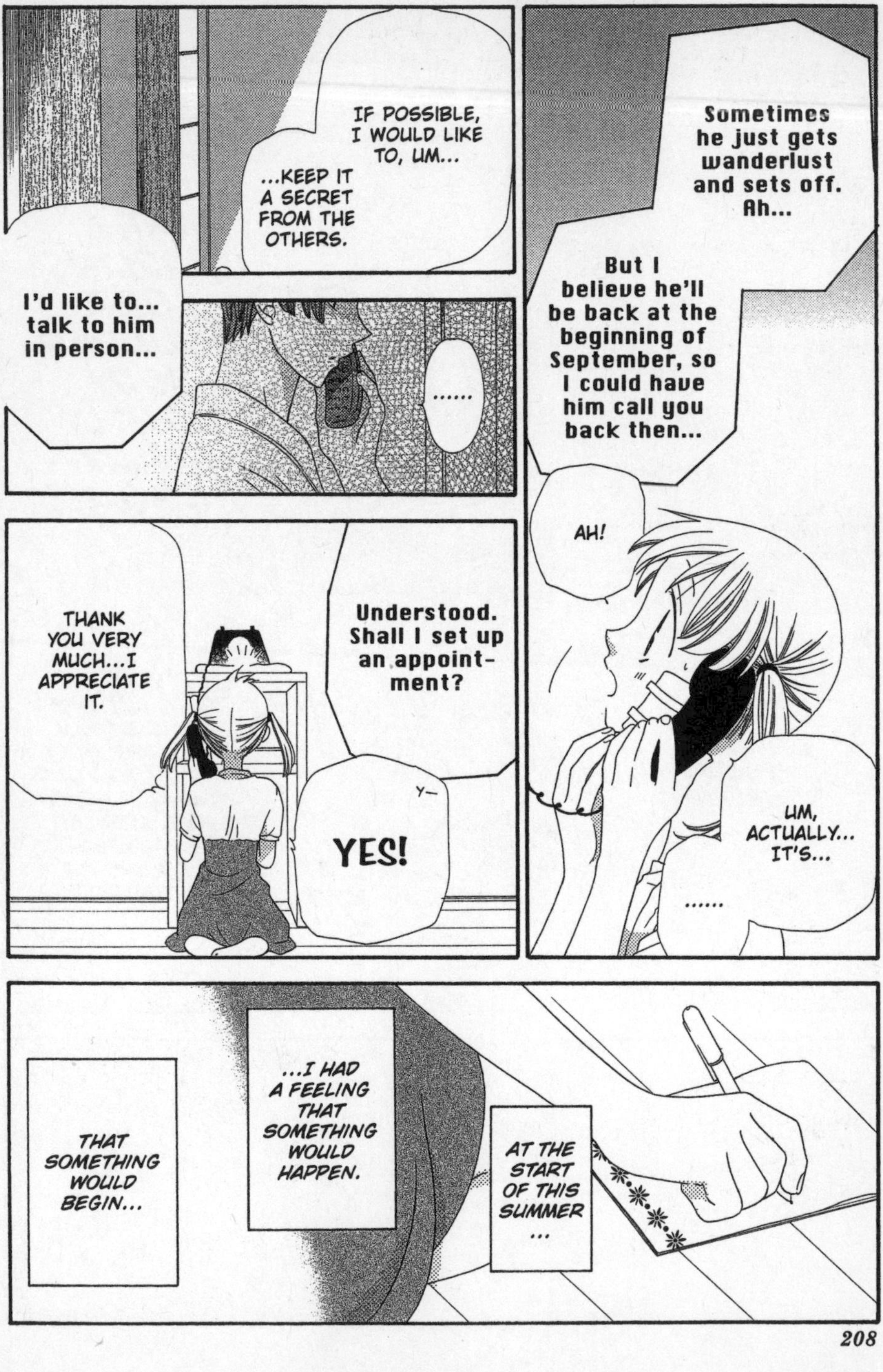

Sometimes he just gets wanderlust and sets off. Ah...
But I believe he'll be back at the beginning of September, so I could have him call you back then...
AH!
UM, ACTUALLY... IT'S...
......
IF POSSIBLE, I WOULD LIKE TO, UM...
...KEEP IT A SECRET FROM THE OTHERS.
I'd like to... talk to him in person...
......
Understood. Shall I set up an appoint-ment?
Y—
YES!
THANK YOU VERY MUCH...I APPRECIATE IT.
AT THE START OF THIS SUMMER...
...I HAD A FEELING THAT SOMETHING WOULD HAPPEN.
THAT SOMETHING WOULD BEGIN...

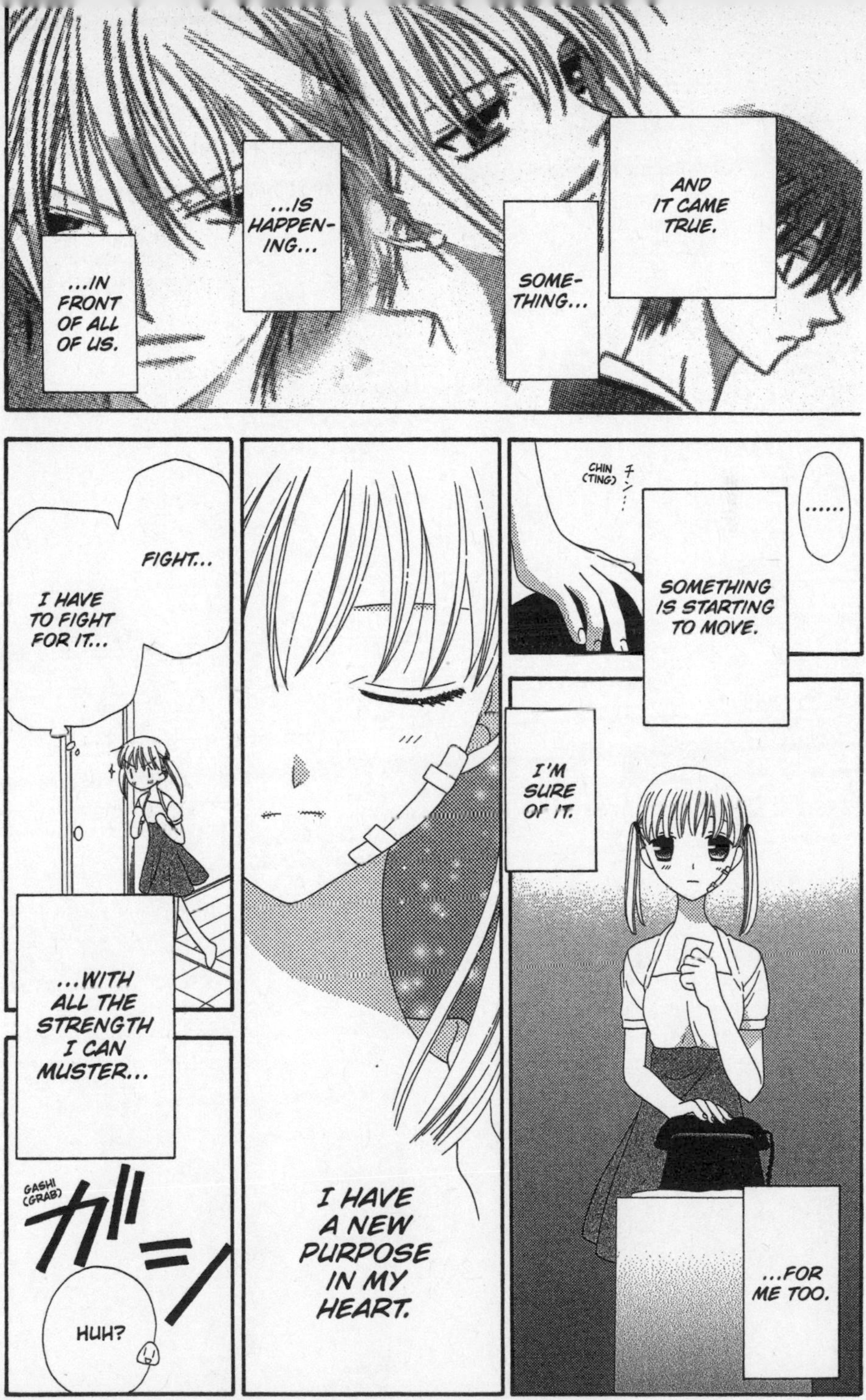
AND IT CAME TRUE.
SOME-THING...
...IS HAPPEN-ING...
...IN FRONT OF ALL OF US.
......
CHIN (TING)
SOMETHING IS STARTING TO MOVE.
I'M SURE OF IT.
...FOR ME TOO.
I HAVE A NEW PURPOSE IN MY HEART.
I HAVE TO FIGHT FOR IT... FIGHT...
...WITH ALL THE STRENGTH I CAN MUSTER...
GASHI (GRAB)
HUH?

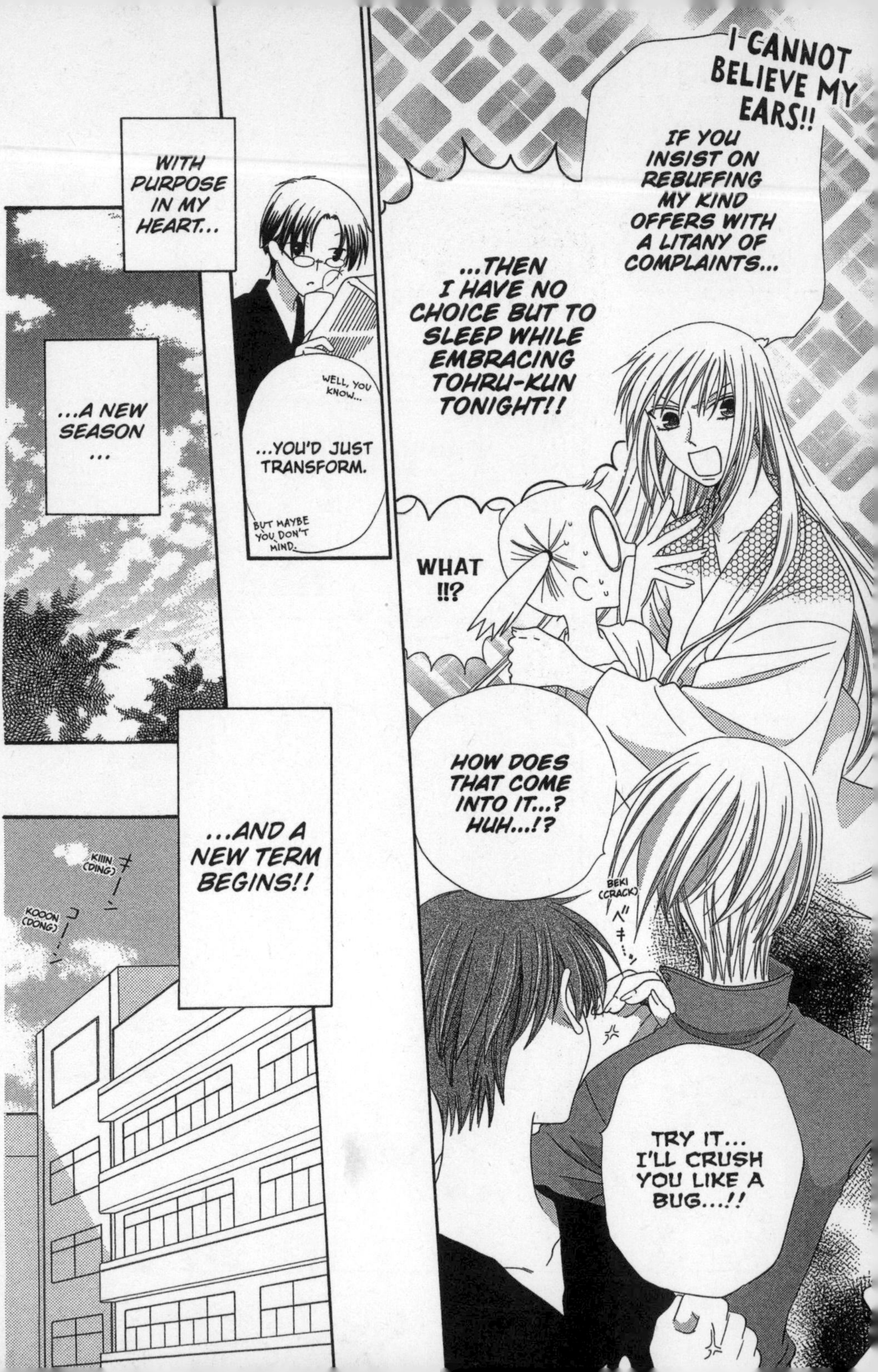
I-CANNOT BELIEVE MY EARS!!
IF YOU INSIST ON REBUFFING MY KIND OFFERS WITH A LITANY OF COMPLAINTS...
...THEN I HAVE NO CHOICE BUT TO SLEEP WHILE EMBRACING TOHRU-KUN TONIGHT!!
WHAT!!?
HOW DOES THAT COME INTO IT...? HUH...!?
BEKI (CRACK)
TRY IT... I'LL CRUSH YOU LIKE A BUG...!!
WITH PURPOSE IN MY HEART...
WELL, YOU KNOW...
...YOU'D JUST TRANSFORM.
BUT MAYBE YOU DON'T MIND.
...A NEW SEASON...
KIIN (DING)
KOOON (DONG)
...AND A NEW TERM BEGINS!!

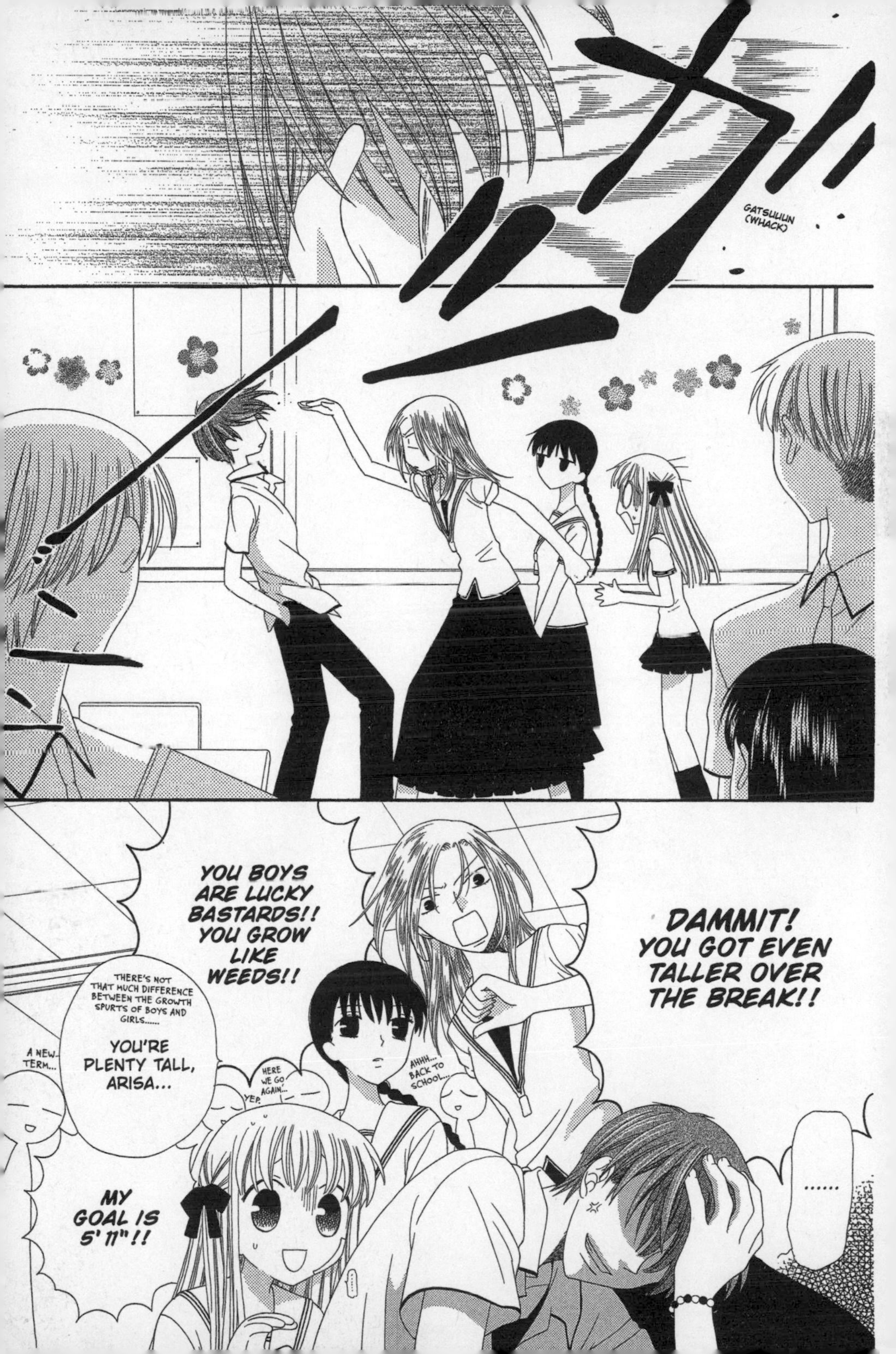
GATSUUUN (WHACK)
DAMMIT! YOU GOT EVEN TALLER OVER THE BREAK!!
YOU BOYS ARE LUCKY BASTARDS!! YOU GROW LIKE WEEDS!!
......
AHHH... BACK TO SCHOOL...
HERE WE GO AGAIN...
YEP.
THERE'S NOT THAT MUCH DIFFERENCE BETWEEN THE GROWTH SPURTS OF BOYS AND GIRLS......
YOU'RE PLENTY TALL, ARISA...
A NEW TERM...
MY GOAL IS 5' 11"!!

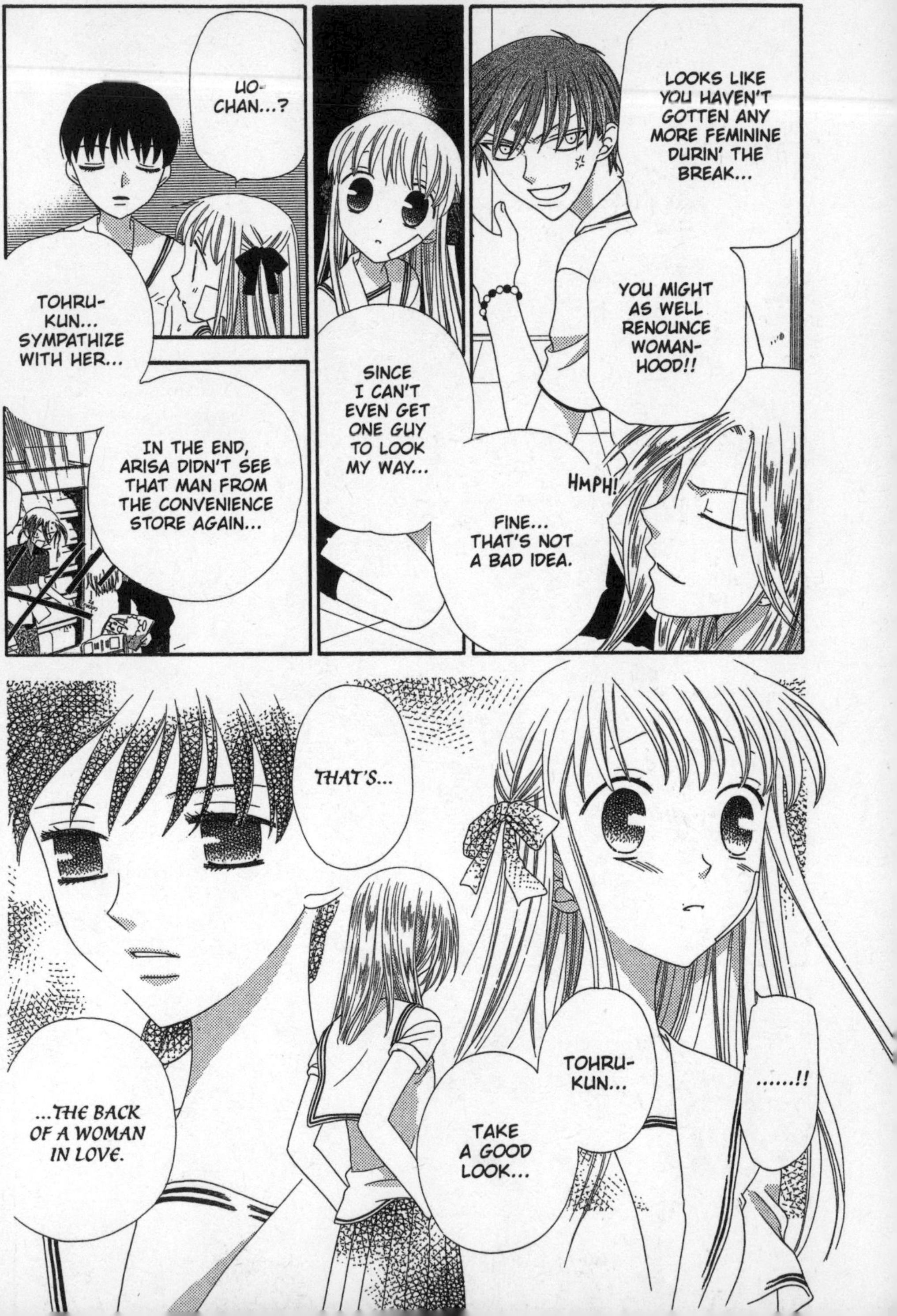
LOOKS LIKE YOU HAVEN'T GOTTEN ANY MORE FEMININE DURIN' THE BREAK...
YOU MIGHT AS WELL RENOUNCE WOMAN-HOOD!!
HMPH!
FINE... THAT'S NOT A BAD IDEA.
SINCE I CAN'T EVEN GET ONE GUY TO LOOK MY WAY...
UO-CHAN...?
TOHRU-KUN... SYMPATHIZE WITH HER...
IN THE END, ARISA DIDN'T SEE THAT MAN FROM THE CONVENIENCE STORE AGAIN...
THAT'S...
......!!
TOHRU-KUN...
TAKE A GOOD LOOK...
...THE BACK OF A WOMAN IN LOVE.

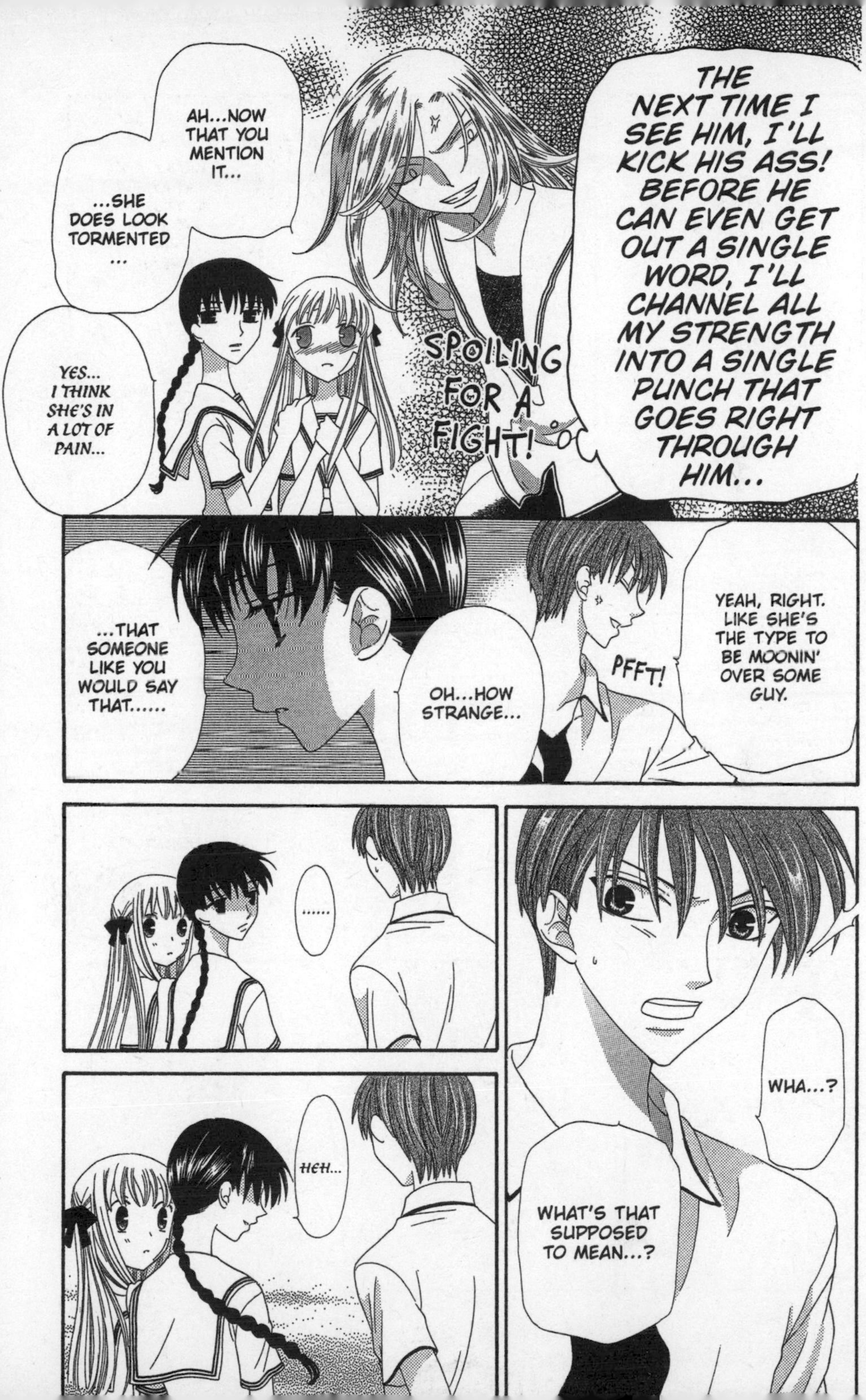
THE NEXT TIME I SEE HIM, I'LL KICK HIS ASS! BEFORE HE CAN EVEN GET OUT A SINGLE WORD, I'LL CHANNEL ALL MY STRENGTH INTO A SINGLE PUNCH THAT GOES RIGHT THROUGH HIM...
SPOILING FOR A FIGHT!
AH...NOW THAT YOU MENTION IT...
...SHE DOES LOOK TORMENTED...
YES... I THINK SHE'S IN A LOT OF PAIN...
YEAH, RIGHT. LIKE SHE'S THE TYPE TO BE MOONIN' OVER SOME GUY.
PFFT!
OH...HOW STRANGE...
...THAT SOMEONE LIKE YOU WOULD SAY THAT......
WHA...?
WHAT'S THAT SUPPOSED TO MEAN...?
......
HEH...

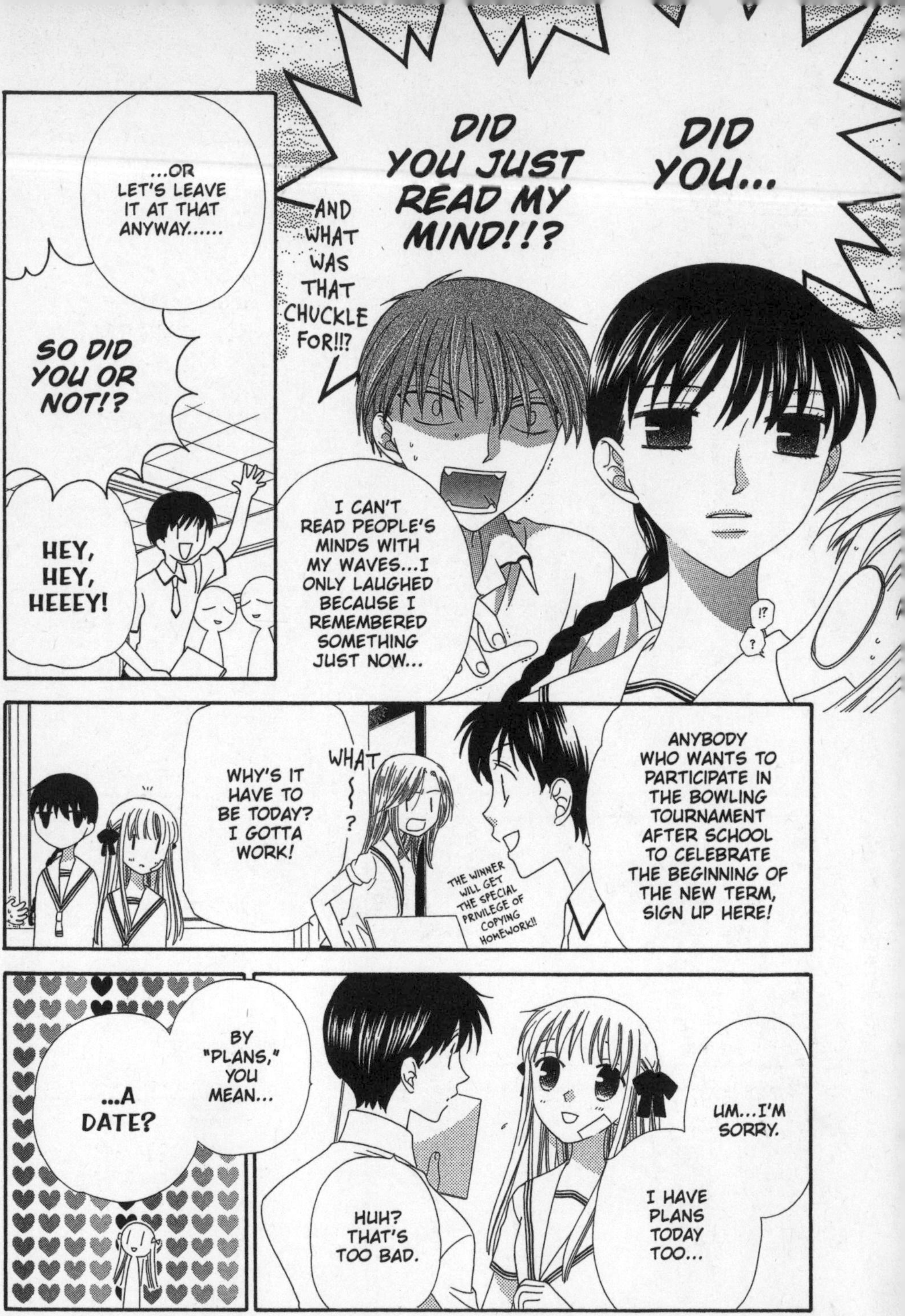
DID YOU...
DID YOU JUST READ MY MIND!!?
AND WHAT WAS THAT CHUCKLE FOR!!?
I CAN'T READ PEOPLE'S MINDS WITH MY WAVES...I ONLY LAUGHED BECAUSE I REMEMBERED SOMETHING JUST NOW...
!?
?
...OR LET'S LEAVE IT AT THAT ANYWAY......
SO DID YOU OR NOT!?
HEY, HEY, HEEEY!
ANYBODY WHO WANTS TO PARTICIPATE IN THE BOWLING TOURNAMENT AFTER SCHOOL TO CELEBRATE THE BEGINNING OF THE NEW TERM, SIGN UP HERE!
THE WINNER WILL GET THE SPECIAL PRIVILEGE OF COPYING HOMEWORK!!
WHAT ~ ?
WHY'S IT HAVE TO BE TODAY? I GOTTA WORK!
UM...I'M SORRY.
I HAVE PLANS TODAY TOO...
HUH? THAT'S TOO BAD.
BY "PLANS," YOU MEAN...
...A DATE?

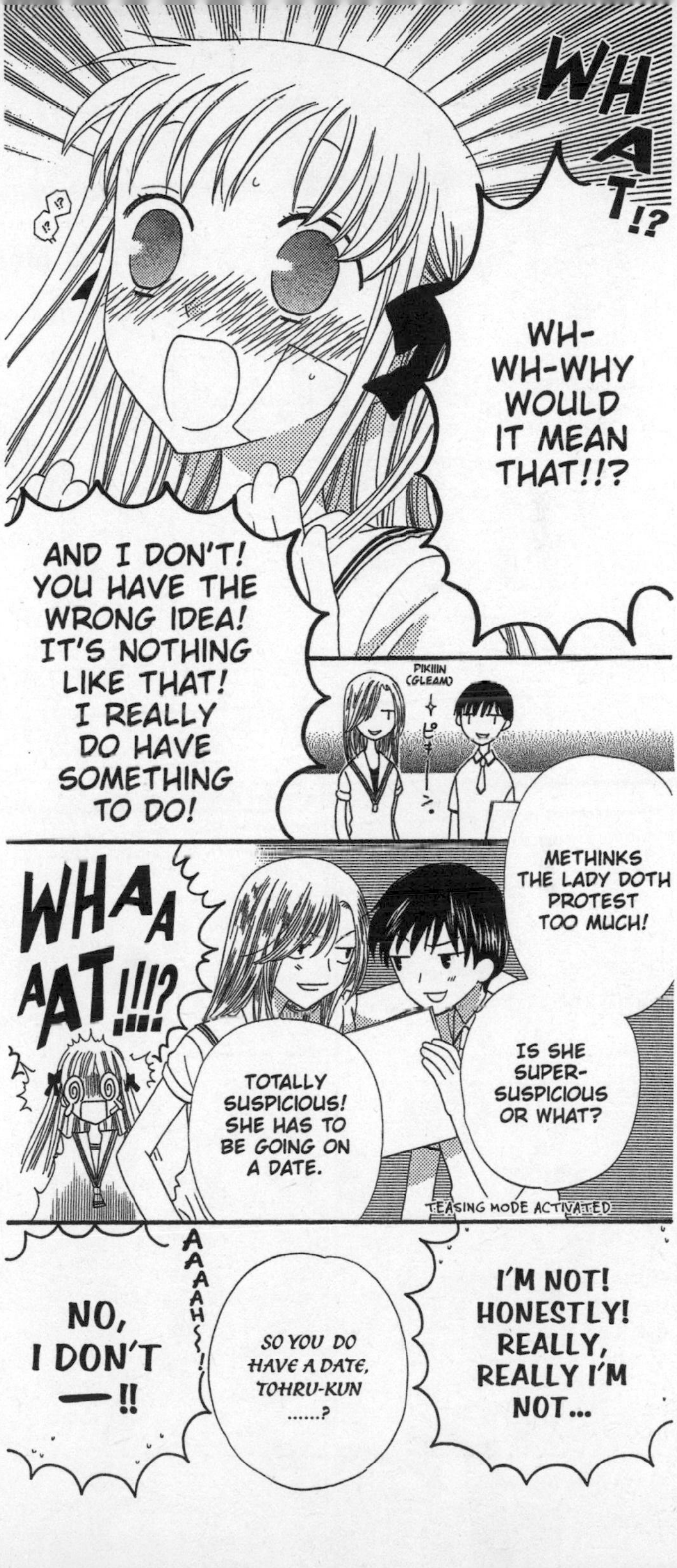
WHAT!?
!? !? !?
WH-WH-WHY WOULD IT MEAN THAT!!?
AND I DON'T! YOU HAVE THE WRONG IDEA! IT'S NOTHING LIKE THAT! I REALLY DO HAVE SOMETHING TO DO!
PIKIIIN (GLEAM)
METHINKS THE LADY DOTH PROTEST TOO MUCH!
IS SHE SUPER-SUSPICIOUS OR WHAT?
TOTALLY SUSPICIOUS! SHE HAS TO BE GOING ON A DATE.
WHAAAAT!!!?
TEASING MODE ACTIVATED
I'M NOT! HONESTLY! REALLY, REALLY I'M NOT...
SO YOU DO HAVE A DATE, TOHRU-KUN ......?
AAAAAH~!
NO, I DON'T—!!
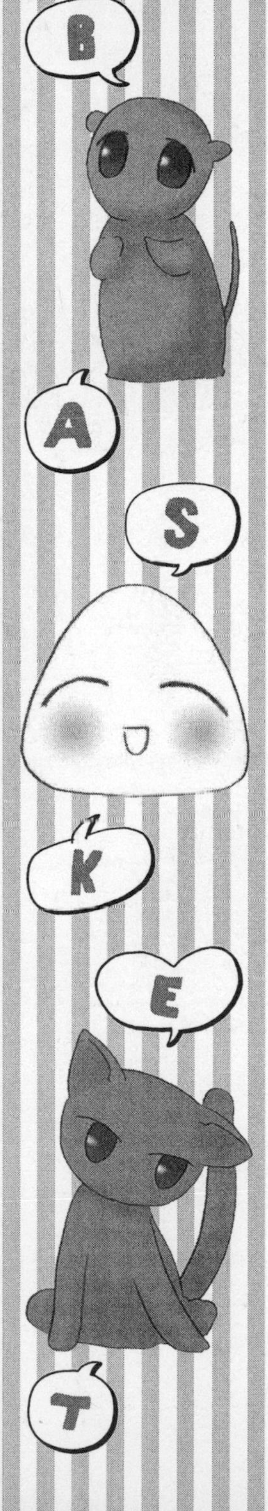
B
A
S
K
E
T

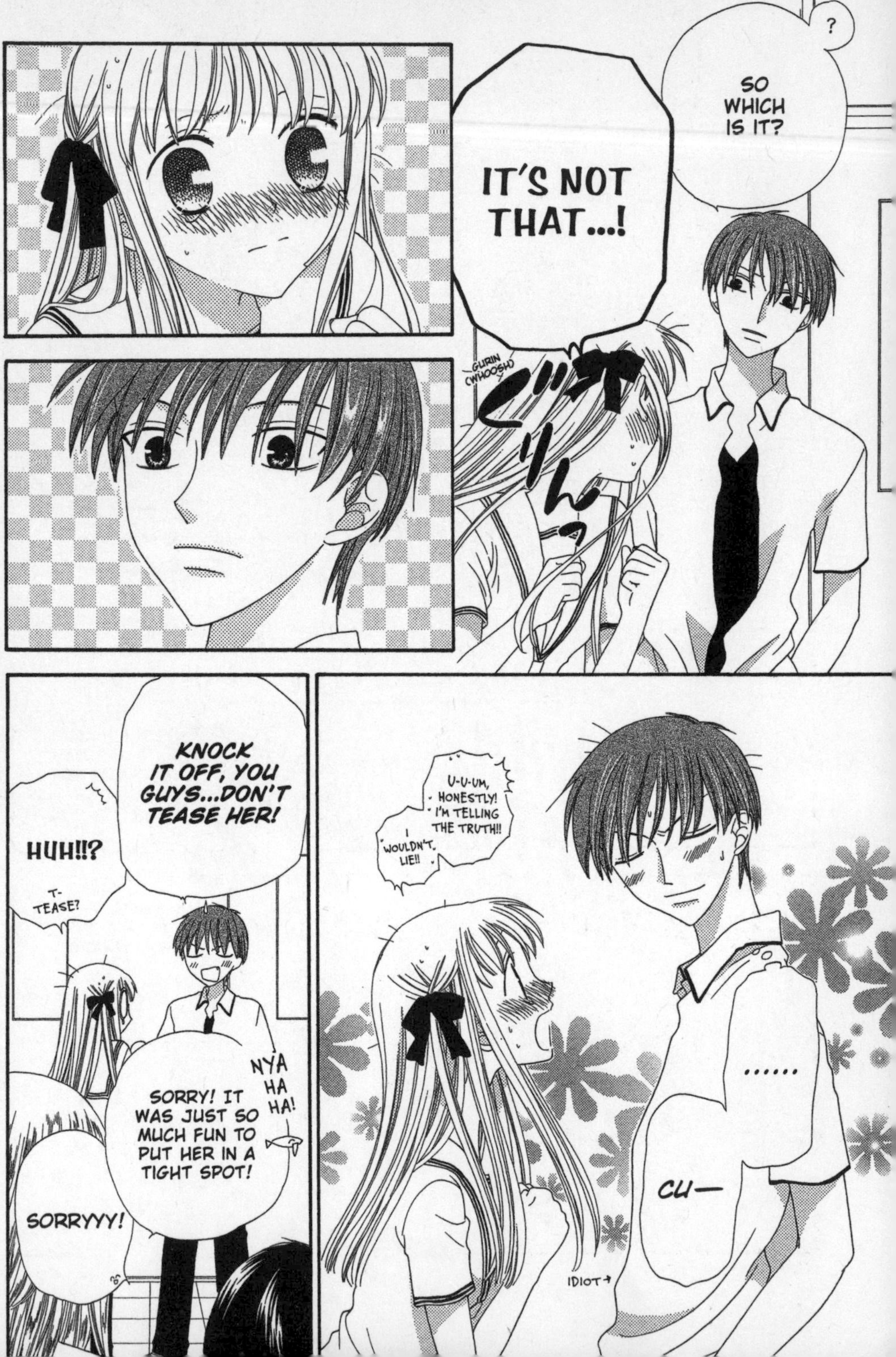
?
SO WHICH IS IT?
IT'S NOT THAT...!
GURIN (WHOOSH)
U-U-UM, HONESTLY! I'M TELLING THE TRUTH!!
I WOULDN'T LIE!!
......
CU—
IDIOT→
KNOCK IT OFF, YOU GUYS...DON'T TEASE HER!
HUH!!?
T-TEASE?
NYA HA HA!
SORRY! IT WAS JUST SO MUCH FUN TO PUT HER IN A TIGHT SPOT!
SORRYYY!

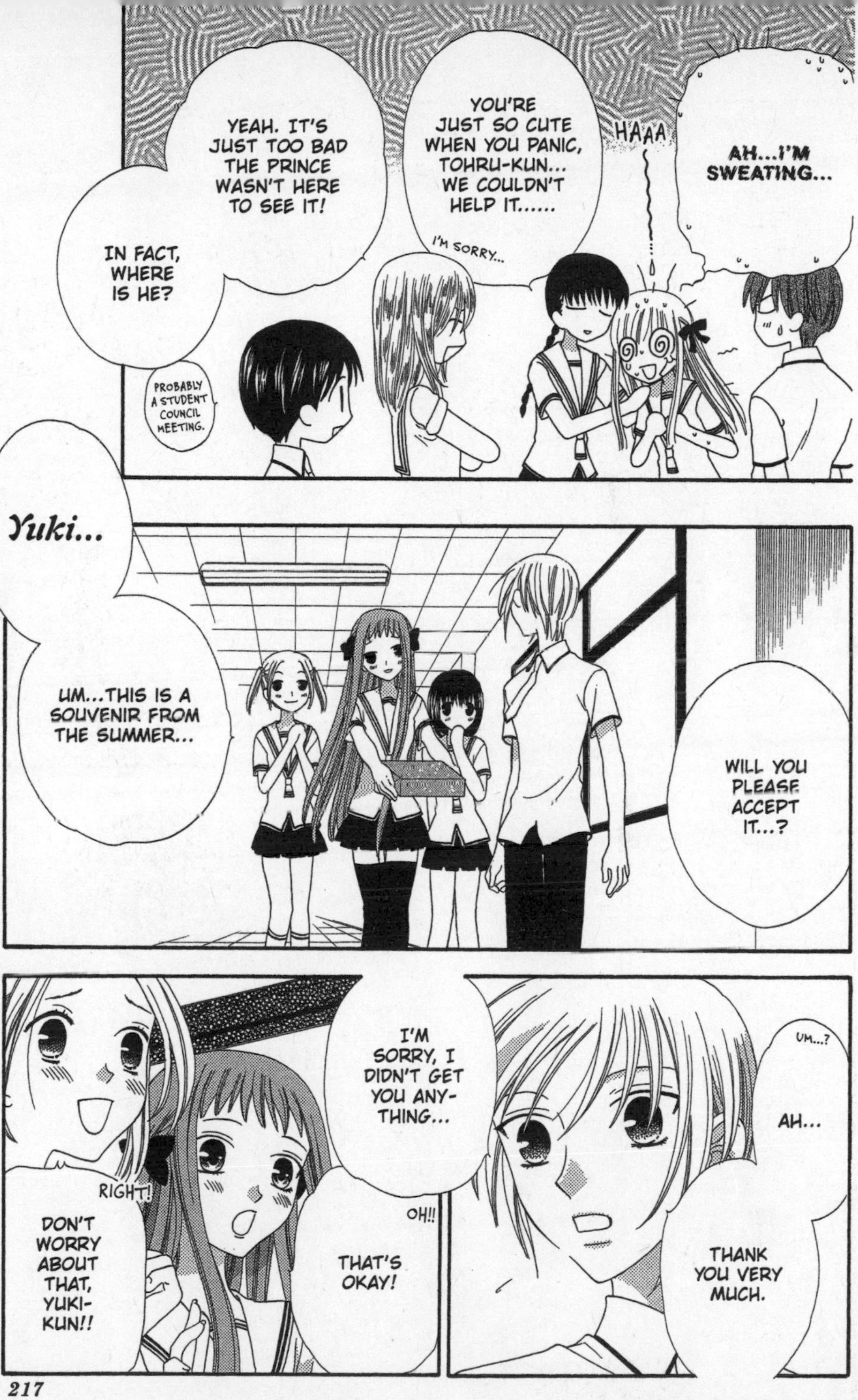
AH...I'M SWEATING...
HAAA
YOU'RE JUST SO CUTE WHEN YOU PANIC, TOHRU-KUN... WE COULDN'T HELP IT......
I'M SORRY...
YEAH. IT'S JUST TOO BAD THE PRINCE WASN'T HERE TO SEE IT!
IN FACT, WHERE IS HE?
PROBABLY A STUDENT COUNCIL MEETING.
Yuki...
UM...THIS IS A SOUVENIR FROM THE SUMMER...
WILL YOU PLEASE ACCEPT IT...?
UM...?
AH...
THANK YOU VERY MUCH.
I'M SORRY, I DIDN'T GET YOU ANY-THING...
OH!!
THAT'S OKAY!
RIGHT!
DON'T WORRY ABOUT THAT, YUKI-KUN!!

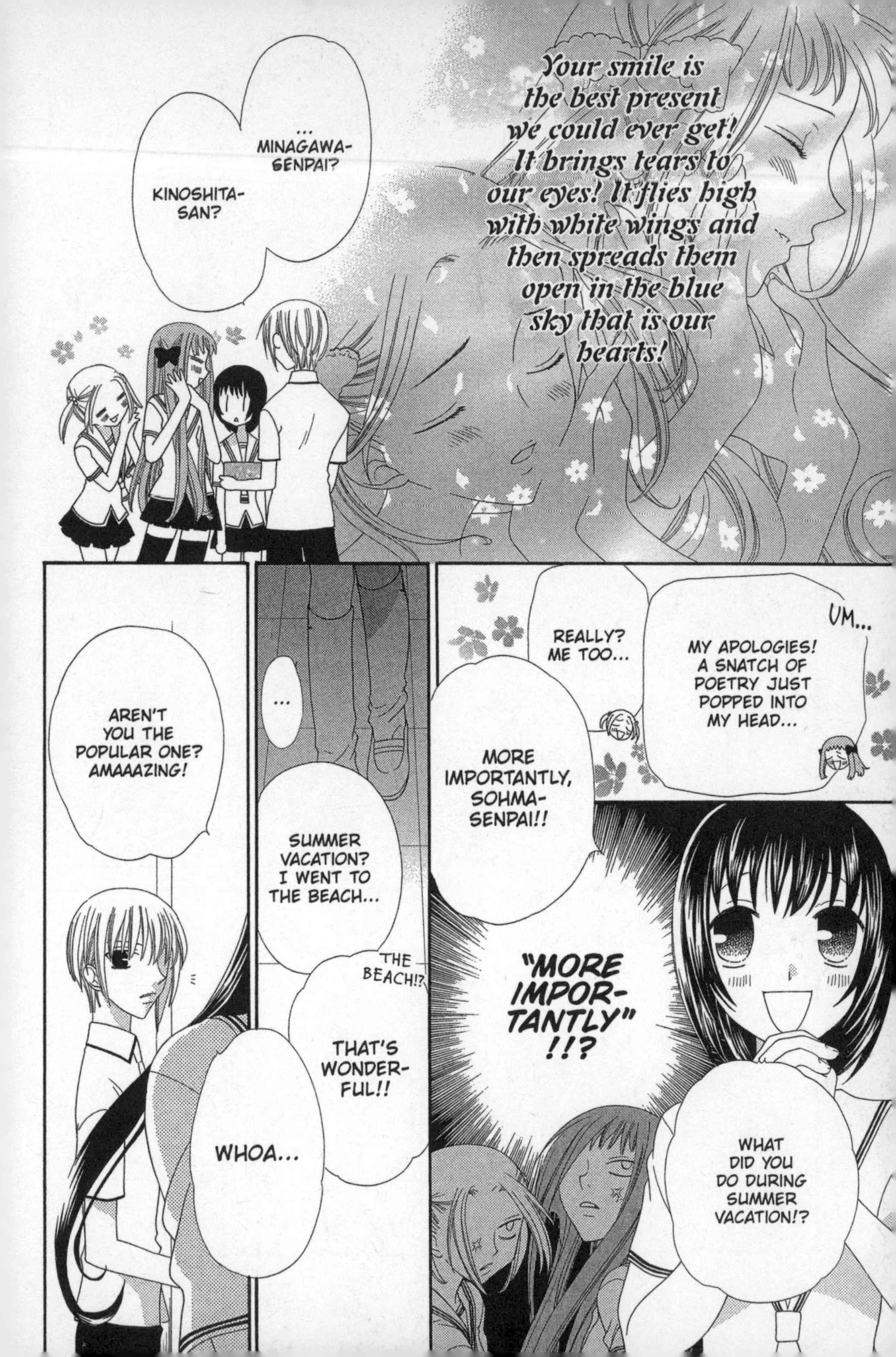
Your smile is the best present we could ever get! It brings tears to our eyes! It flies high with white wings and then spreads them open in the blue sky that is our hearts!
... MINAGAWA-SENPAI?
KINOSHITA-SAN?
UM...
MY APOLOGIES! A SNATCH OF POETRY JUST POPPED INTO MY HEAD...
REALLY? ME TOO...
MORE IMPORTANTLY, SOHMA-SENPAI!!
"MORE IMPOR-TANTLY" !!?
WHAT DID YOU DO DURING SUMMER VACATION!?
...
SUMMER VACATION? I WENT TO THE BEACH...
THE BEACH!?
THAT'S WONDER-FUL!!
WHOA...
AREN'T YOU THE POPULAR ONE? AMAAAZING!

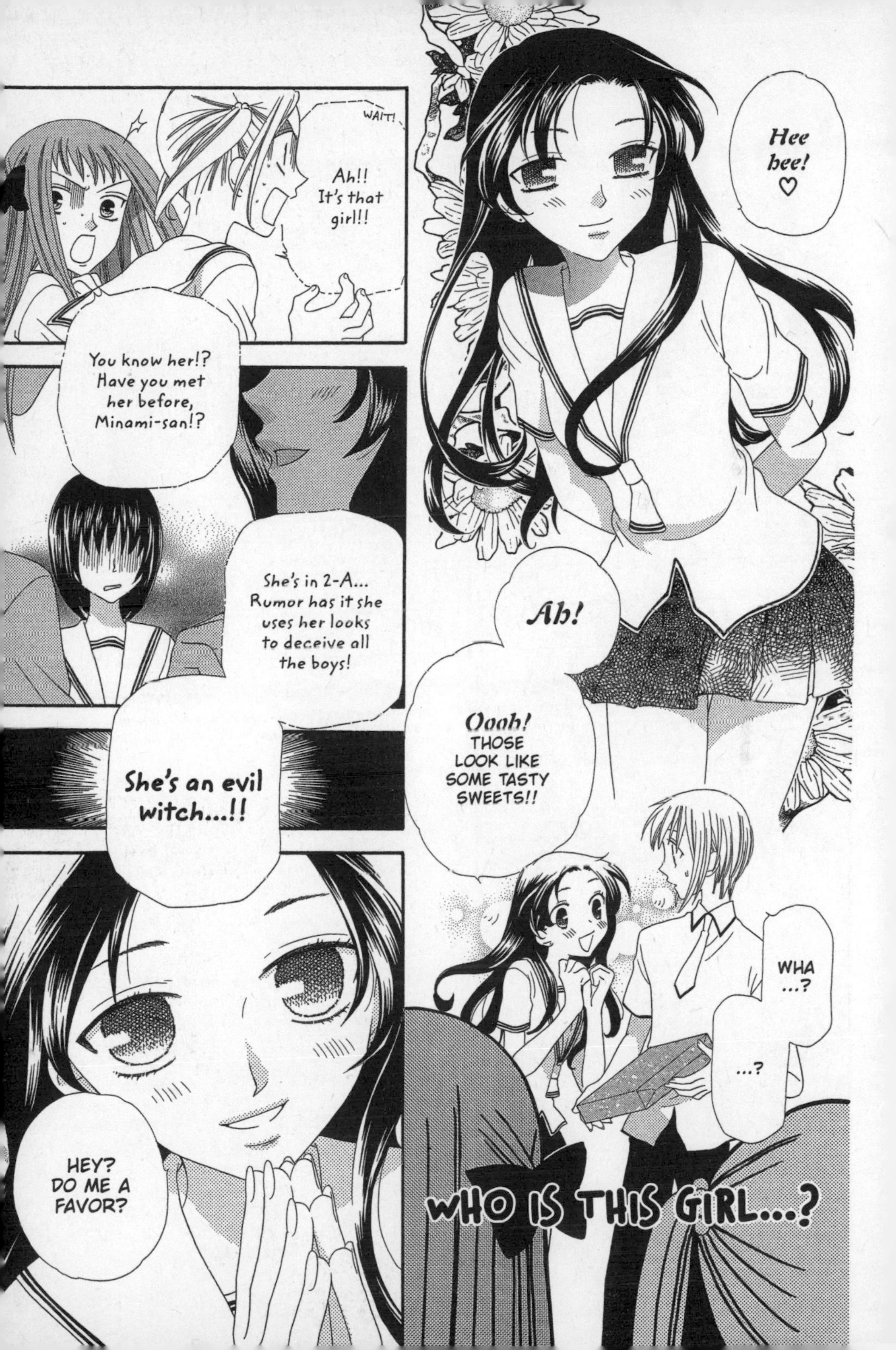
Hee hee! ♡
Ah!
Oooh! THOSE LOOK LIKE SOME TASTY SWEETS!!
WHA ...?
...?
WHO IS THIS GIRL...?
WAIT!
Ah!! It's that girl!!
You know her!? Have you met her before, Minami-san!?
She's in 2-A... Rumor has it she uses her looks to deceive all the boys!
She's an evil witch...!!
HEY? DO ME A FAVOR?

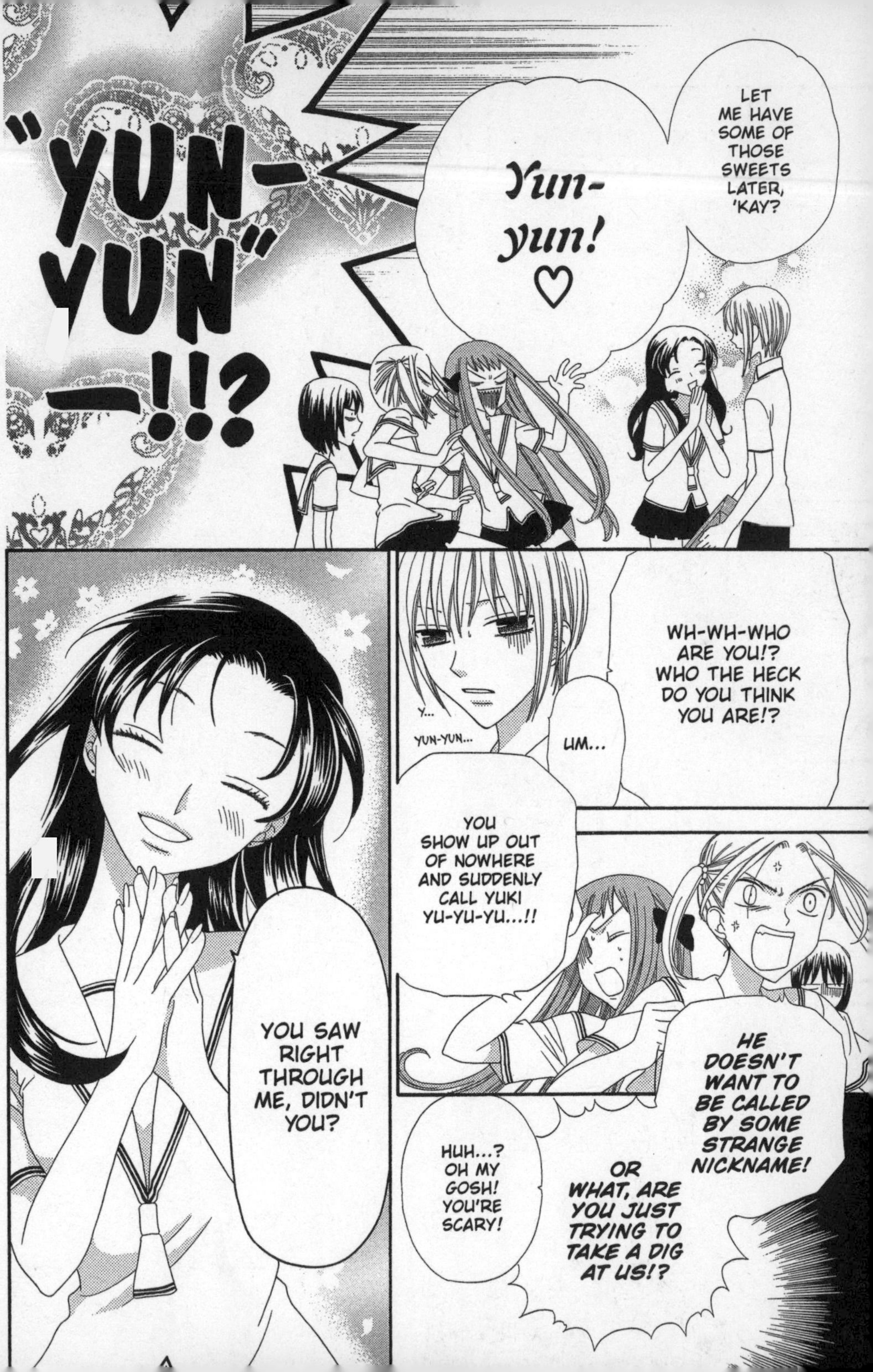
LET ME HAVE SOME OF THOSE SWEETS LATER, 'KAY?
Yun-yun! ♡
"YUN-YUN"—!!?
WH-WH-WHO ARE YOU!? WHO THE HECK DO YOU THINK YOU ARE!?
UM...
Y... YUN-YUN...
YOU SHOW UP OUT OF NOWHERE AND SUDDENLY CALL YUKI YU-YU-YU...!!
HE DOESN'T WANT TO BE CALLED BY SOME STRANGE NICKNAME!
OR WHAT, ARE YOU JUST TRYING TO TAKE A DIG AT US!?
HUH...? OH MY GOSH! YOU'RE SCARY!
YOU SAW RIGHT THROUGH ME, DIDN'T YOU?

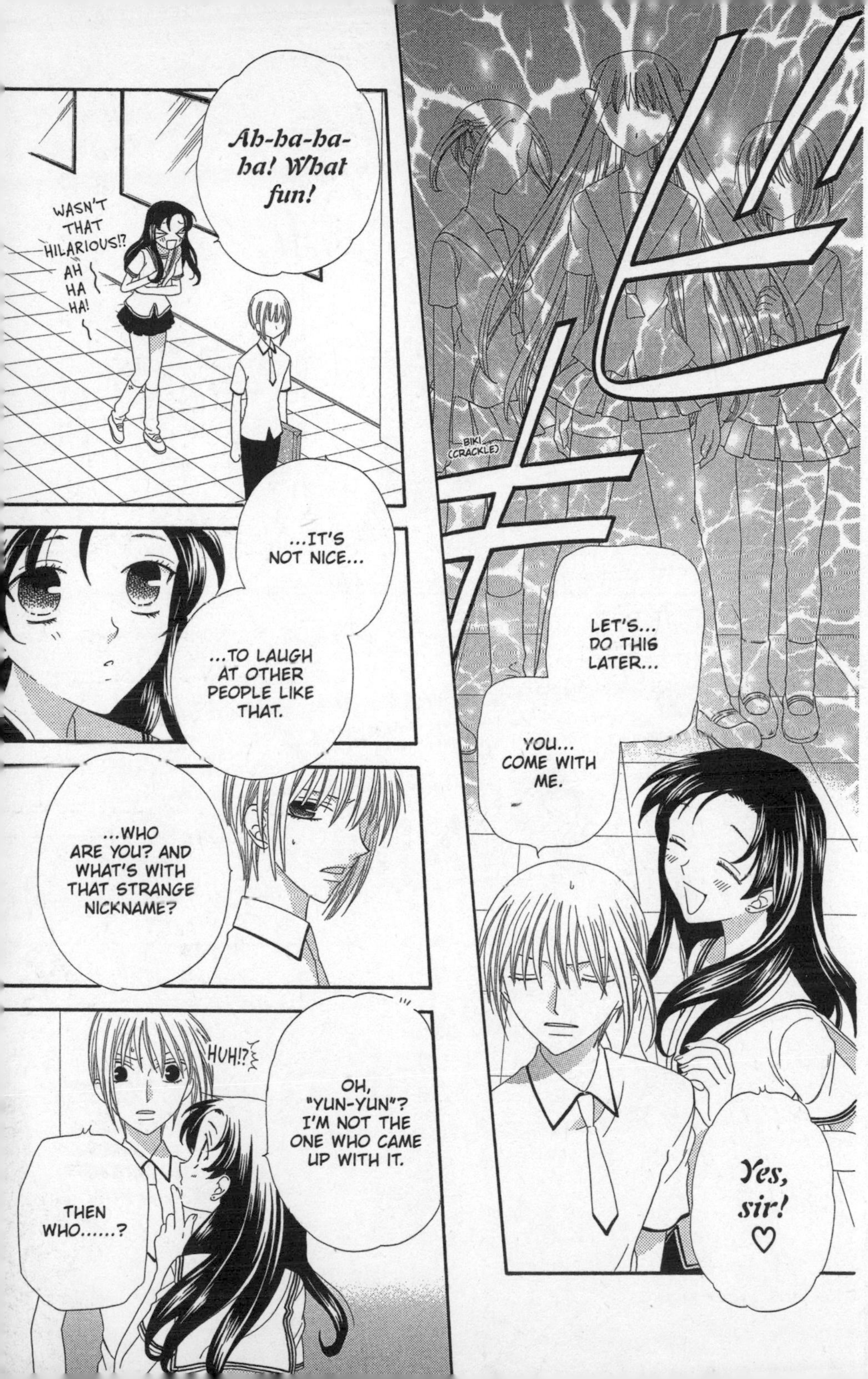
BIKI (CRACKLE)
LET'S... DO THIS LATER...
YOU... COME WITH ME.
Yes, sir! ♡
Ah-ha-ha-ha! What fun!
WASN'T THAT HILARIOUS!?
AH HA HA!
...IT'S NOT NICE...
...TO LAUGH AT OTHER PEOPLE LIKE THAT.
...WHO ARE YOU? AND WHAT'S WITH THAT STRANGE NICKNAME?
OH, "YUN-YUN"? I'M NOT THE ONE WHO CAME UP WITH IT.
HUH!?
THEN WHO......?

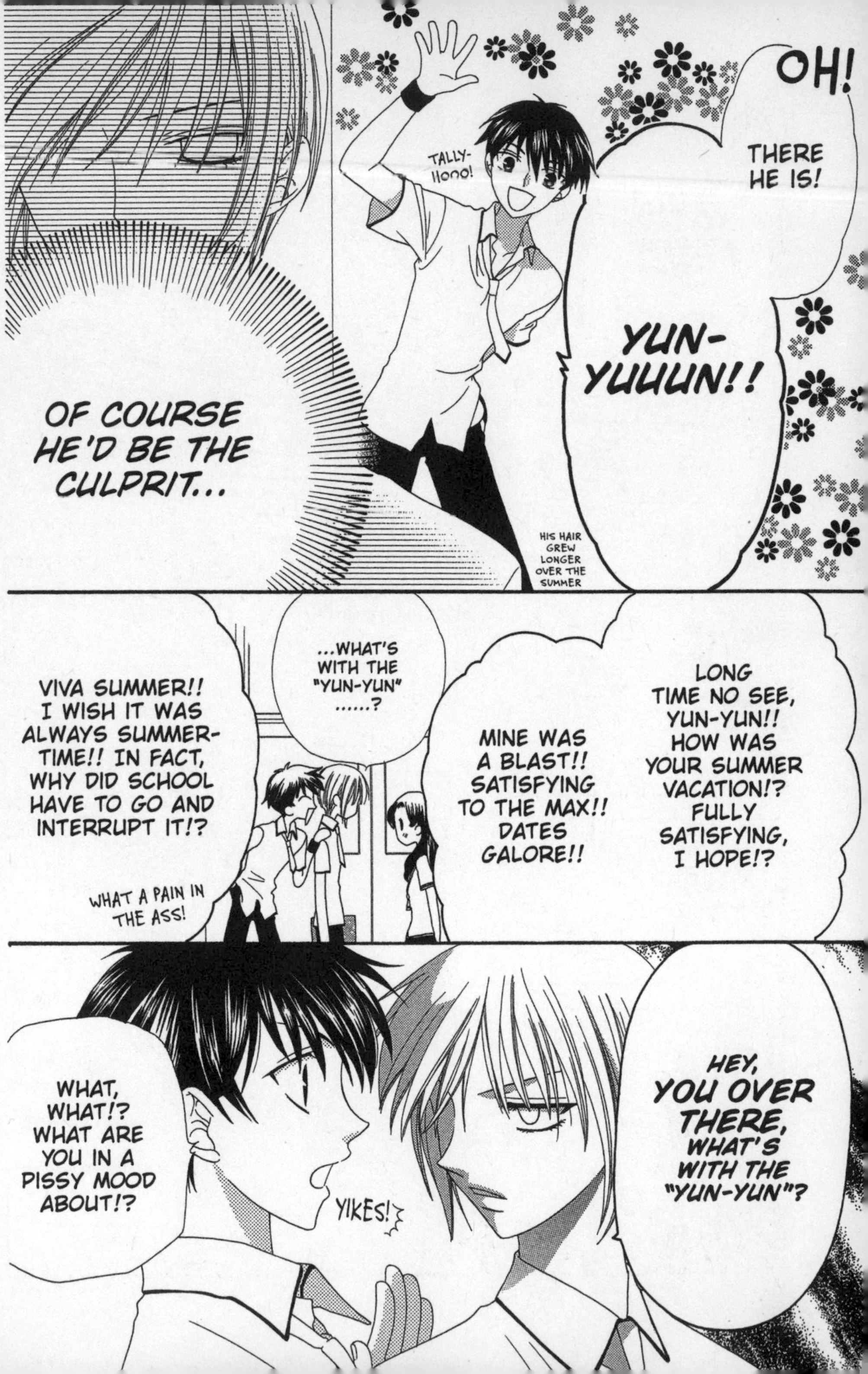
OH!
THERE HE IS!
YUN-YUUUN!!
TALLY-HOOO!
HIS HAIR GREW LONGER OVER THE SUMMER
OF COURSE HE'D BE THE CULPRIT...
LONG TIME NO SEE, YUN-YUN!! HOW WAS YOUR SUMMER VACATION!? FULLY SATISFYING, I HOPE!?
MINE WAS A BLAST!! SATISFYING TO THE MAX!! DATES GALORE!!
...WHAT'S WITH THE "YUN-YUN" ......?
VIVA SUMMER!! I WISH IT WAS ALWAYS SUMMER-TIME!! IN FACT, WHY DID SCHOOL HAVE TO GO AND INTERRUPT IT!?
WHAT A PAIN IN THE ASS!
HEY, YOU OVER THERE, WHAT'S WITH THE "YUN-YUN"?
YIKES!
WHAT, WHAT!? WHAT ARE YOU IN A PISSY MOOD ABOUT!?

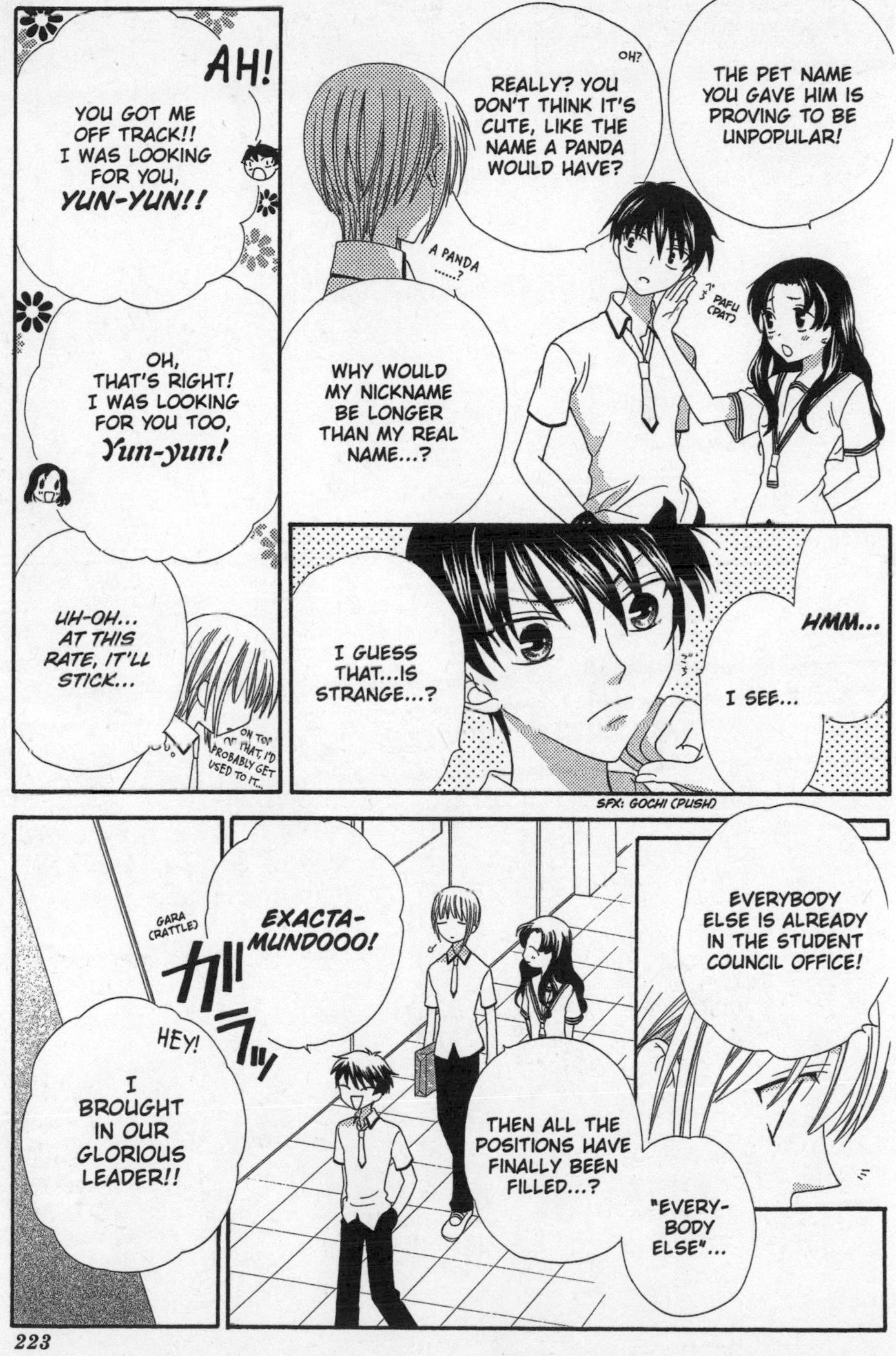

THE PET NAME YOU GAVE HIM IS PROVING TO BE UNPOPULAR!
OH?
REALLY? YOU DON'T THINK IT'S CUTE, LIKE THE NAME A PANDA WOULD HAVE?
PAFU (PAT)
A PANDA ......?
WHY WOULD MY NICKNAME BE LONGER THAN MY REAL NAME...?
HMM...
I SEE...
I GUESS THAT...IS STRANGE...?
SFX: GOCHI (PUSH)
AH!
YOU GOT ME OFF TRACK!! I WAS LOOKING FOR YOU, YUN-YUN!!
OH, THAT'S RIGHT! I WAS LOOKING FOR YOU TOO, Yun-yun!
UH-OH... AT THIS RATE, IT'LL STICK...
ON TOP OF THAT, I'D PROBABLY GET USED TO IT...
EVERYBODY ELSE IS ALREADY IN THE STUDENT COUNCIL OFFICE!
"EVERY-BODY ELSE"...
THEN ALL THE POSITIONS HAVE FINALLY BEEN FILLED...?
EXACTA-MUNDOOO!
GARA (RATTLE)
ガラッ
HEY!
I BROUGHT IN OUR GLORIOUS LEADER!!

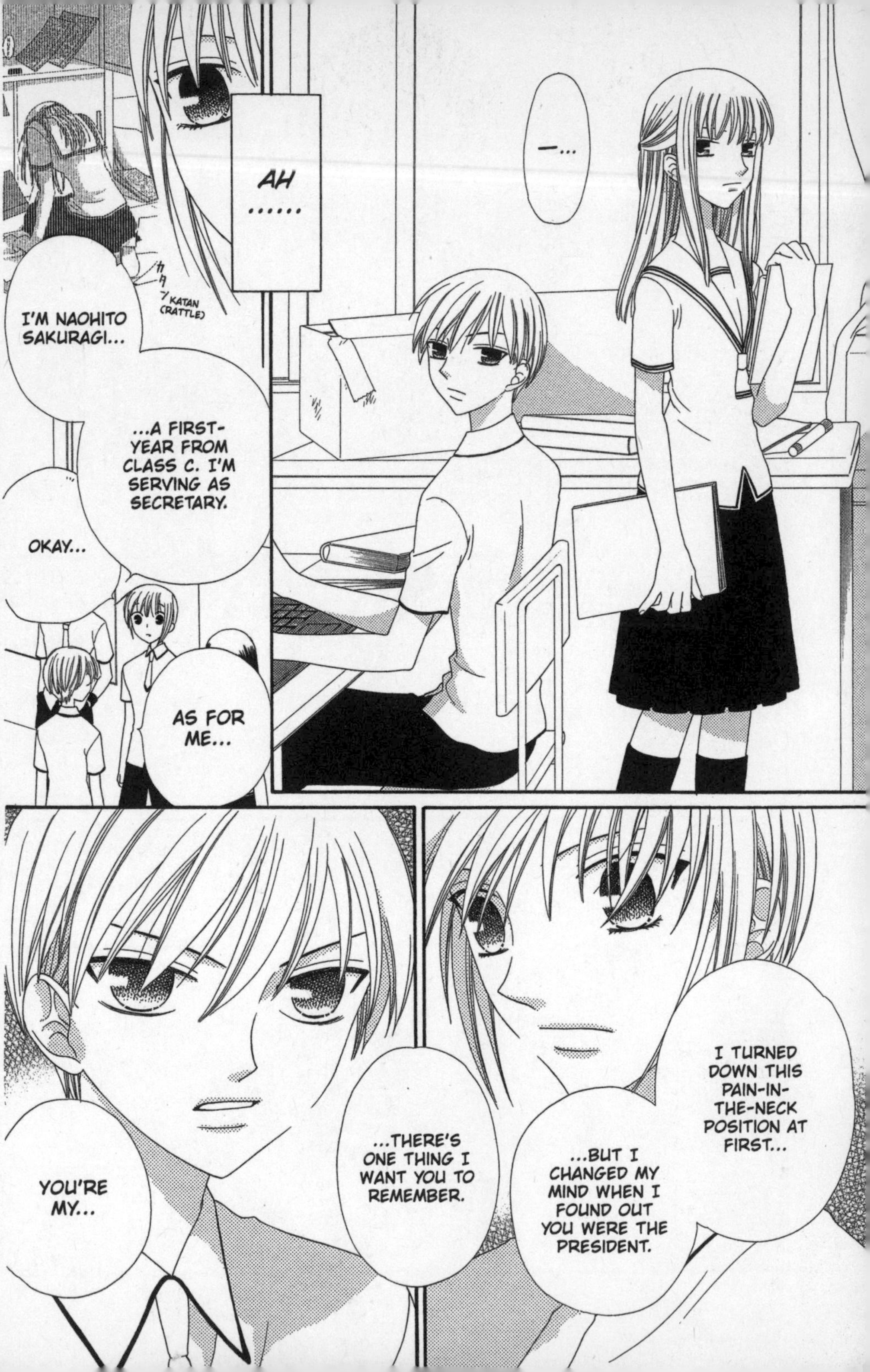
—...
AH ......
カタ
KATAN (RATTLE)
I'M NAOHITO SAKURAGI...
...A FIRST-YEAR FROM CLASS C. I'M SERVING AS SECRETARY.
OKAY...
AS FOR ME...
I TURNED DOWN THIS PAIN-IN-THE-NECK POSITION AT FIRST...
...BUT I CHANGED MY MIND WHEN I FOUND OUT YOU WERE THE PRESIDENT.
...THERE'S ONE THING I WANT YOU TO REMEMBER.
YOU'RE MY...

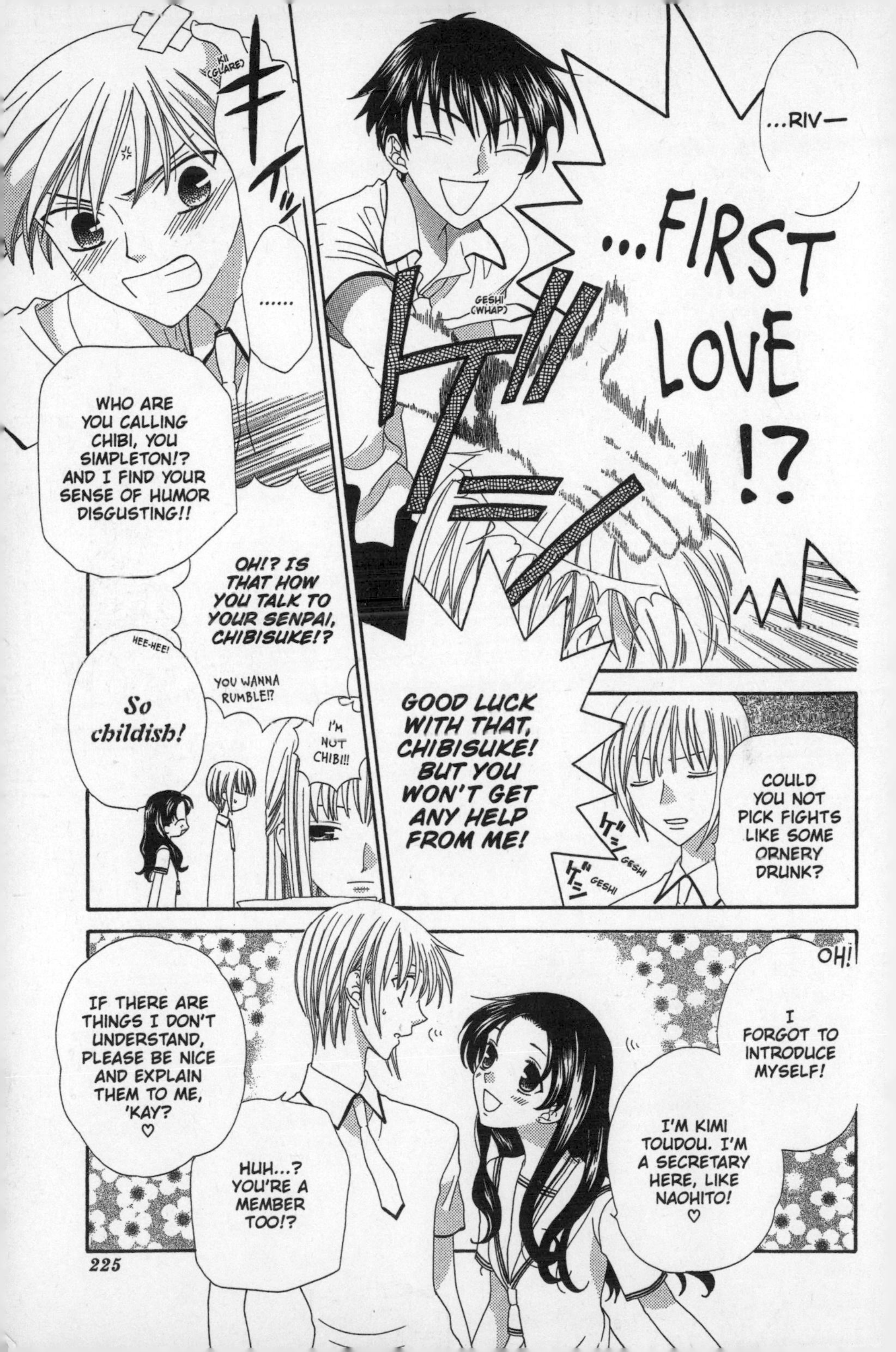
...RIV—
...FIRST LOVE!?
GESHI (WHAP)
KII (GLARE)
......
WHO ARE YOU CALLING CHIBI, YOU SIMPLETON!? AND I FIND YOUR SENSE OF HUMOR DISGUSTING!!
COULD YOU NOT PICK FIGHTS LIKE SOME ORNERY DRUNK?
GESHI
GESHI
GOOD LUCK WITH THAT, CHIBISUKE! BUT YOU WON'T GET ANY HELP FROM ME!
OH!? IS THAT HOW YOU TALK TO YOUR SENPAI, CHIBISUKE!?
YOU WANNA RUMBLE!?
I'M NOT CHIBI!!
HEE-HEE!
So childish!
OH!
I FORGOT TO INTRODUCE MYSELF!
I'M KIMI TOUDOU. I'M A SECRETARY HERE, LIKE NAOHITO! ♡
HUH...? YOU'RE A MEMBER TOO!?
IF THERE ARE THINGS I DON'T UNDERSTAND, PLEASE BE NICE AND EXPLAIN THEM TO ME, 'KAY? ♡

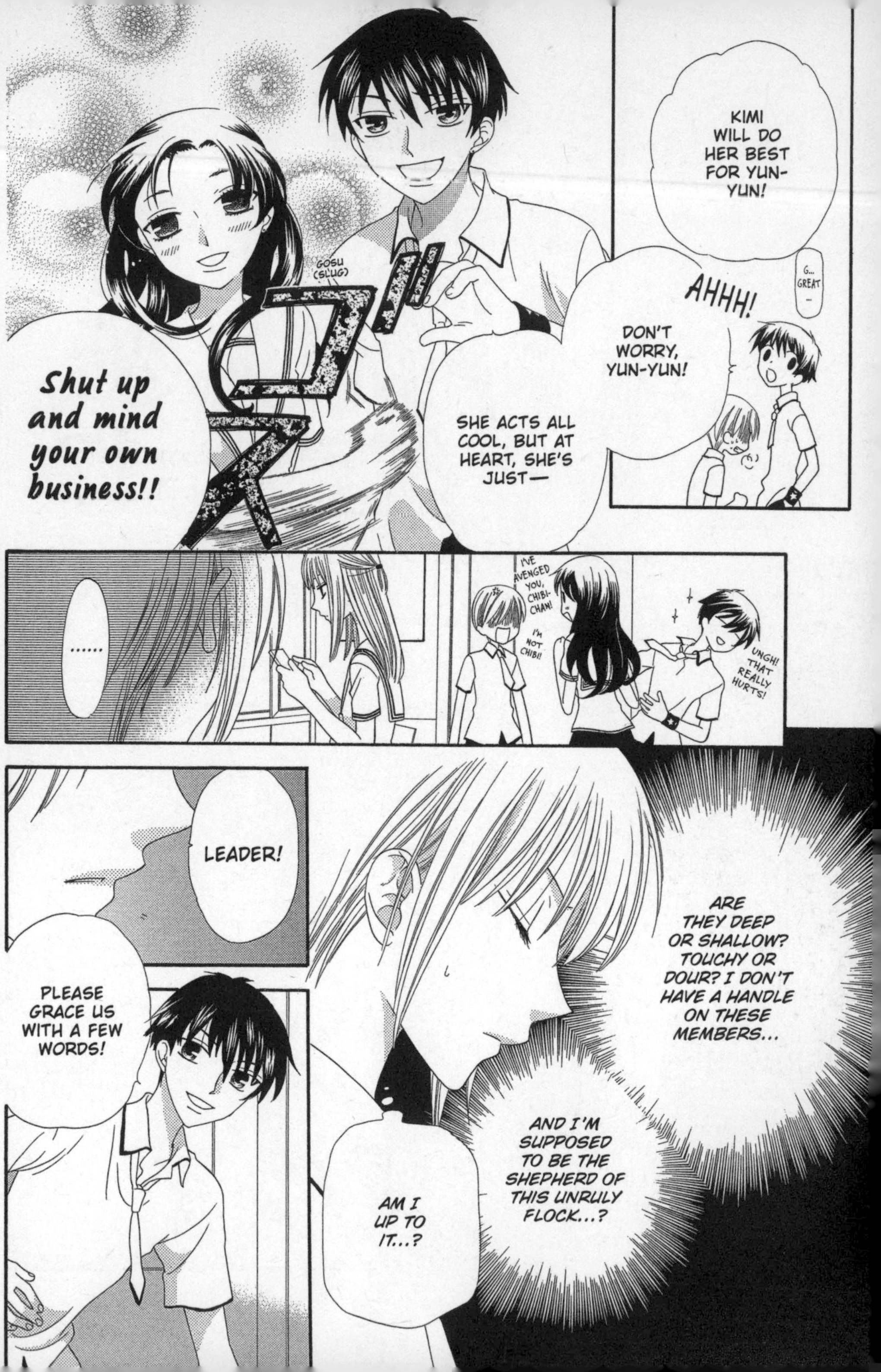
KIMI WILL DO HER BEST FOR YUN-YUN!
G... GREAT...
AHHH!
DON'T WORRY, YUN-YUN!
SHE ACTS ALL COOL, BUT AT HEART, SHE'S JUST—
GOSU (SLUG)
Shut up and mind your own business!!
UNGH! THAT REALLY HURTS!
I'VE AVENGED YOU, CHIBI-CHAN!
I'M NOT CHIBI!
......
ARE THEY DEEP OR SHALLOW? TOUCHY OR DOUR? I DON'T HAVE A HANDLE ON THESE MEMBERS...
AND I'M SUPPOSED TO BE THE SHEPHERD OF THIS UNRULY FLOCK...?
AM I UP TO IT...?
LEADER!
PLEASE GRACE US WITH A FEW WORDS!

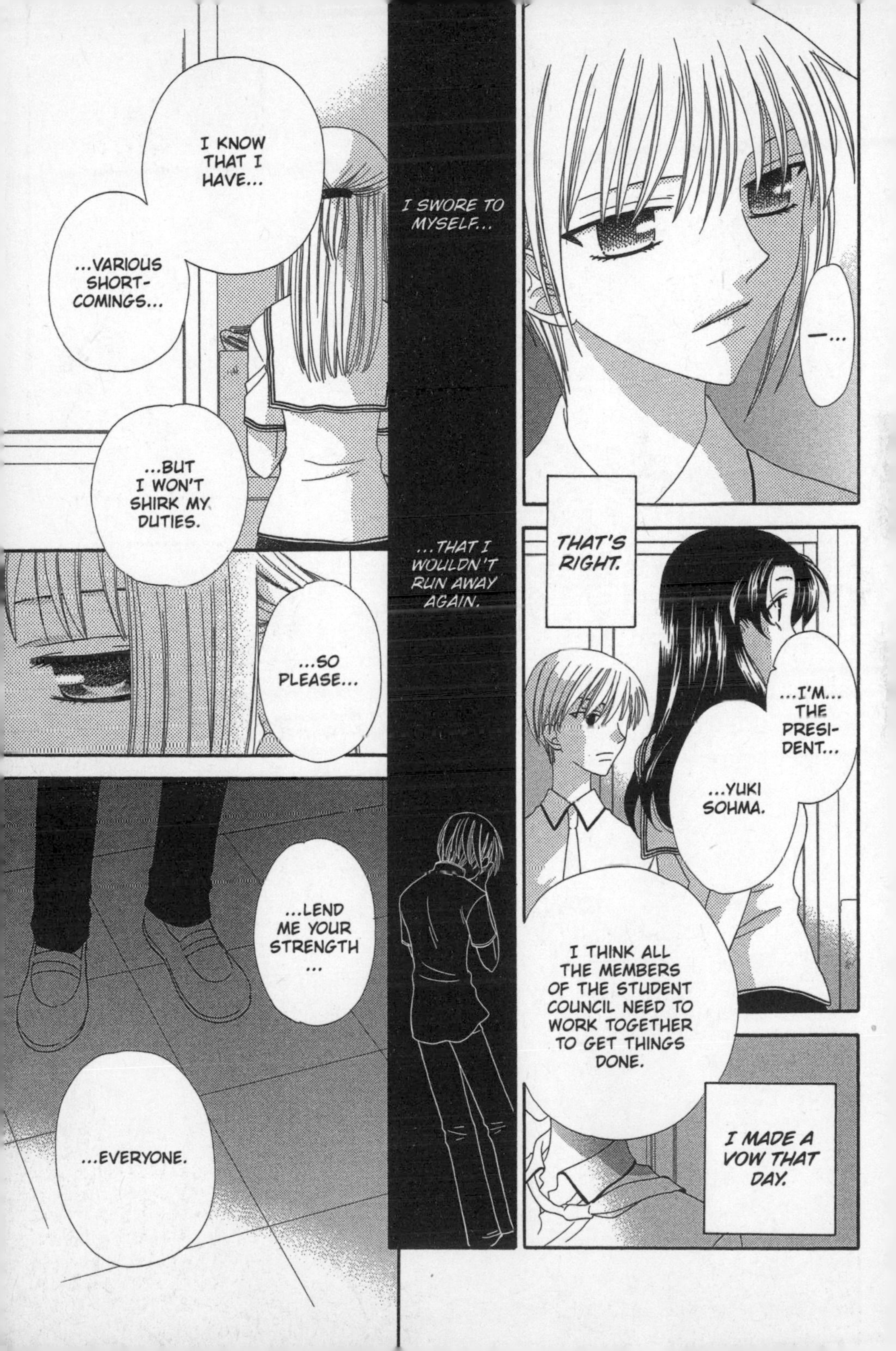
—...
THAT'S RIGHT.
...I'M... THE PRESIDENT...
...YUKI SOHMA.
I THINK ALL THE MEMBERS OF THE STUDENT COUNCIL NEED TO WORK TOGETHER TO GET THINGS DONE.
I MADE A VOW THAT DAY.
I SWORE TO MYSELF...
...THAT I WOULDN'T RUN AWAY AGAIN.
I KNOW THAT I HAVE...
...VARIOUS SHORT-COMINGS...
...BUT I WON'T SHIRK MY DUTIES.
...SO PLEASE...
...LEND ME YOUR STRENGTH ...
...EVERYONE.

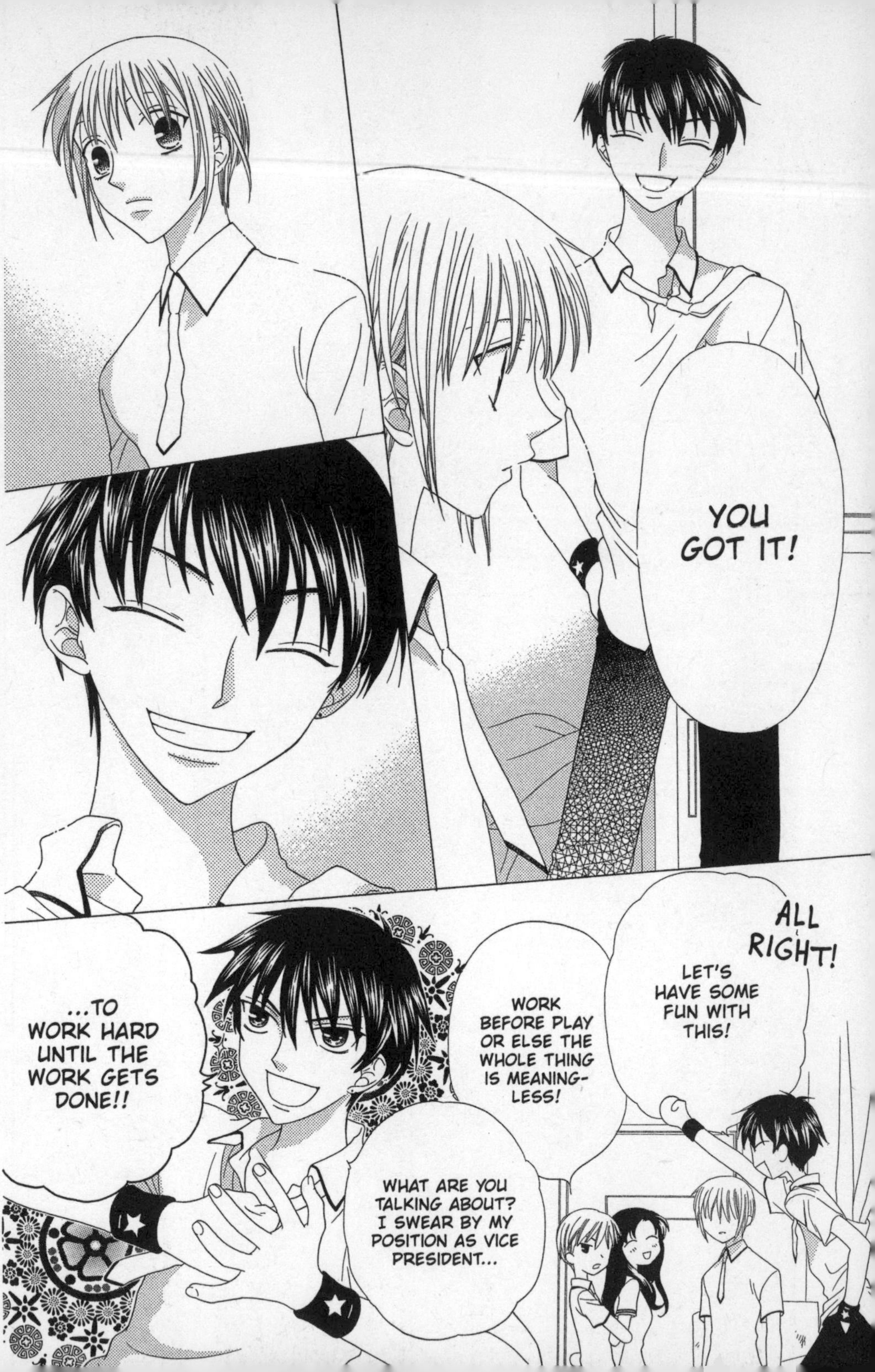
YOU GOT IT!
ALL RIGHT!
LET'S HAVE SOME FUN WITH THIS!
WORK BEFORE PLAY OR ELSE THE WHOLE THING IS MEANING-LESS!
WHAT ARE YOU TALKING ABOUT? I SWEAR BY MY POSITION AS VICE PRESIDENT...
...TO WORK HARD UNTIL THE WORK GETS DONE!!

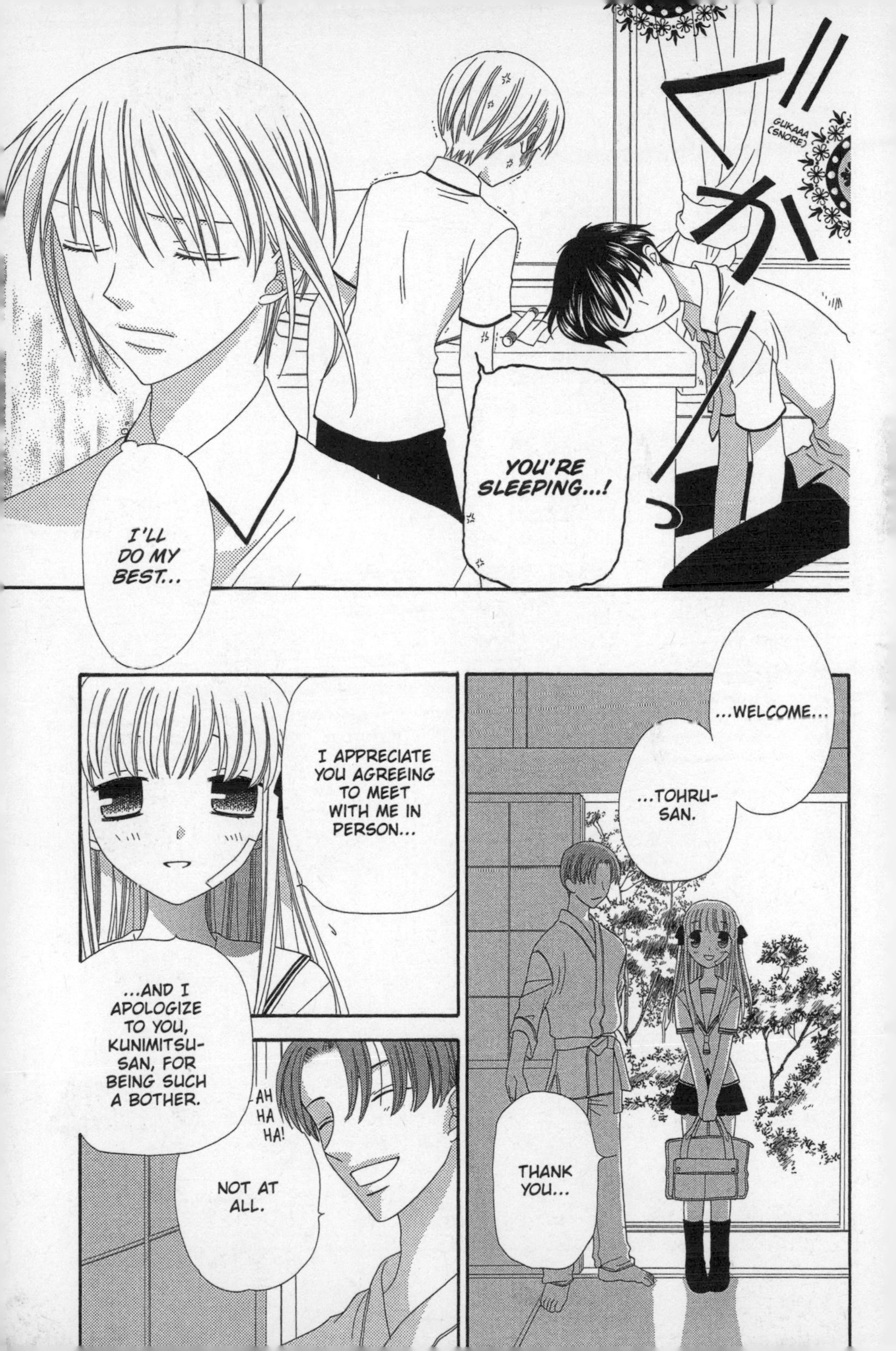
GUKAAA (SNORE)
YOU'RE SLEEPING...!
I'LL DO MY BEST...
...WELCOME...
...TOHRU-SAN.
THANK YOU...
I APPRECIATE YOU AGREEING TO MEET WITH ME IN PERSON...
...AND I APOLOGIZE TO YOU, KUNIMITSU-SAN, FOR BEING SUCH A BOTHER.
AH HA HA!
NOT AT ALL.

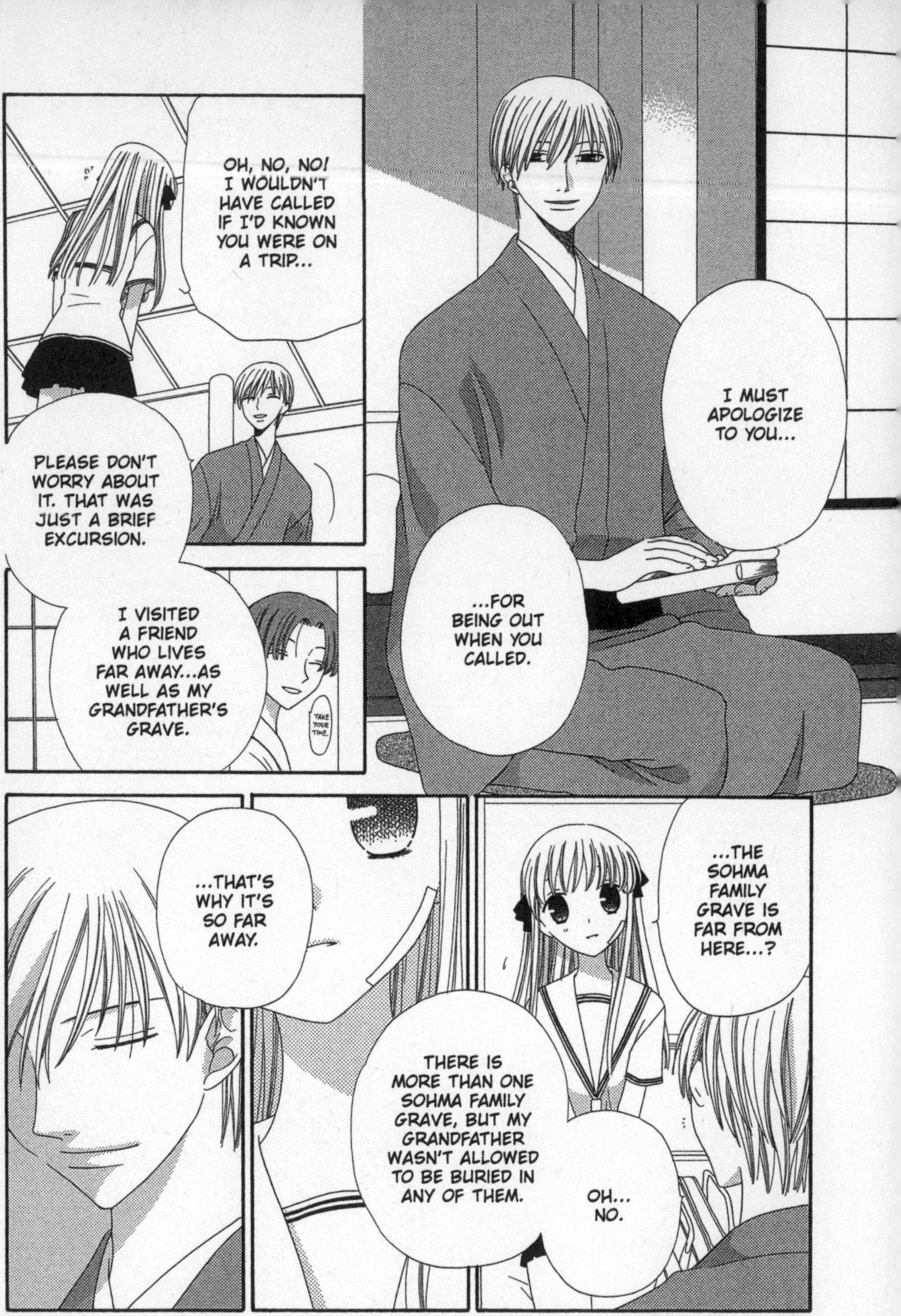
I MUST APOLOGIZE TO YOU...
...FOR BEING OUT WHEN YOU CALLED.
OH, NO, NO! I WOULDN'T HAVE CALLED IF I'D KNOWN YOU WERE ON A TRIP...
PLEASE DON'T WORRY ABOUT IT. THAT WAS JUST A BRIEF EXCURSION.
I VISITED A FRIEND WHO LIVES FAR AWAY...AS WELL AS MY GRANDFATHER'S GRAVE.
TAKE YOUR TIME.
...THE SOHMA FAMILY GRAVE IS FAR FROM HERE...?
THERE IS MORE THAN ONE SOHMA FAMILY GRAVE, BUT MY GRANDFATHER WASN'T ALLOWED TO BE BURIED IN ANY OF THEM.
OH... NO.
...THAT'S WHY IT'S SO FAR AWAY.

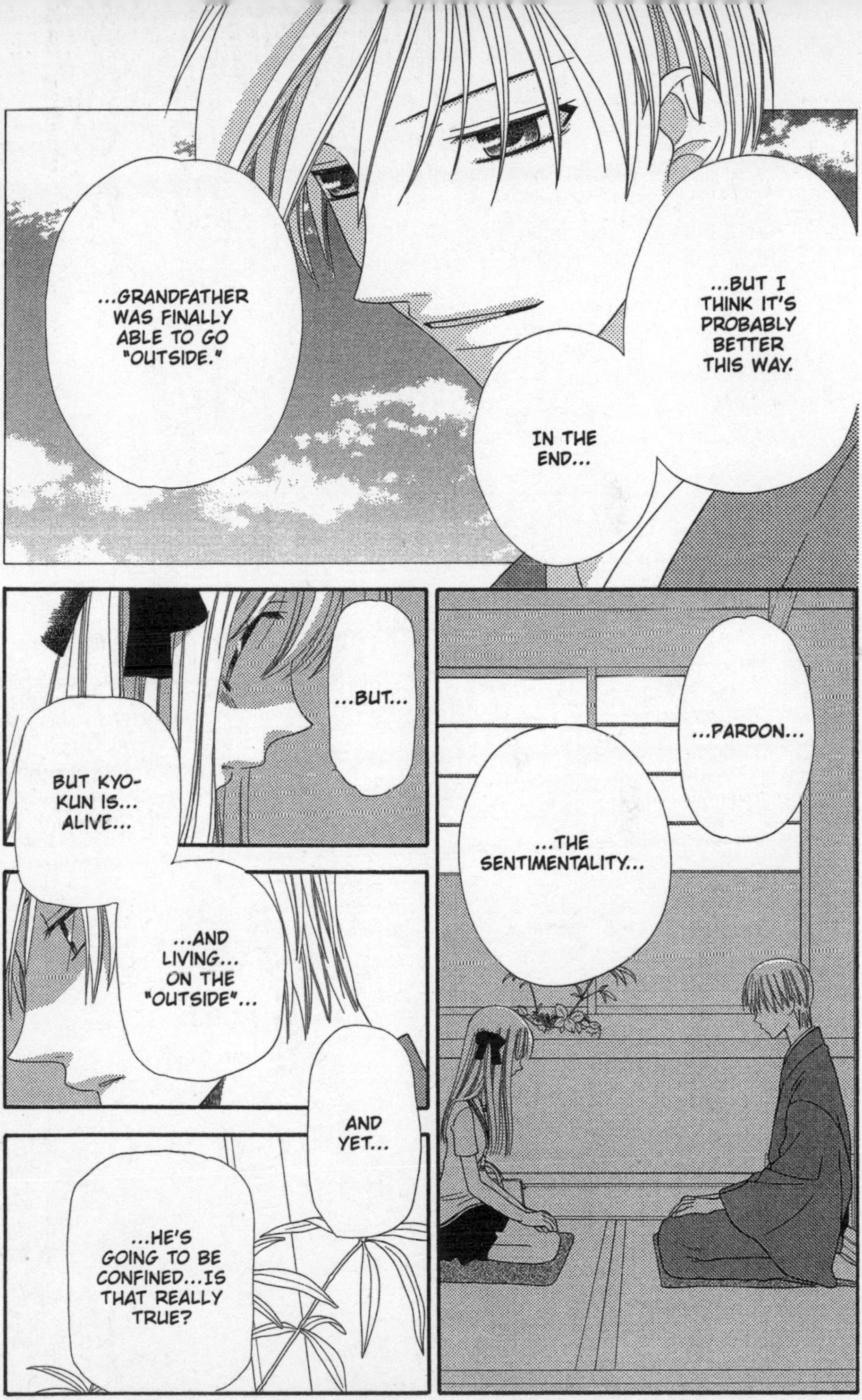
...BUT I THINK IT'S PROBABLY BETTER THIS WAY.
IN THE END...
...GRANDFATHER WAS FINALLY ABLE TO GO "OUTSIDE."
...PARDON...
...THE SENTIMENTALITY...
...BUT...
BUT KYO-KUN IS... ALIVE...
...AND LIVING... ON THE "OUTSIDE"...
AND YET...
...HE'S GOING TO BE CONFINED...IS THAT REALLY TRUE?

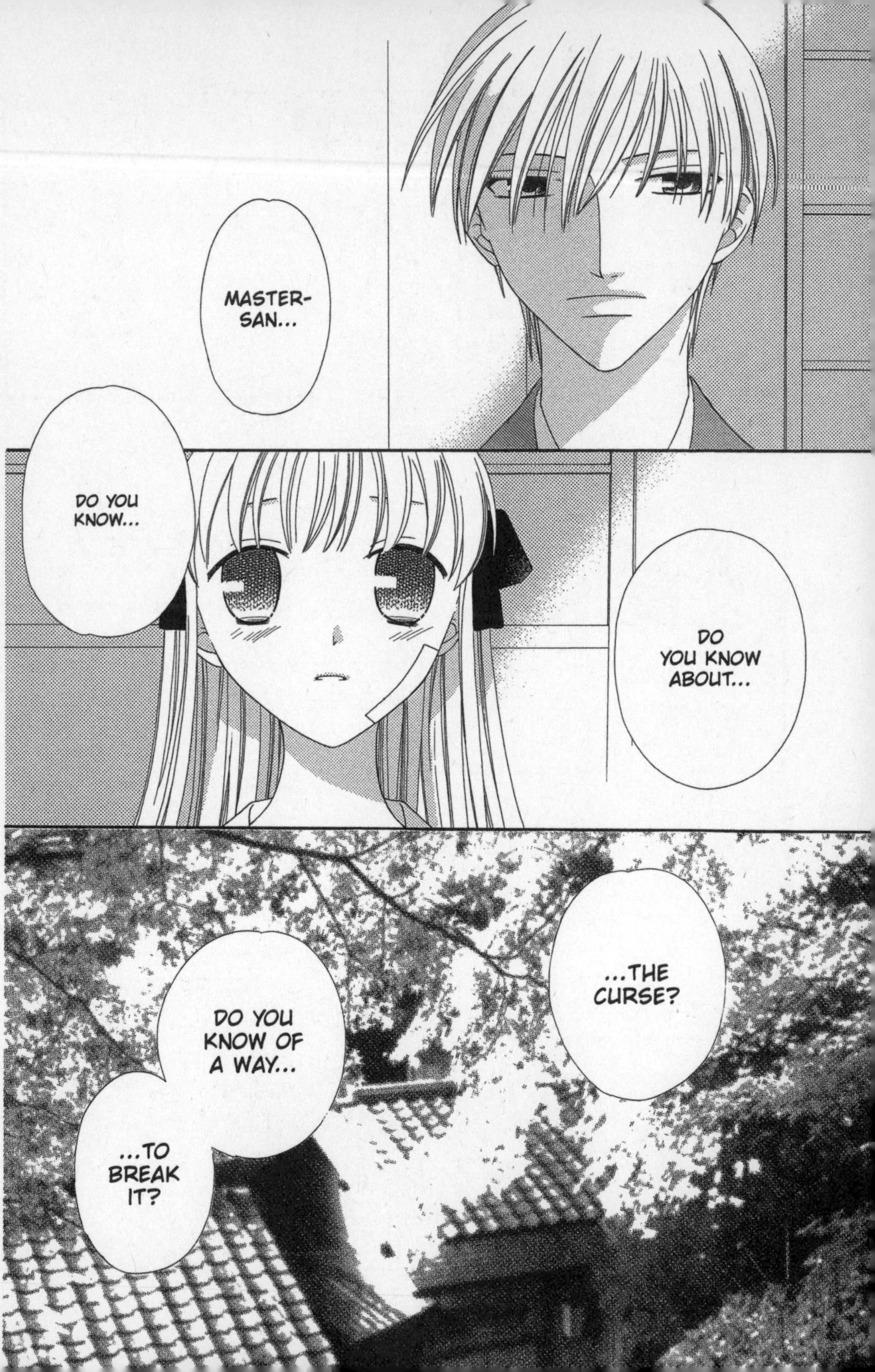
MASTER-SAN...
DO YOU KNOW...
DO YOU KNOW ABOUT...
...THE CURSE?
DO YOU KNOW OF A WAY...
...TO BREAK IT?

Chapter 67

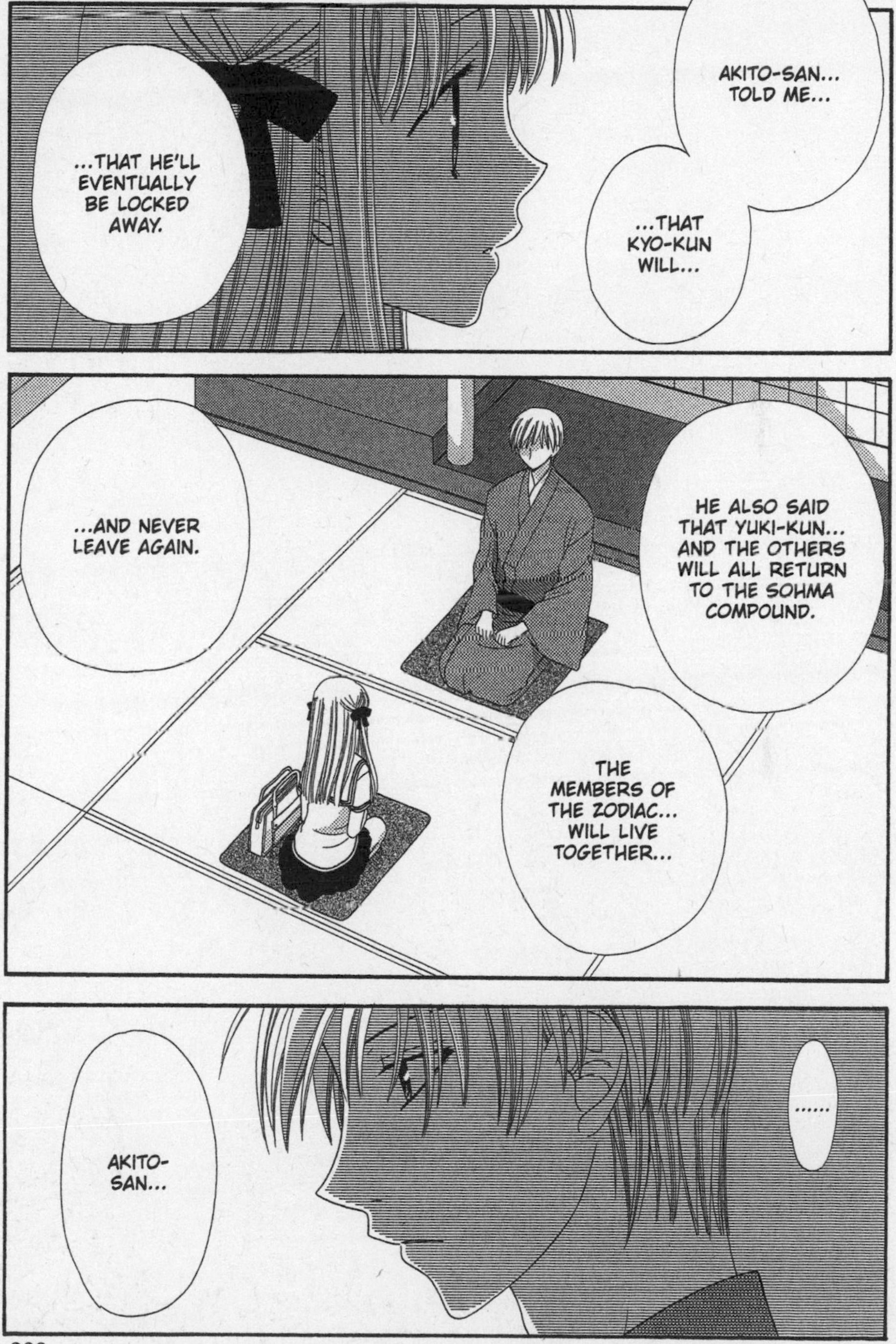
AKITO-SAN... TOLD ME...
...THAT KYO-KUN WILL...
...THAT HE'LL EVENTUALLY BE LOCKED AWAY.
HE ALSO SAID THAT YUKI-KUN... AND THE OTHERS WILL ALL RETURN TO THE SOHMA COMPOUND.
THE MEMBERS OF THE ZODIAC... WILL LIVE TOGETHER...
...AND NEVER LEAVE AGAIN.
......
AKITO-SAN...

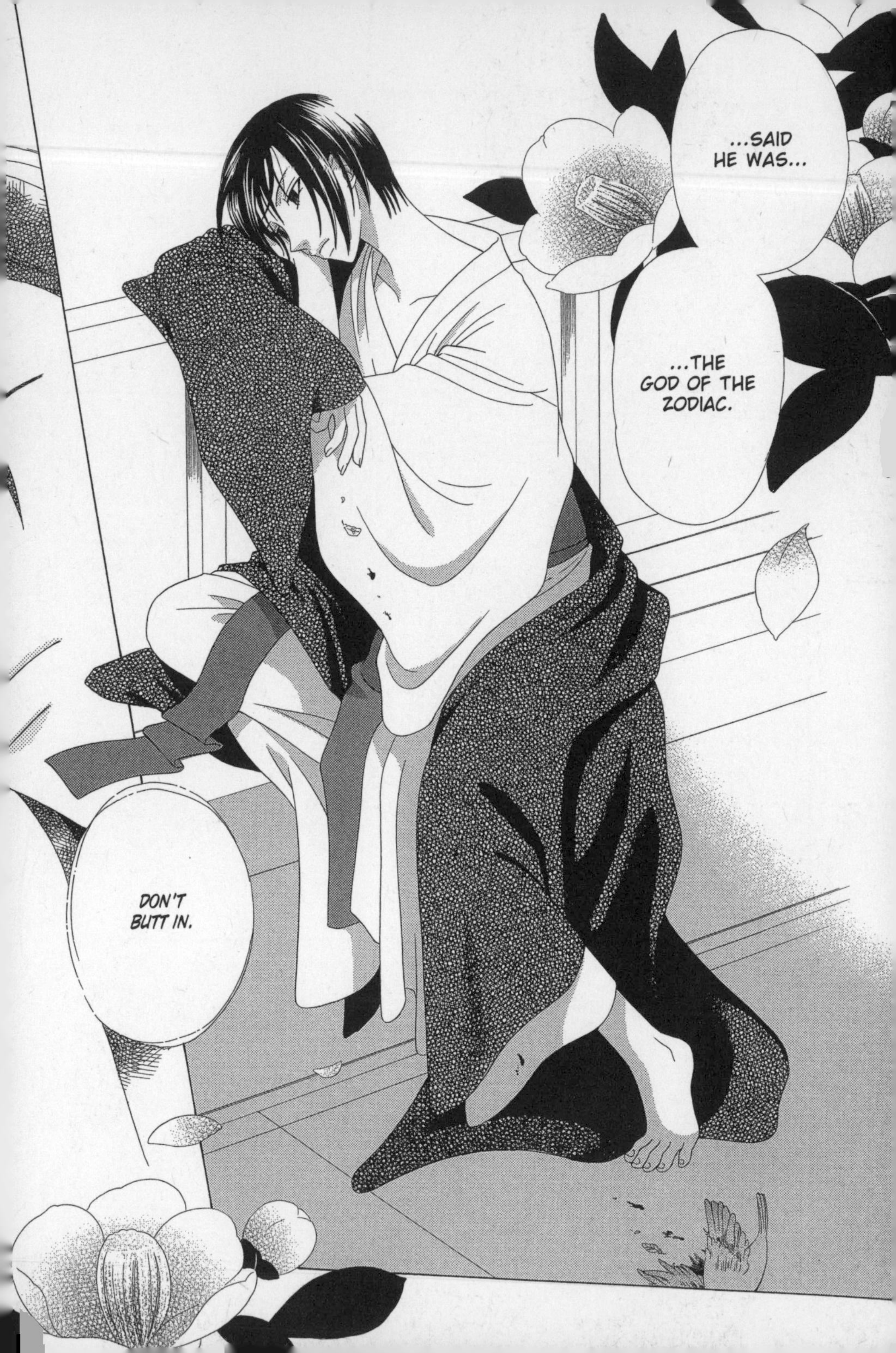
...SAID HE WAS...
...THE GOD OF THE ZODIAC.
DON'T BUTT IN.

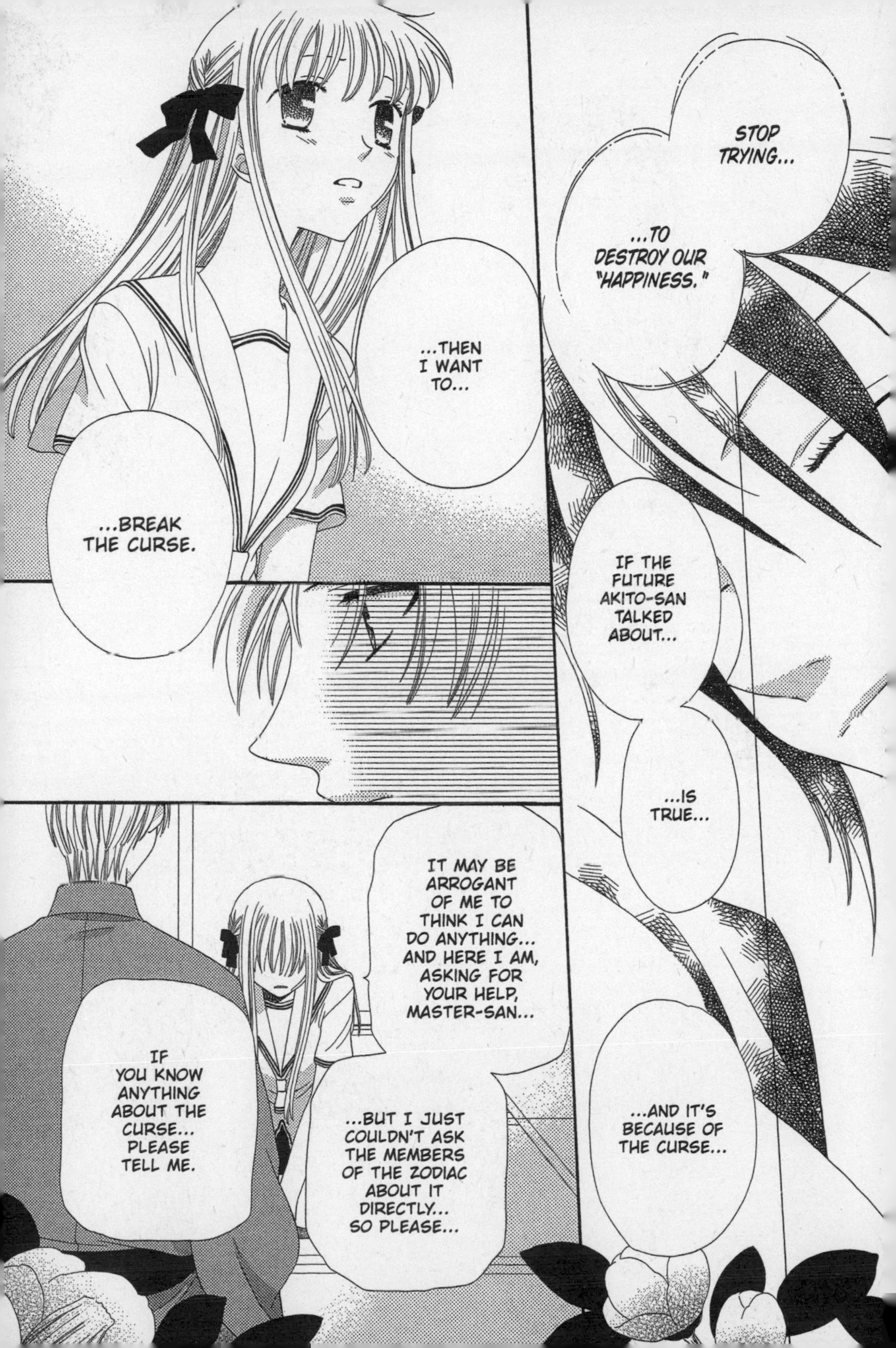
STOP TRYING...
...TO DESTROY OUR "HAPPINESS."
IF THE FUTURE AKITO-SAN TALKED ABOUT...
...IS TRUE...
...AND IT'S BECAUSE OF THE CURSE...
...THEN I WANT TO...
...BREAK THE CURSE.
IT MAY BE ARROGANT OF ME TO THINK I CAN DO ANYTHING... AND HERE I AM, ASKING FOR YOUR HELP, MASTER-SAN...
...BUT I JUST COULDN'T ASK THE MEMBERS OF THE ZODIAC ABOUT IT DIRECTLY... SO PLEASE...
IF YOU KNOW ANYTHING ABOUT THE CURSE... PLEASE TELL ME.

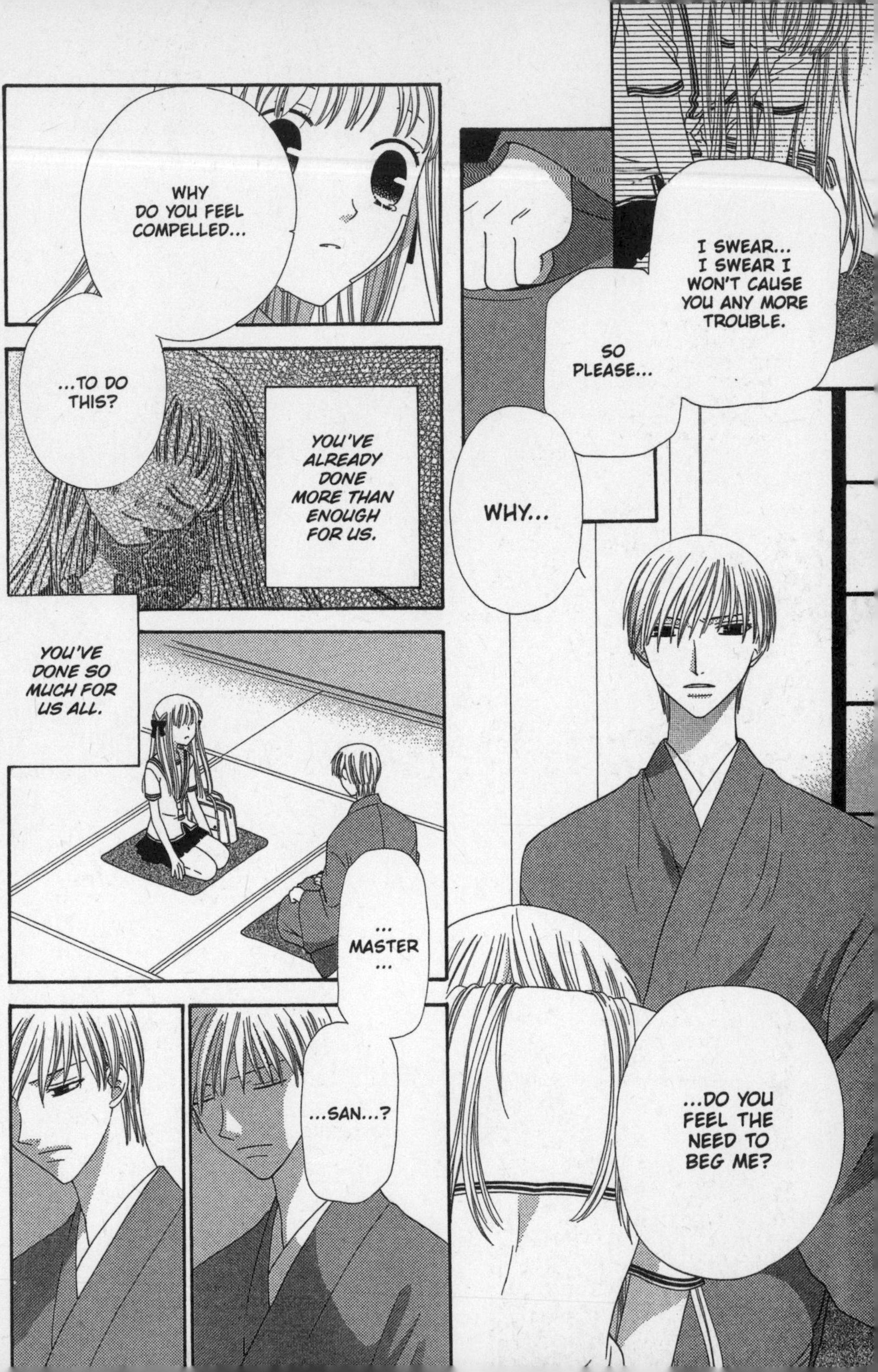
I SWEAR... I SWEAR I WON'T CAUSE YOU ANY MORE TROUBLE.
SO PLEASE...
WHY...
...DO YOU FEEL THE NEED TO BEG ME?
WHY DO YOU FEEL COMPELLED...
...TO DO THIS?
YOU'VE ALREADY DONE MORE THAN ENOUGH FOR US.
YOU'VE DONE SO MUCH FOR US ALL.
...MASTER...
...SAN...?

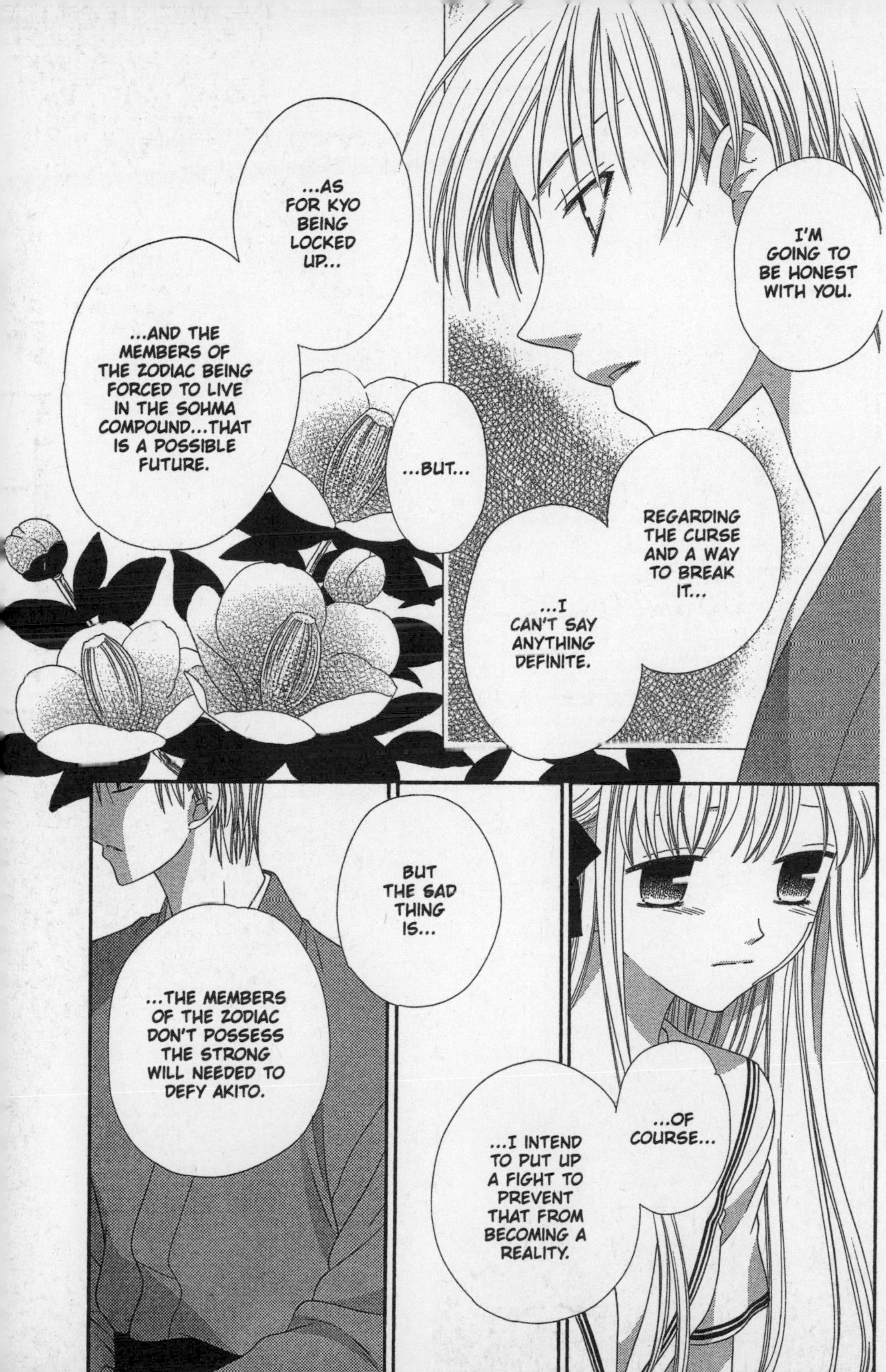

I'M GOING TO BE HONEST WITH YOU.
REGARDING THE CURSE AND A WAY TO BREAK IT...
...I CAN'T SAY ANYTHING DEFINITE.
...BUT...
...AS FOR KYO BEING LOCKED UP...
...AND THE MEMBERS OF THE ZODIAC BEING FORCED TO LIVE IN THE SOHMA COMPOUND...THAT IS A POSSIBLE FUTURE.
...OF COURSE...
...I INTEND TO PUT UP A FIGHT TO PREVENT THAT FROM BECOMING A REALITY.
BUT THE SAD THING IS...
...THE MEMBERS OF THE ZODIAC DON'T POSSESS THE STRONG WILL NEEDED TO DEFY AKITO.

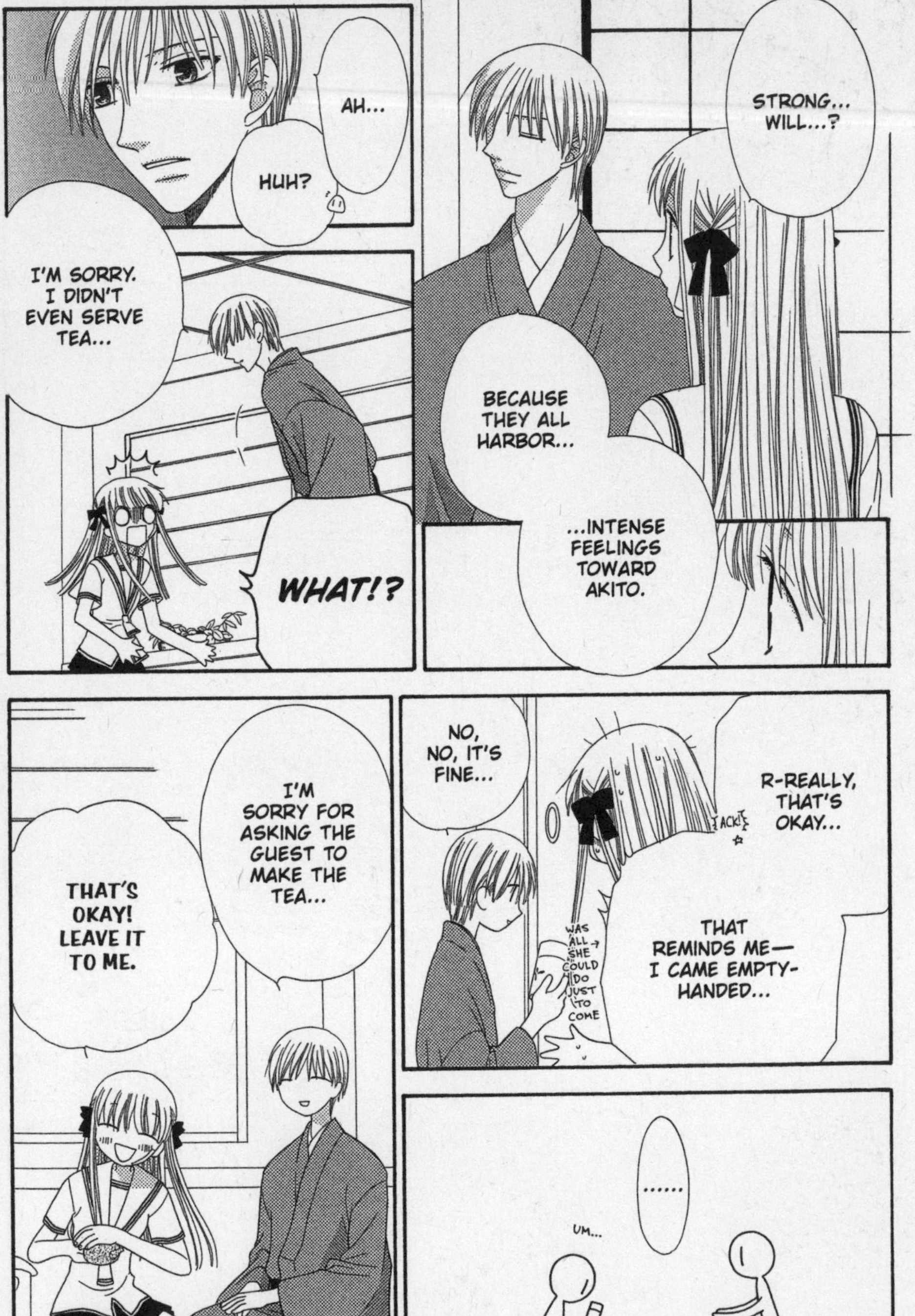
STRONG... WILL...?
BECAUSE THEY ALL HARBOR...
...INTENSE FEELINGS TOWARD AKITO.
AH...
HUH?
I'M SORRY. I DIDN'T EVEN SERVE TEA...
WHAT!?
R-REALLY, THAT'S OKAY...
ACK!
THAT REMINDS ME— I CAME EMPTY-HANDED...
NO, NO, IT'S FINE...
WAS ALL SHE COULD DO JUST TO COME
......
UM...
I'M SORRY FOR ASKING THE GUEST TO MAKE THE TEA...
THAT'S OKAY! LEAVE IT TO ME.

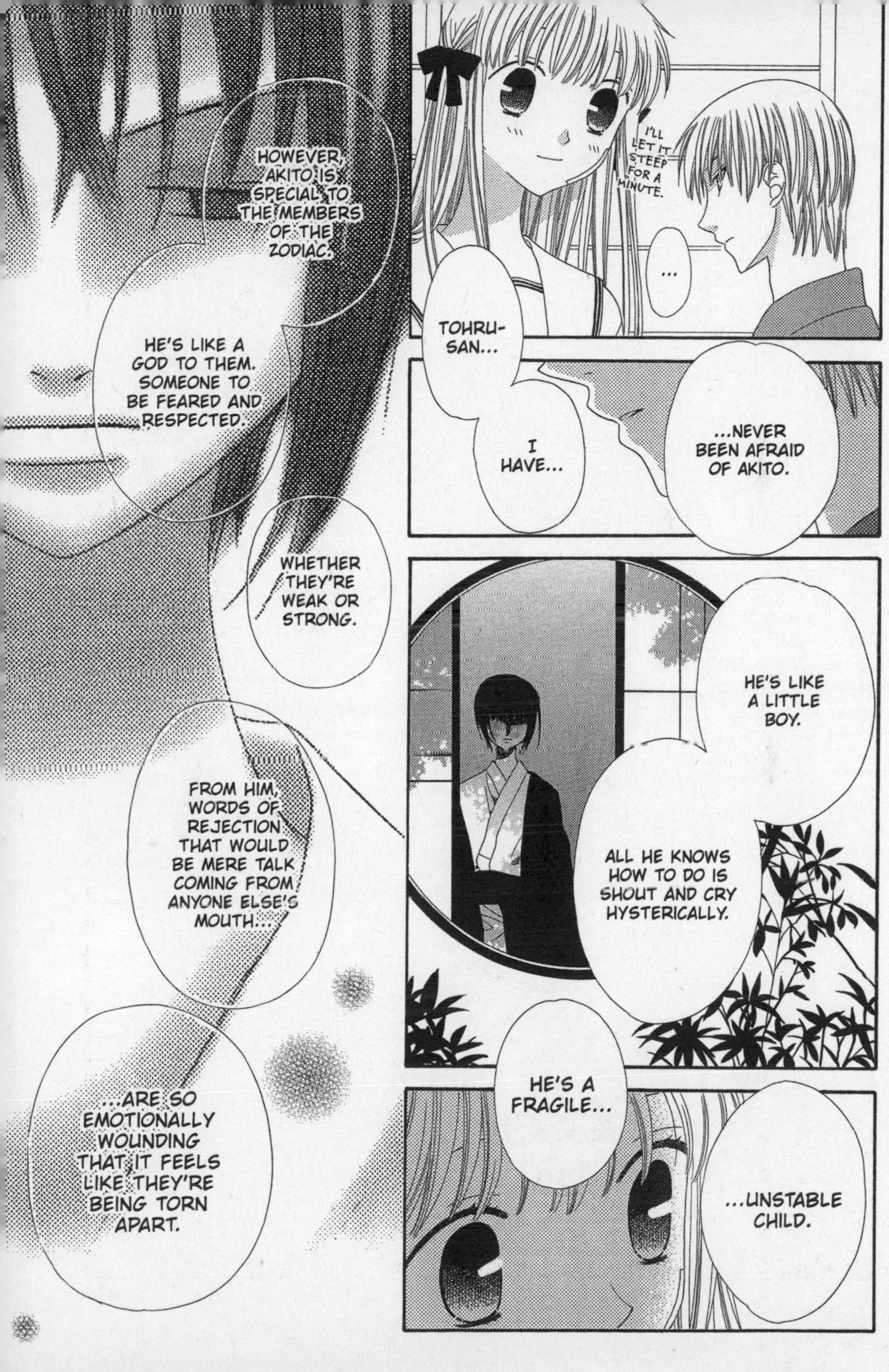
I'LL LET IT STEEP FOR A MINUTE.
...
TOHRU-SAN...
I HAVE...
...NEVER BEEN AFRAID OF AKITO.
HE'S LIKE A LITTLE BOY.
ALL HE KNOWS HOW TO DO IS SHOUT AND CRY HYSTERICALLY.
HE'S A FRAGILE...
...UNSTABLE CHILD.
HOWEVER, AKITO IS SPECIAL TO THE MEMBERS OF THE ZODIAC.
HE'S LIKE A GOD TO THEM. SOMEONE TO BE FEARED AND RESPECTED.
WHETHER THEY'RE WEAK OR STRONG.
FROM HIM, WORDS OF REJECTION THAT WOULD BE MERE TALK COMING FROM ANYONE ELSE'S MOUTH...
...ARE SO EMOTIONALLY WOUNDING THAT IT FEELS LIKE THEY'RE BEING TORN APART.

CIRCLE (CLOCKWISE FROM TOP): RAT, OX, TIGER, RABBIT, DRAGON, SNAKE, HORSE, RAM, MONKEY, ROOSTER, DOG, BOAR

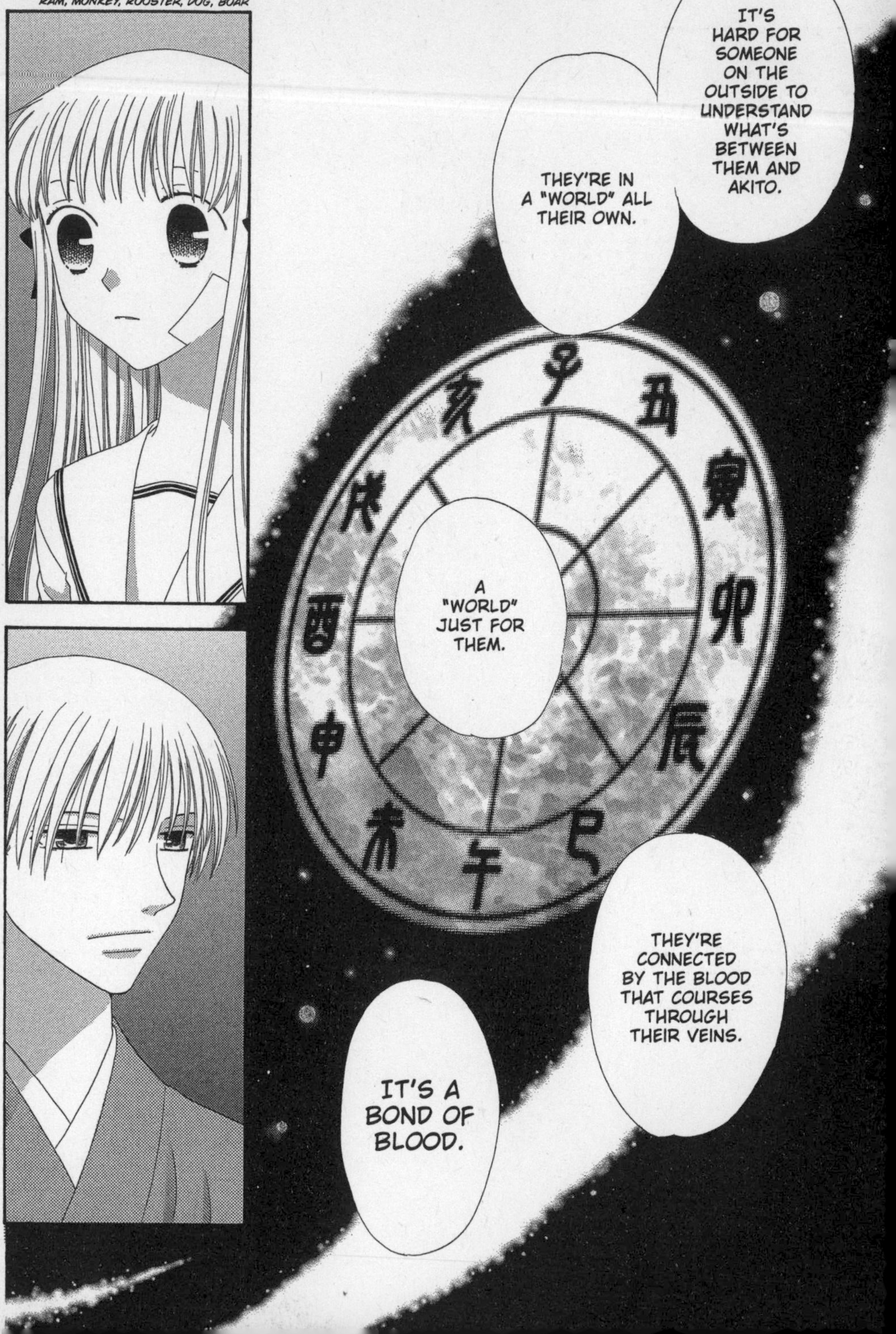
IT'S HARD FOR SOMEONE ON THE OUTSIDE TO UNDERSTAND WHAT'S BETWEEN THEM AND AKITO.
THEY'RE IN A "WORLD" ALL THEIR OWN.
子 丑 寅 卯 辰 巳 午 未 申 酉 戌 亥
A "WORLD" JUST FOR THEM.
THEY'RE CONNECTED BY THE BLOOD THAT COURSES THROUGH THEIR VEINS.
IT'S A BOND OF BLOOD.

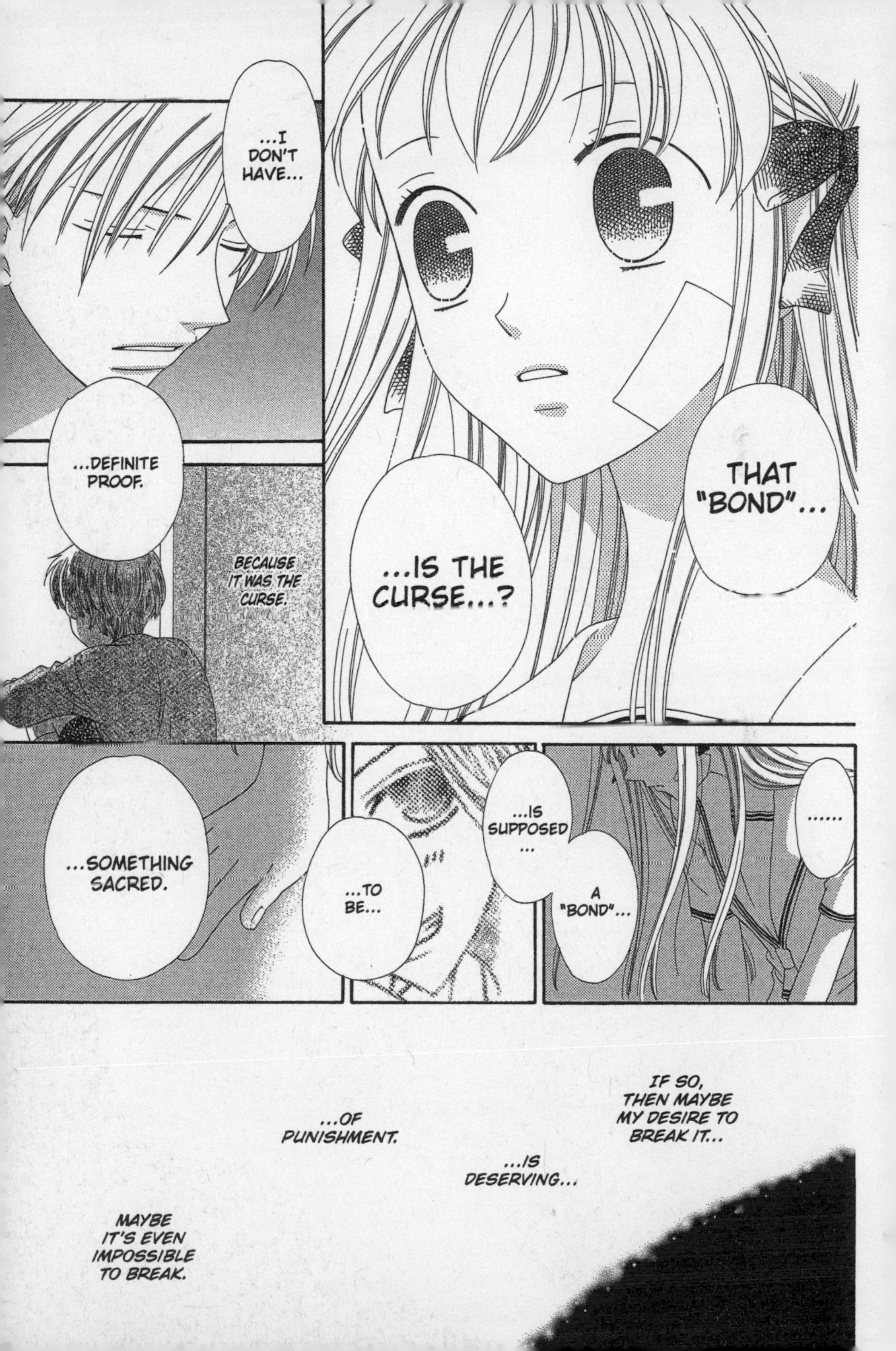
THAT "BOND"...
...IS THE CURSE...?
...I DON'T HAVE...
...DEFINITE PROOF.
BECAUSE IT WAS THE CURSE.
......
A "BOND"...
...IS SUPPOSED...
...TO BE...
...SOMETHING SACRED.
IF SO, THEN MAYBE MY DESIRE TO BREAK IT...
...IS DESERVING...
...OF PUNISHMENT.
MAYBE IT'S EVEN IMPOSSIBLE TO BREAK.

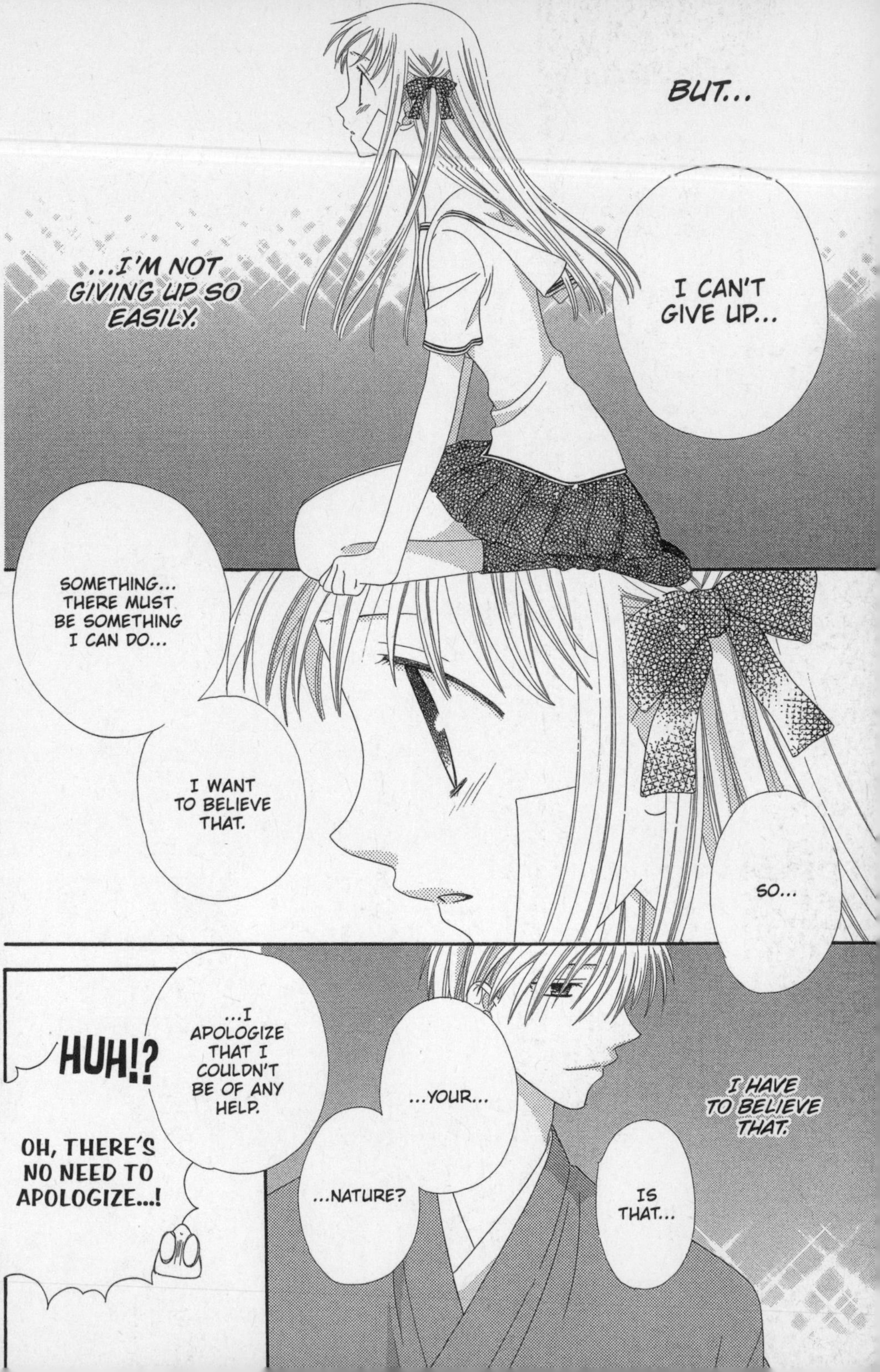
BUT...
I CAN'T GIVE UP...
...I'M NOT GIVING UP SO EASILY.
SOMETHING... THERE MUST BE SOMETHING I CAN DO...
I WANT TO BELIEVE THAT.
SO...
I HAVE TO BELIEVE THAT.
IS THAT...
...YOUR...
...NATURE?
...I APOLOGIZE THAT I COULDN'T BE OF ANY HELP.
HUH!?
OH, THERE'S NO NEED TO APOLOGIZE...!

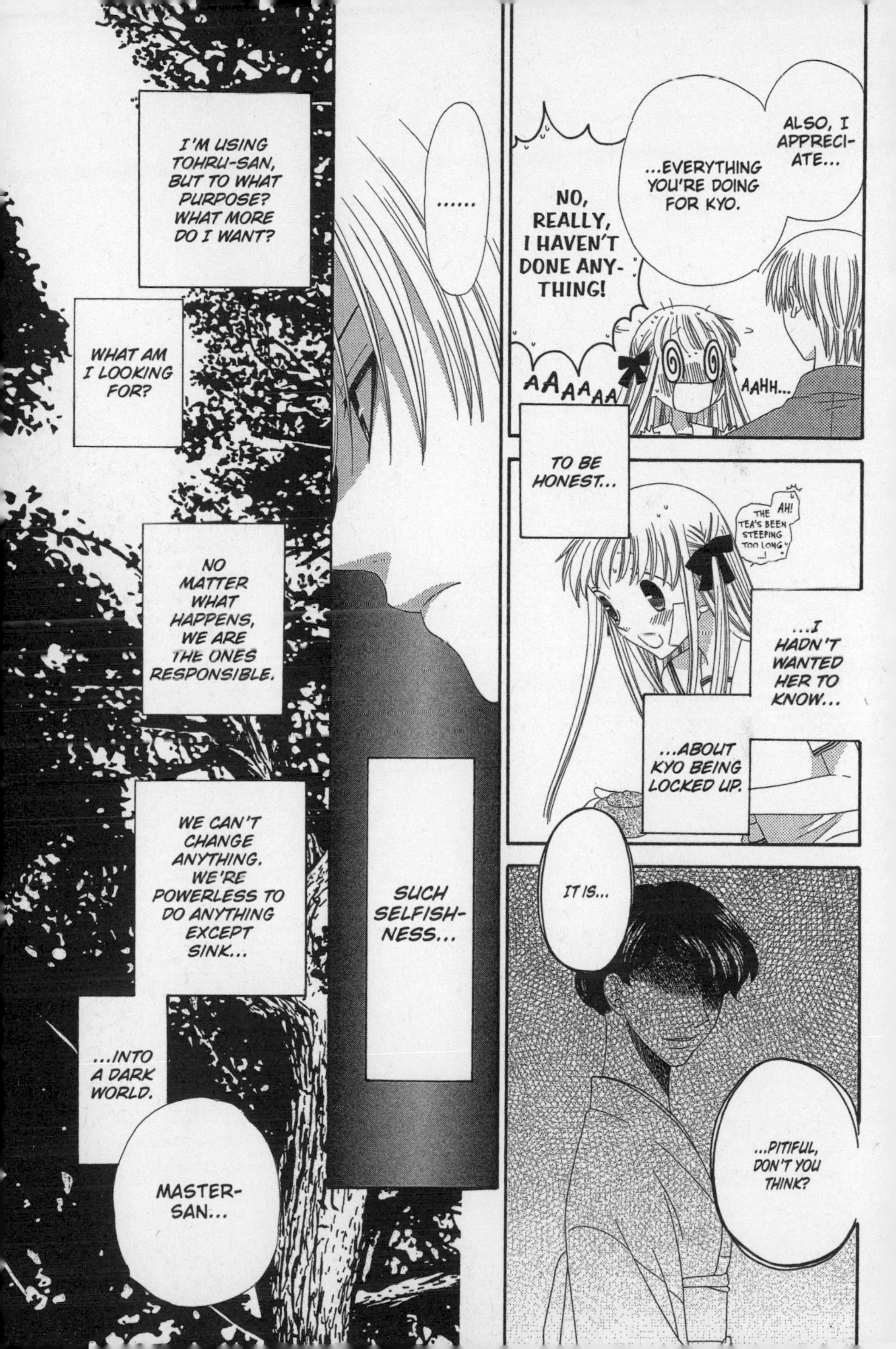

ALSO, I APPRECIATE...
...EVERYTHING YOU'RE DOING FOR KYO.
NO, REALLY, I HAVEN'T DONE ANYTHING!
AAHH...
AAAAAA
TO BE HONEST...
AH!
THE TEA'S BEEN STEEPING TOO LONG...!
...I HADN'T WANTED HER TO KNOW...
...ABOUT KYO BEING LOCKED UP.
IT IS...
...PITIFUL, DON'T YOU THINK?
......
SUCH SELFISHNESS...
I'M USING TOHRU-SAN, BUT TO WHAT PURPOSE? WHAT MORE DO I WANT?
WHAT AM I LOOKING FOR?
NO MATTER WHAT HAPPENS, WE ARE THE ONES RESPONSIBLE.
WE CAN'T CHANGE ANYTHING. WE'RE POWERLESS TO DO ANYTHING EXCEPT SINK...
...INTO A DARK WORLD.
MASTER-SAN...

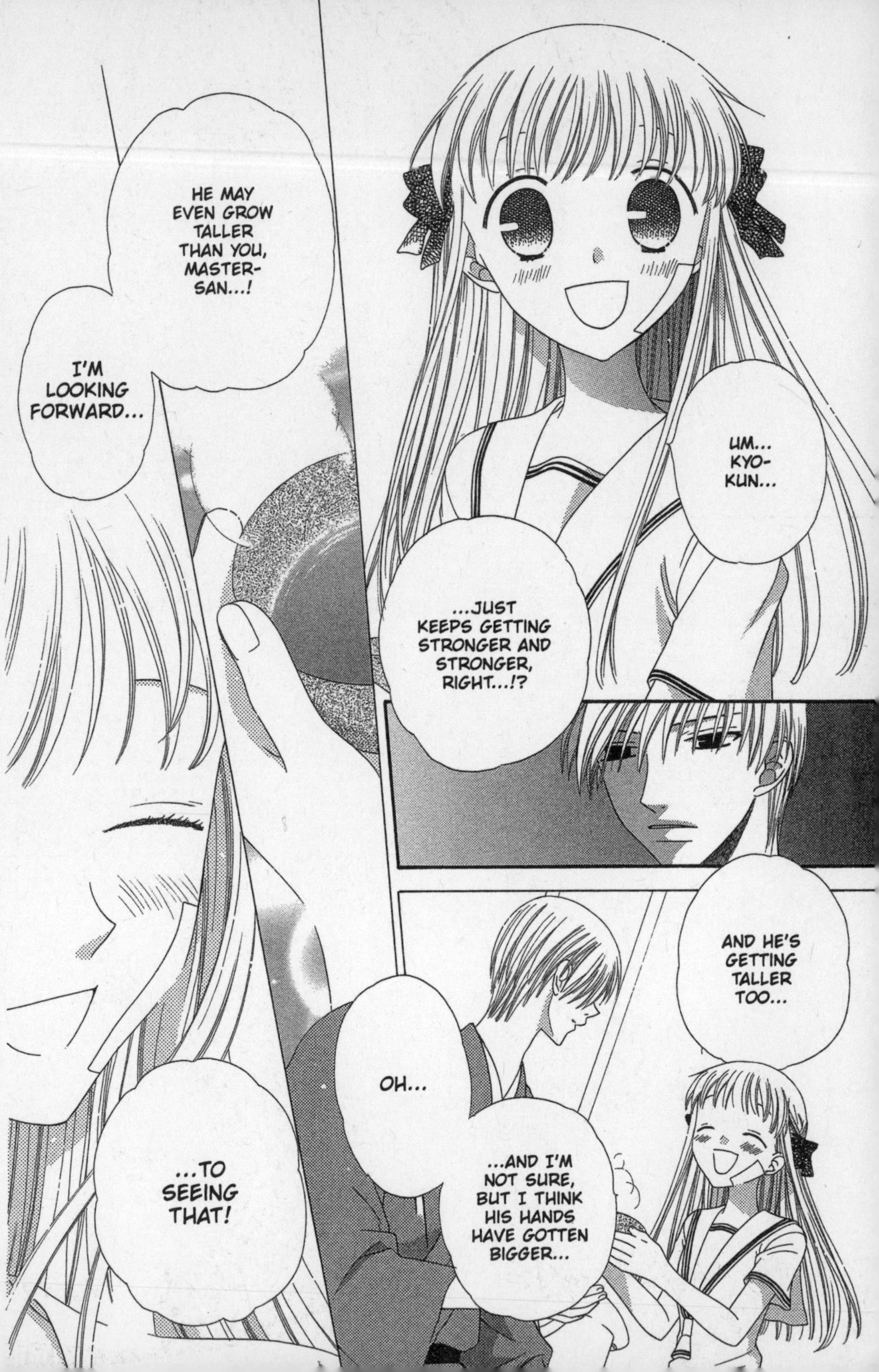
UM... KYO-KUN...
...JUST KEEPS GETTING STRONGER AND STRONGER, RIGHT...!?
AND HE'S GETTING TALLER TOO...
...AND I'M NOT SURE, BUT I THINK HIS HANDS HAVE GOTTEN BIGGER...
OH...
HE MAY EVEN GROW TALLER THAN YOU, MASTER-SAN...!
I'M LOOKING FORWARD...
...TO SEEING THAT!

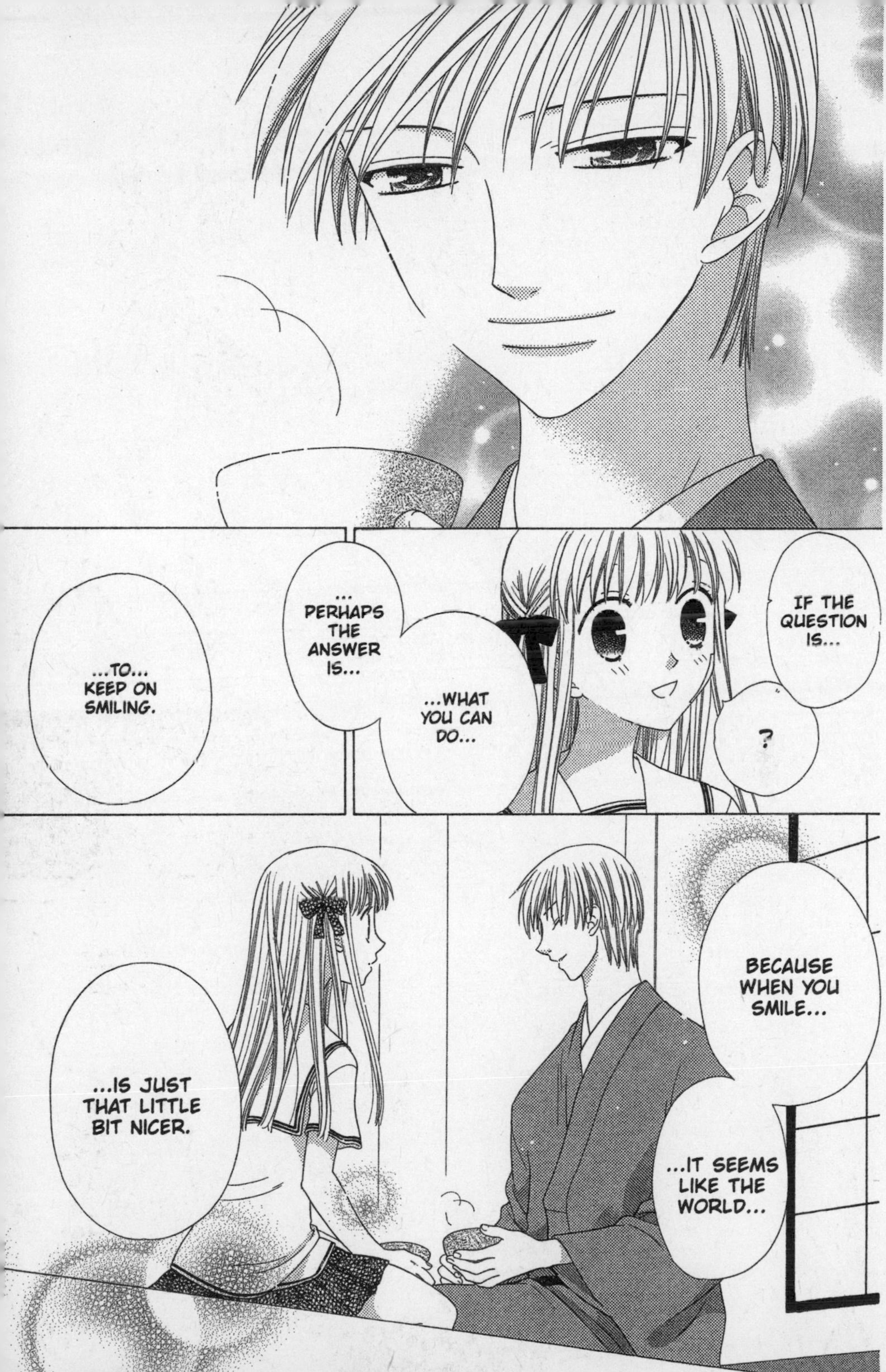
IF THE QUESTION IS...
?
...WHAT YOU CAN DO...
... PERHAPS THE ANSWER IS...
...TO... KEEP ON SMILING.
BECAUSE WHEN YOU SMILE...
...IT SEEMS LIKE THE WORLD...
...IS JUST THAT LITTLE BIT NICER.

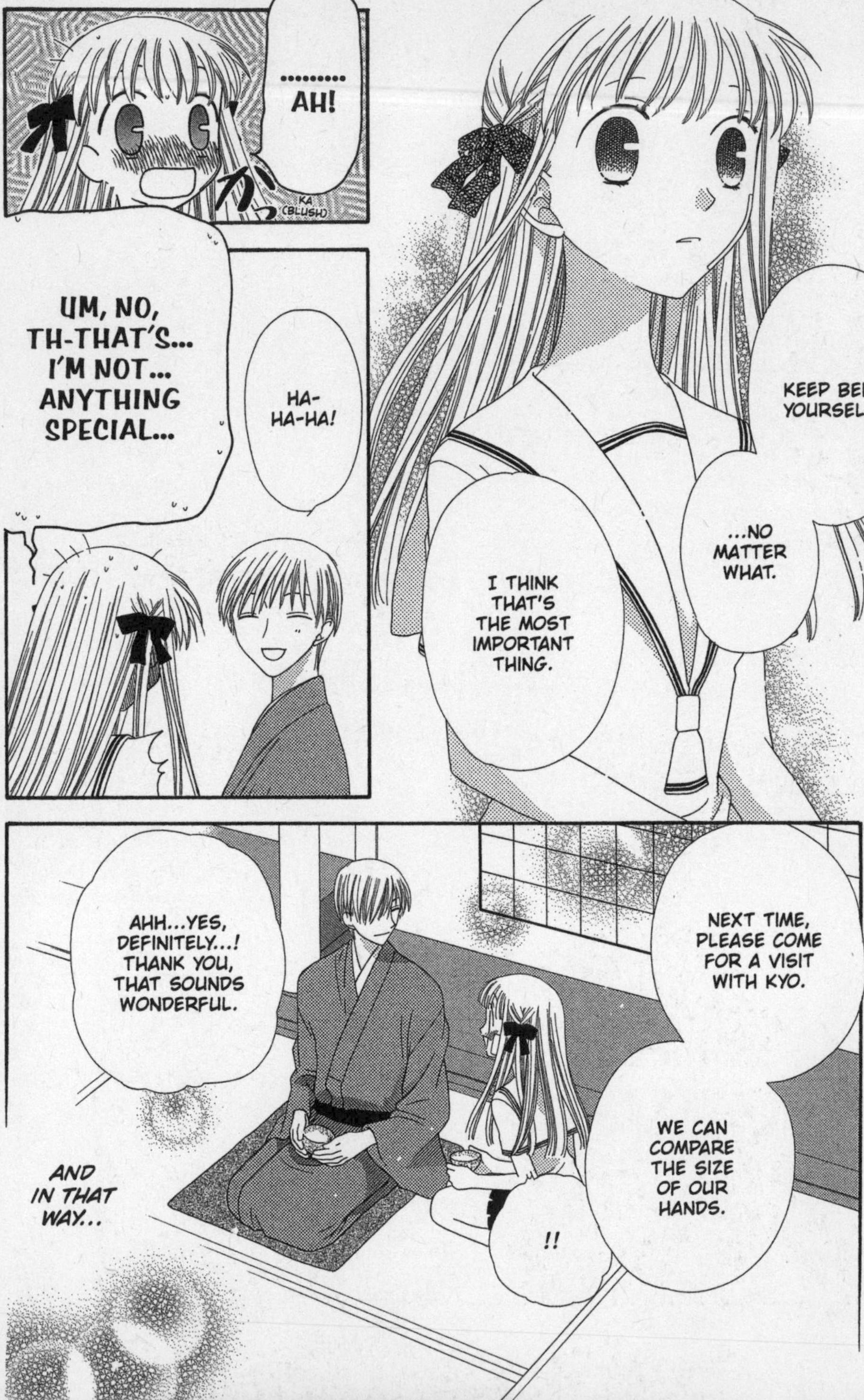
KEEP BEING YOURSELF...
...NO MATTER WHAT.
I THINK THAT'S THE MOST IMPORTANT THING.
....
AH!
かっ
KA (BLUSH)
UM, NO, TH-THAT'S... I'M NOT... ANYTHING SPECIAL...
HA-HA-HA!
NEXT TIME, PLEASE COME FOR A VISIT WITH KYO.
WE CAN COMPARE THE SIZE OF OUR HANDS.
!!
AHH...YES, DEFINITELY...! THANK YOU, THAT SOUNDS WONDERFUL.
AND IN THAT WAY...

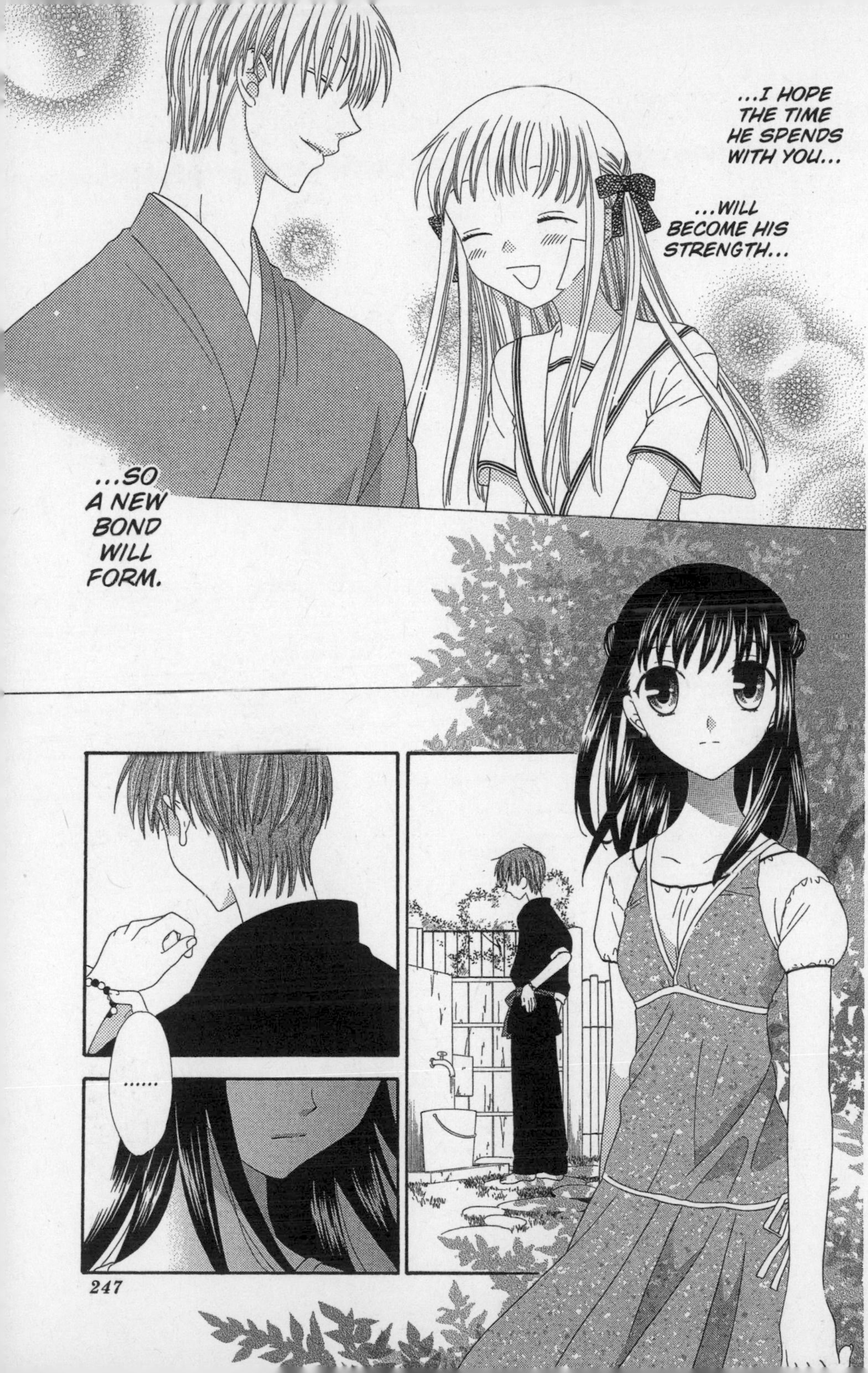
...I HOPE THE TIME HE SPENDS WITH YOU...
...WILL BECOME HIS STRENGTH...
...SO A NEW BOND WILL FORM.
......

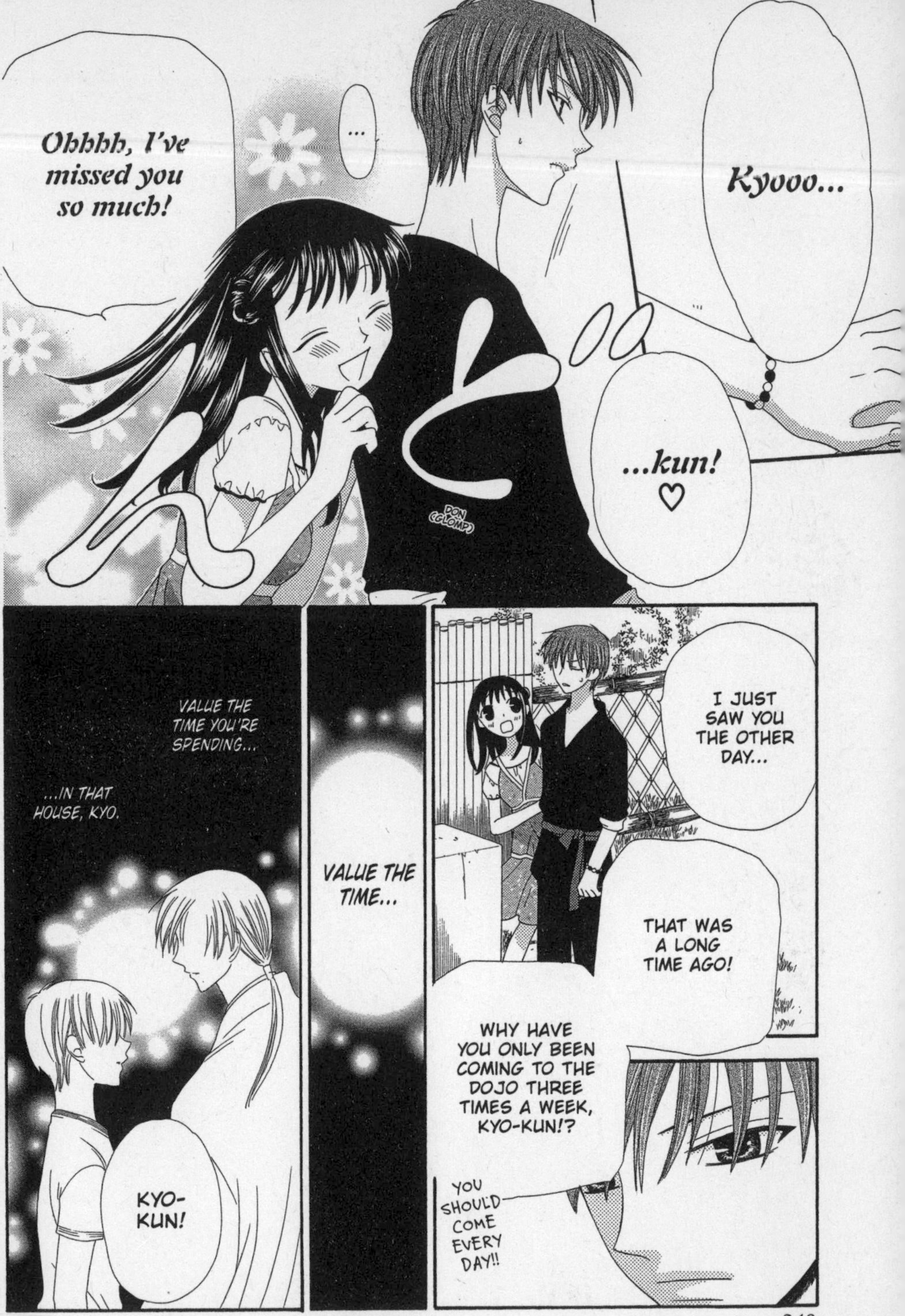

Kyooo...
...kun! ♡
...
Ohhhh, I've missed you so much!
DON (GLOMP)
I JUST SAW YOU THE OTHER DAY...
THAT WAS A LONG TIME AGO!
WHY HAVE YOU ONLY BEEN COMING TO THE DOJO THREE TIMES A WEEK, KYO-KUN!?
YOU SHOULD COME EVERY DAY!!
VALUE THE TIME...
VALUE THE TIME YOU'RE SPENDING...
...IN THAT HOUSE, KYO.
KYO-KUN!

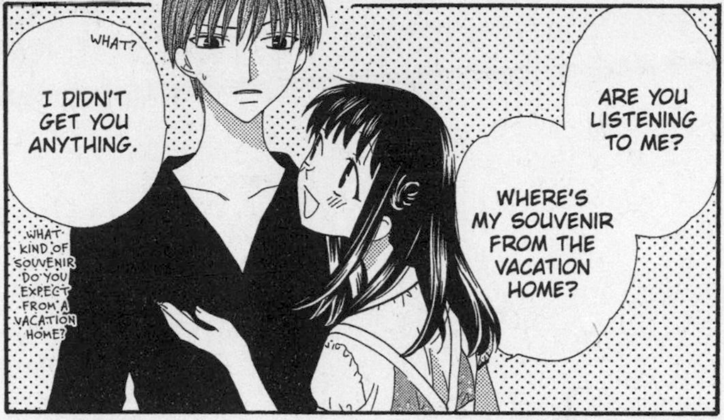
ARE YOU LISTENING TO ME?
WHERE'S MY SOUVENIR FROM THE VACATION HOME?
WHAT?
I DIDN'T GET YOU ANYTHING.
WHAT KIND OF SOUVENIR DO YOU EXPECT FROM A VACATION HOME?
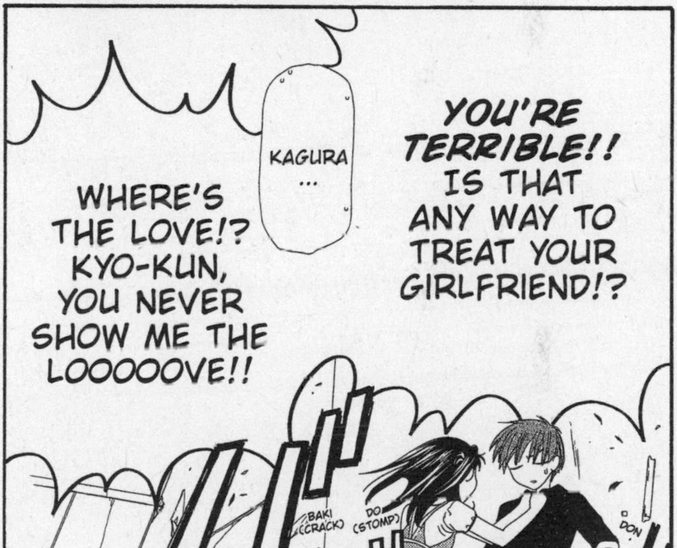
YOU'RE TERRIBLE!! IS THAT ANY WAY TO TREAT YOUR GIRLFRIEND!?
KAGURA ...
WHERE'S THE LOVE!? KYO-KUN, YOU NEVER SHOW ME THE LOOOOOVE!!
DON
DO
DO
DO (STOMP)
BAKI (CRACK)
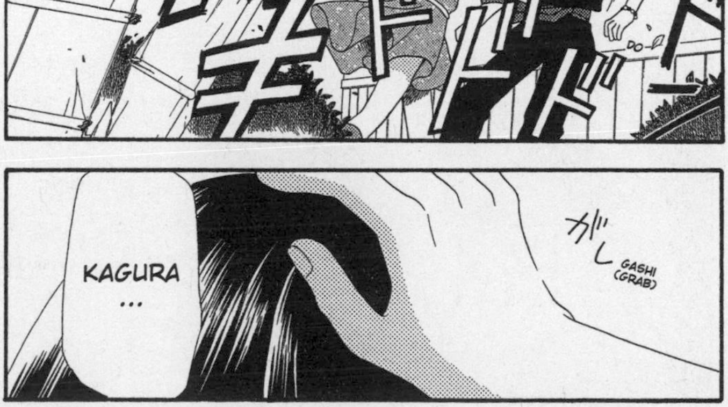
GASHI (GRAB)
KAGURA ...
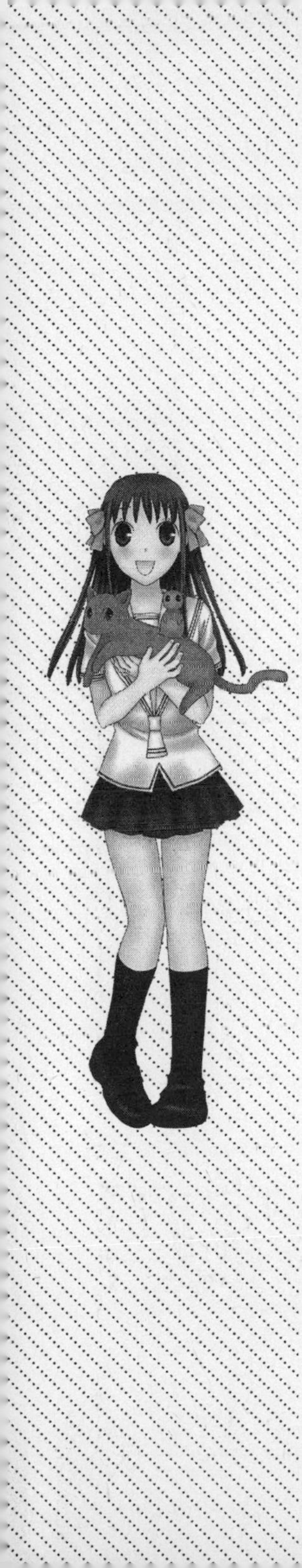

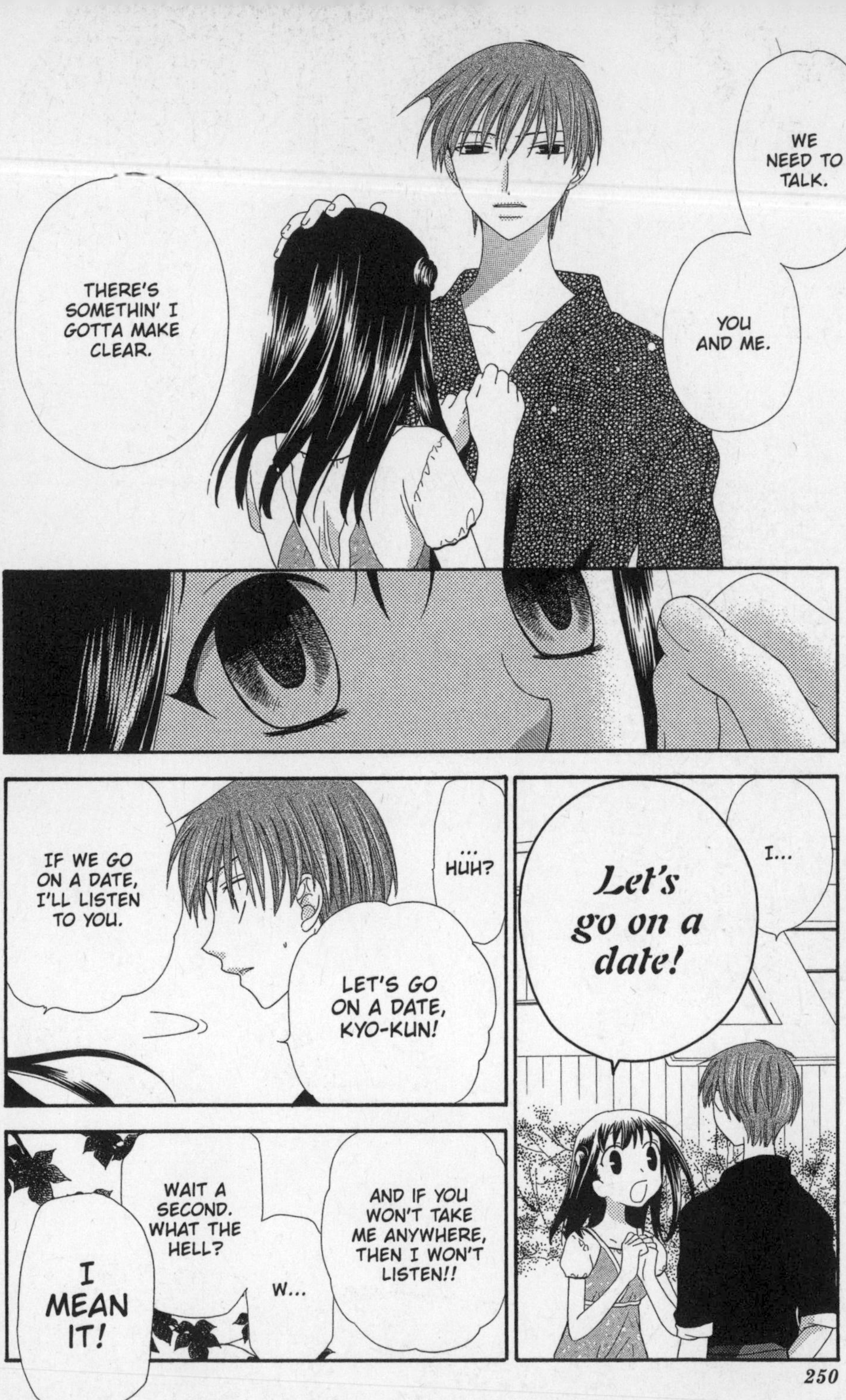
WE NEED TO TALK.
YOU AND ME.
THERE'S SOMETHIN' I GOTTA MAKE CLEAR.
I...
Let's go on a date!
...HUH?
LET'S GO ON A DATE, KYO-KUN!
IF WE GO ON A DATE, I'LL LISTEN TO YOU.
AND IF YOU WON'T TAKE ME ANYWHERE, THEN I WON'T LISTEN!!
W...
WAIT A SECOND. WHAT THE HELL?
I MEAN IT!

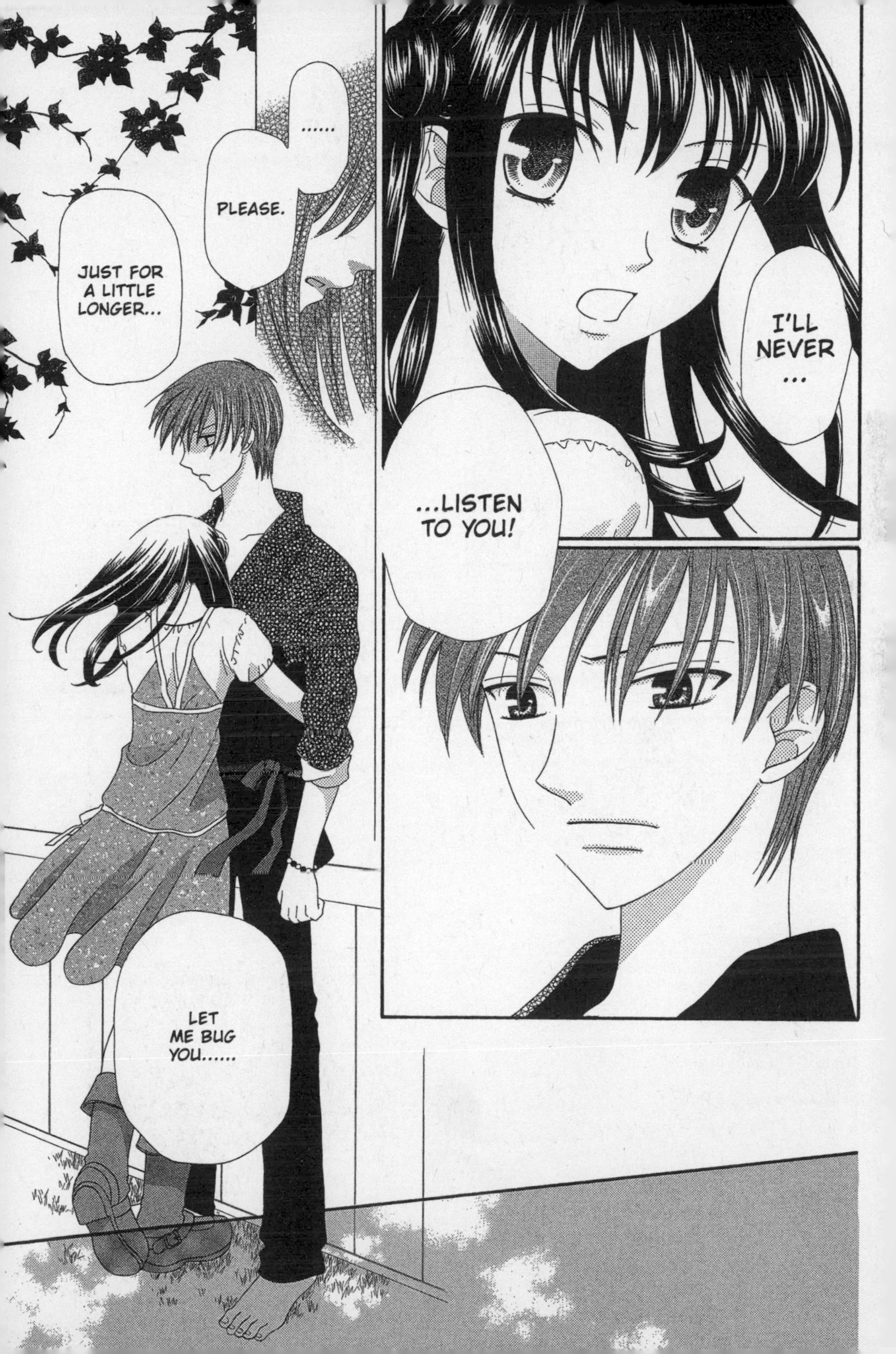
I'LL NEVER ...
...LISTEN TO YOU!
......
PLEASE.
JUST FOR A LITTLE LONGER...
LET ME BUG YOU......

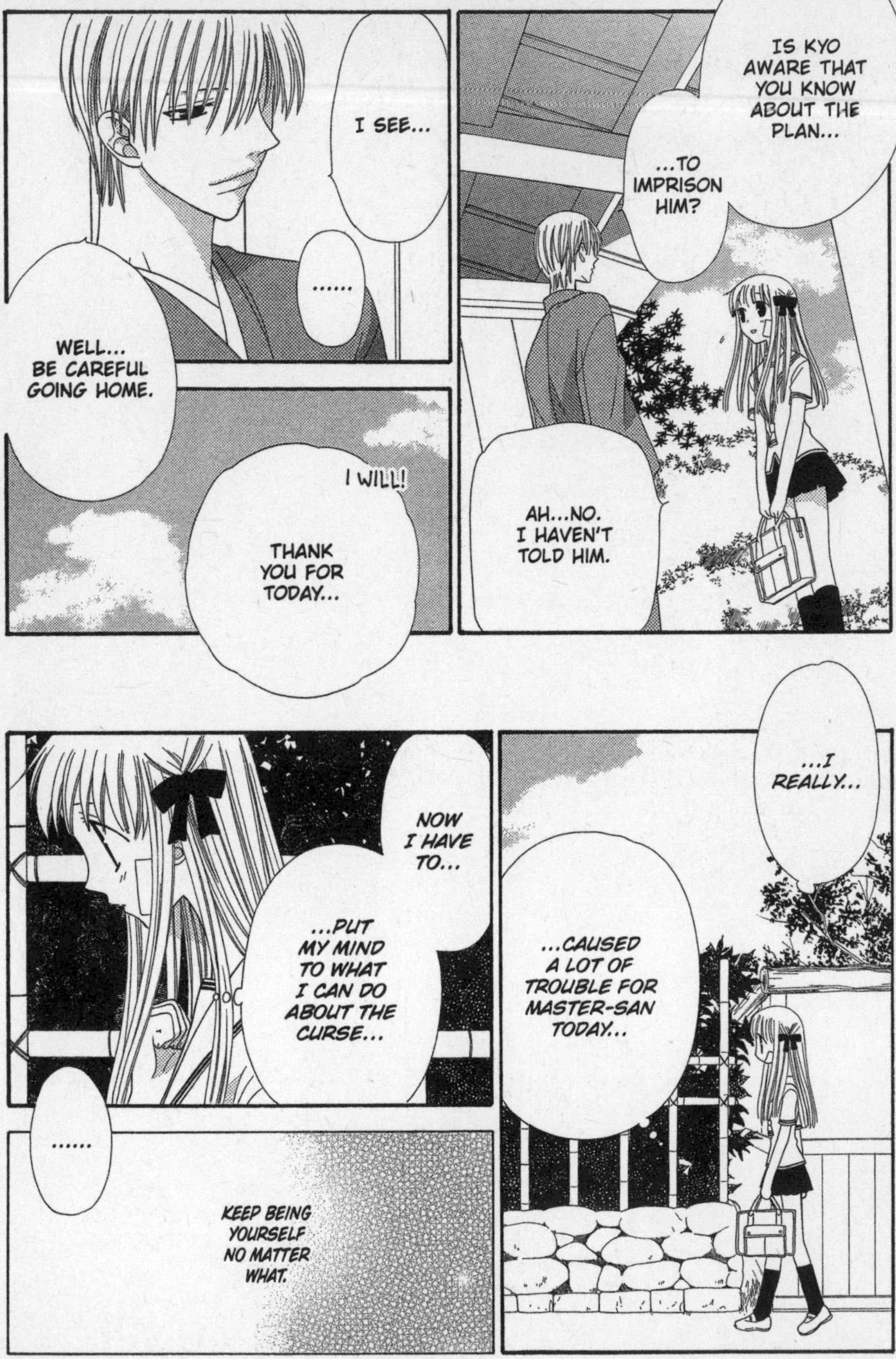
IS KYO AWARE THAT YOU KNOW ABOUT THE PLAN...
...TO IMPRISON HIM?
AH...NO. I HAVEN'T TOLD HIM.
I SEE...
......
WELL... BE CAREFUL GOING HOME.
I WILL!
THANK YOU FOR TODAY...
...I REALLY...
...CAUSED A LOT OF TROUBLE FOR MASTER-SAN TODAY...
NOW I HAVE TO...
...PUT MY MIND TO WHAT I CAN DO ABOUT THE CURSE...
......
KEEP BEING YOURSELF NO MATTER WHAT.

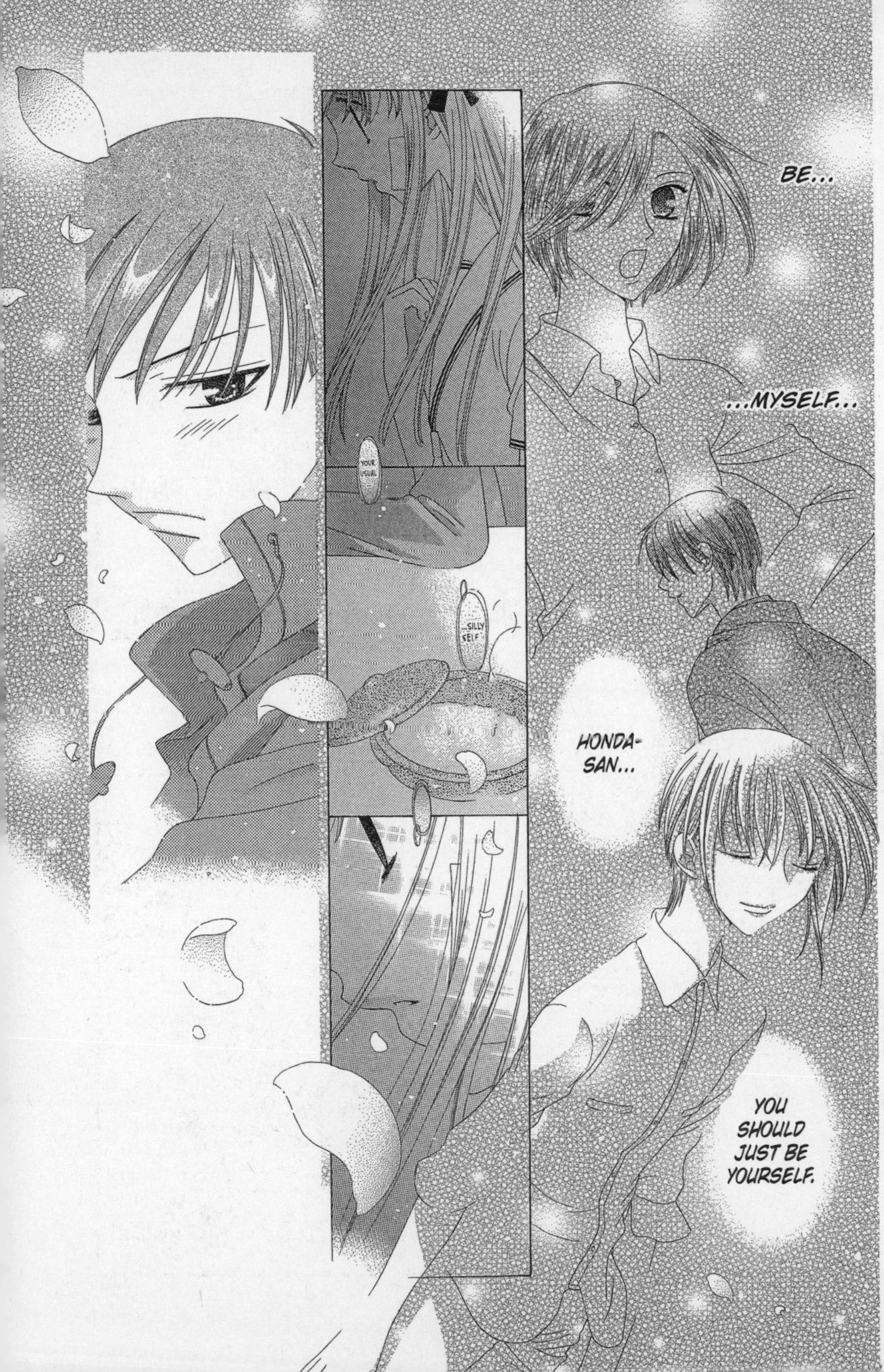
BE...
...MYSELF...
HONDA-SAN...
YOU SHOULD JUST BE YOURSELF.
YOUR USUAL
...SILLY SELF

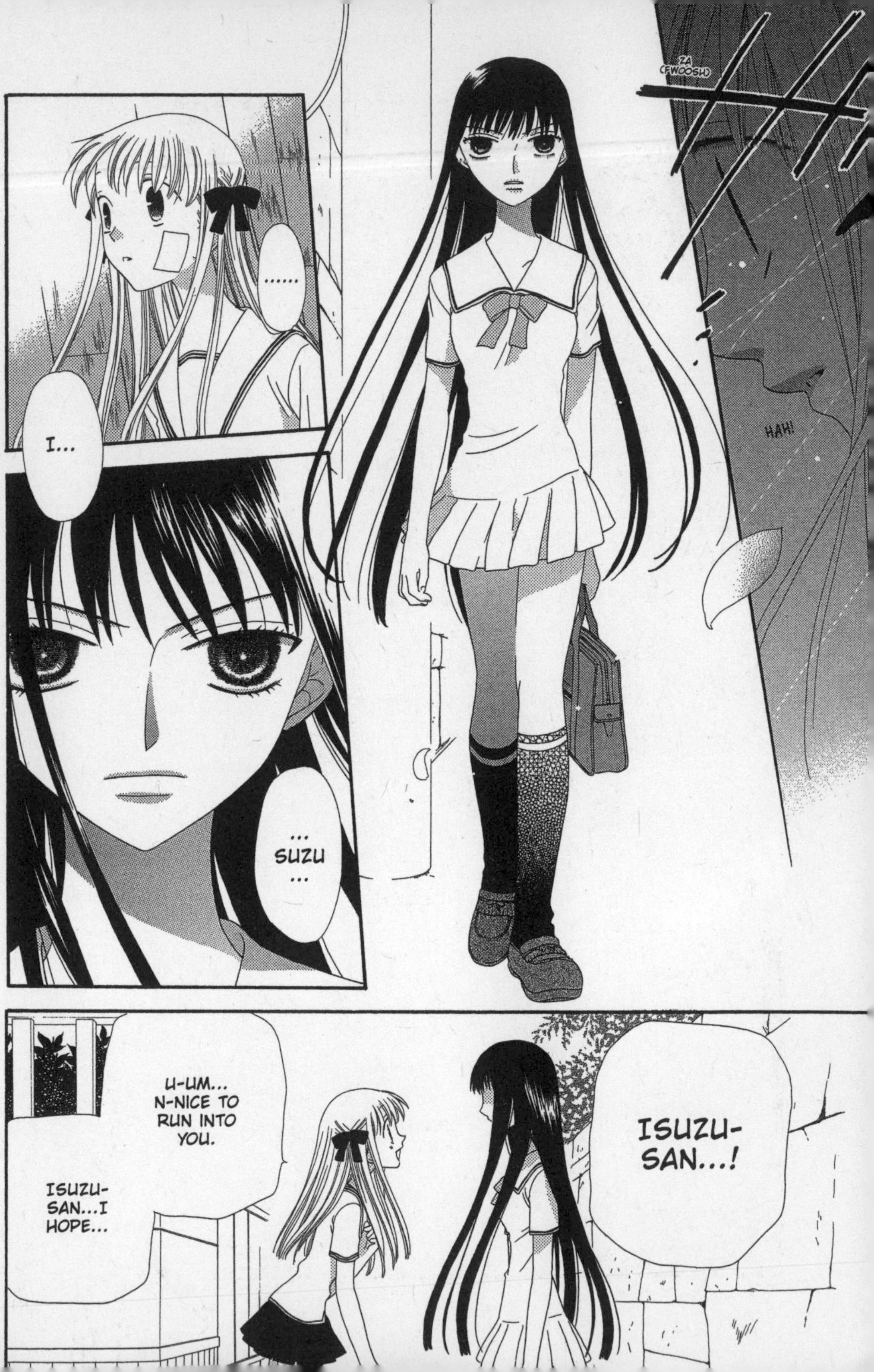

ZA (FWOOSH)
HAH!
......
I...
...SUZU...
ISUZU-SAN...!
U-UM... N-NICE TO RUN INTO YOU.
ISUZU-SAN...I HOPE...

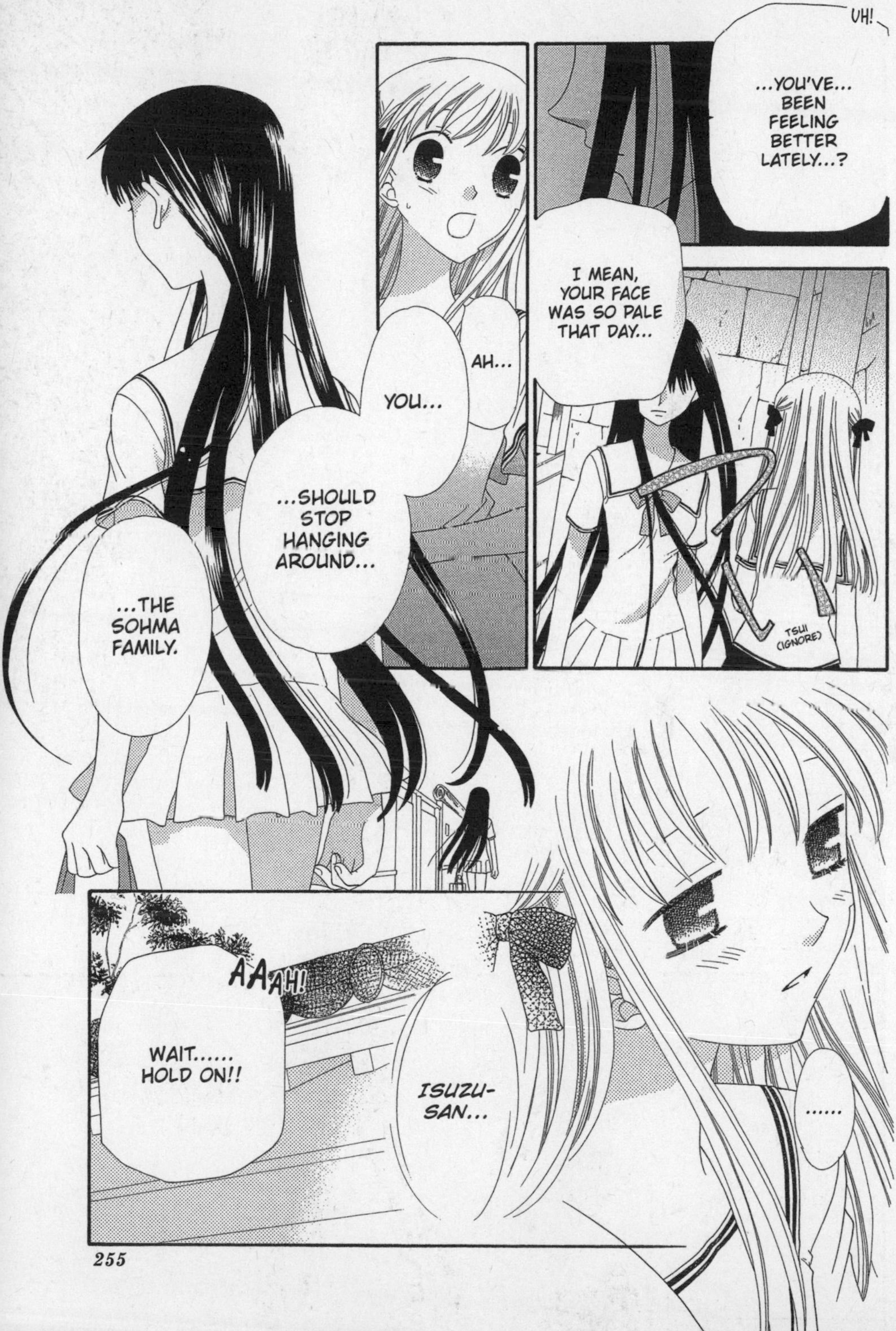

UH!
...YOU'VE... BEEN FEELING BETTER LATELY...?
I MEAN, YOUR FACE WAS SO PALE THAT DAY...
TSUI (IGNORE)
AH...
YOU...
...SHOULD STOP HANGING AROUND...
...THE SOHMA FAMILY.
......
ISUZU-SAN...
AAAH!
WAIT...... HOLD ON!!

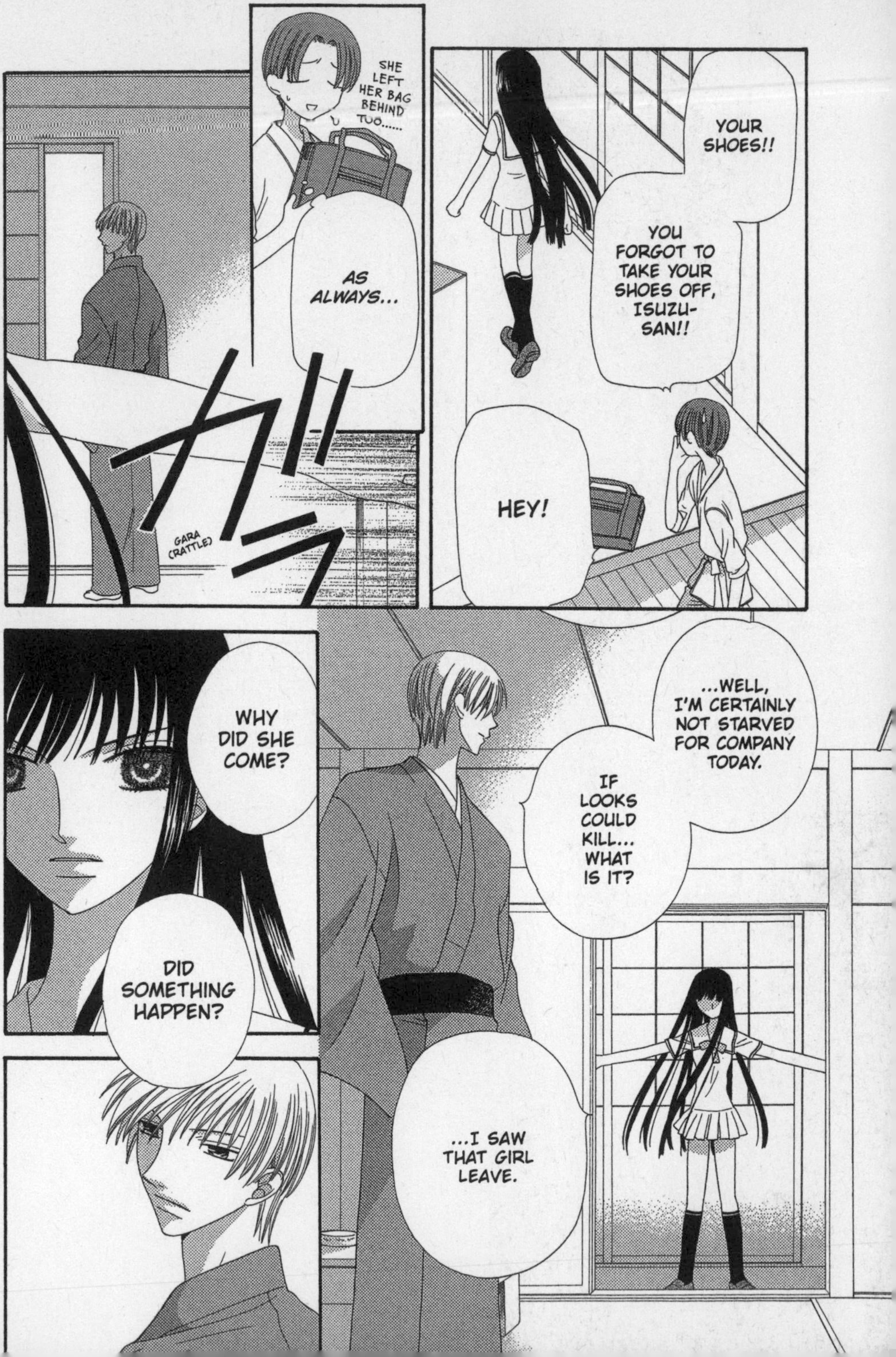
YOUR SHOES!!
YOU FORGOT TO TAKE YOUR SHOES OFF, ISUZU-SAN!!
HEY!
SHE LEFT HER BAG BEHIND TOO......
AS ALWAYS...
GARA (RATTLE)
...WELL, I'M CERTAINLY NOT STARVED FOR COMPANY TODAY.
IF LOOKS COULD KILL... WHAT IS IT?
...I SAW THAT GIRL LEAVE.
WHY DID SHE COME?
DID SOMETHING HAPPEN?

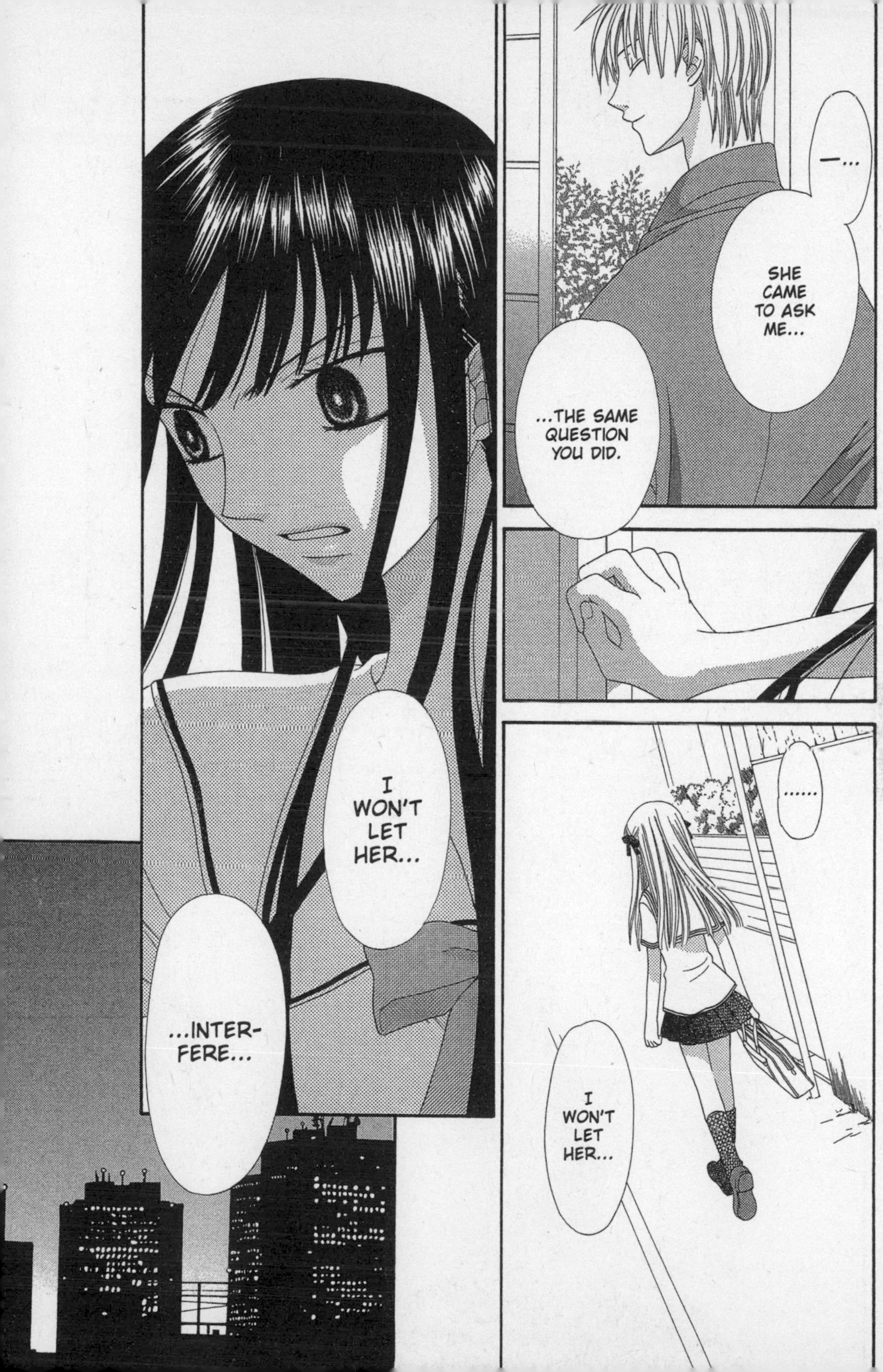
—...
SHE CAME TO ASK ME...
...THE SAME QUESTION YOU DID.
......
I WON'T LET HER...
I WON'T LET HER...
...INTER- FERE...

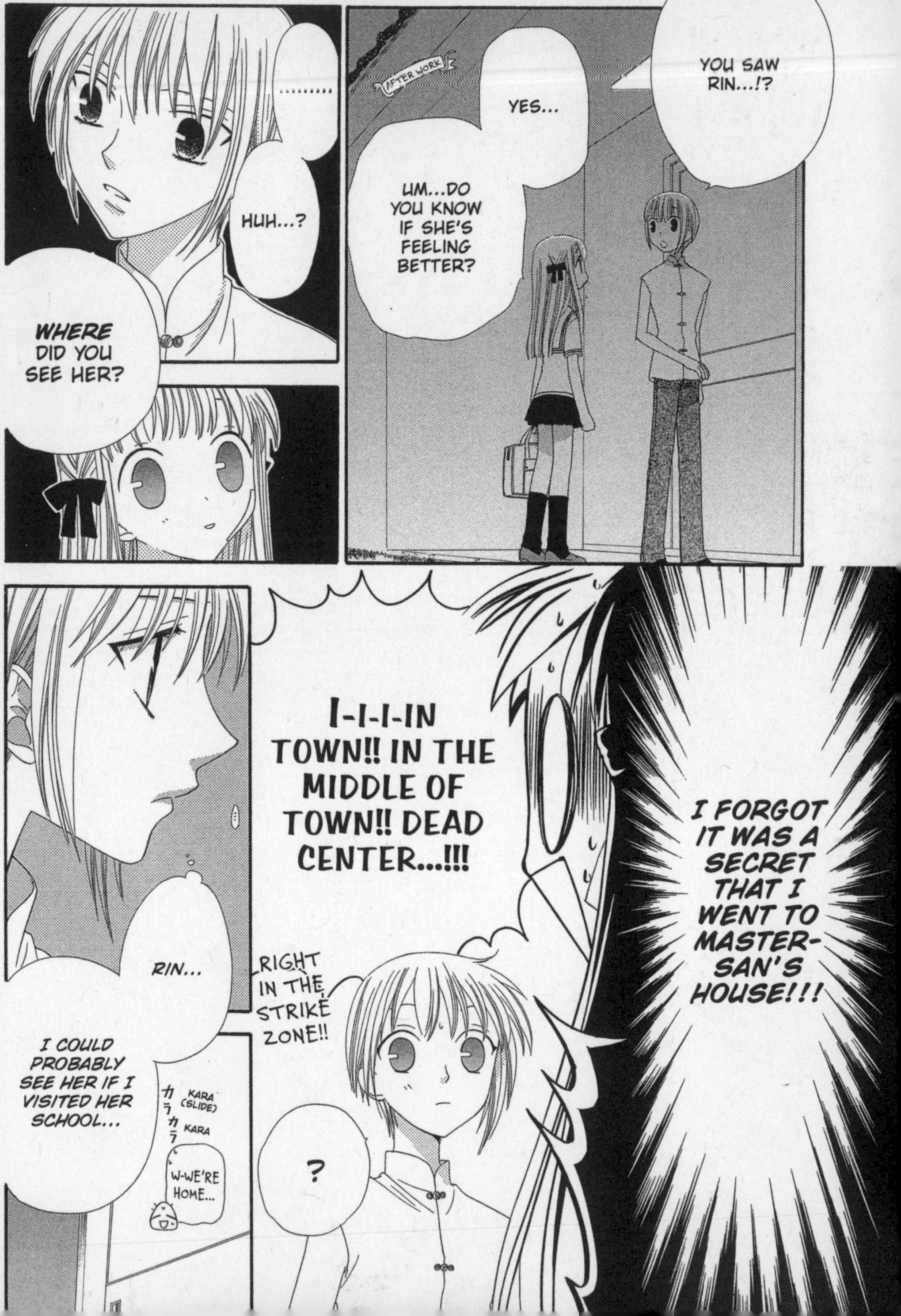
AFTER WORK
YOU SAW RIN...!?
YES...
UM...DO YOU KNOW IF SHE'S FEELING BETTER?
......
HUH...?
WHERE DID YOU SEE HER?
I FORGOT IT WAS A SECRET THAT I WENT TO MASTER-SAN'S HOUSE!!!
I-I-I-IN TOWN!! IN THE MIDDLE OF TOWN!! DEAD CENTER...!!!
RIGHT IN THE STRIKE ZONE!!
?
RIN...
I COULD PROBABLY SEE HER IF I VISITED HER SCHOOL...
カラ KARA (SLIDE)
カラ KARA
W-WE'RE HOME...

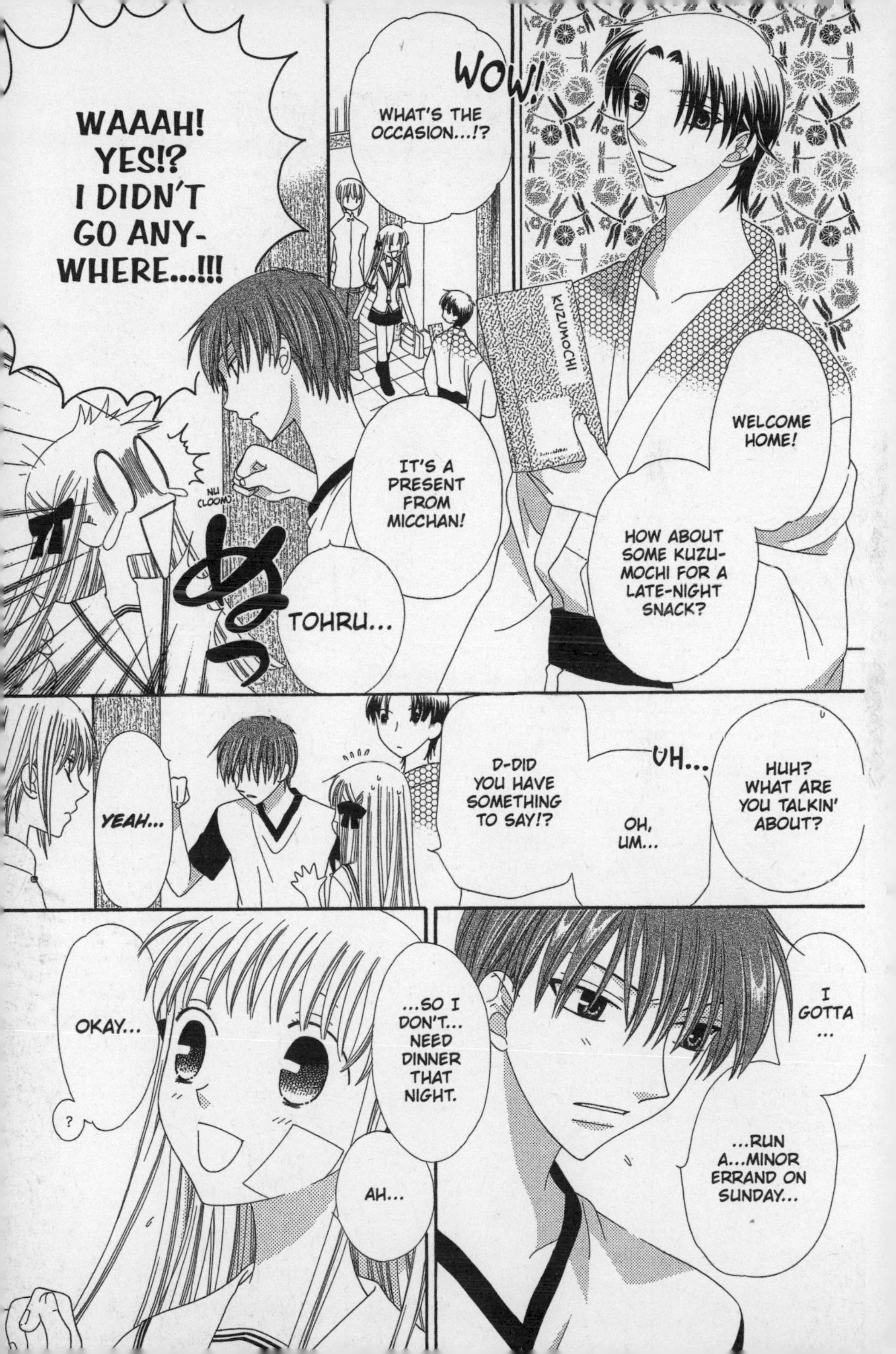
WELCOME HOME!
HOW ABOUT SOME KUZUMOCHI FOR A LATE-NIGHT SNACK?
KUZUMOCHI
WOW!
WHAT'S THE OCCASION...!?
IT'S A PRESENT FROM MICCHAN!
TOHRU...
NU (LOOM)
WAAAH! YES!? I DIDN'T GO ANYWHERE...!!!
HUH? WHAT ARE YOU TALKIN' ABOUT?
UH...
OH, UM...
D-DID YOU HAVE SOMETHING TO SAY!?
YEAH...
I GOTTA ...
...RUN A...MINOR ERRAND ON SUNDAY...
...SO I DON'T... NEED DINNER THAT NIGHT.
AH...
OKAY...
?

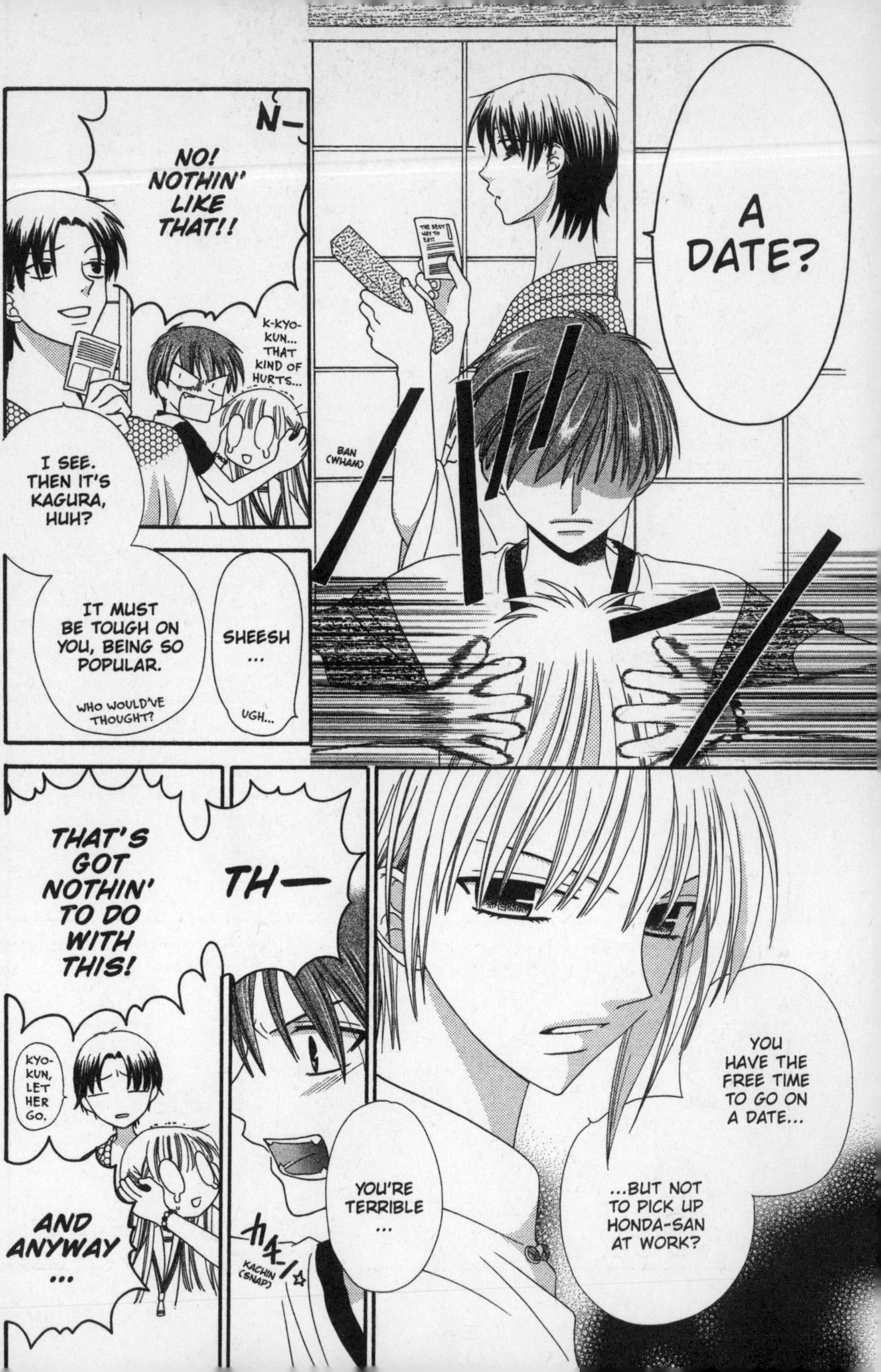
A DATE?
THE BEST WAY TO EAT!
BAN (WHAM)
N—
NO! NOTHIN' LIKE THAT!!
K-KYO-KUN... THAT KIND OF HURTS...
I SEE. THEN IT'S KAGURA, HUH?
SHEESH ...
UGH...
IT MUST BE TOUGH ON YOU, BEING SO POPULAR.
WHO WOULD'VE THOUGHT?
YOU HAVE THE FREE TIME TO GO ON A DATE...
...BUT NOT TO PICK UP HONDA-SAN AT WORK?
YOU'RE TERRIBLE ...
KACHIN (SNAP)
TH—
THAT'S GOT NOTHIN' TO DO WITH THIS!
KYO-KUN, LET HER GO.
AND ANYWAY ...

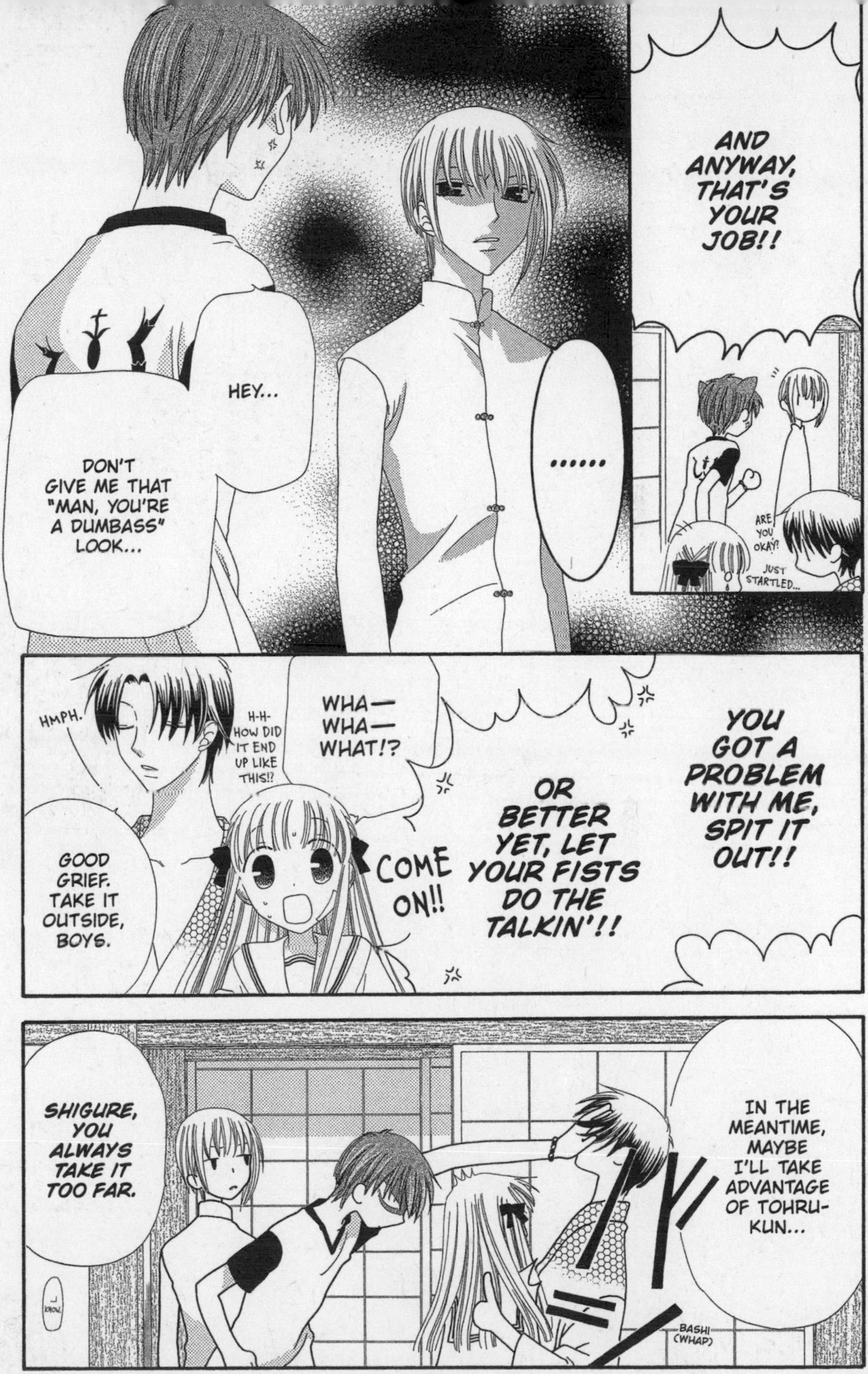
AND ANYWAY, THAT'S YOUR JOB!!
ARE YOU OKAY?
JUST STARTLED...
......
HEY...
DON'T GIVE ME THAT "MAN, YOU'RE A DUMBASS" LOOK...
YOU GOT A PROBLEM WITH ME, SPIT IT OUT!!
OR BETTER YET, LET YOUR FISTS DO THE TALKIN'!!
COME ON!!
WHA— WHA— WHAT!?
H-H-HOW DID IT END UP LIKE THIS!?
HMPH.
GOOD GRIEF. TAKE IT OUTSIDE, BOYS.
IN THE MEANTIME, MAYBE I'LL TAKE ADVANTAGE OF TOHRU-KUN...
BASHI (WHAP)
SHIGURE, YOU ALWAYS TAKE IT TOO FAR.
I KNOW.

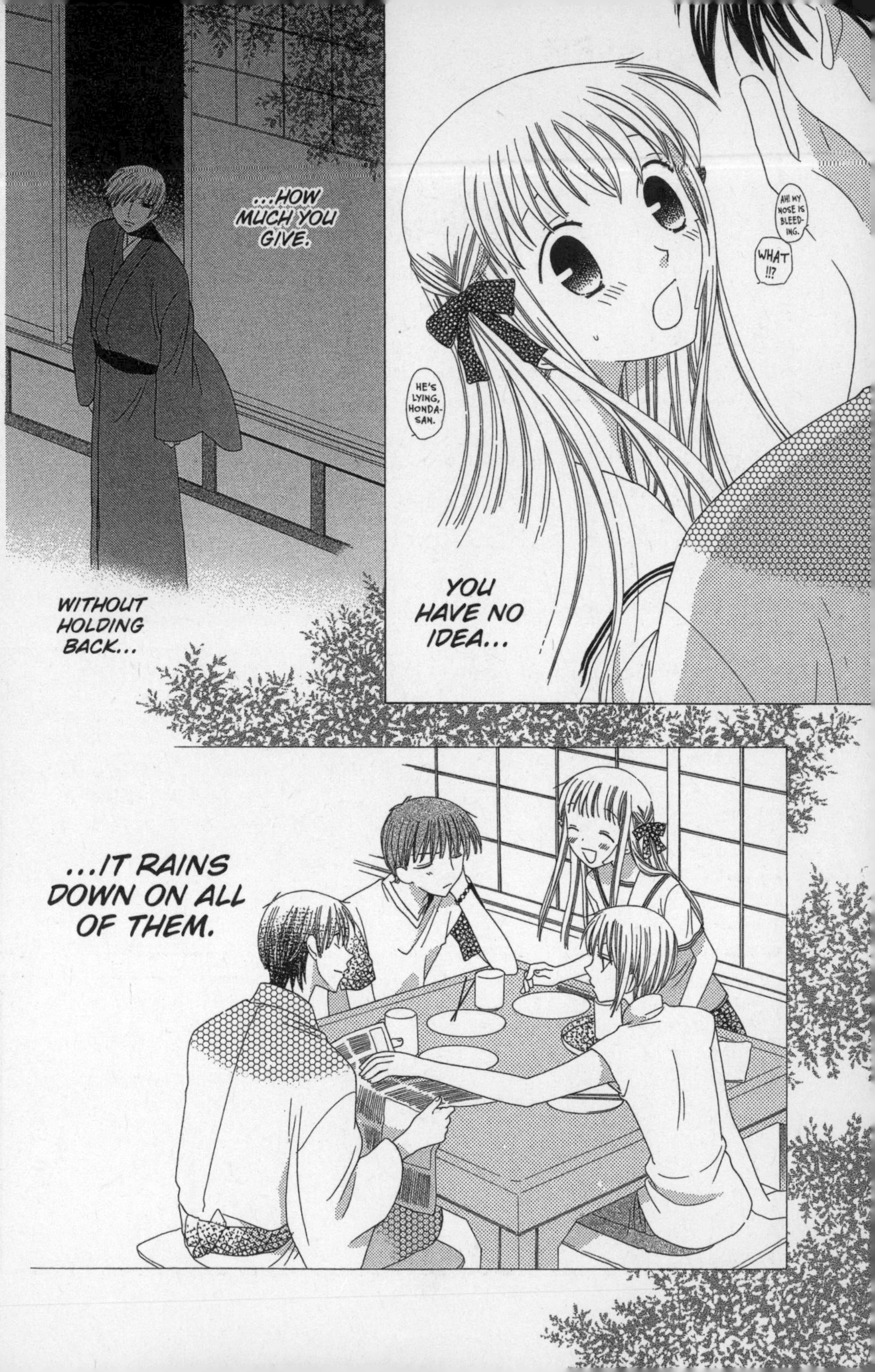
AH! MY NOSE IS BLEED-ING.
WHAT!!?
HE'S LYING, HONDA-SAN.
YOU HAVE NO IDEA...
...HOW MUCH YOU GIVE.
WITHOUT HOLDING BACK...
...IT RAINS DOWN ON ALL OF THEM.

Chapter 68

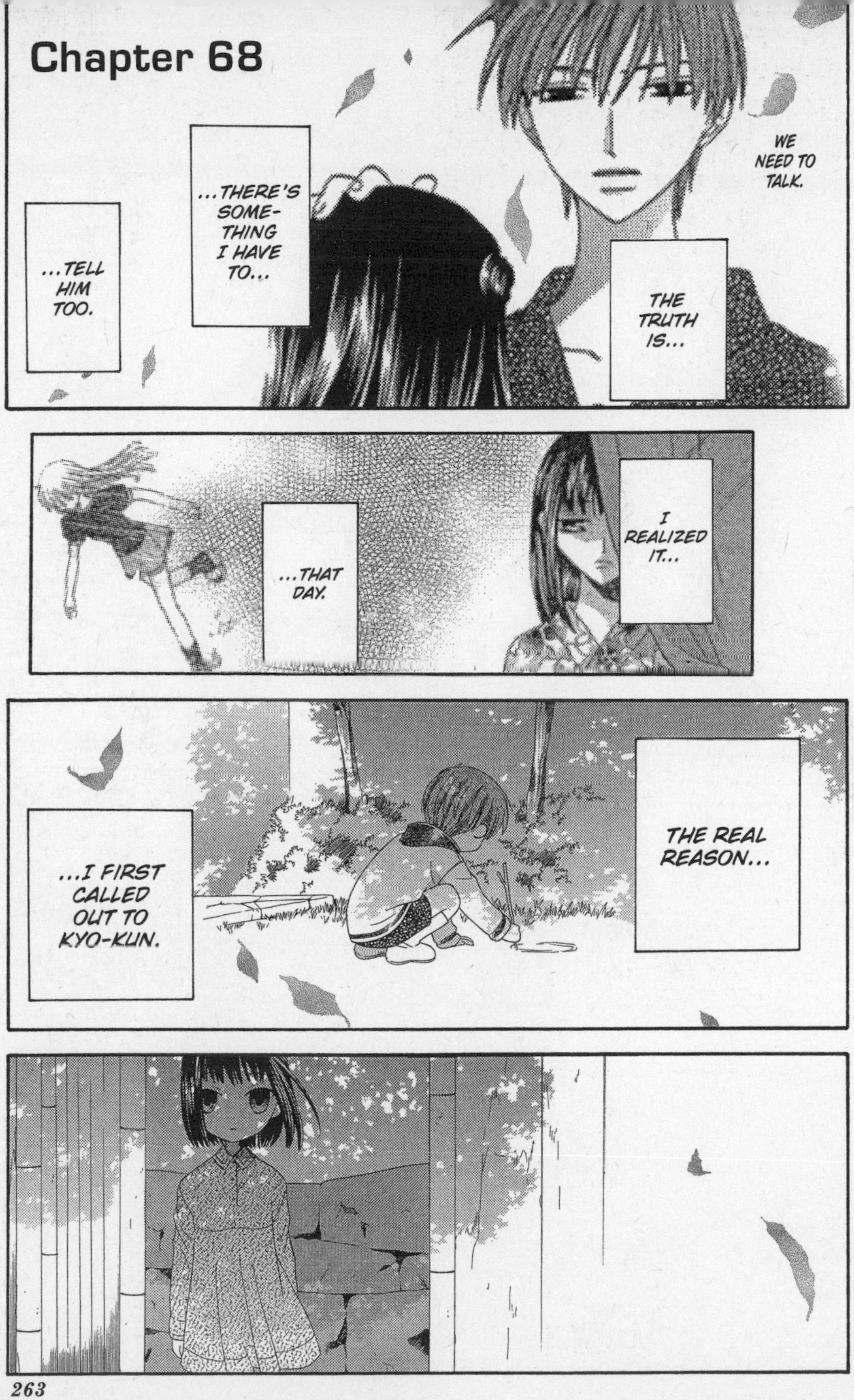
WE NEED TO TALK.
THE TRUTH IS...
...THERE'S SOMETHING I HAVE TO...
...TELL HIM TOO.
I REALIZED IT...
...THAT DAY.
THE REAL REASON...
...I FIRST CALLED OUT TO KYO-KUN.

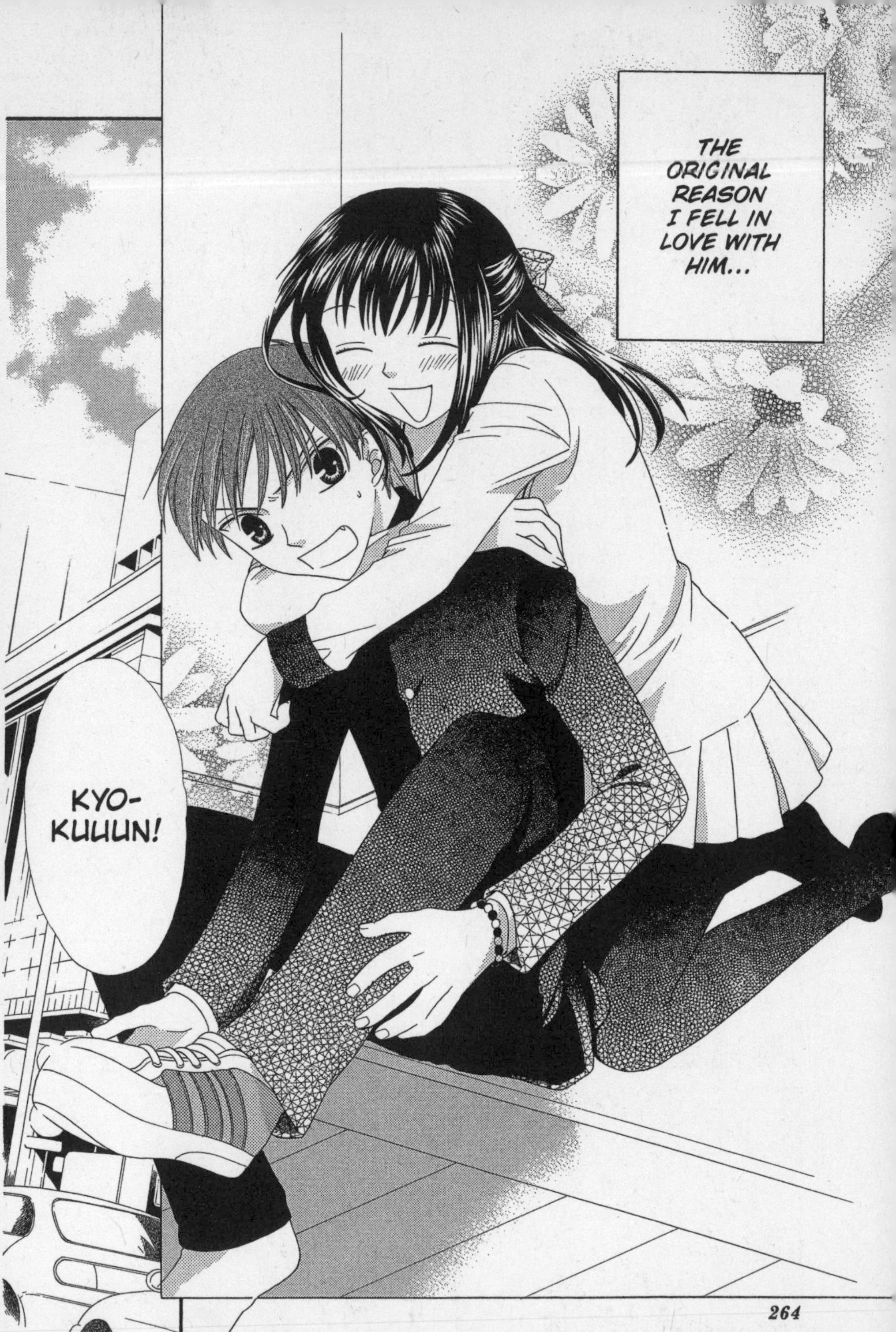
THE ORIGINAL REASON I FELL IN LOVE WITH HIM...
KYO-KUUUN!

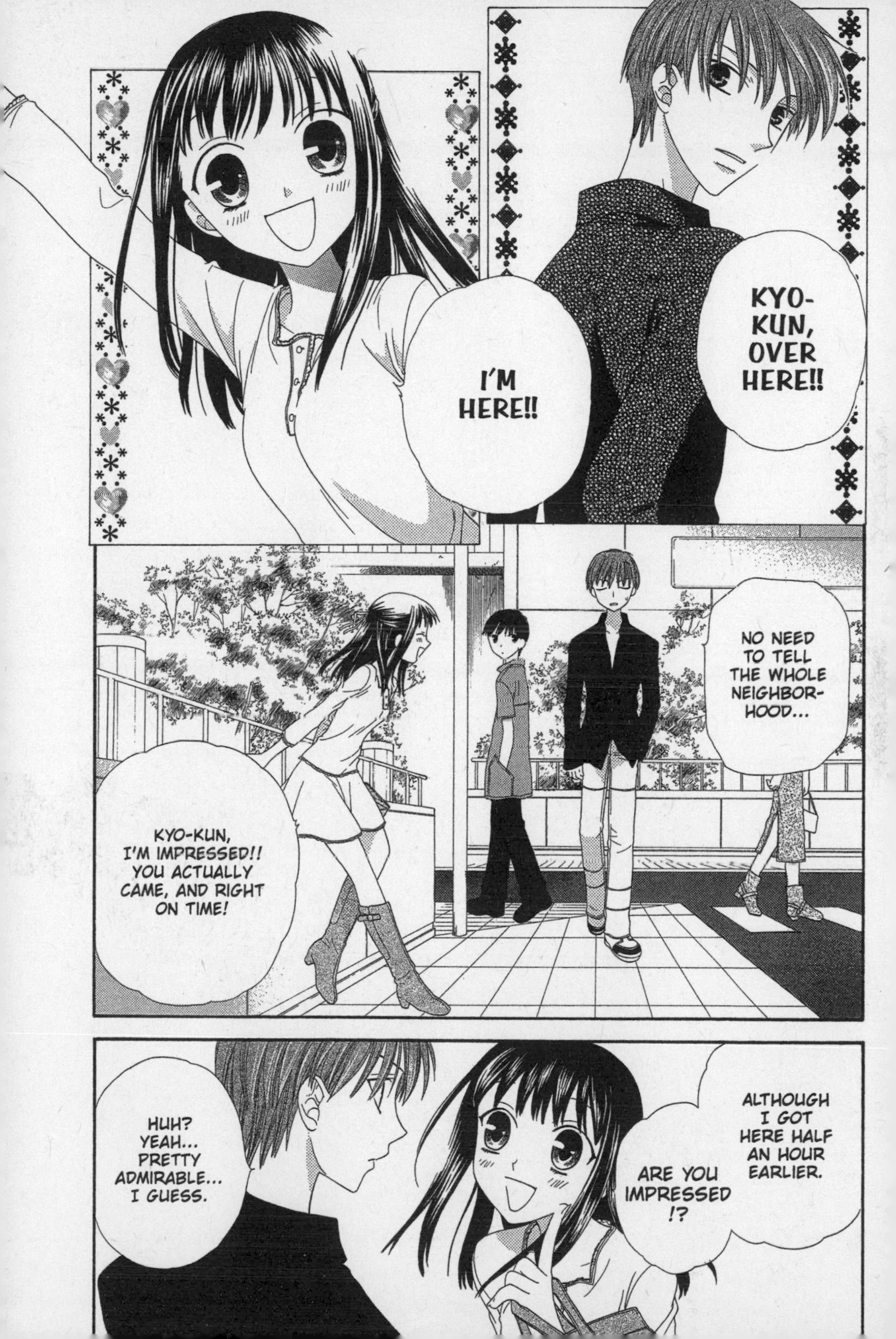
KYO-KUN, OVER HERE!!
I'M HERE!!
NO NEED TO TELL THE WHOLE NEIGHBOR-HOOD...
KYO-KUN, I'M IMPRESSED!! YOU ACTUALLY CAME, AND RIGHT ON TIME!
ALTHOUGH I GOT HERE HALF AN HOUR EARLIER.
ARE YOU IMPRESSED!?
HUH? YEAH... PRETTY ADMIRABLE... I GUESS.

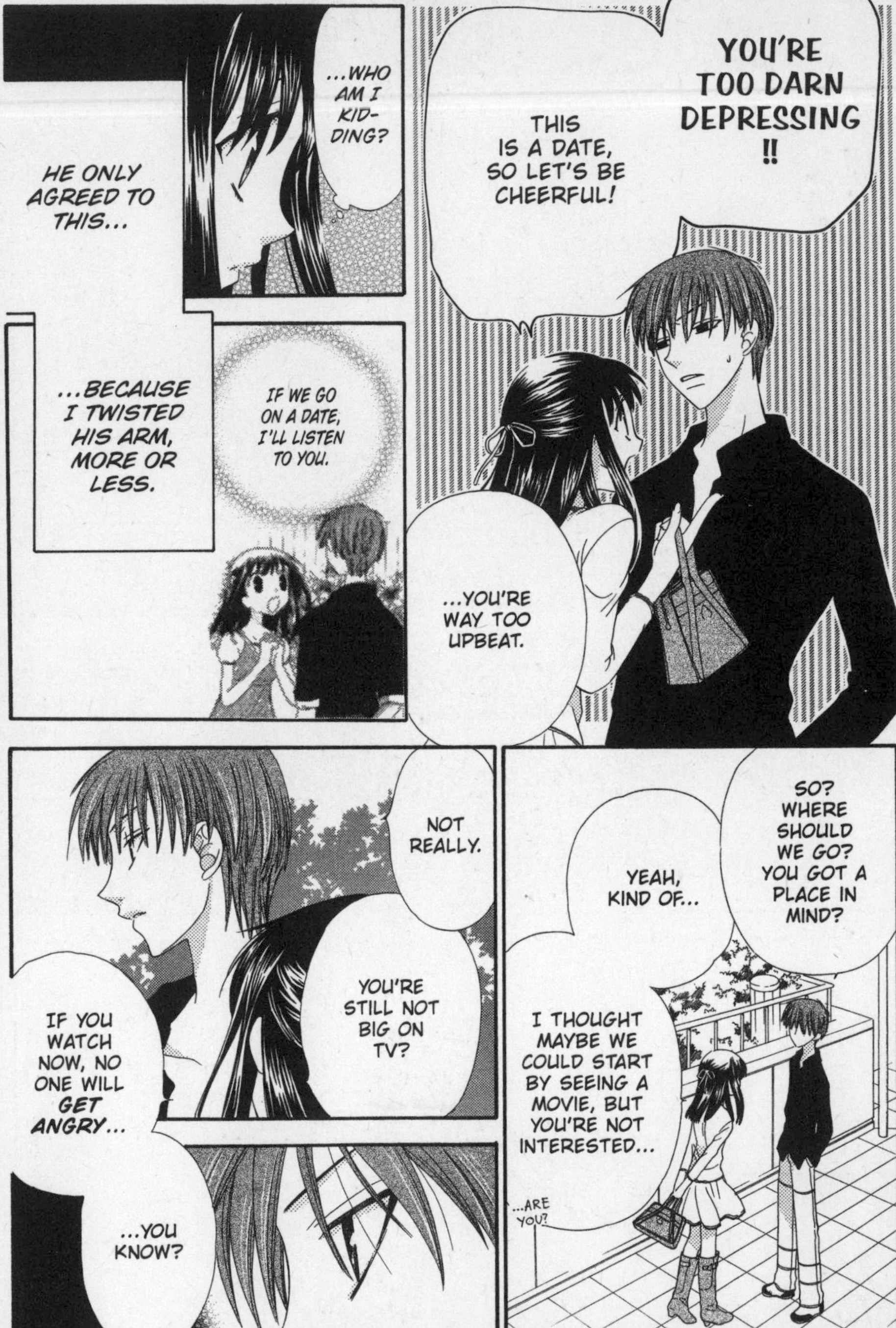
YOU'RE TOO DARN DEPRESSING!!
THIS IS A DATE, SO LET'S BE CHEERFUL!
...YOU'RE WAY TOO UPBEAT.
...WHO AM I KID-DING?
HE ONLY AGREED TO THIS...
...BECAUSE I TWISTED HIS ARM, MORE OR LESS.
IF WE GO ON A DATE, I'LL LISTEN TO YOU.
SO? WHERE SHOULD WE GO? YOU GOT A PLACE IN MIND?
YEAH, KIND OF...
I THOUGHT MAYBE WE COULD START BY SEEING A MOVIE, BUT YOU'RE NOT INTERESTED...
...ARE YOU?
NOT REALLY.
YOU'RE STILL NOT BIG ON TV?
IF YOU WATCH NOW, NO ONE WILL GET ANGRY...
...YOU KNOW?

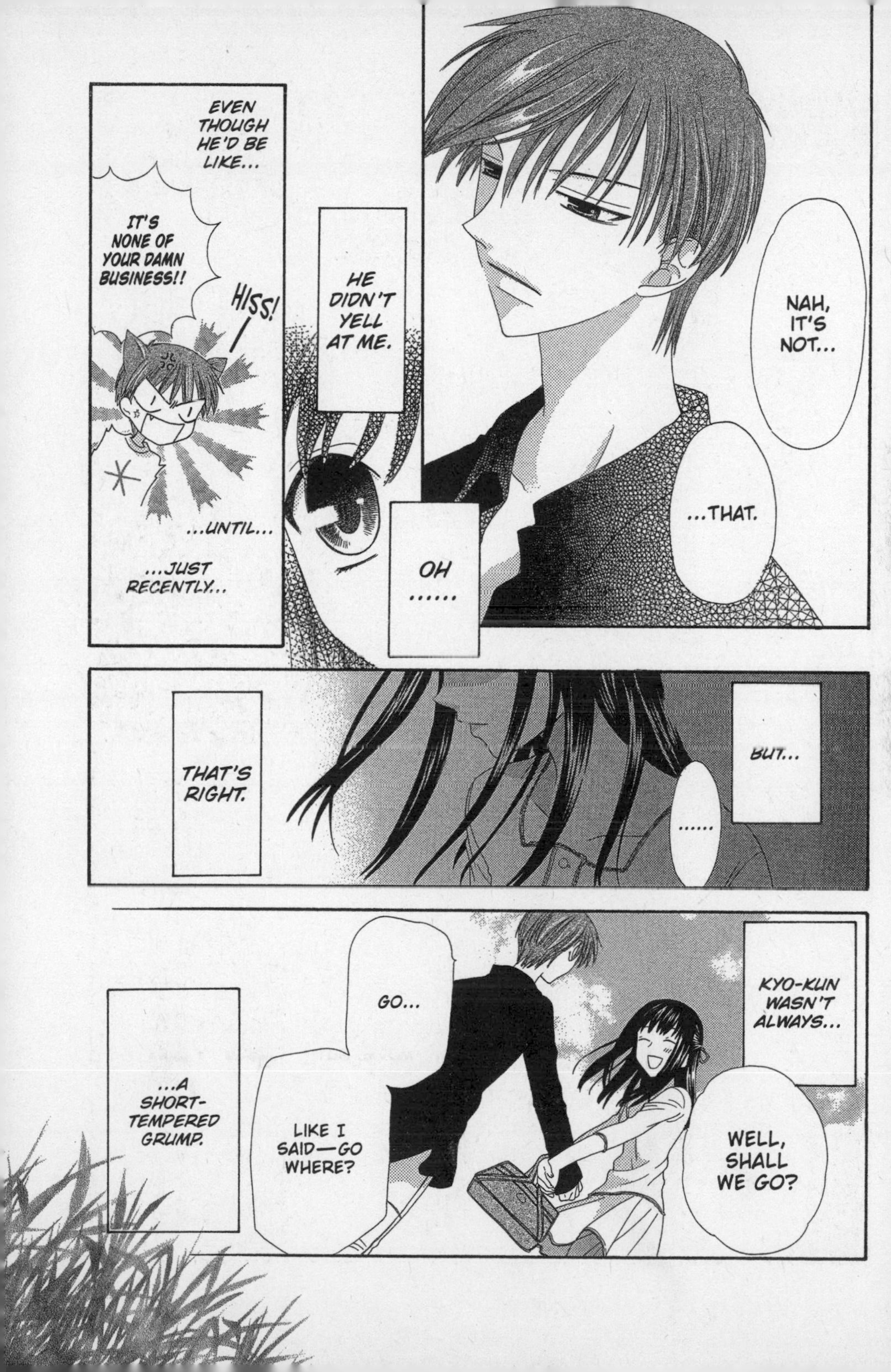
NAH, IT'S NOT...
...THAT.
OH ......
HE DIDN'T YELL AT ME.
EVEN THOUGH HE'D BE LIKE...
IT'S NONE OF YOUR DAMN BUSINESS!!
HISS!
...UNTIL...
...JUST RECENTLY...
BUT...
......
THAT'S RIGHT.
KYO-KUN WASN'T ALWAYS...
WELL, SHALL WE GO?
GO...
LIKE I SAID—GO WHERE?
...A SHORT-TEMPERED GRUMP.

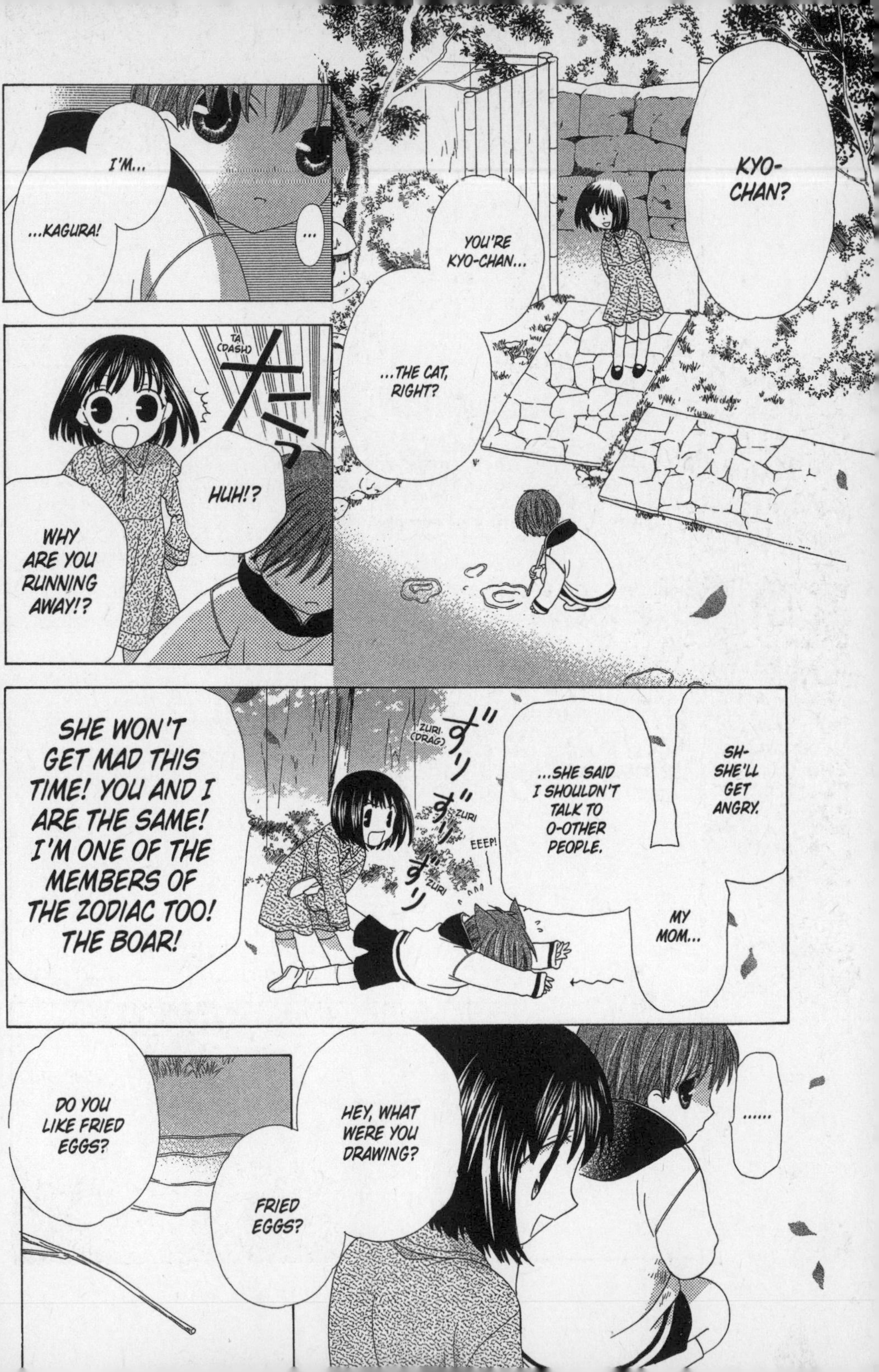
KYO-CHAN?
YOU'RE KYO-CHAN...
...THE CAT, RIGHT?
...
I'M...
...KAGURA!
TA (DASH)
HUH!?
WHY ARE YOU RUNNING AWAY!?
SH-SHE'LL GET ANGRY.
MY MOM...
...SHE SAID I SHOULDN'T TALK TO O-OTHER PEOPLE.
ZURI (DRAG)
ZURI
ZURI
EEEP!
SHE WON'T GET MAD THIS TIME! YOU AND I ARE THE SAME! I'M ONE OF THE MEMBERS OF THE ZODIAC TOO! THE BOAR!
......
HEY, WHAT WERE YOU DRAWING?
FRIED EGGS?
DO YOU LIKE FRIED EGGS?

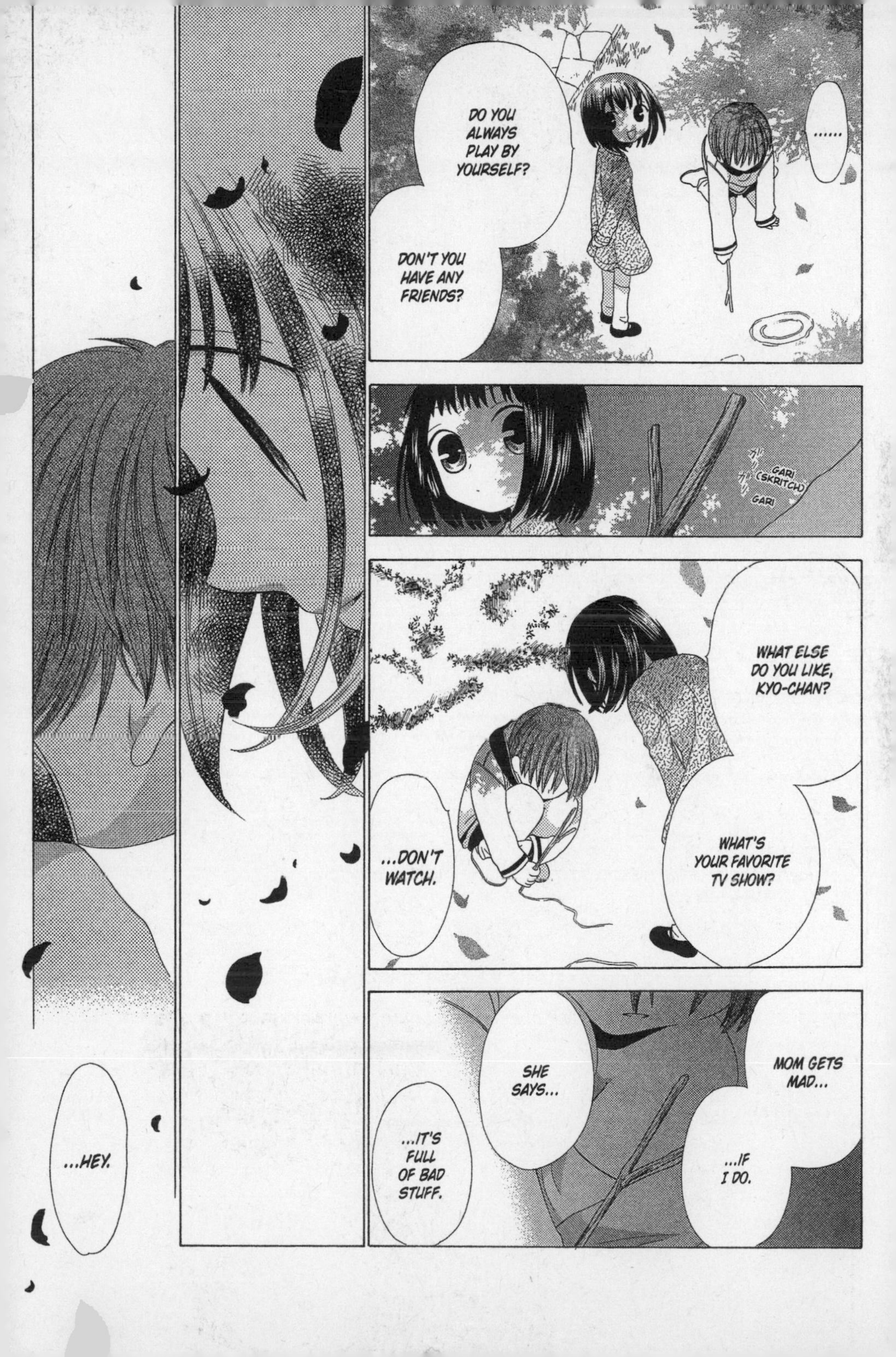
DO YOU ALWAYS PLAY BY YOURSELF?
DON'T YOU HAVE ANY FRIENDS?
......
GARI (SKRITCH) GARI
WHAT ELSE DO YOU LIKE, KYO-CHAN?
WHAT'S YOUR FAVORITE TV SHOW?
...DON'T WATCH.
MOM GETS MAD...
...IF I DO.
SHE SAYS...
...IT'S FULL OF BAD STUFF.
...HEY.

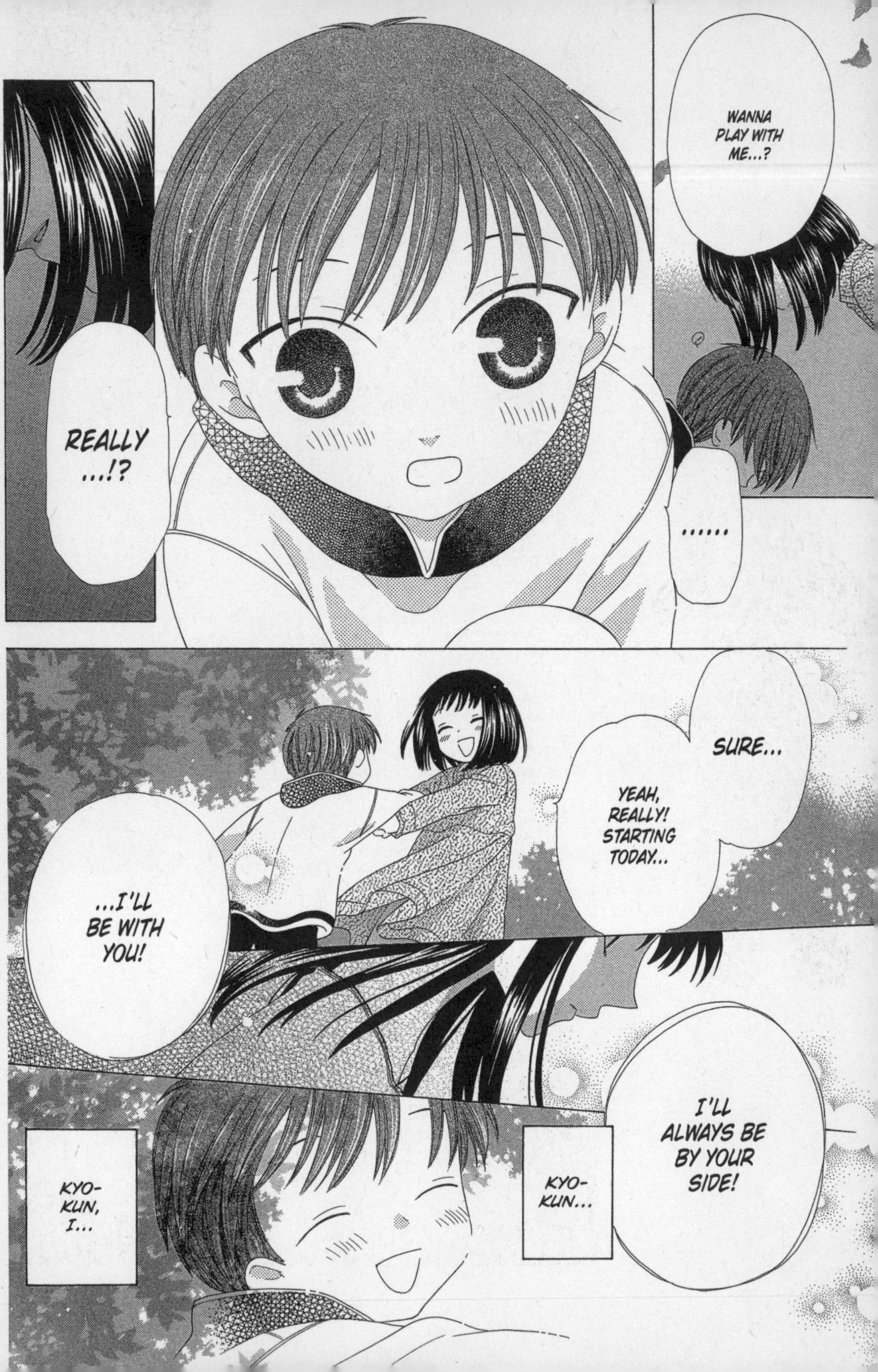
WANNA PLAY WITH ME...?
......
REALLY ...!?
SURE...
YEAH, REALLY! STARTING TODAY...
...I'LL BE WITH YOU!
I'LL ALWAYS BE BY YOUR SIDE!
KYO-KUN...
KYO-KUN, I...

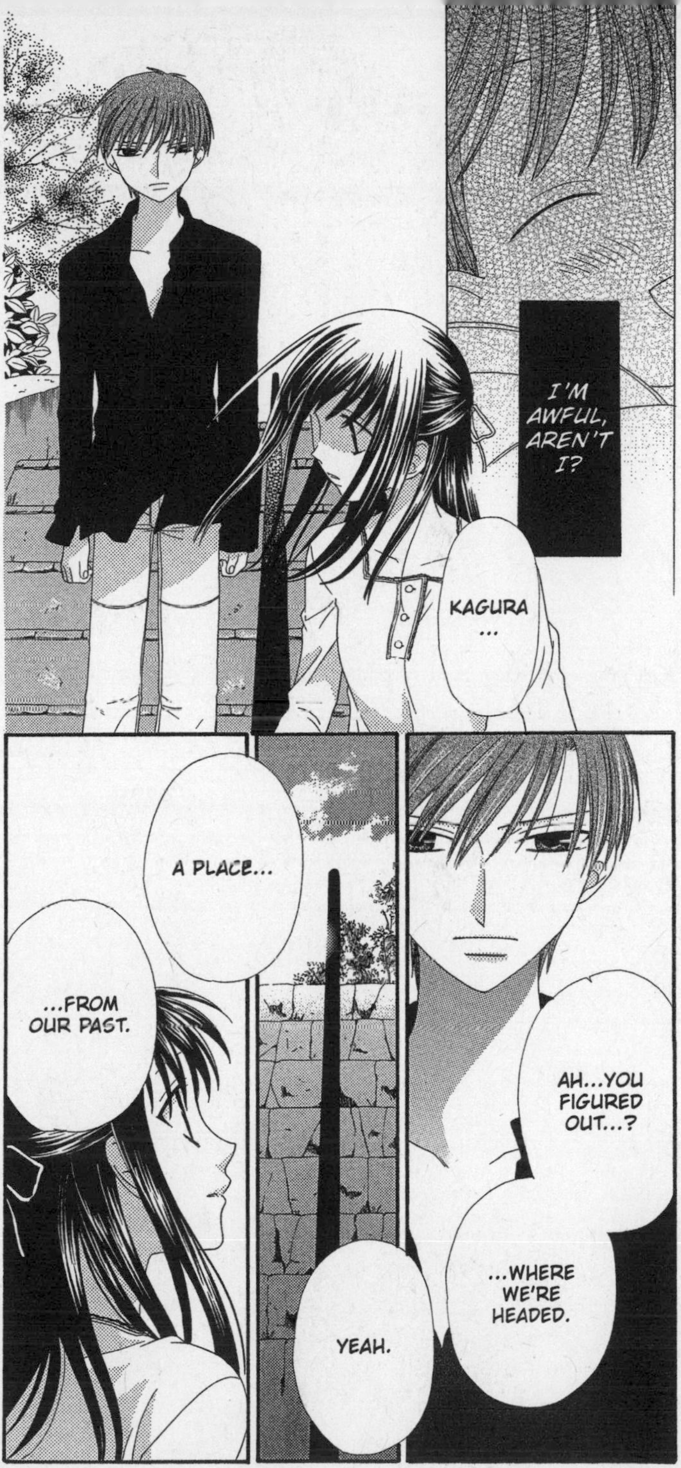
I'M AWFUL, AREN'T I?
KAGURA...
AH...YOU FIGURED OUT...?
...WHERE WE'RE HEADED.
YEAH.
A PLACE...
...FROM OUR PAST.
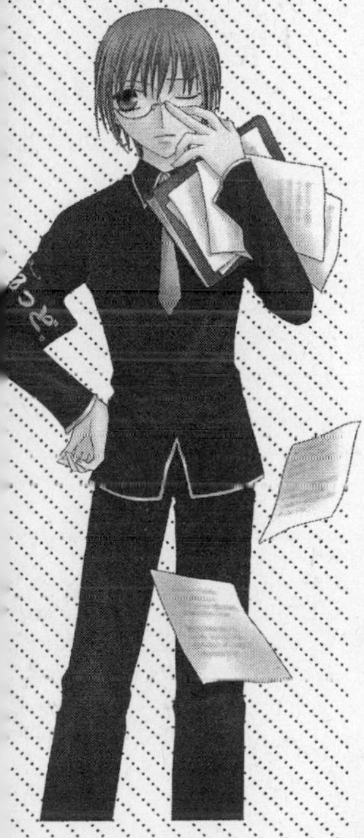

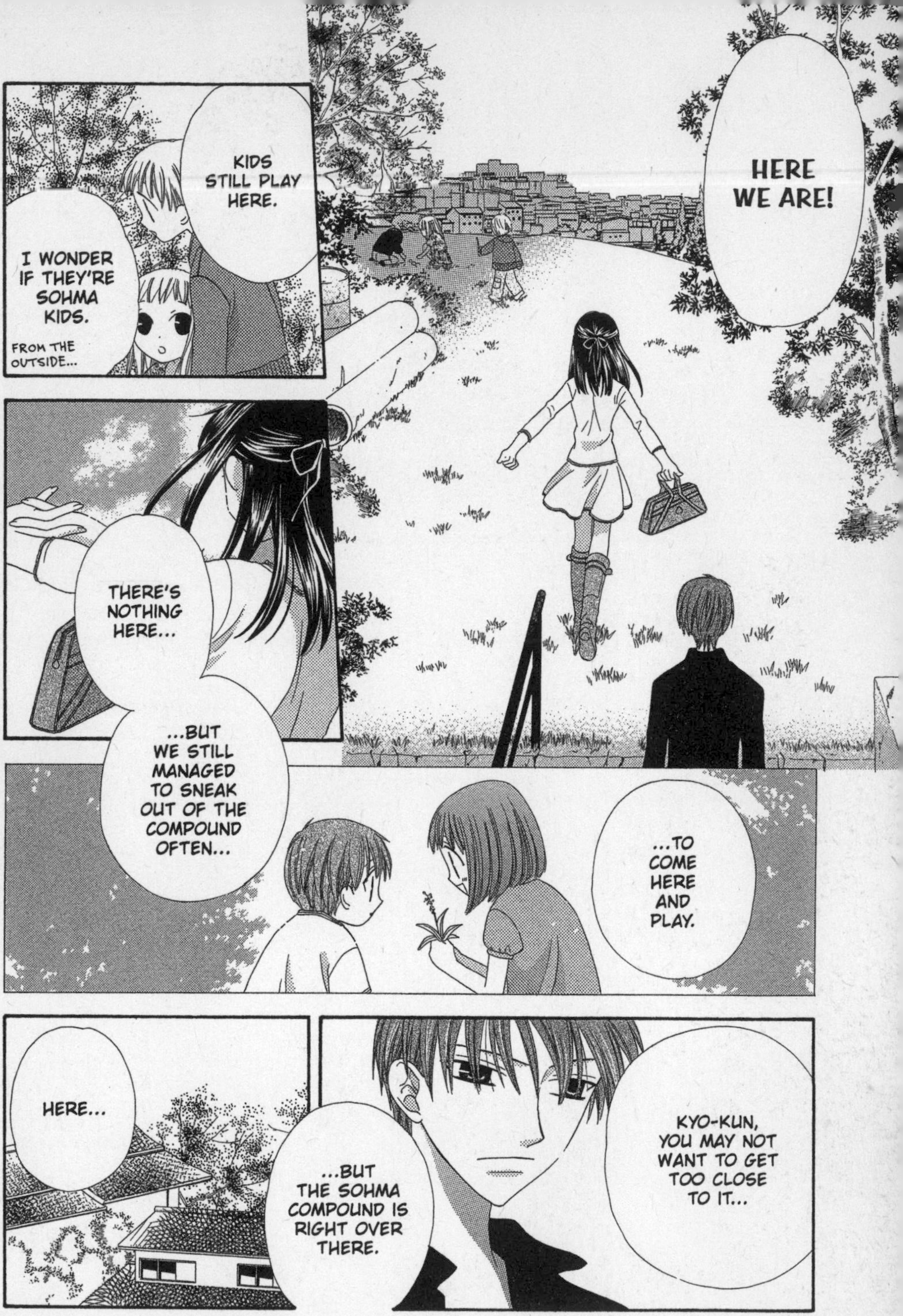
HERE WE ARE!
KIDS STILL PLAY HERE.
I WONDER IF THEY'RE SOHMA KIDS.
FROM THE OUTSIDE...
THERE'S NOTHING HERE...
...BUT WE STILL MANAGED TO SNEAK OUT OF THE COMPOUND OFTEN...
...TO COME HERE AND PLAY.
HERE...
...BUT THE SOHMA COMPOUND IS RIGHT OVER THERE.
KYO-KUN, YOU MAY NOT WANT TO GET TOO CLOSE TO IT...

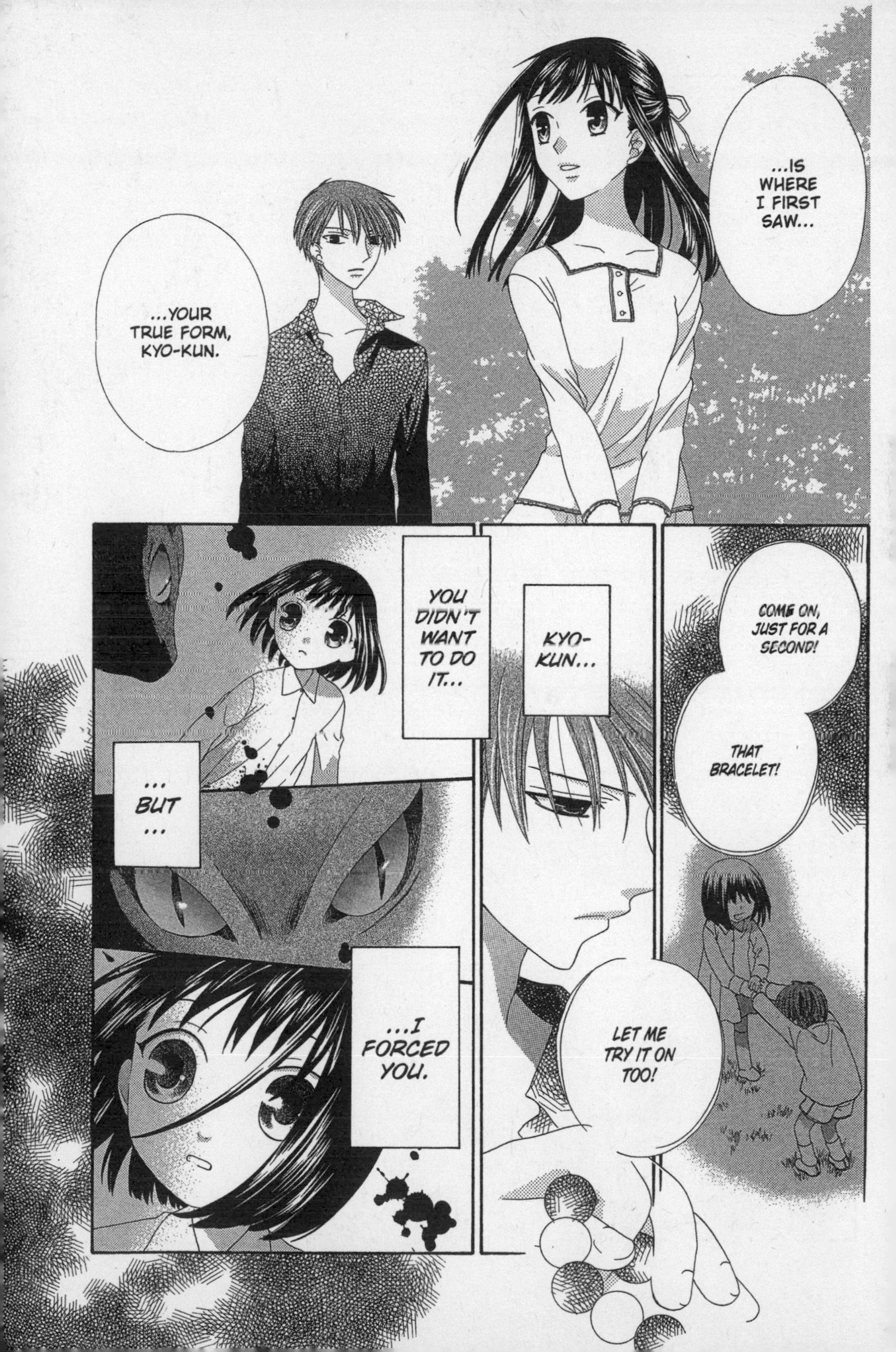
...IS WHERE I FIRST SAW...
...YOUR TRUE FORM, KYO-KUN.
COME ON, JUST FOR A SECOND!
THAT BRACELET!
LET ME TRY IT ON TOO!
KYO-KUN...
YOU DIDN'T WANT TO DO IT...
...BUT...
...I FORCED YOU.

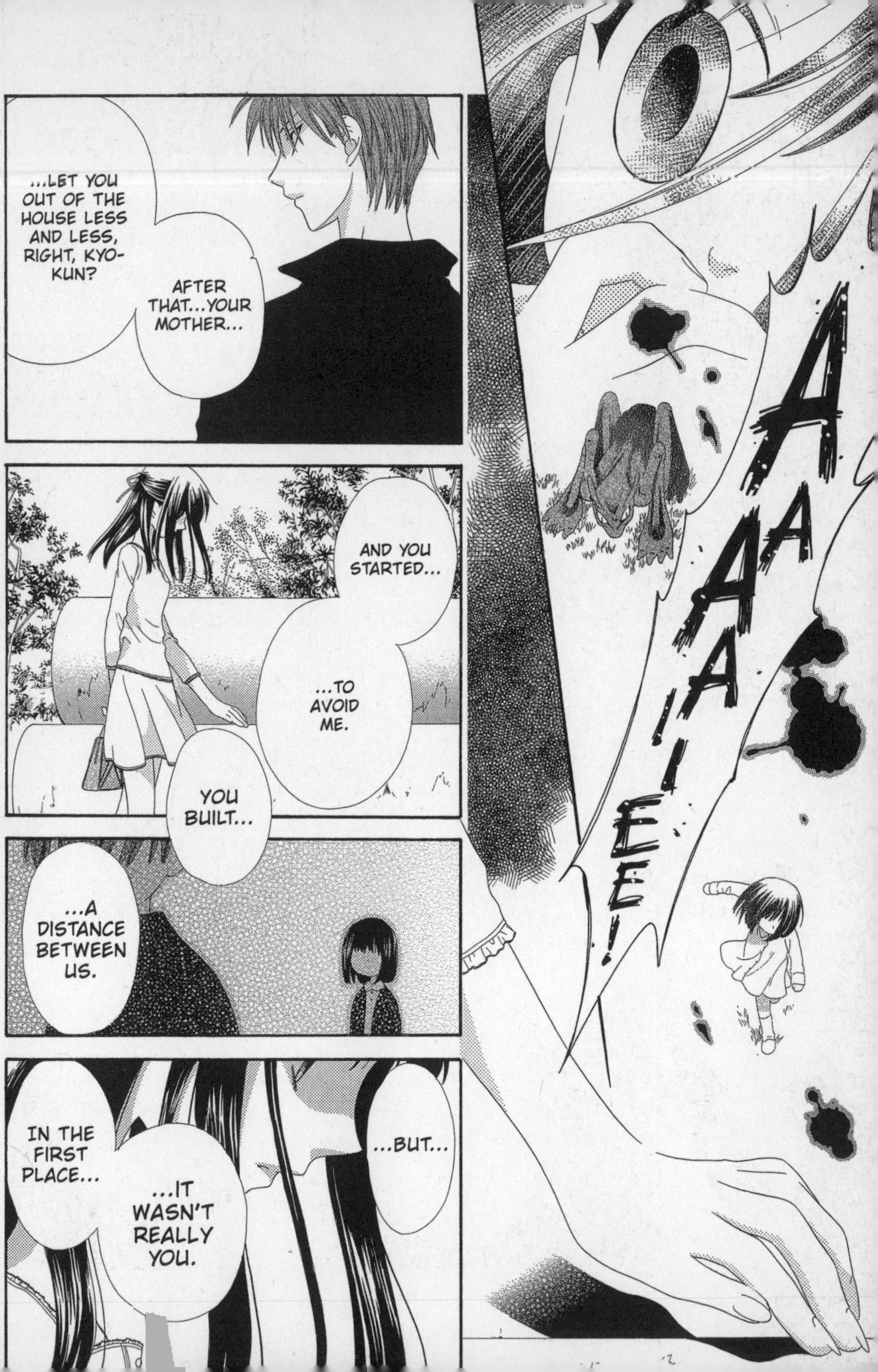
AAAAIIEE!
AFTER THAT...YOUR MOTHER...
...LET YOU OUT OF THE HOUSE LESS AND LESS, RIGHT, KYO-KUN?
AND YOU STARTED...
...TO AVOID ME.
YOU BUILT...
...A DISTANCE BETWEEN US.
...BUT...
IN THE FIRST PLACE...
...IT WASN'T REALLY YOU.

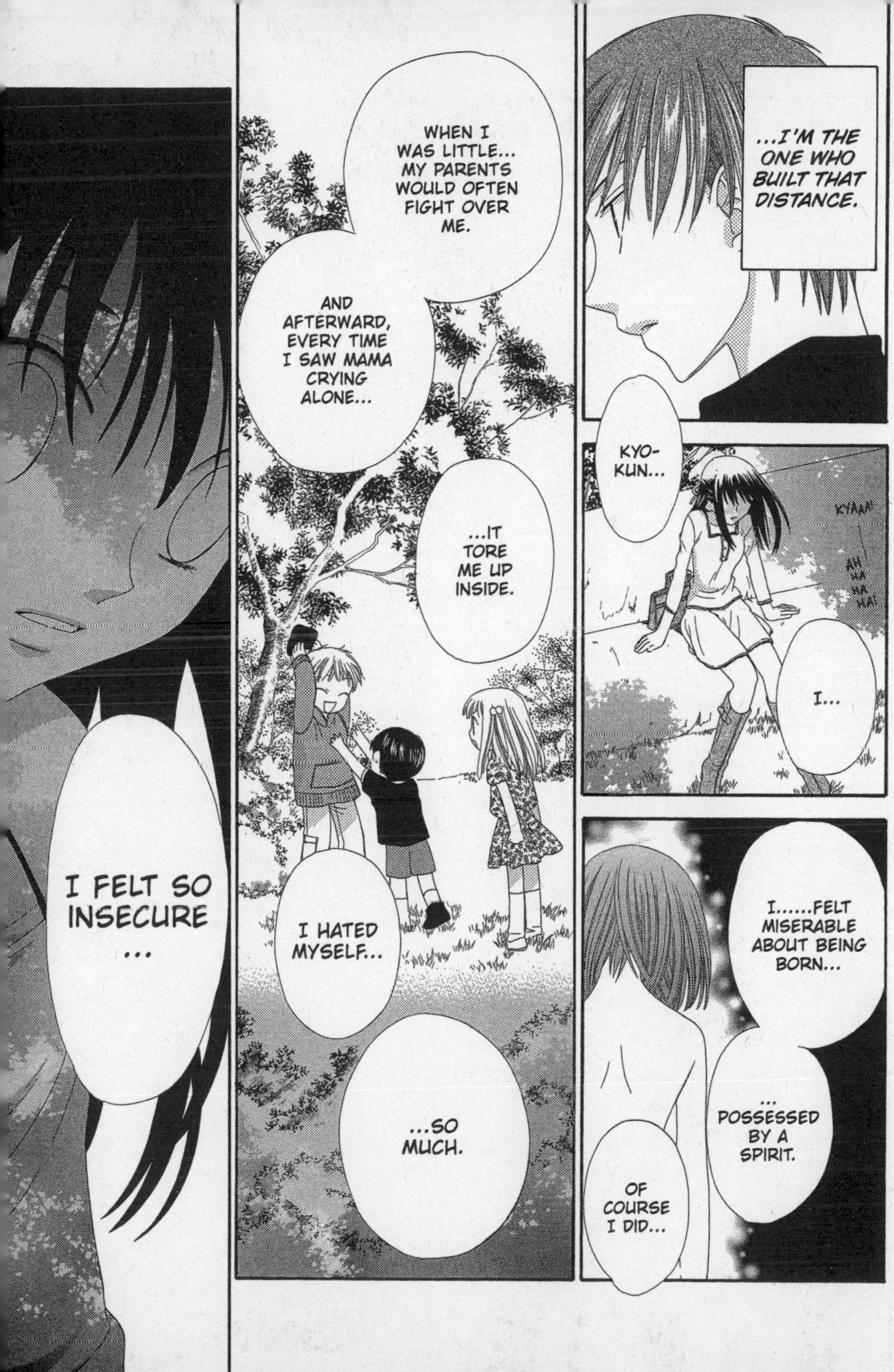
...I'M THE ONE WHO BUILT THAT DISTANCE.
KYO-KUN...
KYAAA!
AH HA HA HA!
I...
I......FELT MISERABLE ABOUT BEING BORN...
...POSSESSED BY A SPIRIT.
OF COURSE I DID...
WHEN I WAS LITTLE... MY PARENTS WOULD OFTEN FIGHT OVER ME.
AND AFTERWARD, EVERY TIME I SAW MAMA CRYING ALONE...
...IT TORE ME UP INSIDE.
I HATED MYSELF...
...SO MUCH.
I FELT SO INSECURE ...

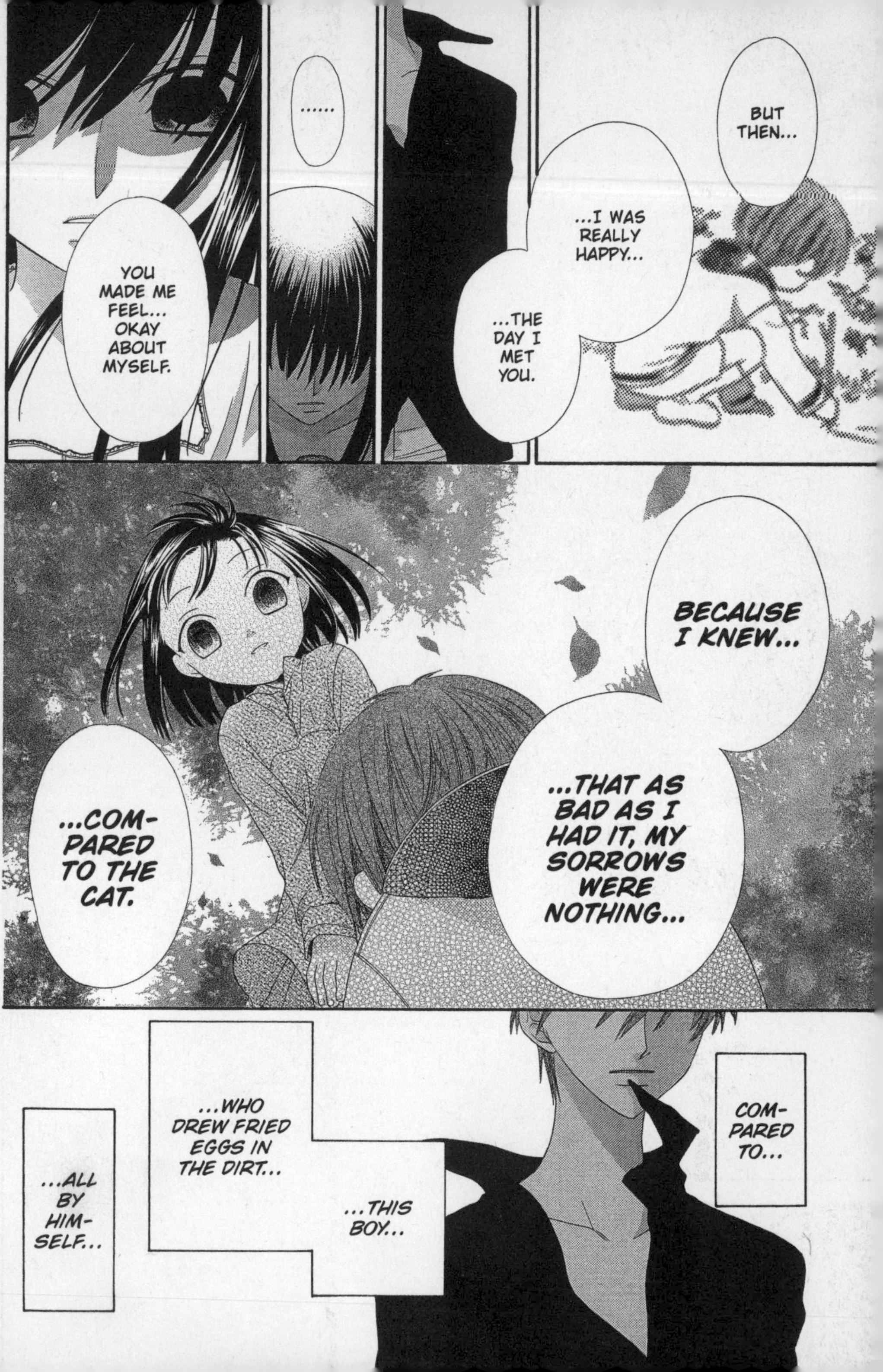

BUT THEN...
...I WAS REALLY HAPPY...
...THE DAY I MET YOU.
......
YOU MADE ME FEEL... OKAY ABOUT MYSELF.
BECAUSE I KNEW...
...THAT AS BAD AS I HAD IT, MY SORROWS WERE NOTHING...
...COMPARED TO THE CAT.
COMPARED TO...
...WHO DREW FRIED EGGS IN THE DIRT...
...THIS BOY...
...ALL BY HIMSELF...

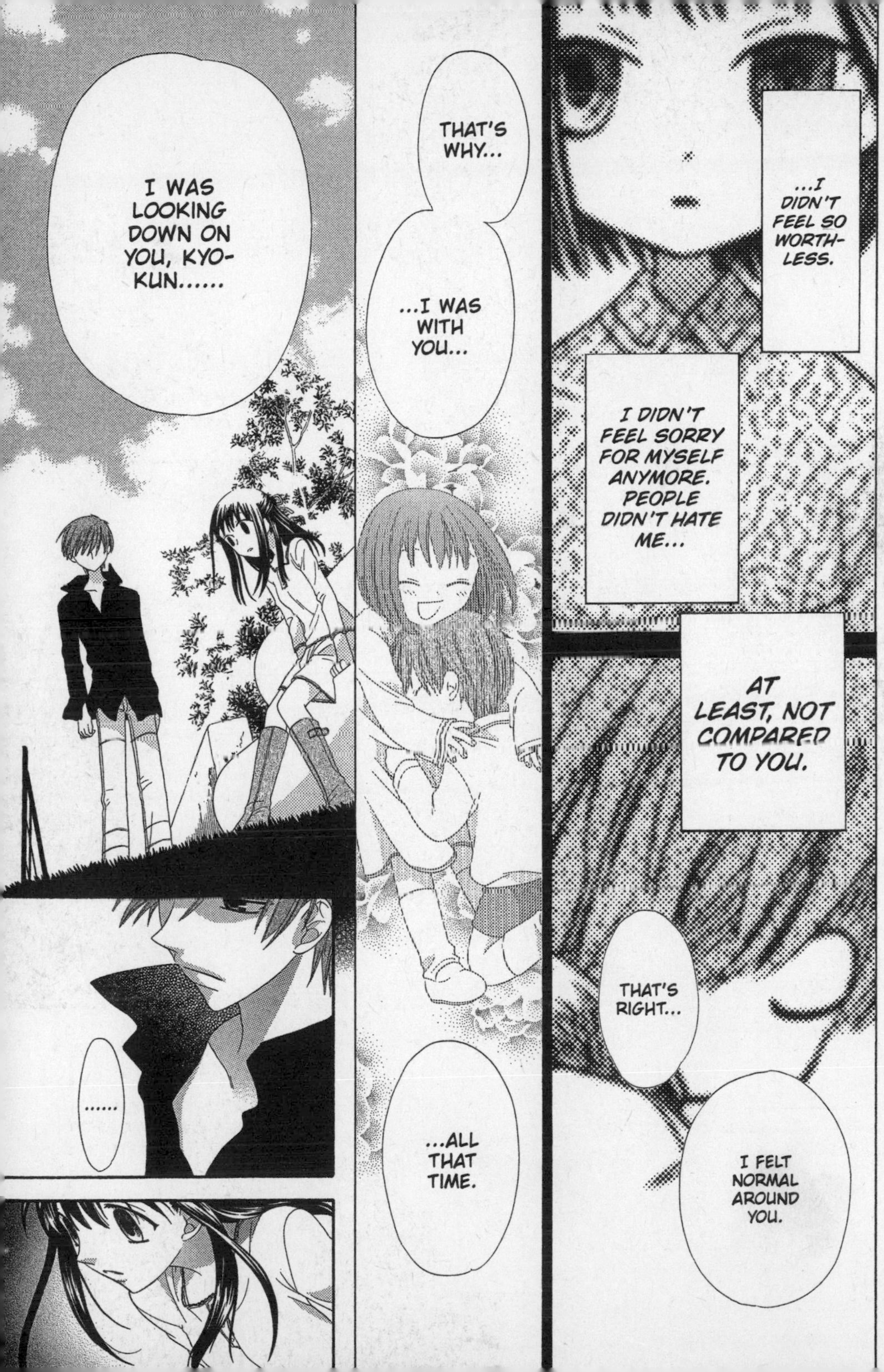
...I DIDN'T FEEL SO WORTH-LESS.
I DIDN'T FEEL SORRY FOR MYSELF ANYMORE. PEOPLE DIDN'T HATE ME...
AT LEAST, NOT COMPARED TO YOU.
THAT'S RIGHT...
I FELT NORMAL AROUND YOU.
THAT'S WHY...
...I WAS WITH YOU...
...ALL THAT TIME.
I WAS LOOKING DOWN ON YOU, KYO-KUN......
......

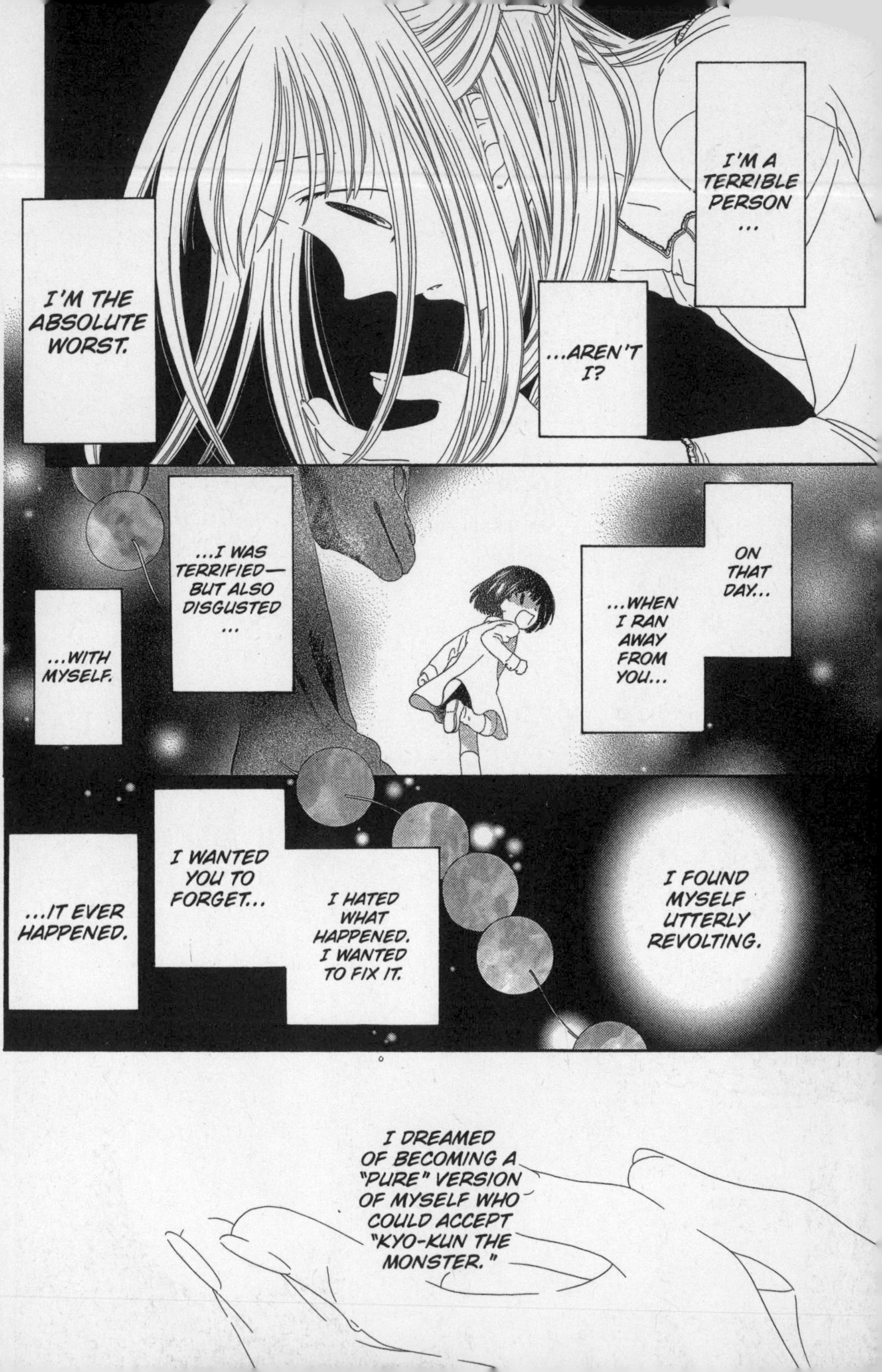
I'M A TERRIBLE PERSON ...
...AREN'T I?
I'M THE ABSOLUTE WORST.
ON THAT DAY...
...WHEN I RAN AWAY FROM YOU...
...I WAS TERRIFIED— BUT ALSO DISGUSTED ...
...WITH MYSELF.
I FOUND MYSELF UTTERLY REVOLTING.
I HATED WHAT HAPPENED. I WANTED TO FIX IT.
I WANTED YOU TO FORGET...
...IT EVER HAPPENED.
I DREAMED OF BECOMING A "PURE" VERSION OF MYSELF WHO COULD ACCEPT "KYO-KUN THE MONSTER."

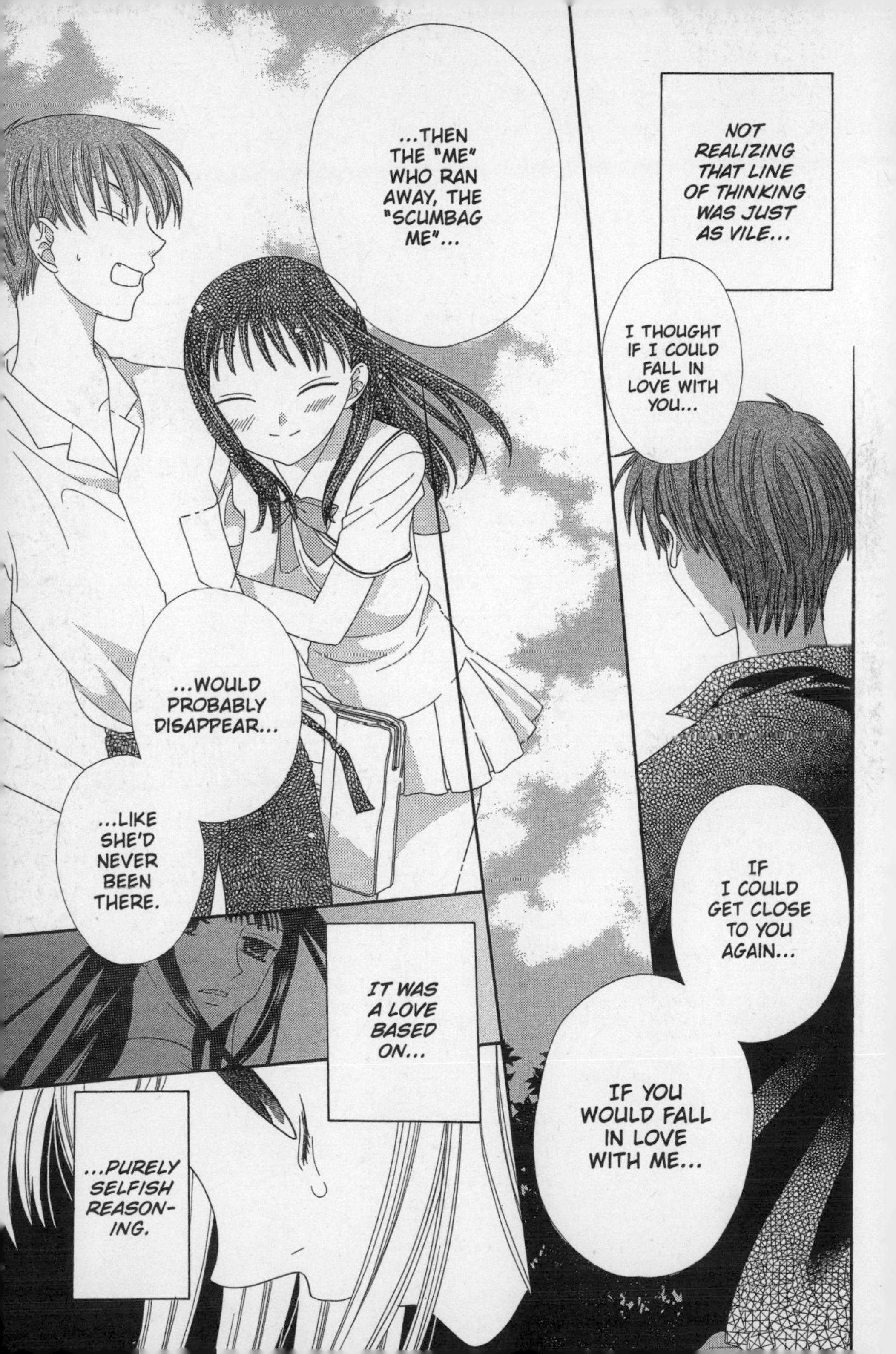
NOT REALIZING THAT LINE OF THINKING WAS JUST AS VILE...
I THOUGHT IF I COULD FALL IN LOVE WITH YOU...
IF I COULD GET CLOSE TO YOU AGAIN...
IF YOU WOULD FALL IN LOVE WITH ME...
...THEN THE "ME" WHO RAN AWAY, THE "SCUMBAG ME"...
...WOULD PROBABLY DISAPPEAR...
...LIKE SHE'D NEVER BEEN THERE.
IT WAS A LOVE BASED ON...
...PURELY SELFISH REASONING.

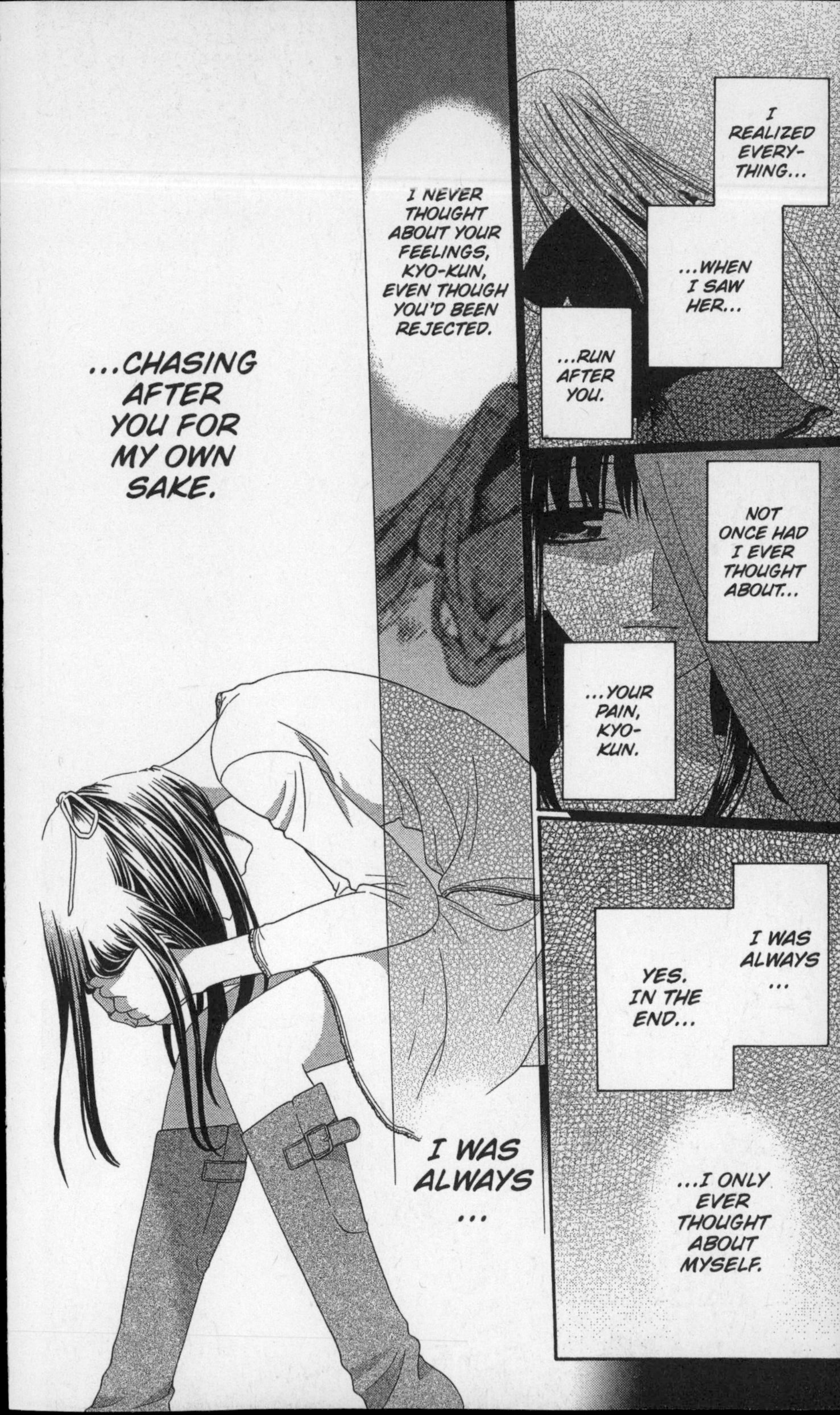

I REALIZED EVERYTHING...
...WHEN I SAW HER...
...RUN AFTER YOU.
NOT ONCE HAD I EVER THOUGHT ABOUT...
...YOUR PAIN, KYO-KUN.
I WAS ALWAYS ...
YES. IN THE END...
...I ONLY EVER THOUGHT ABOUT MYSELF.
I NEVER THOUGHT ABOUT YOUR FEELINGS, KYO-KUN, EVEN THOUGH YOU'D BEEN REJECTED.
I WAS ALWAYS ...
...CHASING AFTER YOU FOR MY OWN SAKE.

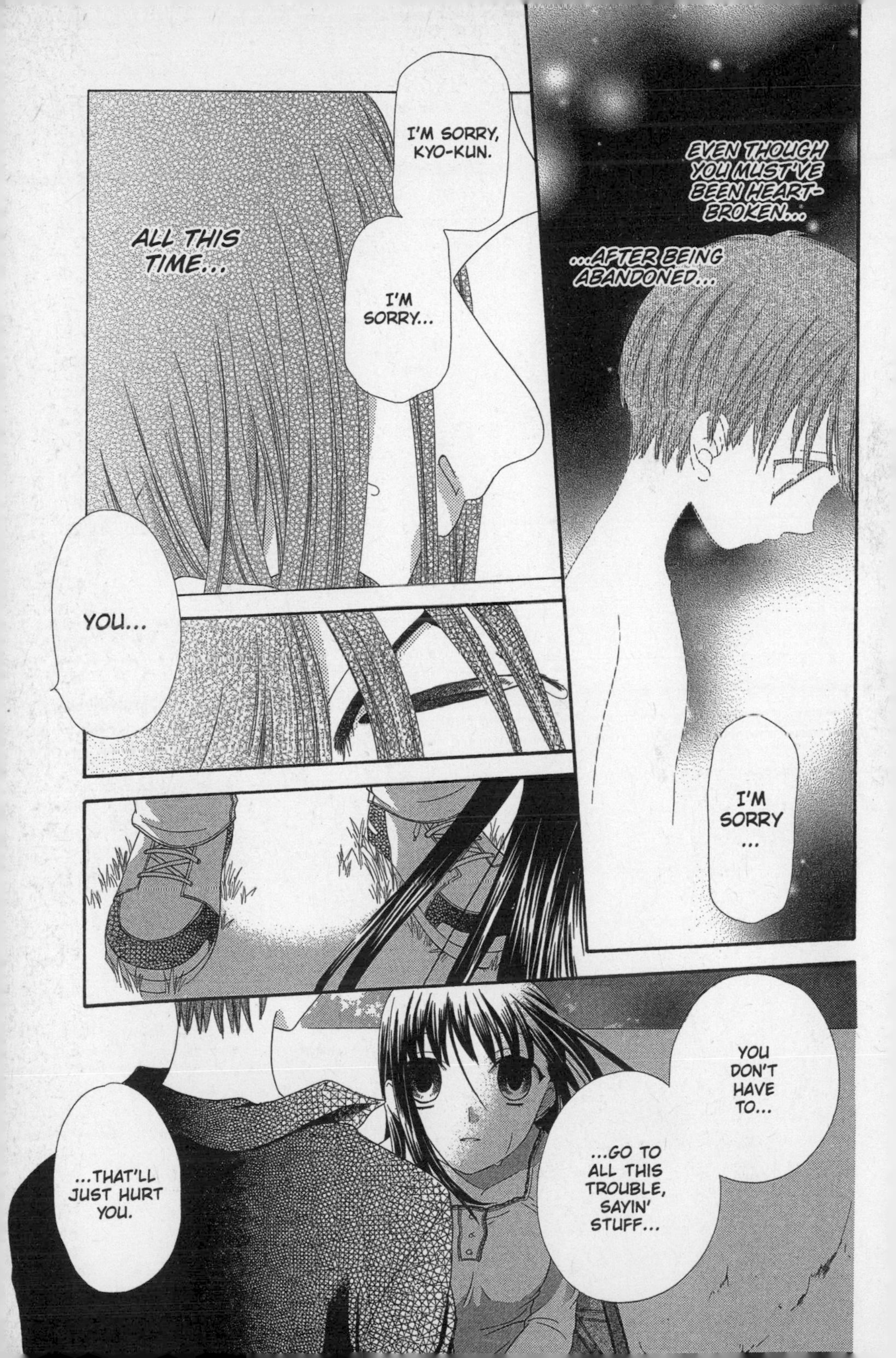
EVEN THOUGH YOU MUST'VE BEEN HEART-BROKEN...
...AFTER BEING ABANDONED...
I'M SORRY ...
I'M SORRY, KYO-KUN.
I'M SORRY...
ALL THIS TIME...
YOU...
YOU DON'T HAVE TO...
...GO TO ALL THIS TROUBLE, SAYIN' STUFF...
...THAT'LL JUST HURT YOU.

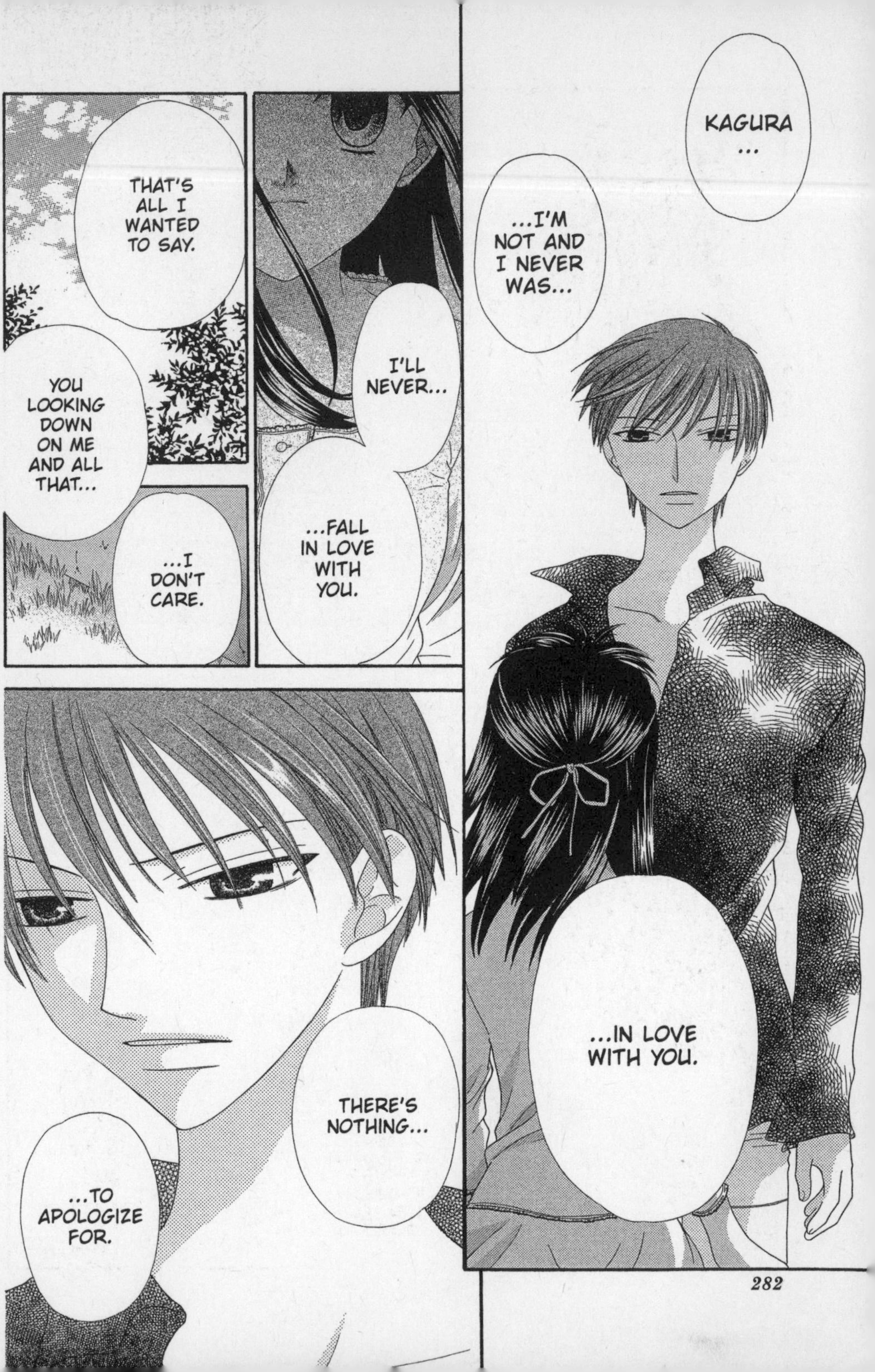
KAGURA...
...I'M NOT AND I NEVER WAS...
...IN LOVE WITH YOU.
I'LL NEVER...
...FALL IN LOVE WITH YOU.
THAT'S ALL I WANTED TO SAY.
YOU LOOKING DOWN ON ME AND ALL THAT...
...I DON'T CARE.
THERE'S NOTHING...
...TO APOLOGIZE FOR.

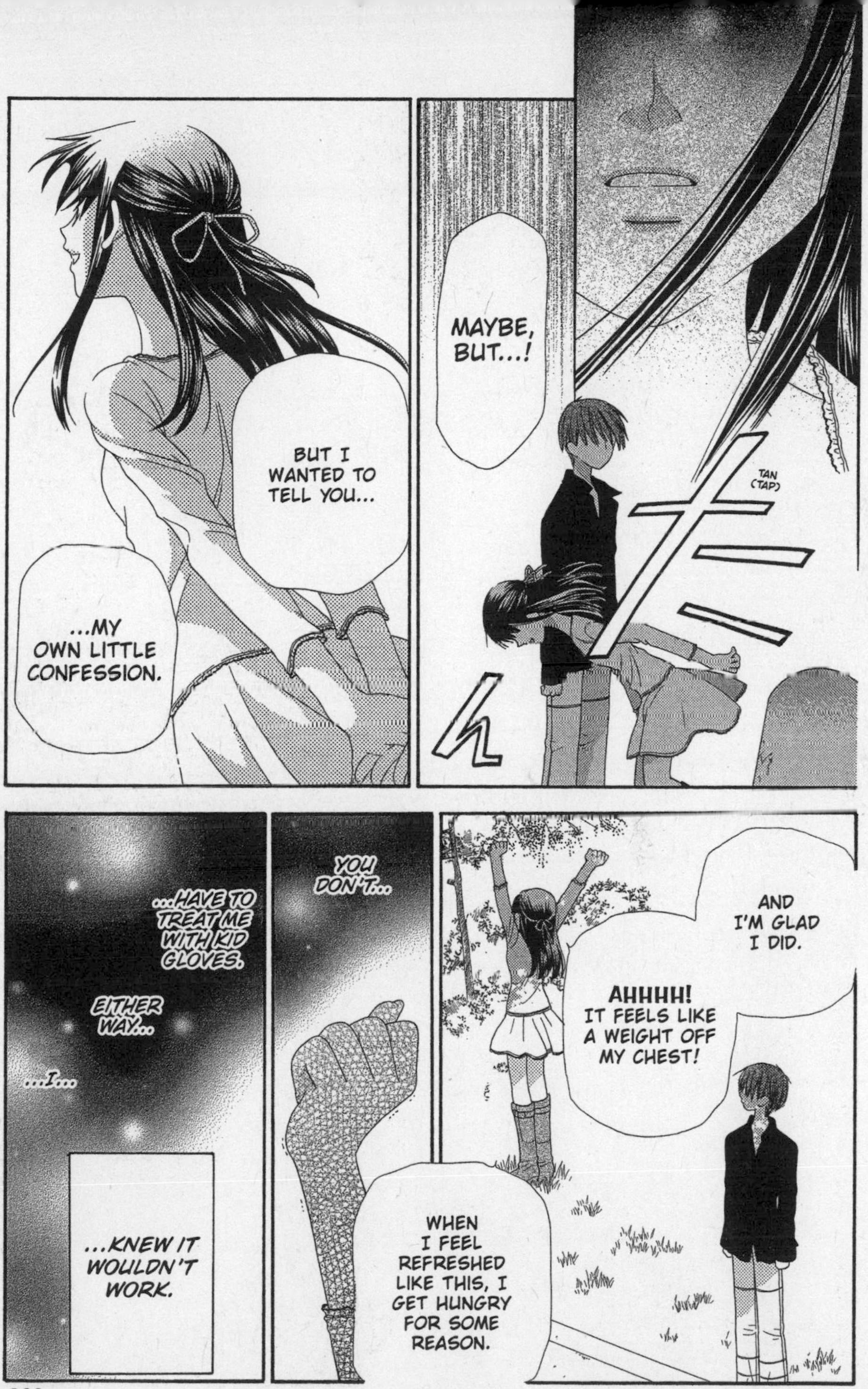
MAYBE, BUT...!
TAN (TAP)
BUT I WANTED TO TELL YOU...
...MY OWN LITTLE CONFESSION.
AND I'M GLAD I DID.
AHHHH! IT FEELS LIKE A WEIGHT OFF MY CHEST!
WHEN I FEEL REFRESHED LIKE THIS, I GET HUNGRY FOR SOME REASON.
YOU DON'T...
...HAVE TO TREAT ME WITH KID GLOVES.
EITHER WAY...
...I...
...KNEW IT WOULDN'T WORK.

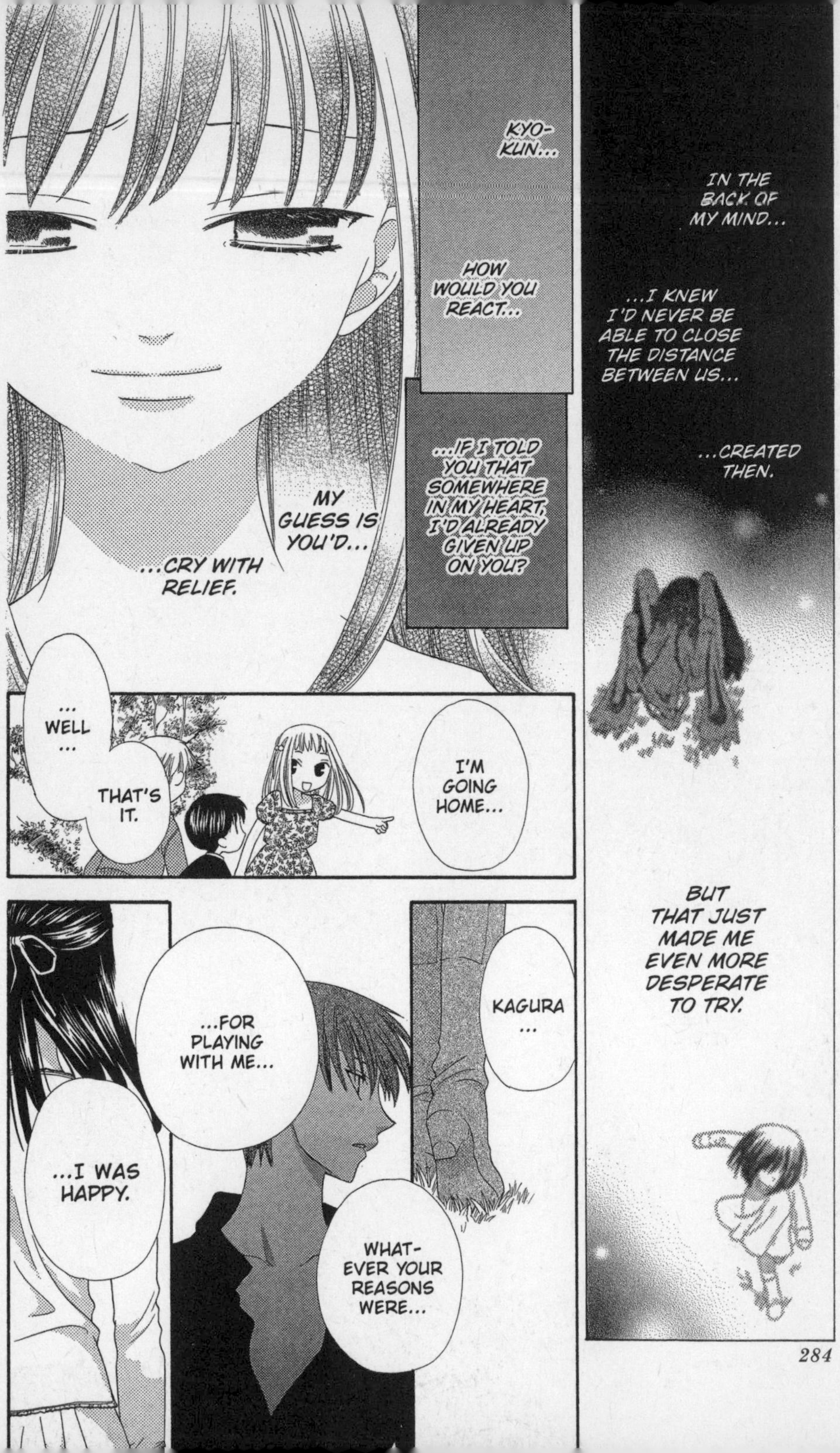
IN THE BACK OF MY MIND...
...I KNEW I'D NEVER BE ABLE TO CLOSE THE DISTANCE BETWEEN US...
...CREATED THEN.
BUT THAT JUST MADE ME EVEN MORE DESPERATE TO TRY.
KYO-KUN...
HOW WOULD YOU REACT...
...IF I TOLD YOU THAT SOMEWHERE IN MY HEART, I'D ALREADY GIVEN UP ON YOU?
MY GUESS IS YOU'D...
...CRY WITH RELIEF.
I'M GOING HOME...
...WELL...
THAT'S IT.
KAGURA...
WHAT-EVER YOUR REASONS WERE...
...FOR PLAYING WITH ME...
...I WAS HAPPY.

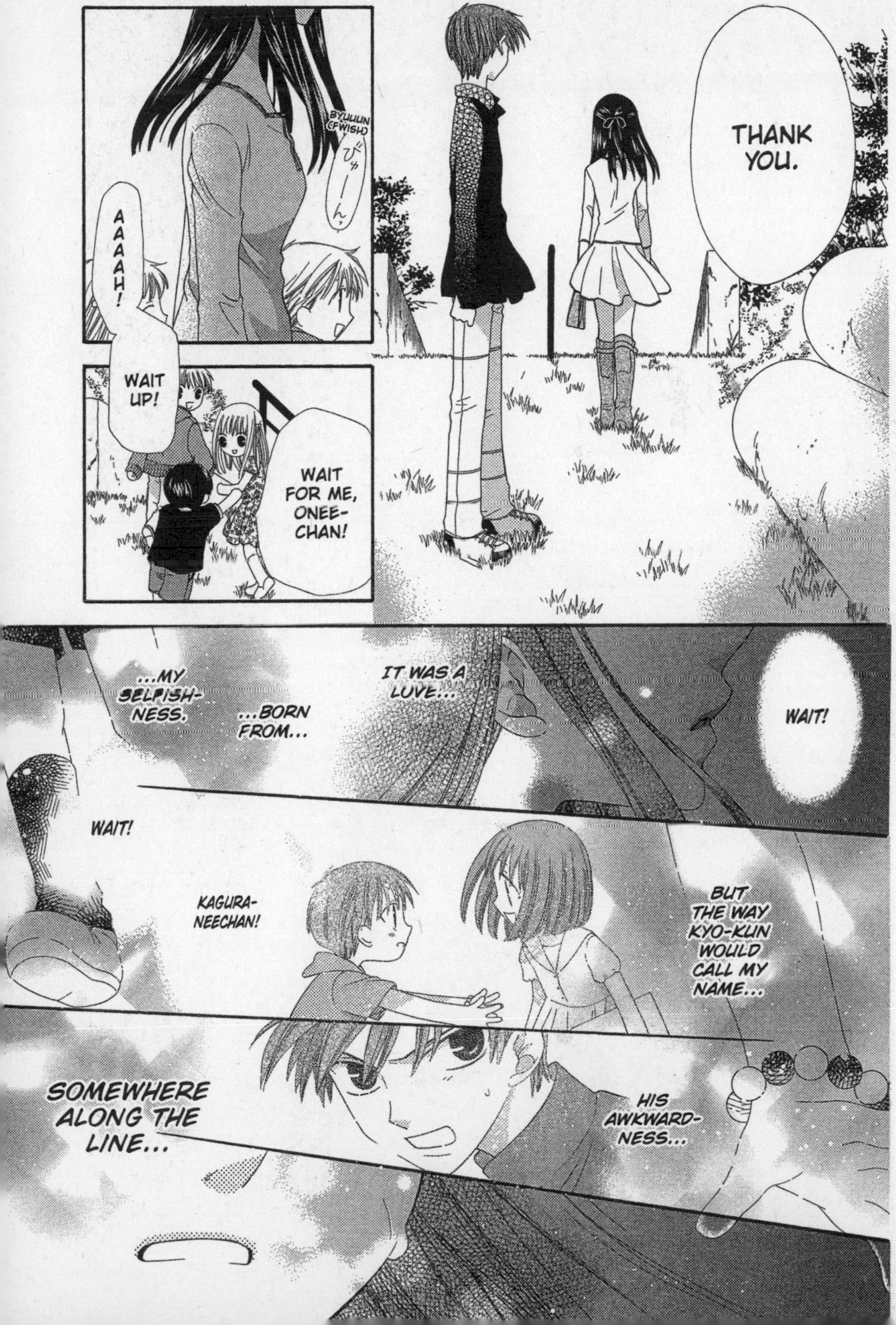
THANK YOU.
BYUUUN (FWISH)
びゅーーん
AAAAAH!
WAIT UP!
WAIT FOR ME, ONEE-CHAN!
WAIT!
IT WAS A LOVE...
...BORN FROM...
...MY SELFISH-NESS.
BUT THE WAY KYO-KUN WOULD CALL MY NAME...
KAGURA-NEECHAN!
WAIT!
HIS AWKWARD-NESS...
SOMEWHERE ALONG THE LINE...

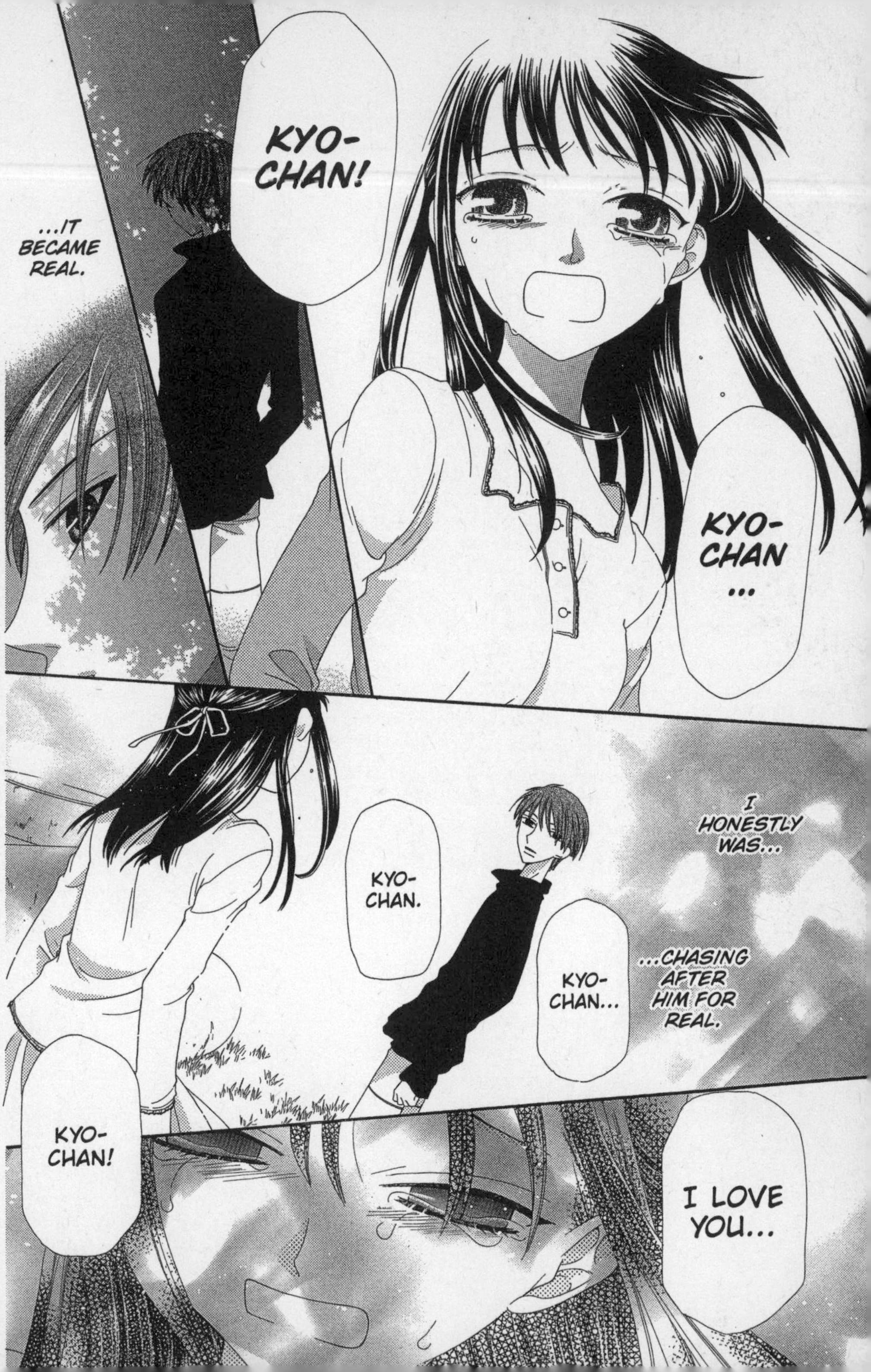
KYO-CHAN!
KYO-CHAN ...
...IT BECAME REAL.
I HONESTLY WAS...
...CHASING AFTER HIM FOR REAL.
KYO-CHAN...
KYO-CHAN.
KYO-CHAN!
I LOVE YOU...

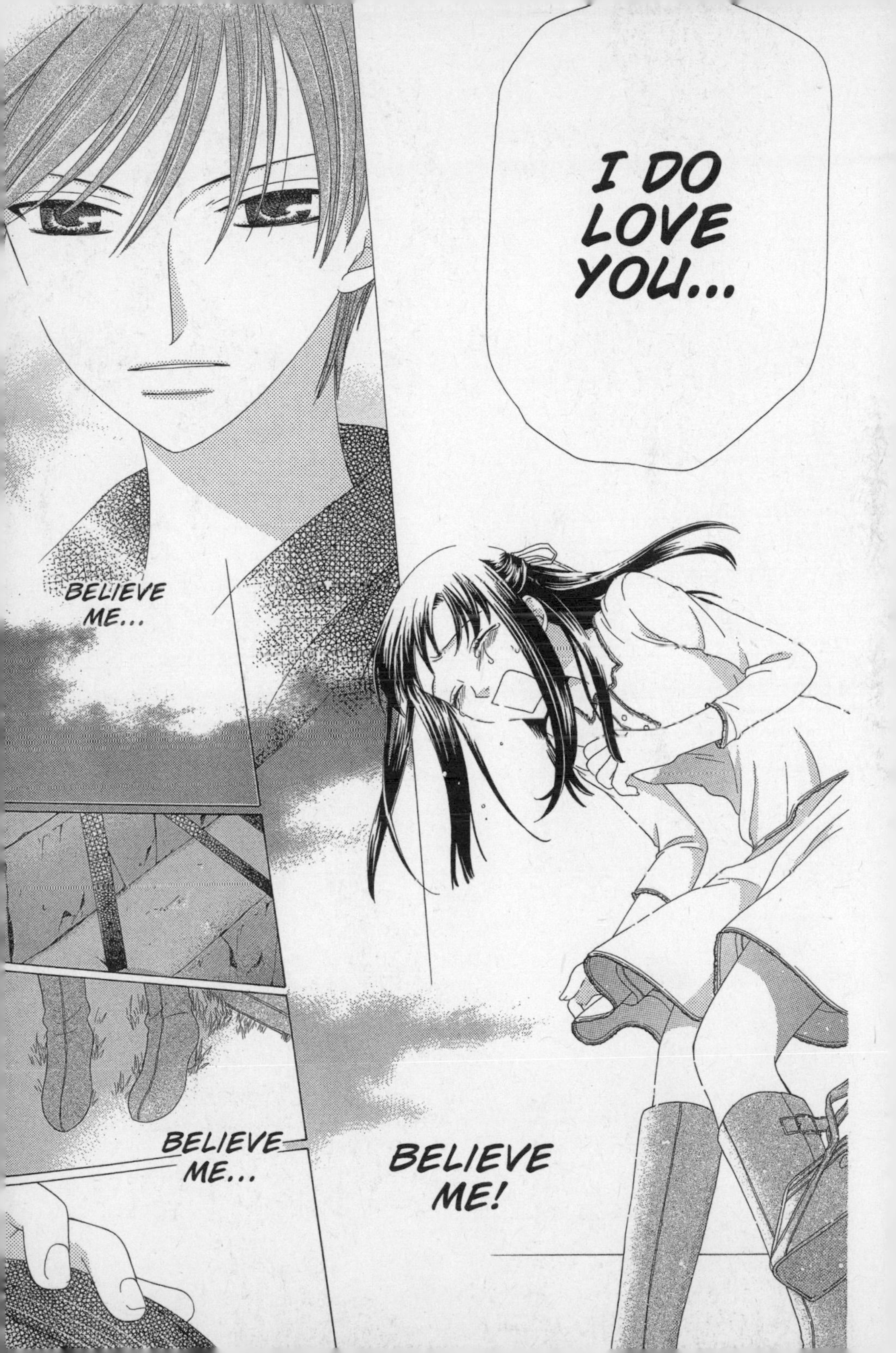
I DO LOVE YOU...
BELIEVE ME...
BELIEVE ME!
BELIEVE ME...

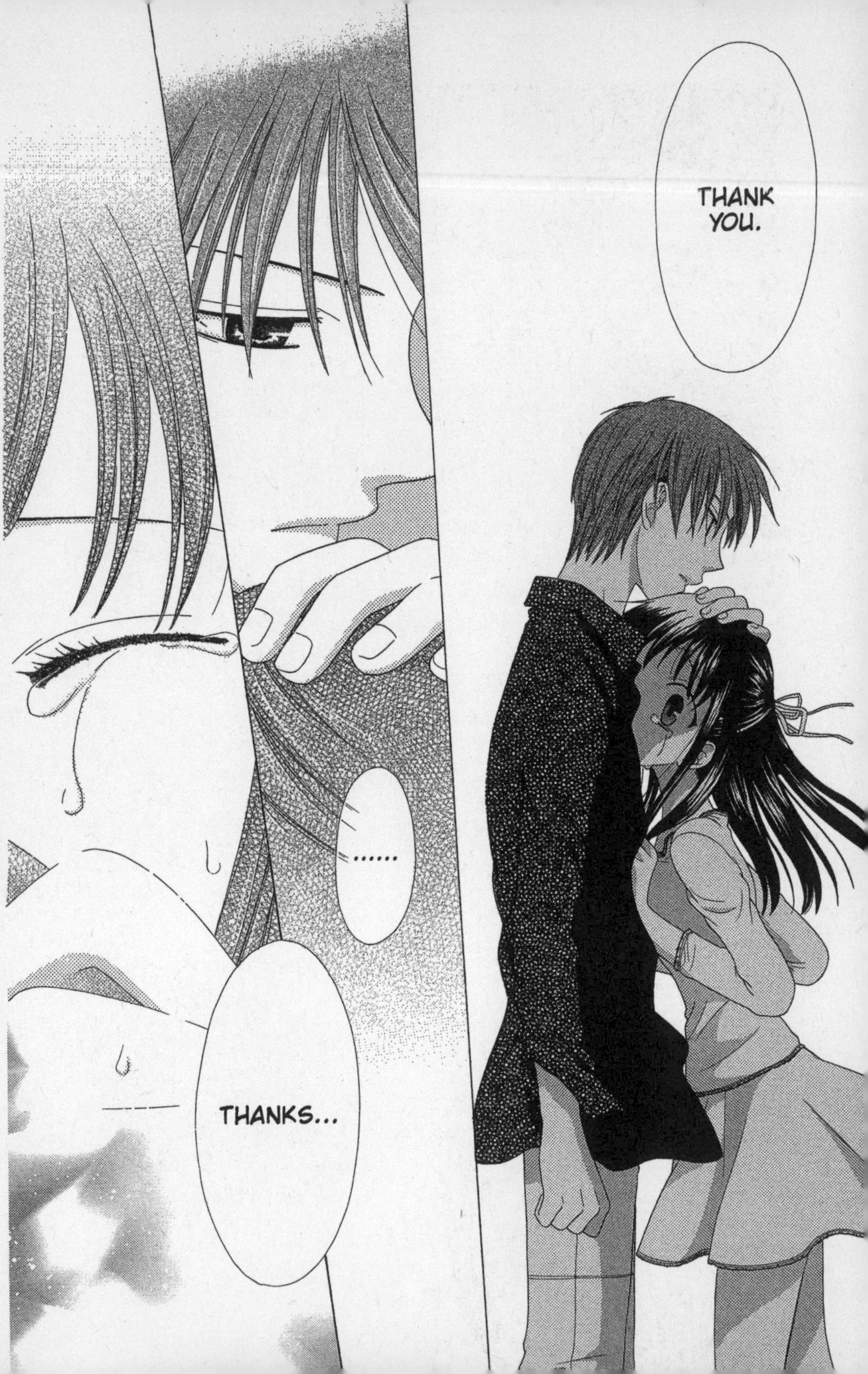
THANK YOU.
......
THANKS...

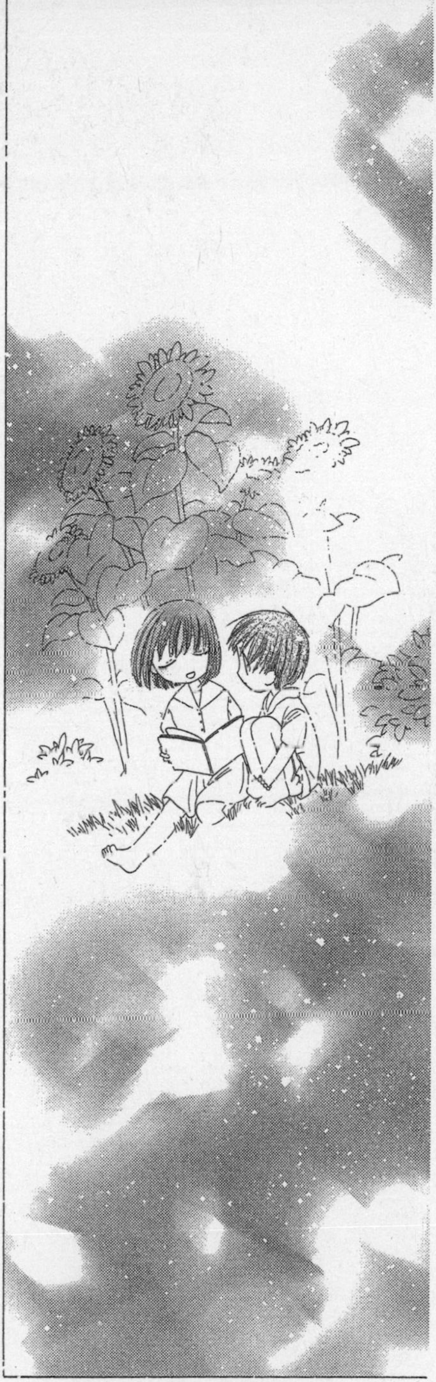
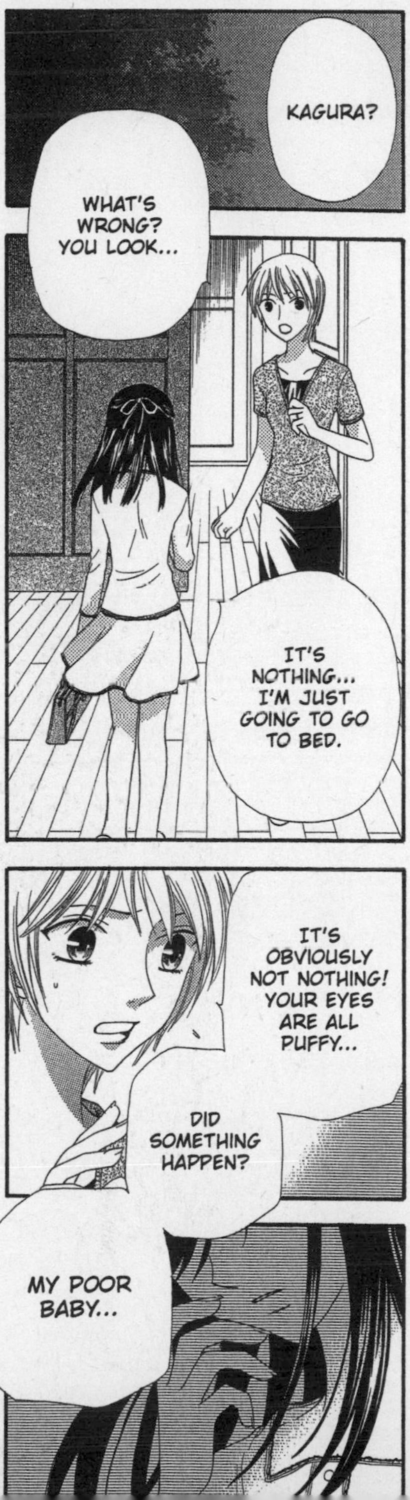
KAGURA?
WHAT'S WRONG? YOU LOOK...
IT'S NOTHING... I'M JUST GOING TO GO TO BED.
IT'S OBVIOUSLY NOT NOTHING! YOUR EYES ARE ALL PUFFY...
DID SOMETHING HAPPEN?
MY POOR BABY...

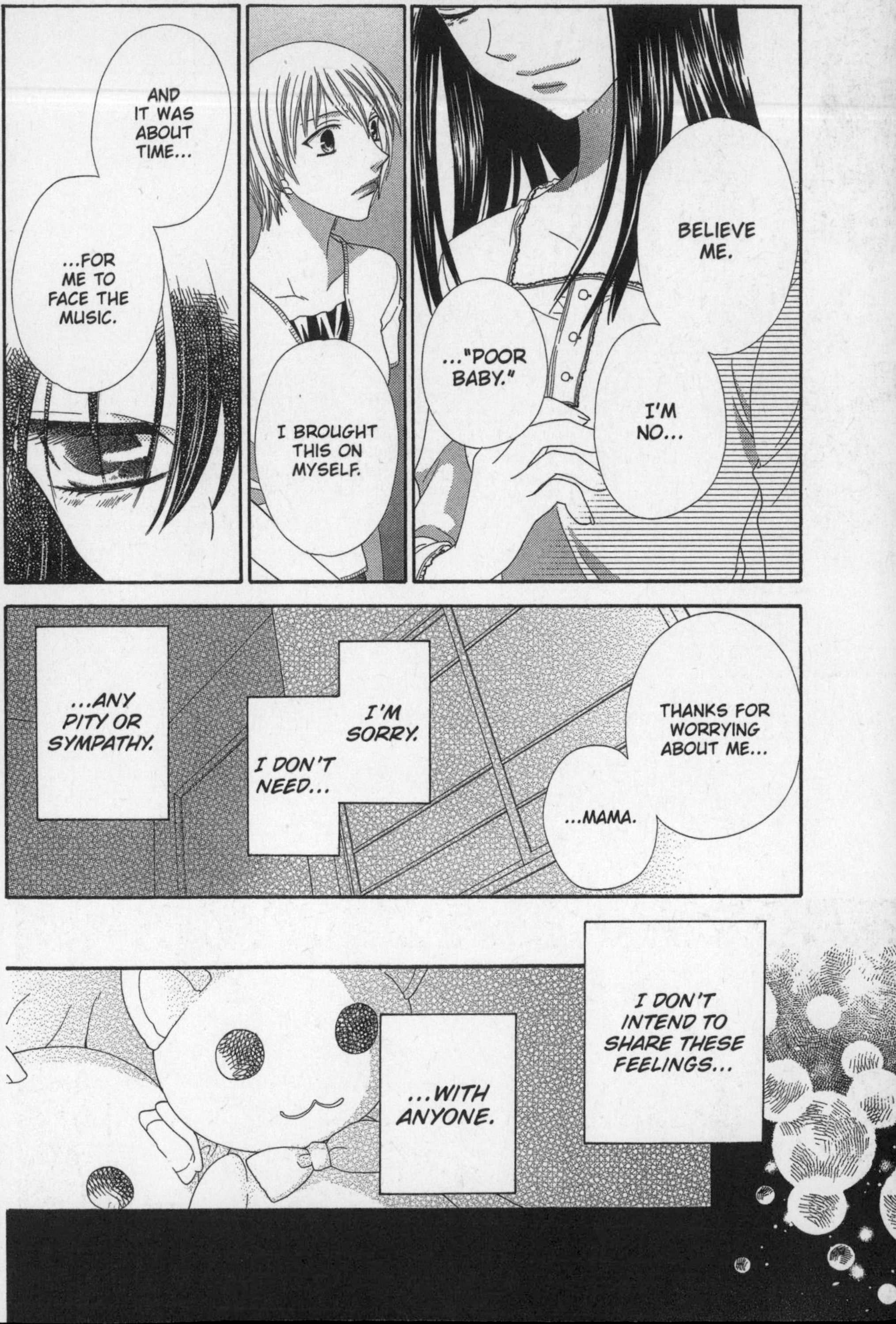
BELIEVE ME.
I'M NO...
..."POOR BABY."
I BROUGHT THIS ON MYSELF.
AND IT WAS ABOUT TIME...
...FOR ME TO FACE THE MUSIC.
THANKS FOR WORRYING ABOUT ME...
...MAMA.
I'M SORRY.
I DON'T NEED...
...ANY PITY OR SYMPATHY.
I DON'T INTEND TO SHARE THESE FEELINGS...
...WITH ANYONE.

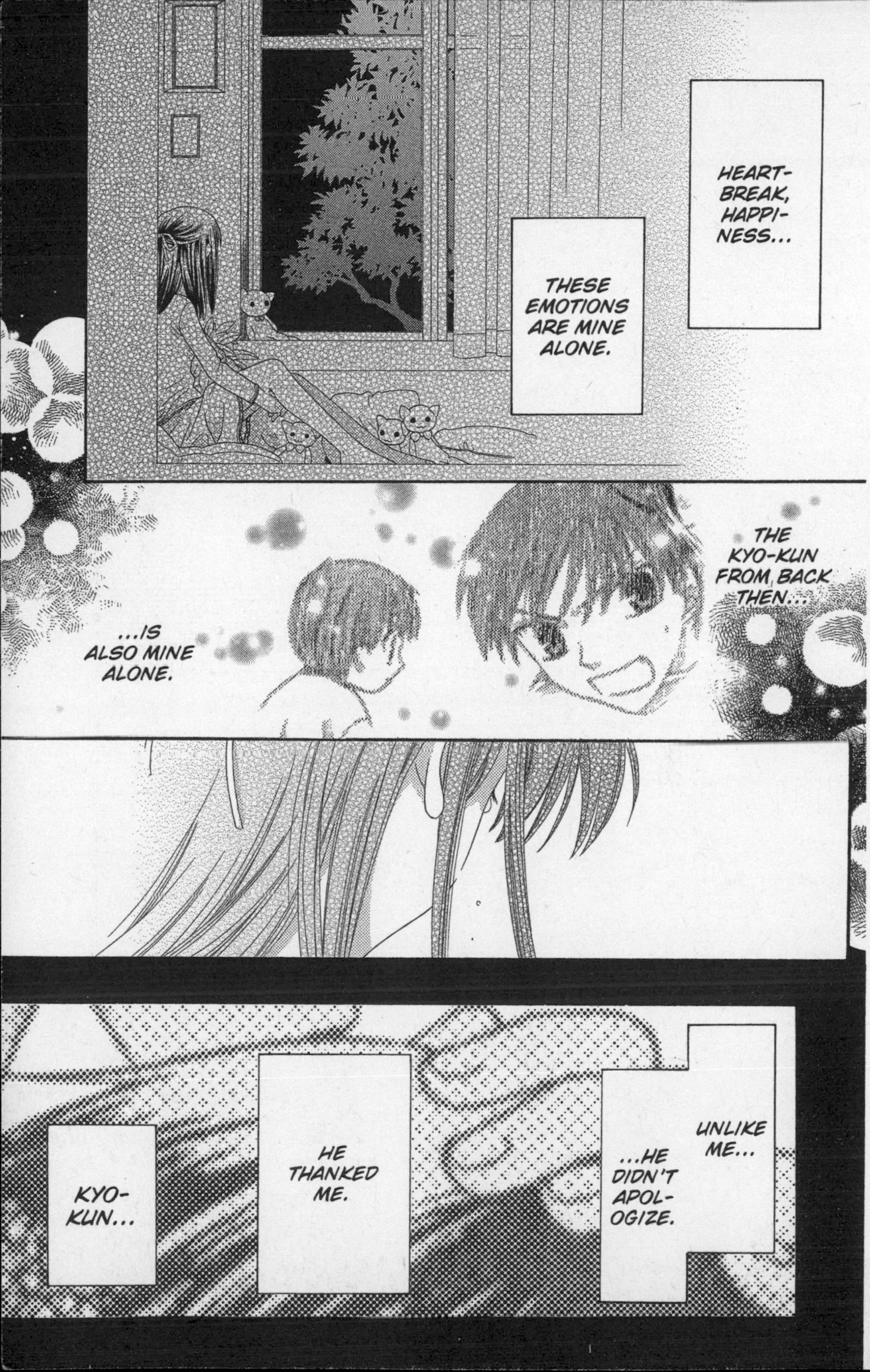
HEART-BREAK, HAPPI-NESS...
THESE EMOTIONS ARE MINE ALONE.
THE KYO-KUN FROM BACK THEN...
...IS ALSO MINE ALONE.
UNLIKE ME...
...HE DIDN'T APOL-OGIZE.
HE THANKED ME.
KYO-KUN...

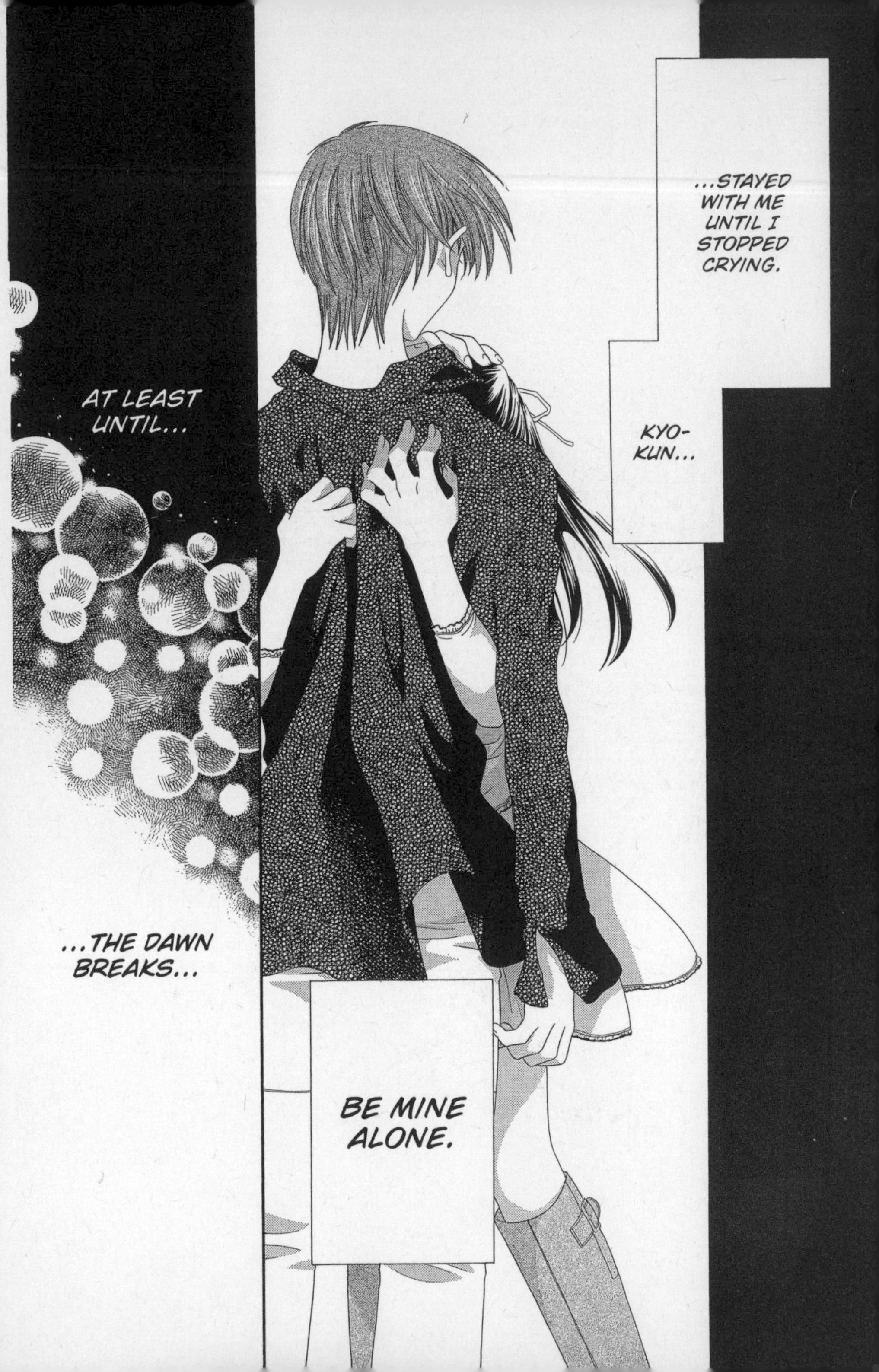
...STAYED WITH ME UNTIL I STOPPED CRYING.
KYO-KUN...
BE MINE ALONE.
AT LEAST UNTIL...
...THE DAWN BREAKS...

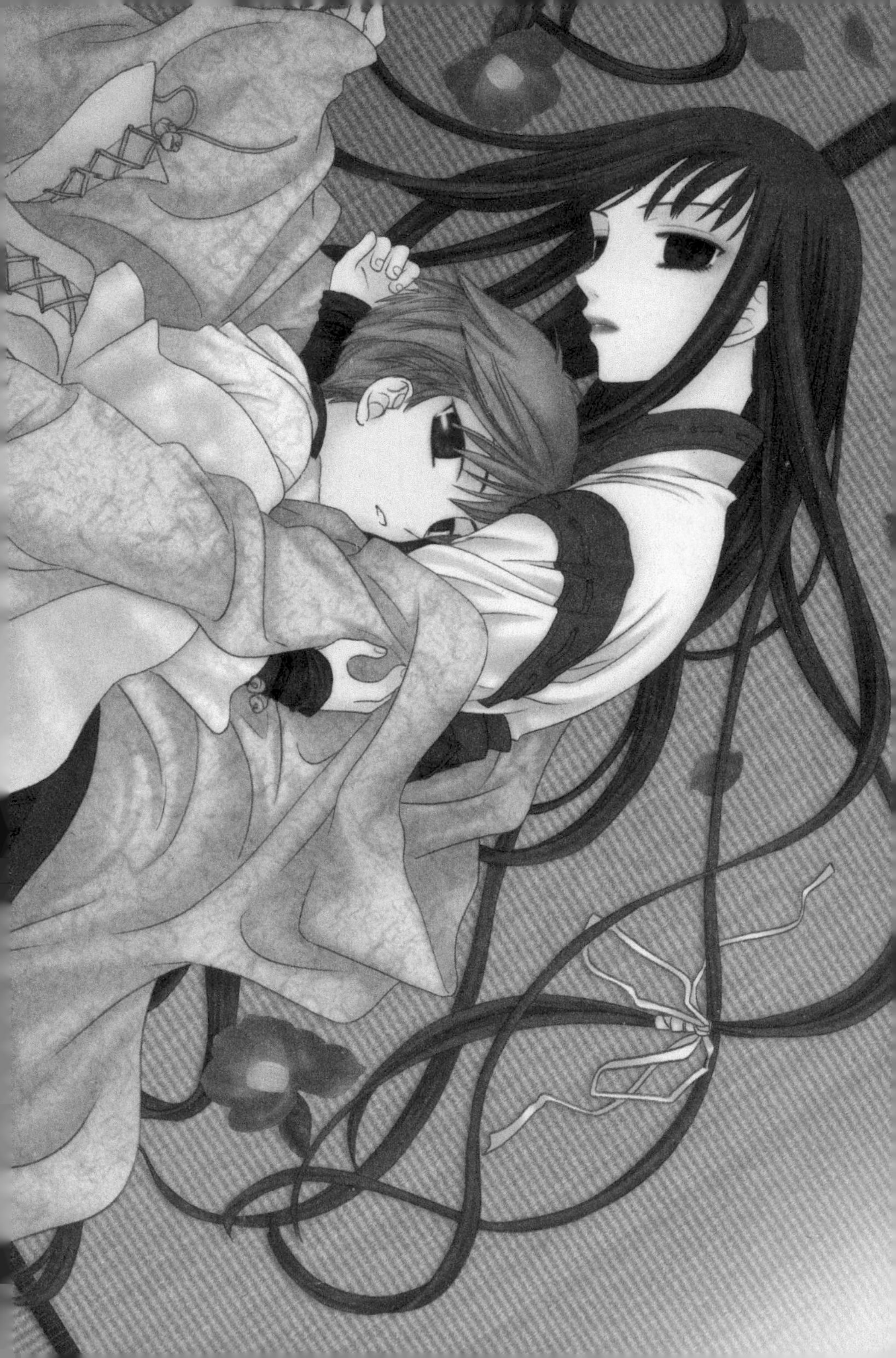

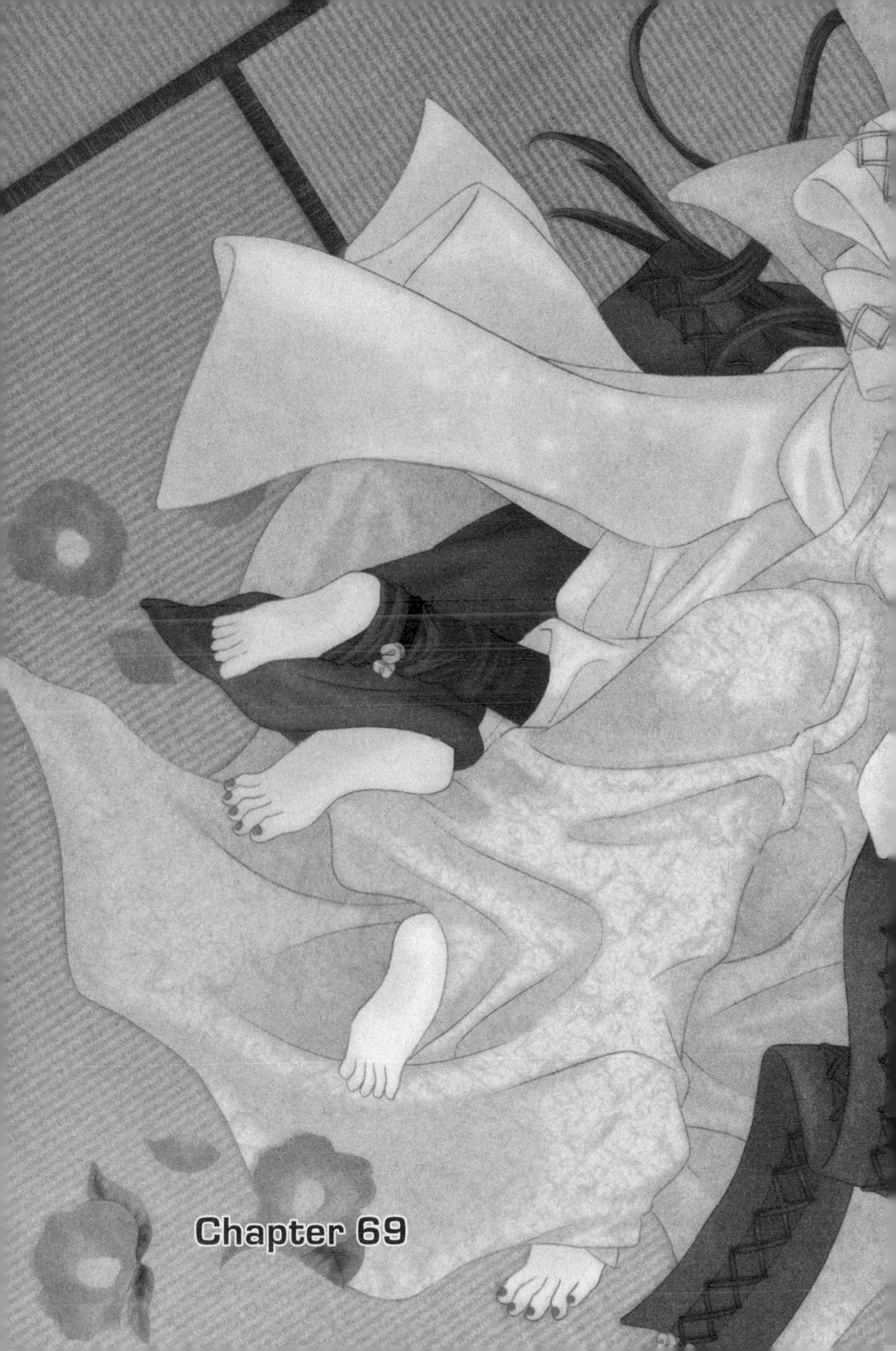
Chapter 69

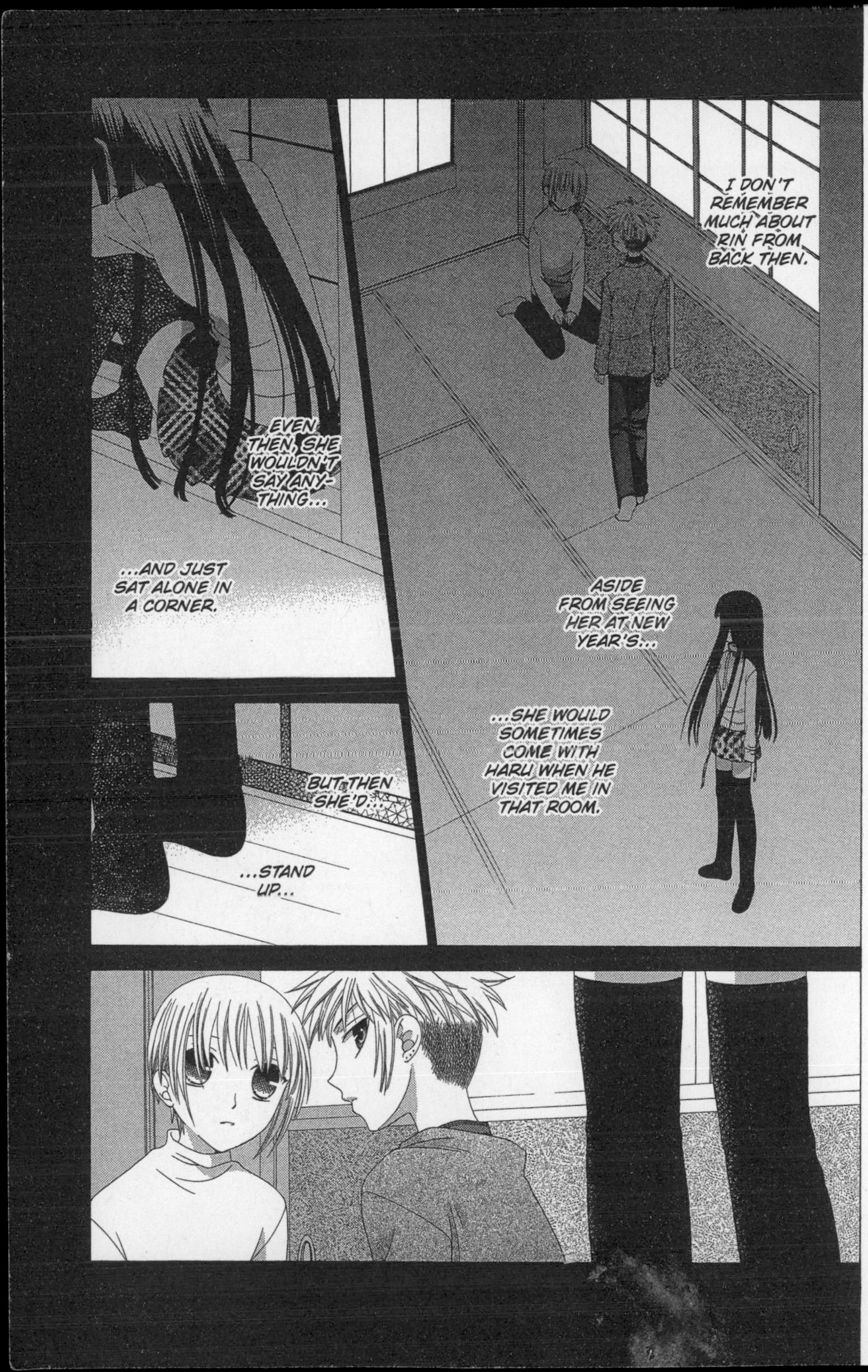
I DON'T REMEMBER MUCH ABOUT RIN FROM BACK THEN.
ASIDE FROM SEEING HER AT NEW YEAR'S...
...SHE WOULD SOMETIMES COME WITH HARU WHEN HE VISITED ME IN THAT ROOM.
EVEN THEN, SHE WOULDN'T SAY ANY-THING...
...AND JUST SAT ALONE IN A CORNER.
BUT THEN SHE'D...
...STAND UP...

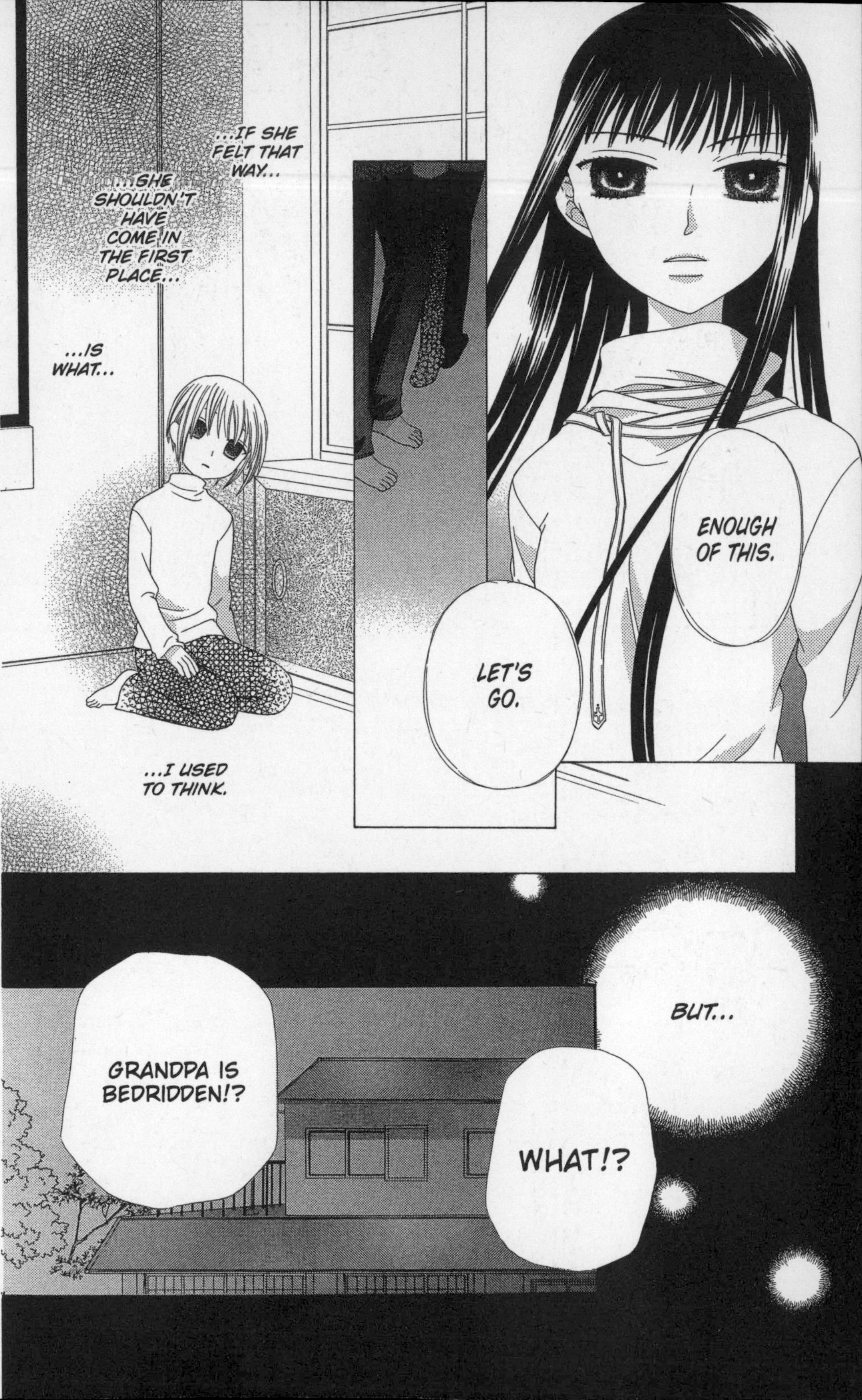
ENOUGH OF THIS.
LET'S GO.
...IF SHE FELT THAT WAY...
...SHE SHOULDN'T HAVE COME IN THE FIRST PLACE...
...IS WHAT...
...I USED TO THINK.
BUT...
WHAT!?
GRANDPA IS BEDRIDDEN!?

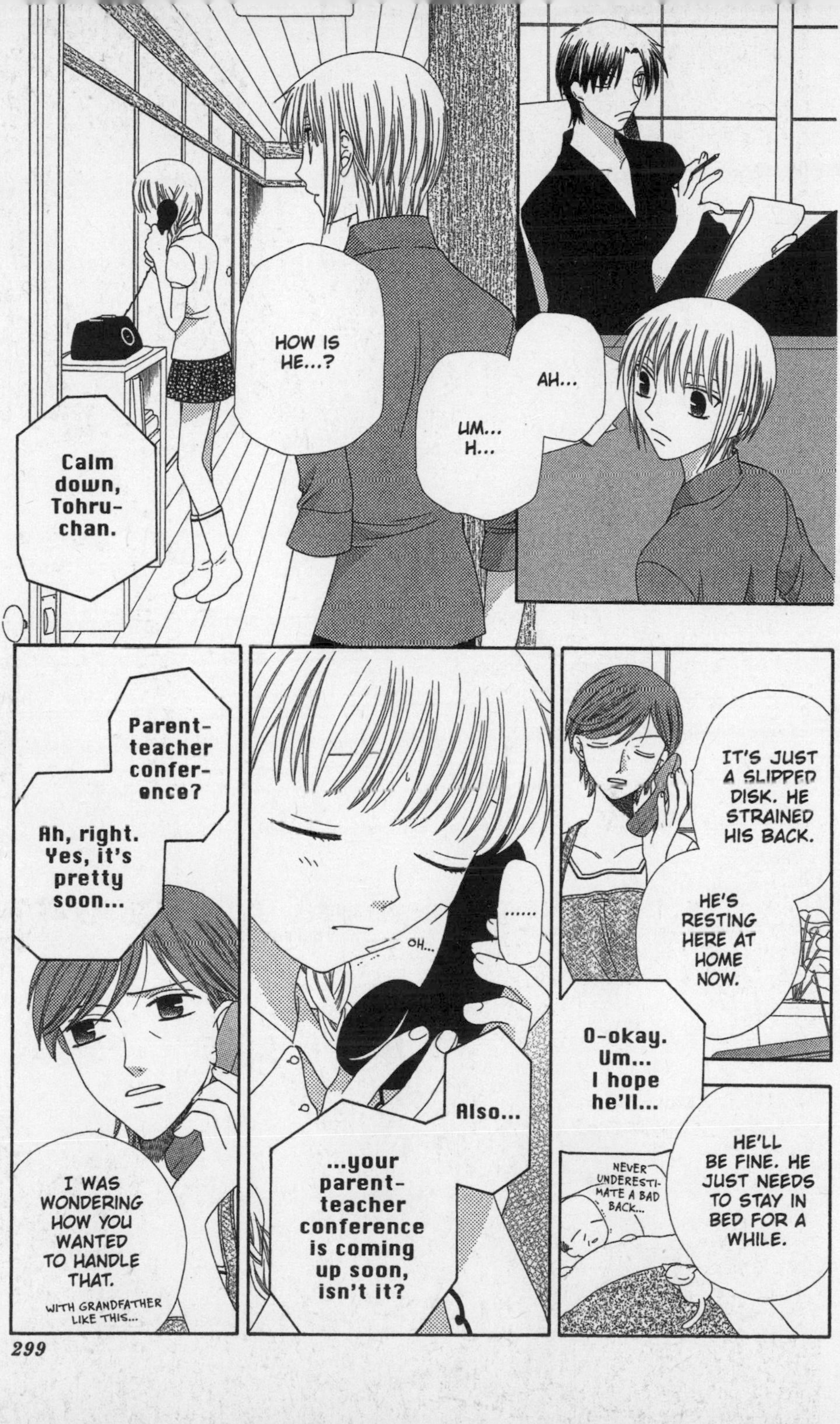
AH...
UM... H...
HOW IS HE...?
Calm down, Tohru-chan.
IT'S JUST A SLIPPED DISK. HE STRAINED HIS BACK.
HE'S RESTING HERE AT HOME NOW.
O-okay. Um... I hope he'll...
HE'LL BE FINE. HE JUST NEEDS TO STAY IN BED FOR A WHILE.
NEVER UNDERESTIMATE A BAD BACK...
......
OH...
Also...
...your parent-teacher conference is coming up soon, isn't it?
Parent-teacher conference?
Ah, right. Yes, it's pretty soon...
I WAS WONDERING HOW YOU WANTED TO HANDLE THAT.
WITH GRANDFATHER LIKE THIS...

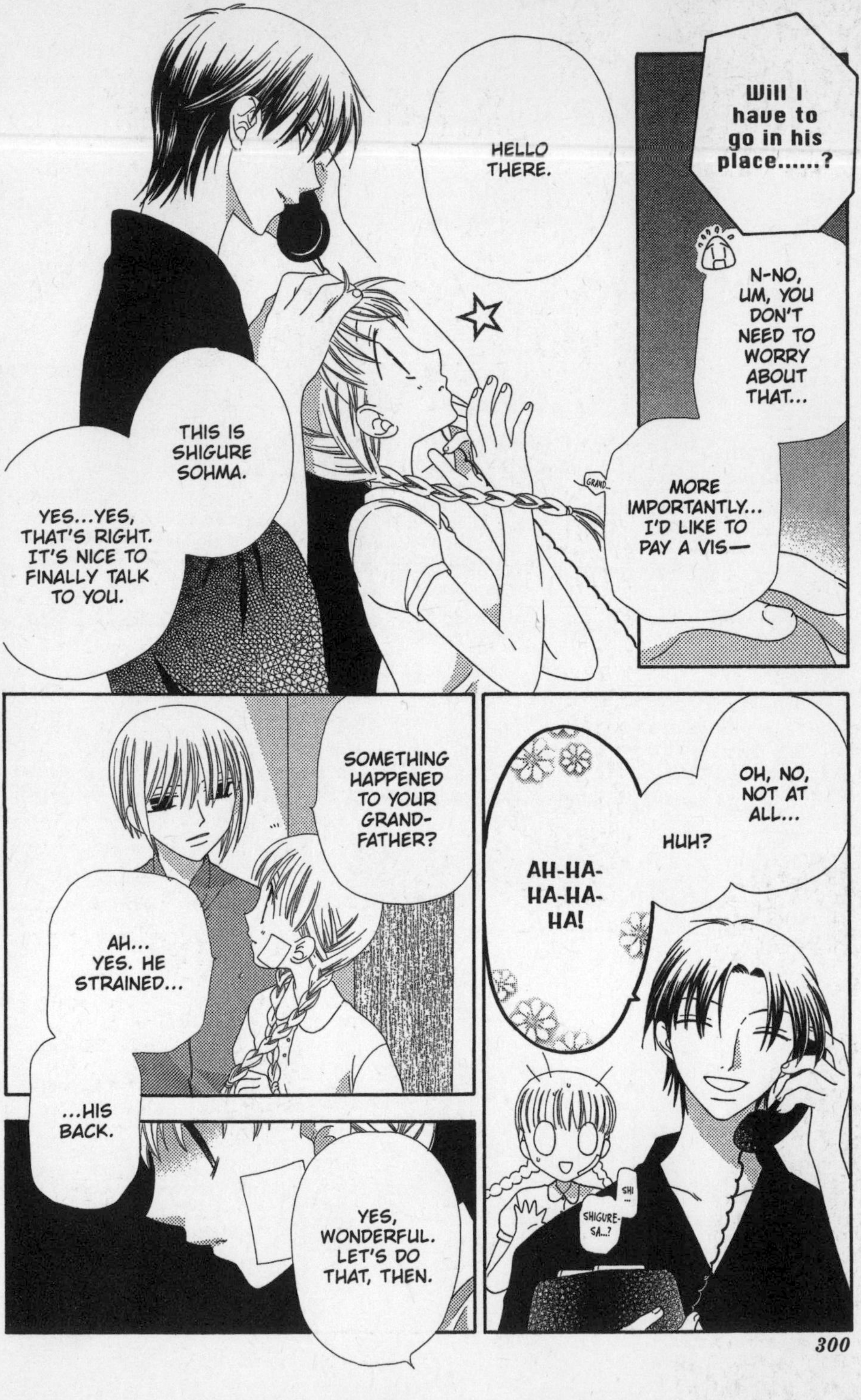

Will I have to go in his place......?
N-NO, UM, YOU DON'T NEED TO WORRY ABOUT THAT...
GRAND...
MORE IMPORTANTLY... I'D LIKE TO PAY A VIS—
HELLO THERE.
THIS IS SHIGURE SOHMA.
YES...YES, THAT'S RIGHT. IT'S NICE TO FINALLY TALK TO YOU.
OH, NO, NOT AT ALL...
HUH?
AH-HA-HA-HA-HA!
SHI...
SHIGURE-SA...?
SOMETHING HAPPENED TO YOUR GRANDFATHER?
...
AH... YES. HE STRAINED...
...HIS BACK.
YES, WONDERFUL. LET'S DO THAT, THEN.

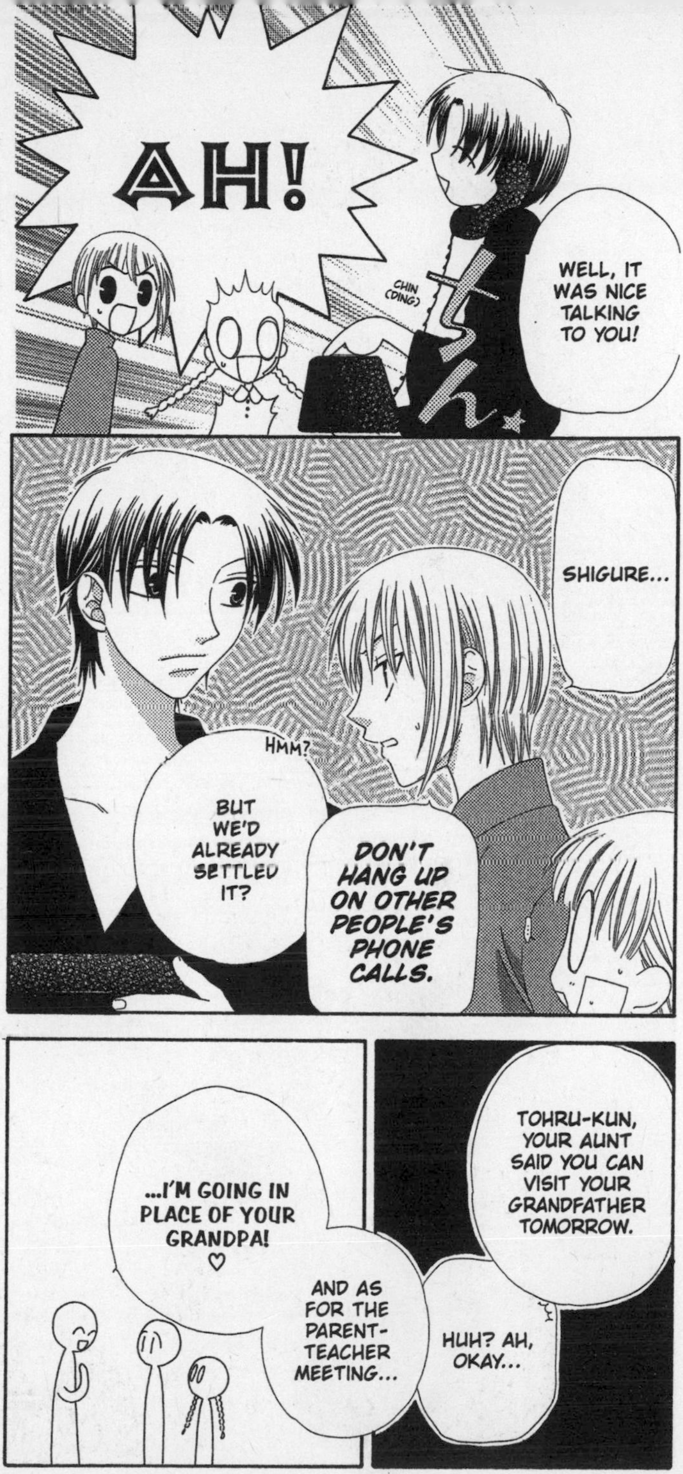
WELL, IT WAS NICE TALKING TO YOU!
CHIN (DING)
AH!
SHIGURE...
DON'T HANG UP ON OTHER PEOPLE'S PHONE CALLS.
HMM?
BUT WE'D ALREADY SETTLED IT?
TOHRU-KUN, YOUR AUNT SAID YOU CAN VISIT YOUR GRANDFATHER TOMORROW.
HUH? AH, OKAY...
AND AS FOR THE PARENT-TEACHER MEETING...
...I'M GOING IN PLACE OF YOUR GRANDPA! ♡

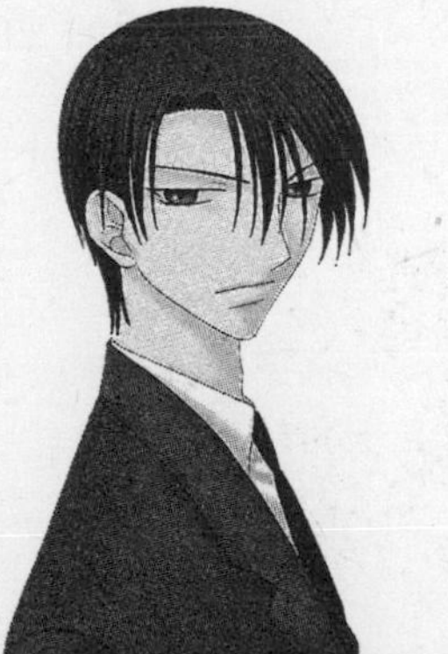

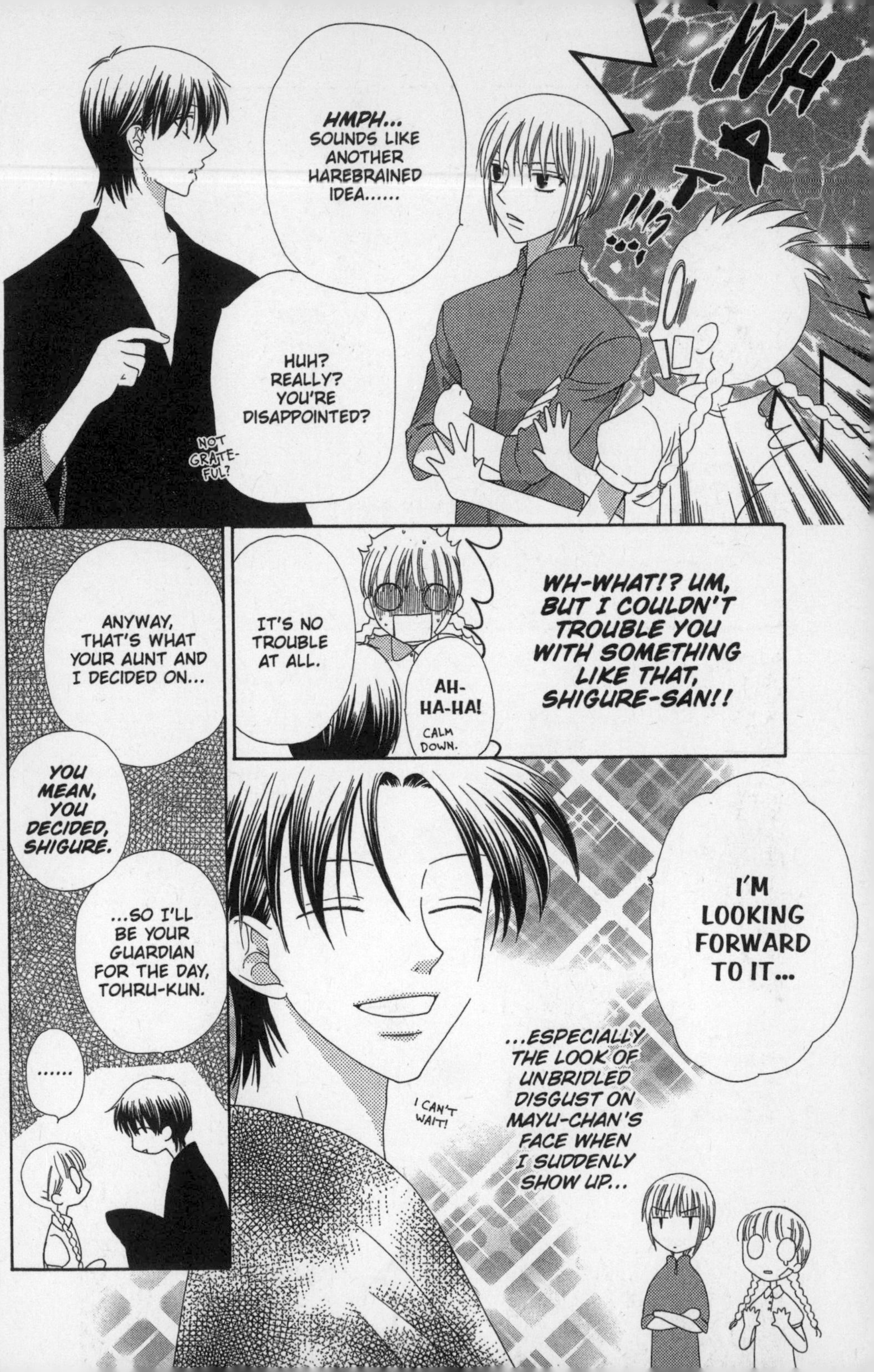
WHAT!!?
HMPH... SOUNDS LIKE ANOTHER HAREBRAINED IDEA......
HUH? REALLY? YOU'RE DISAPPOINTED?
NOT GRATE-FUL?
WH-WHAT!? UM, BUT I COULDN'T TROUBLE YOU WITH SOMETHING LIKE THAT, SHIGURE-SAN!!
IT'S NO TROUBLE AT ALL.
AH-HA-HA!
CALM DOWN.
ANYWAY, THAT'S WHAT YOUR AUNT AND I DECIDED ON...
YOU MEAN, YOU DECIDED, SHIGURE.
...SO I'LL BE YOUR GUARDIAN FOR THE DAY, TOHRU-KUN.
......
I'M LOOKING FORWARD TO IT...
...ESPECIALLY THE LOOK OF UNBRIDLED DISGUST ON MAYU-CHAN'S FACE WHEN I SUDDENLY SHOW UP...
I CAN'T WAIT!

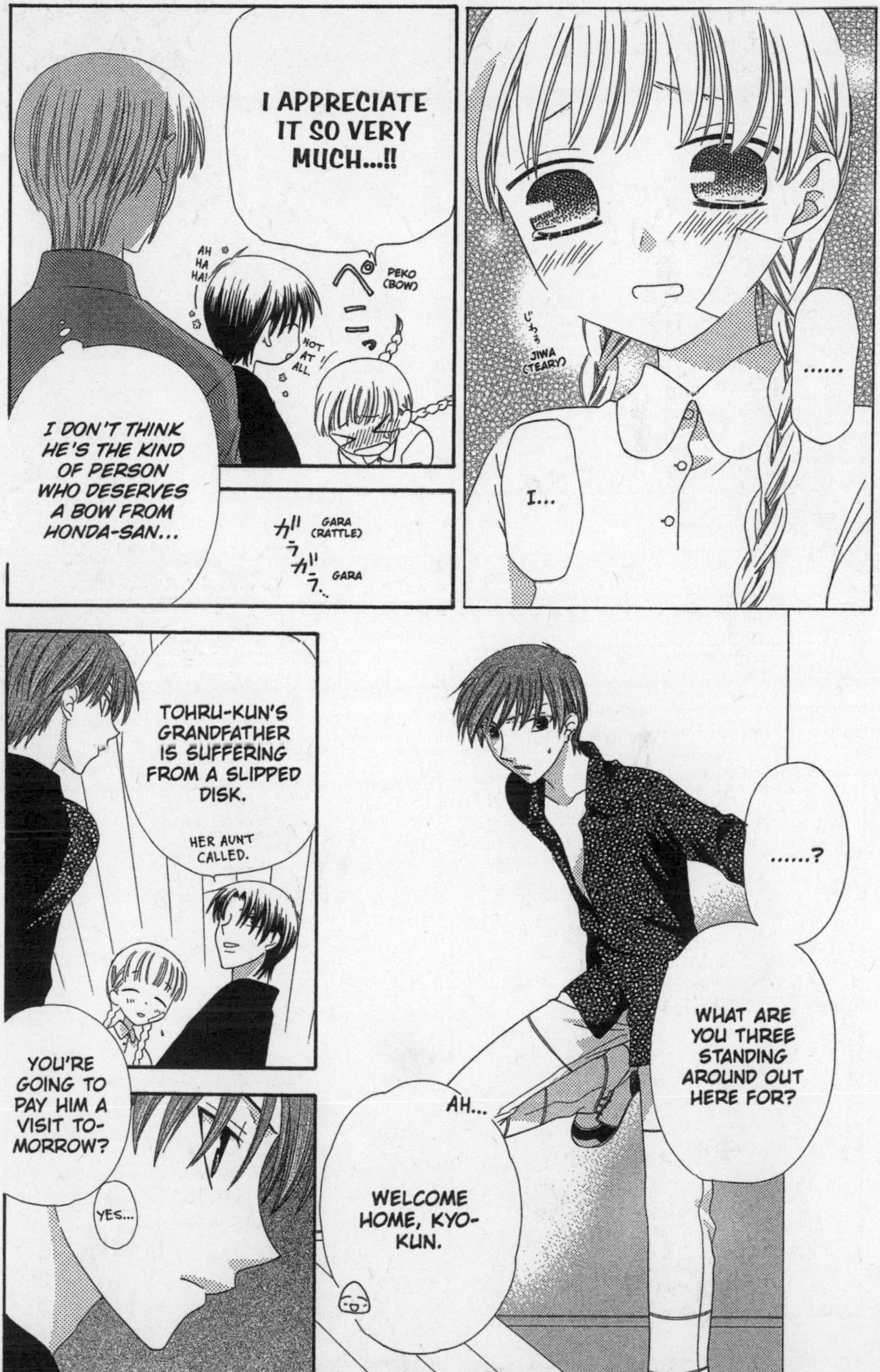

......
I...
JIWA (TEARY)
I APPRECIATE IT SO VERY MUCH...!!
PEKO (BOW)
AH HA HA!
NOT AT ALL.
I DON'T THINK HE'S THE KIND OF PERSON WHO DESERVES A BOW FROM HONDA-SAN...
GARA (RATTLE)
GARA
......?
WHAT ARE YOU THREE STANDING AROUND OUT HERE FOR?
AH...
WELCOME HOME, KYO-KUN.
TOHRU-KUN'S GRANDFATHER IS SUFFERING FROM A SLIPPED DISK.
HER AUNT CALLED.
YOU'RE GOING TO PAY HIM A VISIT TO-MORROW?
YES...

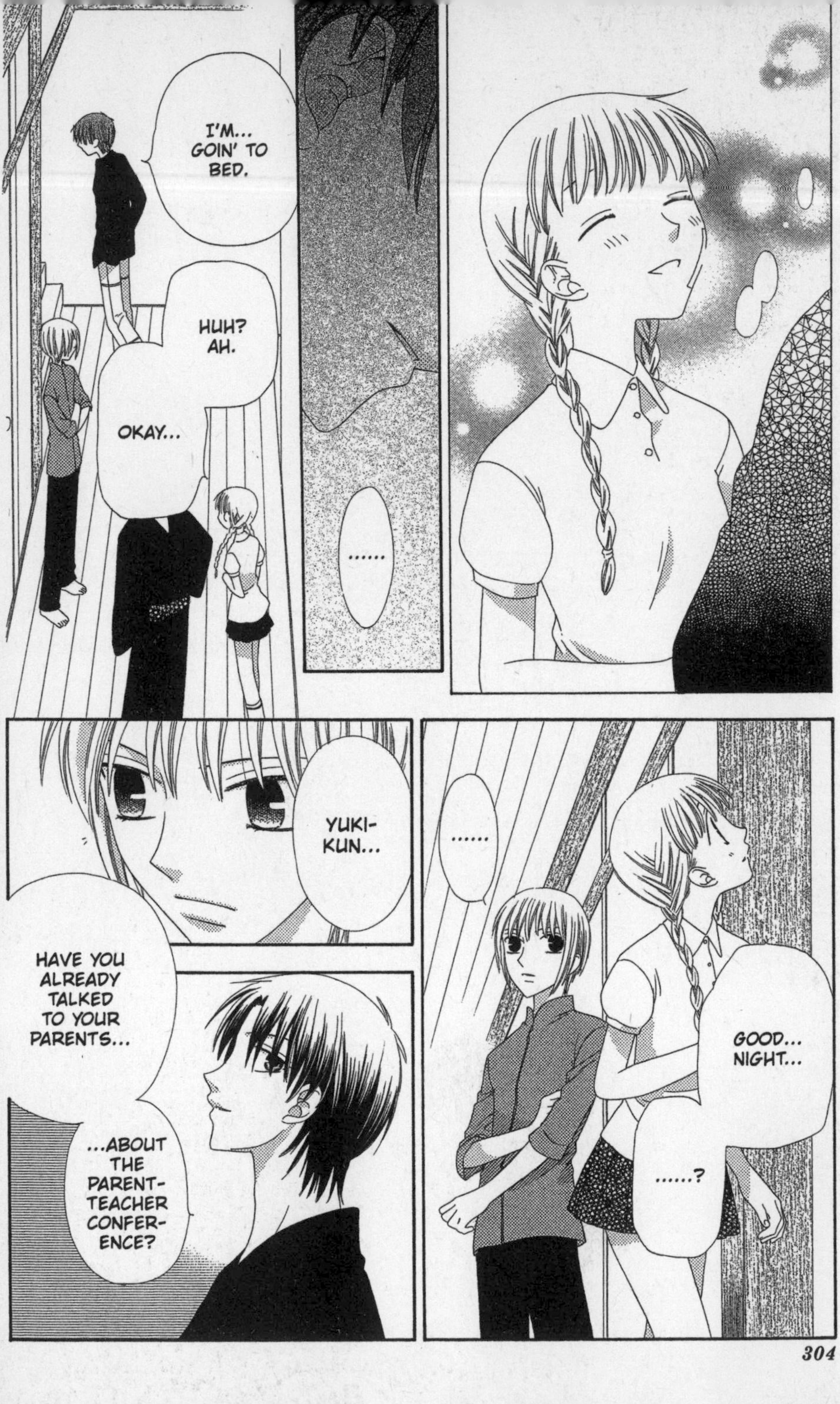
......
I'M... GOIN' TO BED.
HUH? AH.
OKAY...
......
GOOD... NIGHT...
......?
YUKI-KUN...
HAVE YOU ALREADY TALKED TO YOUR PARENTS...
...ABOUT THE PARENT-TEACHER CONFERENCE?

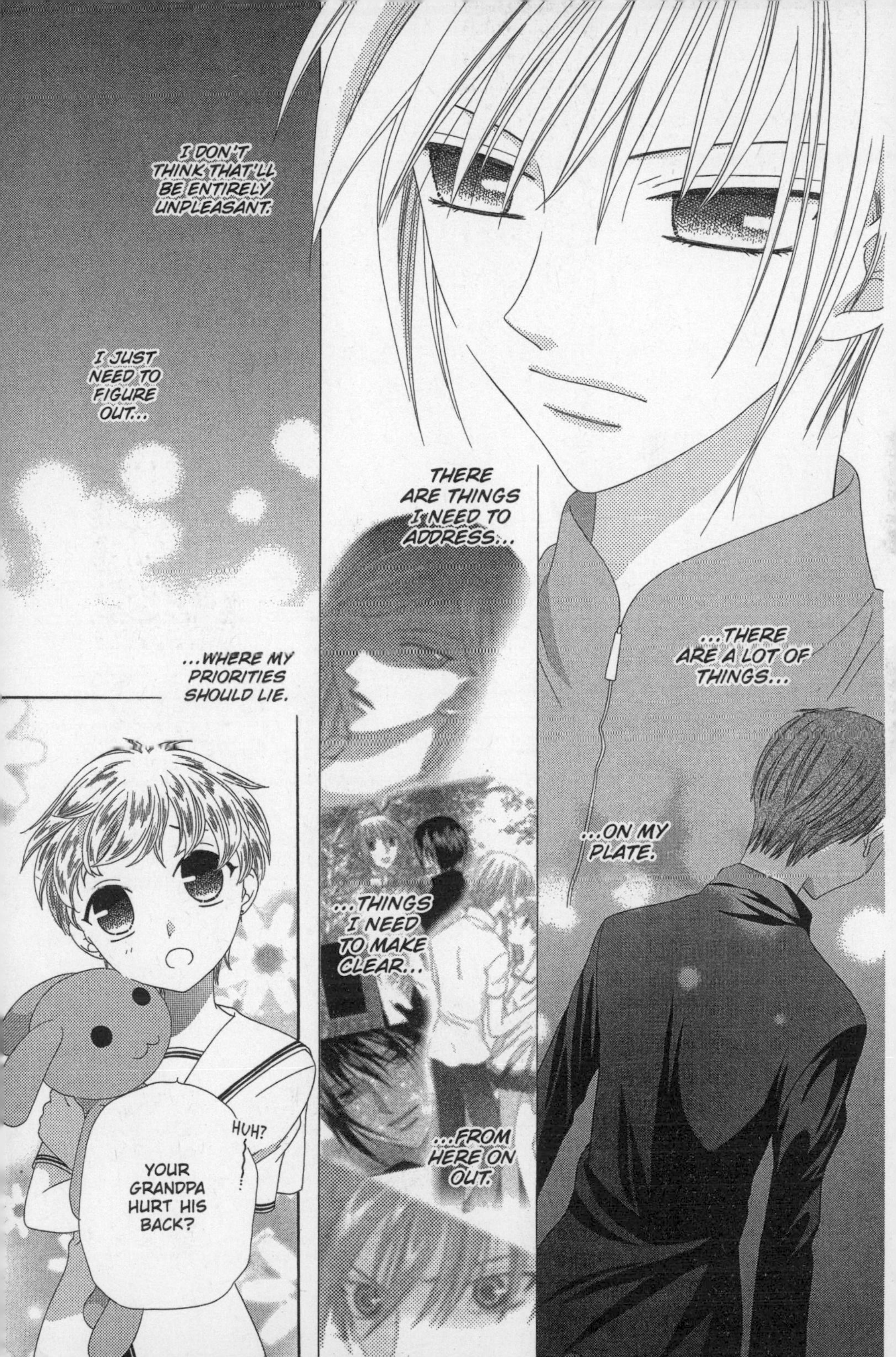
...THERE ARE A LOT OF THINGS...
...ON MY PLATE.
THERE ARE THINGS I NEED TO ADDRESS...
...THINGS I NEED TO MAKE CLEAR...
...FROM HERE ON OUT.
I DON'T THINK THAT'LL BE ENTIRELY UNPLEASANT.
I JUST NEED TO FIGURE OUT...
...WHERE MY PRIORITIES SHOULD LIE.
YOUR GRANDPA HURT HIS BACK?
HUH?

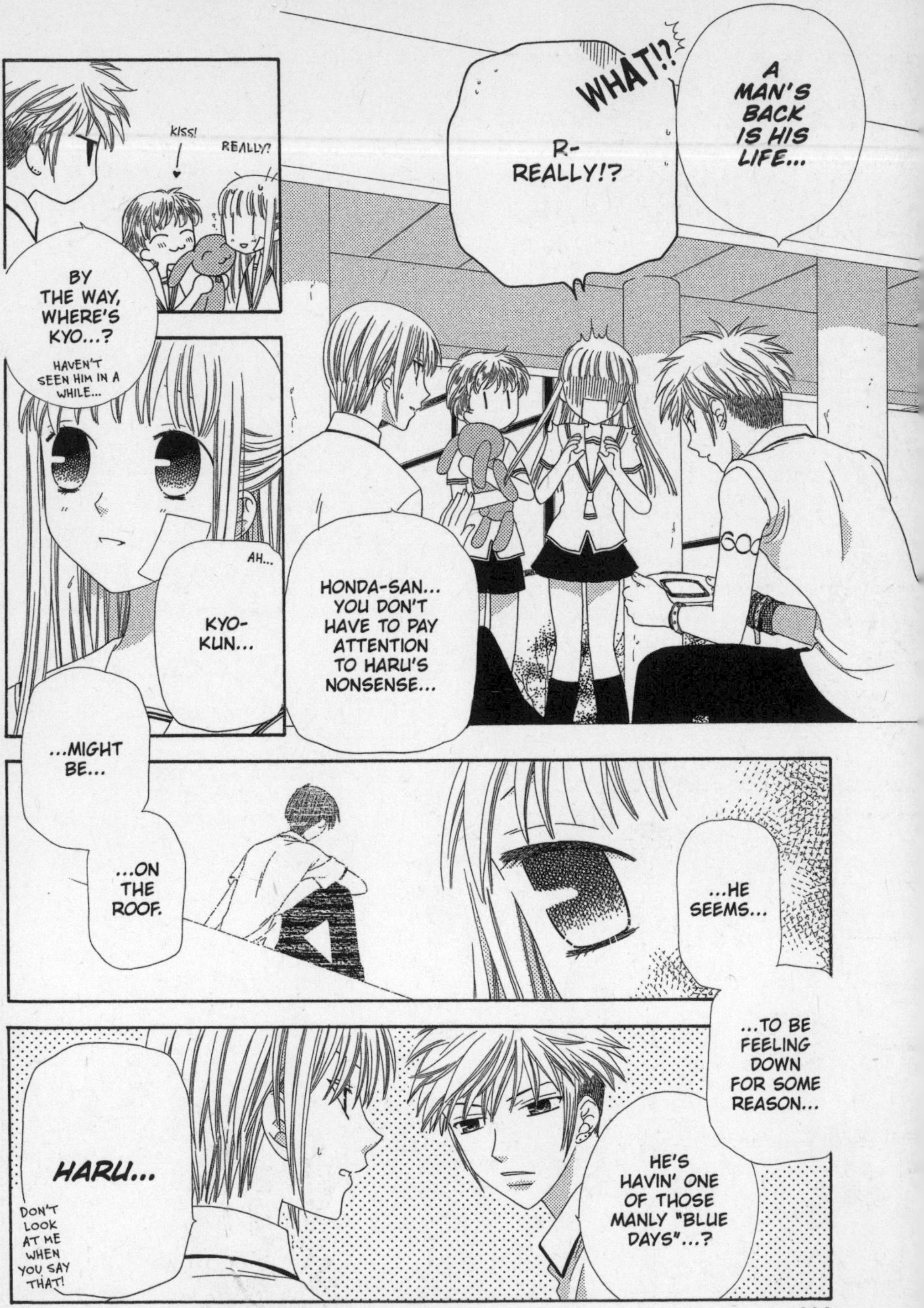
A MAN'S BACK IS HIS LIFE...
WHAT!?
R- REALLY!?
HONDA-SAN... YOU DON'T HAVE TO PAY ATTENTION TO HARU'S NONSENSE...
KISS!
REALLY?
BY THE WAY, WHERE'S KYO...?
HAVEN'T SEEN HIM IN A WHILE...
AH...
KYO-KUN...
...MIGHT BE...
...ON THE ROOF.
...HE SEEMS...
...TO BE FEELING DOWN FOR SOME REASON...
HE'S HAVIN' ONE OF THOSE MANLY "BLUE DAYS"...?
HARU...
DON'T LOOK AT ME WHEN YOU SAY THAT!

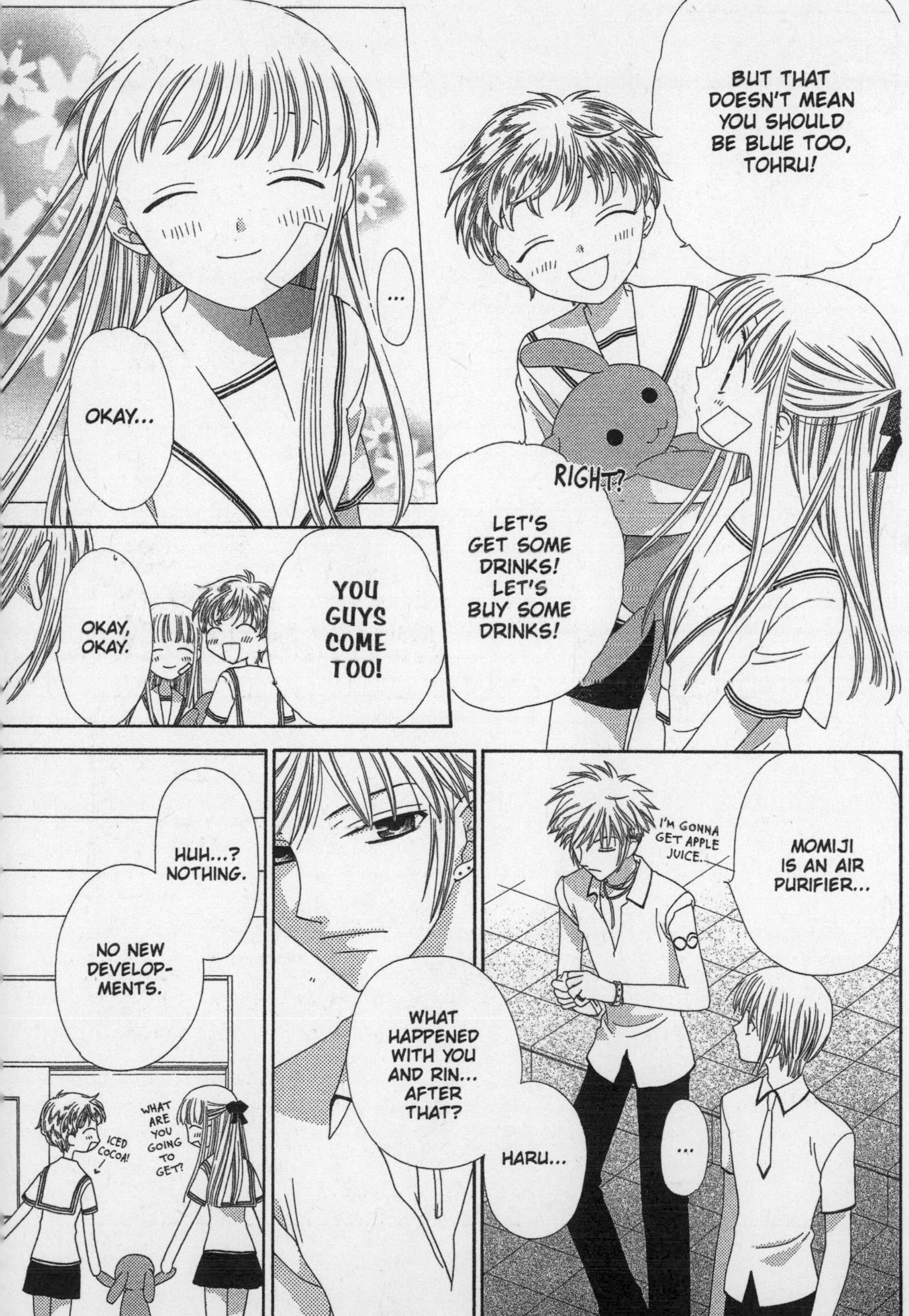
BUT THAT DOESN'T MEAN YOU SHOULD BE BLUE TOO, TOHRU!
RIGHT?
LET'S GET SOME DRINKS! LET'S BUY SOME DRINKS!
...
OKAY...
YOU GUYS COME TOO!
OKAY, OKAY.
MOMIJI IS AN AIR PURIFIER...
I'M GONNA GET APPLE JUICE.
...
HARU...
WHAT HAPPENED WITH YOU AND RIN... AFTER THAT?
HUH...? NOTHING.
NO NEW DEVELOP-MENTS.
WHAT ARE YOU GOING TO GET?
ICED COCOA!

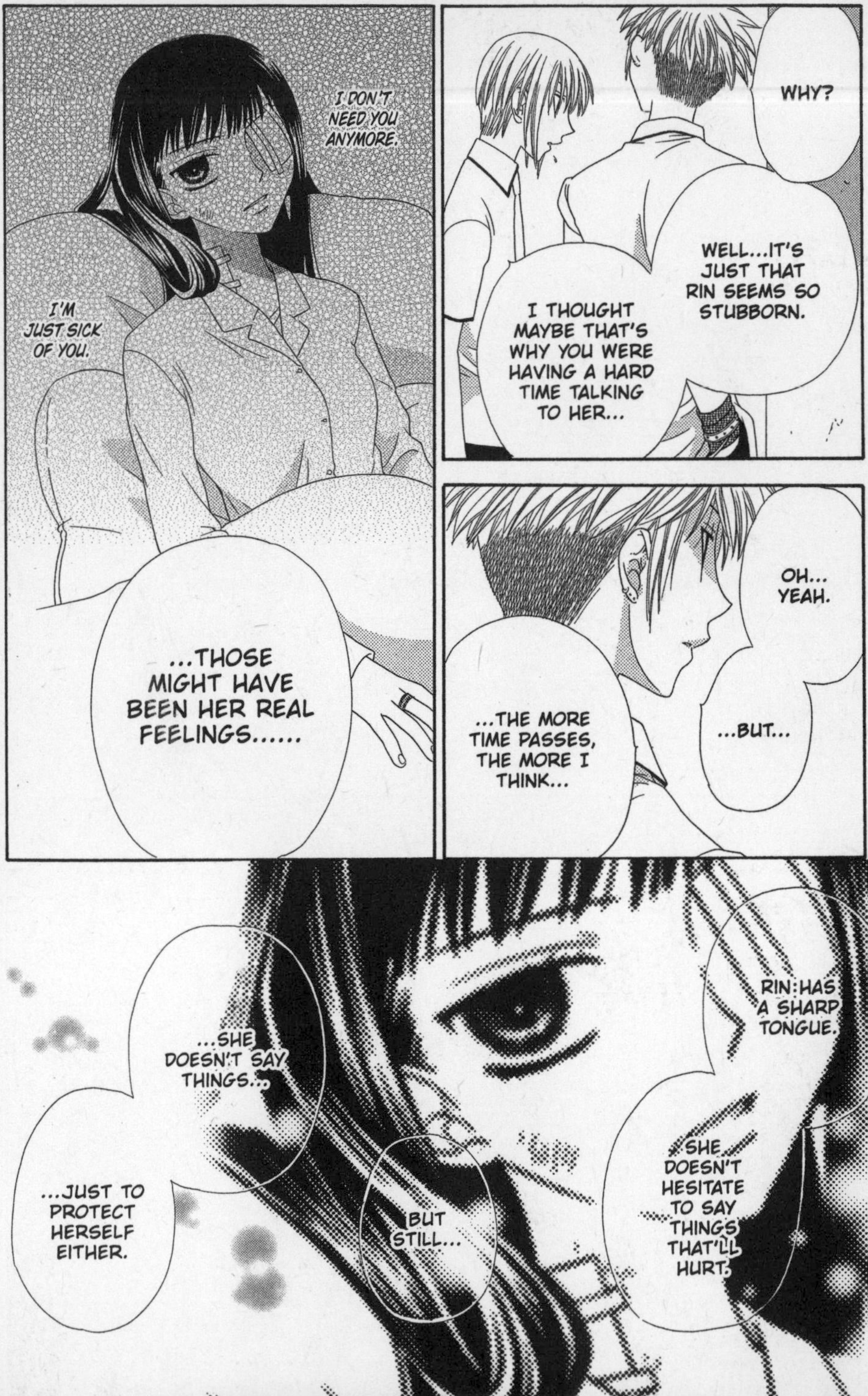
WHY?
WELL...IT'S JUST THAT RIN SEEMS SO STUBBORN.
I THOUGHT MAYBE THAT'S WHY YOU WERE HAVING A HARD TIME TALKING TO HER...
OH... YEAH.
...BUT...
...THE MORE TIME PASSES, THE MORE I THINK...
I DON'T NEED YOU ANYMORE.
I'M JUST SICK OF YOU.
...THOSE MIGHT HAVE BEEN HER REAL FEELINGS......
RIN HAS A SHARP TONGUE.
SHE DOESN'T HESITATE TO SAY THINGS THAT'LL HURT.
BUT STILL...
...SHE DOESN'T SAY THINGS...
...JUST TO PROTECT HERSELF EITHER.

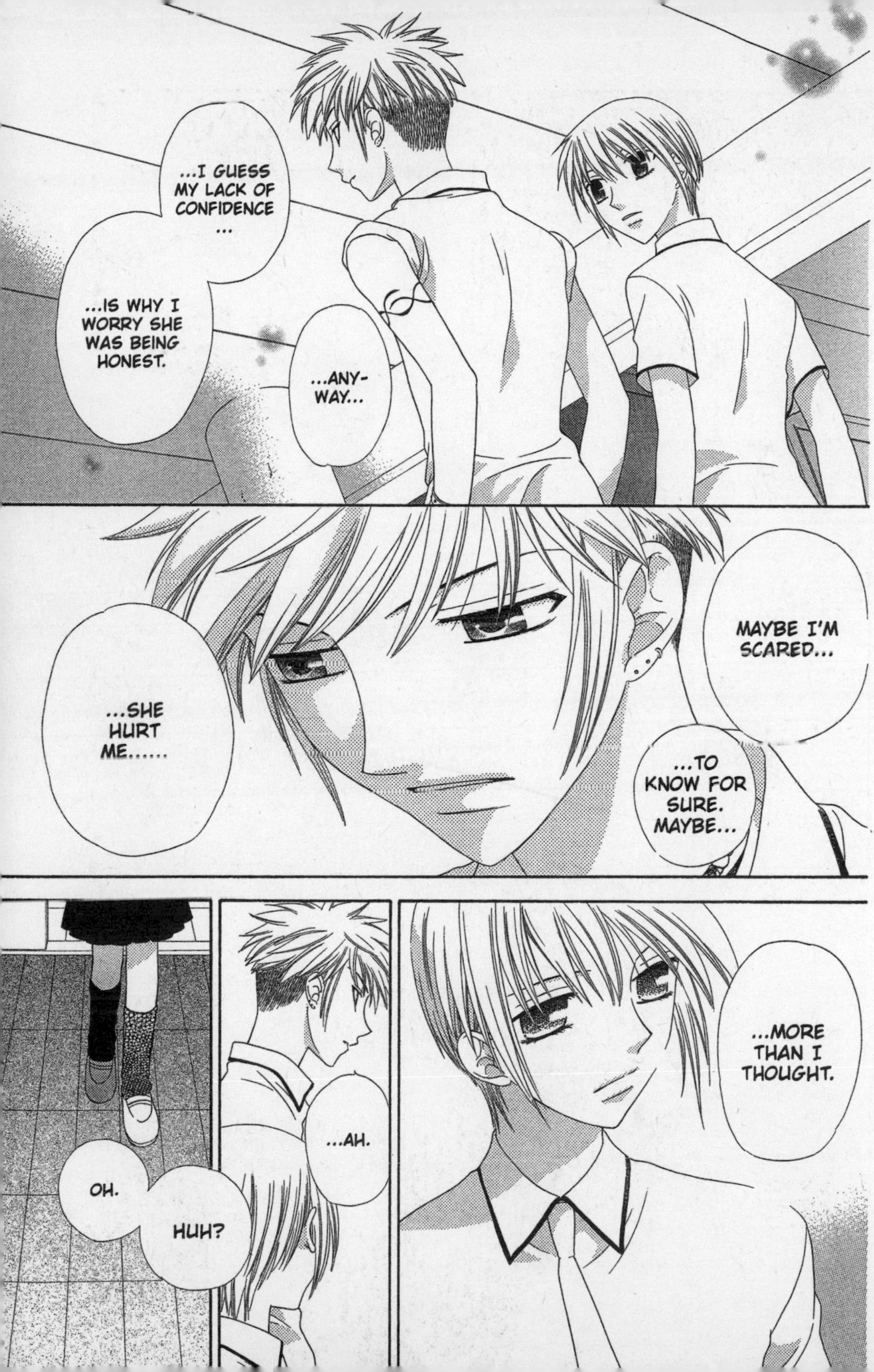
...I GUESS MY LACK OF CONFIDENCE ...
...IS WHY I WORRY SHE WAS BEING HONEST.
...ANY-WAY...
MAYBE I'M SCARED...
...TO KNOW FOR SURE. MAYBE...
...SHE HURT ME......
...MORE THAN I THOUGHT.
...AH.
OH.
HUH?

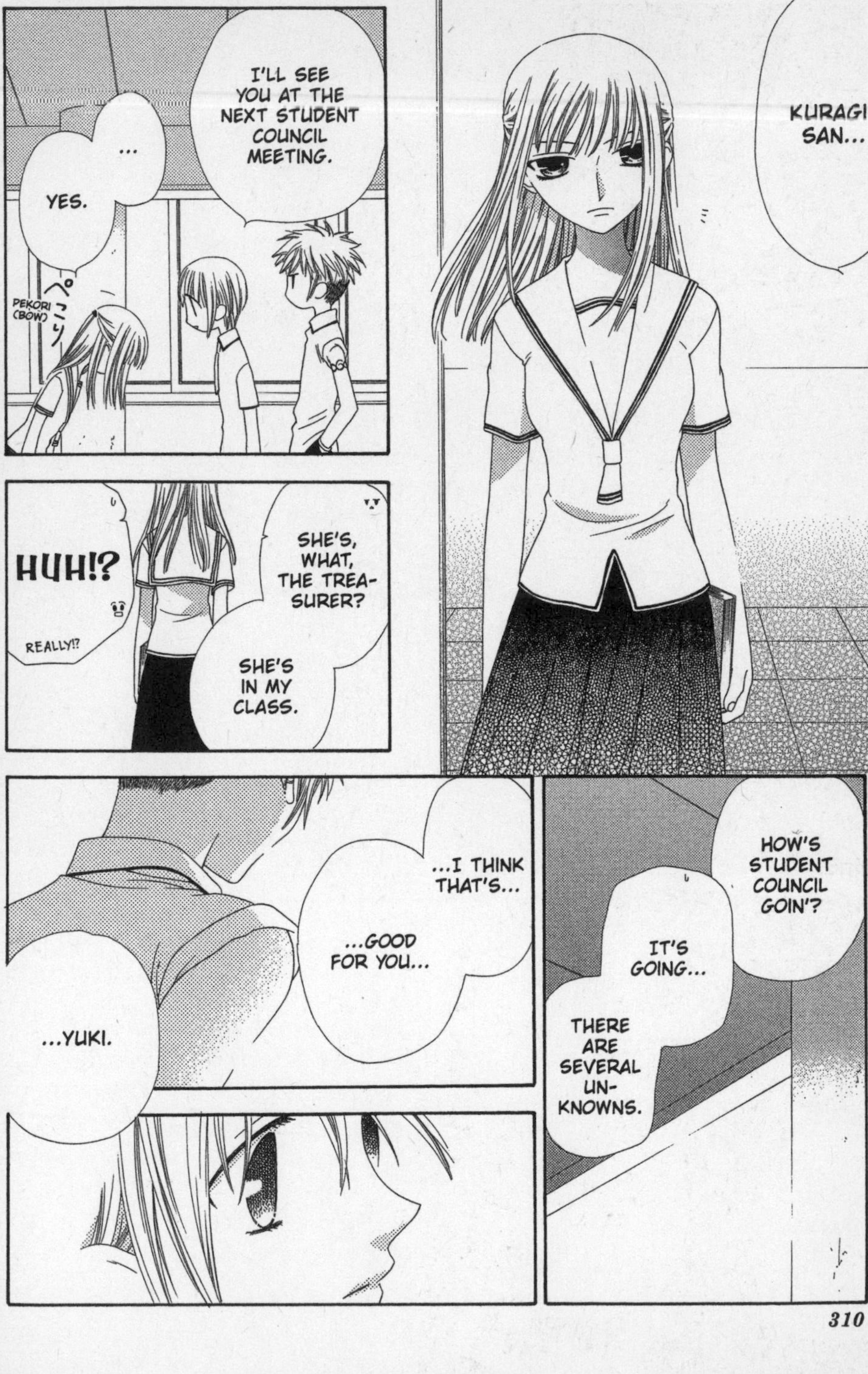
KURAGI-SAN...
I'LL SEE YOU AT THE NEXT STUDENT COUNCIL MEETING.
...
YES.
PEKORI (BOW)
SHE'S, WHAT, THE TREASURER?
SHE'S IN MY CLASS.
HUH!?
REALLY!?
HOW'S STUDENT COUNCIL GOIN'?
IT'S GOING...
THERE ARE SEVERAL UN-KNOWNS.
...I THINK THAT'S...
...GOOD FOR YOU...
...YUKI.

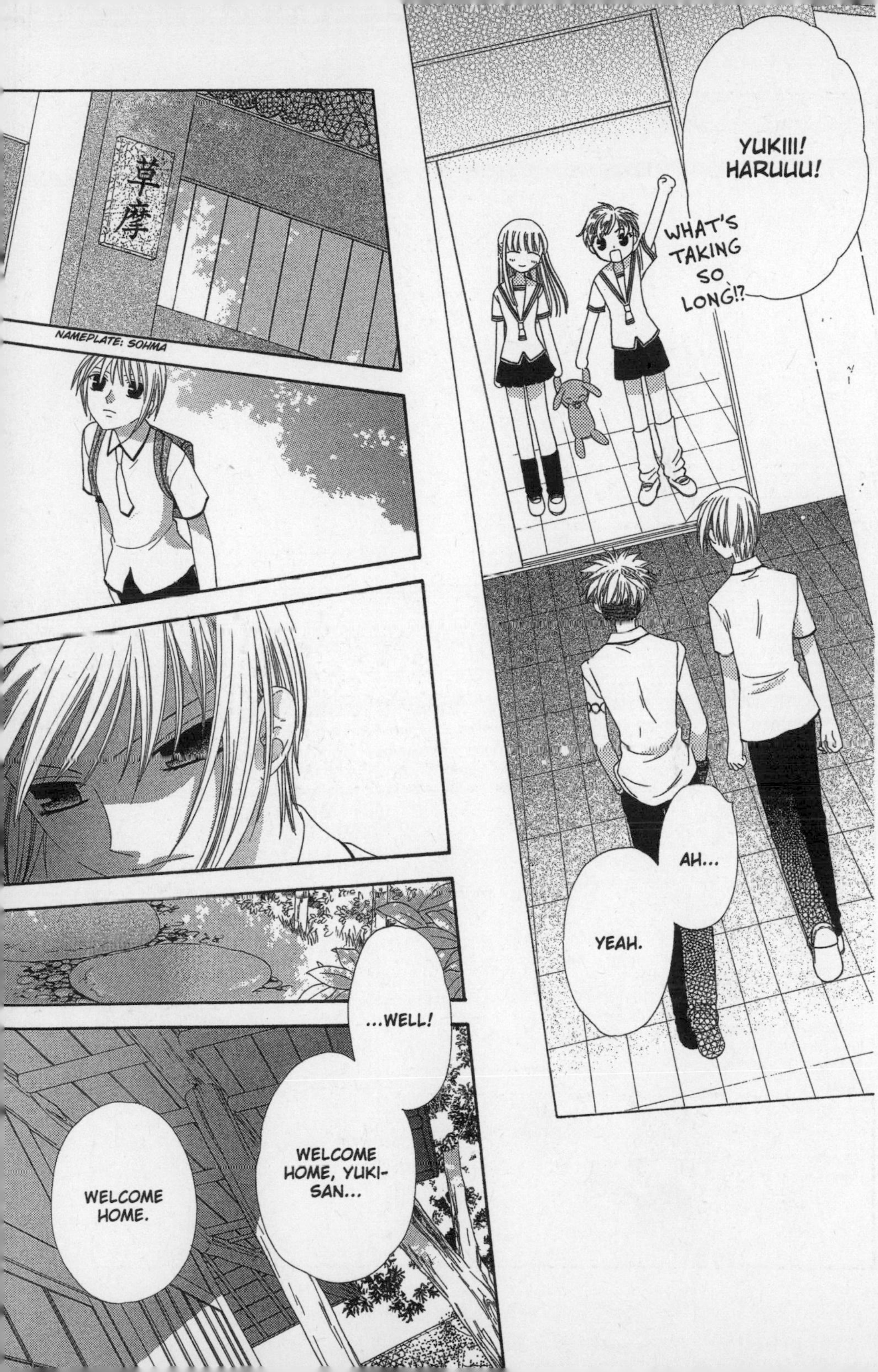
YUKIII! HARUUU!
WHAT'S TAKING SO LONG!?
AH...
YEAH.
草摩
NAMEPLATE: SOHMA
...WELL!
WELCOME HOME, YUKI-SAN...
WELCOME HOME.

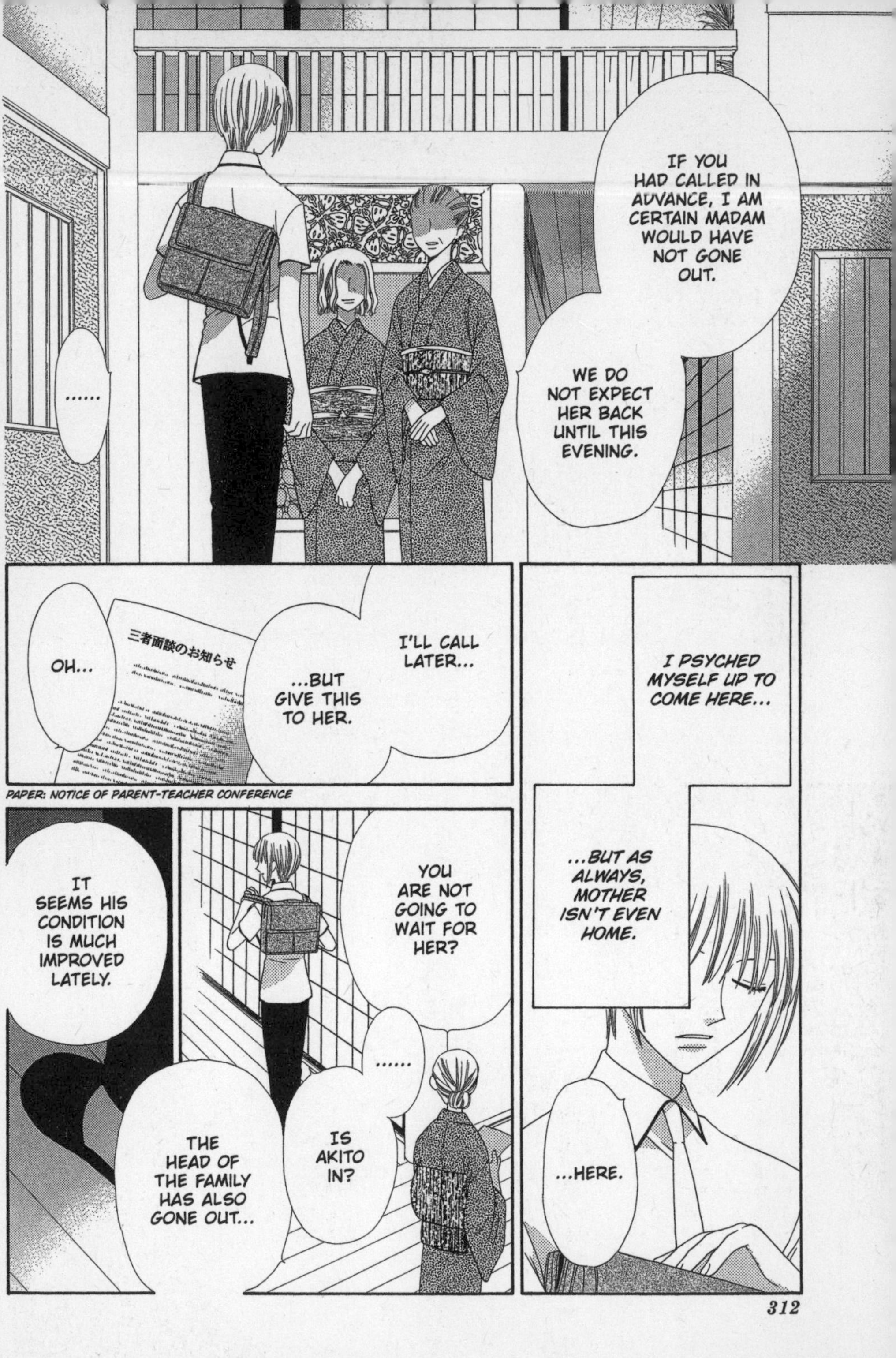
IF YOU HAD CALLED IN ADVANCE, I AM CERTAIN MADAM WOULD HAVE NOT GONE OUT.
WE DO NOT EXPECT HER BACK UNTIL THIS EVENING.
......
I PSYCHED MYSELF UP TO COME HERE...
...BUT AS ALWAYS, MOTHER ISN'T EVEN HOME.
...HERE.
I'LL CALL LATER...
...BUT GIVE THIS TO HER.
OH...
三者面談のお知らせ
YOU ARE NOT GOING TO WAIT FOR HER?
......
IS AKITO IN?
IT SEEMS HIS CONDITION IS MUCH IMPROVED LATELY.
THE HEAD OF THE FAMILY HAS ALSO GONE OUT...
PAPER: NOTICE OF PARENT-TEACHER CONFERENCE

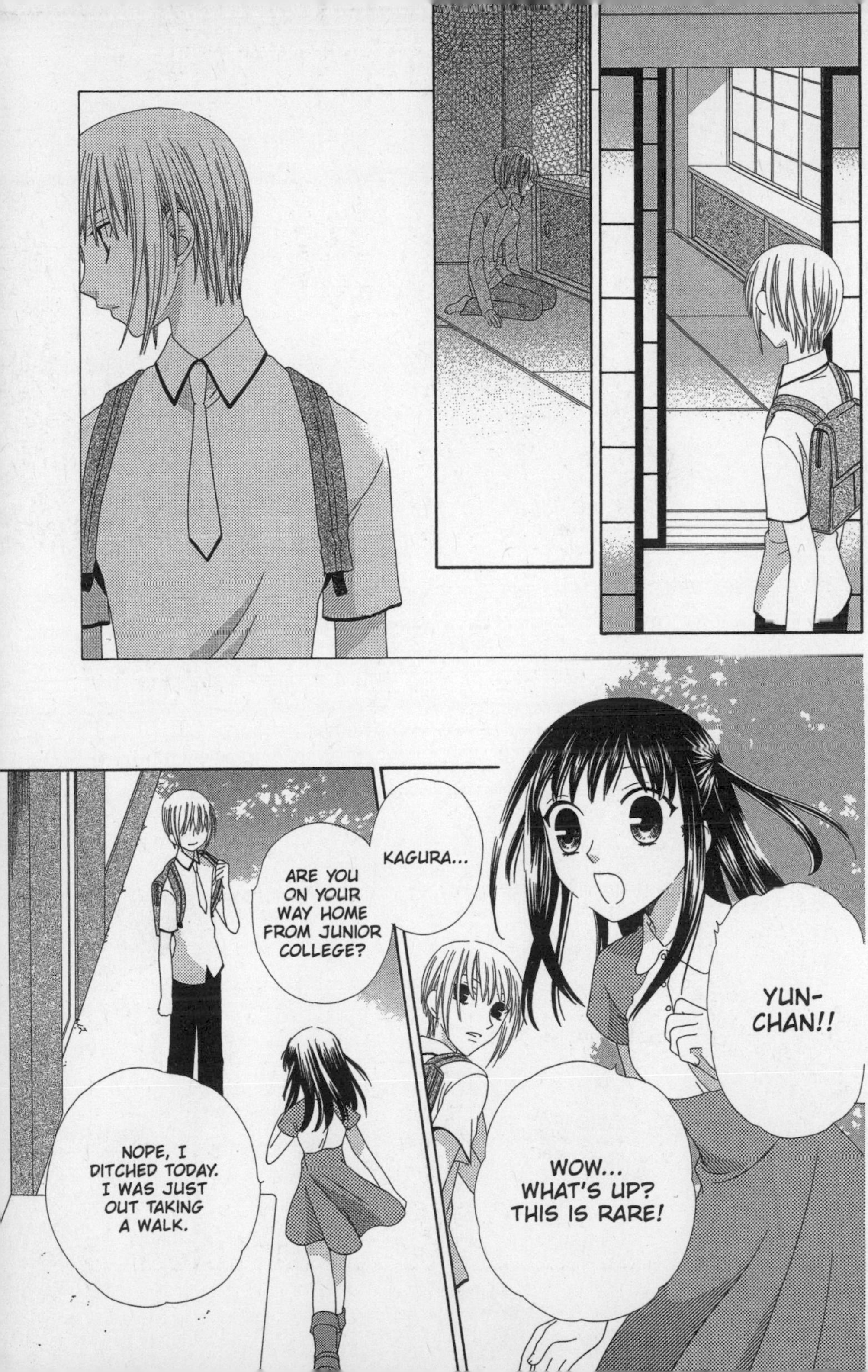
YUN-CHAN!!
WOW... WHAT'S UP? THIS IS RARE!
KAGURA...
ARE YOU ON YOUR WAY HOME FROM JUNIOR COLLEGE?
NOPE, I DITCHED TODAY. I WAS JUST OUT TAKING A WALK.

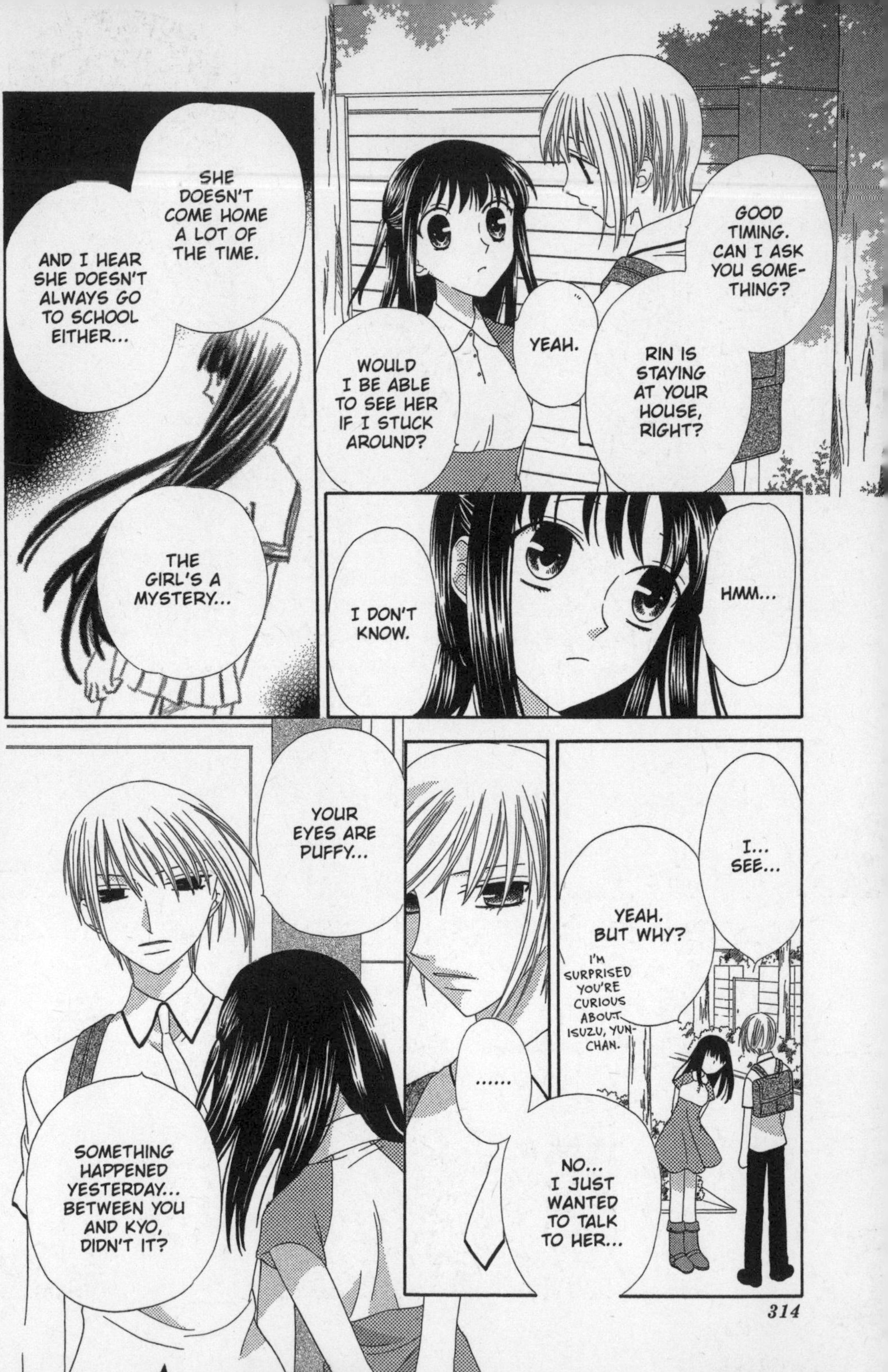
GOOD TIMING. CAN I ASK YOU SOME-THING?
YEAH.
RIN IS STAYING AT YOUR HOUSE, RIGHT?
WOULD I BE ABLE TO SEE HER IF I STUCK AROUND?
HMM...
I DON'T KNOW.
SHE DOESN'T COME HOME A LOT OF THE TIME.
AND I HEAR SHE DOESN'T ALWAYS GO TO SCHOOL EITHER...
THE GIRL'S A MYSTERY...
I... SEE...
YEAH. BUT WHY?
I'M SURPRISED YOU'RE CURIOUS ABOUT ISUZU, YUN-CHAN.
NO... I JUST WANTED TO TALK TO HER...
......
YOUR EYES ARE PUFFY...
SOMETHING HAPPENED YESTERDAY... BETWEEN YOU AND KYO, DIDN'T IT?

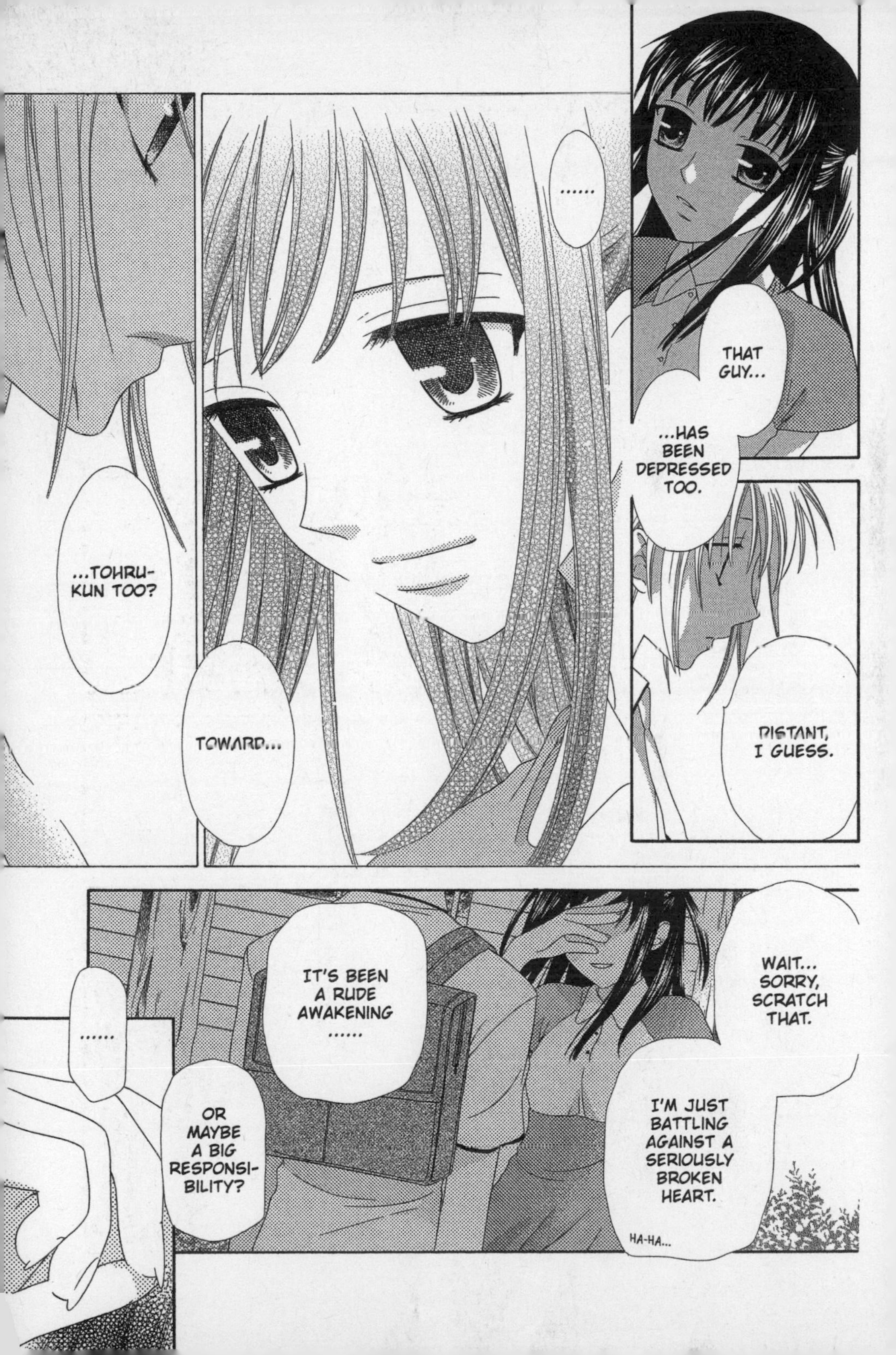
THAT GUY...
...HAS BEEN DEPRESSED TOO.
DISTANT, I GUESS.
......
TOWARD...
...TOHRU-KUN TOO?
WAIT... SORRY, SCRATCH THAT.
I'M JUST BATTLING AGAINST A SERIOUSLY BROKEN HEART.
HA-HA...
IT'S BEEN A RUDE AWAKENING ......
OR MAYBE A BIG RESPONSI-BILITY?
......

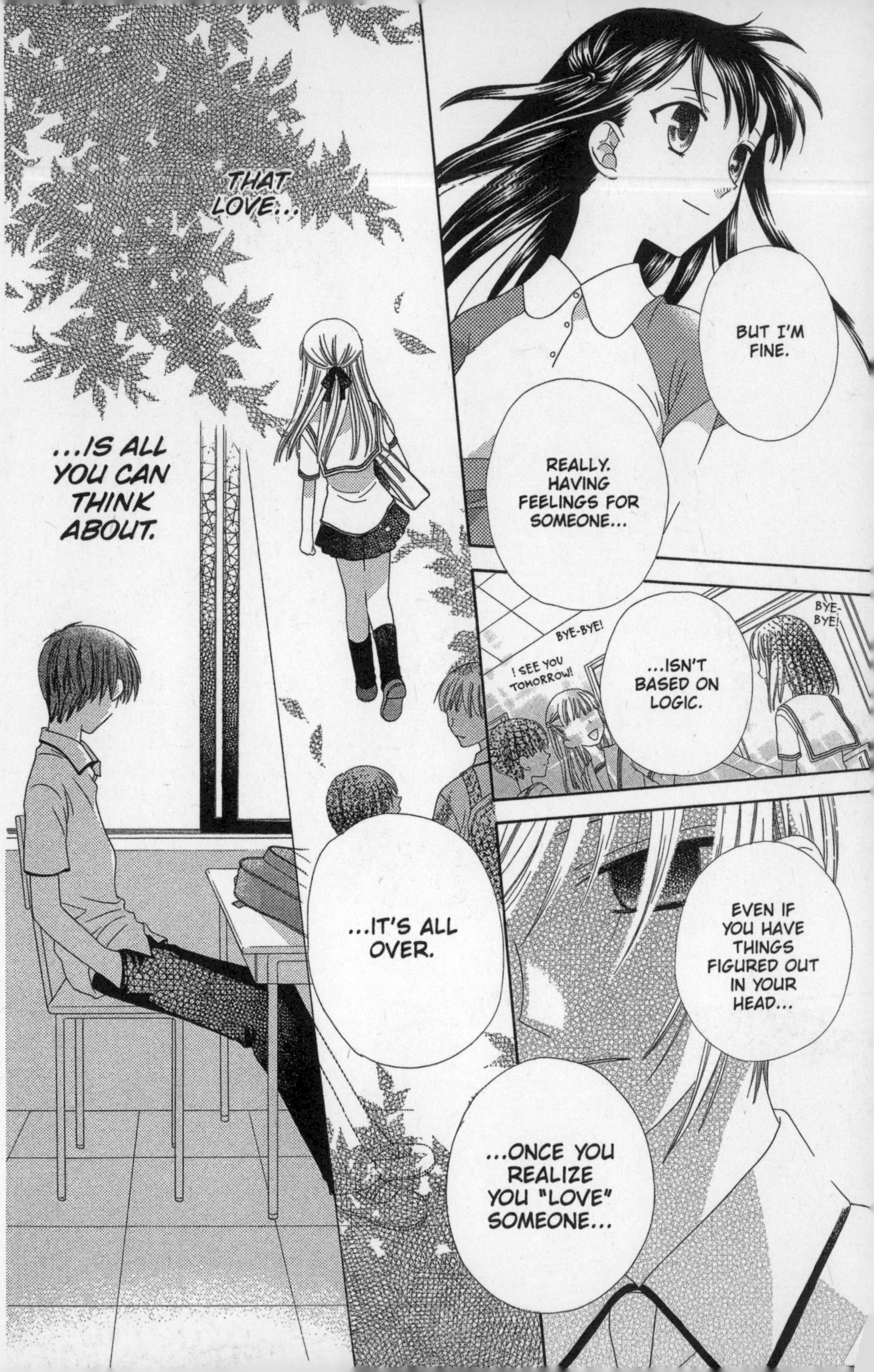
BUT I'M FINE.
REALLY. HAVING FEELINGS FOR SOMEONE...
BYE-BYE!
...ISN'T BASED ON LOGIC.
BYE-BYE!
SEE YOU TOMORROW!
EVEN IF YOU HAVE THINGS FIGURED OUT IN YOUR HEAD...
...ONCE YOU REALIZE YOU "LOVE" SOMEONE...
...IT'S ALL OVER.
THAT LOVE...
...IS ALL YOU CAN THINK ABOUT.

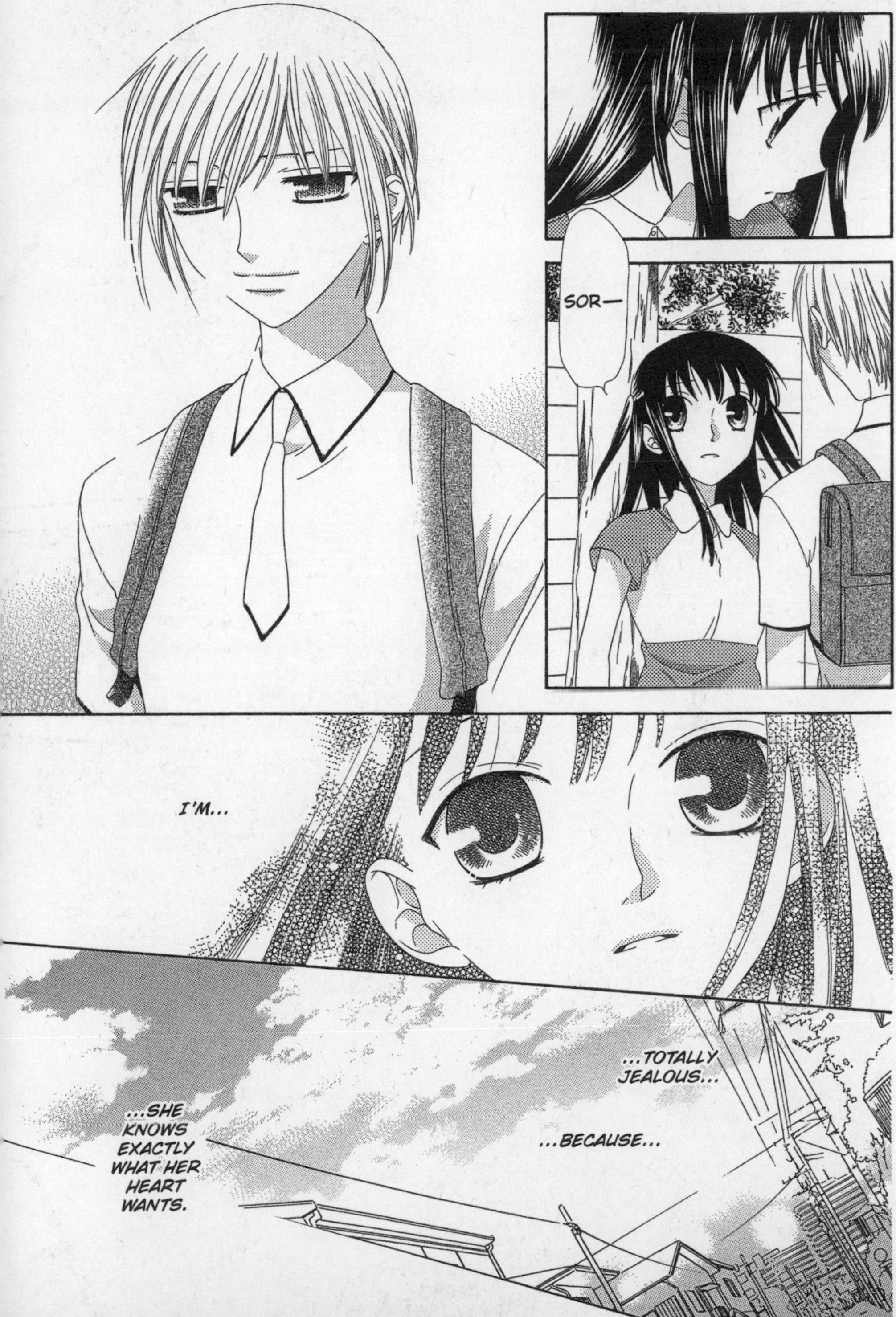
SOR—
I'M...
...TOTALLY JEALOUS...
...BECAUSE...
...SHE KNOWS EXACTLY WHAT HER HEART WANTS.

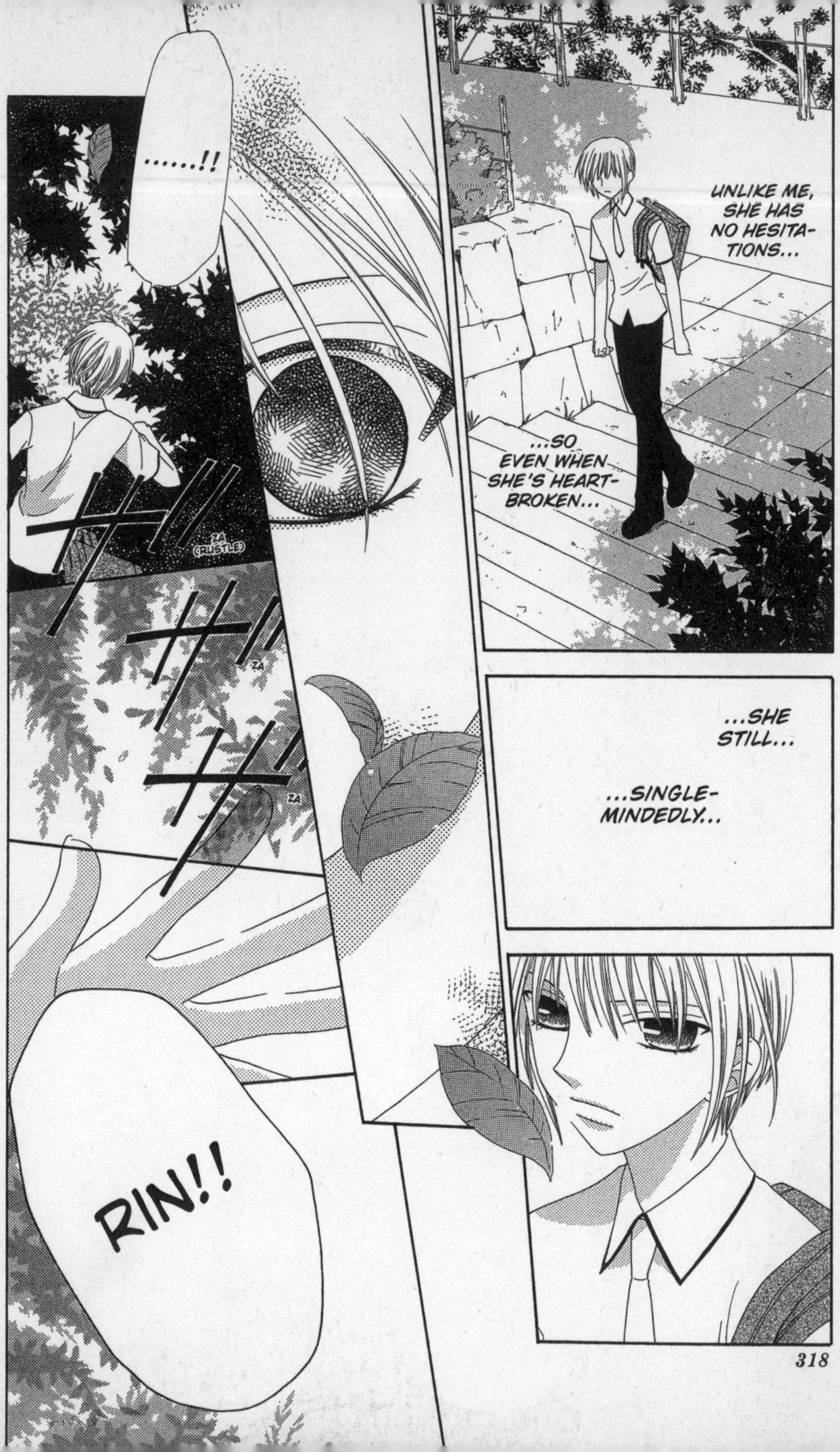
UNLIKE ME, SHE HAS NO HESITATIONS...
...SO EVEN WHEN SHE'S HEART-BROKEN...
...SHE STILL...
...SINGLE-MINDEDLY...
......!!
ZA (RUSTLE)
ZA
ZA
RIN!!

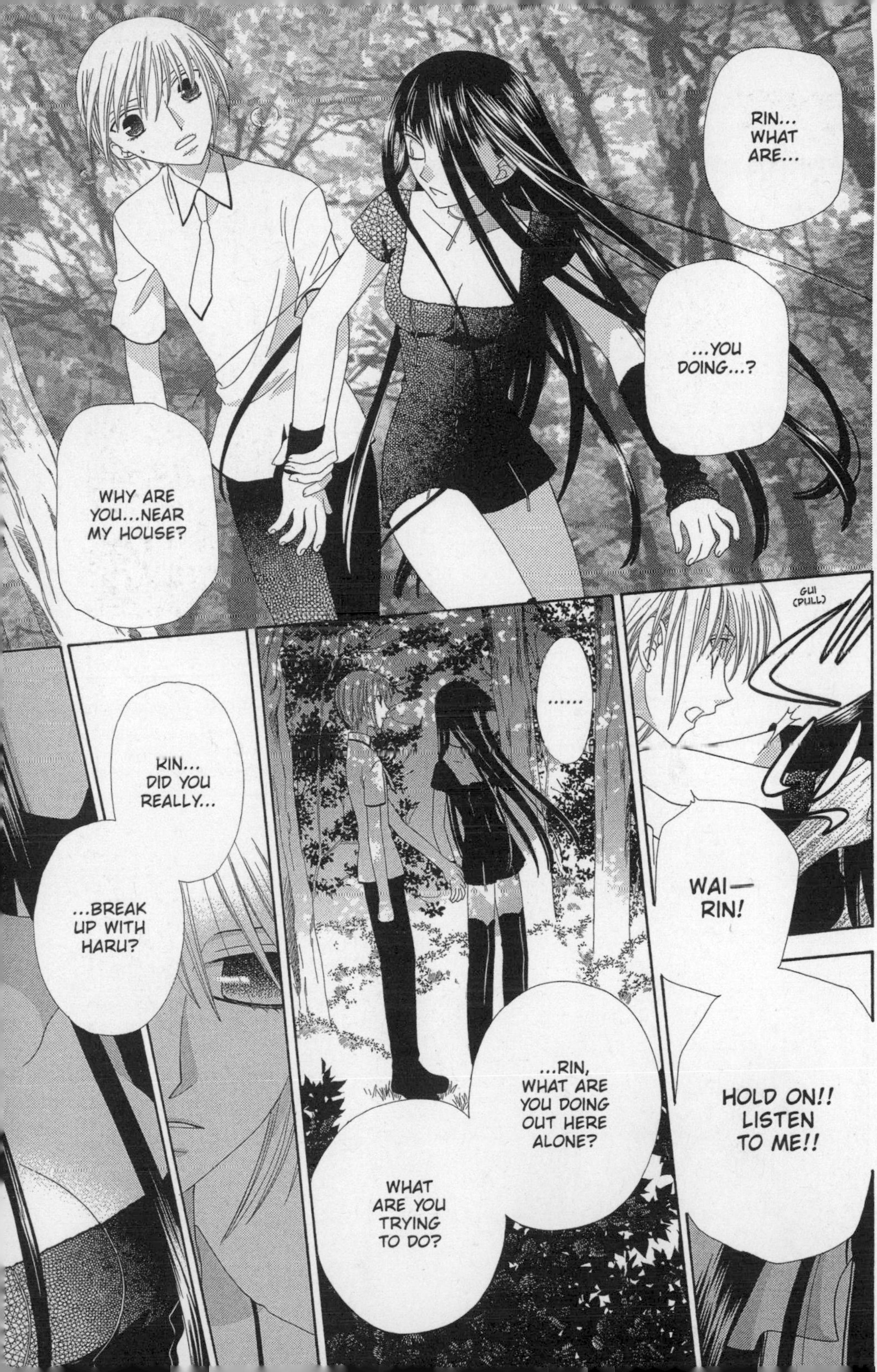
RIN... WHAT ARE...
...YOU DOING...?
WHY ARE YOU...NEAR MY HOUSE?
GUI (PULL)
WAI— RIN!
HOLD ON!! LISTEN TO ME!!
......
...RIN, WHAT ARE YOU DOING OUT HERE ALONE?
WHAT ARE YOU TRYING TO DO?
RIN... DID YOU REALLY...
...BREAK UP WITH HARU?

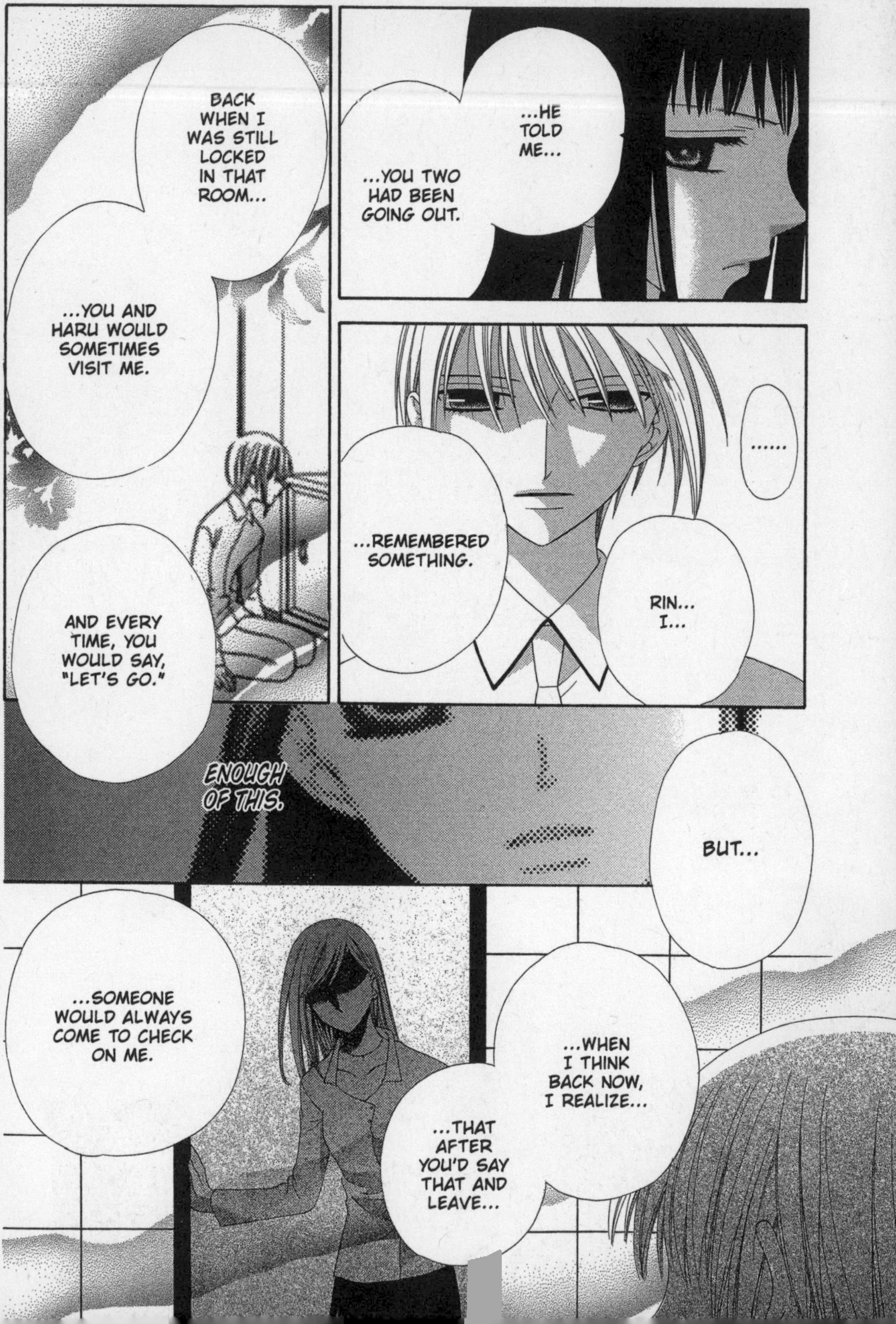

...HE TOLD ME...
...YOU TWO HAD BEEN GOING OUT.
......
RIN... I...
...REMEMBERED SOMETHING.
BACK WHEN I WAS STILL LOCKED IN THAT ROOM...
...YOU AND HARU WOULD SOMETIMES VISIT ME.
AND EVERY TIME, YOU WOULD SAY, "LET'S GO."
BUT...
ENOUGH OF THIS.
...WHEN I THINK BACK NOW, I REALIZE...
...THAT AFTER YOU'D SAY THAT AND LEAVE...
...SOMEONE WOULD ALWAYS COME TO CHECK ON ME.

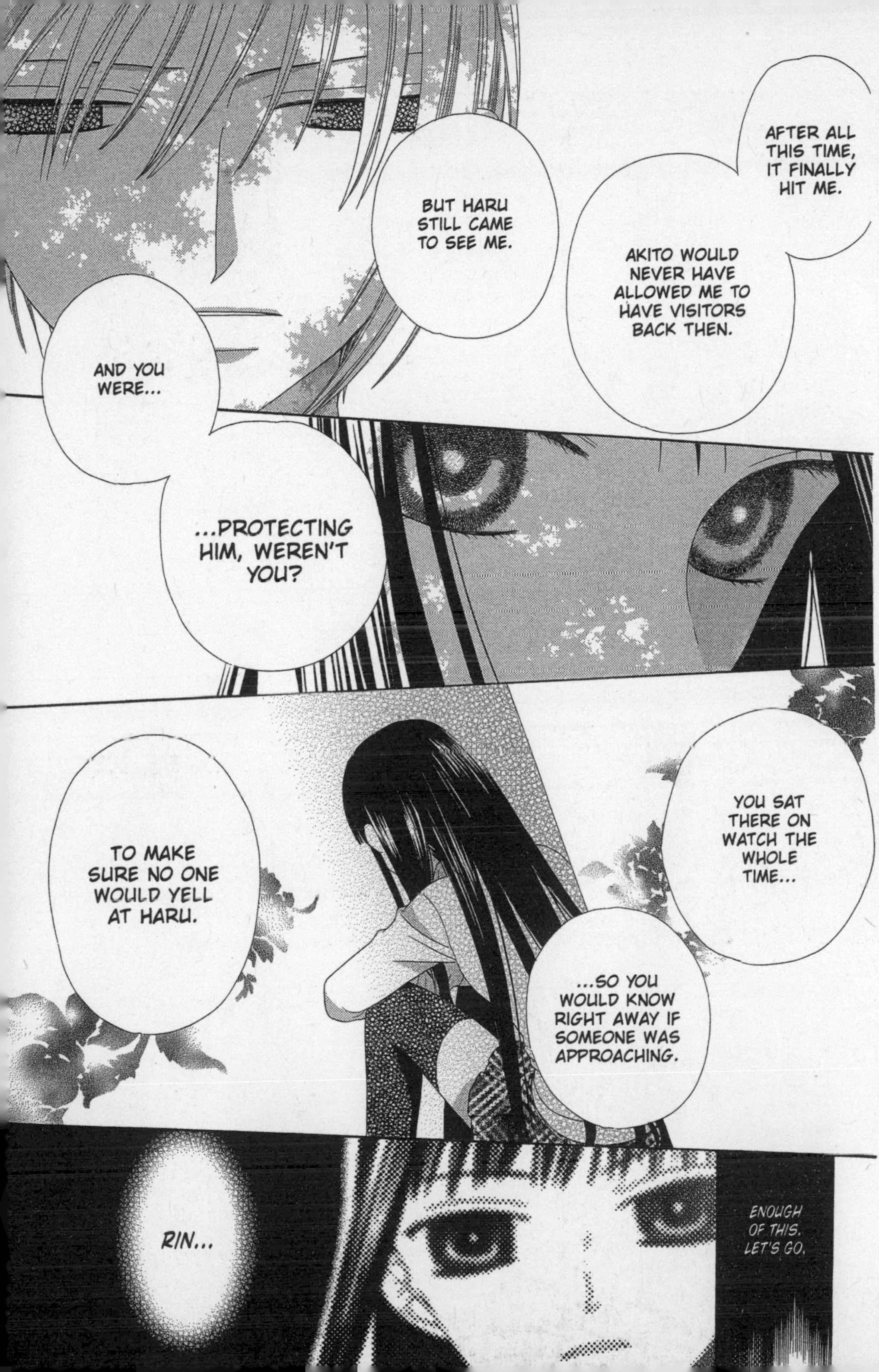
AFTER ALL THIS TIME, IT FINALLY HIT ME.
AKITO WOULD NEVER HAVE ALLOWED ME TO HAVE VISITORS BACK THEN.
BUT HARU STILL CAME TO SEE ME.
AND YOU WERE...
...PROTECTING HIM, WEREN'T YOU?
YOU SAT THERE ON WATCH THE WHOLE TIME...
...SO YOU WOULD KNOW RIGHT AWAY IF SOMEONE WAS APPROACHING.
TO MAKE SURE NO ONE WOULD YELL AT HARU.
ENOUGH OF THIS. LET'S GO.
RIN...

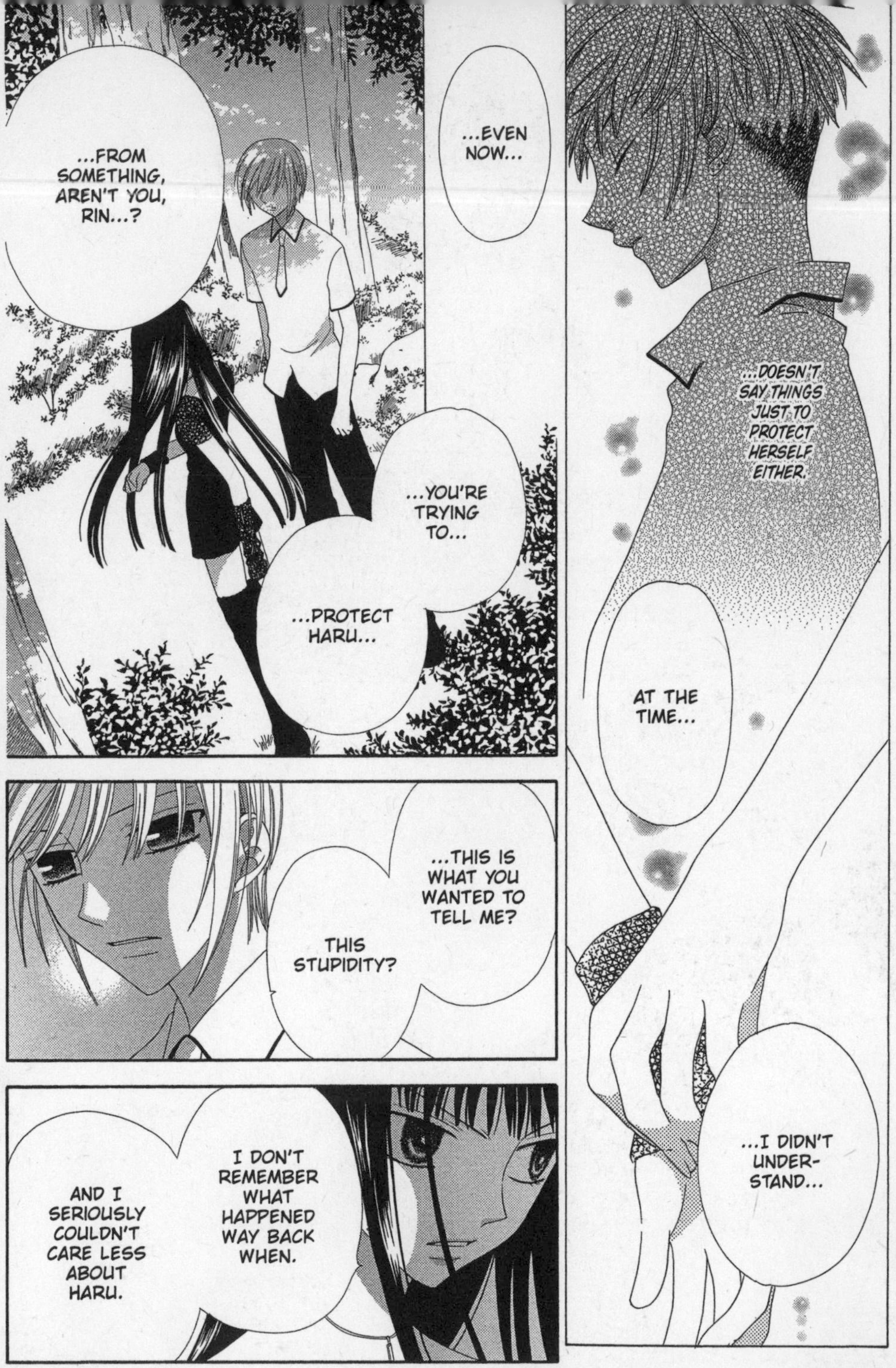
...DOESN'T SAY THINGS JUST TO PROTECT HERSELF EITHER.
AT THE TIME...
...I DIDN'T UNDER-STAND...
...EVEN NOW...
...YOU'RE TRYING TO...
...PROTECT HARU...
...FROM SOMETHING, AREN'T YOU, RIN...?
...THIS IS WHAT YOU WANTED TO TELL ME?
THIS STUPIDITY?
I DON'T REMEMBER WHAT HAPPENED WAY BACK WHEN.
AND I SERIOUSLY COULDN'T CARE LESS ABOUT HARU.

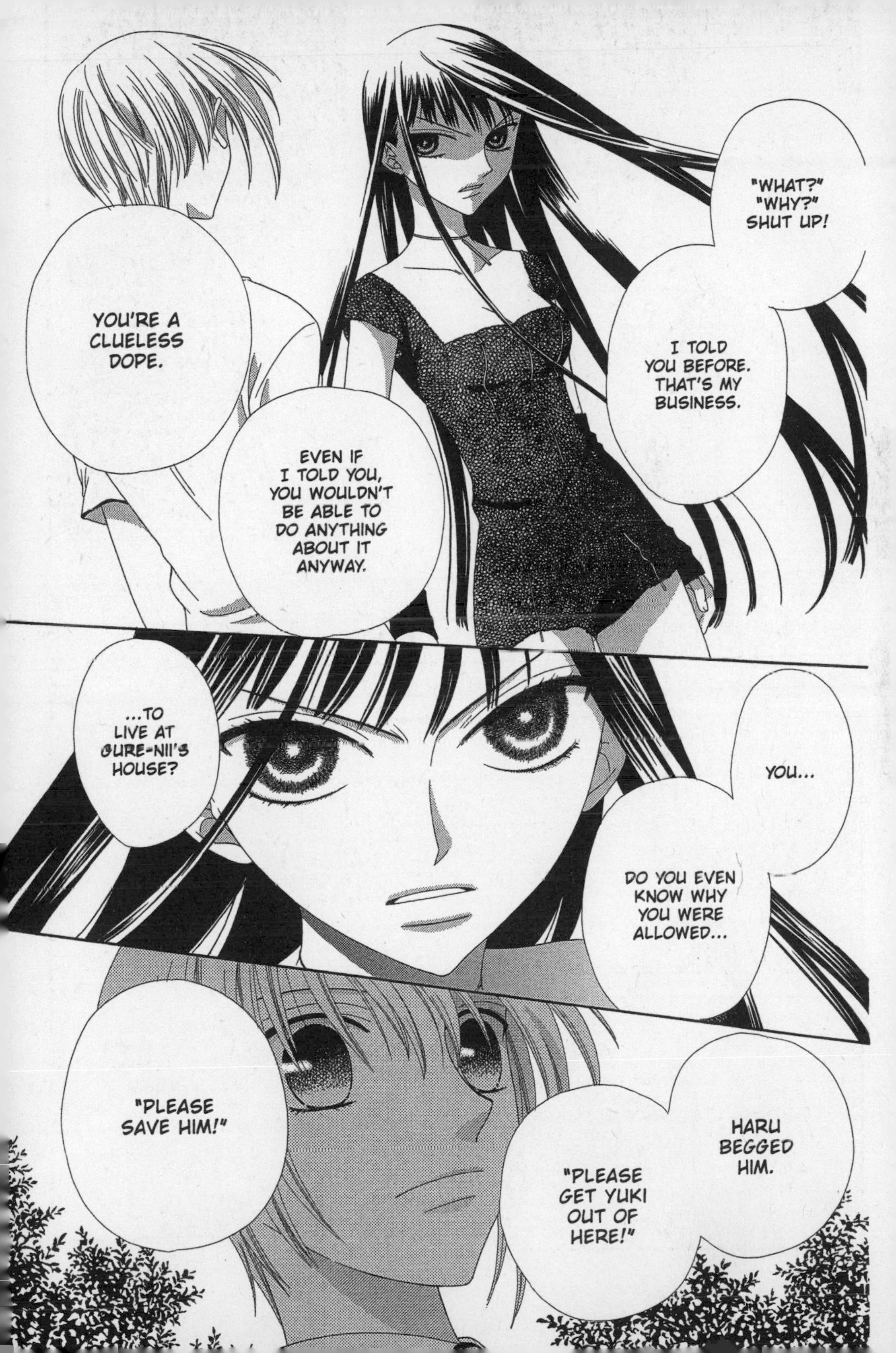
"WHAT?" "WHY?" SHUT UP!
I TOLD YOU BEFORE. THAT'S MY BUSINESS.
EVEN IF I TOLD YOU, YOU WOULDN'T BE ABLE TO DO ANYTHING ABOUT IT ANYWAY.
YOU'RE A CLUELESS DOPE.
YOU...
DO YOU EVEN KNOW WHY YOU WERE ALLOWED...
...TO LIVE AT GURE-NII'S HOUSE?
HARU BEGGED HIM.
"PLEASE GET YUKI OUT OF HERE!"
"PLEASE SAVE HIM!"

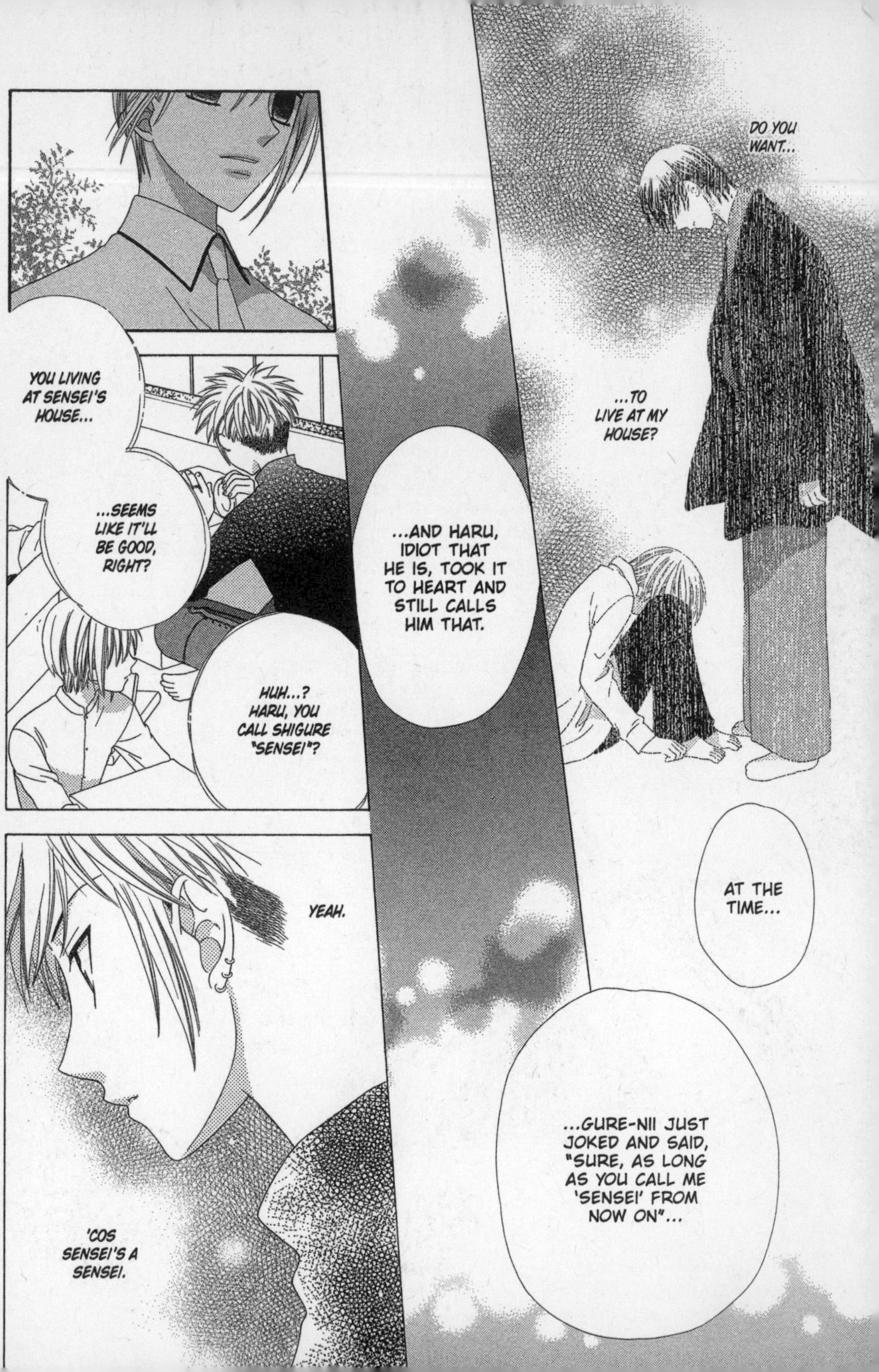
DO YOU WANT...
...TO LIVE AT MY HOUSE?
AT THE TIME...
...GURE-NII JUST JOKED AND SAID, "SURE, AS LONG AS YOU CALL ME 'SENSEI' FROM NOW ON"...
...AND HARU, IDIOT THAT HE IS, TOOK IT TO HEART AND STILL CALLS HIM THAT.
YOU LIVING AT SENSEI'S HOUSE...
...SEEMS LIKE IT'LL BE GOOD, RIGHT?
HUH...? HARU, YOU CALL SHIGURE "SENSEI"?
YEAH.
'COS SENSEI'S A SENSEI.

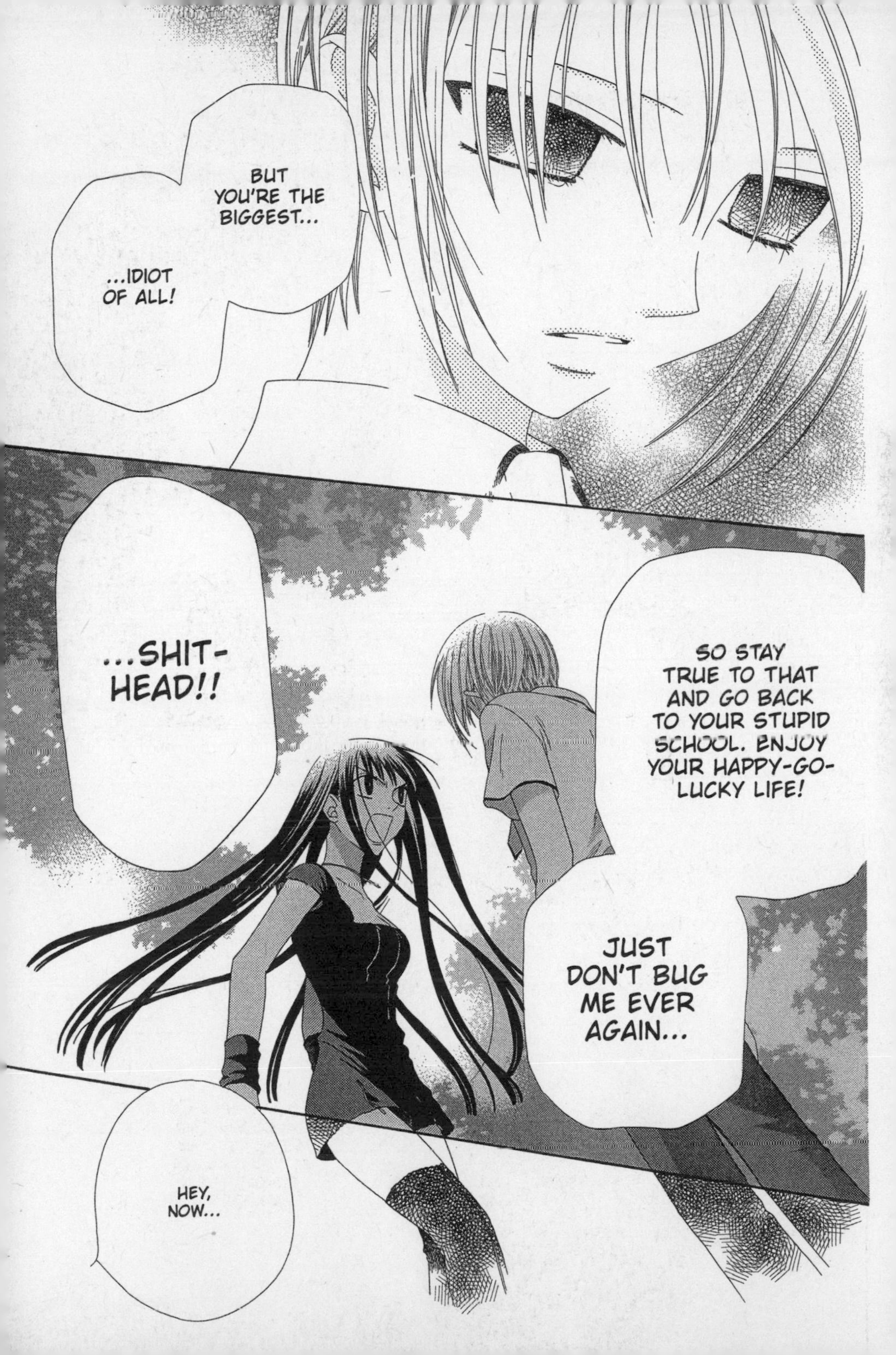
BUT YOU'RE THE BIGGEST...
...IDIOT OF ALL!
SO STAY TRUE TO THAT AND GO BACK TO YOUR STUPID SCHOOL. ENJOY YOUR HAPPY-GO-LUCKY LIFE!
JUST DON'T BUG ME EVER AGAIN...
...SHIT-HEAD!!
HEY, NOW...

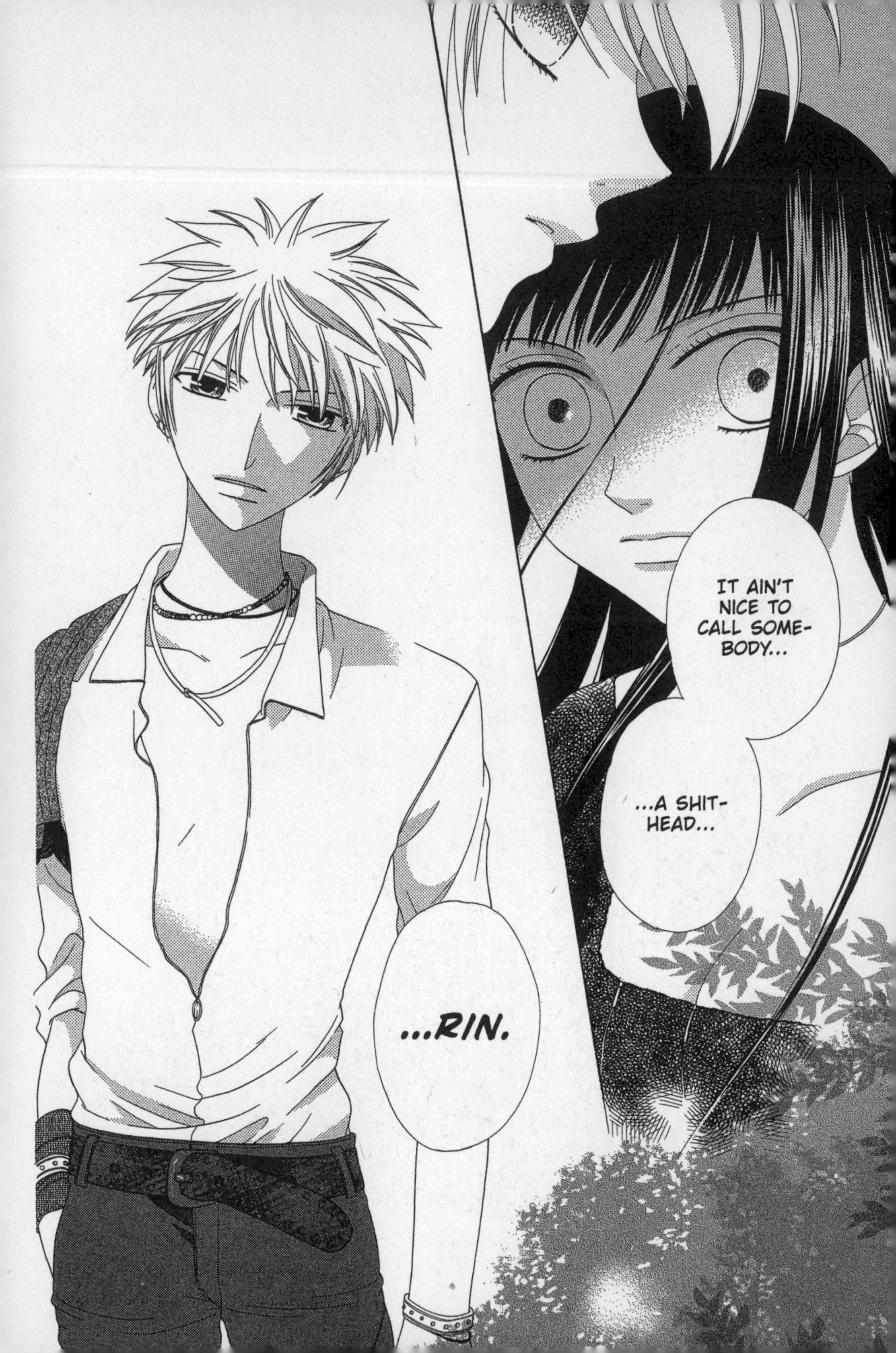
IT AIN'T NICE TO CALL SOME-BODY...
...A SHIT-HEAD...
...RIN.

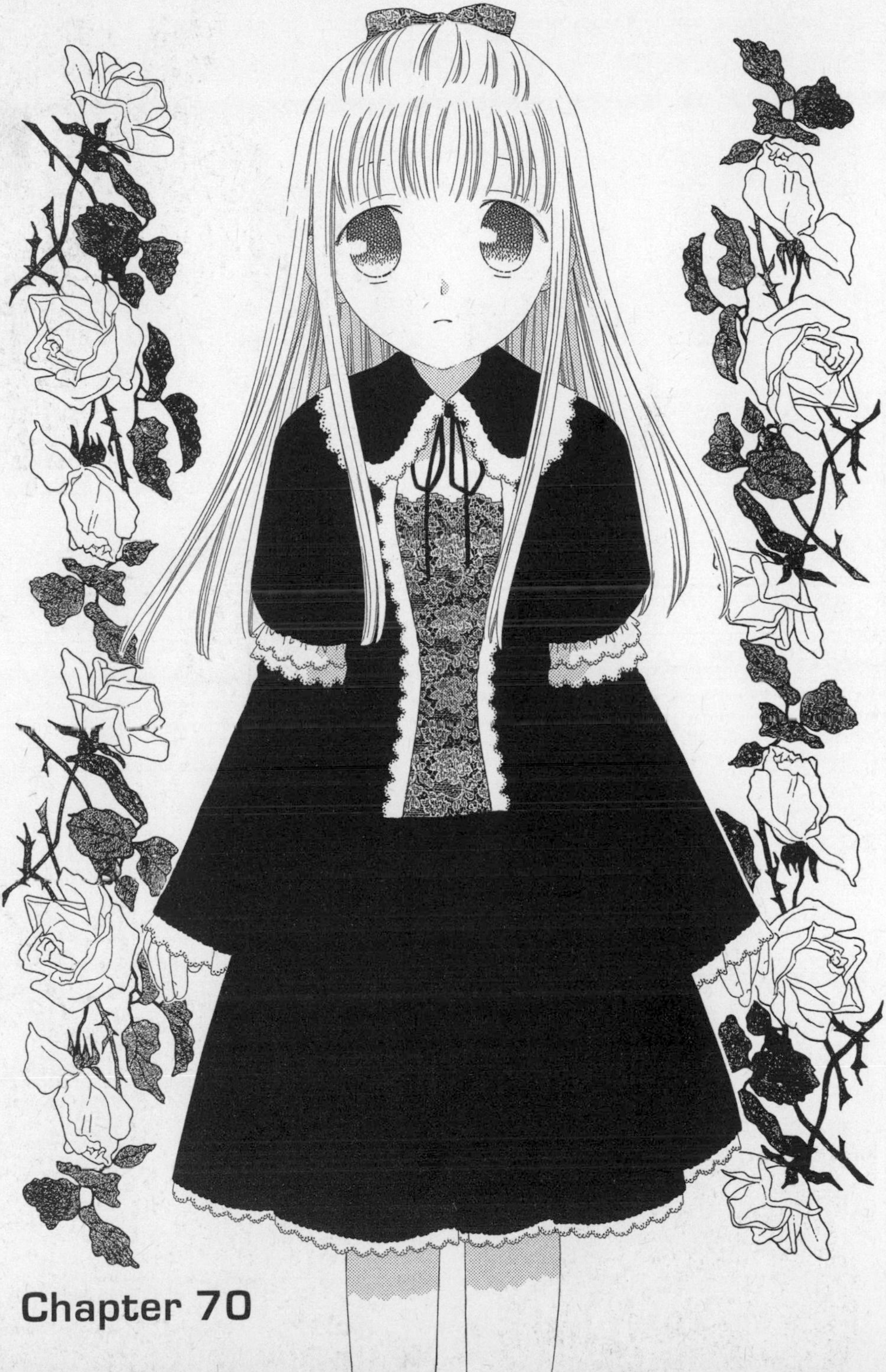

Chapter 70

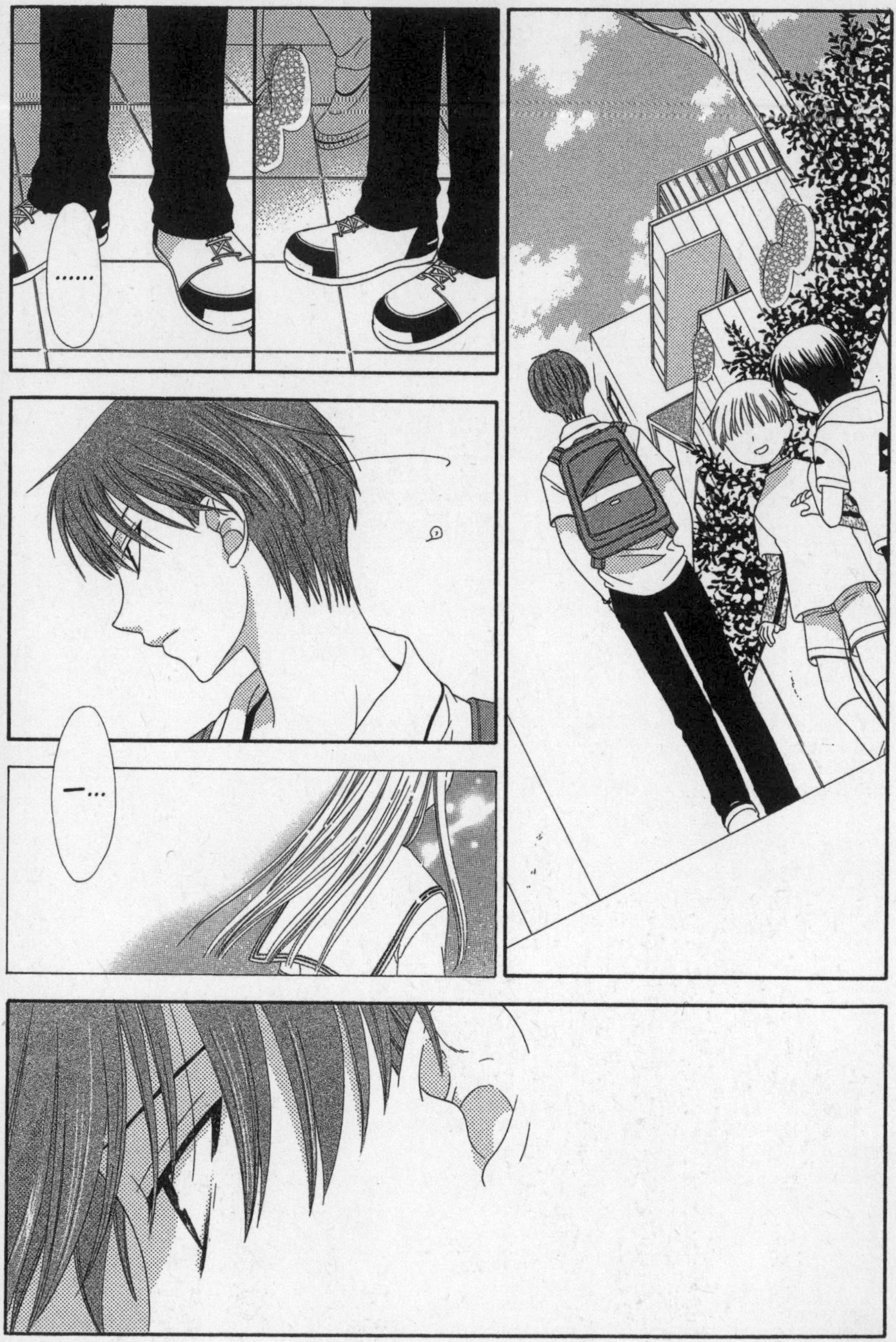
......
—...

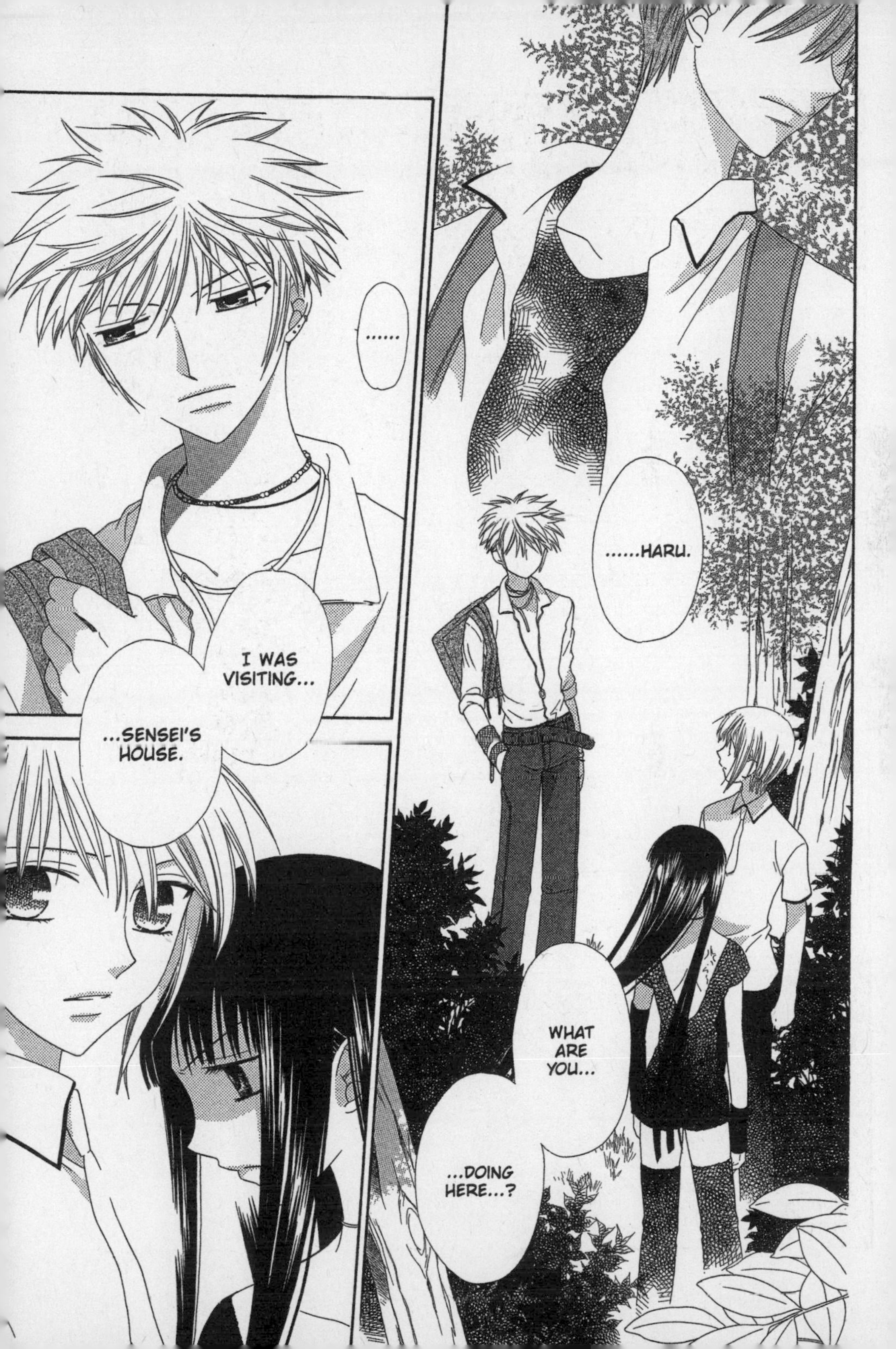
......HARU.
WHAT ARE YOU...
...DOING HERE...?
......
I WAS VISITING...
...SENSEI'S HOUSE.

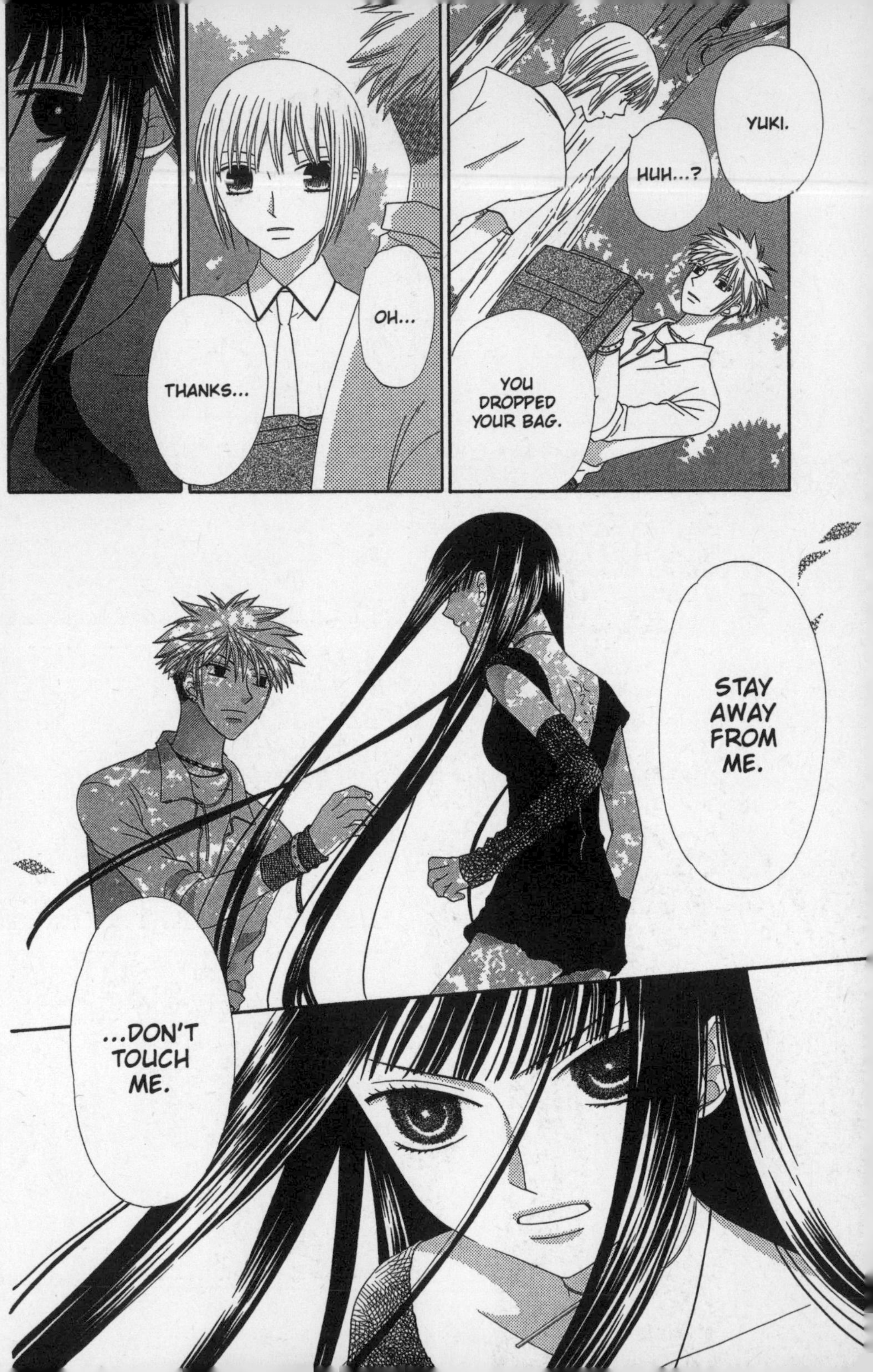
YUKI.
HUH...?
YOU DROPPED YOUR BAG.
OH...
THANKS...
STAY AWAY FROM ME.
...DON'T TOUCH ME.

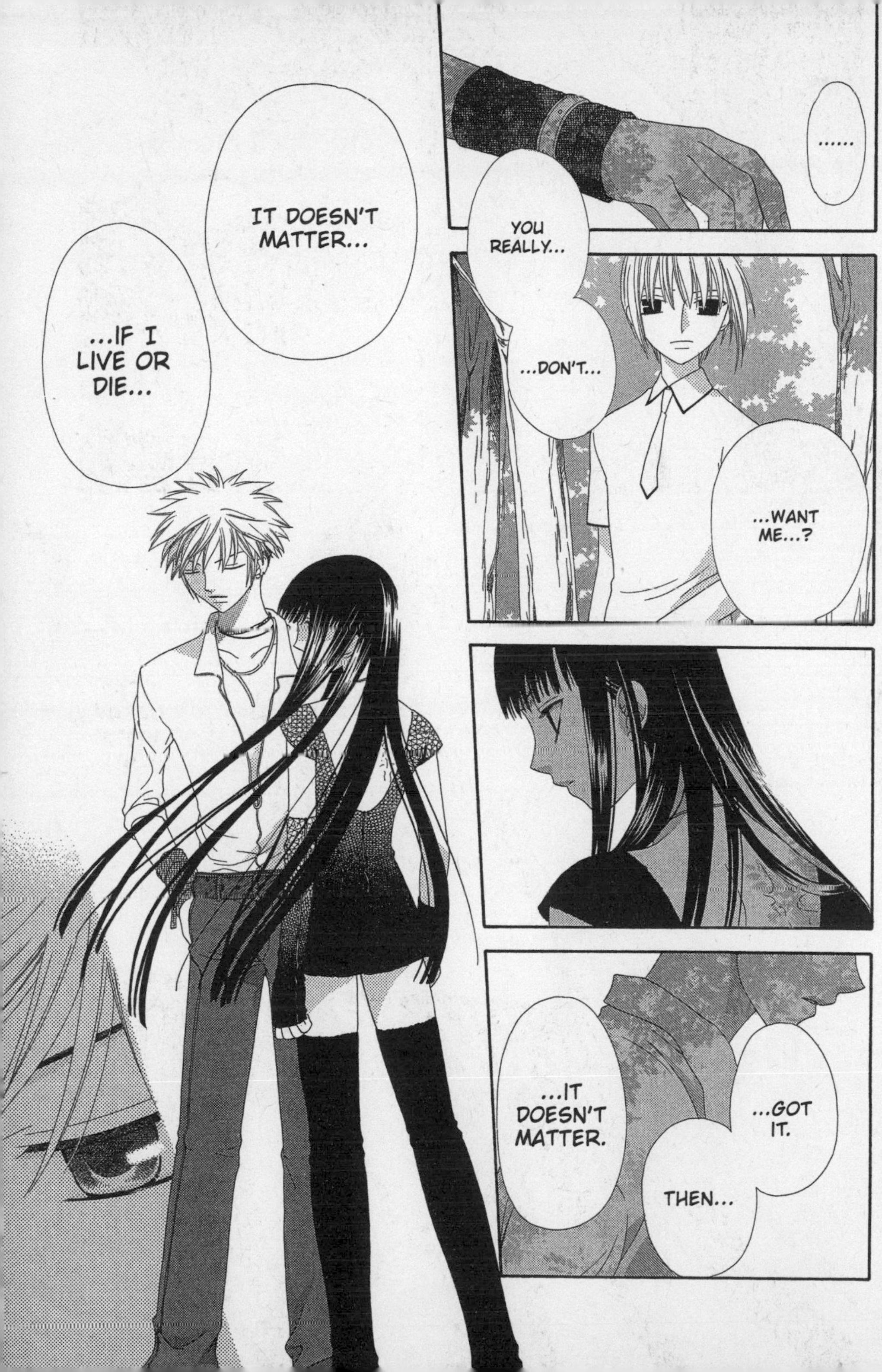
......
YOU REALLY...
...DON'T...
...WANT ME...?
...GOT IT.
THEN...
...IT DOESN'T MATTER.
IT DOESN'T MATTER...
...IF I LIVE OR DIE...

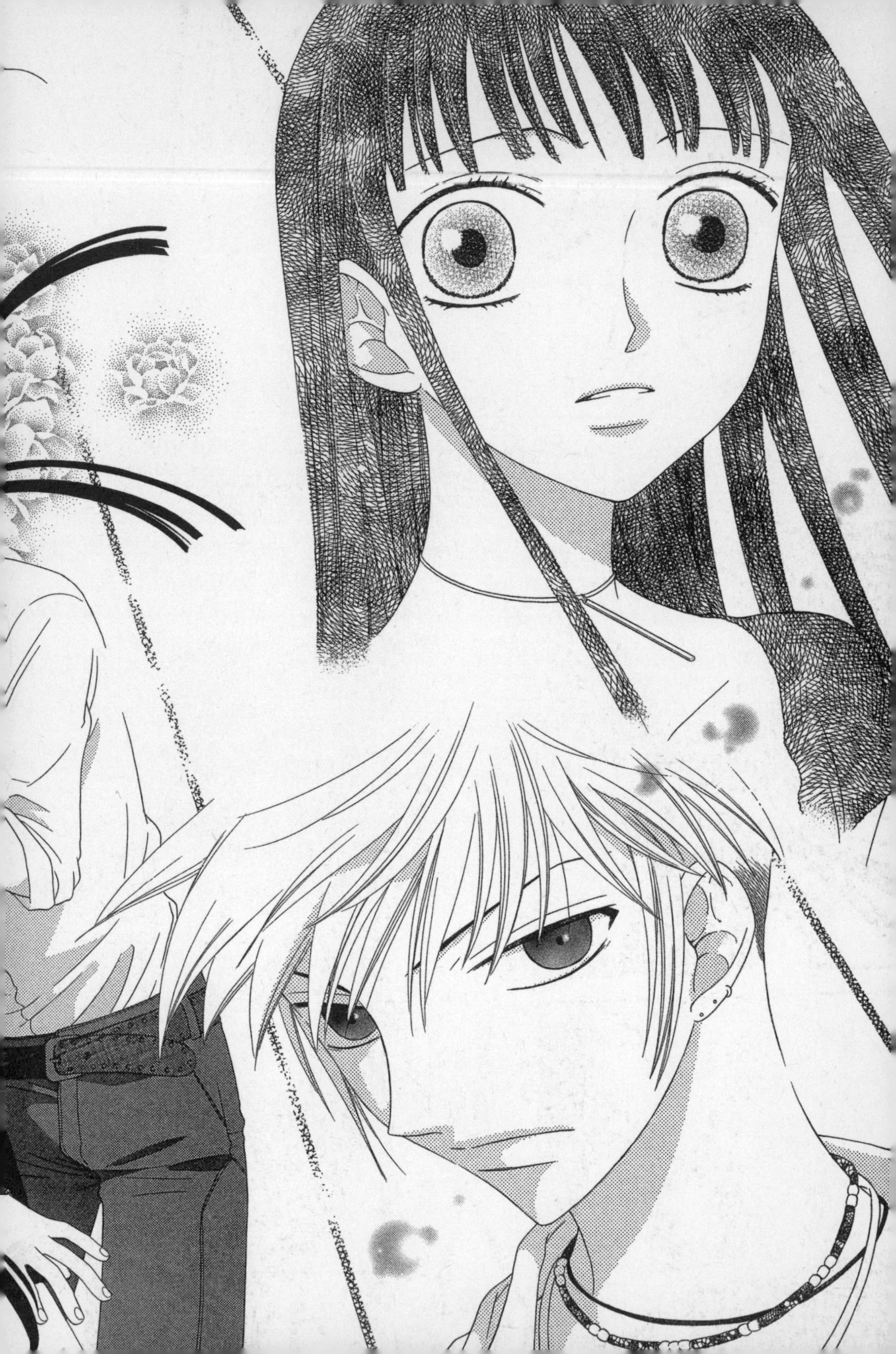

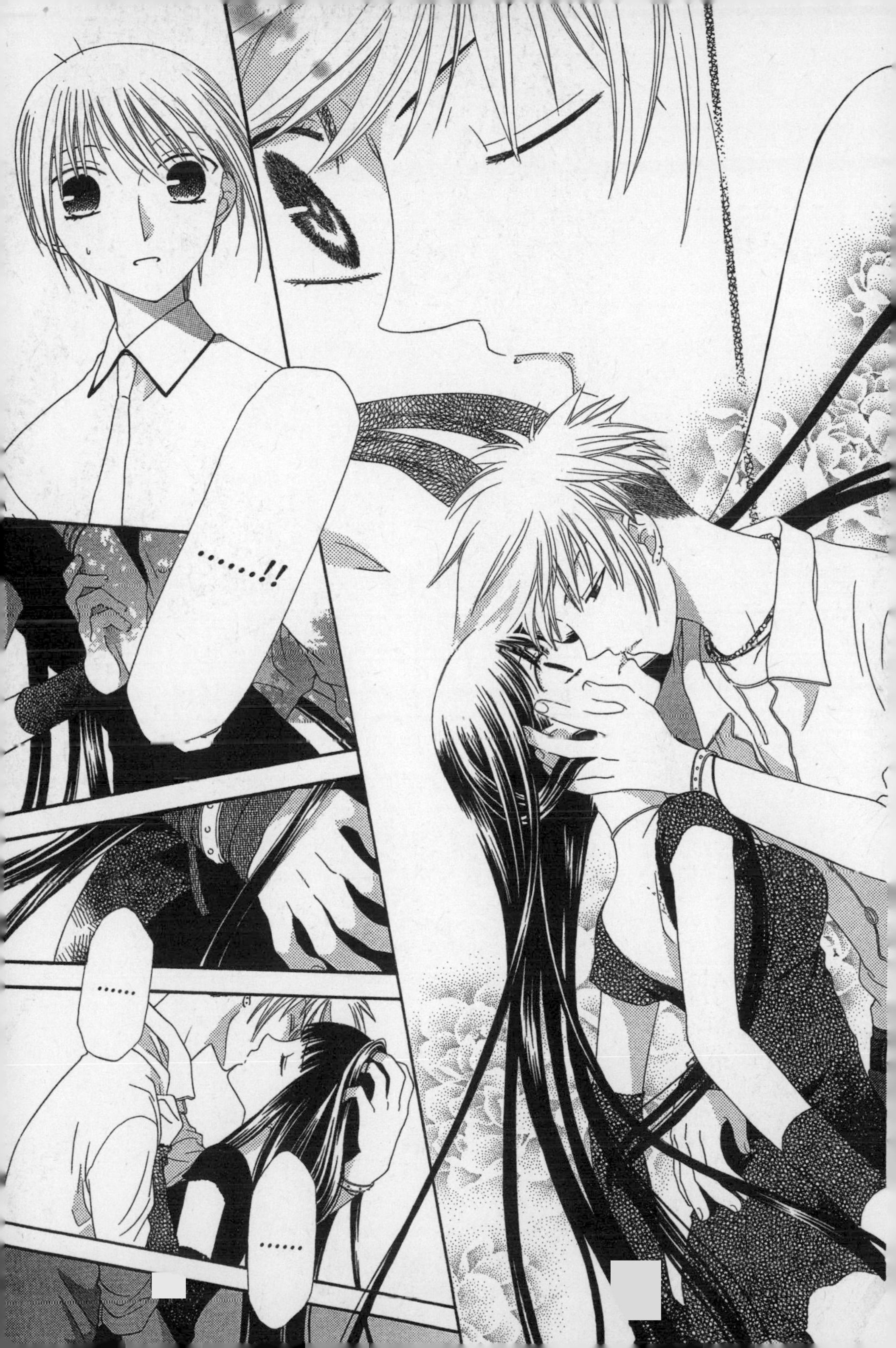
......!!
......
......

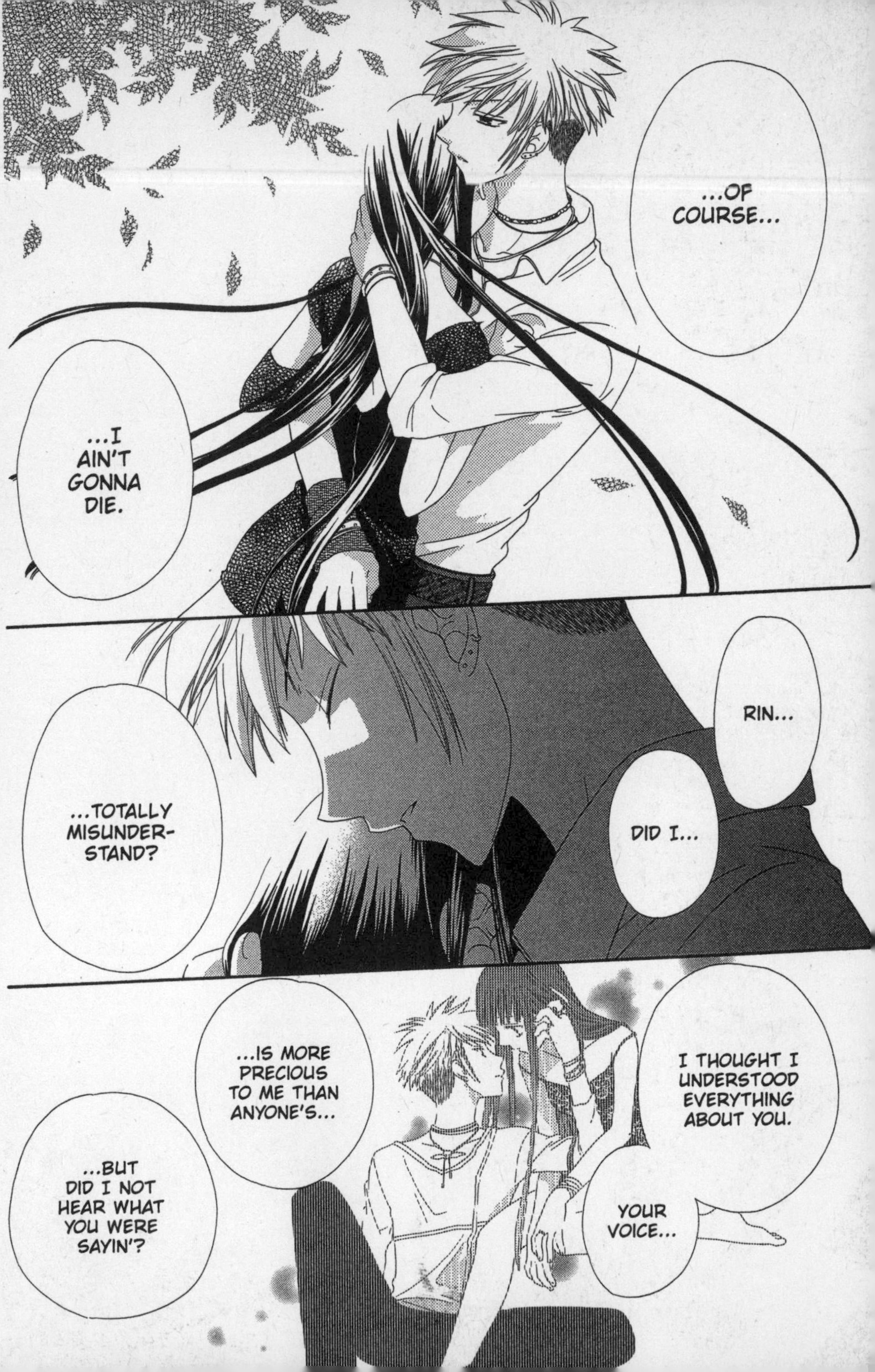
...OF COURSE...
...I AIN'T GONNA DIE.
RIN...
DID I...
...TOTALLY MISUNDER-STAND?
I THOUGHT I UNDERSTOOD EVERYTHING ABOUT YOU.
YOUR VOICE...
...IS MORE PRECIOUS TO ME THAN ANYONE'S...
...BUT DID I NOT HEAR WHAT YOU WERE SAYIN'?

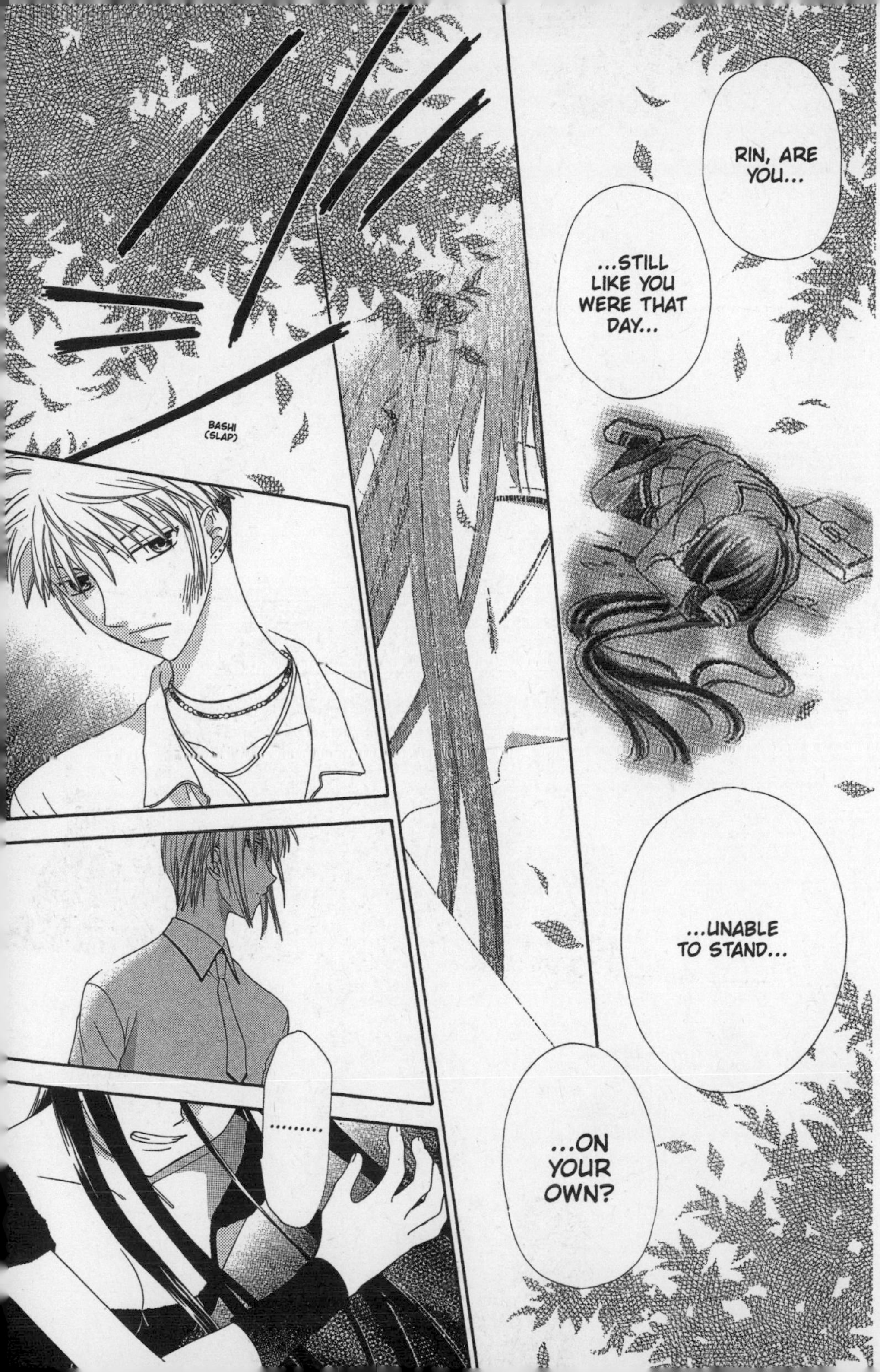
RIN, ARE YOU...
...STILL LIKE YOU WERE THAT DAY...
...UNABLE TO STAND...
...ON YOUR OWN?
BASHI (SLAP)
....

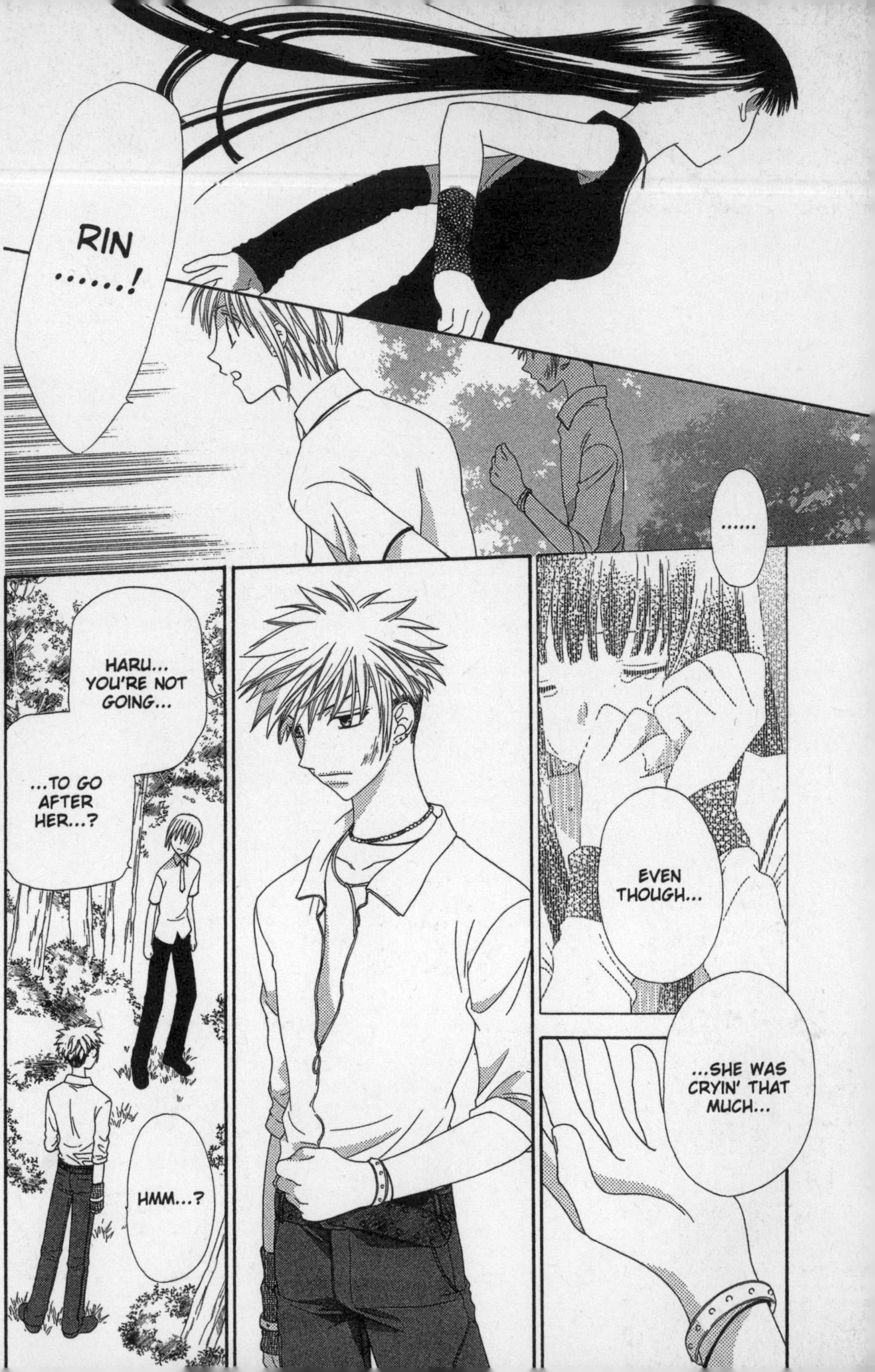
RIN ......!
......
EVEN THOUGH...
...SHE WAS CRYIN' THAT MUCH...
HARU... YOU'RE NOT GOING...
...TO GO AFTER HER...?
HMM...?

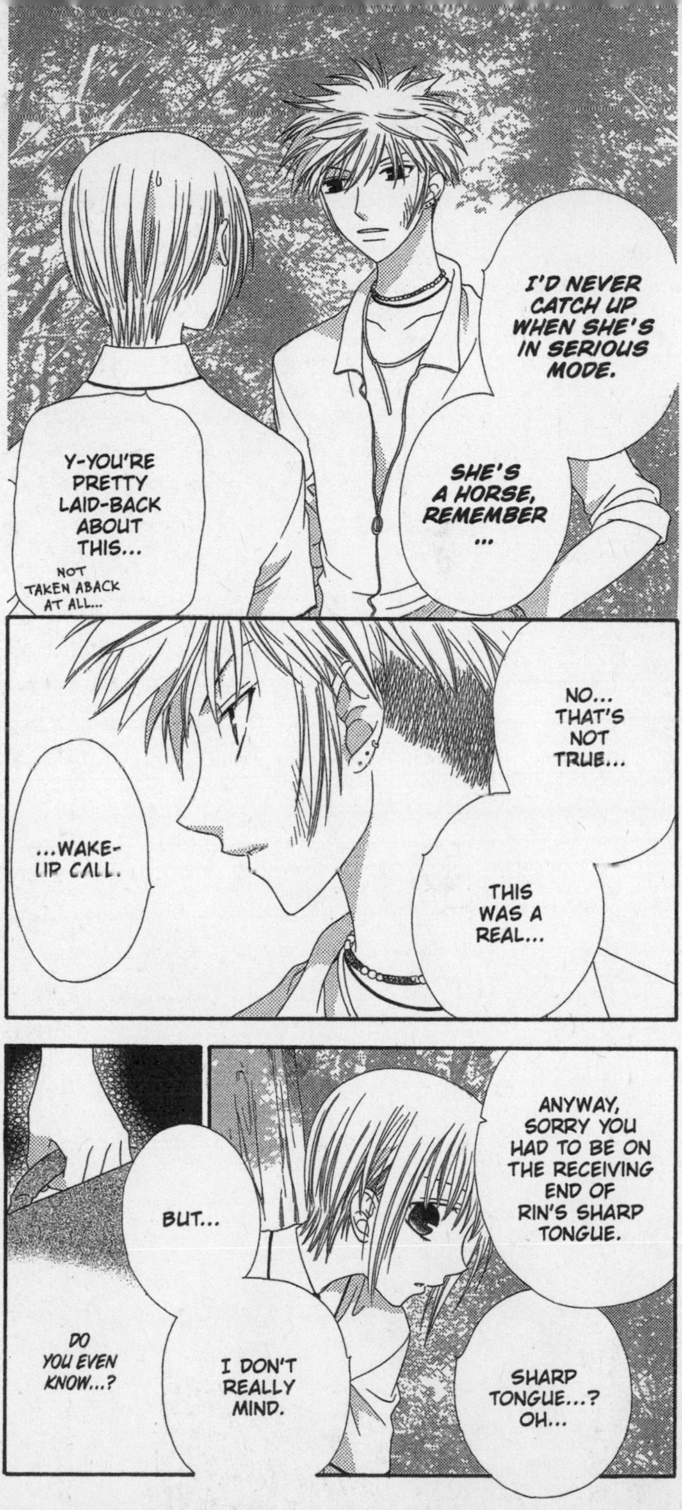
I'D NEVER CATCH UP WHEN SHE'S IN SERIOUS MODE.
SHE'S A HORSE, REMEMBER...
Y-YOU'RE PRETTY LAID-BACK ABOUT THIS...
NOT TAKEN ABACK AT ALL...
NO... THAT'S NOT TRUE...
THIS WAS A REAL...
...WAKE-UP CALL.
ANYWAY, SORRY YOU HAD TO BE ON THE RECEIVING END OF RIN'S SHARP TONGUE.
SHARP TONGUE...? OH...
BUT...
I DON'T REALLY MIND.
DO YOU EVEN KNOW...?

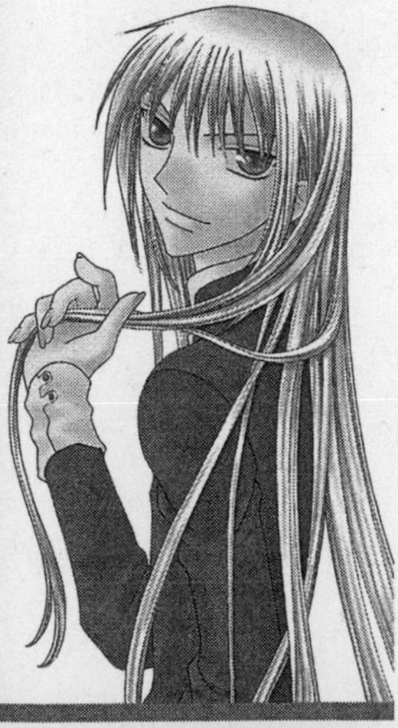

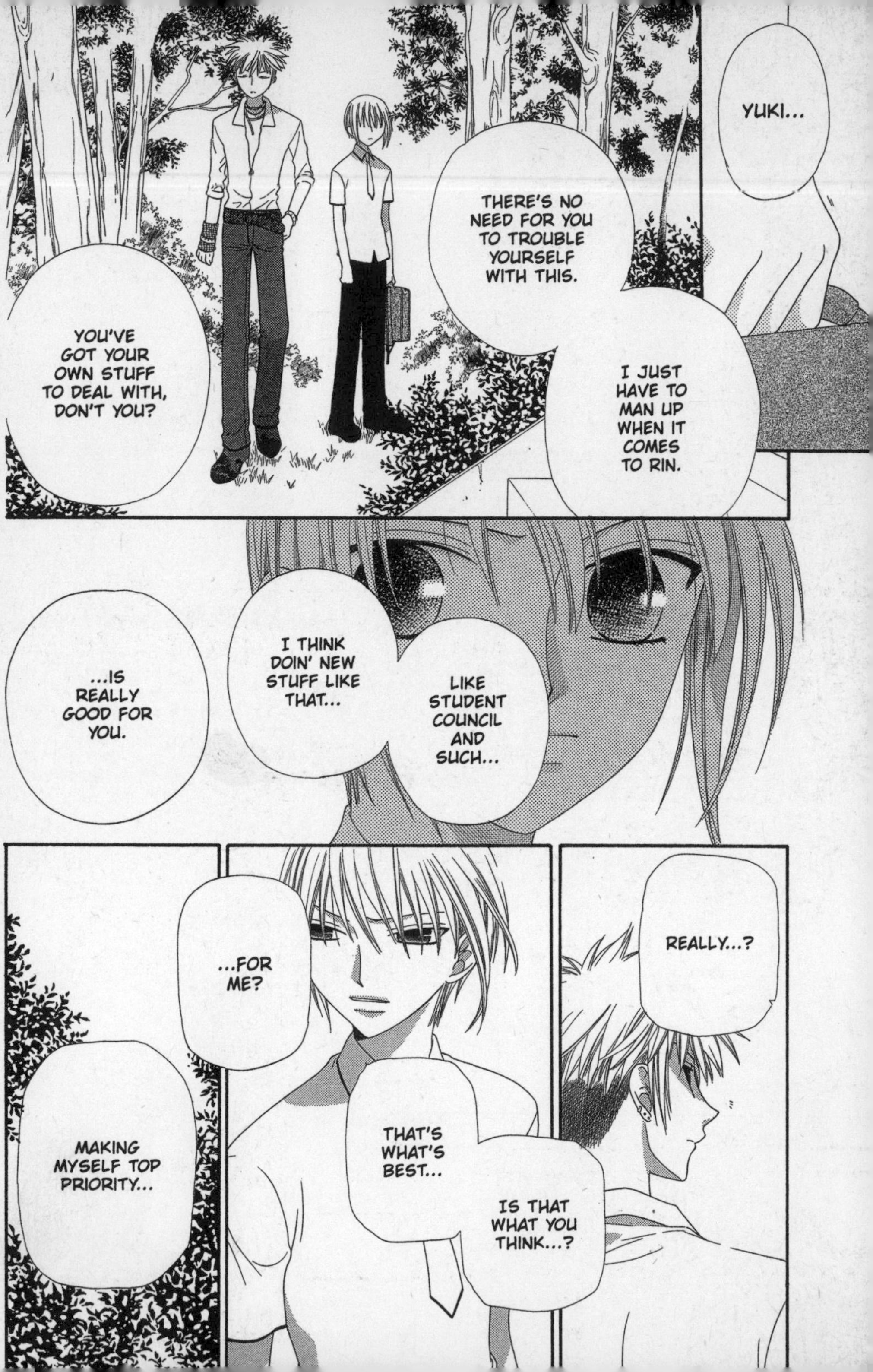
YUKI...
THERE'S NO NEED FOR YOU TO TROUBLE YOURSELF WITH THIS.
I JUST HAVE TO MAN UP WHEN IT COMES TO RIN.
YOU'VE GOT YOUR OWN STUFF TO DEAL WITH, DON'T YOU?
I THINK DOIN' NEW STUFF LIKE THAT...
LIKE STUDENT COUNCIL AND SUCH...
...IS REALLY GOOD FOR YOU.
REALLY...?
...FOR ME?
THAT'S WHAT'S BEST...
IS THAT WHAT YOU THINK...?
MAKING MYSELF TOP PRIORITY...

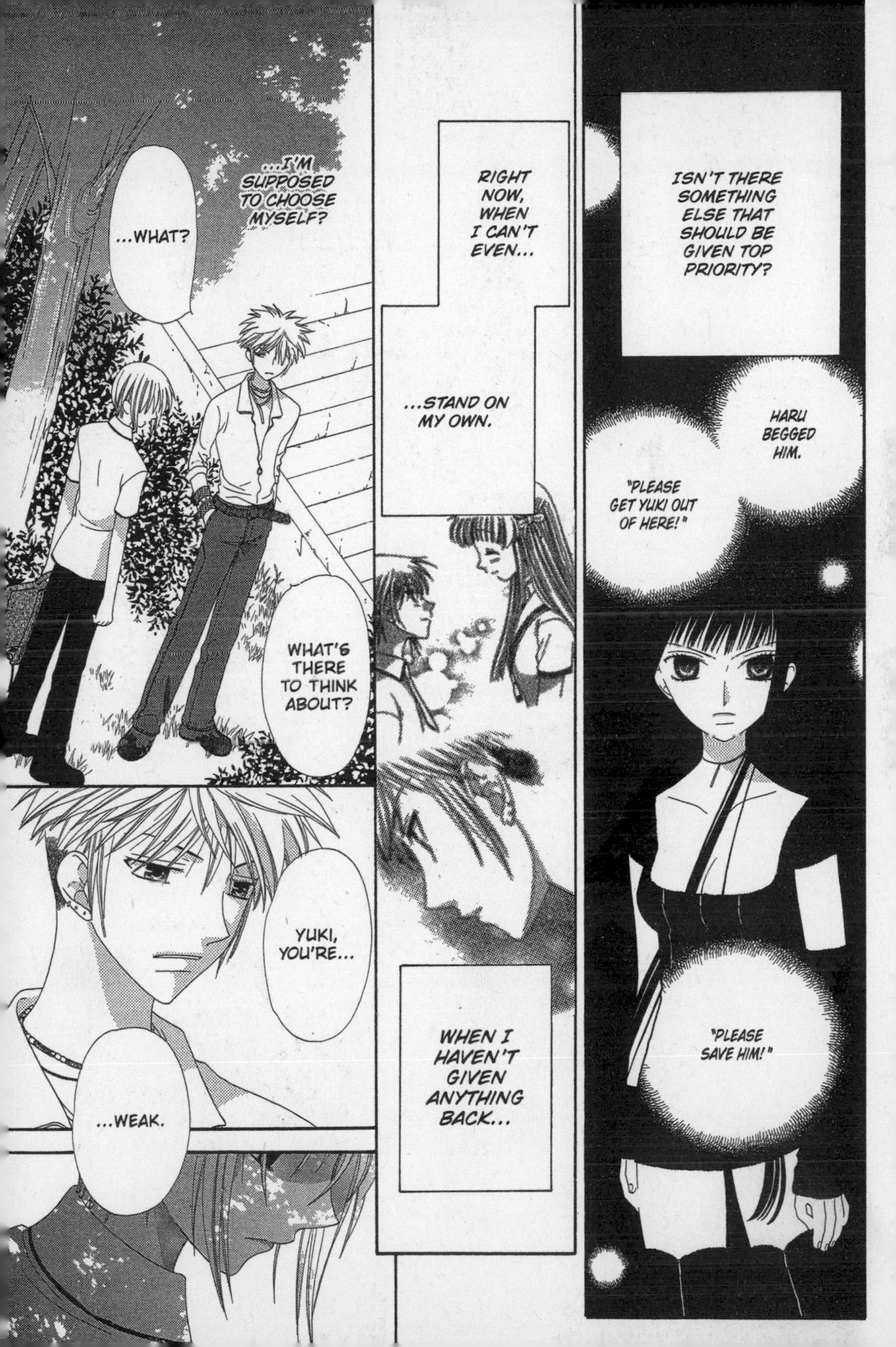
ISN'T THERE SOMETHING ELSE THAT SHOULD BE GIVEN TOP PRIORITY?
HARU BEGGED HIM.
"PLEASE GET YUKI OUT OF HERE!"
"PLEASE SAVE HIM!"
RIGHT NOW, WHEN I CAN'T EVEN...
...STAND ON MY OWN.
WHEN I HAVEN'T GIVEN ANYTHING BACK...
...I'M SUPPOSED TO CHOOSE MYSELF?
...WHAT?
WHAT'S THERE TO THINK ABOUT?
YUKI, YOU'RE...
...WEAK.

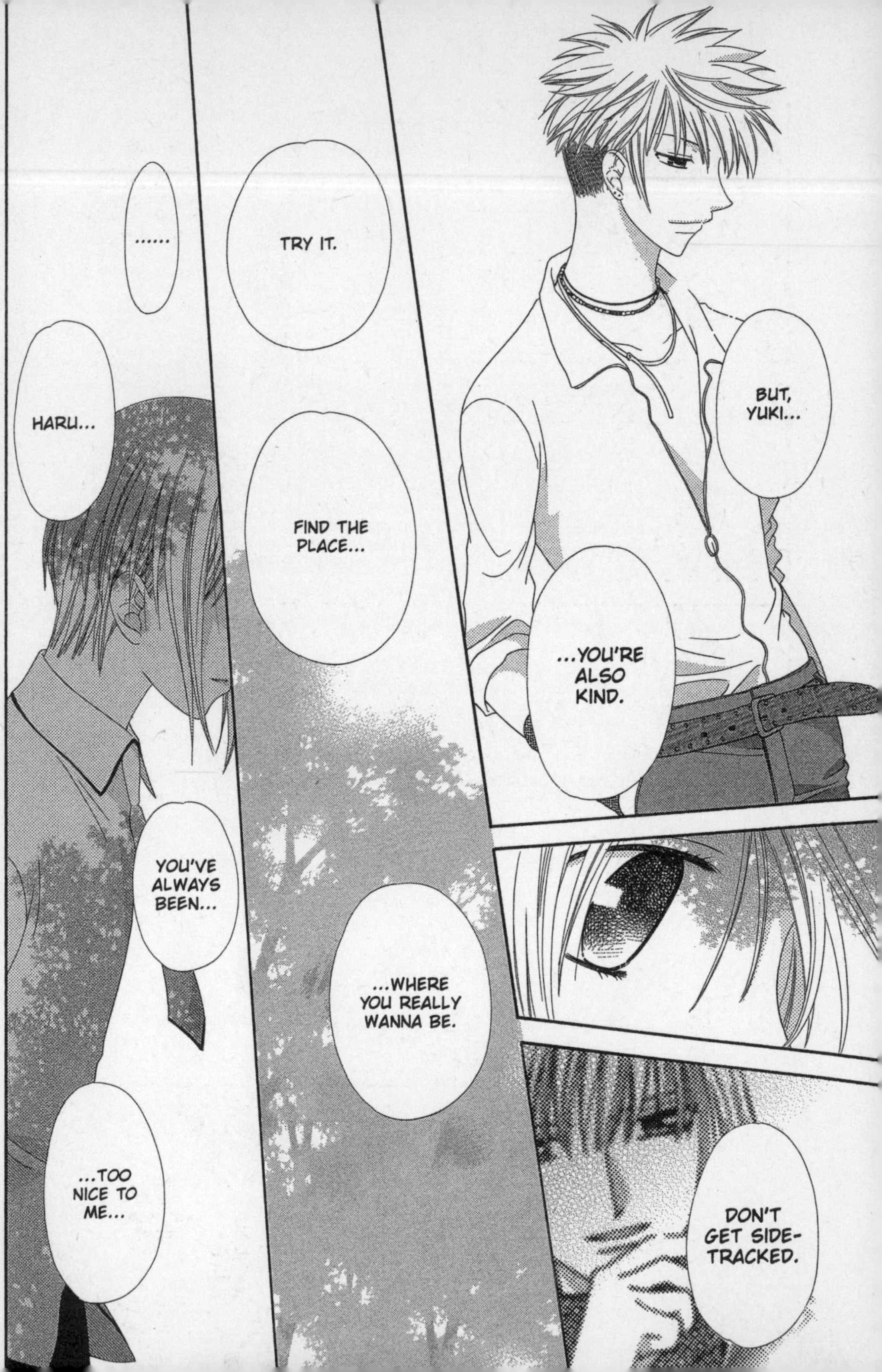

BUT, YUKI...
...YOU'RE ALSO KIND.
DON'T GET SIDE-TRACKED.
TRY IT.
FIND THE PLACE...
...WHERE YOU REALLY WANNA BE.
......
HARU...
YOU'VE ALWAYS BEEN...
...TOO NICE TO ME...

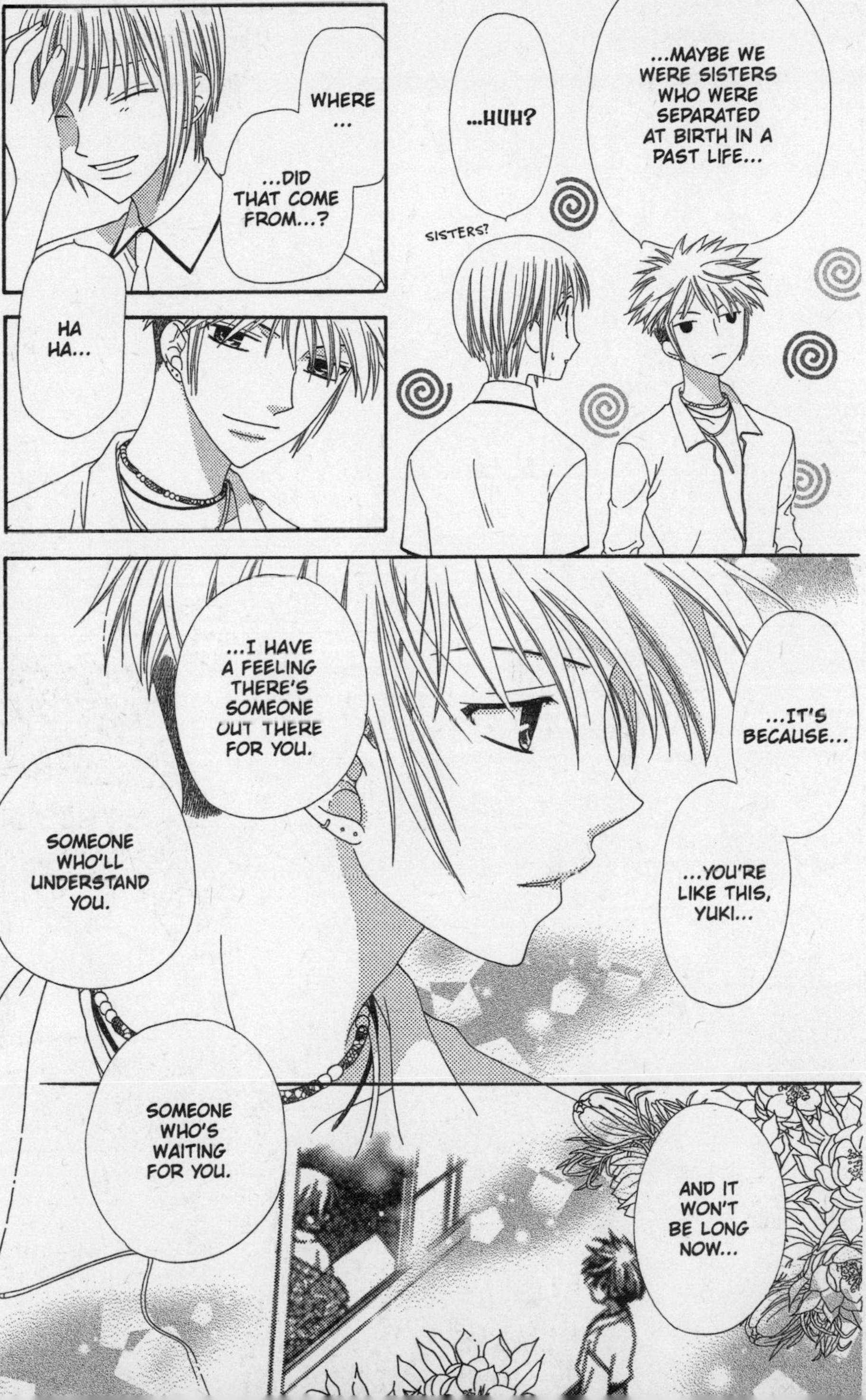
...MAYBE WE WERE SISTERS WHO WERE SEPARATED AT BIRTH IN A PAST LIFE...
...HUH?
SISTERS?
WHERE ...
...DID THAT COME FROM...?
HA HA...
...IT'S BECAUSE...
...YOU'RE LIKE THIS, YUKI...
...I HAVE A FEELING THERE'S SOMEONE OUT THERE FOR YOU.
SOMEONE WHO'LL UNDERSTAND YOU.
SOMEONE WHO'S WAITING FOR YOU.
AND IT WON'T BE LONG NOW...

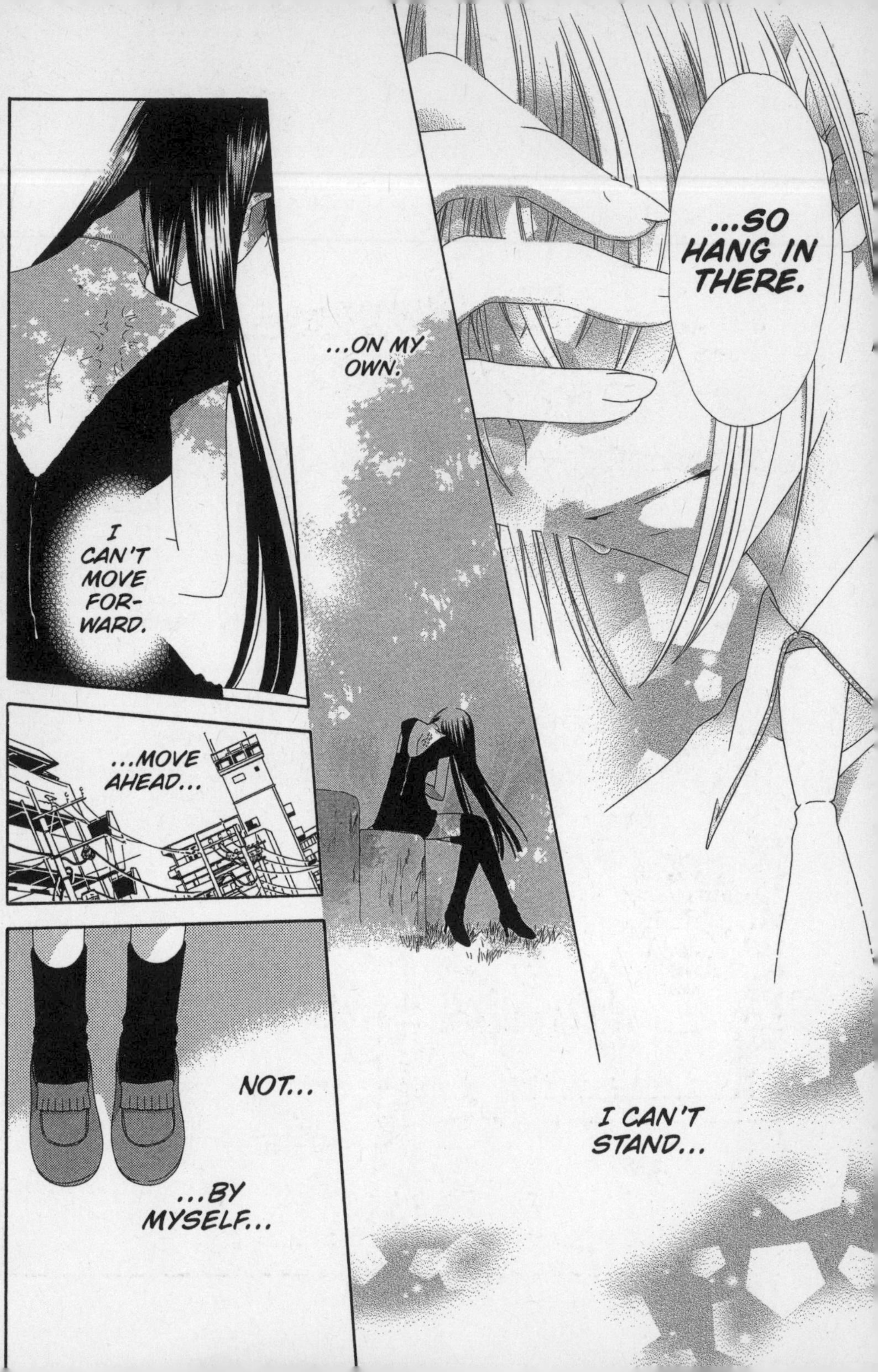
...SO HANG IN THERE.
I CAN'T STAND...
...ON MY OWN.
I CAN'T MOVE FOR-WARD.
...MOVE AHEAD...
NOT...
...BY MYSELF...

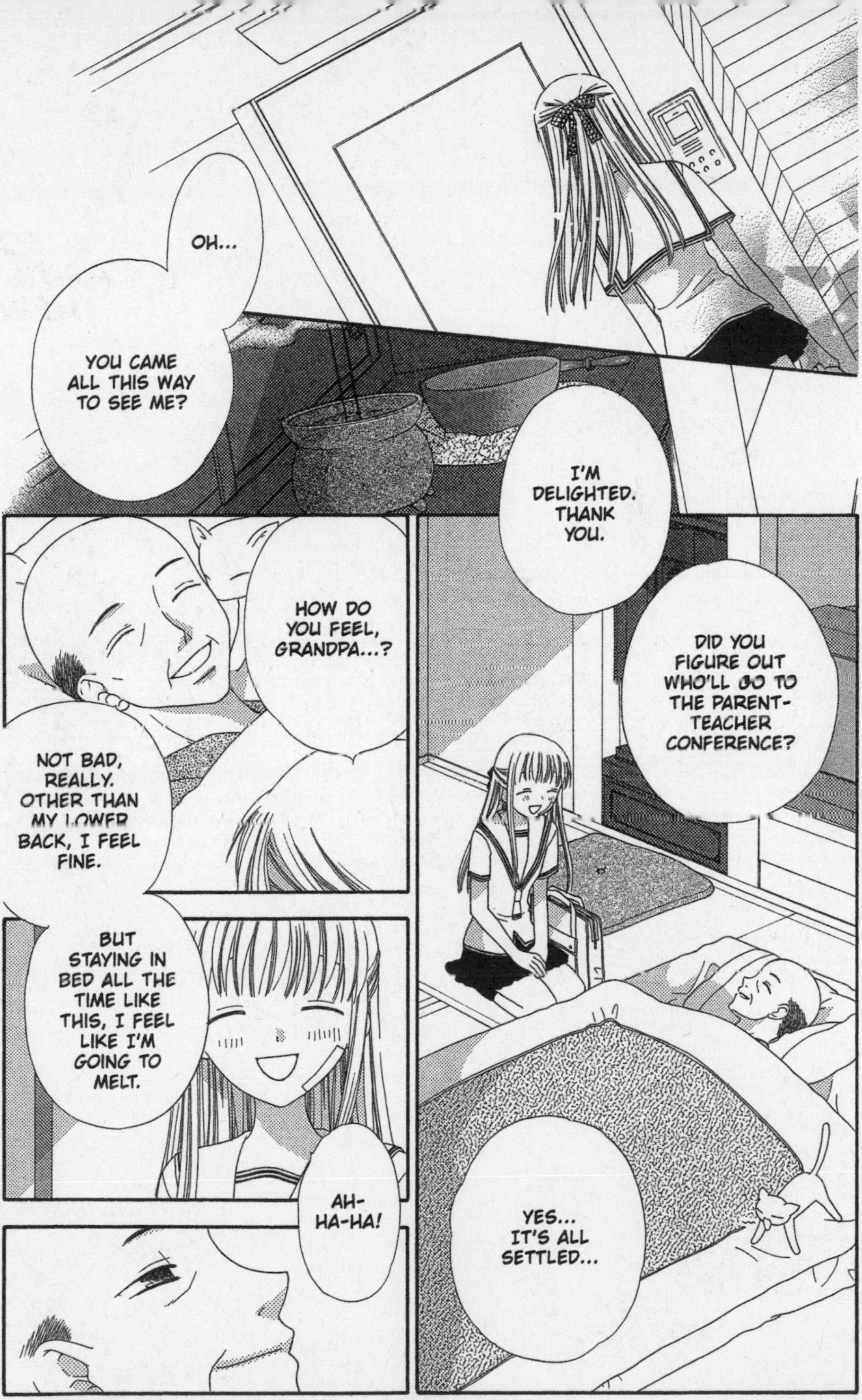
OH...
YOU CAME ALL THIS WAY TO SEE ME?
I'M DELIGHTED. THANK YOU.
DID YOU FIGURE OUT WHO'LL GO TO THE PARENT-TEACHER CONFERENCE?
YES... IT'S ALL SETTLED...
HOW DO YOU FEEL, GRANDPA...?
NOT BAD, REALLY. OTHER THAN MY LOWER BACK, I FEEL FINE.
BUT STAYING IN BED ALL THE TIME LIKE THIS, I FEEL LIKE I'M GOING TO MELT.
AH-HA-HA!

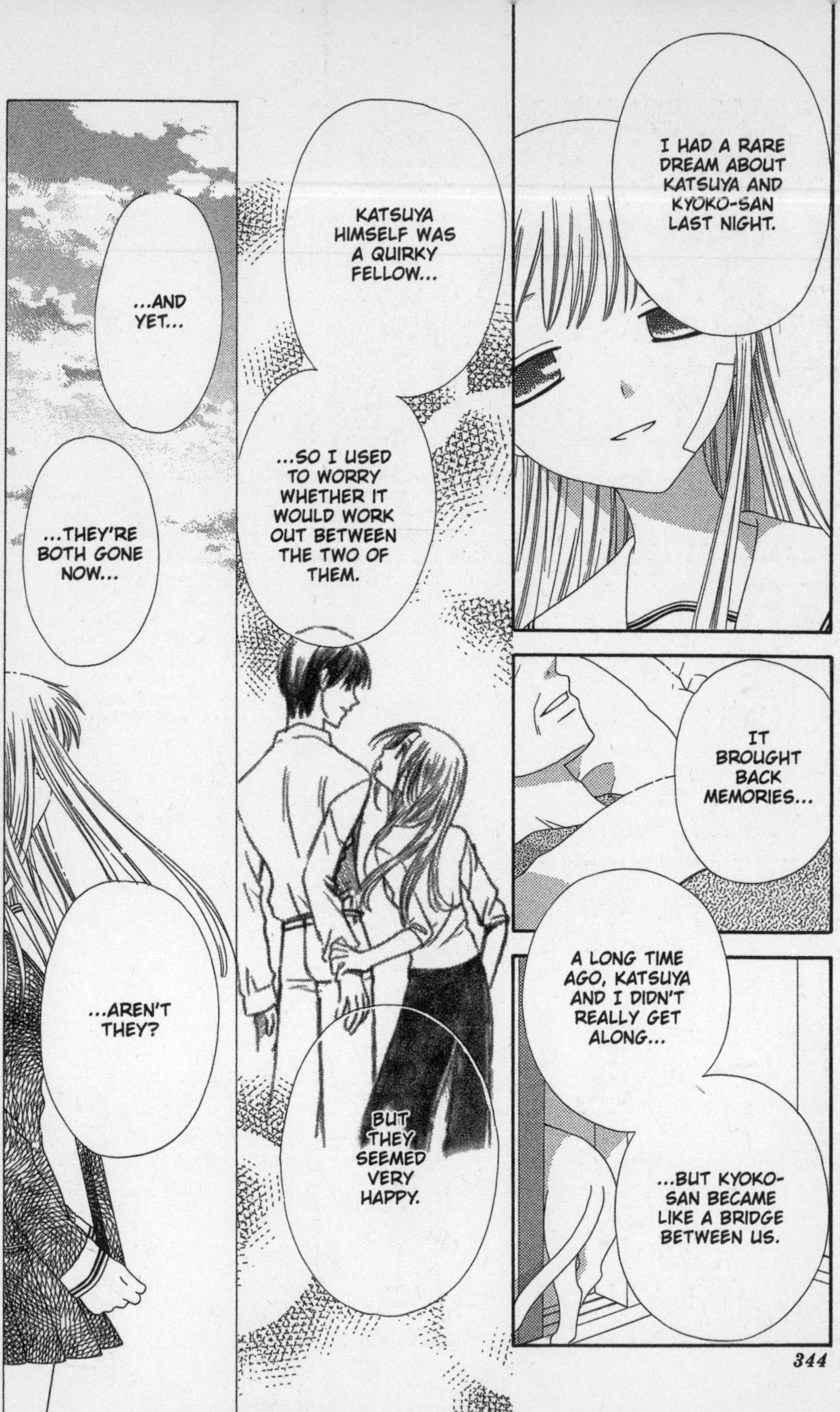
I HAD A RARE DREAM ABOUT KATSUYA AND KYOKO-SAN LAST NIGHT.
IT BROUGHT BACK MEMORIES...
A LONG TIME AGO, KATSUYA AND I DIDN'T REALLY GET ALONG...
...BUT KYOKO-SAN BECAME LIKE A BRIDGE BETWEEN US.
KATSUYA HIMSELF WAS A QUIRKY FELLOW...
...SO I USED TO WORRY WHETHER IT WOULD WORK OUT BETWEEN THE TWO OF THEM.
BUT THEY SEEMED VERY HAPPY.
...AND YET...
...THEY'RE BOTH GONE NOW...
...AREN'T THEY?

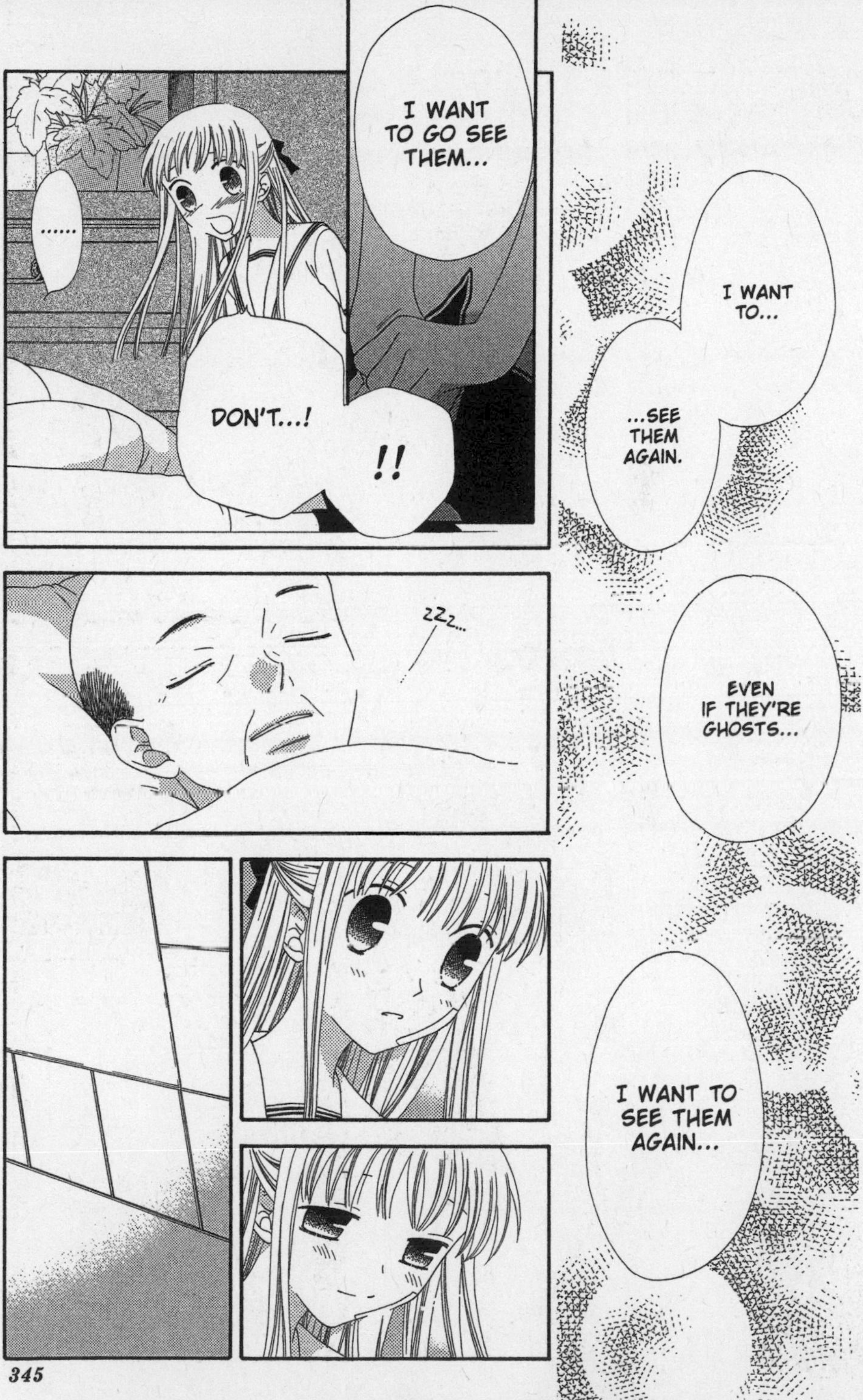
I WANT TO GO SEE THEM...
I WANT TO...
...SEE THEM AGAIN.
DON'T...!
!!
......
EVEN IF THEY'RE GHOSTS...
zZz...
I WANT TO SEE THEM AGAIN...

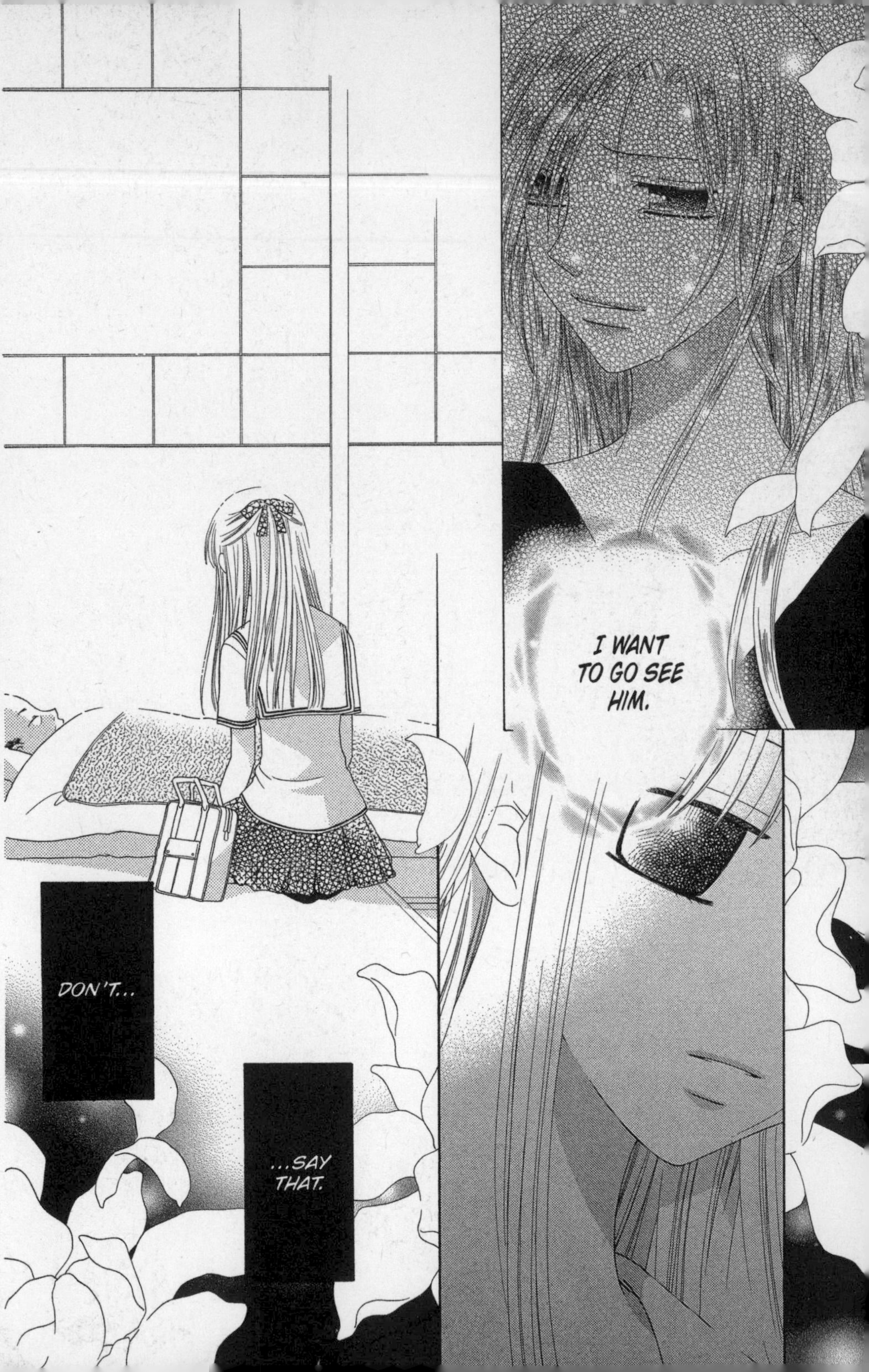
I WANT TO GO SEE HIM.
DON'T...
...SAY THAT.

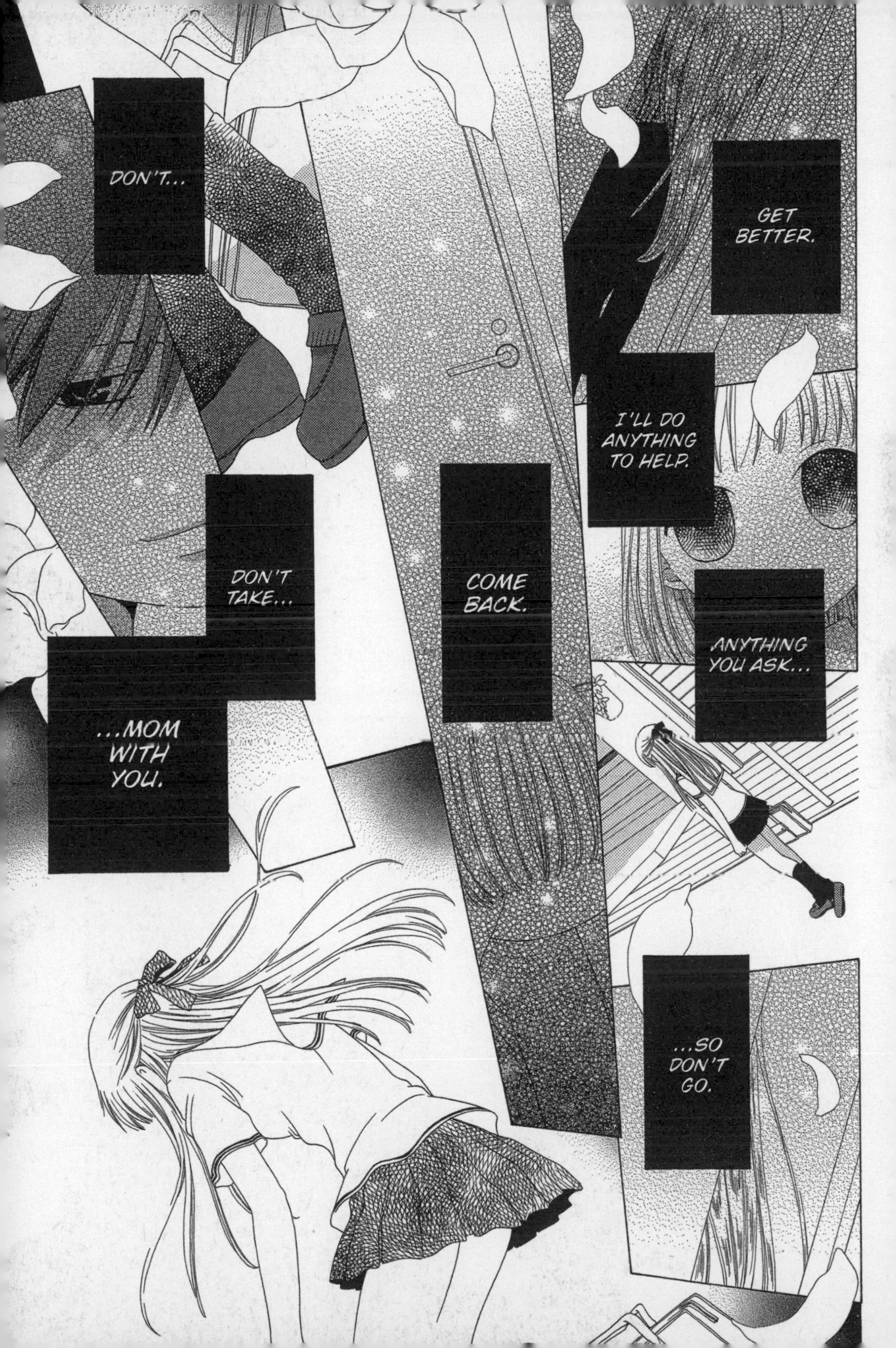
GET BETTER.
I'LL DO ANYTHING TO HELP.
ANYTHING YOU ASK...
...SO DON'T GO.
COME BACK.
DON'T...
DON'T TAKE...
...MOM WITH YOU.

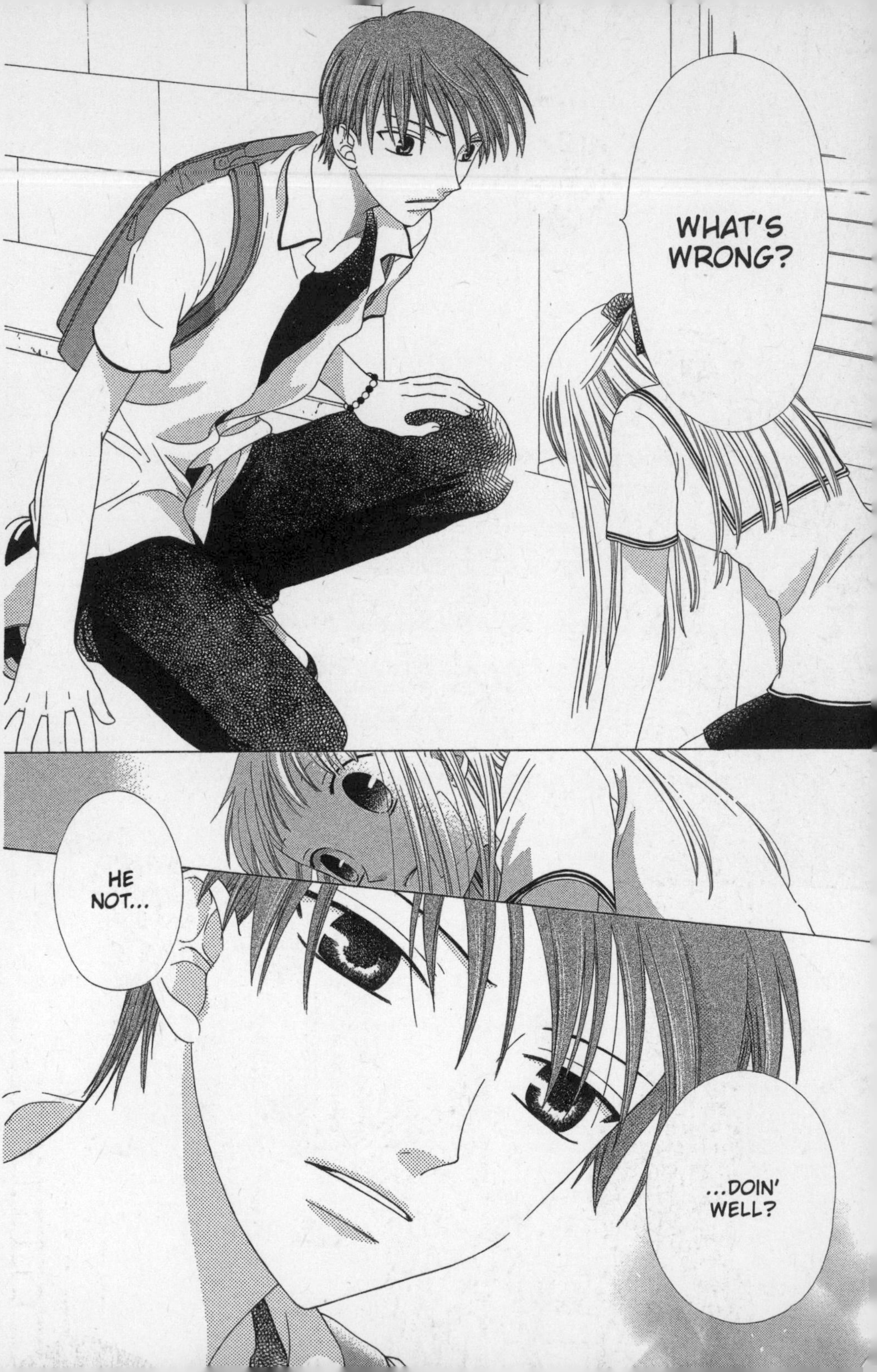
WHAT'S WRONG?
HE NOT...
...DOIN' WELL?

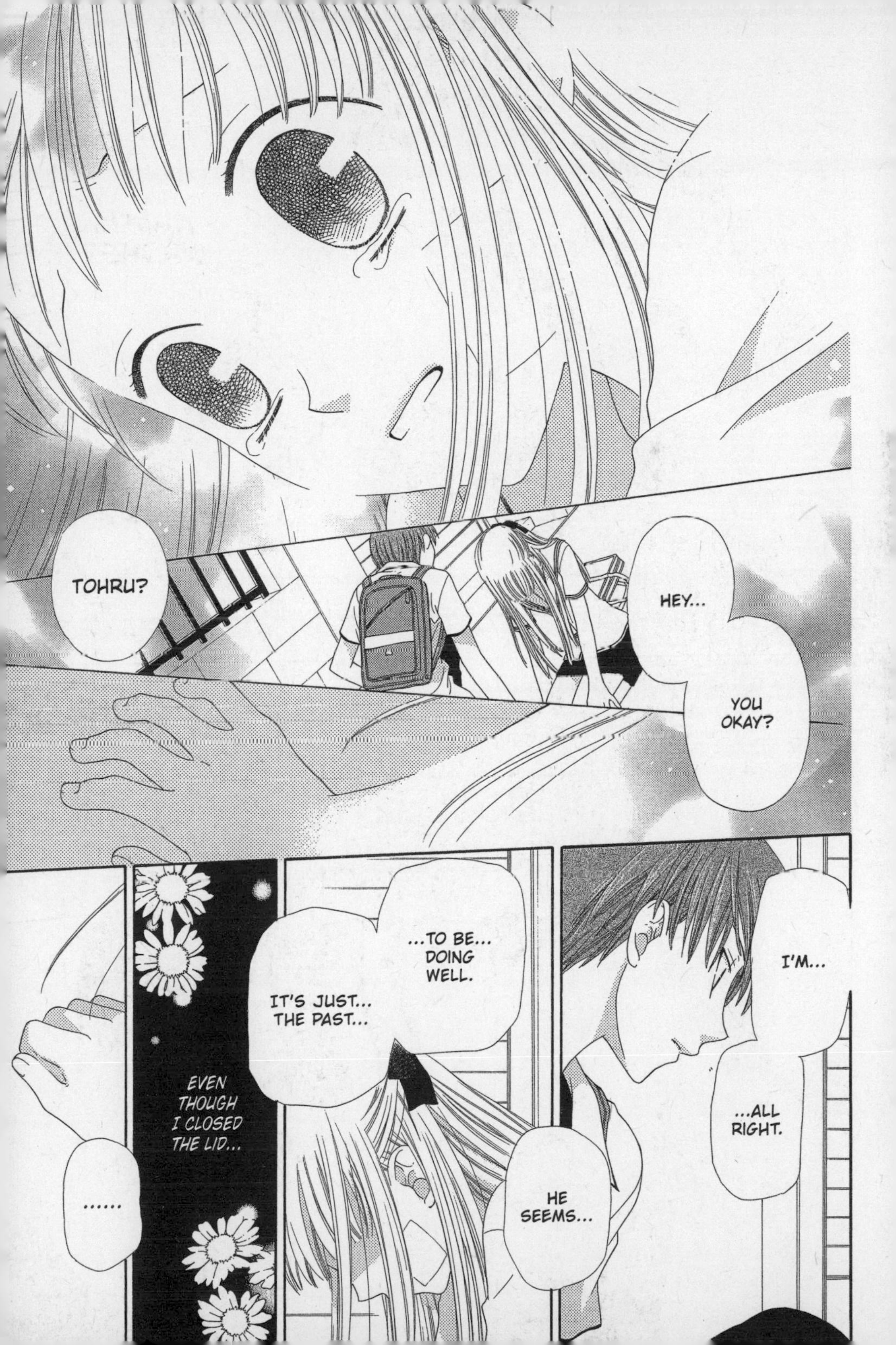
HEY...
YOU OKAY?
TOHRU?
I'M...
...ALL RIGHT.
...TO BE... DOING WELL.
IT'S JUST... THE PAST...
HE SEEMS...
EVEN THOUGH I CLOSED THE LID...
......

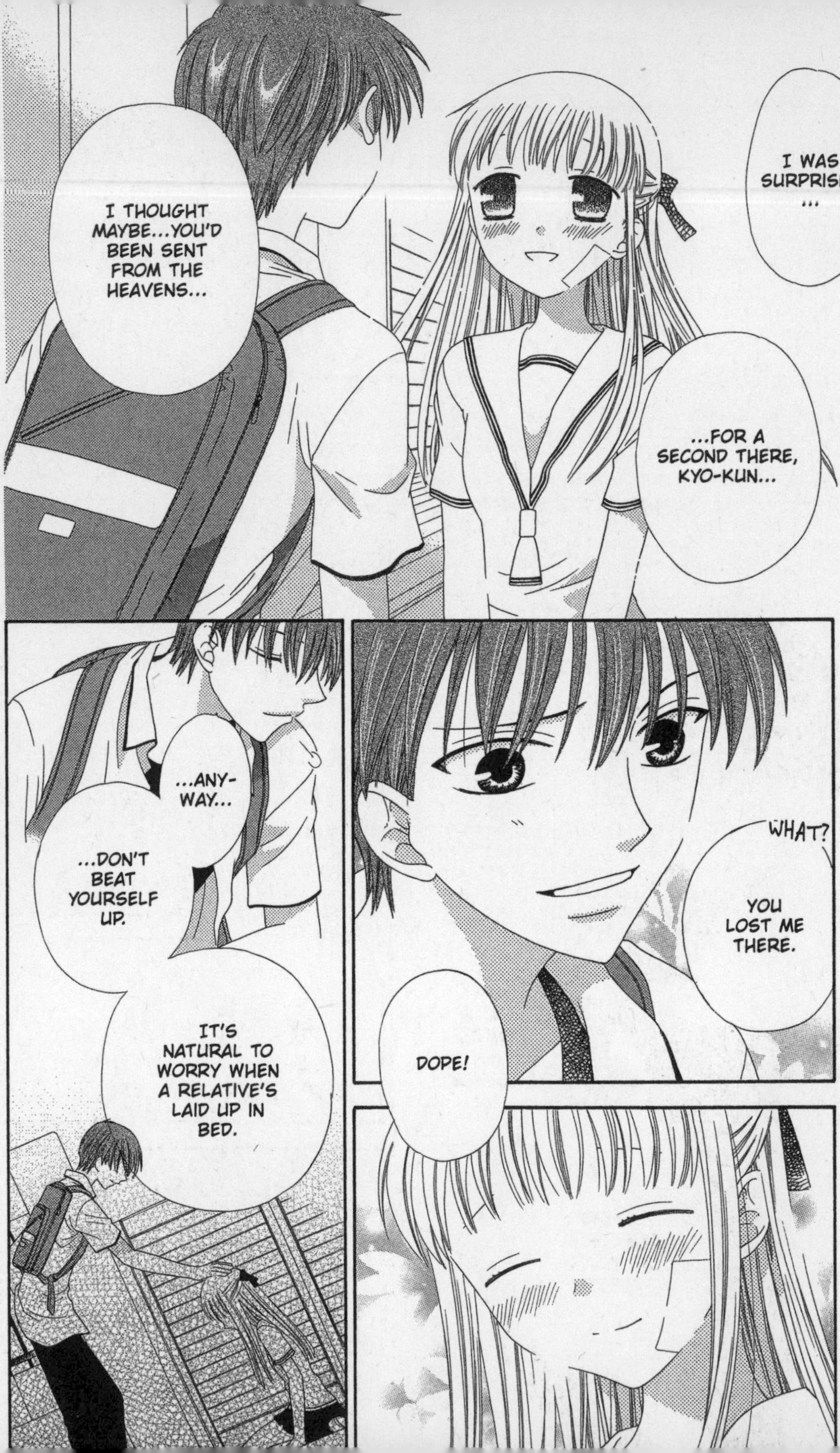
I WAS SURPRISED ...
...FOR A SECOND THERE, KYO-KUN...
I THOUGHT MAYBE...YOU'D BEEN SENT FROM THE HEAVENS...
WHAT?
YOU LOST ME THERE.
DOPE!
...ANY-WAY...
...DON'T BEAT YOURSELF UP.
IT'S NATURAL TO WORRY WHEN A RELATIVE'S LAID UP IN BED.

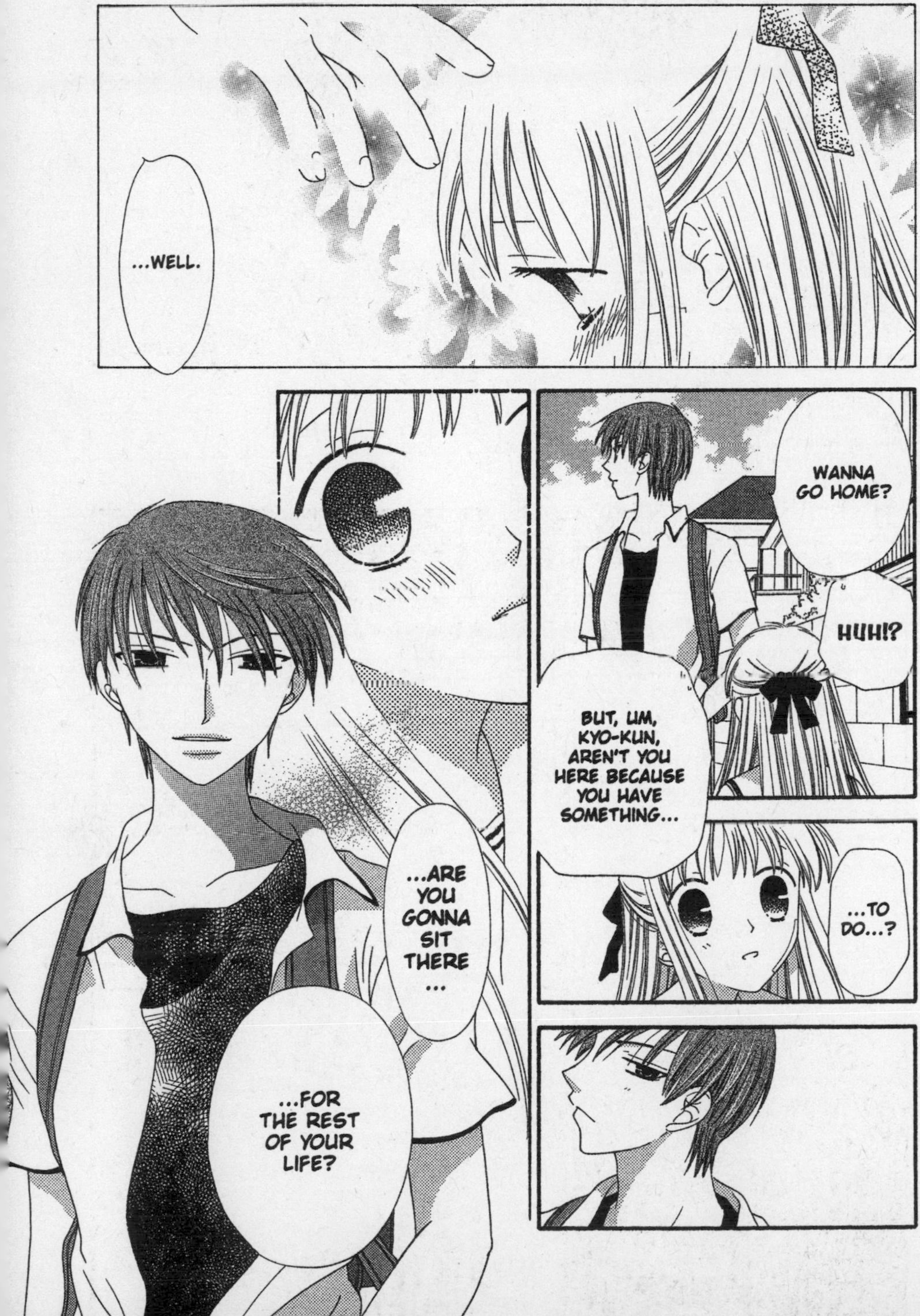
...WELL.
WANNA GO HOME?
HUH!?
BUT, UM, KYO-KUN, AREN'T YOU HERE BECAUSE YOU HAVE SOMETHING...
...TO DO...?
...ARE YOU GONNA SIT THERE...
...FOR THE REST OF YOUR LIFE?

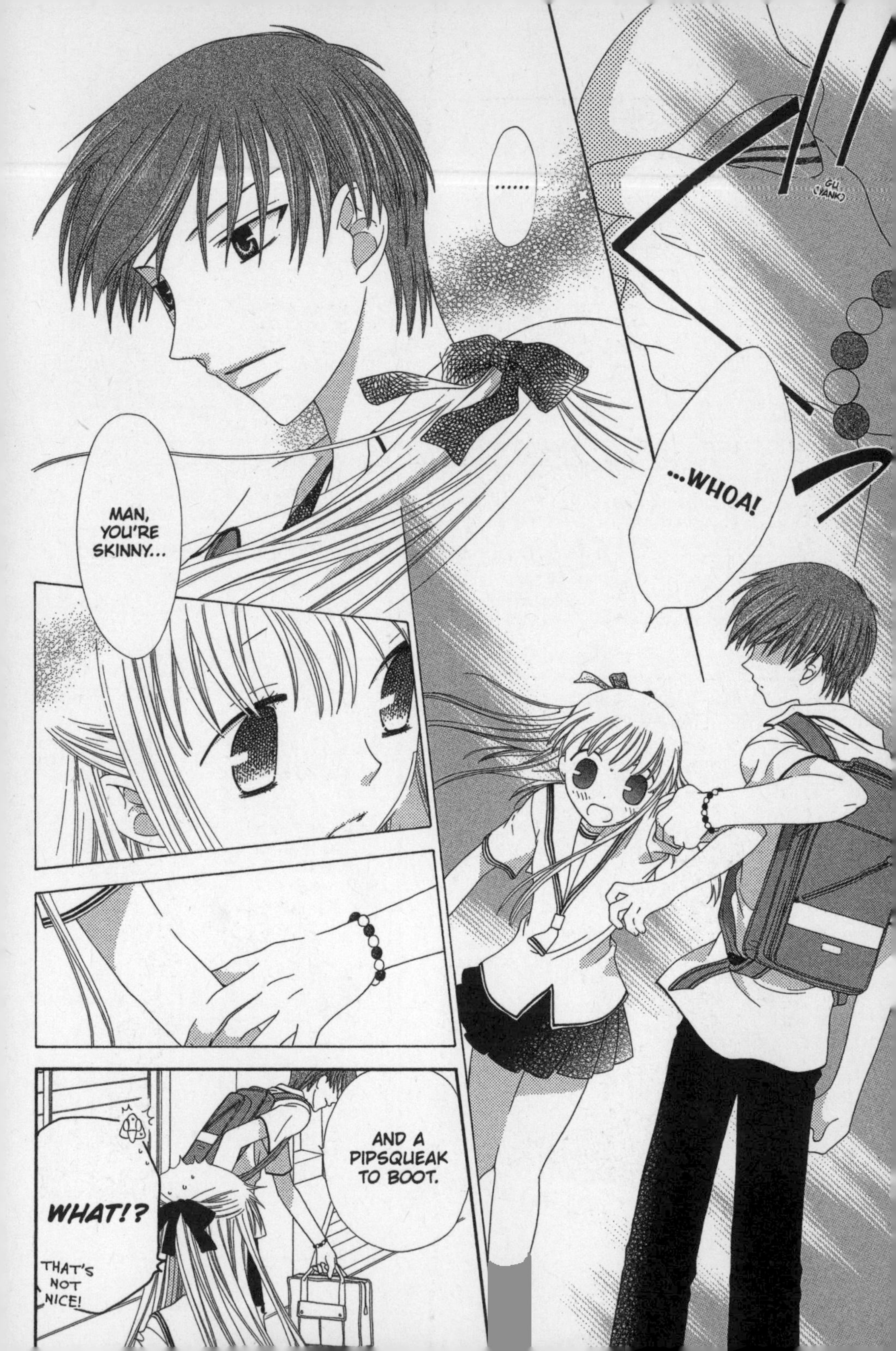

GU (YANK)
...WHOA!
......
MAN, YOU'RE SKINNY...
AND A PIPSQUEAK TO BOOT.
WHAT!?
THAT'S NOT NICE!

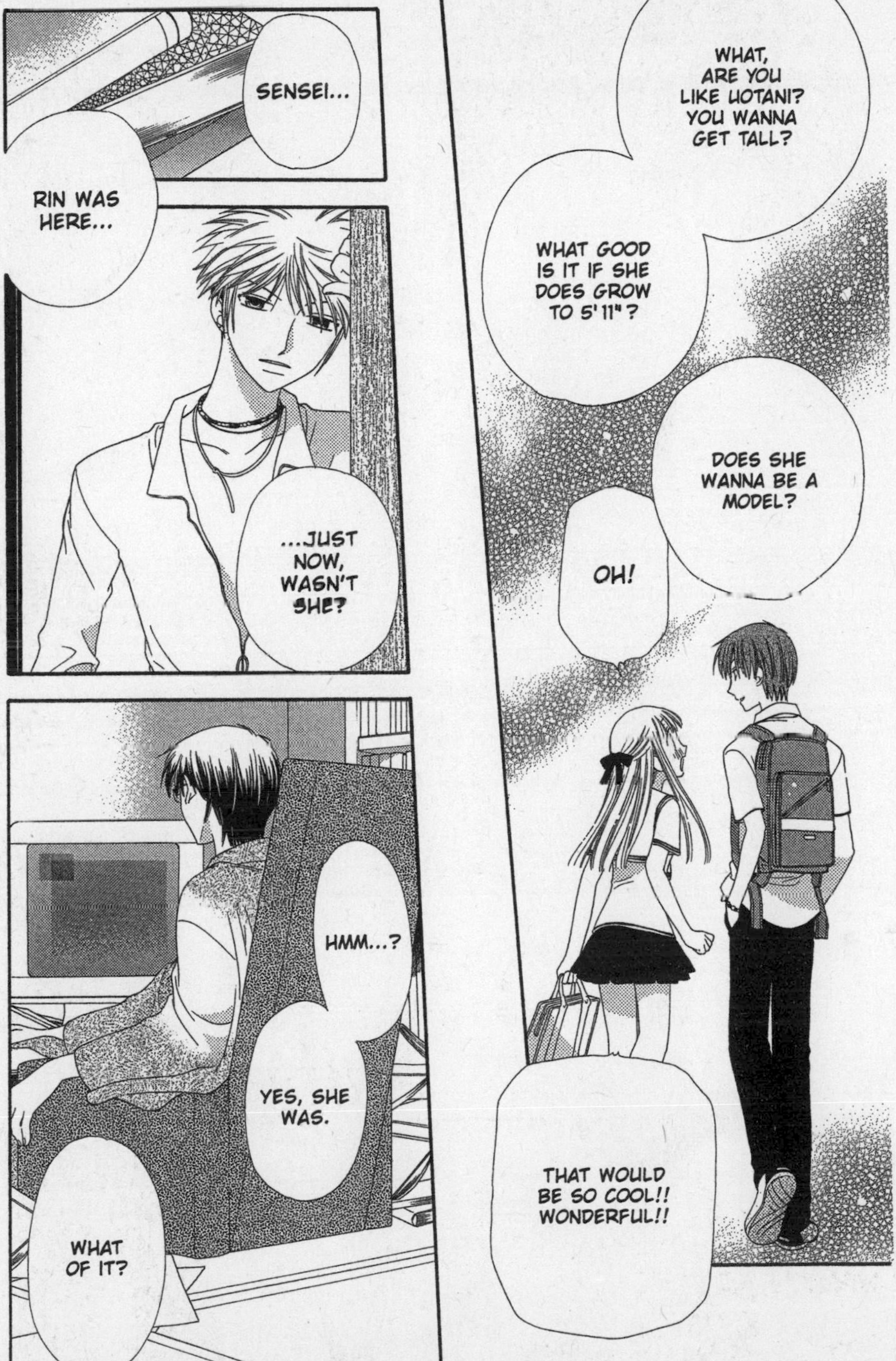
WHAT, ARE YOU LIKE UOTANI? YOU WANNA GET TALL?
WHAT GOOD IS IT IF SHE DOES GROW TO 5'11"?
DOES SHE WANNA BE A MODEL?
OH!
THAT WOULD BE SO COOL!! WONDERFUL!!
SENSEI...
RIN WAS HERE...
...JUST NOW, WASN'T SHE?
HMM...?
YES, SHE WAS.
WHAT OF IT?

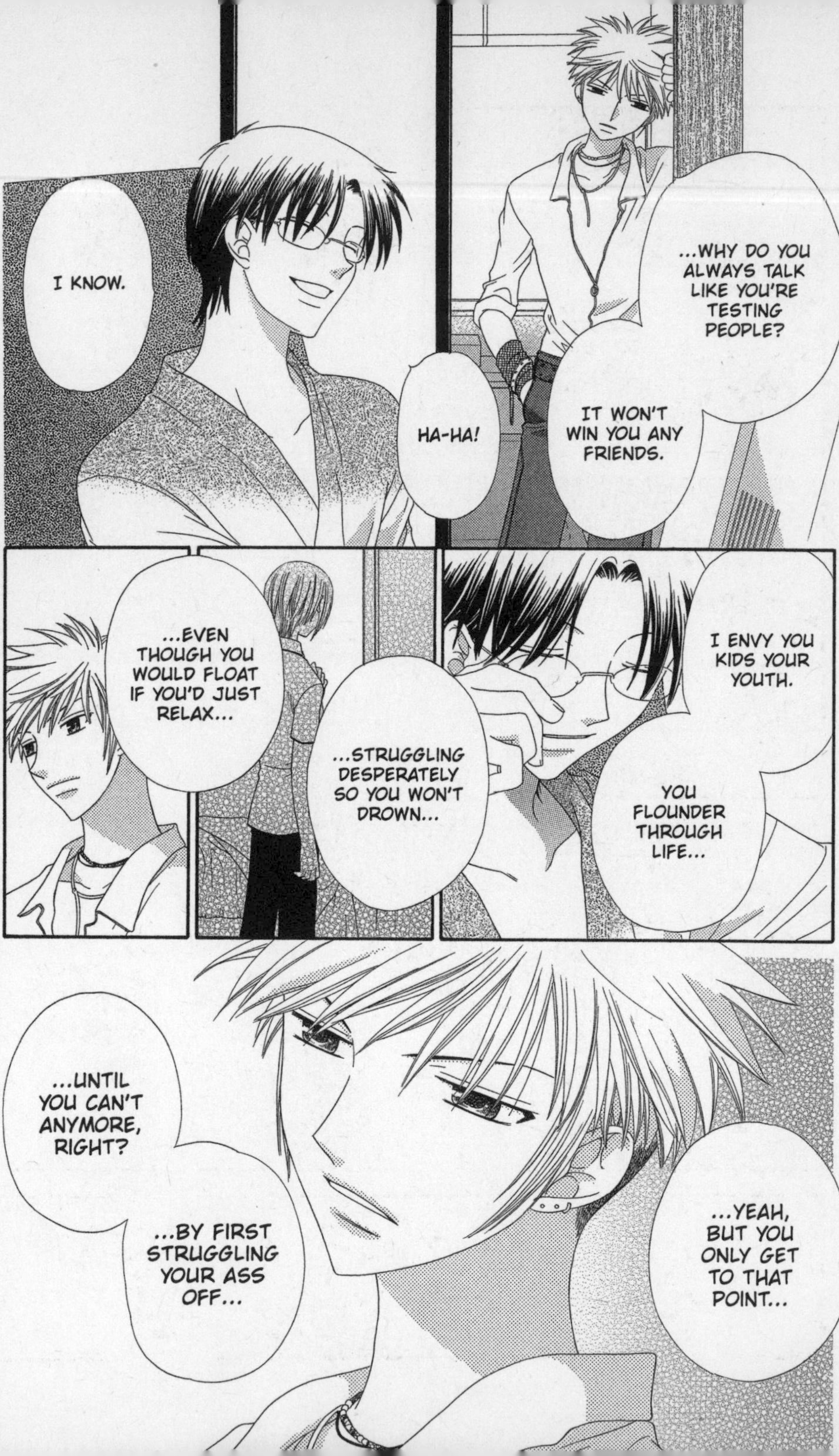
...WHY DO YOU ALWAYS TALK LIKE YOU'RE TESTING PEOPLE?
IT WON'T WIN YOU ANY FRIENDS.
HA-HA!
I KNOW.
I ENVY YOU KIDS YOUR YOUTH.
YOU FLOUNDER THROUGH LIFE...
...STRUGGLING DESPERATELY SO YOU WON'T DROWN...
...EVEN THOUGH YOU WOULD FLOAT IF YOU'D JUST RELAX...
...YEAH, BUT YOU ONLY GET TO THAT POINT...
...BY FIRST STRUGGLING YOUR ASS OFF...
...UNTIL YOU CAN'T ANYMORE, RIGHT?

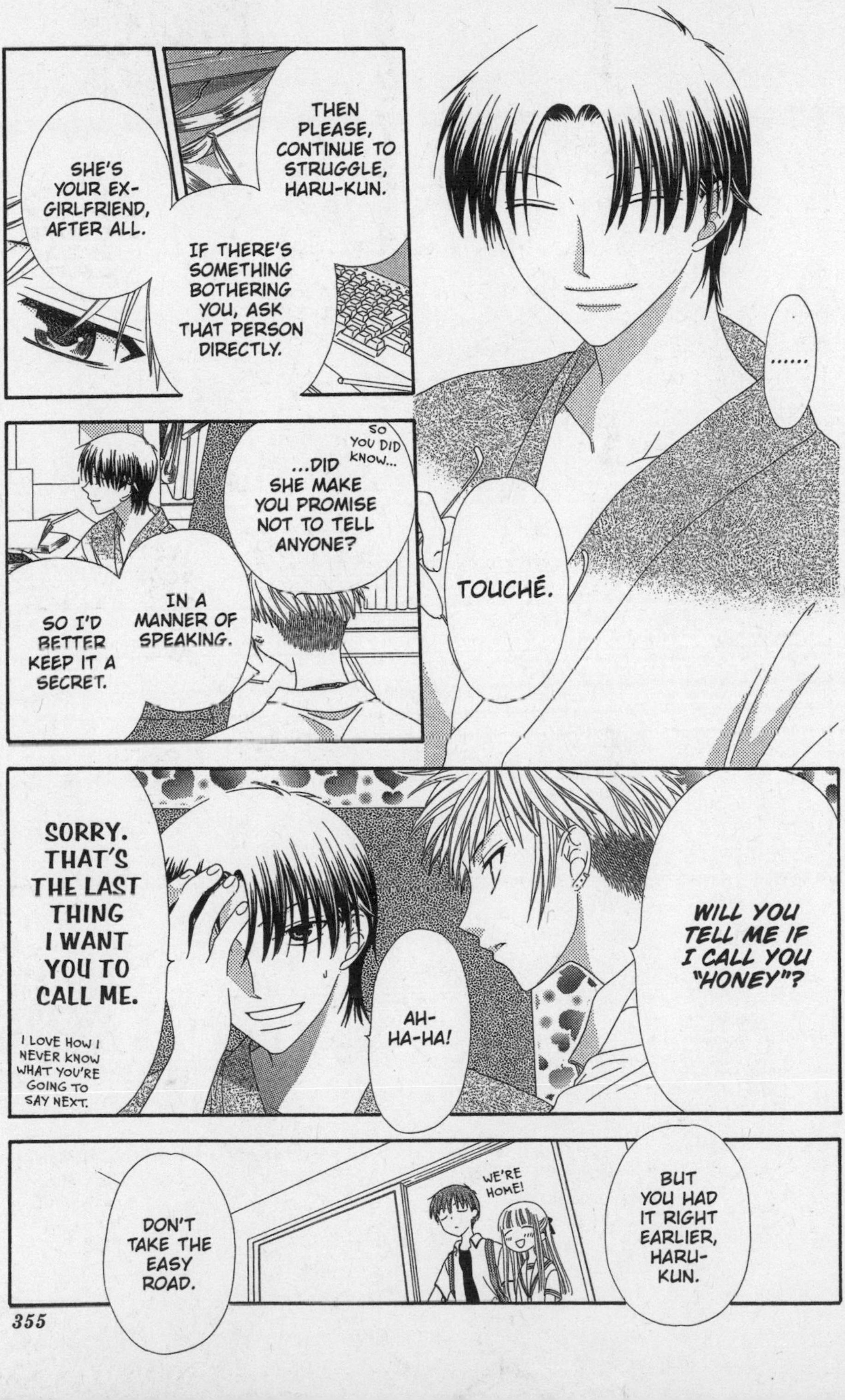

......
TOUCHÉ.
THEN PLEASE, CONTINUE TO STRUGGLE, HARU-KUN.
SHE'S YOUR EX-GIRLFRIEND, AFTER ALL.
IF THERE'S SOMETHING BOTHERING YOU, ASK THAT PERSON DIRECTLY.
SO YOU DID KNOW...
...DID SHE MAKE YOU PROMISE NOT TO TELL ANYONE?
IN A MANNER OF SPEAKING.
SO I'D BETTER KEEP IT A SECRET.
WILL YOU TELL ME IF I CALL YOU "HONEY"?
AH-HA-HA!
SORRY. THAT'S THE LAST THING I WANT YOU TO CALL ME.
I LOVE HOW I NEVER KNOW WHAT YOU'RE GOING TO SAY NEXT.
BUT YOU HAD IT RIGHT EARLIER, HARU-KUN.
WE'RE HOME!
DON'T TAKE THE EASY ROAD.

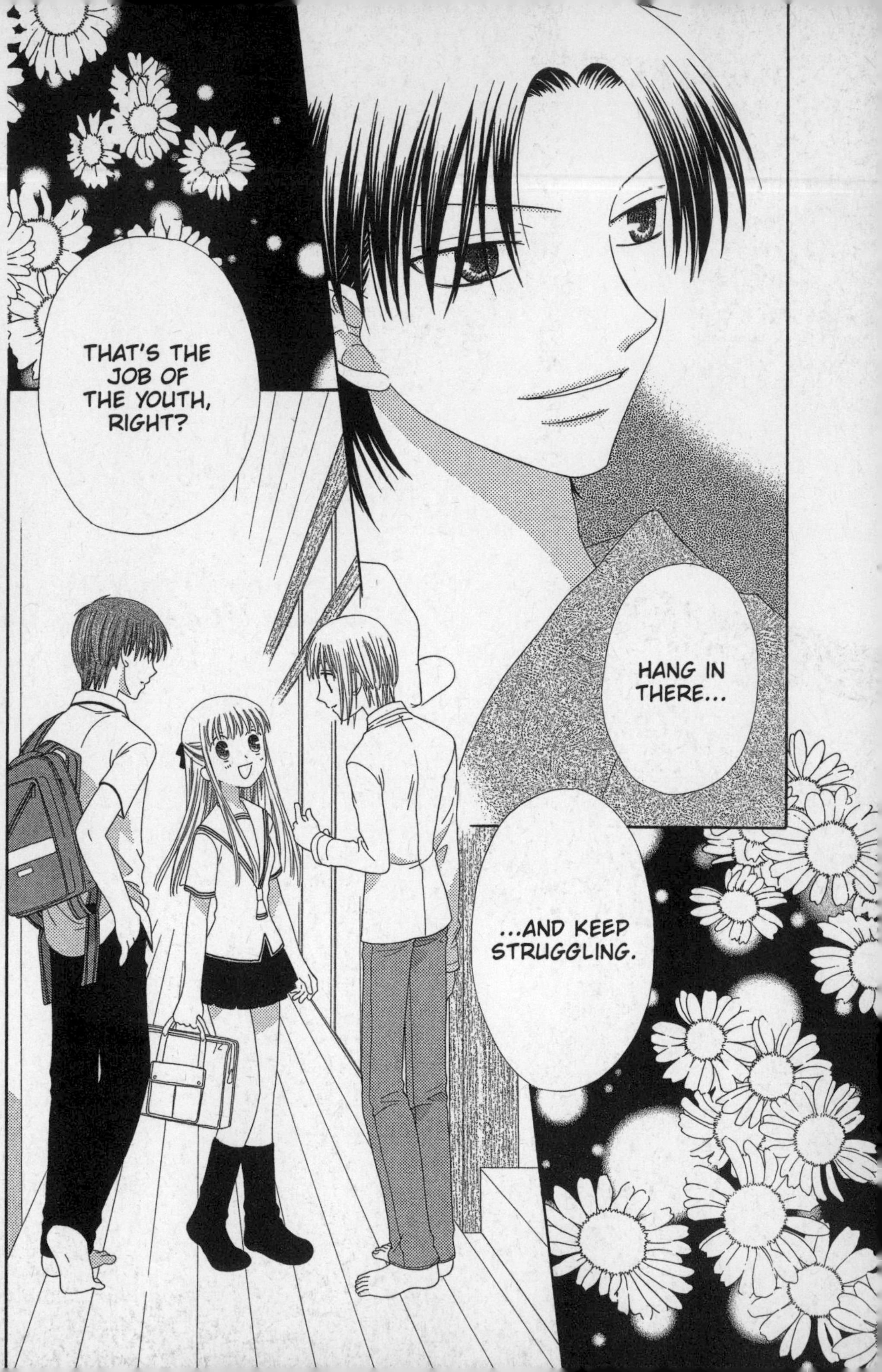
THAT'S THE JOB OF THE YOUTH, RIGHT?
HANG IN THERE...
...AND KEEP STRUGGLING.

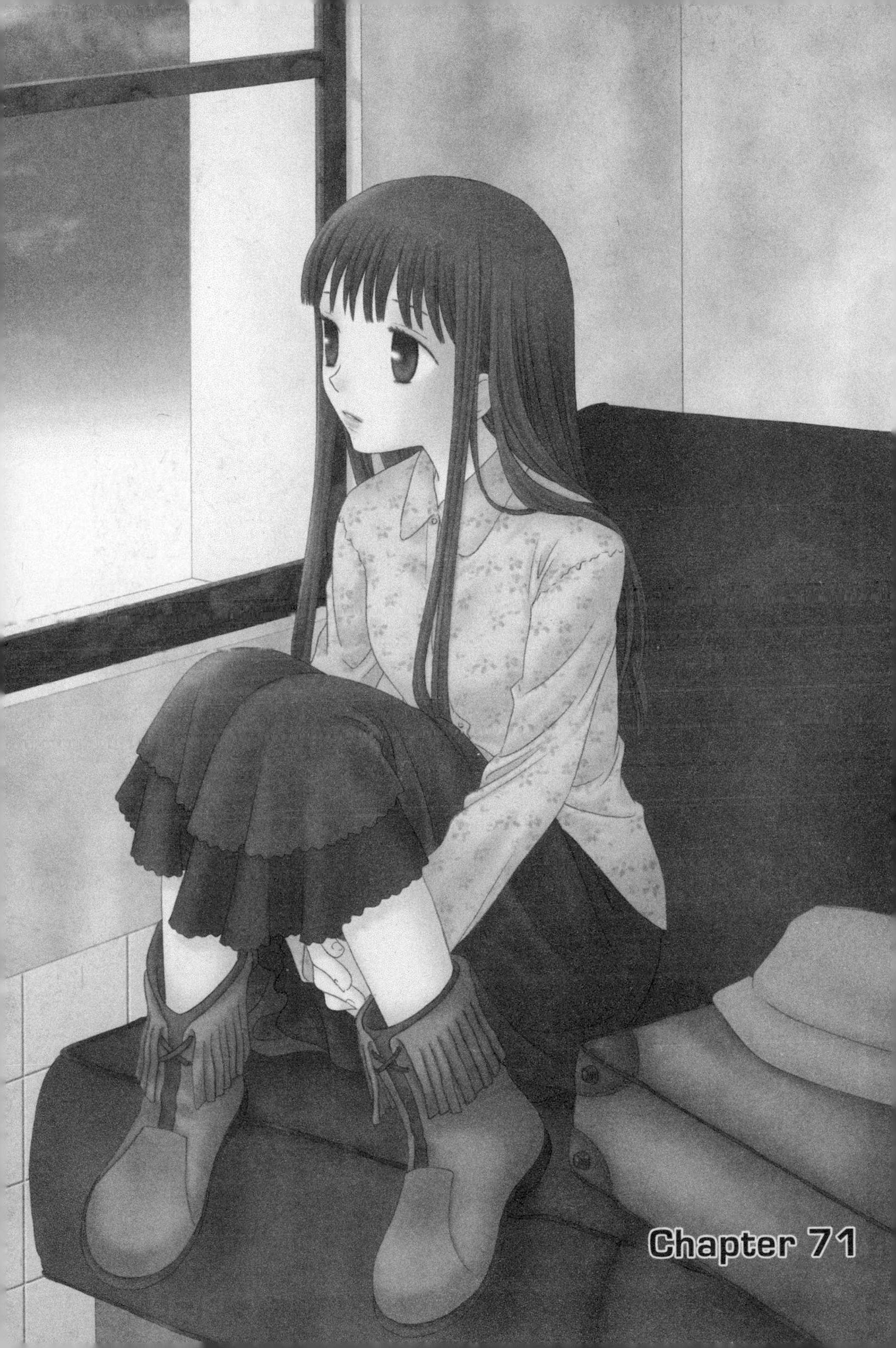

Chapter 71

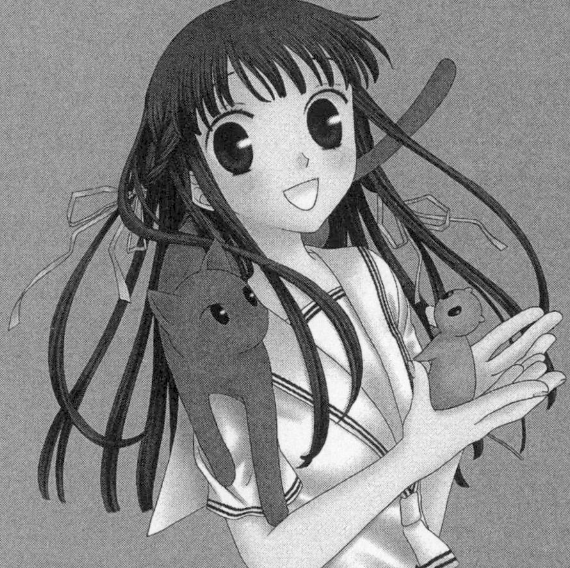

COLLECTOR'S EDITION

Fruits Basket

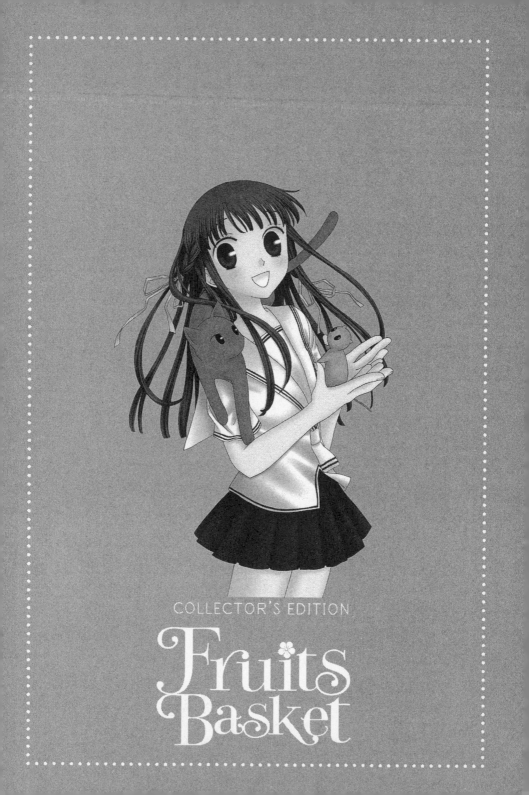

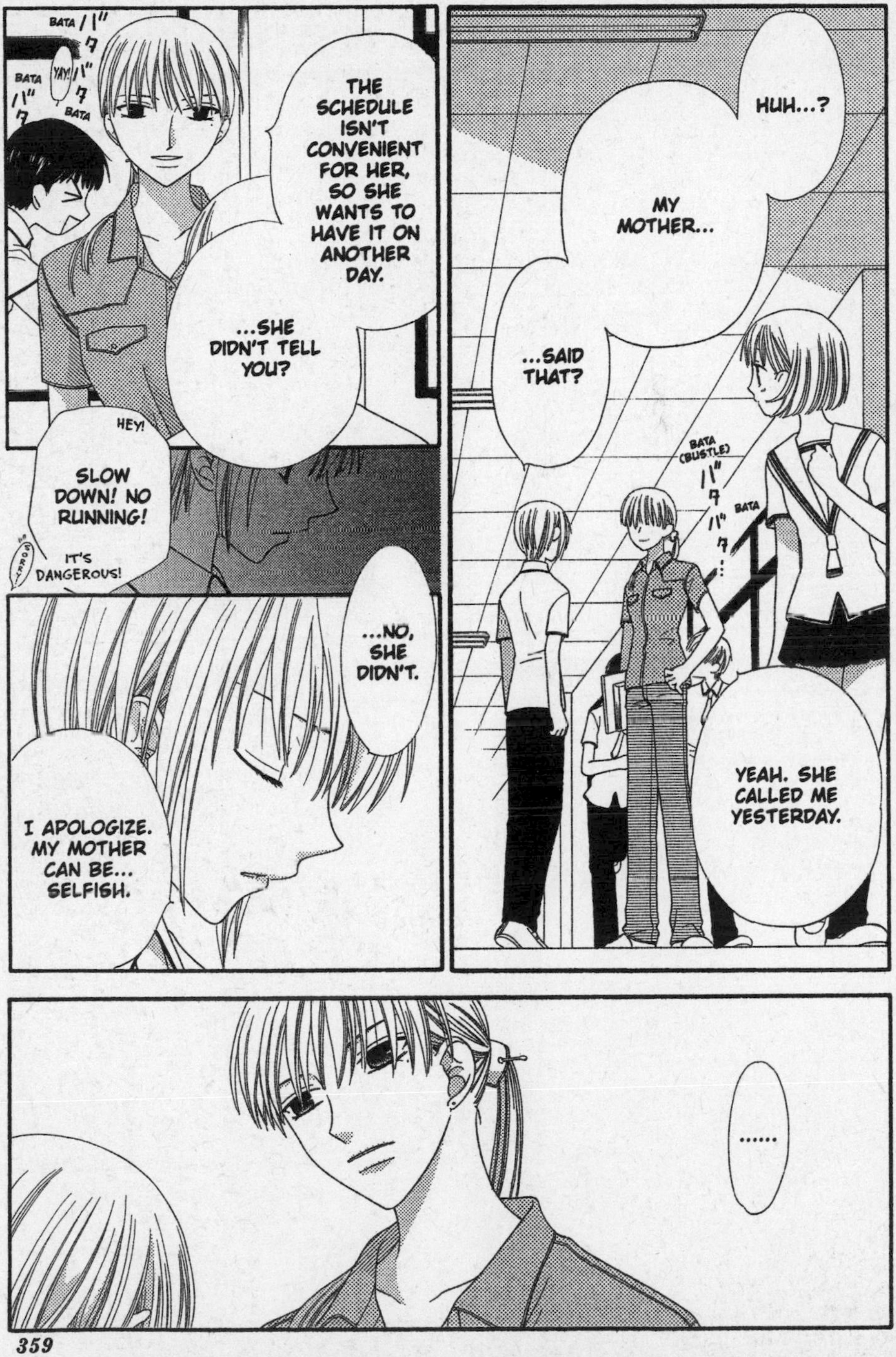
HUH...?
MY MOTHER...
...SAID THAT?
BATA (BUSTLE)
バタバタ…
BATA
YEAH. SHE CALLED ME YESTERDAY.
THE SCHEDULE ISN'T CONVENIENT FOR HER, SO SHE WANTS TO HAVE IT ON ANOTHER DAY.
...SHE DIDN'T TELL YOU?
BATA バタ
YAY!
バタ
BATA バタ
BATA
HEY!
SLOW DOWN! NO RUNNING!
IT'S DANGEROUS!
SORRY!
...NO, SHE DIDN'T.
I APOLOGIZE. MY MOTHER CAN BE... SELFISH.
......

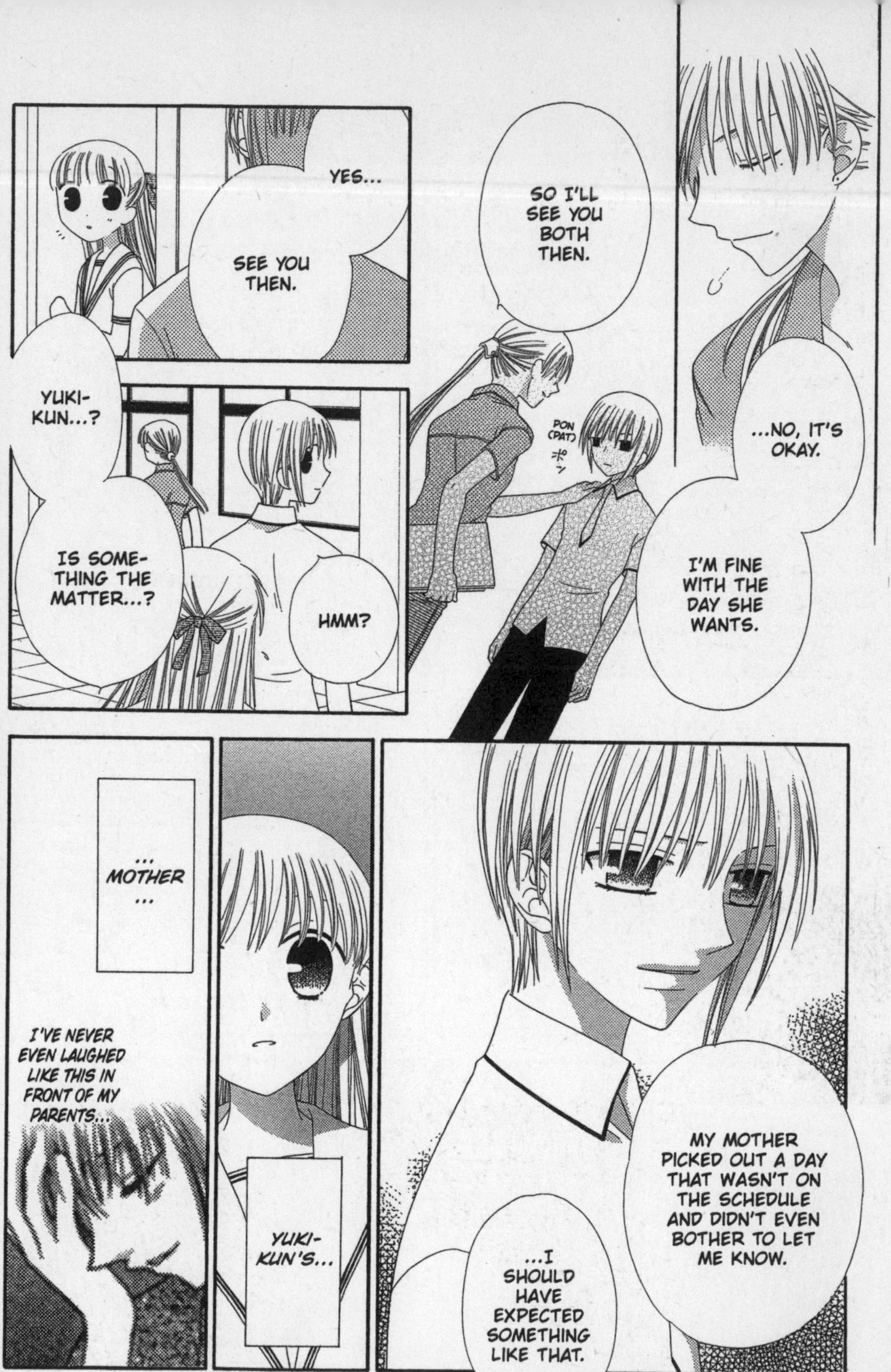
SO I'LL SEE YOU BOTH THEN.
PON (PAT)
ポン
...NO, IT'S OKAY.
I'M FINE WITH THE DAY SHE WANTS.
YES...
SEE YOU THEN.
YUKI-KUN...?
IS SOMETHING THE MATTER...?
HMM?
MY MOTHER PICKED OUT A DAY THAT WASN'T ON THE SCHEDULE AND DIDN'T EVEN BOTHER TO LET ME KNOW.
...I SHOULD HAVE EXPECTED SOMETHING LIKE THAT.
YUKI-KUN'S...
...MOTHER...
I'VE NEVER EVEN LAUGHED LIKE THIS IN FRONT OF MY PARENTS...

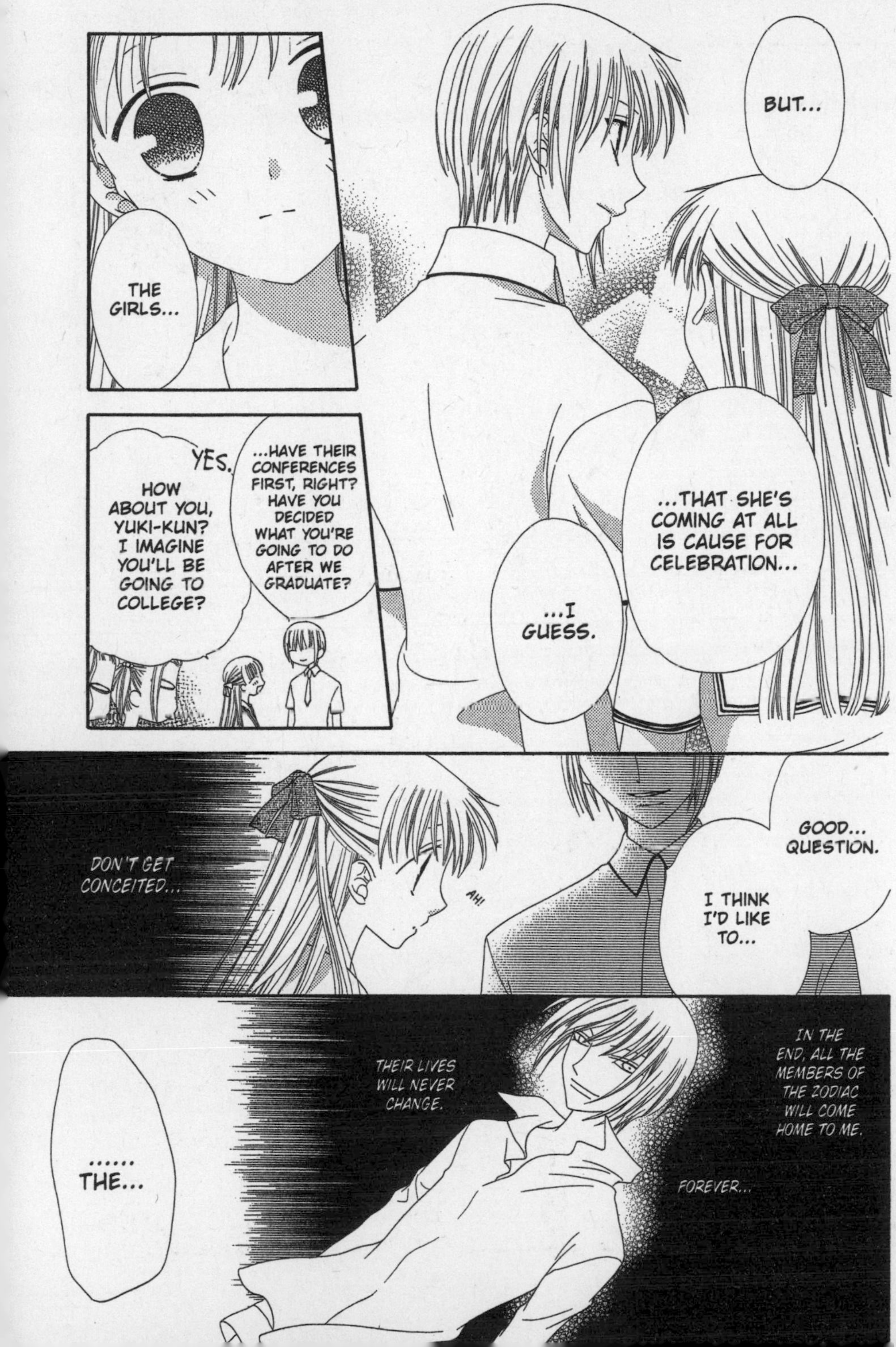
BUT...
...THAT SHE'S COMING AT ALL IS CAUSE FOR CELEBRATION...
...I GUESS.
THE GIRLS...
...HAVE THEIR CONFERENCES FIRST, RIGHT? HAVE YOU DECIDED WHAT YOU'RE GOING TO DO AFTER WE GRADUATE?
YES.
HOW ABOUT YOU, YUKI-KUN? I IMAGINE YOU'LL BE GOING TO COLLEGE?
GOOD... QUESTION.
I THINK I'D LIKE TO...
AH!
DON'T GET CONCEITED...
IN THE END, ALL THE MEMBERS OF THE ZODIAC WILL COME HOME TO ME.
FOREVER...
THEIR LIVES WILL NEVER CHANGE.
...... THE...

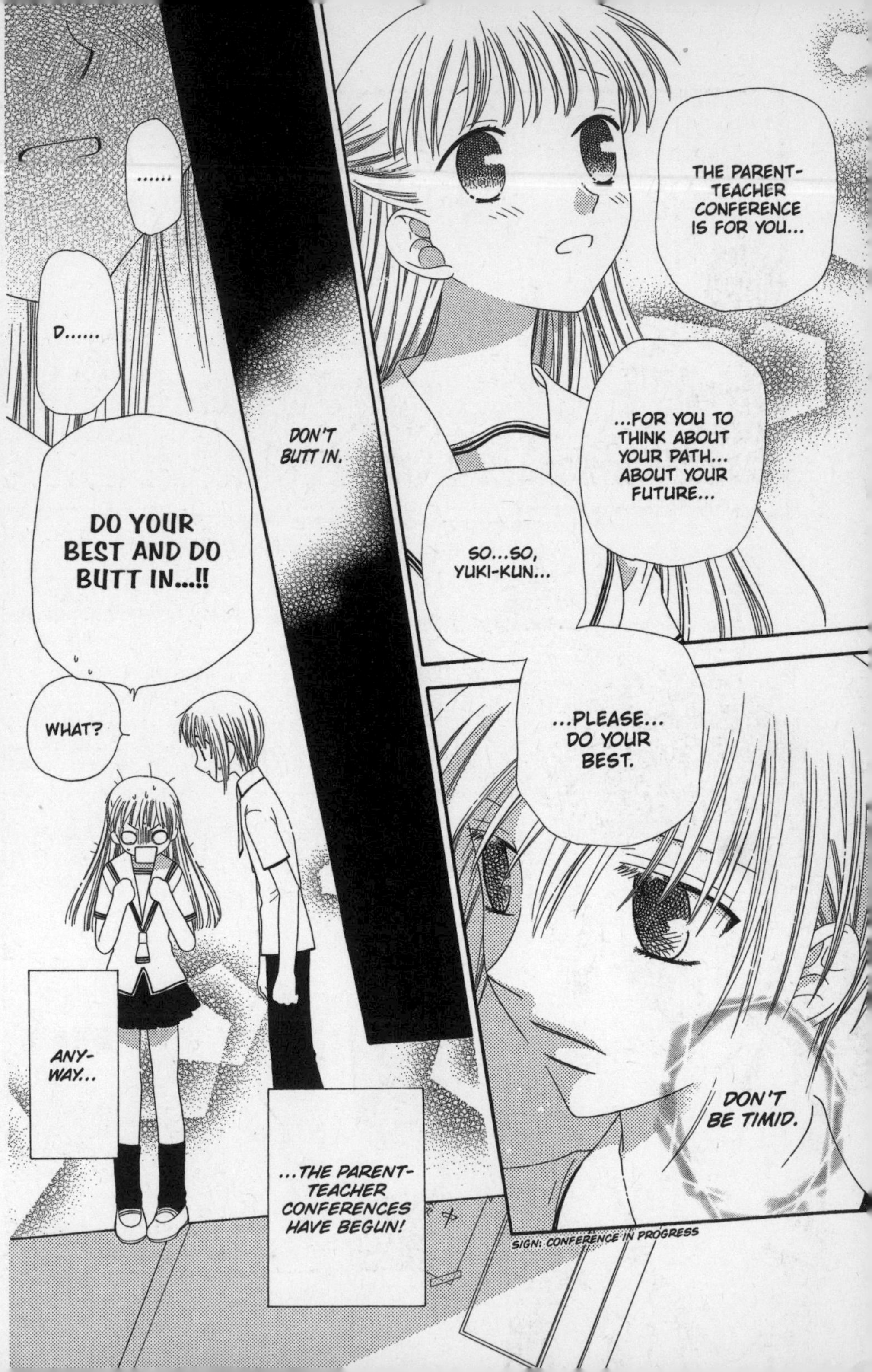
THE PARENT-TEACHER CONFERENCE IS FOR YOU...
...FOR YOU TO THINK ABOUT YOUR PATH... ABOUT YOUR FUTURE...
SO...SO, YUKI-KUN...
...PLEASE... DO YOUR BEST.
DON'T BE TIMID.
SIGN: CONFERENCE IN PROGRESS
DON'T BUTT IN.
......
D......
DO YOUR BEST AND DO BUTT IN...!!
WHAT?
ANY-WAY...
...THE PARENT-TEACHER CONFERENCES HAVE BEGUN!

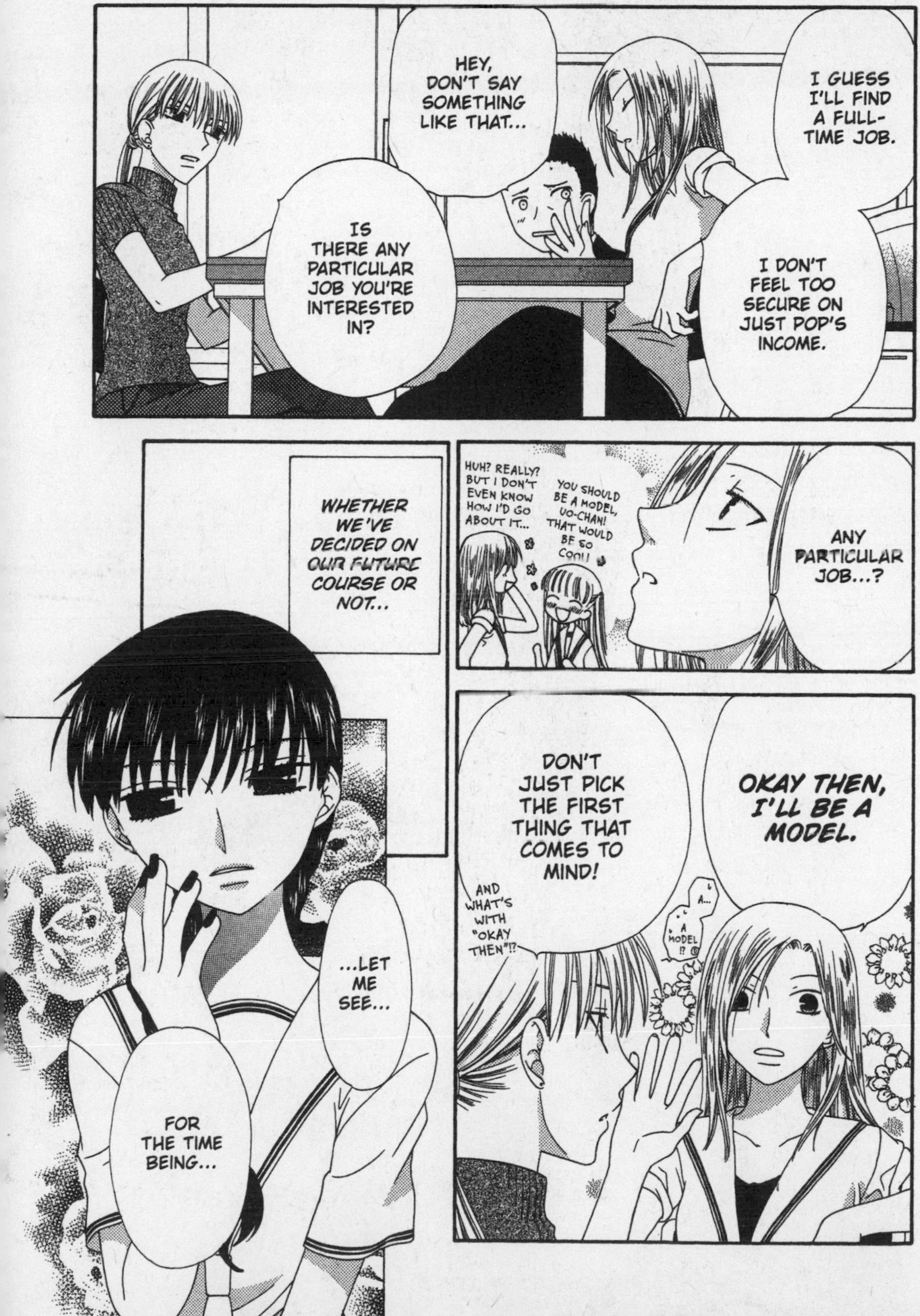
I GUESS I'LL FIND A FULL-TIME JOB.
I DON'T FEEL TOO SECURE ON JUST POP'S INCOME.
HEY, DON'T SAY SOMETHING LIKE THAT...
IS THERE ANY PARTICULAR JOB YOU'RE INTERESTED IN?
ANY PARTICULAR JOB...?
YOU SHOULD BE A MODEL, UO-CHAN! THAT WOULD BE SO COOL!
HUH? REALLY? BUT I DON'T EVEN KNOW HOW I'D GO ABOUT IT...
OKAY THEN, I'LL BE A MODEL.
DON'T JUST PICK THE FIRST THING THAT COMES TO MIND!
A... A MODEL!?
AND WHAT'S WITH "OKAY THEN"!?
WHETHER WE'VE DECIDED ON OUR FUTURE COURSE OR NOT...
...LET ME SEE...
FOR THE TIME BEING...

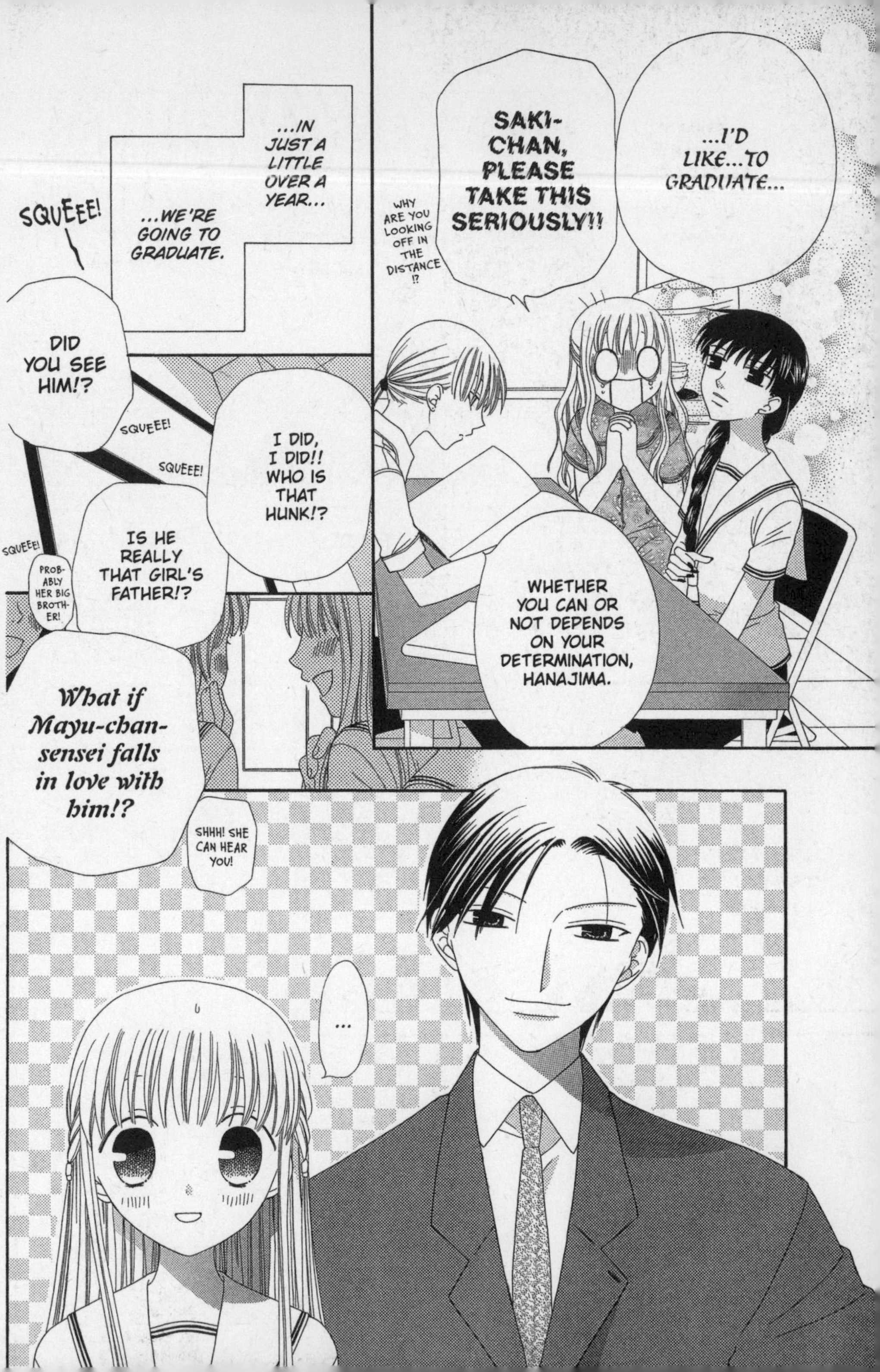
...I'D LIKE...TO GRADUATE...
SAKI-CHAN, PLEASE TAKE THIS SERIOUSLY!!
WHY ARE YOU LOOKING OFF IN THE DISTANCE!?
WHETHER YOU CAN OR NOT DEPENDS ON YOUR DETERMINATION, HANAJIMA.
...IN JUST A LITTLE OVER A YEAR...
...WE'RE GOING TO GRADUATE.
SQUEEE!
DID YOU SEE HIM!?
SQUEEE!
I DID, I DID!! WHO IS THAT HUNK!?
SQUEEE!
IS HE REALLY THAT GIRL'S FATHER!?
SQUEEE!
PROBABLY HER BIG BROTHER!
What if Mayu-chan-sensei falls in love with him!?
SHHH! SHE CAN HEAR YOU!
...

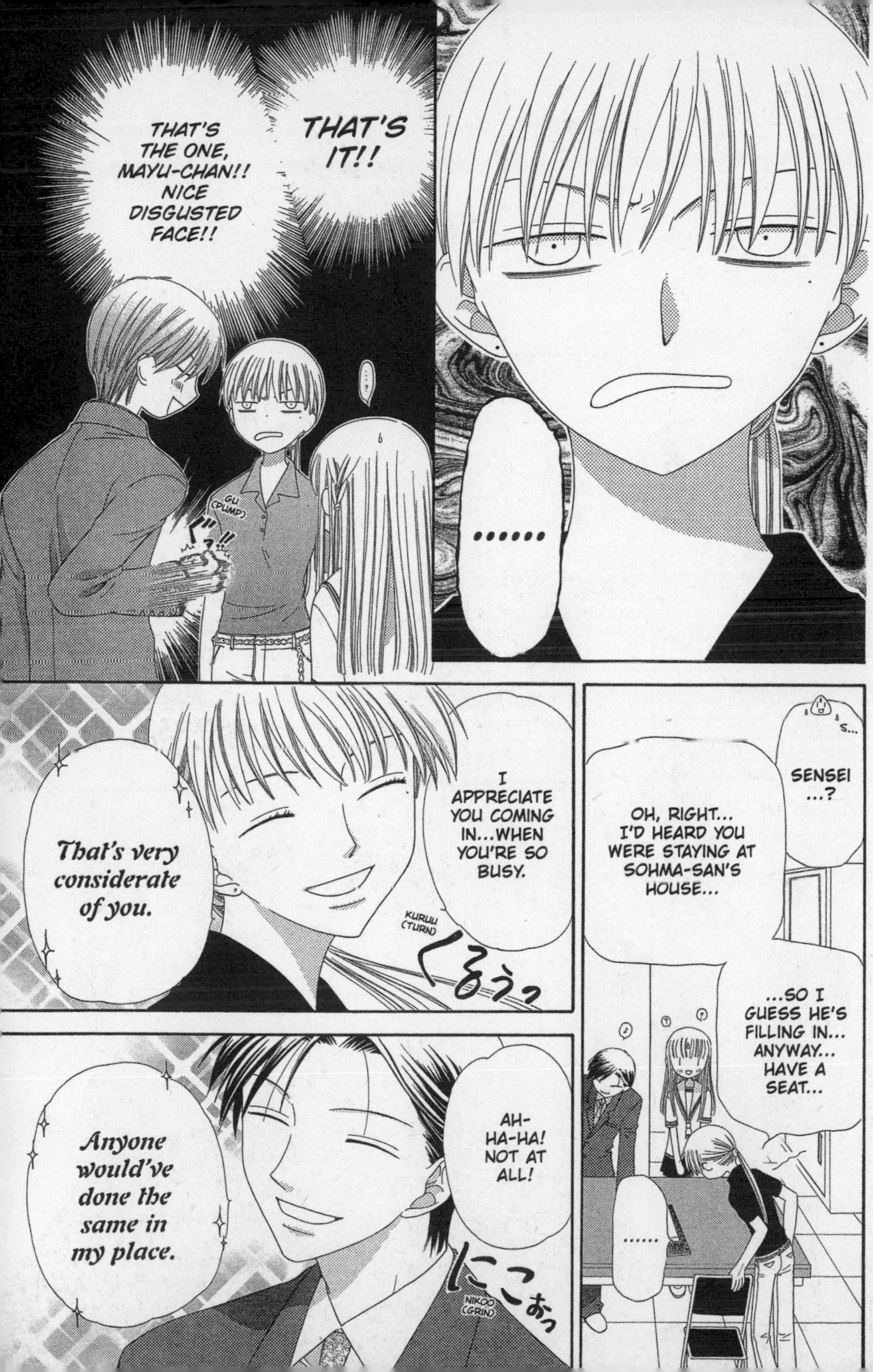
......
THAT'S IT!!
THAT'S THE ONE, MAYU-CHAN!! NICE DISGUSTED FACE!!
...?
GU (PUMP)
S...
SENSEI ...?
OH, RIGHT... I'D HEARD YOU WERE STAYING AT SOHMA-SAN'S HOUSE...
...SO I GUESS HE'S FILLING IN... ANYWAY... HAVE A SEAT...
......
I APPRECIATE YOU COMING IN...WHEN YOU'RE SO BUSY.
That's very considerate of you.
KURUU (TURN)
AH-HA-HA! NOT AT ALL!
Anyone would've done the same in my place.
NIKOO (GRIN)

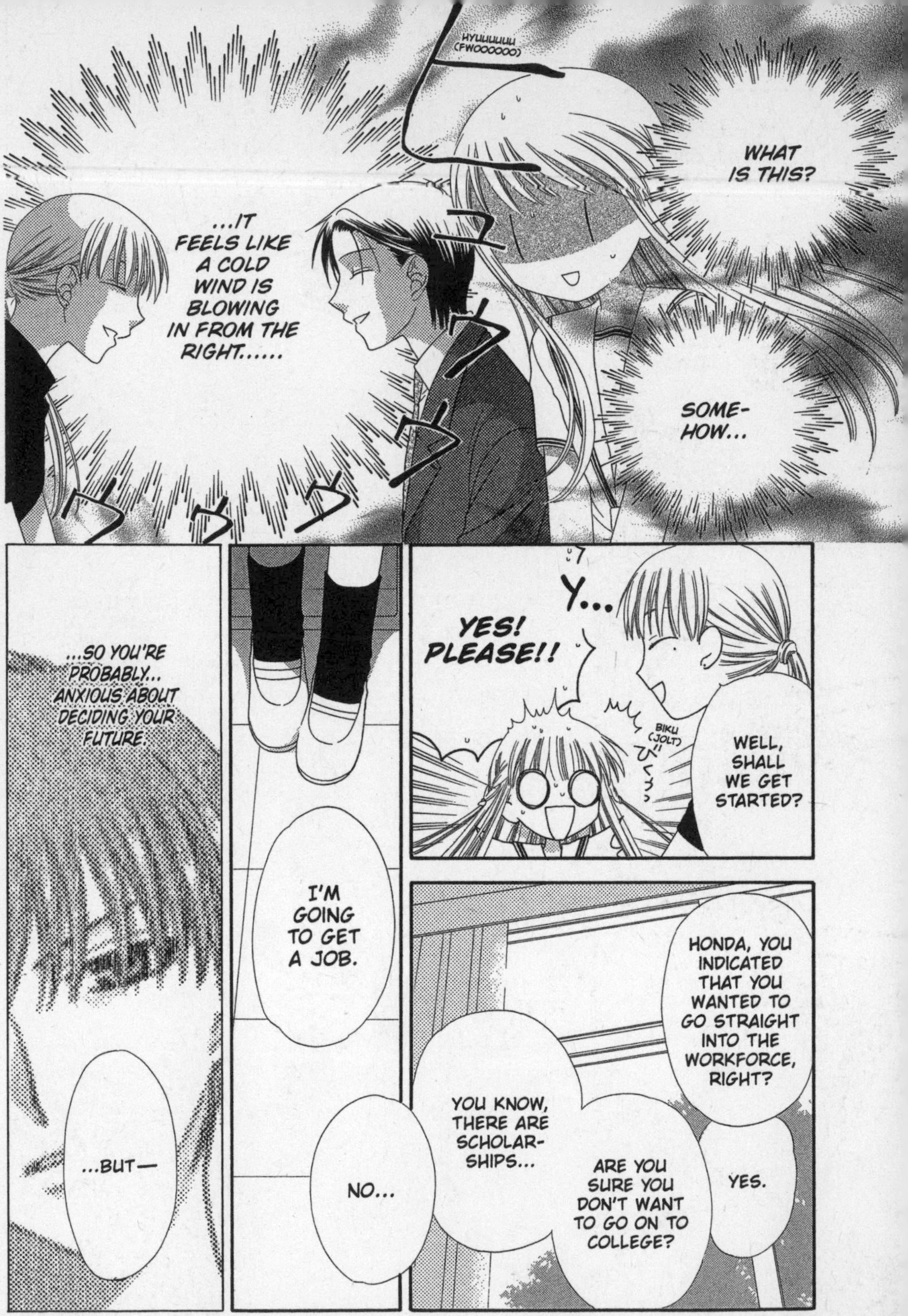
WHAT IS THIS?
SOME-HOW...
HYUUUUUU (FWOOOOOO)
...IT FEELS LIKE A COLD WIND IS BLOWING IN FROM THE RIGHT......
WELL, SHALL WE GET STARTED?
BIKU (JOLT)
Y...
YES! PLEASE!!
HONDA, YOU INDICATED THAT YOU WANTED TO GO STRAIGHT INTO THE WORKFORCE, RIGHT?
YES.
ARE YOU SURE YOU DON'T WANT TO GO ON TO COLLEGE?
YOU KNOW, THERE ARE SCHOLAR-SHIPS...
NO...
I'M GOING TO GET A JOB.
...SO YOU'RE PROBABLY... ANXIOUS ABOUT DECIDING YOUR FUTURE.
...BUT—

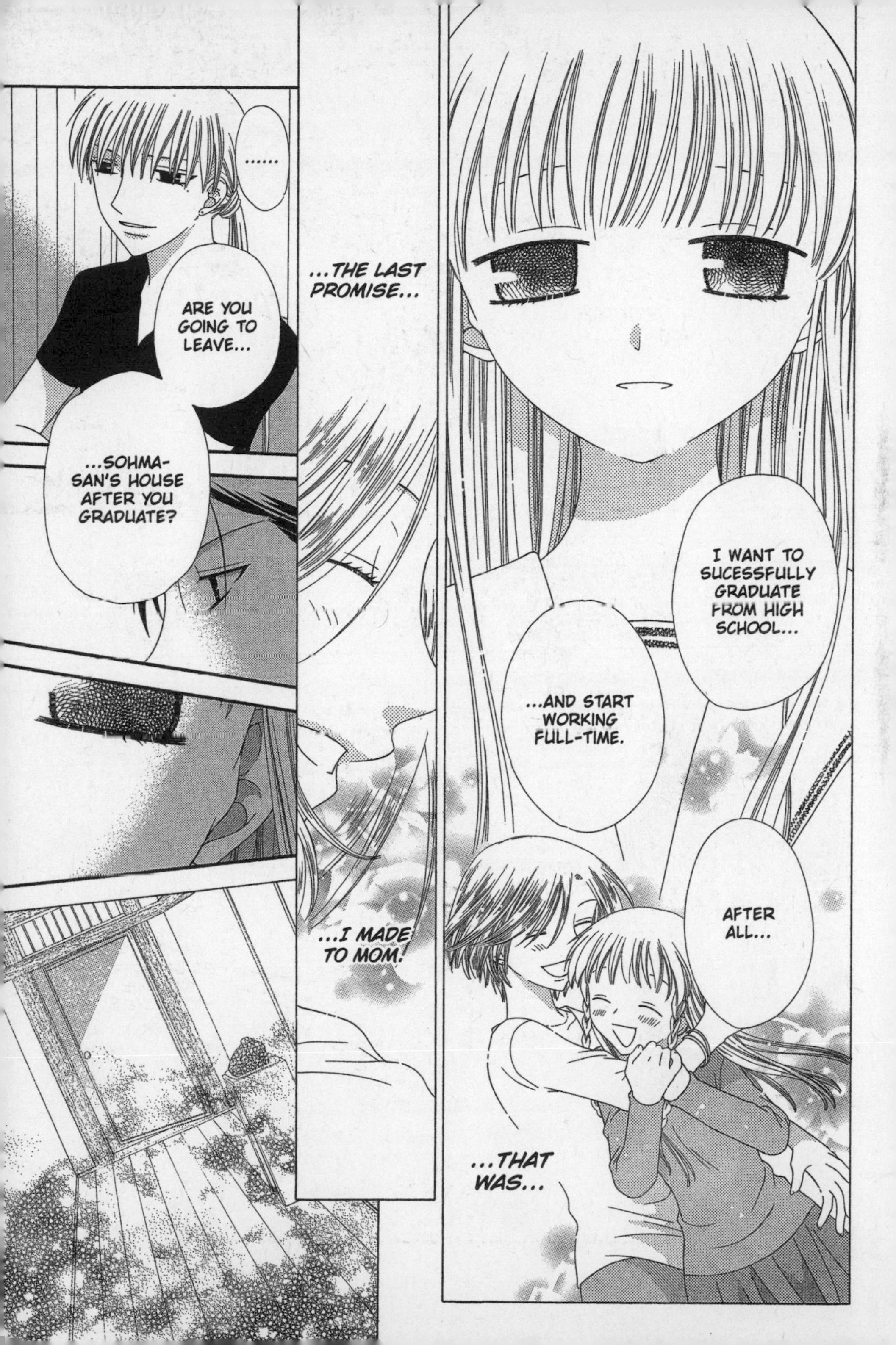

I WANT TO SUCESSFULLY GRADUATE FROM HIGH SCHOOL...
...AND START WORKING FULL-TIME.
AFTER ALL...
...THAT WAS...
...THE LAST PROMISE...
...I MADE TO MOM.
......
ARE YOU GOING TO LEAVE...
...SOHMA-SAN'S HOUSE AFTER YOU GRADUATE?

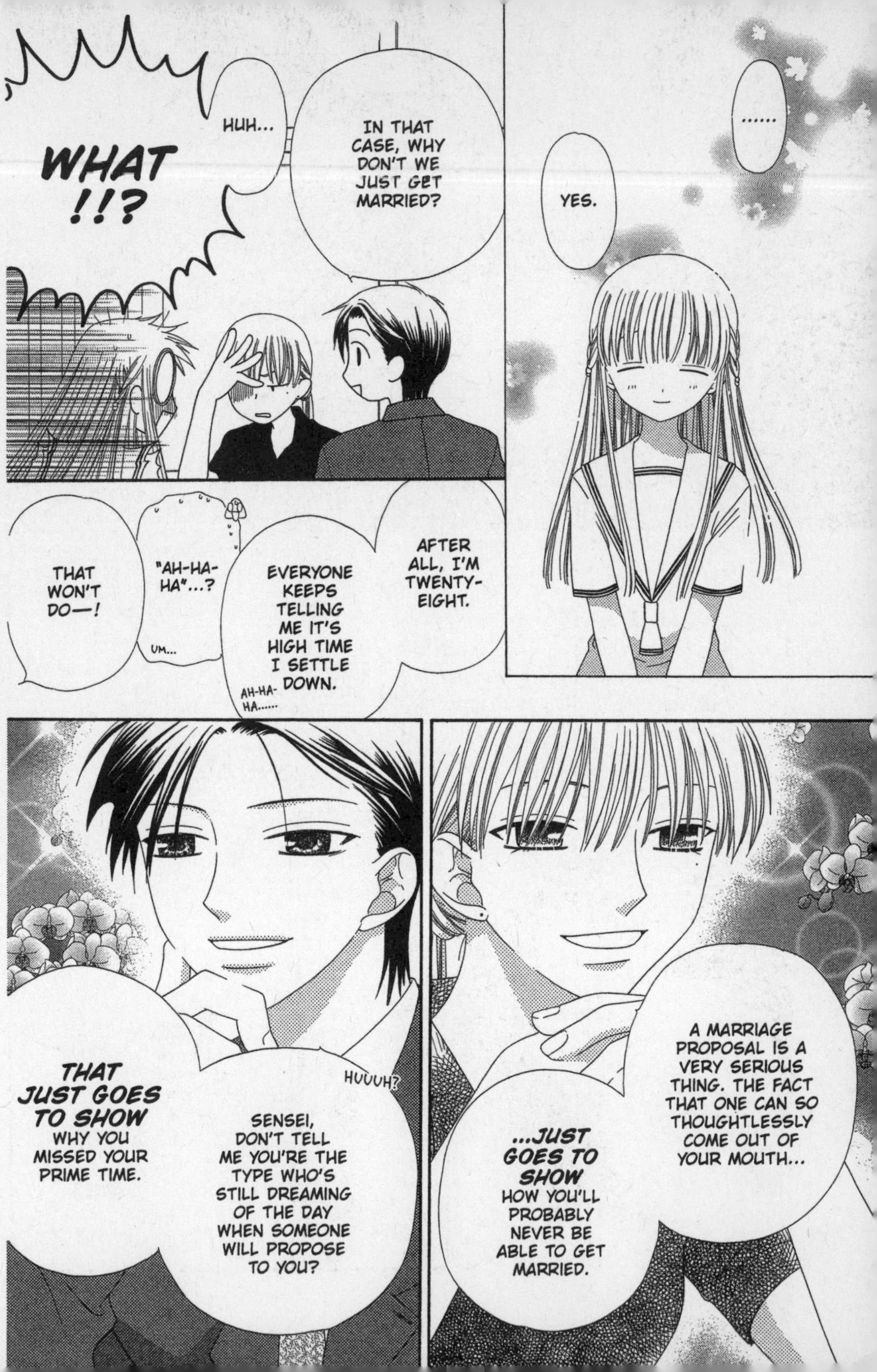
......
YES.
IN THAT CASE, WHY DON'T WE JUST GET MARRIED?
HUH...
WHAT!!?
AFTER ALL, I'M TWENTY-EIGHT.
EVERYONE KEEPS TELLING ME IT'S HIGH TIME I SETTLE DOWN.
AH-HA-HA......
"AH-HA-HA"...?
UM...
THAT WON'T DO—!
A MARRIAGE PROPOSAL IS A VERY SERIOUS THING. THE FACT THAT ONE CAN SO THOUGHTLESSLY COME OUT OF YOUR MOUTH...
...JUST GOES TO SHOW HOW YOU'LL PROBABLY NEVER BE ABLE TO GET MARRIED.
HUUUH?
SENSEI, DON'T TELL ME YOU'RE THE TYPE WHO'S STILL DREAMING OF THE DAY WHEN SOMEONE WILL PROPOSE TO YOU?
THAT JUST GOES TO SHOW WHY YOU MISSED YOUR PRIME TIME.

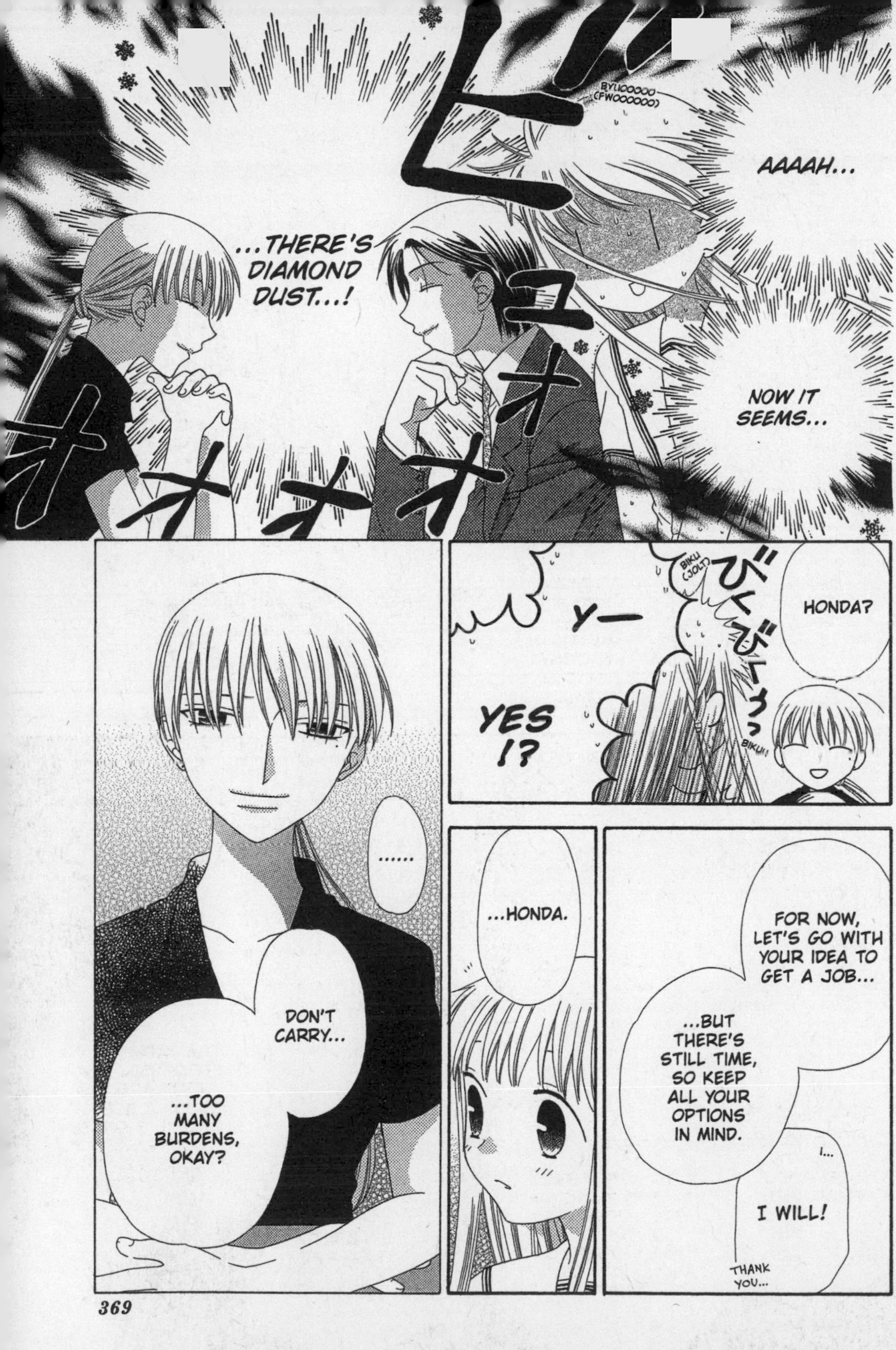
BYUOOOOO (FWOOOOOO)
AAAAH...
NOW IT SEEMS...
...THERE'S DIAMOND DUST...!
HONDA?
BIKU (JOLT)
BIKU!!
YES !?
Y—
FOR NOW, LET'S GO WITH YOUR IDEA TO GET A JOB...
...BUT THERE'S STILL TIME, SO KEEP ALL YOUR OPTIONS IN MIND.
I...
I WILL!
THANK YOU...
...HONDA.
......
DON'T CARRY...
...TOO MANY BURDENS, OKAY?

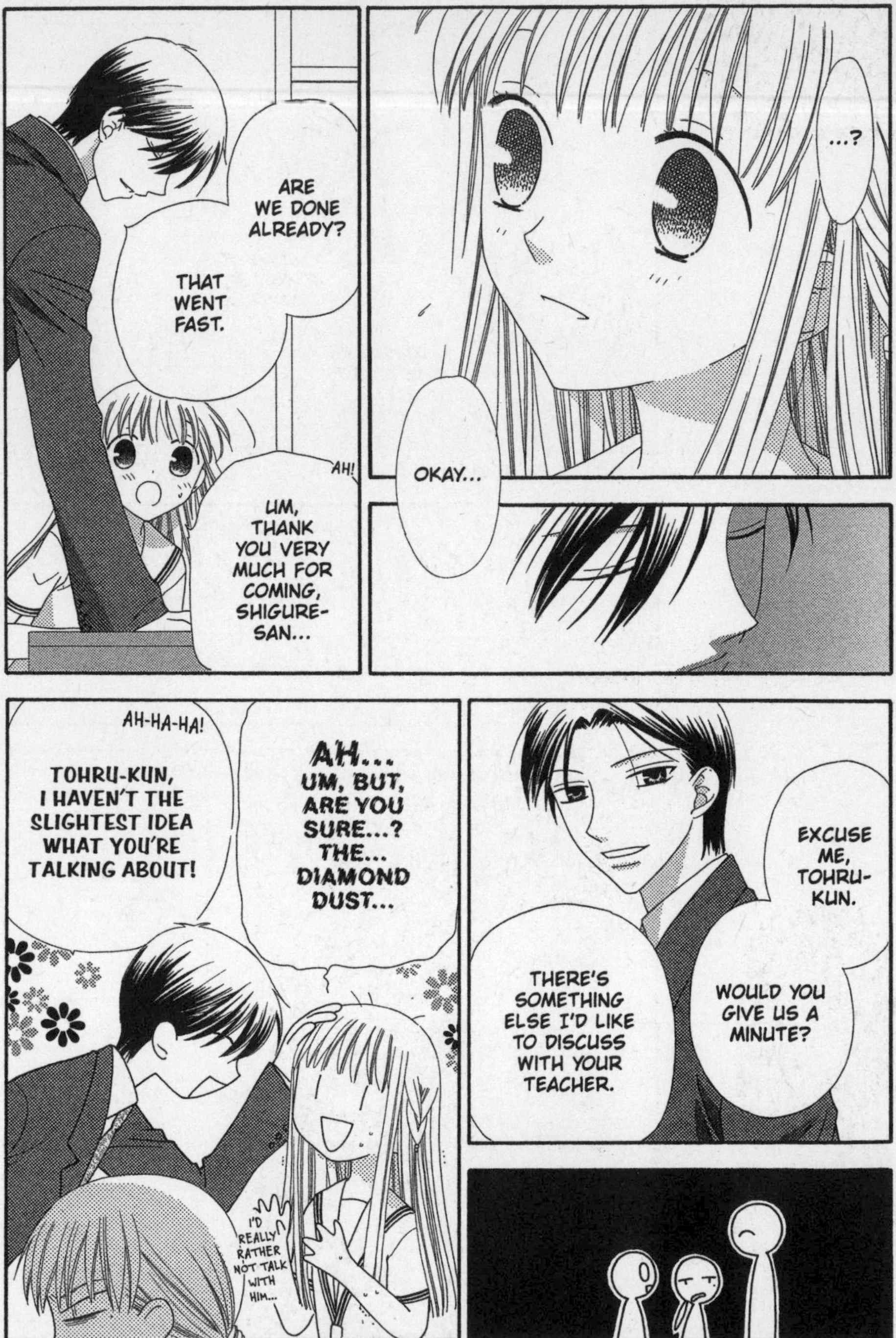
...?
OKAY...
ARE WE DONE ALREADY?
THAT WENT FAST.
AH!
UM, THANK YOU VERY MUCH FOR COMING, SHIGURE-SAN...
EXCUSE ME, TOHRU-KUN.
WOULD YOU GIVE US A MINUTE?
THERE'S SOMETHING ELSE I'D LIKE TO DISCUSS WITH YOUR TEACHER.
AH... UM, BUT, ARE YOU SURE...? THE... DIAMOND DUST...
AH-HA-HA!
TOHRU-KUN, I HAVEN'T THE SLIGHTEST IDEA WHAT YOU'RE TALKING ABOUT!
I'D REALLY RATHER NOT TALK WITH HIM...

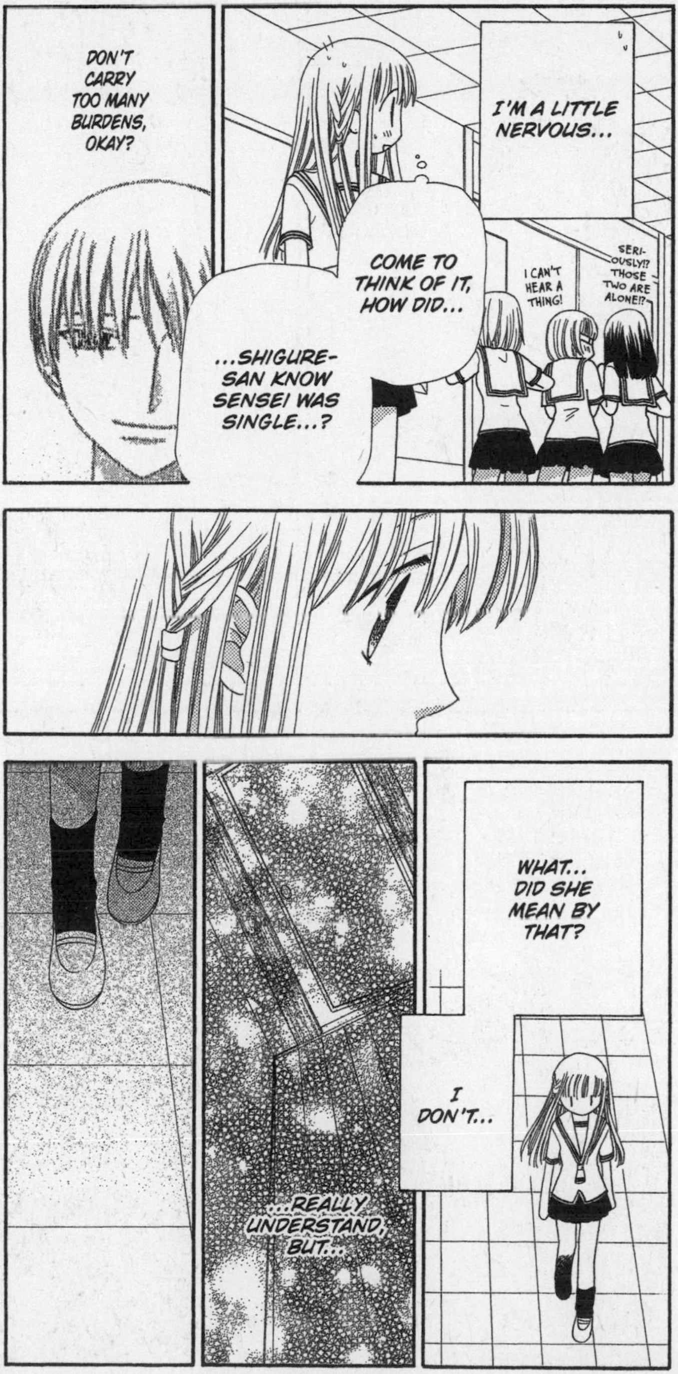
I'M A LITTLE NERVOUS...
SERI-OUSLY!? THOSE TWO ARE ALONE!?
I CAN'T HEAR A THING!
COME TO THINK OF IT, HOW DID...
...SHIGURE-SAN KNOW SENSEI WAS SINGLE...?
DON'T CARRY TOO MANY BURDENS, OKAY?
WHAT... DID SHE MEAN BY THAT?
I DON'T...
...REALLY UNDERSTAND, BUT...

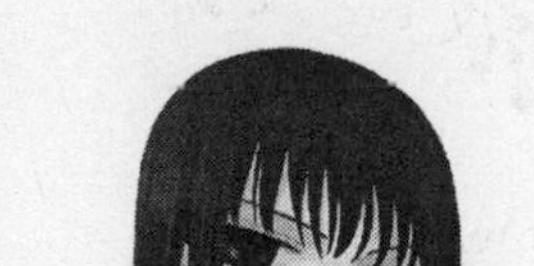

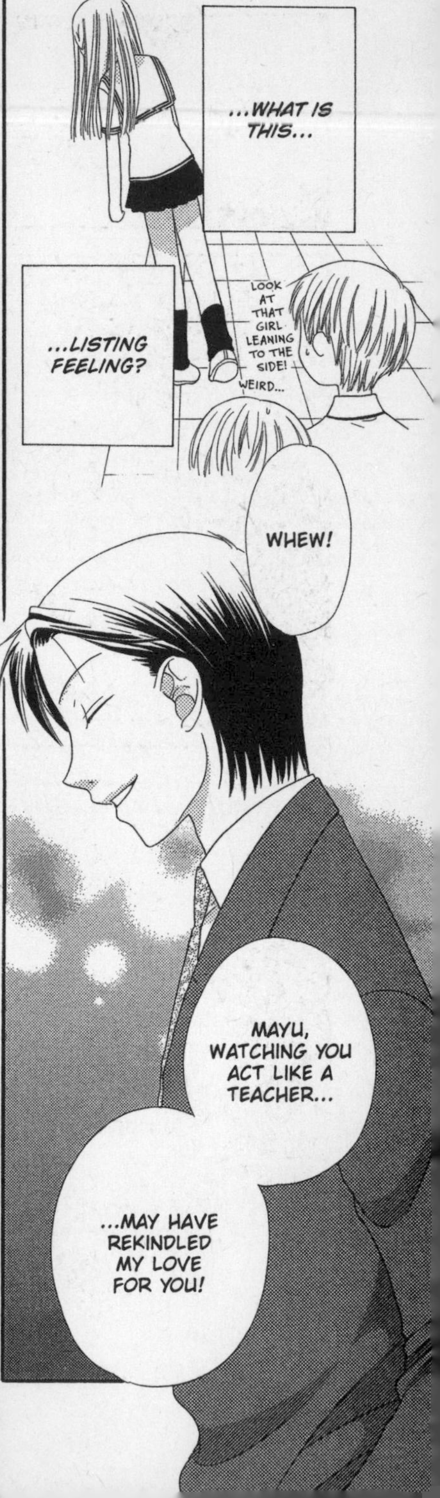
...WHAT IS THIS...
...LISTING FEELING?
LOOK AT THAT GIRL LEANING TO THE SIDE! WEIRD...
WHEW!
MAYU, WATCHING YOU ACT LIKE A TEACHER...
...MAY HAVE REKINDLED MY LOVE FOR YOU!
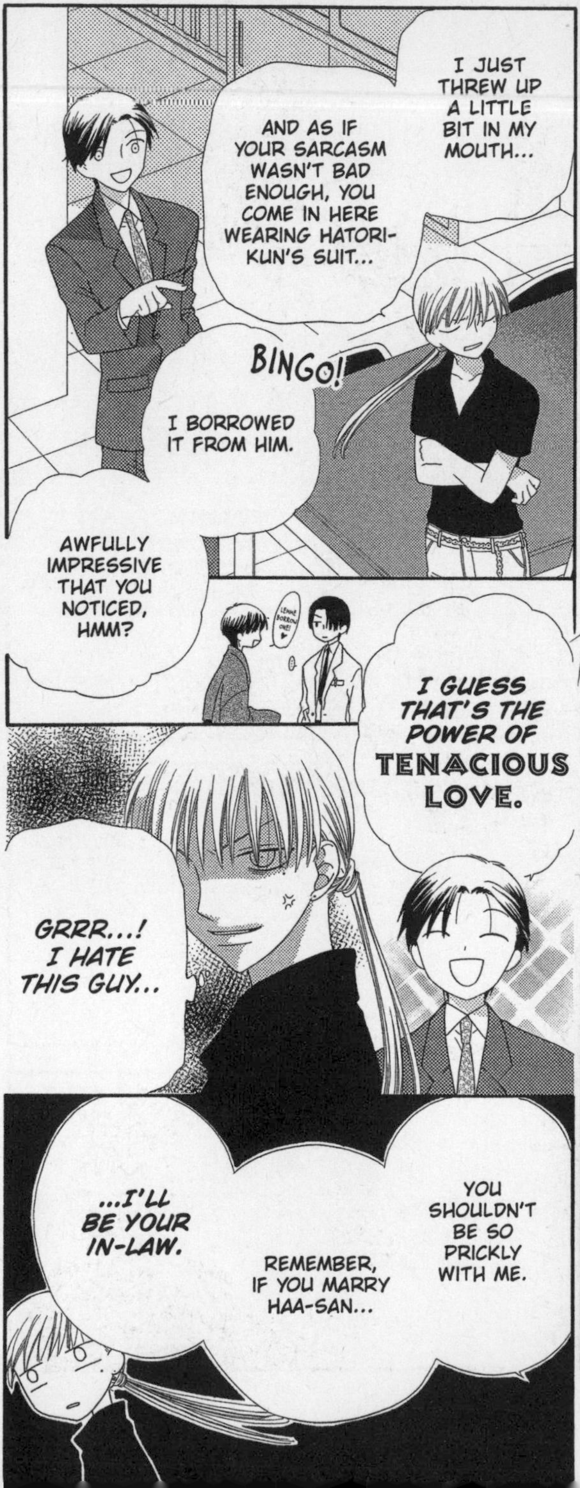
I JUST THREW UP A LITTLE BIT IN MY MOUTH...
AND AS IF YOUR SARCASM WASN'T BAD ENOUGH, YOU COME IN HERE WEARING HATORI-KUN'S SUIT...
BINGO!
I BORROWED IT FROM HIM.
AWFULLY IMPRESSIVE THAT YOU NOTICED, HMM?
LEMME BORROW ONE!
...
I GUESS THAT'S THE POWER OF TENACIOUS LOVE.
GRRR...! I HATE THIS GUY...
YOU SHOULDN'T BE SO PRICKLY WITH ME.
REMEMBER, IF YOU MARRY HAA-SAN...
...I'LL BE YOUR IN-LAW.

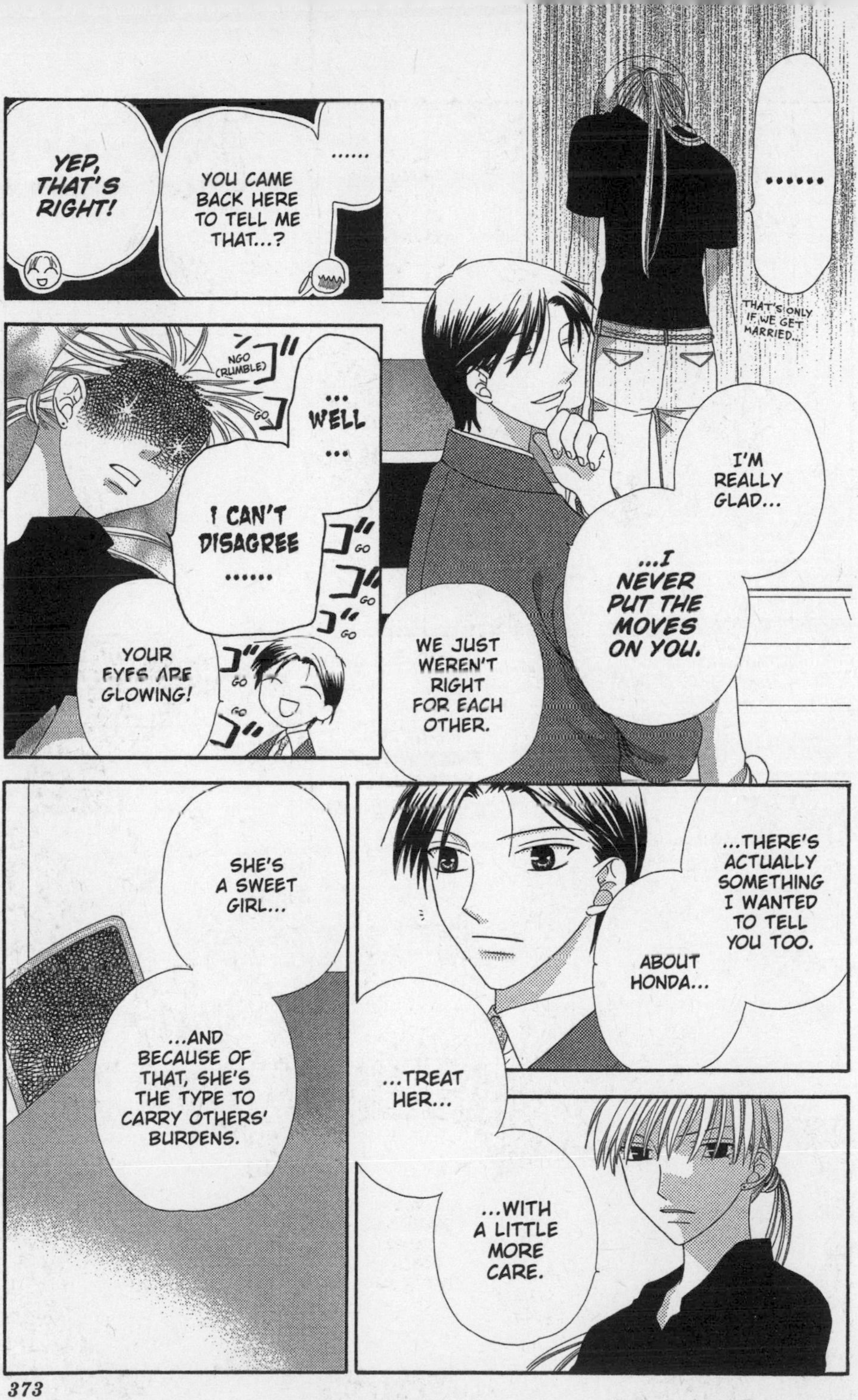
......
THAT'S ONLY IF WE GET MARRIED...
I'M REALLY GLAD...
...I NEVER PUT THE MOVES ON YOU.
WE JUST WEREN'T RIGHT FOR EACH OTHER.
......
YOU CAME BACK HERE TO TELL ME THAT...?
YEP, THAT'S RIGHT!
NGO (RUMBLE)
GO
...WELL...
I CAN'T DISAGREE......
GO
GO
GO
GO
GO
YOUR EYES ARE GLOWING!
...THERE'S ACTUALLY SOMETHING I WANTED TO TELL YOU TOO.
ABOUT HONDA...
SHE'S A SWEET GIRL...
...AND BECAUSE OF THAT, SHE'S THE TYPE TO CARRY OTHERS' BURDENS.
...TREAT HER...
...WITH A LITTLE MORE CARE.

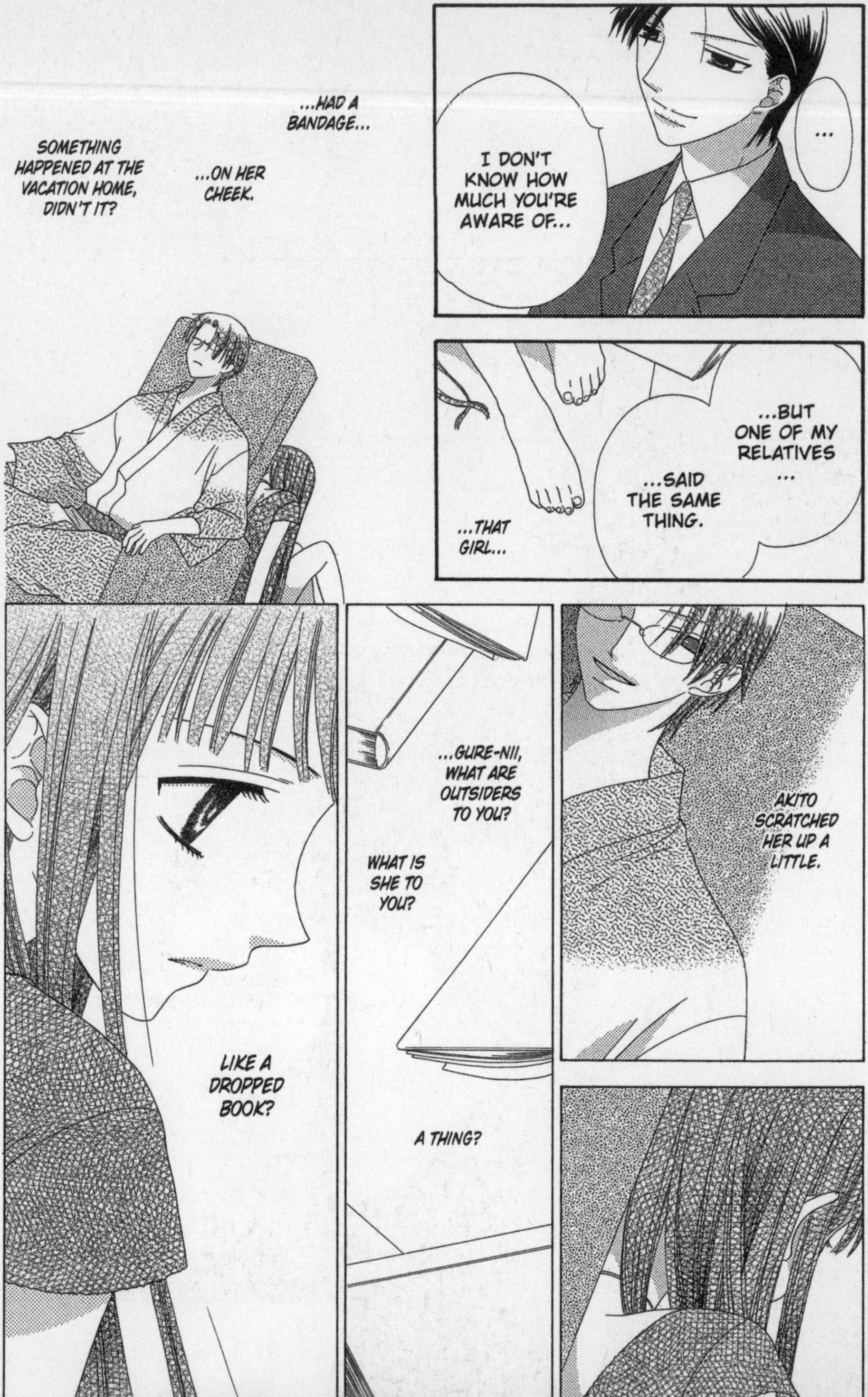
...
I DON'T KNOW HOW MUCH YOU'RE AWARE OF...
...BUT ONE OF MY RELATIVES ...
...SAID THE SAME THING.
...THAT GIRL...
...HAD A BANDAGE...
...ON HER CHEEK.
SOMETHING HAPPENED AT THE VACATION HOME, DIDN'T IT?
AKITO SCRATCHED HER UP A LITTLE.
...GURE-NII, WHAT ARE OUTSIDERS TO YOU?
WHAT IS SHE TO YOU?
A THING?
LIKE A DROPPED BOOK?

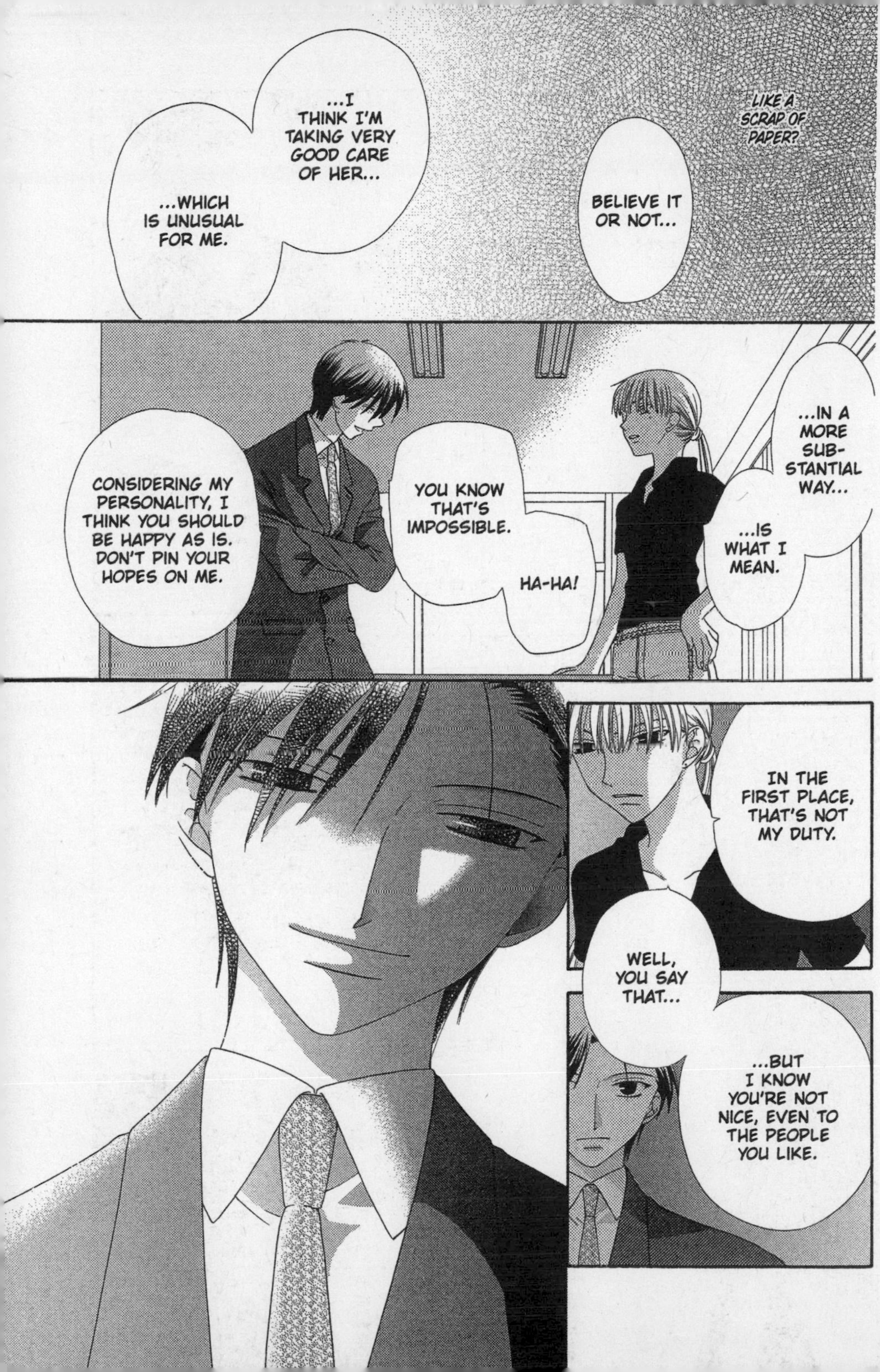
LIKE A SCRAP OF PAPER?
BELIEVE IT OR NOT...
...I THINK I'M TAKING VERY GOOD CARE OF HER...
...WHICH IS UNUSUAL FOR ME.
...IN A MORE SUB-STANTIAL WAY...
...IS WHAT I MEAN.
YOU KNOW THAT'S IMPOSSIBLE.
HA-HA!
CONSIDERING MY PERSONALITY, I THINK YOU SHOULD BE HAPPY AS IS. DON'T PIN YOUR HOPES ON ME.
IN THE FIRST PLACE, THAT'S NOT MY DUTY.
WELL, YOU SAY THAT...
...BUT I KNOW YOU'RE NOT NICE, EVEN TO THE PEOPLE YOU LIKE.

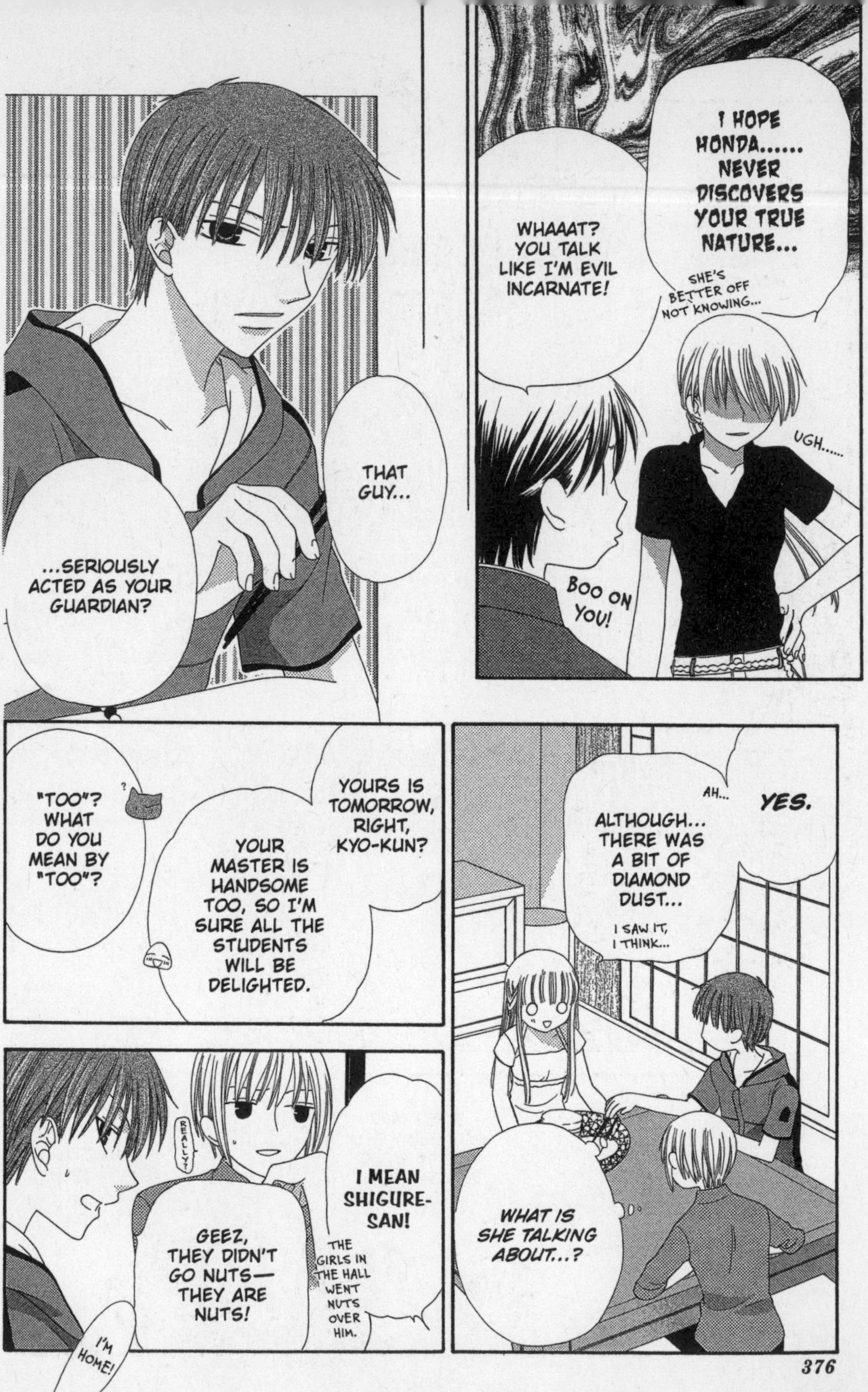
I HOPE HONDA...... NEVER DISCOVERS YOUR TRUE NATURE...
SHE'S BETTER OFF NOT KNOWING...
WHAAAT? YOU TALK LIKE I'M EVIL INCARNATE!
UGH......
BOO ON YOU!
THAT GUY...
...SERIOUSLY ACTED AS YOUR GUARDIAN?
YES.
AH...
ALTHOUGH... THERE WAS A BIT OF DIAMOND DUST...
I SAW IT, I THINK...
YOURS IS TOMORROW, RIGHT, KYO-KUN?
YOUR MASTER IS HANDSOME TOO, SO I'M SURE ALL THE STUDENTS WILL BE DELIGHTED.
"TOO"? WHAT DO YOU MEAN BY "TOO"?
WHAT IS SHE TALKING ABOUT...?
I MEAN SHIGURE-SAN!
THE GIRLS IN THE HALL WENT NUTS OVER HIM.
REALLY?
GEEZ, THEY DIDN'T GO NUTS—THEY ARE NUTS!
I'M HOME!

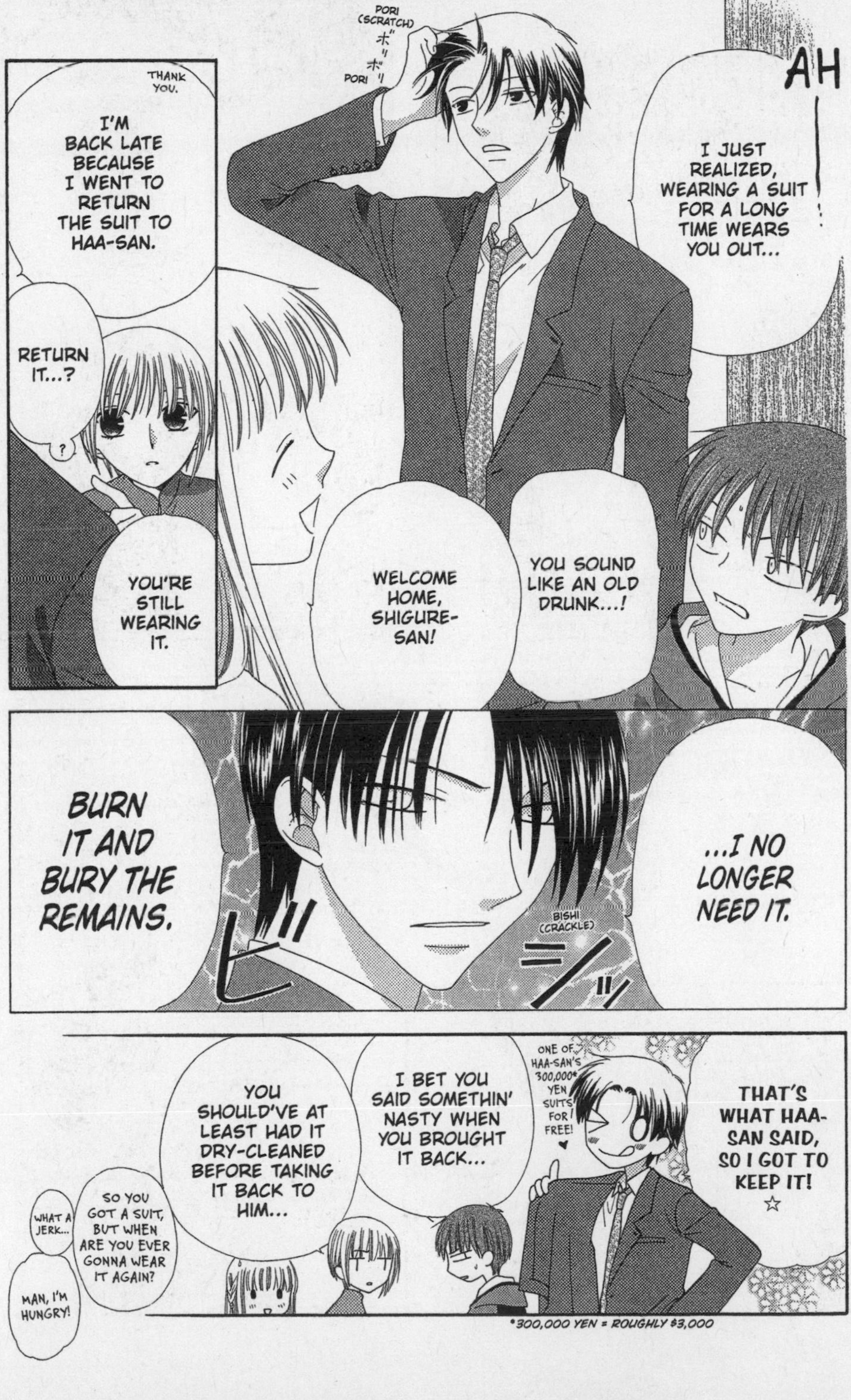
AH
I JUST REALIZED, WEARING A SUIT FOR A LONG TIME WEARS YOU OUT...
PORI (SCRATCH) PORI
YOU SOUND LIKE AN OLD DRUNK...!
WELCOME HOME, SHIGURE-SAN!
THANK YOU.
I'M BACK LATE BECAUSE I WENT TO RETURN THE SUIT TO HAA-SAN.
RETURN IT...?
?
YOU'RE STILL WEARING IT.
...I NO LONGER NEED IT.
BISHI (CRACKLE)
BURN IT AND BURY THE REMAINS.
THAT'S WHAT HAA-SAN SAID, SO I GOT TO KEEP IT! ☆
ONE OF HAA-SAN'S 300,000* YEN SUITS FOR FREE! ♥
I BET YOU SAID SOMETHIN' NASTY WHEN YOU BROUGHT IT BACK...
YOU SHOULD'VE AT LEAST HAD IT DRY-CLEANED BEFORE TAKING IT BACK TO HIM...
SO YOU GOT A SUIT, BUT WHEN ARE YOU EVER GONNA WEAR IT AGAIN?
WHAT A JERK...
MAN, I'M HUNGRY!

*300,000 YEN = ROUGHLY $3,000

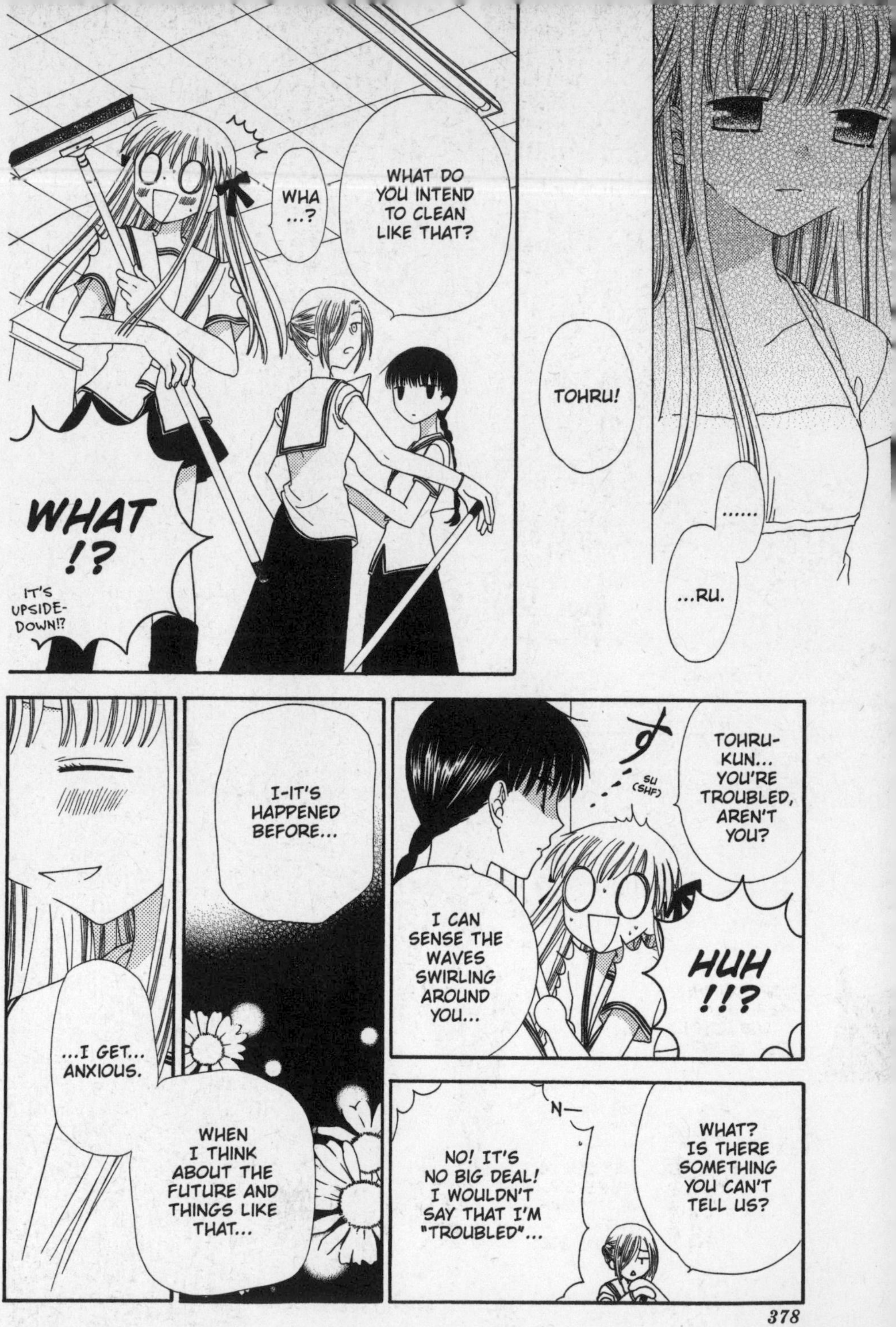
TOHRU!
......
...RU.
WHAT DO YOU INTEND TO CLEAN LIKE THAT?
WHA ...?
WHAT !?
IT'S UPSIDE-DOWN!?
TOHRU-KUN... YOU'RE TROUBLED, AREN'T YOU?
す
SU (SHF)
I CAN SENSE THE WAVES SWIRLING AROUND YOU...
HUH !!?
WHAT? IS THERE SOMETHING YOU CAN'T TELL US?
N—
NO! IT'S NO BIG DEAL! I WOULDN'T SAY THAT I'M "TROUBLED"...
I-IT'S HAPPENED BEFORE...
WHEN I THINK ABOUT THE FUTURE AND THINGS LIKE THAT...
...I GET... ANXIOUS.

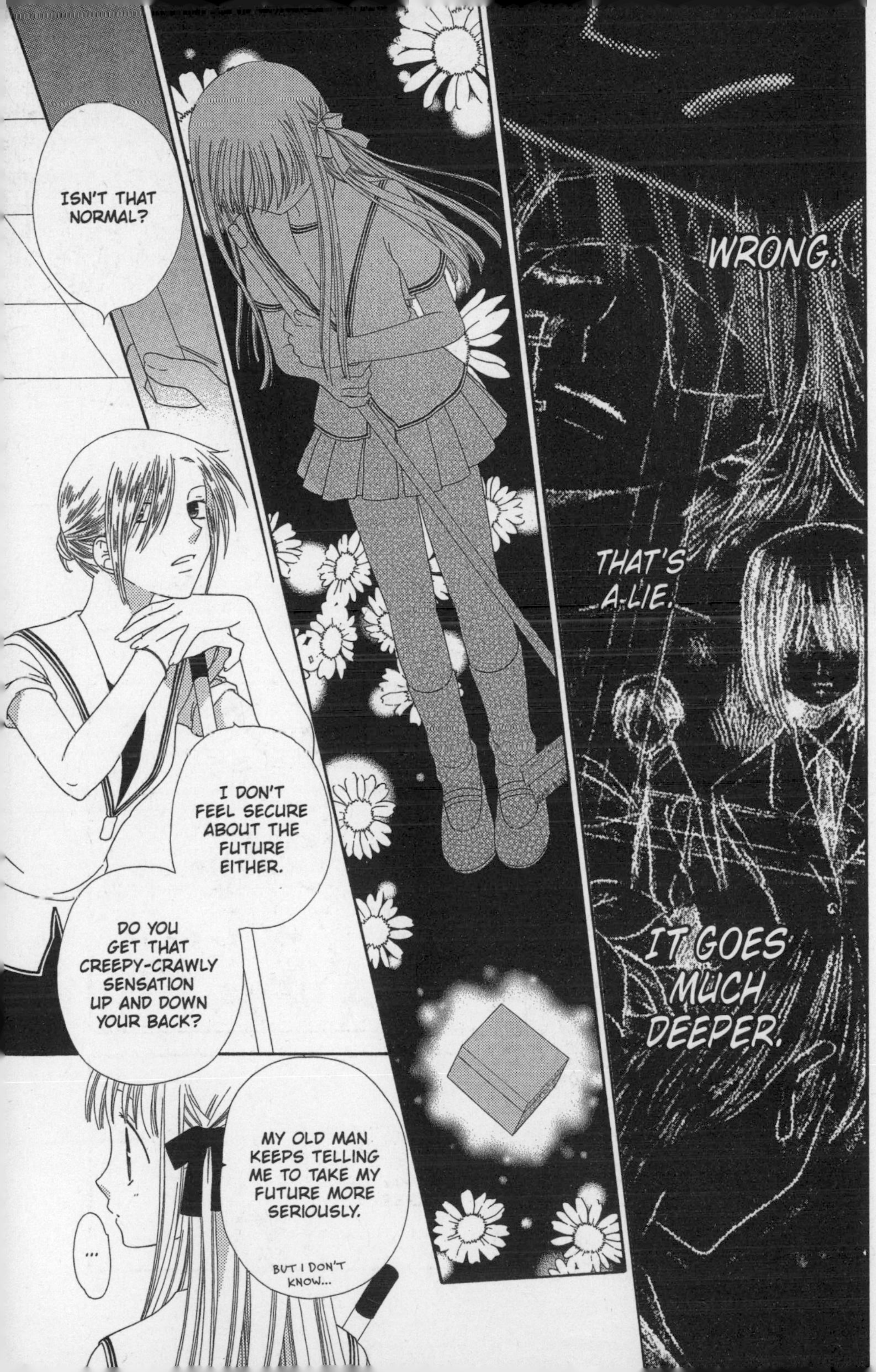
WRONG.
THAT'S A-LIE.
IT GOES MUCH DEEPER.
ISN'T THAT NORMAL?
I DON'T FEEL SECURE ABOUT THE FUTURE EITHER.
DO YOU GET THAT CREEPY-CRAWLY SENSATION UP AND DOWN YOUR BACK?
MY OLD MAN KEEPS TELLING ME TO TAKE MY FUTURE MORE SERIOUSLY.
BUT I DON'T KNOW...
...

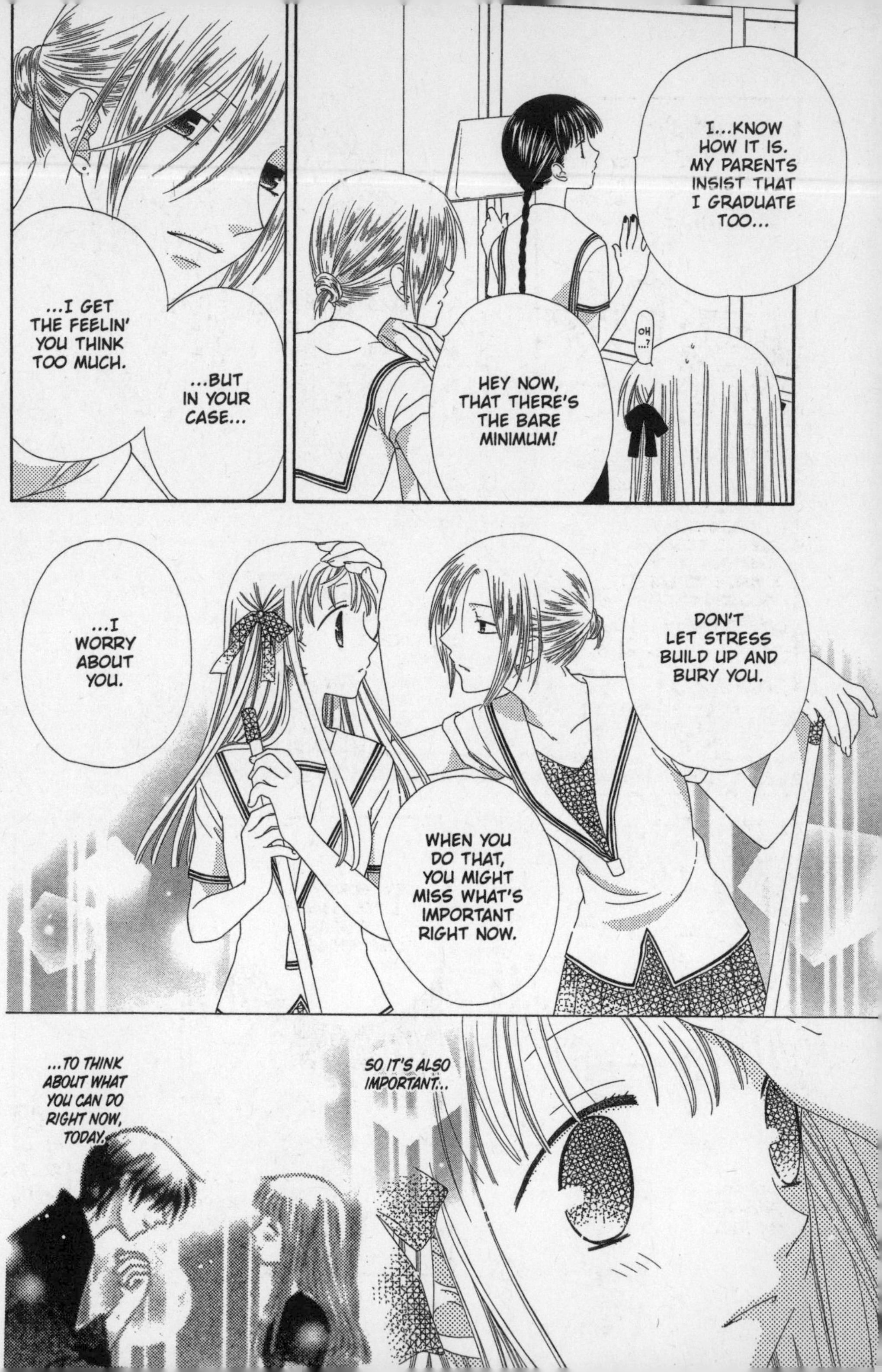
I...KNOW HOW IT IS. MY PARENTS INSIST THAT I GRADUATE TOO...
OH ...?
HEY NOW, THAT THERE'S THE BARE MINIMUM!
...BUT IN YOUR CASE...
...I GET THE FEELIN' YOU THINK TOO MUCH.
DON'T LET STRESS BUILD UP AND BURY YOU.
WHEN YOU DO THAT, YOU MIGHT MISS WHAT'S IMPORTANT RIGHT NOW.
...I WORRY ABOUT YOU.
SO IT'S ALSO IMPORTANT...
...TO THINK ABOUT WHAT YOU CAN DO RIGHT NOW, TODAY.

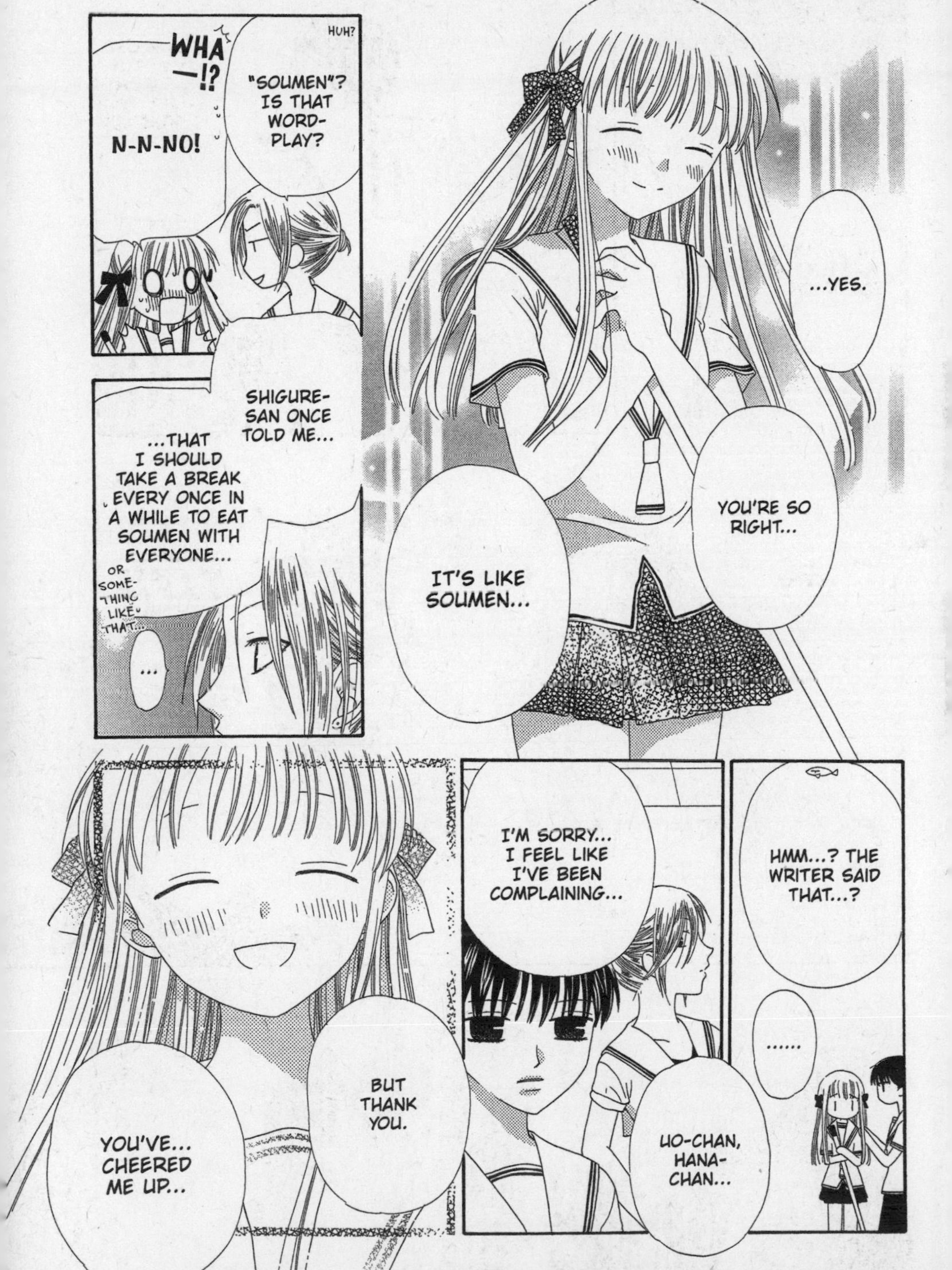
...YES.
YOU'RE SO RIGHT...
IT'S LIKE SOUMEN...
HUH?
"SOUMEN"? IS THAT WORD-PLAY?
WHA—!?
N-N-NO!
SHIGURE-SAN ONCE TOLD ME...
...THAT I SHOULD TAKE A BREAK EVERY ONCE IN A WHILE TO EAT SOUMEN WITH EVERYONE...
OR SOMETHING LIKE THAT...
...
HMM...? THE WRITER SAID THAT...?
......
I'M SORRY... I FEEL LIKE I'VE BEEN COMPLAINING...
UO-CHAN, HANA-CHAN...
BUT THANK YOU.
YOU'VE... CHEERED ME UP...

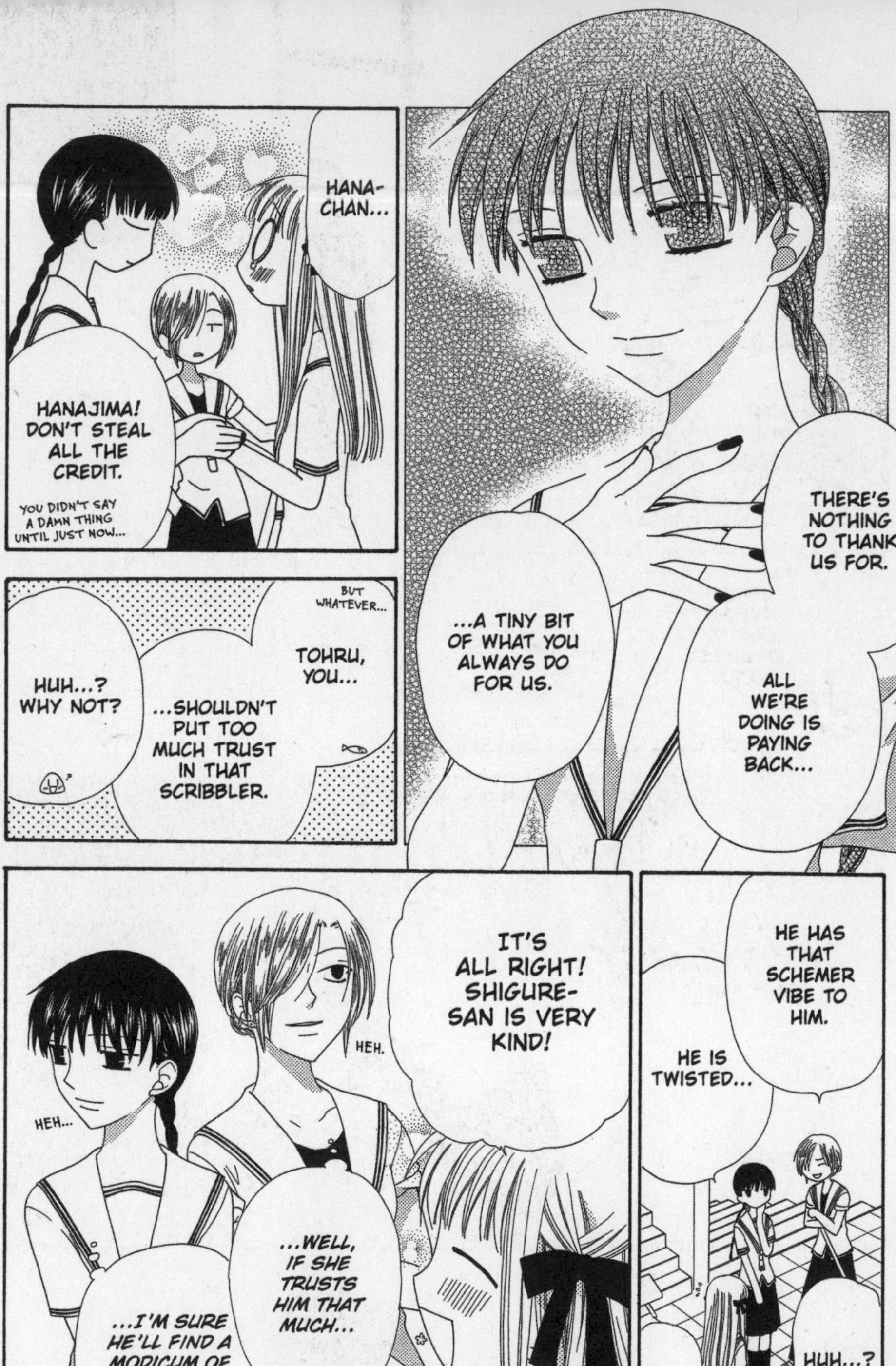

THERE'S NOTHING TO THANK US FOR.
ALL WE'RE DOING IS PAYING BACK...
...A TINY BIT OF WHAT YOU ALWAYS DO FOR US.
HANA-CHAN...
HANAJIMA! DON'T STEAL ALL THE CREDIT.
YOU DIDN'T SAY A DAMN THING UNTIL JUST NOW...
BUT WHATEVER...
TOHRU, YOU...
...SHOULDN'T PUT TOO MUCH TRUST IN THAT SCRIBBLER.
HUH...? WHY NOT?
HE HAS THAT SCHEMER VIBE TO HIM.
HE IS TWISTED...
HUH...?
......
IT'S ALL RIGHT! SHIGURE-SAN IS VERY KIND!
HEH.
HEH...
...WELL, IF SHE TRUSTS HIM THAT MUCH...
...I'M SURE HE'LL FIND A MODICUM OF CONSCIENCE SOMEWHERE ...

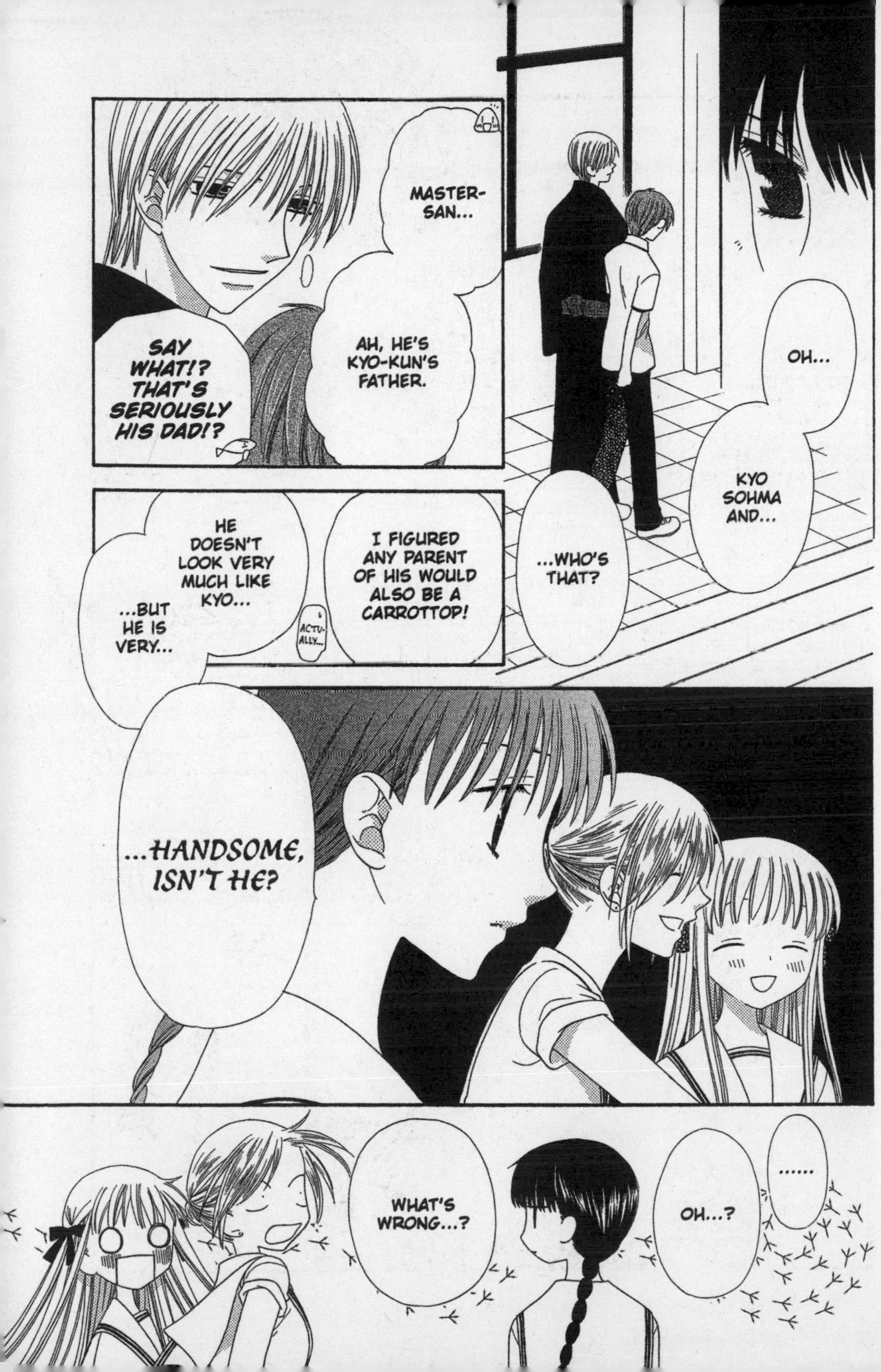
OH...
KYO SOHMA AND...
...WHO'S THAT?
MASTER-SAN...
AH, HE'S KYO-KUN'S FATHER.
SAY WHAT!? THAT'S SERIOUSLY HIS DAD!?
I FIGURED ANY PARENT OF HIS WOULD ALSO BE A CARROTTOP!
ACTUALLY...
HE DOESN'T LOOK VERY MUCH LIKE KYO...
...BUT HE IS VERY...
...HANDSOME, ISN'T HE?
......
OH...?
WHAT'S WRONG...?

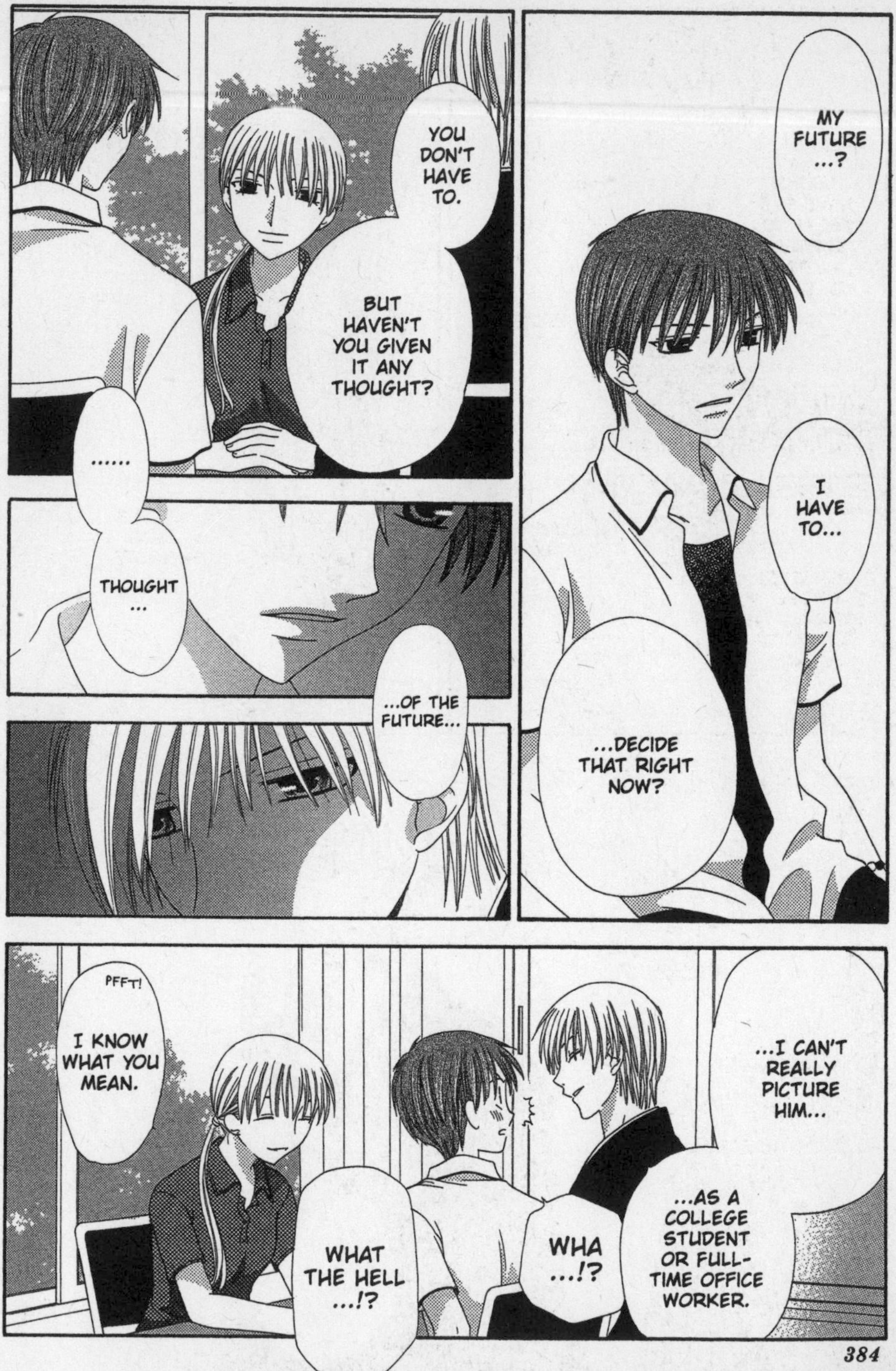
MY FUTURE ...?
I HAVE TO...
...DECIDE THAT RIGHT NOW?
YOU DON'T HAVE TO.
BUT HAVEN'T YOU GIVEN IT ANY THOUGHT?
......
THOUGHT ...
...OF THE FUTURE...
...I CAN'T REALLY PICTURE HIM...
...AS A COLLEGE STUDENT OR FULL-TIME OFFICE WORKER.
WHA ...!?
WHAT THE HELL ...!?
PFFT!
I KNOW WHAT YOU MEAN.

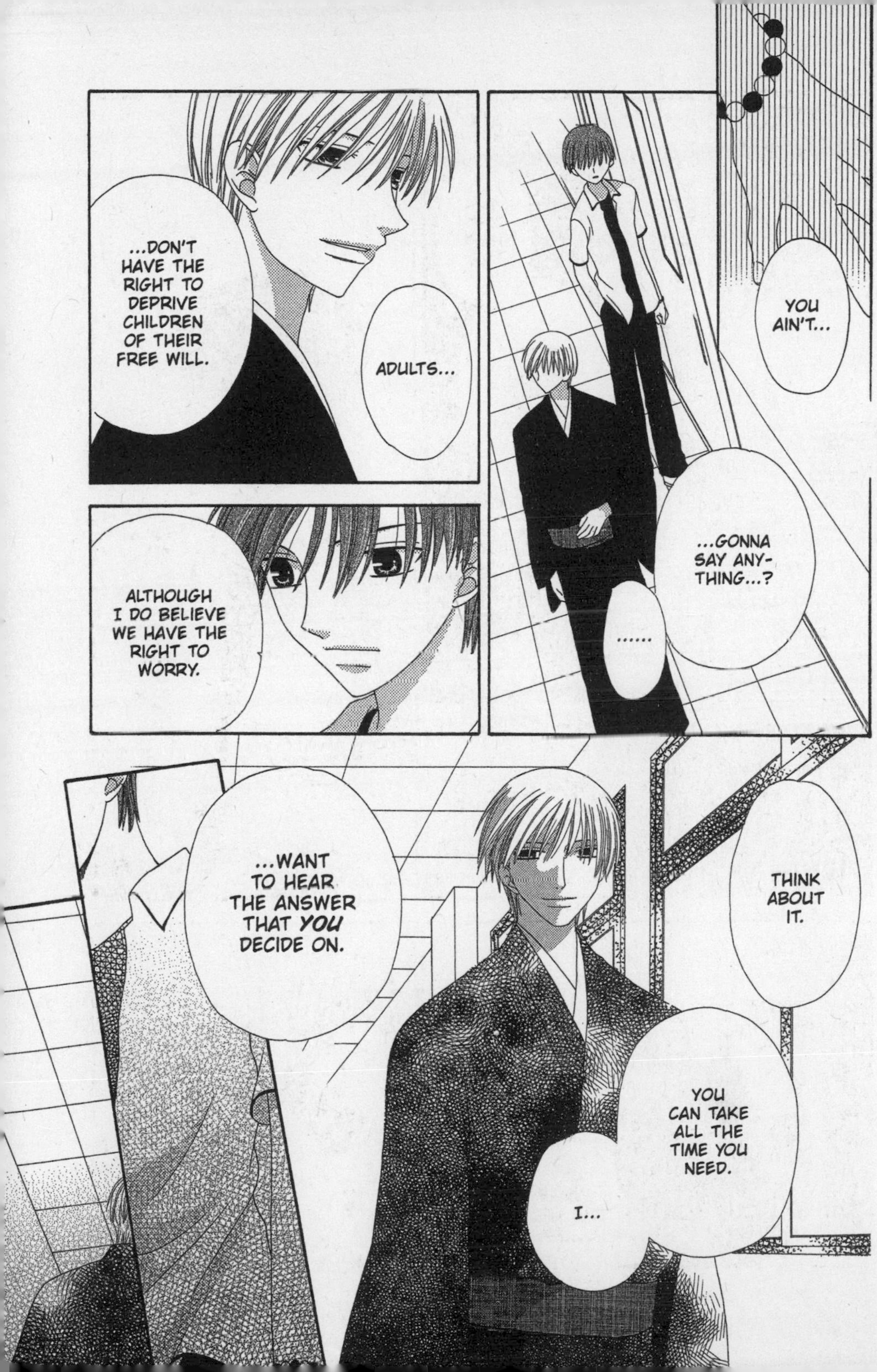

YOU AIN'T...
...GONNA SAY ANY-THING...?
......
ADULTS...
...DON'T HAVE THE RIGHT TO DEPRIVE CHILDREN OF THEIR FREE WILL.
ALTHOUGH I DO BELIEVE WE HAVE THE RIGHT TO WORRY.
THINK ABOUT IT.
YOU CAN TAKE ALL THE TIME YOU NEED.
I...
...WANT TO HEAR THE ANSWER THAT *YOU* DECIDE ON.

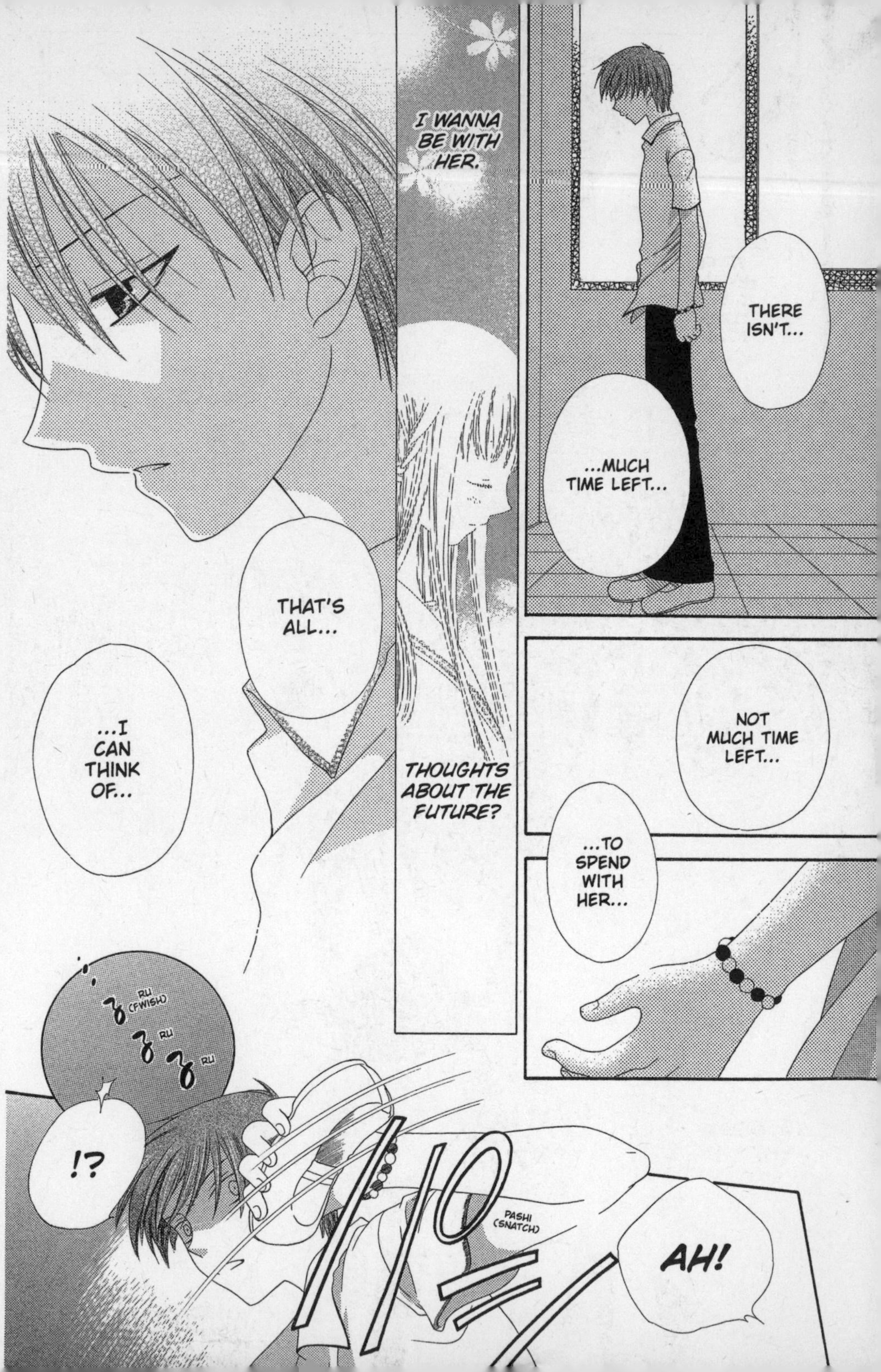

THERE ISN'T...
...MUCH TIME LEFT...
NOT MUCH TIME LEFT...
...TO SPEND WITH HER...
I WANNA BE WITH HER.
THOUGHTS ABOUT THE FUTURE?
THAT'S ALL...
...I CAN THINK OF...
RU (FWISH)
RU
RU
!?
PASHI (SNATCH)
AH!